Praise for Richard Taruskin's *The Oxford History of Western Music*

"There is not a page without insight, and not a chapter that does not fundamentally change the reader's perspective on its subject matter. . .. It is a visionary addition to our understanding of our culture." – Roger Scruton, *Times Literary Supplement*

"Readable, provocative, endlessly challenging and informative, his narrative account of more than a millennium's worth of musical activity represents a virtuoso display of the historian's craft." — Joshua Kosman, *San Francisco Chronicle*

"The most important publishing event in classical music since The New Grove Dictionary of Music and Musicians." — *The New York Times*

"Expresses the magnificence and melancholy of its age. . .. Singular in every possible way." — Paul Griffiths, *The Nation*

"If you want to know how brilliant Richard Taruskin's *Oxford History of Western Music* is, just open the first of its five long volumes and start reading right from page one. I found myself on the edge of my seat, as Mr. Taruskin begins his journey of a thousand years." — Greg Sandow, *The Wall Street Journal*

"Erudite, engaging, and suffused throughout with a mixture of brilliance and delirium. . .a highly personal (and often delightfully prickly) take on musical history from an original and eccentric mind — a mind to which anybody interested in the art of music should be exposed." — Tim Page, *The Washington Post*

"[Taruskin's] analyses are generally both cogent and entertaining, written in a rambunctious style that conveys technical information with great lucidity." — Charles Rosen, *The New York Review of Books*

"Taruskin has created a corpus of scholarship of breathtaking scope and crushing weight." – *Lingua Franca*

"[Taruskin is]. . .one of the most fluent writers on music in modern scholarship." – *The Musical Times*

"Entertaining. Provocative." – *The New York Times Book Review*

"Taruskin's magnum opus is a must-read, and in its way, a real page-turner of detective non-fiction. It's a cinch to become the most discussed music title of the year, if not of the decade." — Robert Everett-Green, *The Globe & Mail*

"It's a must-read for people who love or are curious about what we call western classical music. . .. Suddenly there is a coherent, irresistible narrative, full of delightful, sometimes disturbing surprises that leave you thinking for days. Suddenly, music history lives and breathes." — Tamara Bernstein, *CBC Online*

"Erudite, biased and persuasive; an irresistible survey of a millennium of music. Its ideas, a brillliant distillation of contemporary cultural attitudes, will likely percolate across music studies and other cultural histories." — Pierre Ruhe, *Atlanta Journal-Constitution*

"He is an elegant storyteller whose gifts of explication lead the reader to new levels of understanding, if not always agreement. . .his history is destined to remain intriguing and influential for years to come." — Don Rosenberg, *Cleveland Plain Dealer*

"It isn't likely that anyone, anytime soon, will challenge or replace this huge effort of Taruskin's. . .it is a staggering accomplishment." — Alan Rich, *LA Weekly*

"The book is nothing short of spectacular. . .stellar, worthwhile reading. — Daniel Felsenfeld, *New Music Box*

"One of the liveliest and most remakable books about music. . .. It will give real pleasures and revelations to any music lover, amateur or professional." — Raphael Mostel, *The Forward*

"It is difficult to arrive at a final opinion of so vast and multifarious a work other than to say that few people in the field could have encompassed it with the thoroughness and knowledge of Richard Taruskin." — Patrick J. Smith, *The New Criterion*

"Musicians, students, historians, and other readers wishing a detailed narrative about the career, patronage, musical influences, reception, and creative production of western composers, as well as the development of musical styles, will find this a fascinating and satisfying resource." — *Reference & Research Library Book News*

"Richard Taruskin, the most authoritative controversialist in modern musicology, has written an *Oxford History of Western Music* to rival Gibbon's *Decline and Fall* in ambition, literary distinction and sheer bulk. " — David Gutman, *The Independent*

"There's no doubt. . .that *The Oxford History of Western Music* is an important model of music historiography for some years to come." — Rob Haskins, American Record Guide

"There's no place else to look for such a comprehensive, entertaining overview of this immense subject." — John W. Freeman, *Opera News*

"It's likely to be remembered as the magnum opus of the most stimulating and insightful English-languge writer on music at work today." — Claude Bustard, *Richmond Times-Dispatch*

"A towering achievement." — Melinda Bargreen, *The Seattle Times*

"Taruskin has suceeded in writing a stimulating overview of Western society, setting a standard that will not be surpassed for a very long time." — Timothy J. McGee, *Library Journal starred review*

"Wickedly brilliant." — *BBC Music Magazine*

MUSIC IN THE
EARLY TWENTIETH CENTURY

THE OXFORD HISTORY OF WESTERN MUSIC

The Oxford History of Western Music is a continuous narrative, in five volumes (originally issued with a sixth containing indices and other back matter), covering the history of literate music making in Europe and (eventually) North America from inception, with the introduction of music notation in the ninth century CE, to the dawn of the third millennium. This book, corresponding to Volume 4 of the whole, has been lightly revised for the sake of greater accuracy and self-sufficiency. The indices and back matter have been divided among the several volumes in this edition.

The Earliest Notations to the Sixteenth Century

The Seventeenth and Eighteenth Centuries

The Nineteenth Century

The Early Twentieth Century

The Late Twentieth Century

MUSIC IN THE
EARLY TWENTIETH CENTURY

Richard Taruskin

THE OXFORD HISTORY OF WESTERN MUSIC

OXFORD
UNIVERSITY PRESS
2010

OXFORD
UNIVERSITY PRESS

Oxford   New York

Auckland   Bangkok   Buenos Aires   Cape Town   Chennai
Dar es Salaam   Delhi   Hong Kong   Istanbul   Karachi   Kolkata
Kuala Lumpur   Madrid   Melbourne   Mexico City   Mumbai   Nairobi
São Paulo   Shanghai   Taipei   Tokyo   Toronto

Copyright © 2005, 2010 by Oxford University Press, Inc.

Published by Oxford University Press, Inc.
198 Madison Avenue, New York, New York 10016
http://www.oup.com/us

Oxford is a registered trademark of Oxford University Press

Library of Congress Cataloging-in-Publication Data
Taruskin, Richard.
[Oxford history of western music. 4, Early twentieth century]
Music in the early twentieth century/by Richard Taruskin.
p. cm. — (The Oxford history of western music; v. 4)
Originally published as: Oxford history of western music. Vol. 4, Early twentieth century.
Oxford; New York : Oxford University Press, 2005.
ISBN 978-0-19-538484-0 (alk. paper)
1. Music – 20th century – History and criticism. I. Title.
ML197.T28 2009
780.9′04 – dc22
2008045034

5   7   9   8   6   4
Printed in the United States of America

Contents

Introduction: The History of What?

The argument *is no other than to inquire and collect out of the records of all time what particular kinds of learning and arts have flourished in what ages and regions of the world, their antiquities, their progresses, their migrations (for sciences migrate like nations) over the different parts of the globe; and again their decays, disappearances, and revivals; [and also] an account of the principal authors, books, schools, successions, academies, societies, colleges, orders — in a word, everything which relates to the state of learning. Above all things, I wish events to be coupled with their causes. All this I would have handled in a historical way, not wasting time, after the manner of critics, in praise and blame, but simply narrating the fact historically, with but slight intermixture of private judgment. For the manner of compiling such a history I particularly advise that the matter and provision of it be not drawn from histories and commentaries alone; but that the principal books written in each century, or perhaps in shorter periods, proceeding in regular order from the earliest ages, be themselves taken into consultation; that so (I do not say by a complete perusal, for that would be an endless labour, but) by tasting them here and there, and observing their argument, style, and method, the Literary Spirit of each age may be charmed as it were from the dead.*

— FRANCIS BACON, *DE DIGNITATE ET AUGMENTIS SCIENTIARUM LIBRI IX* (1623)[1]

Mutatis *mutandis*, Bacon's task was mine. He never lived to complete it; I have — but only by dint of a drastic narrowing of scope. My *mutanda* are stated in my title (one not chosen but granted; and for that honor I extend my thanks to the Delegates of the Oxford University Press). For "learning and the arts" substitute music. For "the different parts of the globe" substitute Europe, joined in Volume 3 by America. (That is what we still casually mean by "the West," although the concept is undergoing sometimes curious change: a Soviet music magazine I once subscribed to gave news of the pianist Yevgeny Kissin's "Western debut" — in Tokyo.) And as for antiquities, they hardly exist for music. (Jacques Chailley's magnificently titled conspectus, *40,000 ans de musique*, got through the first 39,000 years — I exaggerate only slightly — on its first page.[2])

Still, as the sheer bulk of this offering attests, a lot was left, because I took seriously Bacon's stipulations that causes be investigated, that original documents be not only cited but analyzed (for their "argument, style, and method") and that the approach should be catholic and as near exhaustive as possible, based not on my preferences but on my estimation of what needed to be included in order to satisfy the dual requirement of causal explanation and technical explication. Most books that call themselves histories of Western music, or of any of its traditional "style periods," are in fact surveys, which cover — and celebrate — the relevant repertoire, but make little effort truly to explain why and how things happened as they did. This set of books is an attempt at a true history.

Paradoxically, that means it does not take "coverage" as its primary task. A lot of famous music goes unmentioned in these pages, and even some famous composers. Inclusion and omission imply no judgment of value here. I never asked myself whether this or that composition or musician was "worth mentioning," and I hope readers will agree that I have sought neither to advocate nor to denigrate what I did include.

But there is something more fundamental yet to explain, given my claim of catholicity. Coverage of all the musics that have been made in Europe and America is obviously neither the aim of this book nor its achievement. A glance at the table of contents will instantly confirm, to the inevitable disappointment and perhaps consternation of some, that "Western music" here means what it has always meant in general academic histories: it means what is usually called "art music" or "classical music," and looks suspiciously like the traditional canon that has come under so much justified fire for its long-unquestioned dominance of the academic curriculum (a dominance that is now in irreversible process of decline). A very challenging example of that fire is a fusillade by Robert Walser, a scholar of popular music, who characterizes the repertoire treated here in terms borrowed from the writings of the Marxist historian Eric Hobsbawm. "Classical music," writes Walser,

> is the sort of thing Eric Hobsbawm calls an "invented tradition," whereby present interests construct a cohesive past to establish or legitimize present-day institutions or social relations. The hodgepodge of the classical canon — aristocratic and bourgeois music; academic, sacred and secular; music for public concerts, private soirées and dancing — achieves its coherence through its function as the most prestigious musical culture of the twentieth century.[3]

Why in the world would one want to continue propagating such a hodgepodge in the twenty-first century?

The heterogeneity of the classical canon is undeniable. Indeed, that is one of its main attractions. And while I reject Walser's conspiracy-theorizing, I definitely sympathize with the social and political implications of his argument, as will be evident (for some — a different some — all too evident) in the many pages that follow. But that very sympathy is what impelled me to subject that impossibly heterogeneous body of music to one more (perhaps the last) comprehensive examination — under a revised definition that supplies the coherence that Walser impugns. All of the genres he mentions, and all of the genres that are treated in this book, are literate genres. That is, they are genres that have been disseminated primarily through the medium of writing. The sheer abundance and the generic heterogeneity of the music so disseminated in "the West" is a truly distinguishing feature — perhaps the West's signal musical distinction. It is deserving of critical study.

By critical study I mean a study that does not take literacy for granted, or simply tout it as a unique Western achievement, but rather "interrogates" it (as our hermeneutics of suspicion now demands) for its consequences. The first chapter of this book makes a fairly detailed attempt to assess the specific consequences for music of a literate culture, and that theme remains a constant factor — always implicit, often explicit — in every chapter that follows, right up to (and especially) the concluding ones. For it is the basic claim of this multivolumed narrative — its number-one postulate — that the literate tradition of Western music is coherent at least insofar as it has a completed shape. Its beginnings are known and explicable, and its end is now foreseeable (and also explicable). And just as the early chapters are dominated by the interplay of literate and preliterate modes of thinking and transmission (and the middle chapters try to cite enough examples to keep the interplay of literate and nonliterate alive in the reader's consciousness), so the concluding chapters are dominated by the interplay of literate and postliterate modes, which have been discernable at least since the middle of the twentieth century, and which sent the literate tradition (in the form of a backlash) into its culminating phase.

This is by no means to imply that everything within the covers of these volumes constitutes a single story. I am as suspicious as the next scholar of what we now call metanarratives (or worse, "master narratives"). Indeed, one of the main tasks of this telling will be to account for the rise of our reigning narratives, and show that they too have histories with beginnings and (implicitly) with ends. The main ones, for music, have been, first, an esthetic narrative — recounting the achievement of "art for art's sake," or (in the present instance) of "absolute music" — that asserts the autonomy of artworks (often tautologically insulated by adding "insofar as they are artworks") as an indispensable and retroactive criterion of value and, second, a historical narrative — call it "neo-Hegelian" — that celebrates progressive (or "revolutionary") emancipation and values artworks according to their contribution to that project. Both are shopworn heirlooms of German romanticism. These romantic tales are "historicized" in volume III, the key volume of the set, for it furnishes our intellectual present with a past. This is done in the fervent belief that no claim of universality can survive situation in intellectual history. Each of the genres that Walser names has its own history, moreover, as do the many that he does not name, and it will be evident to all readers that this narrative devotes as much attention to a congeries of "petits récits" — individual accounts of this and that — as it does to the epic sketched in the foregoing paragraphs. But the overarching trajectory of musical literacy is nevertheless a part of all the stories, and a particularly revealing one.

* * * * *

The first thing that it reveals is that the history narrated within these covers is the history of elite genres. For until very recent times, and in some ways even up to the present, literacy and its fruits have been the possession — the closely guarded and privileging (even life-saving) possession — of social elites: ecclesiastical, political, military, hereditary, meritocratic, professional, economic, educational, academic, fashionable, even criminal. What else, after all, makes high art high? The casting of the story as the story of the literate culture of music turns it willy-nilly into a social history—a contradictory social history in which progressive broadening of access to literacy and its attendant cultural perquisites (the history, as it has sometimes been called, of the democratization of taste), is accompanied at every turn by a counterthrust that seeks to redefine elite status (and its attendant genres) ever upward. As most comprehensively documented by Pierre Bourdieu, consumption of cultural goods (and music, on Bourdieu's showing, above all) is one of the primary means of social classification (including self- classification)—hence, social division—and (familiar proverbs notwithstanding) one of the liveliest sites of dispute in Western culture.[4] Most broadly, contestations of taste occur across lines of class division, and are easiest to discern between proponents of literate genres and nonliterate ones; but within and among elites they are no less potent, no less heated, and no less decisively influential on the course of events. Taste is one of the sites of contention to which this book gives extensive, and, I would claim, unprecedented coverage, beginning with chapter 4 and lasting to the bitter end.

Indeed, if one had to be nominated, I would single out social contention as embodied in words and deeds—what cultural theorists call "discourse" (and others call "buzz" or "spin")—as the paramount force driving this narrative. It has many arenas. Perhaps the most conspicuous is that of meaning, an area that was for a long time considered virtually off limits to professional scholarly investigation, since it was naively assumed to be a nonfactual domain inasmuch as music lacks the semantic (or "propositional") specificity of literature or even painting. But musical meaning is no more confinable to matters of simple semantic paraphrase than any other sort of meaning. Utterances are deemed meaningful (or not) insofar as they trigger associations, and in the absence of association no utterance is intelligible. Meaning in this book is taken to represent the full range of associations encompassed by locutions such as "If that is true, it means that . . . ," or "that's what M-O-T-H-E-R means to me," or, simply, "know what I mean?" It covers implications, consequences, metaphors, emotional attachments, social attitudes, proprietary interests, suggested possibilities, motives, significance (as distinguished from signification). . . and simple semantic paraphrase, too, when that is relevant.

And while it is perfectly true that semantic paraphrases of music are never "factual," their assertion is indeed a social fact—one that belongs to a category of historical fact of the most vital importance, since such facts are among the clearest connectors of musical history to the history of everything else. Take for example the current impassioned debate over the meaning of Dmitry Shostakovich's music, with all of its insistent claims and counterclaims. The assertion that Shostakovich's music reveals him to be a political dissident is only an opinion, as is the opposite claim, that his music shows him to have been a "loyal musical son of the Soviet Union"—as, for that matter, is the alternative claim that his music has no light to shed on the question of his personal political allegiances. And yet the fact that such assertions are advanced with passion is a powerful testimony to the social and political role Shostakovich's music has played in the world, both during his lifetime and (especially) after his death, when the Cold War was playing itself out. Espousing a particular position in the debate is no business of the historian.

(Some readers may know that I have espoused one as a critic; I would like to think that readers who do not know my position will not discover it here.) But to report the debate in its full range, and draw relevant implications from it, is the historian's ineluctable duty. That report includes the designation of what elements within the sounding composition have triggered the associations — a properly historical sort of analysis that is particularly abundant in the present narrative. Call it semiotics if you will.

But of course semiotics has been much abused. It is an old vice of criticism, and lately of scholarship, to assume that the meaning of artworks is fully vested in them by their creators, and is simply "there" to be decoded by a specially gifted interpreter. That assumption can lead to gross errors. It is what vitiated the preposterously overrated work of Theodor Wiesengrund Adorno, and what has caused the work of the "new musicologists" of the 1980s and 1990s — Adornians to a man and woman — to age with such stunning rapidity. It is, all pretenses aside, still an authoritarian discourse and an asocial one. It still grants oracular privilege to the creative genius and his prophets, the gifted interpreters. It is altogether unacceptable as a historical method, although it is part of history and, like everything else, deserving of report. The historian's trick is to shift the question from "What does it mean?" to "What has it meant?" That move is what transforms futile speculation and dogmatic polemic into historical illumination. What it illuminates, in a word, are the *stakes*, both "theirs" and "ours."

Not that all meaningful discourse about music is semiotic. Much of it is evaluative. And value judgments, too, have a place of honor in historical narratives, so long as they are not merely the historian's judgment (as Francis Bacon was already presciently aware). Beethoven's greatness is an excellent case in point because it will come in for so much discussion in the later volumes of this book. As such, the notion of Beethoven's greatness is "only" an opinion. To assert it as a fact would be the sort of historians' transgression on which master narratives are built. (And because historians' transgressions so often make history, they will be given a lot of attention in the pages that follow.) But to say this much is already to observe that such assertions, precisely insofar as they are not factual, often have enormous performative import. Statements and actions predicated on Beethoven's perceived greatness are what constitute Beethoven's authority, which certainly is a historical fact — one that practically determined the course of late-nineteenth-century music history. Without taking it into account one can explain little of what went on in the world of literate music-making during that time — and even up to the present. Whether the historian agrees with the perception on which Beethoven's authority has been based is of no consequence to the tale, and has no bearing on the historian's obligation to report it. That report constitutes "reception history" — a relatively new thing in musicology, but (many scholars now agree) of equal importance to the production history that used to count as the whole story. I have made a great effort to give the two equal time, since both are necessary ingredients of any account that claims fairly to represent history.

* * * *

Statements and actions in response to real or perceived conditions: these are the essential facts of human history. The discourse, so often slighted in the past, is in fact the story. It creates new social and intellectual conditions to which more statements and actions will respond, in an endless chain of agency. The historian needs to be on guard against the tendency, or the temptation, to simplify the story by neglecting this most basic fact of all. No historical event or change can be meaningfully asserted unless its agents can be specified; and *agents can only be people*. Attributions of agency unmediated by human action are, in effect, lies — or at the very least, evasions. They occur inadvertently in careless historiography (or historiography that has submitted unawares to a master narrative), and are invoked deliberately in propaganda (i.e., historiography that consciously colludes with a master narrative). I adduce what I consider to be an example of each (and leave it to the reader to decide which, if any, is the honorable blunder and which the propaganda). The first comes from Pieter C. Van den Toorn's *Music, Politics, and the Academy*, a rebuttal of the so-called New Musicology of the 1980s.

> The question of an engaging context is an aesthetic as well as an historical and analytic-theoretical one. And once individual works begin to prevail for what they are in and of themselves and not for what they represent, then context itself, as a reflection of this transcendence, becomes less dependent on matters of historical placement. A great variety of contexts can suggest themselves as attention is focused on the works, on the nature of both their immediacy and the relationship that is struck with the contemporary listener.[5]

The second is from the most recent narrative history of music published in America as of this writing, Mark Evan Bonds's *A History of Music in Western Culture*.

> By the early 16th century, the rondeau, the last of the surviving *formes fixes* from the medieval era, had largely disappeared, replaced by more freely structured chansons based on the principle of pervading imitation. What emerged during the 1520s and 1530s were new approaches to setting vernacular texts: the Parisian chanson in France and the madrigal in Italy.
>   During the 1520s, a new genre of song, now known as the Parisian chanson emerged in the French capital. Among its most notable composers were Claudin de Sermisy (ca. 1490–1562) and Clément Jannequin (ca. 1485–ca. 1560), whose works were widely disseminated by the Parisian music publisher Pierre Attaingnant. Reflecting the influence of the Italian frottola, the Parisian chanson is lighter and more chordally oriented than earlier chansons.[6]

This sort of writing gives everybody an alibi. All the active verbs have ideas or inanimate objects as subjects, and all human acts are described in the passive voice. Nobody is seen as *doing* (or deciding) anything. Even the composers in the second extract are not described in the act, but only as an impersonal medium or passive vehicle of "emergence." Because nobody is doing anything, the authors never have to deal with motives or values, with choices or responsibilities, and that is their alibi. The second extract is a kind of shorthand historiography that inevitably devolves into inert survey, since it does nothing more than describe objects, thinking, perhaps, that is how one safeguards "objectivity." The first extract commits a far more serious transgression, for it is ideologically committed to its impersonality. Its elimination of human agency is calculated to protect the autonomy of the work-object and actually prevent historical thinking, which the author evidently regards as a threat to the universality (in his thinking, the validity) of the values he upholds. It is an attempt, caught as it were in the act, to enforce what I call the Great Either/Or, the great bane of contemporary musicology.

The Great Either/Or is the seemingly inescapable debate, familiar to all academically trained musicologists (who have had to endure it in their fledgling proseminars), epitomized in the question made famous by Carl Dahlhaus (1928–89), the most prestigious German music scholar of his generation: Is art history the *history* of art, or is it the history of *art*? What a senseless distinction! What seemed to make it necessary was the pseudo-dialectical "method" that cast all thought in rigidly — and artificially — binarized terms: "Does music mirror the reality surrounding a composer, *OR* does it propose an alternative reality? Does it have common roots with political events and philosophical ideas; *OR* is music written simply because music has always been written and not, or only incidentally, because a composer is seeking to respond with music to the world he lives in?" These questions all come from the second chapter of Dahlhaus's *Foundations of Music History*, the title of which — "The significance of art: historical or aesthetic?" — is yet another forced dichotomy. The whole chapter, which has achieved in its way the status of a classic, consists, throughout, of a veritable salad of empty binarisms.[7]

This sort of thinking has long been seen through — except, it seems, by musicologists. A scurrilous little tract — David Hackett Fischer's *Historians' Fallacies* — that graduate students of my generation liked to read (often aloud, to one another) behind our professors' backs includes it under the rubric "Fallacies of Question-Framing," and gives an unforgettable example: "Basil of Byzantium: Rat or Fink?" ("Maybe," the author comments, "Basil was the very model of a modern ratfink."[8]) There is nothing *a priori* to rule out both/and rather than either/or. Indeed, if it is true that production and reception history are of equal and interdependent importance to an understanding of cultural products, then it must follow that types of analysis usually conceived in mutually exclusive "internal" and "external" categories can and must function symbiotically. That is the assumption on which this book has been written, reflecting its author's refusal to choose between *this* and *that*, but rather to embrace this, that, and the other.

Reasons for the long if lately embattled dominance of internalist models for music history in the West (a dominance that in large part accounts for Dahlhaus's otherwise inexplicable prestige) have more than two centuries of intellectual history behind them, and I shall try to illuminate them at appropriate points. But a comment is required up front about the special reasons for their dominance in the recent history of the discipline — reasons having to do with the Cold War, when the general intellectual atmosphere was excessively polarized (hence binarized) around a pair of seemingly exhaustive and totalized alternatives. The only alternative to strict internalist thinking, it then seemed, was a discourse that was utterly corrupted by totalitarian cooption. Admit a social purview, it then seemed, and you were part of the Communist threat to the integrity (and the freedom) of the creative individual. In Germany, Dahlhaus was cast as the dialectical antithesis to Georg Knepler, his equally magisterial East German counterpart.[9] Within his own geographical and political milieu, then, his ideological commitments were acknowledged.[10] In the English-speaking countries, where Knepler was practically unknown, Dahlhaus's influence was more pernicious because he was assimilated, quite erroneously, to an indigenous scholarly pragmatism that thought itself ideologically uncommitted, free of theoretical preconceptions, and therefore capable of seeing things as they actually are. That, too, was of course a fallacy (Fischer calls it, perhaps unfairly, the "Baconian fallacy"). We all acknowledge now that our methods are grounded in and guided by theory, even if our theories are not consciously preformulated or explicitly enunciated.

And so this narrative has been guided. Its theoretical assumptions and consequent methodology — the cards I am in process of laying on the table — were, as it happens, not preformulated; but that did not make them any less real, or lessen their potency as enablers and constraints. By the end of writing I was sufficiently self-aware to recognize the kinship between the methods I had arrived at and those advocated in *Art Worlds*, a methodological conspectus by Howard Becker, a sociologist of art. Celebrated among sociologists, the book has not been widely read by musicologists, and I discovered it after my own work was finished in first draft.[11] But a short description of its tenets will round out the picture I am attempting to draw of the premises on which this book rests, and a reading of Becker's book will, I think, be of conceptual benefit not only to the readers of this book, but also to the writers of others.

An "art world," as Becker conceives it, is the ensemble of agents and social relations that it takes to produce works of art (or maintain artistic activity) in various media. To study art worlds is to study processes of collective action and mediation, the very things that are most often missing in conventional musical historiography. Such a study tries to answer in all their complexity questions like "What did it take to produce Beethoven's Fifth?" Anyone who thinks that the answer to that question can be given in one word — "Beethoven" — needs to read Becker (or, if one has the time, this book). But of course no one who has reflected on the matter at all would give the one-word answer. Bartók gave a valuable clue to the kind of account that truly explains when he commented dryly that Kodály's *Psalmus Hungaricus* "could not have been written without Hungarian peasant music. (Neither, of course, could it have been written without Kodály.)"[12] An explanatory account describes the dynamic (and, in the true sense, dialectical) relationship that obtains between powerful agents and mediating factors: institutions and their gatekeepers, ideologies, patterns of consumption and dissemination involving patrons, audiences, publishers and publicists, critics, chroniclers, commentators, and so on practically indefinitely until one chooses to draw the line.

Where shall it be drawn? Becker begins his book with a piquant epigraph that engages the question head-on, leading him directly to his first, most crucial theoretical point: namely, that "all artistic work, like all human activity, involves the joint activity of a number, often a large number, of people, through whose cooperation the art work we eventually see or hear comes to be and continues to be." The epigraph comes from the autobiography of Anthony Trollope:

> It was my practice to be at my table every morning at 5:30 A.M.; and it was also my practice to allow myself no mercy. An old groom, whose business it was to call me, and to whom I paid £5 a year extra for the duty, allowed himself no mercy. During all those years at Waltham Cross he was never once late with the coffee which it was his duty to bring me. I do not know that I ought not to feel that I owe more to him than to any one else for the success I have had. By beginning at that hour I could complete my literary work before I dressed for breakfast.[13]

Quite a few coffee porters, so to speak, will figure in the pages that follow, as will agents who enforce conventions (and, occasionally, the law), mobilize resources, disseminate products (often altering them in the process), and create reputations. All of them are at once potential enablers and potential constrainers, and create the conditions within which creative agents act. Composers will inevitably loom largest in the discussion despite all caveats, because theirs are the names on the artifacts that will be most closely analyzed. But the act of naming is itself an instrument of power, and a propagator of master narratives (now in a second, more literal, meaning), and it too must receive its meed of interrogation. The very first chapter in Volume I can stand as a model, in a sense, for the more realistic assessment of the place composers and compositions occupy in the general historical scheme: first, because it names no composers at all; and second, because before any musical artifacts are discussed, the story of their enabling is told at considerable length—a story whose cast of characters includes kings, popes, teachers, painters, scribes and chroniclers, the latter furnishing a *Rashomon* choir of contradiction, disagreement and contention.

Another advantage of focusing on discourse and contention is that such a view prevents the lazy depiction of monoliths. The familiar "Frankfurt School" paradigm that casts the history of twentieth-century music as a simple two-sided battle between an avant-garde of heroic resisters and the homogenizing commercial juggernaut known as the Culture Industry is one of the most conspicuous and deserving victims of the kind of close observation encouraged here of the actual statements and actions of human agents ("real people"). Historians of popular music have shown over and over again that the Culture Industry has never been a monolith, and all it takes is the reading of a couple of memoirs—as witnesses, never as oracles—to make it obvious that neither was the avant-garde. Both imagined entities were in themselves sites of sometimes furious social contention, their discord breeding diversity; and paying due attention to their intramural dissensions will vastly complicate the depiction of their mutual relations.

If nothing else, this brief account of premises and methods, with its insistence on an eclectic multiplicity of approaches to observed phenomena and on greatly expanding the purview of what is observed, should help account for the extravagant length of this submission. As justification, I can offer only my conviction that the same factors that have increased its length have also, and in equal measure, increased its interest and its usefulness.

R. T.
El Cerrito, California
16 July 2008

Preface

Of all the volumes in this series, this one, covering the first half of the twentieth century, surely differs the most radically from previous accounts. The reason goes beyond matters of selection and emphasis. The traditional narrative of twentieth-century music history is heavily—though often unwittingly—conditioned by a philosophy of history, conventionally identified as Hegelian, that arose in the nineteenth century in the aftermath of the French Revolution and that was first attached to the history of the arts, and to music in particular, in the 1850s. Unashamedly teleological, this historiographical bias was first enunciated in support of what was known at the time as the New German school, the faction figureheaded by Franz Liszt and Richard Wagner and chiefly promulgated by the music historian Franz Brendel. It is laid out in detail and critiqued in the eighth chapter of the previous volume in this series (*Music in the Nineteenth Century*), to which the reader is referred for a fuller understanding of the many references in the present volume to the philosophy of the New German school and its transformation in the twentieth century into the discourse of modernism.

In brief, the recognition of the continuity between the discourses of romanticism and modernism leads to a novel and (the present author is firmly convinced) truer representation of the evolutionary course of twentieth-century music in the literate (or "art") tradition. This new interpretation is most decisively reflected in a revised subperiodization whereby the early decades of the century, usually represented as marking a violent break with the technical and expressive traditions of the nineteenth century, are cast instead as an intensification—or maximalization, to use the word introduced within—of those very traditions. The true break with tradition came in the 1920s with the movement, often identified as "neoclassicism," which the conventional narrative represents as a return, or regression, to traditional ways.

In common with its companions in this series, this volume resolutely rejects the romantic viewpoint that asserts a fundamental divide between art history and world history. In particular, the fundamental tenet of neo-Hegelian art history—that the arts steadily progress toward a state of ever more perfect autonomy—is discarded as impeding by design the investigation of the actual causes of esthetic and stylistic evolution, which are to be sought within rather than outside the histories of social and political affairs. The narrative thus offers an uncompromising challenge to the viewpoint adhered to by a majority of practicing musicians and composers, even down to the present. It is admittedly and deliberately provocative, and proponents of the conventional narrative have often received it with hostility, but it is not offered in a hostile spirit. Rather, it is offered as a benevolent corrective that, by promoting understanding, can only foster enhanced appreciation of the artistic phenomena it describes.

R. T.
November 2008

CHAPTER 1

Reaching (for) Limits

MODERNISM: MAHLER, STRAUSS, SCHOENBERG

This is the whole flaw of "emotional" music. It is like a drug: you must have more drug, and more noise each time, or this effect, this impression which works from the outside, in from the nerves and sensorium upon the self—is no use, its effect is constantly weaker and weaker.[1]

—EZRA POUND

MODERNISM

Ezra Pound, an American poet living in London, wrote these weary words in 1914. By then he had lots of evidence with which to back his pronouncement up, evidence that we will be tracing in this and the following chapters. The period we will be investigating, from the last decade of the nineteenth century to the year in which Pound made his disillusioned diagnosis of its effects, is sometimes called the early modernist period. It was a time of enormously accelerated stylistic innovation, accompanied by an enormous expansion of technical resources. The two accelerations were symbiotic: neither can be called the effective cause of the other, but each fed the other since both fed off the same underlying drives, drives at which Pound was rather darkly hinting.

Before investigating those drives and their artistic consequences, a word is in order about the term "modernism" and the concepts it embodies. To make an ism out of being modern is on the face of it paradoxical, since if modern simply means "of or pertaining to present and recent time"[2] (as one dictionary defines it), then everyone is modern by default, and always has been, since we cannot live at any other time than the present. To be modernist, then, is more than to be modern. Modernism is not just a condition but a commitment.

It asserts the superiority of the present over the past (and, by implication, of the future over the present), with all that that implies in terms of optimism and faith in progress. It was an optimism that many had begun, under the stress of industrialization and its social discontents, to lose toward the century's end, leading to the malaise that the term *fin de siècle* (end of the century) was coined to evoke. The generation gap that began to widen between disillusioned romantics and young moderns is illustrated by a possibly apocryphal anecdote that, owing to its very aptness, became a veritable legend. Gustav Mahler (1860–1911), one of this chapter's protagonists, was supposedly taking a walk with Johannes Brahms at Bad Ischl, an Austrian spa where Brahms habitually vacationed, in the summer of 1896 (Brahms's last).

In the version of Richard Specht, one of Brahms's biographers,

> Brahms began discoursing, as usual, on the decline and fall of music, but Mahler suddenly took his arm and, pointing down to the river they were passing with his other hand, exclaimed, "Just look, doctor, just look!" "What is it?" Brahms asked. "Don't you see, there goes the last wave!" It was a good symbol for the eternal movement in life and in art, which knows of no cessation. But I seem to remember that it was Brahms who had the last word, thus: "That is all very fine, but perhaps what matters most is whether the wave goes out to sea or into a swamp."[3]

This tension between generations stimulated the modernist penchant to celebrate innovation as a mark of vitality. It further implies exclusivity: all are modern, few are modernist. Some live in the present with resignation; others with indifference; still others in a state of resistance to it. Modernists live in the present with enthusiasm, an enthusiasm requiring audacity, high self-regard and self-consciousness (along with its complement, heightened alertness to the surrounding world), and, above all, *urbanity* in every meaning of the word from "citified" to "sophisticated" to "artificial" to "mannered." All of this sounds like the very opposite of romanticism as originally defined — in terms, that is, of spirituality, sincerity, naturalness, spontaneity, naïveté, authenticity, pastoralism, and transcendence of the worldly, all being aspects or echoes of the original romantic revolt against the militant optimism of Enlightenment. Modernism celebrates every quality that Jean-Jacques Rousseau or Johann Gottfried von Herder reviled — and does it, moreover, with irony (as anything so self-aware must do), so that any attempt to reduce modernism to a set of core beliefs or practices quickly turns into an exercise in chasing one's tail.

But of course we have been observing a symbiotic process of highly self-conscious technical innovation and expanded technical resources over the whole course of the nineteenth century; one carried out, moreover, in the very name of romanticism. The romantic century, after all, was also the great age of industrialization and urbanization. We have already witnessed immense changes in artistic aims and means brought about as by-products of underlying changes in demography, as the populations of Europe and America were increasingly concentrated in cities. Nor are we strangers by now to irony. We know how calculated the impression of romantic spontaneity can be. We know how detached an artist has to be in order to create a complicated artwork, even one that broadcasts immediacy.

FIG. 1-1 Gustav Mahler, bust by Auguste Rodin (1840–1917) at Vienna State Opera.

Indeed, we will find that one of modernism's great ploys is to hide itself behind a mask of pastoral innocence. It is a long time since anyone has dared take anything at face value.

And we may also be wondering what the difference could possibly be between modernism and the "Zukunftism" (future-ism) of the New German School, epitomized in Wagner, which was also predicated on optimism and faith in progress. Haven't we seen it all before? Was there ever a more sophisticated composer than the one who wrote *Tristan und Isolde*? Was there ever a more artificial or mannered technical innovation than the *Tristan*-chord, however elemental and seemingly natural its representational power? Isn't the difference between what we've already seen and anything we're likely to see now just a difference in degree?

Of course it is—with one possible reservation. Consider the implicit paradox that has always attended Wagner and his "future-istic" methods. The most radically innovative composer of the nineteenth century—or at least the man so reputed, however equivocally—was in fact no friend of modernity. On the contrary, the social vision that motivated Wagner's artistic reforms was one of restored premodern harmony. At least by the time he finished composing *The Ring of the Nibelung*, his gargantuan mythological tetralogy, Wagner was not a futuristic utopian but the very opposite, a nostalgic (which is to say, a reactionary) one. The nostalgic vision, widely shared in the nineteenth century in direct reaction to the social discombobulations caused by modernization, informed not only Wagner's spectacular artistry but also his horrid politics. For the very incarnation of modernity in its every threatening aspect was, for Wagner and for every other nostalgic nationalist, the figure of the emancipated, assimilated, urbanized Jew.

And so, inevitably as it might seem, two of the paradigmatic early modernists within the German sphere—two of the leaders in the radical acceleration of stylistic innovation and technological advance that we will now be tracing—are Mahler, whom we have already met, and Arnold Schoenberg (1874–1951), both of them emancipated, urbanized, and assimilated (indeed, converted) Austrian Jews. Their modernism was widely taken—not only by their enemies, but also by their supporters and even by themselves—as the expression of that social emancipation and racial assimilation. Modernism, for them, was a source of optimism in the face of romanticist gloom. As always, what threatened some promised deliverance to others.

But it also expressed withal (and inevitably) their ineradicable sense of outsiderhood and, eventually—for Schoenberg, especially—of social alienation. And so modernism—like the romanticism it in some ways continued, in others supplanted—has always been an ambiguous and ambivalently regarded phenomenon. There is radicalism of ends and radicalism of means; and as Wagner's case already makes clear, the two do not necessarily coincide. Not all radicalism should be regarded as modernism. And not all modernism requires radical means of expression.

But of course the easy association of modernism with Jewry, whether maintained by friend or foe, was illusory. Jews had no lock on modernism. Just as deserving of the name among German composers, at least for a while, was Richard Strauss (1864–1949), who although a gentile was equally at the forefront of stylistic innovation and technological expansion during the rough period 1890–1914. Nor did assimilated Jews necessarily identify themselves consciously as modernists. Some were ardent defenders of tradition, seeing any attempt to upset the social or artistic apple cart as a threat to their precarious status. Even Mahler and Schoenberg showed signs of ambivalence about their modernism. They identified strongly with the distinguished tradition of German music in all its aspects, the Wagnerian one emphatically included. They saw themselves as its heirs and rightful continuers.

To maintain such a divided consciousness meant detaching musical tradition from social and ethnic tradition, and regarding it exclusively as a matter of style and technique. That was the most controversial move of all, and (being the one with which Wagner would have most vehemently disagreed) the most exclusively modernist one. So successful has the modernist viewpoint been in the twentieth century, though, that even Wagner has been assimilated to it. It is the only way in which Jews can love and follow him. And since emancipated Jews have not only been among the strongest creative talents in the twentieth century, but among the most influential historians as well, that is the way Wagner has figured in modernist musical history — worshipped as a stylistic innovator and technical expander, forgotten (or repressed) as a political and social thinker.

The modernist narrative, even though it is at bottom an instrument of social change, has always insisted on representing art as divorced from the social world, subject only to internally motivated stylistic change. In music history that view was most powerfully promulgated by Guido Adler (1855–1941), another emancipated Austrian Jew (a pupil of Bruckner and in his youth an ardent Wagnerian), who succeeded Hanslick as professor of music history at the University of Vienna. In 1885 Adler published a paper entitled *Umfang, Methode und Ziel der Musikwissenschaft* ("Scope, methods, and aim of musicology"), the influence of which can hardly be overestimated.

As the zeal with which its centennial was observed in 1985 made clear, this short article managed to chart the course of the newly recognized academic discipline of musicology for a hundred years, limiting its scope to the study of music in the literate Western tradition as an autonomous discourse (as opposed to "primitive music," which could be studied as a social phenomenon); limiting its methods to those of "style criticism" or stylistic classification; and limiting its aim to that of narrating and justifying the progress of the art toward the autonomous, socially divorced status that warranted the establishment of an independent academic discipline for studying it.[4] The circularity of the project was as momentous as it was paradoxical.

The viewpoint of this book, meanwhile, even though it accepts Adler's definition of the territory it will cover, nevertheless implicitly opposes that divorce, canonized though it has been within the discipline of musicology. Its coverage of modernism will go perforce against the grain, just as (and just because) the advent of modernism made insistence on the divorce explicit. Things will have to be represented here, on occasion, in ways that contradict both the traditional viewpoint of music history and the formulated declarations and explanations of the historical actors. The relationship of the early modernists to tradition will be the first case in point. Though they tried to present it as an unproblematic matter of inheritance, it was a deeply conflicted and contentious relationship. The conflicts, and the tensions to which they gave rise, were themselves among the engines driving the accelerated pace of change.

MAXIMALISM

Within the period 1890–1914, and especially in the German-speaking lands, modernism chiefly manifested itself in the manner to which Pound drew attention in the passage that heads this chapter as an epigraph: as a radical intensification of means toward accepted or traditional ends (or at least toward ends that could be so described). That is why modernism of this early vintage is perhaps best characterized as *maximalism*. The cultural phase we are about to embark upon was called the fin de siècle not only because it happened to coincide with the end of a century, but also because it reflected apocalyptic presentiments — superstitious premonitions of ultimate revelation and possible catastrophe — such as attend any great calendrical divide. The acceleration of stylistic innovation, so marked as to seem not just a matter of degree but one of actual kind, requiring a new "periodization," looks now, from the vantage point of the next fin de siècle, to have been perhaps more a matter of inflated rhetoric than of having new things to say.

What were the traditional ends given radically intensified or maximalized expression? Pound has already mentioned emotional expression, one of the prerequisites of romantic art. Another, from the very beginning of romanticism, was a sense of religious awe in the presence of the sublime. A third, sometimes an ally of the other two but potentially a subversive diversion (hence the most essentially "modernist") was sensuality.

What were the intensified means? One involved the two dimensions in which musical works exist, the temporal and the sonorous, both of them already maximalized to a degree by Wagner. Turning musical works into awe-inspiring mountains — by extending their length, amplifying their volume, and complicating their texture — became an obsession. Another way of amplifying the sense of musical space, as Wagner had also demonstrated, was to increase the range and maneuverability of "tonal navigation," that is, the range of key relationships. Yet another area in which Wagner had set a benchmark to be emulated and, if possible, exceeded, was the sheer level of tolerable (or at least tolerated) dissonance, and even more important, the postponement of its resolution. The former maximized the representation of emotional tension, the latter maximized the listener's participation in it.

The "Brahms line" could also be maximized. Here the benchmark could be described as "motivic saturation" — the loading of the texture with significant motifs to be kaleidoscopically recombined. By thus maximizing its "introversive reference" — the profusion and density of significant internal relationships — the musical texture was made ever more pregnant with potential meaning. That meaning could be harvested either in the domain of transcendence (in which nothing was specified, the imagination left free to organize the received impressions according to its own subjective criteria of relevance) or in the domain of "extroversive reference," where motifs are invested (as in the case of leitmotives) with paraphrasable connotations.

At its peak, the maximalizing tendency in fin-de-siècle or early modernist music gave rise to a body of works to which the German music historian Rudolf Stephan gave the name *Weltanschauungsmusik*[5] — roughly, "music expressive of a world outlook," or even "philosophy-music." Such works, always of hugely ambitious dimensions, attempted, through all the devices broached in the foregoing paragraphs, to deal with and resolve the metaphysical issues — questions that cannot be answered on the sole basis of sensory experience or rational thought — that had preoccupied philosophers (especially German philosophers) throughout the nineteenth century. The belief that music, in its word-transcending expressivity, was the only medium through which eschatological matters — matters of "ultimate reality" — could be adequately contemplated impelled the early modernists on their quest for new horizons.

MAHLER: MAXIMALIZING THE SYMPHONY

The quintessential representative of *Weltanschauungsmusik* and the man whose work most justifies the coining of the term was the composer who professed as his aim the writing of a symphony "so great that the whole world is actually reflected therein — so that one is, so to speak, only an instrument upon which the universe plays."[6] The author of these words was Gustav Mahler, whose ten finished symphonies (the next-to-last disguised as an orchestral song cycle called *Das Lied von der Erde*, "The Song of the Earth", composed between 1908 and 1909), plus a fragmentary eleventh called the Tenth, left unfinished at his death in 1911, brought the line of Austro-German symphonic composition to a climax — and conclusion. After Mahler, as we shall see, there has been no German-speaking symphonist of comparable prominence; the important twentieth-century "schools" of symphony writers have been Scandinavian, Russian, and Anglo-American.

Mahler's career was one of the great success stories of music history. He was born in a small town in what is now the Czech Republic, into the large family of a Jewish distiller and tavern keeper: of his thirteen siblings only six survived into maturity, leaving him the eldest. He first showed talent as a pianist, gave a public recital at the age of ten, and (having landed a sponsor) was sent to the Vienna Conservatory, where he was drawn toward theory and composition and, finally, conducting. At the age of seventeen (having been one of the few to sit out the first performance to its end) he was given the task of preparing the piano-duet reduction of Bruckner's Third Symphony for publication. He also audited a few of Bruckner's lectures at the University of Vienna, but was careful to insist that he was never a pupil of Bruckner's in composition.

Mahler did not begin to make a reputation as a composer until he was already a famous conductor, especially of opera. To scan a resumé of his conducting posts is to witness an astounding, truly meteoric rise to the pinnacle of his profession. It began with an appointment, in the summer of 1880, to direct operettas at a vacation resort. The next summer he was employed at the provincial opera house in Laibach (now Ljubljana in Slovenia) where he conducted his first opera (Verdi's *Il trovatore*). In 1883 he was appointed a staff conductor in another provincial city, Olmütz (now Olomouc in the Czech district of Moravia). From there he went to the central German town of Kassel, a provincial capital, where he served until 1885.

From now on it would be only big cities and major posts: Prague (the German theater, 1885–86); Leipzig (1886–88), where he conducted Wagner's *Ring* for the first time; the Royal Opera at Budapest (1888–91), where he conducted a *Don Giovanni* that aroused the admiration and support of Brahms; the Municipal Theater of Hamburg (1891–97), where he conducted Chaikovsky's *Eugene Onegin* in its non-Russian debut, much to the composer's delight, and from where he began to tour internationally, first in England, later in Russia.

Finally, in 1897, aged thirty-six, Mahler was offered the plum of plums: the directorship of the Vienna court opera, the empire's top musical organization. To take this job he had to accept pro forma baptism in the Catholic faith, but it nevertheless seems extraordinary that a Jew, however emancipated and assimilated, could have been thought as indispensable to the glory of Austrian music-making as Mahler's talent and drive had made him in the eyes of the Viennese arts establishment. (It was not in fact quite as extraordinary as it might seem: the highest aristocratic circles, secure in their supremacy, are relatively tolerant as a rule; Mahler, who certainly knew that he was in for it, was dependably subjected to anti-Semitic attacks in the bourgeois press, the domain of the upwardly mobile — see Fig. 1-2 where, as a "hypermodern conductor," he is caricatured as a "typical" wildly gesticulating Jew.)

Mahler held this post for a decade, leaving it only for an even more prestigious joint appointment at the helm of both of New York's leading musical institutions, the Metropolitan Opera and the New York Philharmonic orchestra. The record he compiled in Vienna made Mahler, by common consent, the world's greatest conductor. It was a record of authoritarian intransigence and perfectionism, in which heavy demands were made not only on singers but on audiences as well (the new kapellmeister zealously reinstating all the

FIG. 1-2 "A hypermodern conductor," caricature by Hans Schliessmann in *Fliegende Blätter*, March 1901. The caption, "Kapellmeister [Conductor] Kappelmann conducts his *Symphonie diabolica*," makes unmistakable reference to Mahler's Jewishness.

customary cuts in Wagner, for example). Identifying as a composer with composers rather than as a performer with performers, Mahler made a fetish of textual fidelity at the expense of singerly display. Yet at the same time he allowed himself the creative liberty to improve Schumann's orchestration and modernize Beethoven's. To adopt a Wagnerian analogy, he made sure that the relationship between the author of the score and the effectuators of the performance paralleled that of the gods and the Nibelungs. Since he himself, the composer-conductor (and yet a Jewish outsider in the eyes of many), claimed godlike power within his interpretive domain, Mahler was widely regarded as a sort of Alberich, the upstart world-destroyer of the *Ring*.

Yet his authoritarian purism set an example, however controversial in his own day, that became the norm in twentieth-century performance practice, and as such another benchmark of modernism. Also prescient was the literalism with which Mahler construed the idea of textual fidelity. He found abhorrent the idea of unwritten performance conventions, such as appoggiaturas in Mozart (something Mozart never dreamed of dispensing with), and tried to stamp them out. His battle cry against performers who insisted on maintaining such conventions in the name of tradition — "Tradition ist Schlamperei!" (Tradition is just sloppiness!) — has become a watchword among conductors in the twentieth century, who in the name of an imagined "historical authenticity" have actually produced a style of performing that is radically new in its amnesiac divorce from historical precedent.

Despite his lifelong association with the opera house, Mahler never wrote an opera. His one attempt, *Rübezahl*, was begun in 1879 and abandoned in 1883. Five years later he undertook to complete Weber's last opera, *Die drei Pintos* — a task Meyerbeer had previously undertaken but failed to complete, and which Mahler, then working in Leipzig, accepted as a love-offering to the wife of Weber's grandson, with whom he was having an affair. That is the extent of Mahler's creative contribution to the musical genre in which he excelled recreatively.

His domain was and — as he claimed — had to be the symphony: the maximalized, philosophical symphony of early modernism. In a letter to Max Marschalk, a friend and colleague, Mahler declared that "we are now standing — I am sure of it — at the great crossroads that will soon separate forever the two diverging paths of symphonic and dramatic music," and, he added, like any truly *contemporary* musician, he was casting his lot on the symphonic side.[7] These statements are often viewed as paradoxical. As we shall see, no composer ever appropriated so many dramatic and otherwise vocally or textually oriented means toward symphonic ends. But Mahler himself acknowledged this apparent contradiction in the letter's very next sentence. "Wagner," he admitted, "appropriated the means of expression of symphonic music, just as now in his turn the symphonist will be justified in helping himself to the new possibilities of expression opened to music by Wagner's efforts and in using them for his own means." And yet he went right on insisting on the categorical generic divide.

The insurmountable difference between the genres, for Mahler or any other practitioner of *Weltanschauungsmusik*, was that one could not truly express a weltan-schauung — a world outlook, or as Mahler would say, a world reflection — through anything so limited as a narrative plot or a dramatic scenario, no matter how metaphorical. One needed the unlimited interpretive space that "absolute music" provided. Then one could load the symphony with as much introversive and extroversive sign-language as one wished, confident that its application would be infinitely extensible, bound only by the listener's powers of imagination.

IS THERE OR ISN'T THERE? (NOT EVEN THE COMPOSER KNOWS FOR SURE)

Perhaps the best possible illustration of these points, and the most vivid model of symphonic maximalism, would be Mahler's Symphony no. 2 in C minor, the actual subject of the letter from which the foregoing quotes were extracted. Composed over a six-year period beginning in 1888, the symphony received its first complete performance under the composer's baton at Berlin in December 1895. On that occasion it bore the subtitle "Auferstehung" ("Resurrection") after the text of its choral finale. Even during Mahler's lifetime the subtitle came and went, betraying an ambivalence that also peeps between the lines of the letter.

Sometimes Mahler acknowledged a programmatic component in the symphony, sometimes he denied it. Sometimes he admitted that he needed some verbal (or "poetic") hook on which to hang the music of a large-scale composition; at other times he claimed that his first two symphonies together recounted the story of his own (inner) life; at still other times he maintained that whatever programmatic content he might agree to describe would be only a sop to the duller members of the audience. "When my style still seems strange and new," he wrote to Marschalk, "the listener should get some road-maps and milestones on the journey — or rather, a map of the stars, that he may comprehend the night sky with its glowing worlds."[8]

What is known for certain is that the programmatic content of the symphony's first movement underwent a metamorphosis. That in itself was nothing new: a well-known precedent was Miliy Balakirev's Overture *1000 Years*, which started out simply as the "Second Overture on the Themes of Russian Folk Songs" and ended up as a symphonic poem entitled *Russia*. With Mahler the dynamic went the other way, from more to less detailed, reflecting his eventual commitment to "absolute music," full of intense but undefined (which is to say undelimited) expression.

Under a stimulus chiefly provided by Franz Liszt, the genres of symphony and symphonic poem had begun to converge toward the end of the nineteenth century, so it will not overly surprise us to learn that the symphony's first movement was initially conceived as a symphonic poem and existed in that form for several years before acquiring its companion movements. (Even more tellingly, what we know as Mahler's First Symphony was given its first performance in 1889 as a "Symphonic poem in five movements" called *Titan* after a novel by the German Romantic author Jean Paul.) The American musicologist Stephen Hefling has established that the Second Symphony's first movement, called *Todtenfeier* ("Funeral Rite") in its symphonic-poem guise, originally followed a scenario adapted from *Dziady* ("Forefathers' eve"), a narrative ballad by the Polish national poet Adam Mickiewicz.[9] One of Mahler's friends had made a German translation of the poem, in which the hero's name happens to be Gustav, and published it under the very title that Mahler would adopt for his symphonic poem.

The fourth part of *Dziady*, the "Gustav poem," is a tale of doomed love and suicide, culminating in the hero's funeral and his soul's subsequent hovering in limbo until his beloved joins him in death. Mahler was attracted to this poem, Hefling suggests, because of the way it paralleled the miserable end of his recent affair with Marion von Weber, for whose sake he had completed *Die drei Pintos*. Hefling has given his hypothesis impressive support by closely reading the music in terms of the poem. But no contemporary listener had that chance. By the time of the first performance the Mickiewicz program had been suppressed—or rather, sublimated—and replaced by another that consisted mainly of questions of an "ultimate" or eschatological character, designed to put the listener in an appropriately "philosophical" frame of mind and stimulate an appropriately lofty response to the symphony's "absolute" content—an endeavor more worthy, in its demands, of what Mahler deemed a truly contemporary art.

As Mahler put it, somewhat mendaciously, in his letter to Marschalk, "In conceiving the work I was never concerned with the detailed description of an *event*, but to the highest degree with that of a *feeling*."[10] The "never" was clearly an exaggeration, but the aim was clear: to transcend what Mahler elsewhere described as "that insipid, erroneous way of composing, which is to choose for oneself a limited, narrowly circumscribed incident, and to follow it programmatically step by step."[11]

Here instead is the version of the program that Mahler actually wrote out for publication as a program note at the premiere:

> We stand by the coffin of a well-loved person. His life, struggles, passions and aspirations once more, for the last time, pass before our mind's eye. — And now in this moment of gravity and of emotion which convulses our deepest being, when we lay aside like a covering everything that from day to day perplexes us and drags us down, our heart is gripped by a dreadfully serious voice which always passes us by in the deafening bustle of daily life: What now? What is this life — and this death? Do we have an existence beyond it? Is all this only a confused dream, or do life and this death have a meaning? — And we must answer this question if we are to live on.[12]

In the end he decided against printing even this much; but that did not prevent him from confiding an even more abstract but at the same time even more urgent version of the program to Marschalk in the famous letter:

> I have named the first movement "Funeral Rite" (*Todtenfeier*), and, if you are curious, it is the hero of my D major Symphony [that is, the "Titan" of the First] that I am burying here and whose life I am gathering up in a clear mirror, from a higher vantage point. At the same time it is the great question: *Why have you lived? Why have you suffered? Is all this merely a great, horrible jest?* — We *must* resolve these questions somehow or other, if we are to go on living — indeed, even if we are only to go on dying! Once this call has resounded in anyone's life, he must give an answer; and that answer I give in the last movement.[13]

And now to the music. In terms of sheer dimensions, its maximalism requires little comment. At more than twenty minutes' length the *Todtenfeier* was by itself longer than most eighteenth-century symphonies, and was outstripped only by the monumental Adagio from Bruckner's Eighth Symphony. (Mahler redressed this shortfall in his next symphony, the Third, in which both the first movement and the last exceed a half hour's duration.) In terms of sonority, a listing of the symphony's roster — not all of it used in the first movement — can speak for itself, for this was the largest orchestra ever specifically demanded by any composer to date:

4 flutes, alternating on 4 piccolos
4 oboes, two alternating on English horns
3 clarinets, one alternating on bass clarinet
2 E♭ clarinets, one alternating on B♭ clarinet, both to be doubled in fortissimos
3 bassoons
contrabassoon

10 horns (four for use offstage)
8 – 10 trumpets (4 – 6 for use offstage)
4 trombones
contrabass tuba

Percussion (requiring seven players):
7 timpani, 6 (3 players) onstage, one offstage
2 pairs of cymbals, one offstage
2 triangles, one offstage
snare drum (more than one if possible)
glockenspiel
3 tubular bells
2 bass drums (one offstage, played with a wooden stick)
2 tam-tams (gongs), high and low

2 harps, several players per part if possible
Organ

Largest possible contingent of all strings

At the first performance the instrumentalists numbered 120, which means that there were between sixty and seventy string players. In addition to this, the last two movements require the participation of two solo singers (soprano and alto) and a large mixed choir. Even before the voices are heard, the symphony had made a decidedly operatic, or at least theatrical impression by virtue of the offstage brass band, previously employed outside of the opera house only by Berlioz and Verdi in their highly theatricalized Requiem Masses. But of course Mahler's symphony was also a requiem of sorts, or at least (as the organ proclaims) a quasi-sacred work, even without taking note of the religiose texts that will be sung in the two last movements in "answer," as Mahler implied, to the questions propounded in the first.

Another sort of maximalism was expressed through the medium of intertextual reference. Like any composer conscious of his late appearance in a canonical succession — or, to put it another way, like every composer of symphonies since Brahms — Mahler was not only enormously conscious of his heritage and the obligations it imposed, but was also aware of the opportunities it afforded him to "signify." By making deliberate references to the works of his great predecessors (but always regarding them as forerunners to be vied with and if possible surpassed), Mahler was able to communicate wordlessly a good deal of the programmatic content that he declined to paraphrase verbally for fear of the limitations such paraphrase imposed on the audience's subjective response.

EX. 1-1   Gustav Mahler, Symphony no. 2, I, first page of the score

The opening page of the score (Ex. 1-1) makes pointed "poetic" reference to no fewer than three Beethoven symphonies — the three that were by tradition the most heavily fraught with meaning. Even before a note is played, of course, reference will have been made to Beethoven's Ninth: the poetic texts in the program and the physical presence of the singers on stage telegraph Mahler's determination to revive the infiltration of oratorio into symphony that Wagner had blessed and Brahms had subsequently anathematized. But the opening string tremolo, disclosing neither tempo nor key, was an equally pointed reference to the famously nebulous beginning of Beethoven's Last.

At the same time the brusque unison motifs given out by the cellos and basses, and the fermata that separates the second of them from what follows, could not help but evoke the peremptory opening of Beethoven's Fifth; and of course so did the key of C minor, throughout the nineteenth century the most "meaningful" (and obliging) of keys. One of the things the key of C minor obliges is a breakthrough to the major in the finale. But anyone responding to the march tempo and the amplifying direction, *Mit durchaus ernstem und feierlichem Ausdruck* ("With grave and solemn expression throughout"), would have been reminded of the *Marcia funebre* in Beethoven's Third Symphony, the *Eroica*—an association that all by itself connotes two of the main components of Mahler's unstated program involving the funeral of a hero. The *Eroica* association contradicts the one to the Fifth insofar as it places the key of C minor in relation not to its parallel but its relative major. And sure enough, Mahler's symphony will end as triumphantly as did Beethoven's Third, Fifth, and Ninth, but in the "Eroica" key of E♭ major.

In Beethoven's day such a key relationship could be expressed only in the middle of a work, not between the two ends. By Mahler's day — thanks in part to his own previous work, notably the song cycle *Lieder eines fahrenden Gesellen* ("Songs of a wayfarer") in which the wayfarer's wandering is symbolized by a "progressive tonality" in which every song ends in a key other than the one in which it began — a tonal metamorphosis or modulation over the full course of a work was no longer necessarily regarded as a contradiction of "organic" form. And so Mahler's symphony both proclaims its loyalty to Beethovenian precedent and announces an advance over it: a perfect testament to the optimistic modernist view of tradition as perpetually self-renewing and inexhaustible.

Nor is the Beethovenian tradition the only one to which Mahler proclaimed allegiance. By the time of his writing, there was another heroic funeral march in C minor to emulate: the one Wagner wrote for Siegfried in *Götterdämmerung*. As we shall see, Mahler paid it as conspicuous a tribute as he could possibly have done, for this was another reference that elucidated (and enhanced) his own secret program. As traditions continue, the store of available subtext accumulates; as potential reference proliferates, actual reference is "maximized."

But of course the most potent area for maximalism was the actual sound surface — the melodic, harmonic, and tonal events that constitute the "purely musical" content of the score. It was not only the most potent area but, as Pound pointed out, also the most necessary; for if Mahler hoped to equal the impact that his great predecessors had achieved in their time, he would actually have to surpass both its intensity and its sublimity. That is, the sounds themselves would have to outstrip their predecessors in pungency, and they would have to duplicate the fascinated bafflement that Beethoven and Wagner had produced in their audiences — and all of this would have to be achieved, moreover, in a manner that could be directly related to the achievements of old, so that it would look like a valid continuation, worthy of inclusion in the "permanent collection." A tall order, this, amounting to a dilemma.

HIGH TENSION COMPOSING

The best place to look to observe Mahler's response to it is the moment that traditionally carried the highest charge in a symphonic first movement: the "retransition" to the recapitulation, where sufficient "dominant tension" had to be generated to motivate a "double return" commensurate in strength to the length and range of the preceding development. Beethoven had already solved this problem in maximalistic fashion in the first movement of the *Eroica*, with the "premature" horn entry with the opening theme in the tonic against an unbearably prolonged dominant pedal in the violins. Mahler's retransition, which begins five bars before 20 with the arrival of the dominant pedal in the bass, builds on Beethoven's precedent, drawing as well on a related precedent in the Ninth.

Ex. 1-2 shows the spot in question as Mahler sketched it in an early draft for the *Todtenfeier*, amounting to a harmonic reduction. The G tremolo in the bass should be understood as continuing as a pedal up to (but not including) the last measure shown. From the beginning Mahler strives for maximum dissonance against the pedal — a semitone in the first measure, a major second in the second measure, a tritone in the fourth. Beginning at m. 6, harmonies that are normally mutually exclusive (that is, normally sounded in succession) are mixed over the dominant pedal, just as they had been ninety years earlier in the *Eroica*. The first mixture pits what looks like a tonic triad against a diminished seventh spelled with F♯ as the root, the two chords having two notes in common. It gives way in m. 7 to an even more dissonant combination, consisting of the same tonic triad over a diminished seventh built on B natural, the leading tone, the two chords having no notes in common. They produce, instead, a seven-note cluster.

Connoisseurs of musical horror will recognize this cluster as the very chord Beethoven had used in the finale of the Ninth for the intensified repetition of the *Schreckensfanfaren*, the "horror fanfares" (as Wagner called them) that precede the Ode to Joy and set it in relief. Over the course of the intervening seventy years, this harmony had been regarded as a one-time curiosity to be explained only in terms of its immediate expressive context. Not until Mahler's time did anyone see it as a benchmark to be exceeded; that is evidence both of Mahler's consciousness of continuity with tradition, and of the difference between his early modernist attitude and those of Beethoven's earlier progeny.

But whereas Beethoven's *Schreckensfanfaren* functioned more as a peremptory noise than as a harmony (even if, by moving to the dominant, it acquires a harmonic function retrospectively), Mahler's equally dissonant chord is set in a progression that assigns it an unbearably tense dominant function. Remembering that the bass G continues to sound throughout Ex. 1-2, we may construe the two harmonies in m. 6 as, on the one hand, a tonic $^6_4$, and, on the other, a diminished seventh built on the leading tone to G, hence functioning as a "V of V." In other words, we have a mixture of two chords that in the present context can be assigned the same function — namely, that of "predominant," or dominant preparation. The dissonance produced by the mixture of two chords of similar function intensifies or maximizes the function, lending it an ever greater need for resolution.

The next move is to hold the tonic $^6_4$ as a pedal and replace the first diminished seventh chord with another that, because it is built on the leading tone of the tonic scale, now reinforces the function of the dominant pedal, producing a "dominant ninth." In Mahler's version of the *Schreckensfanfare* chord, then, the C and the E♭, while nominally part of the tonic chord, are actually functioning as a dissonant suspension over a dominant ninth. Since they can be represented in notation as an additional pair of thirds (an "eleventh" and a "thirteenth") stacked atop the dominant-ninth chord, and since such chords (following Mahler's precedent and faithfully continuing the tradition in which he participated) became increasingly common during the early modernist period, many musicians trained during or after that period would call the harmony in m. 7 a "dominant- thirteenth" chord, here making what amounts to its symphonic debut.

EX. 1-2   Gustav Mahler, sketch for *Todtenfeier*

But unless we remember that two of its members are functional suspensions, we will not appreciate the effect of the harmony in m. 8 of Ex. 1-2, in which the C is palpably resolved to B natural, a chord tone, leaving only the E♭ suspended, hence putting additional pressure on it to resolve and upping the level of "dominant tension" beyond anything previously experienced by the audience who heard the symphony at its premiere. The tonic to which this amplified dominant is cataclysmically resolved — via a bass descent through a full chromatic scale and then some! — in the movement's most "maximal" single gesture is expressed as a pair of eighths: a Wagnerian double drumbeat that makes absolutely explicit the already implicit reference to Siegfried's heroic C-minor funeral music.

And yet for all the familiar resonances and the absolute clarity of the cadential function these maximalized harmonies perform, their novelty was widely perceived not merely as a difference in degree of intensity, but as an absolute difference in stylistic kind. This we may learn from the testimony of a highly qualified witness, none other than Guido Adler, who wrote that in the Second Symphony,

> the bold power of combination builds up to harmonies previously not to be found in the literature. In this respect [Mahler] oversteps the boundary previously accepted in our time for the purely beautiful. It is not impossible, and not improbable — indeed surmise based on the experience of history suggests — that the progressive artist leads his own age and especially posterity to another way of

viewing and understanding sounds. Whether an enduring advance results, only the future can decide.[14]

One may suspect that Adler's question was somewhat disingenuous. His critique was so solidly informed by the old "New German" insistence on "progressive" art as to remove any doubt that, for Adler (as for any early modernist), Mahler's "unprecedented cacophonies" were in large part responsible for his value as an artist. Nor would anyone but a "philistine" have insisted by the 1890s that the domain of art was limited to the "purely beautiful." The whole history of nineteenth-century music was a history of the creeping encroachment of the "great" (or the sublime) upon the traditional domain of the beautiful. To put it another way, composers of "great" music, beginning with Beethoven, had long been sacrificing ingratiating pleasure on the altar of edifying pain. This process, too, was undergoing a maximalizing acceleration as late romanticism shaded into early modernism, and here, too, Mahler was in the vanguard.

HALF-STEPS OVER FIFTHS

But moments of dramatic horror must be kept rare so as to retain their potency, and also so that they may lend focus and compelling shape to what otherwise might merely be a sprawling temporal span. Unprecedented buildups of harmonic tension toward cataclysmic, cacophonous resolution can only occur once or twice per piece. Elsewhere, what made Mahler's harmonic idiom seem new and disorienting was precisely his avoidance of powerful root motions by fifth. Such motions, formerly "tonality's" bread and butter, were now special effects. For purposes of ordinary harmonic navigation, half steps continued their progress toward domination — a progress that can be traced back to Schubert, and that had reached a previous peak in Wagner and Bruckner, Mahler's most immediate mentors.

We can view this process with telling clarity by tracing the modulatory path within the *Todtenfeier*'s exposition section. The movement begins, harmonically speaking, in a state of near-immobility. The combination of the dominant pedal, held *tremolando* for nineteen measures (and maintained thereafter, with only momentary interruptions, for another sixteen) and the stark unison writing that only yields to an almost equally stark two-part counterpart after twelve bars, prevent any but the most primitive sense of tonal orientation to emerge. The first complete tonic triad is not sounded until the downbeat of m. 28. (Until then, the predominating "linear" texture had permitted some pretty excruciating part-writing dissonances to occur, like the parallel seconds on the last beat of m. 23.) Not until m. 41 is a tonic triad preceded by a fully expressed dominant, and when it finally happens, its rarity is underscored by a great climactic explosion of brass and percussion.

So far we have been witnessing a maximalization of an effect first encountered in the *Eroica* (although it had had some precedents in Beethoven even by then): the "achievement," through effort and stress, of the first tonic cadence — an effect that in itself enacts or symbolizes a kind of ethically fraught, heroic deed. Once Mahler has achieved the tonic, however, he quits it with equally maximalized dispatch: in a span of eight bars he manages to traverse a virtual light-year of tonal space, to the key of E major, the domain of the "second theme." And in another fifteen bars he has reached the exposition's closing tonality, an equally unexpected, tonally distant Eb minor.

This passage of harmonic sleight of hand is reduced and summarized in Ex. 1-3. It is all done with half steps. First the tonic C-minor triad is expanded, in the third bar after fig. 2, by half steps in contrary motion: its fifth ascends to Ab and its root descends to Cb while the third, held constant, acts as an anchor. The Ab minor $^6_3$ chord thus achieved is inflected two bars later, at 3, by another half-step motion whereby the Eb in the middle voice (reconceptualized as D♯) resolves as a leading tone to the new tonic, E. It is almost as if Mahler had set himself a kind of musical chess problem: white to get from C minor to E major in two moves.

EX. 1-3   Gustav Mahler, *Todtenfeier*, modulatory progression to secondary theme area

Of course the tonic triad of E major has been expressed so far only in the $^6_4$ position, which (being a cadential preparation) is more a promise of the new key than a fulfillment. The dominant (B major, preceded by *its* dominant) arrives in confirmation after eight more bars, and is tantalizingly surrounded with chromatic neighbors before sinking back to Bb while its companion notes, respelled as Eb and Gb, join it in a new cadential $^6_4$ that promises final resolution not to E but to Eb. We have been through a passage that could not have been more definitely in E major, yet one in which the tonic had failed to appear even once in stable, cadentially supported form.

Mahler has one more half-step inflection up his sleeve. The Gb of the Eb-minor triad, shorn of its companion notes, is peremptorily altered to G natural to prepare a modified repetition of the exposition at fig. 4. As soon as the cellos and basses break in with their explosive recall of the first theme, the G tremolo is retrospectively reconfigured as the fifth of C minor rather than the third of Eb; but for a moment Mahler had allowed a direct inflection of a minor triad to its parallel major. And in so doing he set up one of the symphony's most important leitmotifs — one that will resonate in his oeuvre far beyond this symphony, in fact.

The primitive inflection of minor to major or vice versa functions in Mahler as an elemental barometer of moods. The resolute upward inflection of Gb to G at the exposition repeat is mournfully mirrored at the analogous point at the exposition's close (eleven after fig. 6) by the downward inflection of B natural, the dominant's leading tone, to Bb (Ex. 1-4a). Even more pointed is the repetition of the mournful mirror in the recapitulation (seventeen after 23), where G♯ is inflected downward to the same G that had been produced the first time around by an upward inflection (Ex. 1-4b).

The reversal of direction links the motif with a much older symbolic use of the semitone — the ancient *Seufzer* or "sigh-figure" first described at the beginning of the seventeenth century by Joachim Burmeister, a theorist of musical rhetoric, who had

EX. 1-4A   Gustav Mahler, Symphony no. 2, I, mm. 107–108

EX. 1-4B   Gustav Mahler, Symphony no. 2, I, mm. 381–386

deduced it from the music of Lassus. (Also compare the sigh-figure that takes place within the tonic triad seven measures before the movement's end, precipitating the *Todtenfeier*'s last shudder.) The sigh-figures before fig. 6 and after fig. 23 serve to trigger the closing sections of the exposition and recapitulation respectively, in which another age-old half-step device, the basso ostinato reiterating a chromaticized descending fourth or *passus duriusculus* (a staple of the earliest operas), is conjured up to perform its appointed task as an emblem of lament. Needless to say, Mahler's immediate model was no seventeenth-century Venetian like Monteverdi or Cavalli, but rather the exactly analogous spot—the first-movement coda—in Beethoven's Ninth. And another simultaneous reverberation of ancient and recent pasts occurs in the midst of the development section (e.g., eight before fig. 17), when the Dies Irae, evoking not only primeval funerary rites but also the fantastical dream visions of Hector Berlioz's Symphonie fantastique (1830), rears up in the horns, marked *sehr bestimmt* (very distinct).

Digging up the most ancient of traditional expressive devices—here, affect-laden semitones and ritual cantus firmus tunes—and displaying them alongside the most modern variations of those same devices was another sort of maximalism, here recalling a maneuver associated with such works as Brahms's Haydn Variations, in which near and remote ancestors are "timelessly" associated and equated. Brahms dug back to the late seventeenth century for his remotest forebears; Mahler digs almost a century further back and juxtaposes his ancient trophies with even more up-to-the-minute modern equivalents. His "tradition" dwarfs Brahms's at both ends.

LYRISCHES INTERMEZZO

There remains one more aspect of maximalism to describe, and that is the colossally underscored contrast in mood, tempo, key, and orchestration that sets the *Todtenfeier*'s E-major "second theme" off from the first. (The use of scare quotes around "second theme" here signals that the theme so designated is not by any means literally the second melody to be heard, but rather the melody that expresses or embodies the movement's main secondary tonality.) This was a characteristic of late-nineteenth-century symphonic writing that Mahler seems deliberately to have enhanced so as to magnify the impression of a world-encompassing reach, or a reach into the inner world, where Weltanschauungs originate.

The history of the nineteenth-century symphony, or at least of one of its major strains, might well be told in terms of the progressive growth of the second theme to the point of virtual elephantiasis, such as now we find in Mahler. Beginning in Haydn as just a little touch-down on the dominant (for which purpose a repetition of the first theme might do just as well, as in Haydn's "London" Symphony, no. 104), the second theme had grown from the time of Schubert to that of Bruckner into a virtual "lyrisches Intermezzo," to put it in poetic terms borrowed from the title of a famous book of poems by Heine: a "lyrical interlude" signaling a retreat into a Schubertian "music trance," a state of subjective reverie in which the quality of time is radically transformed from one of purposeful progress to one of virtual suspension. Rhythm becomes less pulsatile, tempo is usually decreased. But even when the tempo is not explicitly relaxed, recourse to long-sustained notes, legato phrasing, and dilatory harmonic rhythm produce a subjective or psychological relaxation all the same.

Even Mozart's symphonies exhibit this lyrical tendency in distinction to Haydn's; even at the end of the eighteenth century the symphony could be seen as branching off into two strains that contrasted ever more radically over the course of the nineteenth. The previous lyrical benchmark had been set by Chaikovsky, in the first movement of his Sixth Symphony, the "Pathétique," already widely performed by the time Mahler's Second was first heard, and hence received by audiences as a precedent for it, even though Mahler's first movement was composed earlier. Chaikovsky's second theme — an expansive Andante displacing a nervous Allegro non troppo — takes the form of a fully self-sufficient, potentially detachable composition in its own right, preceded and followed by silence, with its own internal structure (involving subsections and subthemes) and its own fully articulated conclusion, completely dwarfing the rest of the exposition.

Mahler's second theme goes Chaikovsky's one better in that, while it is less fully developed in its initial expository statement, it continues to haunt the movement, lending the form a layer of strophic balladry (shades, after all, of Mickiewicz?) that crosscuts and complicates its linearly progressing "sonata form." Mahler, sketching, called the theme the *Gesang* — "the song" or "the singing" — as if to emphasize its Chaikovskian quality of lyrical intrusion. Its first (E major) appearance is cut off, as we have seen, after a mere fifteen bars. It unexpectedly reappears, having been cut out of the exposition repeat, at fig. 7, a sort of no-man's-land between exposition and development, in the key of C major (foreshadowing Elysium, as someone thinking of Beethoven's Ninth might guess), and lasting twice as long. Unlike most "second themes," it intrudes "dialectically" upon the development section at fig. 13, with a tempo marking (*etwas drängend*, "somewhat hurried") that contradicts its earlier character of respite and therefore seems all the more oppressively to signal anxiety.

The final appearance of the *Gesang*, ten bars after 22, restores its original character and key, and adds a few plagal cadences reminiscent of the final "redemptive" pages of Wagner's *Götterdämmerung*. But the major-minor inflection in Ex. 1-4b, encompassing two voices in imitation (G♯ to G in the horn, E to E♭ in the first violin), dispels all promise of redemption, and the movement ends in a bellow of despair.

What now follows is the most "maximal" moment of all: a command from the composer, "Here there must be a pause of at least five minutes' duration." Requiring of the audience that they sit still and contemplate what they have heard for five minutes is explicitly to require that they behave as they would in church. The *Todtenfeier* has stopped being a representation of a solemn rite and has actually become such a rite. Never had the sacralization of art — another process that can be traced over the course of the whole preceding century — been so graphically asserted and enforced.

While in terms of the sheer emphasis accorded it, Mahler's second theme is comparable to Chaikovsky's, its mood is quite different. Rather than passionately expressive it is vividly pastoral, even bucolic in quality, owing to the use of such additional stock illustrative "figures" as pedal tones (evocative of drones, hence of bagpipes) and "horn fifths" (evocative of rustic or primitive "natural brass"). In later symphonies like the Sixth (1904) and the Seventh (1905), Mahler reinforced the pastoral imagery of his "second themes" by actually including "cowbells" (*Heerdenglocken*), the bells placed since ancient times around the necks of cattle to prevent straying from the herd, among the percussion instruments in the orchestra.

This obsession with the pastoral and the primitive — and the association of such images with fleeting interludes of lyrical contemplation — is a common feature of early modernist art. It betokens the wistful irony of the thoroughly modern, thoroughly urban spirit, conscious of its separation from the "natural" world and alienated by that consciousness from its own stressful environment. This nostalgic obsession ran like a thread through Mahler's work over the course of his whole career — alas, a somewhat stunted career, since Mahler was very much the victim of its stresses, succumbing to heart disease shortly before his fifty-first birthday.

FOLKLORE FOR CITY FOLK

Another manifestation of that perennial obsession was Mahler's infatuation with *Des Knaben Wunderhorn* ("The youth's magic horn"), an anthology of German folk lyrics edited by two early romantic poets — Achim von Arnim (1781–1831) and his brother-in-law Clemens Brentano (1778–1842) — and published in three installments between 1805 and 1808. Between 1887 and 1901 Mahler set some two dozen *Wunderhorn* texts to music, some with full orchestral accompaniments, and even more tellingly, incorporated some of the same songs, and some newly composed ones, into the symphonies composed during the same period, namely the Second, Third, and Fourth.

It is sometimes wondered why no composer before Mahler took a comparable interest in the often exquisite poems in *Des Knaben Wunderhorn*, given that *Volkstümlichkeit* (folksiness), with its implied wisdom of innocence, was from the beginning such an important value for the German romantics. There are a few pre-Mahler settings of

Wunderhorn poems — by Carl Maria von Weber, Carl Loewe, Felix Mendelssohn, Robert Schumann, and Brahms among others — but Mahler practically specialized in them. To ask the question another way, why did so many composers of lieder, beginning with Franz Schubert or even his "Berlin School" predecessors, so avidly set Goethe's or Herder's artistic imitations of folk balladry and lyricism to music, but not "the real thing"? The answer seems to be that only the heightened sense of distance from the land and from its denizens brought on by the advent of modernism created the demand for an "authenticity" that only the folk original could supply; only modernity's quickened sense of loss (of innocence, of goodness, of well-being and peace) demanded the undiluted restorative powers of actual, rather than artistically adapted, folklore. That demand, sometimes called neoprimitivism, was another aspect of modernity that maximalized the romantic heritage.

Mahler's Second Symphony makes two references to the *Wunderhorn* collection. The third movement, the first of Mahler's famously grotesque scherzos, while an instrumental movement, is based throughout on the song *Des Antonius von Padua Fischpredigt* ("St. Anthony of Padua's sermon to the fishes"), composed in 1893 — or rather, on the song's madcap accompaniment (with only scattered references to the sung tune). And between the scherzo and the grandiose choral finale, Mahler interpolated in its entirety an orchestral song from the *Wunderhorn* set entitled *Urlicht* ("Primordial light"), a setting for alto solo that expresses a child's faith in salvation — the first of the promised "answers" to the oppressively urgent philosophical questions propounded by the *Todtenfeier*.

To anticipate a remark made by Claude Debussy, a French contemporary of Mahler's whom we will meet in the next chapter, about a work by Igor Stravinsky, a Russian neoprimitivist of the next generation, Mahler's *Urlicht* is "primitive music with all modern conveniences."[15] The harmony and orchestration that clothe its studied melodic simplicity are of an extreme sophistication, as are the subtly calculated metrical dislocations that lend an air of "spontaneity" to the performance. A piece like this one communicates a deeply ironic double message, proclaiming at once the urgent need for a return to simple values and the utter impossibility, at this late date, of ever achieving simplicity. The theatrical reconstruction of paradise lost contradicts the faith in progress that had led musical style to such a level of technical complexity. The naive sentiments wishfully manifested *in* the choice of text are contradicted by the shameless self-consciousness manifested *by* the choice. Nostalgia is perhaps the most modern and complicated — or in one word, the most modernist — of all emotions.

The symphony's finale is an all-stops-out attempt to surpass the finale of Beethoven's Ninth in every dimension: in length, in sonorous magnitude, and especially in philosophical depth. After a wild orchestral fantasy standing in lieu of Beethoven's *Schreckensfanfare*, a solo trombone sings a recitative (Ex. 1-5a), like the cellos and basses in the Ninth, that will later be repeated by a singer, with a text. It begins, fittingly enough, with a pair of bare *Seufzern* or sigh-figures.

After the chorus sings the *geistliche Lied* or sacred hymn — *Aufersteh'n*, "Resurrection" — by the religious poet Friedrich Klopstock (1724–1803), from which the

EX. I-5A Gustav Mahler, Symphony no. 2, V, trombone solo at fig. 21

EX. I-5B Gustav Mahler, Symphony no. 2, V, alto solo at fig. 39

O glau - be, mein Herz——— o glau - be

symphony draws its occasional subtitle, the alto soloist returns to re-sing the trombone's recitative to words of Mahler's own (Ex. 1-5b), which begin with an exhortation: "O glaube, mein Herz, o glaube!" (Believe it, my heart, believe it!). The admonition to believe puts Mahler's own verses at a great distance from Beethoven or Klopstock, to say nothing of the anonymous poets in *Des Knaben Wunderhorn*, who needed no such instruction.

But then they had never been faced with a set of questions like those propounded by the *Todtenfeier*. By the age of early modernism, mankind's lot was doubt. The symphony's apocalyptic conclusion, in which Mahler's verses pass in a steady crescendo from the alto to the soprano, thence to the chorus, and finally to a colossal orchestral tutti augmented by the organ, can be experienced either as an ecstatic renewal of faith in spite of everything or as a desperate effort to drown out doubt. But there can be no innocence. Nothing—least of all style or rhetoric—will ever again be taken for granted. Tradition is aging. It will not age gracefully. Rather, it will become preoccupied with what the great early-modernist novelist Marcel Proust (1871–1922), in the all-encompassing title of a long series of novels, called "la recherche du temps perdu." Literally the phrase means "the quest for lost time." What it really amounts to is the doomed attempt to reexperience youth. As well as any single phrase could hope to do, it encapsulates the whole history of music in the twentieth century.

WHAT THEN?

The ultimate failure of maximalism as a means of renewal, however great or valuable its products, was implicit in its very premises. Eventually limits are discovered. The maximalist boundary for symphonies (according to the authority in such matters, the *Guinness Book of World Records*) was set by the English composer Havergal Brian (1876–1972). His Symphony no. 2 (later renumbered as no. 1), the "Gothic," completed in 1927, lasts somewhere over 100 minutes and requires 55 brass instruments in four antiphonal bands; 31 woodwinds; six kettle-drummers playing 22 drums; additional percussion including wind machine, thunder machine, and rattling chains; four vocal soloists; four large mixed choruses; a children's chorus; and an organ. The last movement is an oratorio in itself—a complete setting of the Te Deum, the Christian hymn of victory. It was not performed until 1961, when the composer was eighty-five, and has had only two performances since then, which already suggests one of the pitfalls of maximalism.

Mahler himself exceeded his Second Symphony in length only once, in the Third, which requires a boys' choir (the very symbol of "lost time"!) on top of everything else and lasts more than ninety minutes (the first movement alone clocking over three-quarters of an hour). His Eighth Symphony (1906), known as the "Symphony of a Thousand," was the biggest in terms of performing medium. An oratorio in all but name, scored for a full complement of vocal soloists, plus chorus and orchestra, it contains no purely instrumental music at all. Rather, its two movements consist respectively of a setting of the medieval Latin hymn *Veni, creator spiritus* and a setting of the mystical closing pages of the second part of Goethe's *Faust*. But even before composing it, Mahler had called off the maximalist quest, at least in terms of dimensions. His Fourth Symphony, lasting about fifty minutes and requiring only a soprano soloist in addition to the orchestra, was by Mahlerian standards a miniature. Except for the Eighth, it was also his last numbered symphony to employ voices.

There were, however, many ways of being maximalist, and some of them could not be so easily called off. Maximalism of emotional intensity, the aspect that exercised Pound, continued to preoccupy Mahler to the end. Consider the Tenth Symphony in F♯ major, his last. It was left unfinished at his death, with only the first movement, a lengthy Adagio, fully scored. Often interpreted, owing in part to its pervadingly homophonic texture (and to some marginalia discovered by its posthumous editors), as a love song to the composer's wife, the movement alternates between dulcet and agonized extremes — as did the marriage, apparently: as much a part of the Mahler legend as his walk with Brahms was a later walk he took in Amsterdam with Sigmund Freud, the founder of psychoanalysis, in which his marital problems were the main topic of conversation.

The most turbulent interlude is one near the end, in A♭ minor. In itself the key is not as outlandish as it may seem: it is just the ordinary supertonic of F♯ major spelled enharmonically. The passage that links this episode with the movement's last section, in the original tonic, functions as a "retransition," which means that it must provide a modulatory link between ii and I.

That link is obviously going to be V — but what a V! The passage is given in Ex. 1-6a in orchestral score. Ex. 1-6b is nothing but a single-staff transcription of the functional dominant chord, presented as Mahler presents it, in two stages, with all the parts for transposing instruments rendered "in C" for ease of reading. The bottom five notes consist of an ordinary "dominant ninth" on C♯, the ordinary fifth degree. But to convey an affect sufficient to the composer's expressive needs, a thirteenth (spelled A natural), a "diminished fifteenth" (C natural), a "diminished seventeenth" (E♭) and even a "diminished nineteenth" (G natural) are piled atop the chord, producing a searingly dissonant dominant harmony containing nine different pitches. Who knows what Guido Adler, for whom the Second and Third Symphonies already contained "unprecedented cacophonies," might have called it?

EX. 1-6A Gustav Mahler, Symphony no. 10, Adagio, fig. 27 to fig. 29

EX. 1-6A (*continued*)

EX. I-6B   Gustav Mahler, Symphony no. 10, Adagio, fig. [27] to fig. [29], analytical reduction

Even within Mahler's own output, then, we can observe the pressure to maximalize, to exceed all limits and precedents. Where a "dominant thirteenth" had sufficed as a point of maximum tension in the Second Symphony, the Tenth required a "dominant nineteenth." How much further could this procedure go? In one sense the answer is easy: three more notes can be added to the chord before all the available pitches (or "pitch classes") in the tuning system of Western classical music will have been used up. Then what?

Moreover, as Mahler's omissions from his "V_{19}" suggest, the remaining three pitches might not have produced any further maximalization of the dominant function within the key of F♯ major. Omitted (along with E) are F♯ itself and A♯, the essential definers of the tonic triad; include them in the preceding chord and there can be no sense of progression to them, whether by fifth or by semitone. In the event, of course, the actual progression linking the maximalized dominant chord with the tonic turns on a semitone—A (the "thirteenth") to A♯—rather than a fifth. We can say "of course" because we have seen its like before, in the first movement of the Second Symphony, the *Todtenfeier*. There, too, we recall, the V – I progressions, few and far between, were mainly reserved for big rhetorical effects, or to provide formal signposts. The real harmonic work was done by semitone progressions.

So we are not surprised to find that, having made its rhetorical and form-defining point, the gigantic V_{19} in the Tenth Symphony is gradually "liquidated," leaving only the A in the trumpet and a D natural in the cellos (nominally the ninth of the chord) to resolve outward in contrary motion to a tonic $^6_4$ that returns along with the main theme in the violins to signify tonal relaxation. This is hardly a conventional usage for a $^6_4$ chord, and tonal relaxation has a way to go before the piece can end. But the truly effective and *functional* harmonic move has been the one executed by semitones, not fifths. Fifths, by now, have had their day.

The A – A♯ link is all the more efficacious because it is "motivic." Ex. I-7 shows the very beginning of the Adagio, an enigmatically chromatic "recitative" for the violas ending on the same A natural, which then resolves cadentially into the A♯ with which the first violins' "aria" begins. Comparison with Mahler's *particell* draft (Fig. I-3) shows that the editor who prepared the Adagio for posthumous publication, thinking primarily of the players' ease in reading, failed to respect Mahler's fastidious orthography, according to which both the A natural and the G natural that precedes it are notated as "tendency tones," namely the sixth and seventh degrees (F𝄪 and G𝄪) of a putative "melodic minor" scale on A♯.

The long-held A natural that makes cadential resolution to A♯ in Ex. I-6 is likewise conceptually a G𝄪. Throughout the score, and cumulatively over the course of his career, Mahler had been executing a retreat from the circle of fifths toward the unmediated chromatic scale as the generator and governor of harmonic functions. With that move went a concomitant one that located essential harmonic relations on the melodic surface rather than assigning them to the bass. These moves were not Mahler's

EX. 1-7 Gustav Mahler, Symphony no. 10, Adagio, mm. 1–24

alone. They were pervasive among Germanic composers of "emotional" music (to recall Pound's terminology). German composers increasingly became "semitone composers," fascinated to the point of obsession with what the critic Theodor Wiesengrund Adorno called the "smallest link."[16]

The heightened subjective expressivity that these harmonic devices were developed to serve — a maximalized romanticism that would eventually be dubbed "expressionism" — led to one more stylistic feature of which Mahler was a pioneer. That is the lyric or "singing" line that transcends the human singing range by means of huge melodic leaps to tensely expressive appoggiaturas — that is, "tendency tones" in need of resolution by semitone. The violin "aria" in Mahler's Adagio, shown in both Ex. 1-7

EX. 1-7   (*continued*)

FIG. 1-3   Adagio from Mahler's Tenth Symphony, first page of *particell* or sketch score.

and Fig. 1-3, is an epitome of the technique. Listeners had never before encountered so thoroughly disjunct a melody, nor such large leaps to "nonharmonic" tones (or the complementary move, resolutions accompanied by octave displacements). This is the familiar "yearning" (*Sehnsucht*) of romanticism, long associated with Schubert, already given a famous maximalization by Wagner, and now, in Mahler and his contemporaries, entering a phase that was widely described as "decadent."

DECADENCE

The novel use of semitonal adjacencies gave easy access to (formerly) exotic or recondite harmonies and tonal relations. Ultimately they became commonplace, hence no longer exotic or recondite: the extraordinary, so to speak, became ordinary. And that is a fine way of approaching musically the notoriously slippery term and concept of "decadence."

It was introduced in the mid-1880s into discussions of art and life and their interrelationship, most notably in the novel *À rebours* ("Against the grain", sometimes translated as "Against Nature", 1884) by Joris-Karl Huysmans (1848–1907), a French writer of Dutch descent, whose sickly aristocratic artist-hero Des Esseintes was the very embodiment of rarefied, artificial, esoteric, exacting taste. His favorite music, we learn in one revealing aside, was the "emaciated" Gregorian chant, from which everything afterward (excepting only Schubert's lieder, or some few of them) has been a comedown, an "impurity." There was something of the "Brahmin" in him, too, as that term was used during the fin de siècle to denote snobbishly discriminating taste, recalling as it did both the ultra-sophisticated music of Brahms and the highest caste of Hindu society. Des Esseintes avoided secular music because it was

> a promiscuous art, in that you cannot enjoy it at home, by yourself, as you can a book; to savor it he would have had to join the mob of inveterate theater-goers that fills the Cirque d'Hiver, where under a broiling sun and in a stifling atmosphere you can see a hulking brute of a man waving his arms about and massacring disconnected snatches of Wagner to the huge delight of an ignorant crowd. He had never had the courage to plunge into this mob-bath.[17]

But compared with him a mere Brahmin was incorrigibly bourgeois and conventional. Fatally jaded and misanthropic, Des Esseintes is repelled by anything "natural" (meaning anything vigorous or "normally" healthy) and fatally attracted to risky behavior of all kinds — "substance abuse" (as we would call it now), including nightly expurgation with enemas; nightmarish sexual encounters ("unnatural loves and perverse pleasures"); defiance of conventional ("bourgeois") hygiene. In 1886 the German psychiatrist Richard von Krafft-Ebing, in a famous treatise called *Psychopathia Sexualis* ("Mental illness related to sex"), coined the term *masochism* from the name of Leopold von Sacher-Masoch (1836–95), a popular novelist whose characters exhibit many "inversions," including the inversion of hedonism to which the medical term referred: like Des Esseintes, Masoch's characters experience pleasure or sexual arousal on being subjected to pain or humiliation, which they therefore seek out.

Friedrich Nietzsche, who described himself intermittently as a decadent, defined the condition in 1888 as that of "instinctively choosing what is harmful for oneself."[18] But of course he was jesting; instinct had nothing to do with it. To be decadent was to revel in artificiality and affectation, in "learned behavior" and "acquired taste," in doing things "on purpose" and fastidiously avoiding anything that was immediately pleasurable or popular.

The Picture of Dorian Gray, a novella by the Irish esthete Oscar Wilde (1854–1900), contains a tribute to an unnamed *À rebours* and the effect it made on its readers. As the title character describes it, "it seemed to him that in exquisite raiment and to the delicate sound of flutes, the sins of the world were passing in dumb show before him: things that he had dimly dreamed of were suddenly made real to him; things of which he had never dreamed were gradually revealed."[19] The book, formerly passed from hand to hand in rarefied artistic circles, became scandalously famous when Wilde was forced by the prosecutor to identify it during his 1895 trial for homosexuality. It was then that "decadent" subject matter became a selling point for artworks appealing to the broad "bourgeois" public. Decadence was opened up, so to speak, for the tourist trade, and that is where the musicians came in.

For preliminary—mild and pretty—illustrations we can turn to two very early works by Strauss and Schoenberg respectively. They are tiny pieces, showing that maximalism, in the form of concentrated effect, can coexist perfectly well with brevity—indeed, as we will see later, there was eventually a race toward the limits of compression, just as there had previously been one toward the limits of extension.

Maximalism is above all a highly competitive phenomenon, as was decadence once it went public. As to compression, Wilde said it best when describing a cigarette as "the perfect pleasure: it is exquisite, and it leaves one unsatisfied."[20] Strauss's little *Rêverie* (or *Träumerei*) for piano, op. 9, no. 4 (Ex. 1-8), comes from a set of pieces called *Stimmungsbilder* ("Mood pictures"), composed between 1882 and 1884, when the precociously gifted composer was in his late teens. It would be his last published work for piano. Except for lieder, which he produced abundantly throughout his career, Strauss's primary media were the largest: first the symphonic poem (which he rechristened *Tondichtung*, "tone poem," a term that has taken firm hold in English), of which he wrote ten between 1886 and 1915; and later opera, of which he wrote fifteen between 1892 and 1941.

The main thematic substance of the *Rêverie* consists not of a tune but of a chord progression, announced at the very beginning of the piece and endlessly repeated until it sounds "normal." It is an oscillation between an arpeggiated tonic triad and a chord consisting entirely of semitonal adjacencies—"chromatic neighbors"—over a tonic pedal. As a "vertical" entity the chord cannot be classified, but as a contrapuntal event

EX. 1-8   Richard Strauss, *Rêverie*, Op. 9, no. 4

EX. 1-8   *(continued)*

its function (which means its immediate future) could not be clearer: it's got to go back where it came from, and nowhere else.

As the Russian composer Rimsky-Korsakov once told a disciple who asked him the name of a similarly unclassifiable chromatic chord in one of his works, "I don't actually know what kind of chord this is exactly; I only know that it has three resolutions . . . ."[21] Harmony is as harmony does. It has become contextual rather than strictly functional. It governs only immediate connections, not overall coherence (which must be supplied, if desired, by other means). Imagine a harmonic texture in which all or most of the connections are like the one at the beginning of Strauss's *Rêverie* and you will understand "decadence." You will have imagined, in fact, the harmonic texture of Strauss's early operas.

Before turning to them, let us stop to admire Schoenberg's *Erwartung* ("Anticipation"), op. 2, no. 1 (Ex. 1-9), written in 1899 (when the composer was twenty-three) to a poem by Richard Dehmel (1863–1920), a writer who by virtue of his risqué subject matter and extravagant imagery also enjoyed a reputation as a "decadent." The poem Schoenberg selected depicts a man, hoping for a sexual encounter, standing amid an exotic, possibly "oriental," landscape; his senses are quickened in anticipation, strangely alive to shifting lights and colors, darting movements, tactile sensations. The poem's explicit play of complementary colors — green against red, the implied black of a dead oak against the implied white of the moon — stimulates the reader's own sensory awareness, fulfilling the poet's aim to "make poetic technique more sensuous by incorporating painterly and musical effects."[22] The strategy for capturing a sensually charged moment of erotic arousal like the one evoked in *Erwartung* was to "associate a color word with a particularly strong upwelling of a psychological state."

To achieve a comparably sensual effect in his music Schoenberg resorts to a technique almost identical to the one Strauss had used in his *Rêverie* (which Schoenberg almost certainly knew), but in a slightly more radical (yes, maximalized) manner. The first two colors named in the poem are accompanied by an ear-tingling "color-chord" — an unclassifiable, mildly dissonant, but still triadic harmony consisting of semitonal neighbors to the tones of the initial E♭-major tonic triad, plus a tonic pedal. In m. 4, where the black/white pair is mentioned, the color-chord is inverted and transposed down a fifth, and cleverly "resolved" to a dominant ninth on G that can function as an applied dominant to a new tonic, so that the whole color-progression can be repeated on C, a Lisztian minor third away (Ex. 1-9).

The play between the purely coloristic (or static) variant of the novel chord and the semi-"functional" (or progressing) one gives the music a restlessness that adds significantly (and beyond the power of words) to the affect of the poem. The whole middle section (mm. 11–17), in which the darting reflections of green and red in the man's opal ring are described, consists musically of a sequence of semifunctional progressions from the color chord to dominant ninths, only some of which are allowed to resolve functionally.

The return to the tonic is made not by way of the dominant, but by way of a seemingly "remote" dominant seventh on B major (enharmonically contained in the color-chord) that resolves in mm. 17–18 by "outward" semitonal resolution in the fashion of an augmented-sixth chord. The long-sustained tonic $^6_4$ harmony in mm. 21–22 does not proceed to the tonic by way of the dominant, but by way of the color-chord, which returns unexpectedly in m. 23 to accompany the longed-for apparition at the window of the lover's hand. The music almost palpably tickles.

The affect, and the musical techniques that evoke it, are (perhaps needless to say) related to those in *Tristan und Isolde*; but Schoenberg's sensuality, unlike Wagner's, no longer needs the mask (or excuse) of philosophy or religion. Like its sister arts at the fin de siècle, music has begun to shed its shame over sex. The world is sexy, it seems to imply, as did the creators of a highly decorative and curvaceous pictorial approach called *Jugendstil* or "youth style" (named after *Jugend*, a Munich arts magazine—see Fig. 1-4). That sexiness, *Jugendstil* implied, need not carry a heavy

EX. 1-9   Arnold Schoenberg, *Erwartung*, Op. 2, no. 1, mm. 1–23

EX. 1-9 (continued)

burden of passion or spirituality. Delight in it, as modern psychologists now say, can be "polymorphously perverse"—unrestricted to those sexual functions and acts that straightforwardly promote procreation, just as chords do not have to connect in ways that straightforwardly produce a functional cadence, so long as their succession gives pleasure.

FIG. 1-4 *Jugenstil*: Theodor Thomas Heine, *Serpentinentänzerin* (Dancing Girl Doing Wavy Figures, 1900). The dancer depicted is the American Loie Fuller, who made a specialty of "serpentine dancing" and created a sensation in fin-de-siècle Europe.

A lessening of shame and an acceptance of perversity together constituted another definition of "decadence," of course, especially popular with the many who equated it then and since with moral (or in extreme cases, with genetic) degeneracy. We might approach an understanding of decadence — or at least perversity — by imagining a child at play with an "erector set." For a while, if intelligent and interested, or at least well-behaved, the child will follow the instruction book and connect the pieces "structurally," producing the expected buildings and bridges. Later, however, in order to maintain interest, the child might start connecting the pieces with one another in ways the instruction book does not prescribe, creating weird shapes that have no practical application, but give pleasure (to the maker, at least). Really curious children might even stick the pieces in places their mothers might not care to hear about.

And so it was with harmonic connections. Where the instruction books continued to prescribe the circle of fifths, composers happily experimented with semitones or other "interval cycles," producing progressions that evoked sensations, as one composer proudly put it, of "iridescent silk"[23] (shades of Dehmel's opals!), or as his father complained, of having "your trousers full of crawling June bugs."

STRAUSS: MAXIMALIZING OPERA

The composer was Richard Strauss, describing the music of his one-act (but full-evening) opera *Salome* (1905), a verbatim setting of a preexisting play by Oscar Wilde (1893), originally written in French and published in Paris. That the play, and consequently the music, had a lot to do with perverse sex — and that the task of representing sexual perversity motivated the musical innovations — can go practically without saying. Wilde's play — one of many representations of the celebrated dancing princess in many artistic media that cropped up at the fin de siècle — was already a benchmark of decadence by the time Strauss set it. That is precisely what attracted the composer, whether in the disinterested pursuit of new musical beauties or (as many insinuated) in pursuit of reichsmarks. (But of course, and as usual, the only evidence of his venality was his commercial success.) The basis of the play, ironically enough, was the Holy Bible. Two of the Gospels contain the story of Herod the king and John the Baptist, given here in the somewhat shorter version of Matthew (14:3–12), according to the New English Bible:

> Now Herod had arrested John, put him in chains, and thrown him into prison, on account of Herodias, his brother Philip's wife [whom he desired for himself]; for John had told him: "You have no right to her." Herod would have liked to put him to death, but he was afraid of the people, in whose eyes John was a prophet. But at his birthday celebrations the daughter of Herodias danced before the guests, and Herod was so delighted that he took an oath to give her anything she cared to ask. Prompted by her mother, she said, "Give me here on a dish the head of John the Baptist." The king was distressed when he heard it; but out of regard for his oath and for his guests, he ordered the request to be granted, and had John beheaded in prison. The head was brought in on a dish and given to the girl; and she carried it to her mother.

The name Salome (in history Herod's daughter-in-law) was attached by tradition to his dancing niece. In Wilde's version she is a breathtakingly beautiful maiden over whom desperate men are shown committing suicide, but who cares for no one — that is, until she spies the filthy, emaciated John the Baptist in his cell and conceives an enormous desire for him. She asks for a kiss and is angrily rebuffed. After her "Dance of the Seven Veils" (that is, her striptease) before the king, she asks for the prophet's head not so much to avenge her mother's honor (or her own) as to slake her passion. She dances orgiastically with the bloody severed head and, delirious with desire, kisses it on the mouth (Fig. 1-6); upon which Herod, scandalized and nauseated by her necrophilia, has her put straightaway to death.

Strauss's music raised eyebrows even higher than the play, both for the obvious ways in which it intensified the play's challenge to conventional morality, and for the novelty of its technical procedures — at once inscrutable and yet uncannily effective, hence (like *Tristan*) disquieting, but (unlike *Tristan*) depicting a passion no one in the audience could admit to identifying with. applied for permission to give the premiere in Vienna, but was refused by the city fathers in the name of public morals. (The actual premiere took place on 9 December 1905 in Dresden.) Mahler made Schoenberg the gift of the vocal score, and one of Schoenberg's pupils, Egon Wellesz, happened in on him while he was taking his first look at the opening pages (Ex. 1-10), and heard him marveling that it

FIG. 1-5 Richard Strauss working on his opera *Die schweigsame Frau* (The Silent Woman) at his villa outside Munich, 1932.

FIG. 1-6 Aubrey Beardsley (1872–1898), *The Climax*, illustration for Oscar Wilde's *Salome* (1893).

would be twenty years before anyone would be able to figure out by what principle they were composed.[24]

In all likelihood Schoenberg figured out what we are about to discover in twenty minutes, not twenty years, but by then Wellesz had left and the story stood. On the face of it, the chord progressions seem altogether arbitrary, though sensuously alluring in the extreme, suitably expressing the first lines of the text: first the lovesick Narraboth's exclamation, "How fair is the princess Salome tonight," immediately juxtaposed with the Page's comparison of the pale moon (shades of Richard Dehmel!) with a woman rising from a tomb, a vision a true decadent—but only a true decadent—would surely find voluptuous.

The four-sharps signature defines the key as C♯ minor, and that is indeed the first harmony we hear; but in m. 2 a sixth is added and in m. 3—lo!—both the third and the sixth are transformed ("like iridescent silk") into the major to accompany Narraboth's rapture. In m. 4, the top note of the chord pushes up to a seventh, creating a need for resolution; but the next measure evades the expected closure with a curious deceptive cadence in which not only the root and fifth but also the seventh(!) move up a semitone in parallel motion. At the same time, the E♯ in m. 4 moves down to E natural, providing the new chord with a ninth. A semitonal expansion in the outer voices of m. 6—top up to C♯, bottom down to A♭—produces a dissonant harmony with no traditional classification but definitely with somewhere to go (that is, with a "function"): resolving by a further outward expansion, the augmented third moves to a perfect fifth, and G is established as the chord root.

By the downbeat of m. 8, that chord has been replaced by a rootless augmented triad (albeit with the seventh of the G chord hanging on to produce a sort of whole-tone cluster, and the fifth continuing as a sort of pedal). Measure 9 brings a strange surprise: resolution to B minor, perhaps the last destination anyone could have expected, but justified (or at least made consistent with the rest) by the voice leading—a semitonal expansion hidden among the inner voices: F to F♯ vs. E♭ to D. Nor could anyone have expected the arrival of F major in m. 11, but its root is the result of an ascending semitone, and the D♭ in the highest part, while ostensibly not a chord tone, is approached via a complementary descending semitone, from D. So while anyone attempting to relate the ostensible triadic root progression thus far—C♯–D–G–B–F—to the tonic of C♯ minor will inevitably end up as bewildered as Schoenberg apparently was when

EX. I-IOA   Richard Strauss, *Salome*, mm. 1–16

Wellesz discovered him, there is indeed a consistent principle of voice leading driving the harmonic succession.

That principle is "semitonal expansion/contraction" as we may somewhat clumsily dub it, and it operates in other places on the first page as well, including the voice parts. Note Narraboth's ostensible A-minor arpeggio on a rather significant word ("Salome!") in m. 5, proceeding to a rising sixth ("heute Nacht") from Ab to F — that is, from a semitone below to a semitone above the limits of the triad. And now look at mm. 13–16, where the Page's image of the woman rising from the tomb is accompanied by a harmonic progression proceeding in the opposite direction, from F minor (subsuming the Ab and the F from above) to A minor. We have witnessed the derivation of a leitmotif, in fact: a chord progression that will accompany future associations of "sex object" and "death." The first such explicit association comes shortly afterward when the Page compares Salome's pale complexion to that of a corpse, and the orchestra obliges with the F minor/A minor progression (Ex. 1-10b).

The opening harmonies are also a leitmotif. They return to accompany Salome's first entrance (Ex. 1-11a), at a quicker harmonic rhythm that exposes even more clearly the chromatic lines in contrary motion that generate the harmony: on successive downbeats, the top voice in the orchestra part proceeds E♯–E–E♭–D–C♯ and the bass proceeds C♯–D–E♭–E, lacking only a concluding E♯ to produce a complete and literal criss-cross (or in fancy terminology, a "chiasmus," from the Greek). A complementary representation of the chiasmus (complete in the bass, lacking one member in the soprano) comes at the point where the teasing Salome inveigles the lovesick Narraboth to produce the imprisoned John the Baptist for her inspection (Ex. 1-11b). Counting by pairs of measures, the tops of the sustained orchestral chords yield E♯–E–E♭–D (the last note notated in the vocal score under an F♯ coming from an orchestral countermelody), and the bass goes the full distance: C♯–D–E♭–E–E♯(F).

The longest semitonal chiasmus in the score (Ex. 1-12a) goes through nine progressions out of a possible twelve. It takes place during the scene of flirtation between Herod and Salome leading up to her dance. The intervals here expand rather than contract (so that the chiasmus goes in the opposite direction), and it begins and ends on intervals we have not yet observed in such a context. But beginning with the

EX. 1-10B   Richard Strauss, *Salome*, mm. 24–26

EX. I-IIA   Richard Strauss, *Salome*, Salome's first entrance (fig. 20)

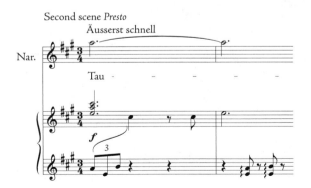

EX. I-IIB Richard Strauss, *Salome*, Salome teases Narraboth (two before fig. 57)

second chord it reproduces in reversed order all the "simultaneities" we have already witnessed: E/D, E♭/E♭, D/E, D♭/F (=C♯/E♯). In short, it is an especially long segment of what we might take hypothetically to be the "master array" of intervals, all linked by semitonal expansion/contraction, that served Strauss as a harmonic blueprint for constructing this masterpiece of maximalized decadence (Ex. 1-12b).

EX. 1-12A   Richard Strauss, *Salome*, Herod flirts with Salome (4 before fig. 179)

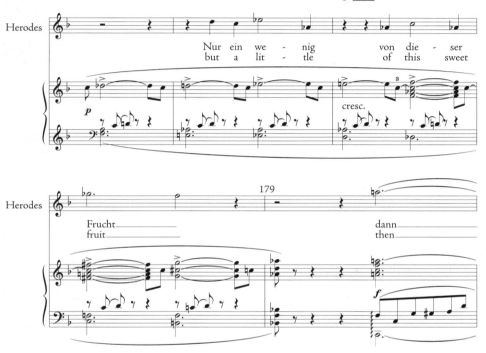

EX. 1-12B   Harmonic abstract of semitonal chiasmus (the "master array")

Minute analysis of the score will confirm the hypothesis: our "master array" is indeed the opera's harmonic plan, one that owes nothing at all to the circle of fifths, but that, while maintaining the "phonology" or sound-vocabulary of triadic functional harmony, connects the chords in polymorphously perverse fashion by variously "filling in" the semitonally linked intervals in the array. Authentic ("V–I") cadences in *Salome* are in fact exceedingly rare, and mainly serve a "ceremonial" function—as a symbol for decisive action, for example, or of resoluteness or rectitude in contrast to the pervading lasciviousness. (Needless to say, Saint John the Baptist gets most of them.) The As and E♭s in Ex. 1-12b are represented as "whole notes" as opposed to the black note-heads otherwise employed, because they are the points at which the master array "resolves" to perfect consonances (unisons or octaves). The intervals formed between the voices on either side of the E♭ are precisely the same, but the relationship between the voices is inverted and the order is reversed. Thus the two octave pitches form a potential tonal axis (or axis of symmetry) at the tritone, the exact midpoint of the chromatic scale. Strauss does not exploit this feature to any very appreciable degree in *Salome*, but he will exploit it to the hilt in his next opera, which is therefore, and to that precise extent, a more radical or maximalistic work than its predecessor. The race to the patent office continues. Modernists and maximalists compete not only with each other but with themselves. Each work must show "progress."

CONSUMMATION

What little there is of "axis music" in *Salome* is found, of course, in the last scene. "Of course," because the music for this scene, in which the title character gets her man — or at any rate the desired part of him — and gets to consummate her "unnatural love" and reap "perverse pleasure" to the full, will have to reach its own maximum in musical perversity, which is to say in illicit but pleasurable connections. It all reaches a head in the last half-dozen pages of the score, Salome's perverted *Liebestod*.

The music we are about to examine consists almost entirely of material drawn from the "Dance of the Seven Veils," presented in a maximalistically distorted form, even as the parent material had itself been an "orientalist" distortion of a few significant leitmotifs, some of them by now familiar. The harmonic background to the oboe's "snake-charmer" tune at the beginning of the Dance, for example, recalls the A minor/F minor oscillation that we have been taught to associate with linked thoughts of sex and death; but the F-minor component has been transformed into a voluptuous four-note whole-tone cluster (the augmented triad G-B-E♭ hovering over an octave-doubled bass F) that straddles the ground between a dominant ninth and a French sixth (Ex. 1-13a).

EX. 1-13A   Richard Strauss, *Salome*, Salome's dance, beginning

EX. 1-13B   Richard Strauss, *Salome*, Salome's dance, first violins at 3 before [L]

(John the Baptist motif)

EX. 1-13C   Richard Strauss, *Salome*, Salome's dance, first violins at 3 after [R]

Thereafter the Dance consists of a number of linked sections at increasingly fast tempos, each initiated by the dropping of another layer of clothing. Three motifs, derived from the themes of two of these sections, are slated for recapitulation in the climactic scene (Exx. 1-13b, 1- 13c).

The first place to look, perhaps, to see what Strauss is up to in the final pages, is the exchange (a typical "mad scene" exchange, redolent of familiar precedents in favorite Italian operas like Donizetti's *Lucia di Lammermoor*) between Salome and the high wood-winds in Ex. 1-14a. Both phrases are derived from motif "c" in Ex. 1-13. They are pitched a tritone apart, according to an axis of symmetry like the one illustrated in Ex. 1-12b. If we take them to be arpeggios, the roots of the triads they describe are B♭ and E, respectively.

And now compare the accompanying harmony: as notated in the organ part, on which Ex. 1-14a is based, the basic harmony is C♯ minor, significant for two reasons. First, because it was the tonality that opened the opera, showing Strauss to be still sensitive, perhaps surprisingly, to the requirement for traditional tonal closure. But second (and in local terms perhaps more important), C♯ is equidistant from E and B♭, the two axis tones. It bisects their difference, just as the tritone itself bisects the octave. And the two remaining tones in the organ part, F✗ and A♯, though camouflaged here as an appoggiatura and an "added sixth" respectively, can be read as the root and third of a G-minor triad, standing at the tritone from, and thus challenging, the "basic harmony," and also bisecting the E-B♭ "axis tritone" on the other side, as it were.

EX. 1-14A   Richard Strauss, *Salome*, final scene, adaptation of organ part at "Auf deinen Lippen"

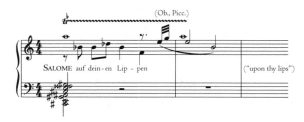

EX. 1-14B   Richard Strauss, *Salome*, final scene, "Was tut's?"

The four roots, E – G – B♭ – C♯, could be said to describe a diminished seventh chord; perhaps more pertinently, they describe a symmetrically apportioned division of the octave of a kind that will become exceedingly prevalent in the music of the "maximalist" or early modernist period, challenging and (in the work of quite a few composers) eventually supplanting diatonic scales and circles of fifths as primary avenues of harmonic navigation. To the ear, especially when its components are distinguished, as here, by timbres, symmetrical arrays can present themselves as mixtures of conventional harmonies, a device now often referred to as "polytonality" (although the term was not coined until the 1920s). Such mixtures can either clash, to produce violent effects, or blend, to produce effects of uncanny bittersweetness.

Strauss employs both kinds of mixture in the final pages of *Salome*. When, in her necrophiliac ecstasy, she actually sings of the bitter taste of love on the sweet lips of the severed head, Strauss actually pits motif "b" from Ex. 1-13 in imitation with itself at the tritone (on D♯[E♭] and A, the original axis pair!) over an F♯ root, against which the pitches of the three-note pickups (A♯[B♭] and E, the other axis pair) are heard as the third and seventh respectively. The combination (Ex. 1-14b) produces a sort of F♯ seventh chord that bears a lot of affect-laden freight reminiscent of the opera's opening: a double-inflected (major/minor) third and an added sixth. Whether it is "truly" a polychord, or a contrapuntal relationship colored by a pedal, is not something that can be (or need be) decided. Both readings of the harmony isolate particular elements that only in their unique conjunction (or *Gestaltung*, "configuration," to use the word Strauss might have used) create the weird affect of perversity in which the listener is being invited to participate.

The strongest stuff comes last. After Salome's final line ("I've kissed you on your mouth"), as she stands in a passion-trance with the bloody head pressed to her lips (and, according to the stage directions, with the moon lighting up her pale cadaverous form with a greater intensity than ever of white light, the sex-death color), the orchestra screams out motif "a" from Ex. 1-13b in a final orgiastic cadence. It reaches its earsplitting dynamic peak immediately before the unmistakable resolution to C♯ major at 361, on a chord about which more ink has been spilled than about any other single harmony in the opera. What has made it so seemingly inscrutable (yet compelling!) can be immediately apprehended by looking at the bottom two staves of the full score (Ex. 1-15a) and noting the A♯ in the cellos, playing the melody (doubled at the octave by the violins and various winds and brass), and the A natural in the double basses (also massively doubled by tuba, bass trombone, contrabassoon) against which it so violently clashes.

EX. 1-15A   Richard Strauss, *Salome*, ending in full score

EX. 1-15B   Richard Strauss, *Salome*, ending in piano reduction

Here the piano reduction (Ex. 1-15b) will tell us more than the full score, or at least tell us more quickly, because it represents the harmony the way in which Strauss's hands on the keyboard probably discovered it: F♯ major in the right hand against an incomplete dominant seventh on A in the left. These chords can be related to one another by invoking the "master array" in Ex. 1-12b. The F♯ bisects the distance between the "whole notes" (A and E♭). But such an analysis, while certainly demonstrable, may in this case be gratuitous; for it does not take the obvious and powerful cadential function of the chord into account. Applied to the tonic to which it proceeds, the F♯ major triad is IV, the ordinary subdominant. If the harmony were unmixed, we would call the cadence "plagal."

And maybe we should call it plagal anyway, since the left-hand component also has a time-honored cadential relationship to C♯ major: respell the G as F𝄪 and we are dealing with an "Italian" augmented sixth chord, whose normal cadential function would be registered as ♭VI. Both IV and ♭VI normally move to V; they are "predominants" in authentic cadences. Since they have the same tonal function, since (to put it another way) they are functionally interchangeable in preparing an authentic cadence, then their mixture can be understood, just like the mixed harmonies in Mahler's Second Symphony, as an intensification of the function in question. Thus Strauss's mixed harmony, like Mahler's, is no "polytonal" configuration but rather a maximalized cadence that achieves the appropriate syntactical purpose—and does so with greater power than ever before. In effect it provides the opera with its orgiastic Tristanesque (or Isoldesque) final cadence, after which the quick killing of Salome is a tonally insignificant (though dramatically shattering) appendage. But Strauss's climax does full justice to the difference between the spiritual sublimation of Isolde's sex drive and the kinky gratification of Salome's.

ANOTHER MADWOMAN

In Strauss's next opera, *Elektra* (1908), these harmonic mixtures are more the rule than the climactic exception. The story is again an ancient one that embodies in its plot the transgression of age-old taboos, namely matricide and incestuous love (to which the opera added a scene of lesbian seduction between the title character and a sister unknown to Greek mythology). Elektra (or Electra, as the name is rendered in English) was the daughter of Agamemnon, the victorious commander in the Trojan War, who was murdered by Clytemnestra, his wife and the mother of Electra, with the help of

Clytemnestra's lover Aegisthus. Electra longs for the return from exile of her brother Orestes, who alone can avenge the crime. He appears incognito; she recognizes him; they rejoice in their love and plot vengeance. He kills their mother as she looks on in ecstasy.

This gruesome tale had been dramatized by all three of the great Greek tragedians: Aeschylus, Sophocles, and Euripides. The version that Strauss set was the one "rewritten for the German stage," chiefly after Sophocles, by Hugo von Hofmannsthal (1874–1929), a distinguished poet and playwright who collaborated enthusiastically with Strauss on the adaptation of his play, and went on to create five more operas with the composer, right up to the end of his life. This hugely cultured and aristocratic gentleman, whom the composer, though ten years older, came to regard as something of a mentor, undoubtedly played a part in eventually moderating Strauss's modernist zeal.

The grisly *Elektra*, at the very beginning of their collaboration, was Strauss's maximalist extreme. Their next work, *Der Rosenkavalier* ("The cavalier of the rose," 1911) was a romantic comedy set in eighteenth-century Vienna. There is still a fair share of fin-de-siècle kinkiness in the treatment of the plot — the opera opens with two women in bed (one of them playing a boy), the music before curtain having graphically portrayed his/her ejaculation — but the music has begun to substitute extremes of virtuosity in handling traditional assignments (an ideal often described as "classicism") for extremes of innovation.

By the time of his death at the age of eighty-five, Strauss was stylistically perhaps the most conservative European composer of major stature. He certainly regarded himself as such: most of his late works were self-conscious valedictories or farewells to older, supposedly better, times. And yet the fact that by the mid-twentieth century stylistic conservatism was as conscious a stance, and as deliberate a choice, as stylistic radicalism is powerful testimony to the triumph of modernism as the dominant worldview for twentieth-century artists. The only choice was to be modernist or antimodernist, just as for a time one could only be Communist or anti-Communist. (Another testimony is the way in which Strauss's career has often been described by twentieth-century historians. Extreme but not untypical is the remark by one writer that the composer's development "from a historical point of view, must be viewed as 'backward,' "[25] rendering all

FIG. I-7 Strauss, *Der Rosenkavalier*; photo from act II of a performance by the Königliche Oper, Berlin, 1911, with Elisabeth Boehm van Endert as Oktavian and Erna Denera as Sophie.

of Strauss's music after *Elektra* "curiously 'unhistorical.'"[26] It would be an excellent exercise to deduce the very special philosophy—or definition—of "history" that informs this assessment.)

At the time of *Elektra*, though, Strauss was still an ardent modernist, which inevitably meant a maximalist. And his own former achievements were the ones he now had to maximalize. He began exactly where *Salome* left off. Indeed, the two operas had so much in common in plot and even in dramatic structure, and the two title characters were so similar in disposition and behavior, that the possibility of "continuing" *Salome* into *Elektra* must have been a paramount consideration in the choice of subject, one plainly dictated by the maximalist ideal.

The opera begins with a D-minor arpeggio motif that fairly blares the name "AgaMEMnon!" (Ex. 1-16), as Elektra will confirm when she appropriates it in her first monologue. And the opening motif seems to be followed in mm. 7–8 by a corresponding arpeggio on the dominant. But before the implied cadence can close, at m. 10 (coinciding with the title character's first appearance on stage) Strauss begins surrounding D with chords remote from it according to the circle of fifths, but closely related to it in the parallel universe (the symmetrical circle of minor thirds) that he had begun exploring in the last scene of *Salome*. For fully five bars triads on B minor (a minor third below D) alternate with triads on F minor (a minor third above), describing the "axis" relationship of a tritone.

EX. 1-16   Richard Strauss, *Elektra*, mm. 1–18 in vocal score

EX. 1-16 (continued)

The strange chord at m. 15 will eventually become Elektra's "leitharmonie": it inhabits another circle of minor thirds, being a mixture of major triads on E and D♭(C♯), with A♭(G♯), the melody note, doing double duty as fifth of one and third of the other. When the chord returns to accompany Elektra's first monologue (Ex. 1-17a), it will take on additional freight: a B♭ major triad, complementing E on the other side of D♭(C♯) and describing another tritone-axis of harmonic symmetry. As for the triads on B and F, they too return in maximalized (i.e., mixed) form to launch the first scene between Elektra and her sister Chrysothemis (Ex. 1- 17b).

EX. 1-17A   Richard Strauss, *Elektra*, Elektra's first lines

In addition to the circle of minor thirds, Strauss continues to exploit "arrays" of semitones in contrary motion like the ones we observed in *Salome*. Ex. 1-16 already contains a telling example: the progression in the last bar from a segment of the "*Elektra* chord" (B-Db-F) "outward" to an augmented triad (Bb-D-F♯). The use of semitonal arrays will reach its zenith in the final scene (consisting—again like *Salome*!—of the heroine's triumphant dance in celebration of a murder), where the semitone progressions will entirely preempt the circle of fifths as the director of the harmony.

Ex. 1-18a shows how Strauss gets from Eb major to E major along a semitonal matrix that has one of its octave-points on C, the tonality that will eventually end the opera. More conventional keys are occasionally adumbrated—but never by full cadence, only the sounding of a $^6_4$ chord that suffices to imply the rest of a cadence that never comes. In Ex. 1-18b, a descending semitone progression in the bass that had covered more than an octave finally zeroes in (in the fifth measure of the example) on F♯, harmonized as the bass of a $^6_4$ chord whose root, B, promises a cadence in that key. Unlike most of Strauss's $^6_4$ chords, this one is followed by its expected dominant. But at the point of expected arrival on the tonic, Strauss substitutes another $^6_4$ chord (falsely promising G), and a new semitone progression, ascending this time, gets underway in the bass.

The very end of the opera deserves comment, since it appears to end in two keys at once. Ex. 1-19 shows the last thirty-six measures of the opera, beginning with the tail end of the last appearance of the semitonal array shown in Ex. 1-18a. Contrary motion in the outer voices has produced a juxtaposition of Eb against A, the sort of tritonal opposition that had generated so much of the opera's harmony. The harmony that accompanies this last tritonal confluence, a diminished seventh, is liquidated, leaving

EX. 1-17B   Richard Strauss, *Elektra*, Chrysothemis calls Elektra

only the E♭, tremolando and still *fortississimo*, which finally picks up another harmony, the minor triad of which it is the root, when Elektra finishes her dance in a heap.

That E♭ is now subjected to a tug of war between the E♭ minor triad (henceforth played softly) and bellowing reminiscences of the "Agamemnon" leitmotif in which it is the highest note, so that the other notes of the arpeggio associate it with the implied tonic of C minor. Even the final measure fails to resolve this deadlock, merely giving out both putative tonics at a renewed *fortississimo*.

This deadlocked ending of course implies that the tragedy of the house of Agamemnon has not come to an end. (Classicists will know why — Orestes, called upon in vain by Chrysothemis, is already being pursued by the Furies!) It replays the famous ending device in Strauss's most grandiose tone poem, *Also sprach Zarathustra* ("Thus spake Zarathustra," 1896) after Nietzsche, his most impressive contribution to the heady literature of *Weltanschauungsmusik*. To conclude on a properly speculative note, or in acknowledgment that the last questions will never be answered, the final word never said, Strauss contrived an ending that seemed to die away on an oscillation between tonics on B and C, with C (as in *Elektra*) getting the last word (Ex. 1-20).

EX. 1-18A   Richard Strauss, *Elektra*, another intervallic "array"

EX. 1-18B   Richard Strauss, *Elektra*, Elektra tells Chrysothemis to "Shut up and dance!"

Had B been given the last word, or were the extreme registers reversed, the ploy would not have worked. It would then have been obvious that the C (though placed many octaves lower than its rival, in a register the ear is used to associating with the fundamental bass) was, in functional terms, making a *descent* to the tonic B as part of a "French sixth" chord (itself a decorative substitute for a very plain "Phrygian" cadence that normally identifies a dominant, not a tonic). Rather than an ending in two keys, we are dealing with a registrally distorted, interrupted, yet functionally viable cadence on B.

All right. A lot of philosophical music (like a lot of philosophy) may look like flimflam when subjected to a close grammatical analysis. But that is a logical objection, not an "esthetic" one. The effect of "polytonality," artificial though it may be, gives the music an uncanny—that is, a "sublime"—aura in keeping with advanced contemporary views of art and its value in life. That is the effect achieved at the end of *Elektra* as well—a suitable atmosphere for the modern revival of a myth. There can't be anything wrong with artifice in art.

EX. 1-19   Richard Strauss, *Elektra*, end

EX. I-19   (*continued*)

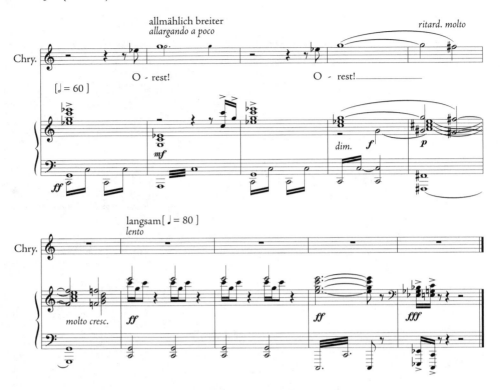

EX. I-20   Richard Strauss, *Also sprach Zarathustra*, ending (with harmonic reduction)

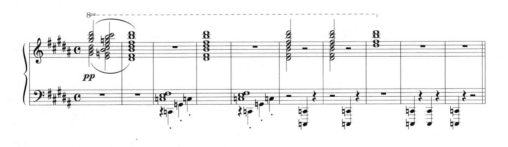

Harmonic (voice-leading) reduction

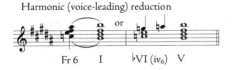

HYSTERIA

But now we are broaching a far more important reason why the end of *Elektra* deserves comment — one that has little or nothing to do with the artifices of musical maximalism per se, but lots to do with their pretext. Within the modernist narrative itself, the pretext of artistic innovation is always progress, liberation, and the authentic value that only the renewal of methods and resources can confer. In the case of *Elektra*, and perhaps even more in that of *Salome*, the destructive power the title characters wield over the men in their lives, read in the context of the contemporaneous social emancipation of women, is nowadays often read as a feminist allegory as well.

Yet both of Strauss's maximalist operas end with the deaths of their title characters; and in both cases these deaths were imported deaths, the product of their fin-de-siècle adaptations, not the original stories. In the Bible we do not learn of Salome's fate. It was Wilde and Wilde alone who had Herod turn to Herodias and say, "She is a monster, that daughter of yours, a monster!" before ordering his soldiers to "Kill that woman!" In Greek mythology, Electra, having expiated her father's death, married Orestes's friend Pylades and bore him two sons. It was Hofmannsthal, and Hofmannsthal alone, who had her dance so strenuously in triumph as to split a gut (or something) and fall dead in a heap. It is hard not to see these alterations as the modern authors' commentary on feminine monstrousness, and the deaths as a modern male vengeance on the threatening effigy of the emancipated — that is, newly empowered — modern female.

Voyeuristic fantasies of feminine evil were so rampant in fin-de-siècle culture that Bram Dijkstra, a professor of comparative literature, had no trouble filling a four-hundred-page book, to which he gave the title *Idols of Perversity*, with dozens of pictorial reproductions, verses, and plot summaries suggesting the extent to which the artistic maximalism of the period may have been a vicariously violent male response to the earliest stirrings of female emancipation.[27] The last exhibit in the book, after countless Judiths, Jezebels, and Turandots, is of course Salome, the ultimate "headhuntress," the subject (by Dijkstra's count) of ten scandalous pictures and a dozen bloodcurdling works of literature produced between 1876 and 1901. Needless to say, Des Esseintes, the outlandish hero of Huysmans's *À rebours*, found Salome as irresistible as she found John the Baptist. Contemplating the famous picture of Salome's dance by the eerie decadent painter Gustave Moreau (1826 – 98), he exults at seeing at last

> the Salomé, weird and superhuman, he had dreamed of. No longer was she merely the dancing-girl who extorts a cry of lust and concupiscence from an old man by the lascivious contortions of her body; who breaks the will, masters the mind of a King by the spectacle of her quivering bosoms, heaving belly and tossing thighs; she was now revealed in a sense as the symbolic incarnation of world-old Vice, the goddess of immortal Hysteria, the Curse of Beauty supreme above all other beauties by the cataleptic spasm that stirs her flesh and steels her muscles, — a monstrous Beast of the Apocalypse, indifferent, irresponsible, insensible, poisoning, like Helen of Troy of the old Classic fables, all who come near her, all who see her, all who touch her.[28]

Critics had already diagnosed a degree of misogyny in the operas of Giacomo Puccini (1858 – 1924) with their wilting heroines suffering their protracted agonies. Conventional music historiography might attribute the difference between Puccini's relatively gentle, noninnovative style, which no one would ever call maximalistic, and the furious modernistic frenzy of Strauss/Wilde and Strauss/Hofmannsthal to a difference in kind — modernist (boldly progressive, historically significant) vs. traditional (timidly backward, "unhistorical"). Yet from the point of view we are now exploring the difference might appear to be more one of degree, perhaps conditioned less by factors intrinsic to artistic media and more by matters of public and social currency.

Surely it is significant that Dijkstra's gallery of horrors contains virtually nothing by Italians. It was in the economically developed and (except for France) largely Protestant countries of northern Europe and America that the "new woman" posed the greater threat to male security and aroused the greater backlash. Consequently, it was the English, French, and German artists who invested their response to her with what Des Esseintes pinpointed as *hysteria* — a marvelously ironic term to use in this context, since its root is the Greek for uterus, so that aggressive male behavior is cast as stereotypically female. The greater social ferment produced a misogynistic response of greater vehemence, greater spite, greater ugliness, and in stylistic terms, greater novelty. Did that make it greater art?

CHAPTER 2

Getting Rid of Glue

SATIE, DEBUSSY, FAURÉ, RAVEL, LILI BOULANGER

Who amongst us has not, in his ambitious days, dreamed of the miracle of a poetic prose — musical without meter and without rhyme, flexible enough and sufficiently accented to correspond to the lyrical impulses of the spirit and to the undulations of the world of dreams?[1]

— CHARLES BAUDELAIRE (1862)

As to the kind of music I want to make, I would like it to be flexible enough and sufficiently accented to correspond to the lyrical impulses of the spirit and to the capriciousness of dreams.[2]

— CLAUDE DEBUSSY (1886)

DENATURING DESIRE

Ars gallica, the "truly French" art promised in 1871 by the Société Nationale de Musique in reaction to military humiliation at the hands of the Prussians, finally began rather bashfully to show its face toward the end of the next decade. Rather than attempt to vie with the Germans in loftiness and profundity, which merely encouraged "epigonism," the newer French impulses were at first modest and unthreatening. They aimed at the deflation of rhetoric — an especially pointed gesture in the face of German expressive maximalism — and placed a renewed premium on immediate physical sensation.

The French composers of Strauss's and Mahler's generation no longer sought (or no longer said they sought) musically to embody "the Will," as Arthur Schopenhauer would have said. Rather than use their music to represent and stimulate strong desire — for sexual union, for union with God, or for that mixture of the two known as the "erotic sublime" (less reverently, as "sacroporn") — they sought to restore "decorative" values to a place of honor. They revived "applied" or utilitarian genres; or rather, they sought to recultivate and reanimate esthetic genres that were based on the utilitarian genres of the past. Rather than a source of power, they sought in music a source of pleasure; rather than the sublime, they sought beauty.

In short, stimulated in part by antagonism toward Germany, in part by an interest in neglected indigenous traditions, and in part by concurrent literary and painterly movements, French musicians began to cultivate a very different sort of modernism from the Germans, and a very different musical technique for embodying it. Like all modernisms, the French version was characterized by a suddenly accelerated rate of stylistic change and innovation. Like all modernisms, it was highly self-conscious, reflective, ironic, and urbane. But where the Germans sought a maximalized emotional or psychological content — which implies a maximum human and expressive "presence" — and would go on seeking it far beyond the point to which we have traced their quest so far, the French modernism that began stirring in the 1880s sought to minimize, and ideally to eliminate, everything the Germans were trying to maximize. To use a term coined around 1925 by the Spanish philosopher José Ortega y Gasset (1883–1955) to describe it in retrospect, the French modernists whom we are about to survey sought "the dehumanization of art."[3]

The term can sound rather frightening at the other end of a century so full of social alienation and inhuman deeds. But as Ortega intended it, it had nothing to do with robots or concentration camps. Rather, it stood for an effort to purge art of all those "human, all too human"[4] concerns that threaten to turn it into a sweaty, warty human document of only ephemeral value (since emotions are fleeting and desire can be satiated) instead of an elegant or exquisite object of pleasure. "Frivolous!" comes the German retort; to which the French, unperturbed, come right back: "Pretentious!"

To view the opposition as a battle of frivolity vs. pretension is of course to trivialize both positions, as ideological antagonists usually manage to do. Another way of trivializing it, at once more objectionable and more illuminating because it is more alert to the underlying social issues, would be Ortega's own way. He called the esthetic controversies he was diagnosing in retrospect a war between "two different varieties of the human species," which he further characterized as "a privileged aristocracy of finer senses" and "the masses."[5] Even more contentiously, he cast the split as one between an art that denied its status as art in the name of irrelevant social ambitions or obligations and an art purified of such impertinences: "an art which can be comprehended only by people possessed of the peculiar gift of artistic sensibility — an art for artists and not for the masses, for 'quality' and not for *hoi polloi*."[6] Or as Anatoliy Lyadov, a Russian composer of the fin de siècle, put it, "Everyone is born with a stomach, but with a soul — one in a thousand."[7]

That is going way beyond "Brahminism," which was a staunchly bourgeois snobbery of education, into "estheticism," a snobbery of sensibility, ultimately of breeding. The strong manner in which Ortega expressed it reflected the right-wing political attitudes of the 1920s, with their violent recoil against democratic politics. To that extent Ortega's diagnosis can be criticized as anachronistic. But in milder, less overtly politicized terms the accuracy of Ortega's diagnosis can be confirmed at the very earliest stages of French modernism: in particular, in a trivial musical genre that did indeed fight pretension with frivolity, and from which French modernism can fairly be said to have taken its bearings.

That genre was the Wagner satire, practiced as a conscious resistance to the dread mage of Bayreuth, even as a sort of exorcism, by a generation of French composers who were, many of them, helplessly in thrall to him in their serious work. In some cases one can juxtapose passages of serious (helpless) Wagner-imitation and frivolous (conscious) Wagner-mockery in the work of a single composer. Take Alexis-Emmanuel Chabrier (1841–94), a founding member of the Société Nationale (hence a proponent of ARS GALLICA) who nevertheless made regular pilgrimages to Bayreuth, worshipped *Tristan und Isolde* and *Parsifal*, and could never get out from under Wagner's thumb as an operatic composer. As a result, his operas have largely vanished from the stage, leaving Chabrier to be represented in active repertoire by a few piano pieces and a single orchestral work, a brilliantly scored exotic "rhapsody" called *España* (1883).

Example 2-1a, from the Entr'acte before the third act of his comic opera *Le roi malgré lui* (King in spite of Himself) shows one of the many unconscious — or even worse, perhaps, obsessive — plagiarisms from the *Tristan* prelude that haunt Chabrier's work as they do the work of so many of his contemporaries, like César Franck (who, perhaps for this reason, stuck a "poison" label on his *Tristan* score), Vincent d'Indy (whose opera *Fervaal* became known as "the French *Parsifal*"), or Ernest Chausson. Example 2-1b/c, by contrast, show a couple of hilarious spots from Chabrier's *Souvenirs de Munich*, a quadrille or suite of ballroom dances for piano four-hands on themes from *Tristan und Isolde*, composed in 1885–86 after one of his Wagnerian pilgrimages.

E X. 2-1A   Emmanuel Chabrier, *Le roi malgré lui*, III (Entr'acte)

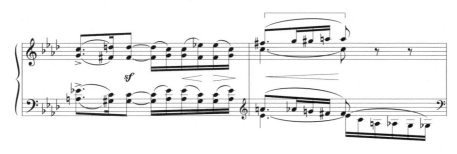

E X. 2-1B   Emmanuel Chabrier, *Souvenirs de Munich*, refrain (*Ecstasies*)

EX. 2-1B   (continued)

EX. 2-1C   Emmanuel Chabrier, *Souvenirs de Munich*, "Death Song"

Wagner spoofs in a similar vein were composed by Gabriel (Urbain) Fauré (1845–1924), André Messager (1853–1929), and others. They always took the form of utilitarian dance pieces, in maximum contradiction to Wagner's completely "emancipated" and "autonomous" art, and always forced Wagner's "endless melody" into incongruous clunky cadences after the standard eight or sixteen bars required by the dance figure. The sheer vengeful satisfaction of doing violence to a composer whose music takes such violent possession of one's responses no doubt contributed to the pleasure of the joke; but perhaps more significant was the reminder that even Wagner's music is, after all, just music. Putting Wagner's powerful symbols of desire into contexts where they remain recognizable but are prevented from achieving their uncanny effects reassuringly denatured them, put them in their place. And by extension, art is put in its place — as an enhancer of the quality of life, neither a vicarious lived experience nor a substitute for religion.

That may seem a heavy load of philosophical freight to read into such trifling pieces, and nothing so completely ruins a joke as an explanation, but the same homely genres and the same implicit philosophy (or antiphilosophy) surface in French music around the same time in contexts less directly attached to Wagner. Many French composers, not by conscious collusion but by a shared sense of mission, became preoccupied with similar technical concerns, amounting to a common technical project. That project can be described as one of neutralizing (or perhaps just "neutering") the Wagnerian desire-symbolism then entering its decadent phase in Germany. The overt Wagner-spoofing was only the jesting public face of a more serious job of exorcism.

To see the project in a more pristine guise we can turn to another set of dances for piano, composed the year after Chabrier's *Souvenirs*. Erik Satie (1866 – 1925) was a twenty-one-year-old Paris Conservatory dropout when he wrote his *Trois sarabandes*, of which the first is sampled in Ex. 2-2. He was pursuing *la vie de Bohème*, the "Bohemian life," in Montmartre (Martyrs' Hill), the highest point in Paris, then a semirural district where (on account of the steep slopes that had to be climbed on foot) rents were cheap and struggling artists could afford to live. The district's main industry was its nightlife, and Satie earned his living as the second-string pianist at Le Chat Noir (the Black Cat), a local pub.

A complete nobody as far as the musical establishment was concerned, dubbed "the laziest student in the Conservatoire"[8] by his exasperated piano teacher, Satie maintained some small notoriety by applying repeatedly (upon learning of the deaths of distinguished members like Charles Gounod or Ambroise Thomas, the Conservatory's director) for membership in the Académie

FIG. 2-1 Erik Satie ca. 1892, by Suzanne Valadon (1867 – 1938).

des Beaux Arts, France's most prestigious artistic honor society, just as a way of riling the surviving members. He was, in short, a "countercultural" type. Eighty years later he might have been called a hippie.

EX. 2-2A   Erik Satie, first *Sarabande* for Piano, mm. 1–21

EX. 2-2B   Erik Satie, first *Sarabande* for Piano, mm. 100–end

Satie was not the first French post-Wagnerian to write a sarabande. Proclaiming one's disaffection for the "music of the future" by making an end run around the recent past was already a time-honored—even a shopworn—strategy among the would-be Wagner resisters of the Société Nationale. The Society's very first concert in 1871 had included a suite for piano by Alexis de Castillon (1838–73), the organization's first secretary, called *Cinq pièces dans le style ancien* ("Five pieces in the olden style"). By the end of the century just about every French composer had a work "dans le style ancien" in his or her portfolio: *Le roi s'amuse, six airs de danse dans le style ancien* for orchestra by Delibes (1882); *Suite dans le style ancien*, in D, for wind septet by d'Indy (1886); *Pièce dans le style ancien* for piano (1893) by Cécile Chaminade (1857–1944), to name just a few. The most famous composition of this type was Saint-Saëns's Septet for trumpet, string quintet, and piano (1881). It did not carry the explicit "olden style" label, but its contents were ostentatiously archaic: "Prélude," "Menuet," and so on, and, to conclude, a "Gavotte en final" that contained a bit of fugato, and sported a theme that parodied the sort of leaping, "string-crossing" melodies one found in old violin music (Ex. 2-3).

EX. 2-3   Camille Saint-Saëns, Septet for trumpet, string quintet, and piano, "Gavotte en final"

Satie's *Trois sarabandes* differed from these efforts, however. While faithfully cast in old "baroque" dance forms (two or three repeated "strains," with repetitions fully if needlessly written out rather than marked with repeat signs), their musical style was at once more up-to-date and more pseudoarchaic, showing how notions of the ancient and the ultranovel had been joined in an anti-Wagnerian amalgam. The latest novelty in French music was the "consonant" seventh or ninth chord, in which tones normally treated as dissonances in need of resolution functioned instead as sensuous enrichments of an ordinary triad. Chabrier's music, especially, luxuriated in this effect. A passage from the prelude to *Le roi malgré lui* (Ex. 2-4), first performed in May 1887, echoes clearly in the opening phrases of Satie's first Sarabande, composed four months later.

EX. 2-4   Emmanuel Chabrier, *Le roi malgré lui*, Prelude

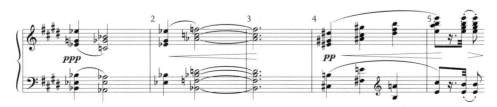

The second chord in the Chabrier passage contains a ninth that is both approached and quitted by leaps, and a seventh that is approached and quitted by chromatic inflection rather than actual resolution to a different scale degree. In the fourth measure, a dominant-ninth chord on C♯ moves in strict parallel motion to another chord of identical structure, showing the sevenths and ninths to be (functionally speaking) every bit as consonant as the thirds and fifths; and the insouciance with which Chabrier continues the parallel fifths and sevenths through another progression shows to what extent he conceived of his harmonies as sheer "sonorities," altogether apart from any vestige of linear voice leading.

The chords themselves may be regarded as "Wagnerian"; the love music from *Tristan und Isolde*, to pick only the most obvious example, is saturated with them. But the whole point of Wagnerian harmony was the prolongation of dissonance to the point of pain — a pain arising precisely out of the thwarted need for resolution. Moving such chords in parallel à la Chabrier, or leaping from ninth to ninth, denies and eventually neutralizes this need. As formerly dissonant chords become consonant through such uses (or abuses, as any conservatory professor would contend), the "cadential imperative" is weakened — and with it, the power of music to represent desire.

The closest antecedent to Chabrier's passage was not in Wagner but in the Coronation bells from Modest Musorgsky's opera *Boris Godunov*, where the oscillation of two dominant-seventh chords with roots a tritone apart effectively cancelled the need for that tritone to resolve. It is altogether likely that Chabrier's harmonic fancy had been stimulated by Musorgsky's experiments. Saint-Saëns had brought back a vocal score of *Boris Godunov* from a Russian tour in 1874, and thinking it no more than a curiosity, showed it around to his friends, some of whom it unexpectedly captivated with its revelation that there could still be music that was neither Wagnerian nor anti-Wagnerian, but simply a-Wagnerian. Satie stands in this line of reception. Every chord in the first seven measures of Ex. 2-2a contains at least a seventh, and five of them contain a ninth as well. But not one of these intervals resolves according to traditional rules of voice leading. They are harmonically stable, making the music they inhabit harmonically static.

The B♭♭ major chord in m. 8 is the first unsullied triad in the Sarabande. That must be what gives it its cadential quality. Surely it is not the progression that leads to it that marks it so. The bass moves by fifth, all right, but the leading tone — it would have been A♭ rather than A♭♭ — has been suppressed. At a time when German composers were making a fetish out of half-step relations, and when (in the sarcastic words of a Russian critic) a character in an opera "cannot ask for a glass of water without using a fistful of sharps or flats,"[9] this French composer was purging his music of functional semitones. In effect, he was ridding his music of its harmonic glue.

Of course, sharps and flats remained in use: depending on the key, they are needed for diatonic as well as chromatic music. And as sheer notational features — rather than emblems of emotional intensity, as the Russian critic implied — they proliferated outlandishly in these early works of Satie. Satie's penchant for overly complicated note-spellings is probably best viewed as an aspect of the preference for the esoteric and the *recherché* that we have already learned to associate with "decadence."

But the truly subversive aspect of the Sarabande was not the superficial outlandishness of its appearance. The truly ticklish thing about it was that all of its important cadential functions have been tonally denatured. The dominant triad in m. 20, the normal "binary" half-cadence, is preceded by a B♭-minor triad: merely a "ii" chord rather than a "V of V." The final cadence in the piece (Ex. 2-2b) very demonstratively replaces the leading tone (G in m. 100) with a "flat seventh" (G♭ in m. 101, held over in the next bar as the third of a minor-seventh chord on the fifth degree) that maintains the ban on leading-tone resolutions (and hence the suppression of a true dominant function) to the bitter end.

This kind of harmony was often described as "modal" and compared with that of the French music of the sixteenth century and earlier — a music that just then, and not at all by coincidence, was starting to be published in quantity, especially by Satie's contemporary the nationalistic antiquarian Henry Expert (1863–1952) in a huge series called *Les maîtres musiciens de la Renaissance* ("The master musicians of the Renaissance"). In fact, however, it was only a pseudomodal style and it was altogether modern. (It, too, had a Russian counterpart in the folk song harmonizations of Balakirev and other Russian nationalists; what Balakirev sought among the peasantry the French were seeking in their musical past — namely, novelty that could claim the pedigreed authority of "authenticity.") In actual practice, even when the "medieval" or "church" mode in which a piece of old polyphonic music was written contained no leading tone, the leading tone was nevertheless supplied at cadences, just as it is in the modern "harmonic minor," by applying the rules of what was known as *musica ficta*. The chaste, charmingly antiquated cadences of Balakirev and Satie conformed to no ancient model. They were a classic case indeed (or, as it came to be called, a "neoclassic" case) of the new passing itself off as old. And for a final irony, this newly manufactured "modal" harmony was quickly and widely adopted as the "authentic" French manner of harmonizing the newly revived and popularized Gregorian chant.

The stable sevenths and ninths and the "modal" cadences in Satie's Sarabande were two aspects of a single effect, that of purging the music of desire. The leading-tone progressions that filled German music with emotional strain, and that were proliferating like kudzu in the music of Mahler and Strauss, were inhibited in the new French music just as the harmonic texture was being enriched. Where the maximalism of Mahler and Strauss gave one a case — as Strauss's father complained, according to his son's famous boast — of bugs in one's pants, the sonorously opulent yet harmonically inert atmosphere of the Sarabandes "imbue the music," in the well-chosen words of Alan M. Gillmor, Satie's biographer, "with a timeless calm."[10]

Satie's next step was to purge the music of that rich harmonic texture and rely on the suppression of leading tones to make possible a "new diatonicism" — music that despite (or even because of) the virtual absence of sharps and flats seemed not merely artless but strangely fresh and rare, as if stripped of memory. What became Satie's most famous composition, the *Trois gymnopédies* for piano (1888), was of this type. The curious name was another pseudoclassical affectation. Satie probably found it in a popular music dictionary of the time, such as Dominique Mondo's *Dictionnaire de musique* (Paris, 1839), which defined *gymnopédie* (from the Greek *gymnopaidia*) as "a nude dance, accompanied by song, which youthful Spartan maidens danced on specific occasions." (The definition has been traced back to Jean-Jacques Rousseau's *Dictionnaire de musique* of 1768.) The slow waltzes that Satie came up with in response to this description surely bore scant resemblance to any ancient model, but they bequeathed a minor genre to later composers (Peggy Glanville-Hicks and John Adams, to name two) who have occasionally written "gymnopedies" on the Satie model.

All three Gymnopédies begin with "vamps"—accompaniments awaiting their tunes—consisting of a pair of chords in a simple alternation suggesting tonic and dominant (Ex. 2-5). In all three cases, however, the tonal "functionality" of the progression is attenuated. In the first, the two harmonies are both "major-seventh" chords, so that a constant level of mild "stable dissonance" is maintained. In the second, the ostensible "I" chord has a sixth (E) in place of its fifth (D), and the ostensible "V" is a minor seventh, stripped of its leading tone (hence of its potency as a dominant). In the third, if the first chord is taken as the tonic, the second can only be construed as some sort of weird "minor v_2^4" (hence not a true dominant), devoid of a leading tone and with its seventh in the bass.

By the time the tune enters in the third Gymnopédie, the second vamping chord is abandoned, to return only at other vamping spots (one in the middle, the other at the end). It is thus exposed as a completely arbitrary sonority without any "inherent" or mandated tonal function. Just as arbitrary is the occasional light chromaticism that impinges from time to time on the strictly diatonic melody. And so, the composer seems to suggest, so are all of our familiar chords, even the ones we consider basic to our "tonal

EX. 2-5A   Erik Satie, *Trois gymnopédies*, no. 1, mm. 1–8

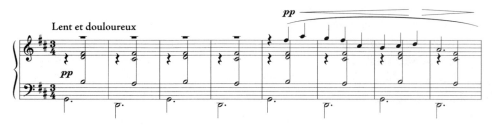

EX. 2-5B   Erik Satie, *Trois gymnopédies*, no. 2, mm. 1–8

EX. 2-5C   Erik Satie, *Trois gymnopédies*, no. 3, mm. 1–8

system." We respond to their functional relationships only because we are conditioned so to do. But we could free ourselves from that conditioning if we wished, and view the field of harmony afresh. Gentle and pretty — and innocuous — though they seemed, Satie's little dances for piano were radical stuff. They already fully exemplified the esthetic position that Ortega, the later theorist of the avant-garde, would spell out in the 1920s in his famous "seven points."[11] Rather than attempting to provide its audience with a vicarious emotional or spiritual life, the ascetic "new artistic sensibility" Ortega described tended:

1. to dehumanize art
2. to avoid living forms
3. to see to it that the work of art is nothing but a work of art
4. to consider art as play and nothing else
5. to be essentially ironical
6. to beware of sham and hence to aspire to scrupulous realization
7. to regard art as a thing of no transcending consequence.

When one considers that these early benchmarks of anti-Teutonic modernism were written ten years before the death of Brahms, Satie's little Sarabandes and Gymnopédies can seem, despite their primitive innocence bordering on infantilism, positively amazing.

HALF-STEPLESSNESS

But that is mainly because we know now how influential Satie's subversive message eventually became, and what an important role these seemingly dehistoricized pieces eventually played in history. It took them a long time, though, to infiltrate the thinking of any but a narrow circle of the composer's friends. Although written in 1887, the Sarabandes were not published until 1911. The Gymnopédies were issued in a tiny edition by a friend of the composer in the year of their composition, but were not effectively placed on the market until 1898; and when they were finally published for actual market distribution, they were accompanied by a pair of orchestrations (of nos. 1 and 3) by a friend of the composer who had in the meantime become famous and fashionable, and who thereby became the chief conduit through which the implications of Satie's somewhat awkward "counterculturalisms" made fruitful contact with the established culture.

FIG. 2-2   Claude Debussy at the piano in the home of the composer Ernest Chausson, Luzancy, August 1892.

It was a situation comparable in its way to the one three hundred years earlier, when a band of Florentine aristocrats theorized about the revival of Greek drama, and even tried putting their ideas into practice at a few royal weddings, but only made a real dent in the history of music when they won a major professional composer, Claudio Monteverdi, to their cause and midwifed the birth of opera. In a like manner, had Satie not managed to impress and creatively affect the work and thinking of his friend Claude Debussy (1862–1918), a composer of prodigiously honed technique who had finished the Conservatory course with distinction and won every prize in sight, and who (though he never taught) occupied a place of real and increasing cultural authority in French musical life, his work might never have been taken seriously at all.

It was Debussy whose 1896 orchestrations of the Gymnopédies put their composer on the map. And a Sarabande that he composed in 1894, later published as part of the *Suite: Pour le piano 1894–1901* (1901), shows that he knew Satie's *Trois sarabandes* at a time when only a personal friend of the composer could have known them. Their friendship dates from 1891, though an earlier acquaintanceship has often been speculated on, since they had so much background in common. Both of them were living in penury in Montmartre, Debussy having returned a few years earlier from Italy, where he had been sent by the Académie des Beaux-Arts in 1885 as the recipient of the prestigious Prix de Rome. He began playing the rebel, refusing to supply a conventional overture for the concert at which his *envois* (things sent back), the creative fruits of his Roman sojourn, were to have been performed, as a result of which the concert was canceled and he was officially reprimanded. He found in the somewhat younger Satie a natural ally and, at first, something of a preceptor.

Debussy, who had spent several summers in Russia as music tutor to the children of Mme von Meck, Chaikovsky's patron, began to declare his allegiance to Russian music, especially that of Musorgsky, as representing in its unschooled (and therefore liberated) primitivism a countercultural ideal. (As late as 1911 he would tell an interviewer that Musorgsky, uncouth as he was, was "something of a god in music."[12]) In conversations with a sympathetic former professor from the Conservatory that took place in 1889 and 1890 and were transcribed stenographically by an eavesdropping Conservatory pupil, Debussy delivered himself of a brash countercultural credo: "There is no theory. You have only to listen. Pleasure is the law!"[13] He illustrated the point at the keyboard with some desultory chord progressions (Ex. 2-6) that used some of the same parallelisms he would shortly discover in the work of Satie, plus a passage of whole-tone harmony of a sort that he may well have discovered first in Russian music (most likely Glinka or Rimsky-Korsakov), where it had by 1889 nearly half a century's worth of precedents. (It is worth noting by the way that, precisely in 1889, Rimsky-Korsakov had conducted a pair of concerts of the newest Russian music at the World Exposition held in Paris to celebrate the centenary of the French Revolution.)

EX. 2-6   "Debussy at the piano strikes these chords" (comment by Maurice Emmanuel, the stenographer)

When his interlocutor, Ernest Guiraud (best known for the recitatives he composed for Bizet's *Carmen* so that it could be performed as a grand opera), commented that "It's all very meandering," Debussy at first responded with patronizing indignation. But then, as if remembering Ortega's last three points above, he broke down and laughed at his own pretension, admitting in effect that esthetic edicts like the ones he was issuing were as often spouted by fools as by geniuses. "I feel free because I have been through the mill," he admitted to his former teacher, "and I don't write in the fugal style because I know it."

The 1894 Sarabande (Ex. 2-7), composed when he had a model in view (Satie's), shows how Debussy was attempting to discipline his vision and subject his rule of pleasure to a bit of theoretical scrutiny. The piece does not meander. Like Satie's, it abides by the formal and tonal conventions of its genre, but does so in the same novel, tonally attenuated fashion that Satie had pioneered, if with far greater technical finesse.

From the point of view of Wagner exorcism, the first measure of Debussy's Sarabande would be hard to beat. Its very first chord, a half-diminished seventh, is aurally tantamount to a *Tristan*-chord; but its dissonances are not treated as something to be resolved. Instead, the chord is moved up a minor third in strict diatonic parallel motion to a minor-seventh chord, whose dissonances are treated similarly. In effect, both chords have been treated as consonances, floating freely in musical space, liberated from the constraints of voice leading. There is no sense that the necessary resolution of the dissonance is being deferred, and consequently there is no provocation of desire. In Ortega's terms, the chords are drained of their "human" content. The harmony no longer analogizes or incites emotion, save the emotion of delight in sheer sensuous gratification. Debussy has "seen to it that the work of art is nothing but a work of art," because he "considers art as play and nothing else." Beauty, in short, has made a comeback.

Thereafter, one will look in vain for the dominant of C♯ minor—which is to say, one will look in vain for a B♯ acting as a leading tone. That half-step relation, being the sort of harmonic "glue" that arouses desire, is everywhere avoided. In mm. 2 and 4 the "minor v" is invoked. In m. 8 a triad on B natural fairly trumpets the fact that B♯ has been banished. In mm. 20–22 harmony is avoided altogether, and the cadential approach to C♯ is made by way of a "plagal" F♯. At the very end (Ex. 2-7b), a chord that would normally be prepared and resolved as a suspension dissonance—its intervals, counted up from the bottom in figured-bass style, could be represented as 7/5/4—is thrice transposed up a third in strict parallel motion, so as to reach a highly demonstrative B natural (i.e., *not* a B♯) in the soprano, which then moves in Satie-esque "pseudomodal" fashion to the tonic.

Ex. 2-7c shows the only fully expressed authentic cadence in the piece, replete with resolving leading tone (and hence the emotional climax). Needless to say, it is not applied to the tonic but to G♯ minor, the antidominant.

EX. 2-7A   Claude Debussy, Sarabande from *Pour le piano*, mm. 1–22

EX. 2-7A   (continued)

EX. 2-7B   Claude Debussy, Sarabande from *Pour le piano*, mm. 67–72

EX. 2-7C   Claude Debussy, Sarabande from *Pour le piano*, mm. 54–57

For a "maximalized" version of the harmonic idiom exemplified by Satie's and Debussy's Sarabandes, a good place to look would be a celebrated piano piece of Debussy's composed a decade and a half later: "Voiles" (1909), the second in a set of twelve *Préludes* for piano published in 1910 (Ex. 2-8). The idea of a set of freestanding preludes, independent aphoristic compositions for the keyboard, obviously stems from Chopin, a composer Debussy worshipped and claimed as a forerunner. Unlike Chopin's, Debussy's preludes carry descriptive subtitles; but unlike most titles, Debussy's are given not at the heads of the pieces, but at the ends, modestly enclosed in parentheses, and preceded by dots of ellipsis, as if to demote them to the rank of whispered interpretive suggestions or "teasers," rather than explicit prescriptions. In the case of "Voiles," the teasing is exaggerated by the ambiguity of the word. "Le voile," with masculine article, means "veil" or "mask"; "la voile," with feminine article, means "sail" or "sailboat." In the plural, the word can mean either.

EX. 2-8A   Claude Debussy, "Voiles" (Préludes, Book I), mm. 1–13

Leaving the implications of the title aside for the moment, we are struck by a different sort of ambiguity. The first forty-one measures of the piece are composed entirely out of the notes of a whole-tone scale, which excludes half-steps by definition (except for a single tiny whiff of decorative chromaticism shown in Ex. 2-8b), and which therefore has no degree functions at all. (It cannot have them: the degree functions in diatonic music are identified by the placement of the half-steps; when all the step intervals are of equal size, degrees cannot be meaningfully differentiated.) Previously to this piece, whole-tone harmony had functioned in Debussy's music the way it had in Russian music: that is, in interaction with diatonic harmony, creating momentary blurs. Now it is the sole point of reference.

As long as all the notes in play are derived from a single whole-tone scale (or "collection," which just means a referential set of pitches whether or not they are played in a particular order), there can be no sense at all of harmonic progression. There is nothing to establish "attraction" between the harmonic elements: neither

EX. 2-8B Claude Debussy, "Voiles" (*Préludes*, Book I), m. 31

circle-of-fifth progressions nor leading tones are possible, since the collection contains neither perfect intervals (except the octave) nor half steps. Instead, everything coexists in relative harmoniousness, and in what seems a single extended instant of time. Debussy accentuates the static quality of the harmony, and at the same time gives it an anchor of sorts, by accompanying the whole piece (from m. 5 on) with a B♭ pedal. A sense of unfolding is achieved not through harmonic variety (which is unavailable) but by an accumulation of melodic ideas (or motifs) in counterpoint.

Slightly past the middle a radical change takes place (Ex. 2-8c): a key signature of five flats suddenly appears, and the whole-tone collection gives way to a "pentatonic" one, the familiar scale on the piano's black keys. The ear is refreshed. Since the pentatonic scale, like the diatonic scale, has intervals of two different sizes (whole steps and minor thirds), the harmony seems to come into sharper focus. But harmonic functions nevertheless remain in abeyance, since the pentatonic collection has the crucial element of "half-steplessness" in common with its whole-tone counterpart: in more formal terminology, both scales are *anhemitonic*, lacking in semitones. The two collections have three tones in common—evidently the criterion governing their choice—and the B♭ pedal sounds right on through the new section. Sensuous values have been varied; functional or syntactical matters remain more or less as they were.

EX. 2-8c Claude Debussy, "Voiles" (*Préludes*, Book I), mm. 41–48

EX. 2-8C   (*continued*)

When the whole-tone collection is reasserted (see the last measure of Ex. 2-8c), a new motif is introduced that imitates the foregoing black-key glissandos and provides a sort of synthesis to mediate and soften the contrast between the two previous sections of the piece. The melodic content of the first section is recapitulated, but in a new registral disposition: whole-tone counterpoint is inherently "invertible." The very end of the piece is somewhat enigmatic. The B♭ pedal falls out three bars before the end, and the closing harmony (the dyad C/E, first heard in m. 5), while perhaps not predictable, and while impossible to justify as a conventional tonic, nevertheless seems right. Why? Possibly because of the way it had ended the first melodic statement, before the pedal had been introduced; or possibly because it provided the midpoint (that is, the axis of symmetry) in the initial scalar descent through which the whole-tone collection had been introduced at the very outset (mm. 1–2). In an altogether new and literal sense, the dyad C/E may be said to act as a tone *center*.

That is probably the best explanation—or at least the "right" one in terms of the composer's actual technique. Increasingly drawn to symmetrical pitch collections (that is, collections that may be represented, as in Ex. 2-9, by scales that are intervallically identical when inverted), Debussy came increasingly to regard the middle of such an array as its most stable element. We will confirm this observation in a moment by examining another piece, but first let us return to the curious title of Debussy's prelude and its implications.

IMPRESSIONISM

If *voiles* is taken to mean "sails," Debussy's music can seem "painterly"—that is, concerned in its subtly calibrated timbres (=colors) and blurry harmony with depictions of outdoor scenes or, more generally, with establishing correspondences between the aural and the visual. That is how many viewed him during his lifetime. As early as 1887, the term "Impressionism" was applied to his music, on an analogy with the famous school of French painters that had begun to flourish somewhat earlier, and which took its name from a painting by Claude Monet (1840–1926) called *Impression: Sunrise*, first exhibited in 1872 (Fig. 2-3).

Like many style-identifying terms in the history of the arts (such as "baroque," to pick the most widely accepted example), "impressionism" was at first a pejorative label.

EX. 2-9   Whole tone and pentatonic collections represented as symmetrical scales

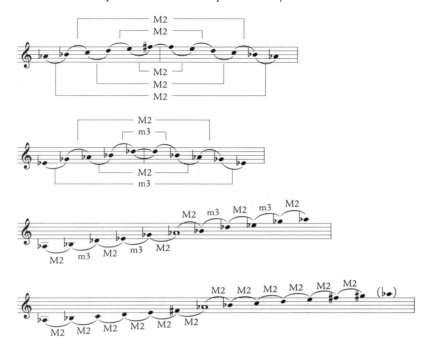

FIG. 2-3   Claude Monet, *Impression: Sunrise* (1872), the painting that gave impressionism its name.

Certainly the critic who coined the term in response to Monet's painting meant it as no compliment. Misunderstanding the intention, which was to capture transitory visual impressions (such as the play of light on a surface) naturalistically and with extreme precision, the critic implied that the broken colors and indistinct outlines in Monet's painting were the result of sloppy technique. Similarly, the secretary of the Académie des Beaux Arts, who first applied the term to Debussy in evaluating the latter's second *envoi* from Rome (a suite called *Le Printemps* or "Springtime," for a wordlessly humming women's chorus and orchestra), used it as a synonym for what he took to be the young Debussy's chief liability: "a strong feeling for color in music which, when exaggerated, causes him to forget the importance of clarity in design and form."[14] Not surprisingly, Debussy found the word annoying, "a convenient term of abuse,"[15] or at least (like any stereotype) a term of confinement. One did not use it to his face. But as in the case of the artists, the term "stuck" despite their resistance, and eventually lost its disapproving connotation. Instead, it came to name a quality that did seem to link the expressive aims of the new styles in French painting and music, and (perhaps even more important at the time) that strongly distinguished them from contemporaneous trends in Germany. The common ingredients, which critics have always found hard to specify in words however keenly they are "felt," might be said to include such things as calculated effects of spontaneity; fascination with subtle gradations in color and texture that produced a nebulous, highly suggestive surface; and a greater interest in sensuousness than in psychology or strongly declared emotion. (Naturally, all of these traits could be easily translated into failings by German or Germanophile critics: vagueness, confusion, lack of expressivity.)

Even the strikingly static effect of Debussy's harmony — the absence of "progression" or forward drive that we have already observed — could be viewed as "painterly," an effort to lessen the discrepancy between an art that unfolds in time and one that extends in space. His frequent use of visually-oriented titles like "Voiles" — its companions in the first book of *Préludes* include "Les collines d'Anacapri" ("The Hills of Anacapri") and "Ce qu'a vu le vent d'ouest" ("What the West Wind Saw") — confirm the parallel. The second book of *Préludes* (published 1913) include a couple — "Bruyères" ("Mists") and "Feuilles mortes" ("Dead Leaves") — that almost seem to parody the titles of typical "impressionist" paintings.

Most revealing of all, perhaps, is the absence of people, or rather of personalities, among Debussy's subjects. One finds representations aplenty in his music of the sea, of the wind, of gardens in the rain and balconies in the moonlight, but of humans few unless viewed *en masse* and from afar ("Fêtes," or festivals, one of three *Nocturnes* for orchestra completed in 1899), or unless mythical (fauns, sirens), artificial ("Golliwogg," his daughter's Negro doll, portrayed in his *Childrens' Corner* suite for piano), or already embodied in art ("Danseuses de Delphes" or Delphic dancers, the first of the *Préludes*, which title evokes not the dancers themselves but the Greek vase on which they are painted). His landscapes are uninhabited, even if they bear traces of former habitation, as in "Des pas sur la neige" ("Footprints in the snow," yet another *Prélude*). In sum, like impressionist painting, Debussy's art was not an art of empathy. Music, he felt, was "not the expression of feeling but the feeling itself."

He scoffed at "expressive" art like Italian opera, comparing it with the cheap music one heard in the streets. "There you can have your emotions-in-melody for a couple of sous!"[16] he exclaimed in 1902, while his own sole completed opera, *Pelléas et Mélisande*, was being readied for the stage. Instead, like the painter Elstir, the fictional stand-in for Monet in Marcel Proust's massive retrospective novel *In Search of Lost Time* (1913–20), Debussy aspired "to accustom his eyes not to recognize any fixed frontier, or absolute division between earth and ocean on a day when light had, as it were, destroyed reality," thus to capture "boats [i.e., *voiles*] as if vaporized by an effect of sunlight," or "churches that, seen from afar in a shimmering haze of sunlight and waves, seem to rise out of the water, as if molded in alabaster or foam, and enclosed within the arc of a multicolored rainbow, forming a picture of mysterious unreality."[17] Amazingly enough (or so it would seem had Proust not known it all along), Debussy actually called one of his *Préludes* "La cathédrale engloutie" ("The submerged cathedral").

This side of Debussy is epitomized in *Nuages* ("Clouds"), the first of the orchestral *Nocturnes*. To speak of illustration would be futile: what do clouds sound like? Everything is suggestion, analogy, *impression* — of shifting shapes, darkening or lightening, perhaps at the very end some distant thunder in the timpani (in homage, no doubt, to the middle movement of Berlioz's seventy-year-old *Symphonie fantastique*).

As is often the case with Debussy, the overall musical shape is simple and conventional: an ordinary ABA, articulated by a modulation (from two to six sharps and back again). Tonally, however, the music is as unconventional as can be. The only "normally" (if weakly) articulated cadence in it is the one between the first and second measures (Ex. 2-10a), in which a leading tone (A♯) is applied to B to establish it at the outset as the tonic. The fact that only two voices (doubled pairs of clarinets and bassoons) are in play eliminates the possibility of full triads here: thus the single unambiguous tonal gesture is characteristically attenuated, stripped down to a minimum (or what some might consider not even the minimum), reduced, in short, to a fleeting "impression."

Beginning in m. 5 (Ex. 2-10b), the tonic note is given two mysterious shadows: first a G that sounds continuously, albeit in fluctuating colors (clarinet/bassoon, flute/horn, violins *divisi*) over the next four measures, and then an F that is introduced by an arching phrase in the English horn that falls back to B (mm. 5–8), but that is later reinforced by the two bassoons at the octave (mm. 7–8). Under normal "tonal" conditions, the three notes thus implicated, G-B-F, would constitute a dissonant harmony ("incomplete dominant seventh") in need of resolution. Here, factors of timbre and register conspire to promote a sense of unperturbable calm that overrides the impulse to resolve. Parts of the configuration come and go. On the downbeat of m. 7 all three notes are present

EX. 2-10A   Claude Debussy, *Nuages*, mm. 1–3

EX. 2-10B   Claude Debussy, *Nuages*, mm. 5–10

(plus a C♯—notated, of course, as G♯—in the English horn to provide a momentary whiff of "French sixth").

The kettledrum has stolen in to reinforce the tonic B in the bass, however; and the first violins have stolen in with the same note at the opposite registral extreme. B thus dominates the chord, even though it is not, by standard reckoning, the functional root. After the downbeat of m. 8 the F is "cleared" from the chord; and on the next downbeat the G cleared, not by removing it altogether, but by nudging it up to G♯. That is obviously no cadential half-step, just an inflection or "tilt" away from G-ness so that B can be left to continue undisturbed in m. 10. There has been no "tonal motion" at all, just a sort of tonal inertia or lethargy that pulls everything back to B.

Following the English horn part through the entire composition will put another kind of Debussyan inertia on display. The English horn's second entrance is identical to the first. And so is the third, except that the C♯ has been replaced by a grace-note D. That is all the variation that will be allowed, however: the next time it comes in, the English horn will repeat the same pair of variants: just as the second solo exactly reproduced the first, so the fifth exactly reproduces the fourth. Toward the end, the English horn plays a series of "petites reprises" (as French composers had been calling them since the seventeenth century) of the last three (cadential?) notes of its characteristic phrase. And its last solo exactly reproduces its whole vocabulary — two variants, *petites reprises*, and all.

The English horn music, in other words, has been *hypostatized*, to use a term (from the Greek *hypostasis*, "substance" or "essence") that music analysts sometimes employ to call attention to an unchanging association of pitch, register, and timbre that remains constant throughout a piece. To put the matter more in structural terms, one could also say that the tritone F-B has been hypostatized in the English horn music, thus freezing into a constant one of the "shadow" pitches noted near the beginning of the piece. That shadowing effect, which became increasingly prominent in early-twentieth-century music, often involved the tritone, the interval that exactly bisects the octave. It is the "first cut," so to speak, if one wishes to apportion the notes of the chromatic scale into a symmetrical, rather than a tonally functional, distribution. The notes in a bare tritone (which when inverted remains a tritone) cannot be functionally differentiated. What gives B its de facto priority in the texture of *Nuages* is not its tonal function but its registral and timbral predominance.

Eventually, B is given a sort of functional priority as well, but it is the new kind of functional priority foreshadowed in our discussion of "Voiles," above. Right before the "B" section, Debussy allows the harmonic focus to go "soft," first by interpolating a string of parallel $\frac{4}{2}$ chords, and then by calling in the whole-tone scale, expressed "maximalistically" as a six-note chord (also describable as a pair of simultaneous augmented triads) that exhausts the whole collection. The effect might be compared with that of a little breeze that nudges the sonic clouds into a new region of the aural sky.

That region (Ex. 2-10c) is D♯ minor, the key whose tonic lies the same distance from B (a major third) as did G, its "shadow" in the first section of the piece, but in the opposite "direction." Like the C/E dyad at the end of "Voiles," B has been located at the center of a symmetrically apportioned tonal space. Counting by semitones, that apportionment could be represented abstractly as 0 4 8. Any of the three functional tones — B, G, D♯ — could be conceptualized as "zero," in which case the other two will occupy the remaining positions. The reasons for regarding B as the "zero pitch" or "center tone" include (once again) its timbral and registral prominence; the fact that it was established first (and also — to peek at the end — sounded last), and is frequently held out in lengthy pedal points; and the fact that it participates in two symmetrical apportionments: the 0 4 8/with G and D♯ just traced, and the/0 6 octave-bisecting tritone relationship with F, periodically invoked by the English horn (and frequently seconded by the horns).

An especially subtle touch is the oboe part in Ex. 2-10d. Clearly an imitation (or transposition) of the horn tritones in mm. 82–83, it has the effect of surrounding B with D and G♯, pitches a minor third away on either side. In other words, the major-third shadowing of B (with D♯ and G) has been shrunk by a semitone, but with B still located at the center, as if "zeroing in." Rather than a strong progression toward B, in which

EX. 2-10C Claude Debussy, *Nuages*, mm. 64–68

EX. 2-10D Claude Debussy, *Nuages*, mm. 82–83 (third horn); mm. 86–87 (oboe)

B is perceived as an object of active desire, the zeroing-in technique establishes B as the fulcrum of a static tonal equilibrium, evocative not of the high-strung striving of contemporary German music, but of a sublime immobility (Ex. 2-11).

EX. 2-11   Zeroing in on the tone center in Claude Debussy, *Nuages*

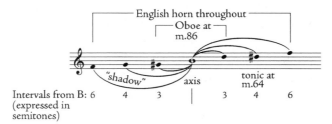

The tonality of the middle section (Ex. 2-10c) is colored by the use of pentatonic melody — or (as mentioned in connection with "Voiles") a melody drawn from an "anhemitonic" pitch collection, to call it by a name that keeps in mind its status as a "half-stepless" counterpart to (and tonal coconspirator with) the whole-tone scale — and also by the use of "modal" chord progressions. The minor triad heard at the outset is qualified as the tonic of "D♯ Dorian" at the end of the third measure, when it proceeds to a major subdominant chord containing B♯, the "raised sixth degree." Later on the tonic reappears in the major (respelled as E♭ in the strings), but alternates with B♭ minor (the "minor v"), which invokes the "Mixolydian" seventh degree in place of the too-focused (or too-focusing) leading tone. Harmonic focus is also avoided at the end of the piece, where no real cadence takes place, just a "liquidation" whereby significant harmony notes (the shadow G and tritone F at m. 99, plus the third of the tonic triad) simply drop out one by one, leaving B alone onstage when the curtain falls.

SYMBOLISM

If, on the other hand, the word *voiles* in the title of Debussy's piano prelude is taken to mean "veils," connoting mystery and concealment, Debussy's music can seem "literary" — concerned, that is, in its reluctance to draw explicit connections or maintain a strongly linear narrative thrust, with issues being raised in the literary domain by the

FIG. 2-4   Title page of Charles Baudelaire's *Richard Wagner et Tannhäuser à Paris* (1861).

poets and other "littérateurs" (literary hangers-on) who belonged to the "Symbolist" school. "Symbolism" was a somewhat older movement than "impressionism" in painting. It goes back to the work of the poet and critic Charles Baudelaire (1821–67), the first of the "decadents" and one of the obvious models for Des Esseintes, the hero of Huysmans's *À rebours*, discussed in the previous chapter. Baudelaire claimed to derive his artistic ideas on the one hand from the music and writings of Richard Wagner, and on the other from the American poet and literary theorist Edgar Allan Poe (1809–49). He lived the role of decadent to the tragic hilt, dying penniless in drug-induced insanity.

All literary Symbolists agreed in tracing their movement to a specific poem of Baudelaire's, the sonnet "Correspondances," published in 1857 in a collection called *Les fleurs du mal* ("Flowers of evil," sometimes translated "Poison blossoms"):

> La Nature est un temple où de vivants piliers
> Laissent parfois sortir de confuses paroles:
> L'homme y passe à travers des forêts de symboles
> Qui l'observent avec des regards familiers.
>
> Comme de longs échos qui de loin se confondent
> Dans une ténébreuse et profonde unité
> Vaste comme la nuit et comme la clarté,
> Les parfums, les couleurs et les sons se
> répondent.
>
> Il est des parfums frais comme des chairs
> d'enfants,
> Doux comme les hautbois, verts comme
> les prairies,
> —Et d'autres, corrompus, riches et triomphants,
>
> Ayant l'expansion des choses infinies,
> Comme l'ambre, le musc, le benjoin et l'enscens,
> Qui chantent les transports de l'esprit et des sens.

[Nature is a temple where living pillars at times send out muddled words: There, man passes through forests of symbols that watch him with familiar looks. Like long echoes that blend from afar in a deep penumbral wholeness as vast as the night and the light, aromas, colors and sounds give answer. There are aromas, cool as baby flesh, sweet as oboes, green as the fields—and others, tainted, rich and thriving, having the power of infinite expansion, like amber, musk, balsam and incense—that sing of the transports of spirit and sense.]

The crucial ideas here are two: *synesthesia*, the equivalence and interchangeability of sense experiences (the whole poem being a sort of gloss on Baudelaire's avowal that "my soul travels through scents the way the souls of others do through music"[18]); and the *occult* knowledge that synesthesia imparts. To see symbols in all things is to lend them a hidden meaning and (as the initial comparison of nature to a temple suggests) to approach the sensory as if it were the spiritual and vice versa. In part, Symbolism was a revival of what modern historians call the "premodern" or magical world view, an outlook that sought the hidden resemblances of all in all. As summarized by the French intellectual historian Michel Foucault, the premodern worldview and its ways of knowing

> tell us how the world must fold in upon itself, duplicate itself, reflect itself, or form a chain with itself so that things can resemble one another. They tell us what the paths of similitude are and the directions they take; but not where it is, how one sees it, or by what mark it may be recognized. These buried similitudes must be indicated on the surface of things; there must be visible marks for the invisible analogies. There are no resemblances without signatures. The world of similarity can only be a world of signs[19]

—which is to say, of symbols. And hence the virtual obsession among symbolist artists with medieval or pseudo-medieval subjects and settings. They not only enabled but positively demanded the adoption of a magical worldview that regarded nature as a gateway to a superior reality.

Factoring Wagner (and what he had come to mean to his numberless enthusiasts) into the equation turned symbolism into a universal "musicalization" of experience, for the relationship between the sensory and the spiritual was strongest in music, where the presence of conceptual objects (concrete "things") was less of an impediment to free association than in any other art, and where the experience of "objectless desire," especially strong in Wagner, had accustomed artists to the idea that all objects of desire were interchangeable. An enthusiastic French Wagnerian, the mystical writer Edouard Schuré (1841–1929), in a typically slanted history of the "music drama" published in 1882, made the strongest case that music, by its very nature, was the art of symbolism par excellence:

> If from the world of visible forms and ideas peculiar to poetry and the plastic arts we enter the world of sounds and harmony, our first impression is that of a man passing suddenly from the light into deepest darkness. In the former everything can be explained, follows logically and creates an image; in the latter everything seems to spring from unplumbed depths where darkness and mystery reign. In the one we find fixed outlines and the inflexible logic of immutable forms; in the other the flux and re-flux of a liquid element, perpetually in motion and metamorphosis, and containing an infinity of possible forms. In this impenetrable night-darkness into which music plunges us, we feel strongly the vibrations of life, but it is impossible for us to see or distinguish anything. But as the soul gradually becomes accustomed to this strange region, it begins to acquire a kind of second sight, rather like a somnambulist who, sinking deeper and deeper into his sleep, becomes submerged in his dream until real objects disappear from sight. But while the outer aspect of things is effaced, their inner content is revealed in a marvelous light.[20]

At its most extreme and musical, then, Symbolism promised knowledge through the senses of the spiritual, or a way *via* art of seeing past the appearances of the phenomenal world into the higher reality of the *au-delà*, the world "beyond" the senses. Art or literature that drew connections too explicitly—that said what it meant and meant what it said—only set limits on its power of evocation, thus frustrating its highest potential goal, that of occult revelation. "By describing what is [and only what is], the poet degrades himself and is reduced to the rank of schoolmaster," wrote Baudelaire; "by telling us what is possible he remains faithful to his vocation."[21] Or as Stéphane Mallarmé (1842–98), the leading Symbolist poet of the next generation, once exclaimed when an editor complimented him on the lucidity of an essay he had just submitted, "Give it back! I need to put in more shadows."

Now whereas drawing connections between Debussy and the impressionist painters was itself an exercise in impressionism, ringed with caveats (including the composer's expressed discomfort with the idea), his connections with Symbolism are biographical facts of major import to the conception of many of his most significant works. The orchestral composition that won him his first réclame, for example, the *Prélude à L'après-midi d'un faune* (Prelude to "The Afternoon of a Faun"), first performed in 1894, was inspired by (and was in some sense an interpretation of) the most famous poem of Mallarmé. Even earlier, he had composed a major song cycle, *Cinq poèmes de Baudelaire* (1890), to words by the spiritual father of the Symbolist movement. As the epigraphs at the top of this chapter attest, moreover, Debussy had read his Baudelaire well, and was given to paraphrasing him when talking "esthetics." His one completed opera, *Pelléas et Mélisande*, on which he worked from 1893 to 1902, was a practically verbatim setting (only slightly abridged) of what was widely taken to be the quintessential Symbolist drama, the work of Count Maurice Maeterlinck (1862–1949), a Belgian writer who after Mallarmé's death was regarded as the movement's leader. Two other operatic projects of Debussy's — *Le diable dans le beffroi* ("The devil in the belfry"), on which he worked from 1902 to 1911, and *La chute de la maison Usher* ("The fall of the house of Usher"), on which he worked from 1908 to 1917 — were based on works by Poe, Baudelaire's acknowledged mentor. The list of symbolists whose work Debussy set, or on which he contemplated basing orchestral or dramatic projects, could be extended manyfold.

Pelléas et Mélisande is not only a Symbolist drama; it is a drama "about" Symbolism; and as Debussy was thrilled to realize, it is a drama about music, as Symbolists like Schuré understood it. Neither Pelléas nor Mélisande, the pair of "operatic lovers" in the title (recalling Tristan and Isolde), is the play's central character. The central character is Golaud, Pelléas's brother and Mélisande's husband, the play's tragic hero. Although left alive at the end of the drama while Pelléas and Mélisande have perished, it is Golaud who is crushed in consequence of a fatal flaw. That flaw is his inability to accept things as they are, in all their infinite mysteriousness and ambiguity, their inaccessibility to reason, their indifference to human designs.

Incapable of accepting reality as "the flux and re-flux of a liquid element, perpetually in motion and metamorphosis, and containing an infinity of possible forms," to recall the words of Schuré, insisting rather on a realm of light and sharp outline in which "everything can be explained, follows logically and creates an image," Golaud finds himself alienated from all the other characters, who have "acquired the second sight of a somnambulist who, sinking deeper and deeper into his sleep, becomes submerged in his dream," of which the medium is music. Because of his philistine ("unmusical") insistence that things mean one thing and one thing only, and because he tries to force

F I G. 2-5   *Pelléas et Mélisande*, Act IV, scene 4, in the original production (Paris, Opéra Comique, 1902),
as printed in the periodical *Le Théâtre*.

the world into conformity with his limited vision, Golaud becomes a destroyer, and
is destroyed.

Here is a brief synopsis of the action, the paragraphs corresponding roughly to
Debussy's five acts:

> Out hunting, Golaud, the grandson of Arkel, king of Allemonde (a French/German
> pun meaning "all the world") comes upon a beautiful young woman weeping by a
> well. She is lost, having fled a place she will not name. Noticing her gold crown
> glittering in the well, Golaud makes as if to retrieve it, but she restrains him, saying
> she would rather die than have it back. She gives her name as Mélisande. She
> agrees to go with him. They marry against Arkel's wishes, but Arkel bows to the
> hand of fate and gives his blessing.
>
> Pelléas, Golaud's younger brother, befriends Mélisande. Seeking relief from
> summer's heat one day, they stray into a shady garden containing a well. He
> admires her long hair, which has fallen into the well. He asks her how she met
> Golaud. In answer, Mélisande takes her wedding ring off her finger to show him,
> but, playfully tossing it in the air, loses it in the well. That night she begins to sob
> and asks Golaud to take her away from the castle where they live. He notices the
> ring missing. He questions her. She lies about its whereabouts, saying she left it in
> a cave. He orders her to go immediately with Pelléas to the cave and retrieve it.
> While in the cave, she and Pelléas are startled by the sight of a starving family.
>
> Pelléas finds Mélisande sitting in a tower window, combing the hair he so
> admires and singing. He asks her to lean out so that he can see it. She leans out
> too far; the hair falls all over the enraptured Pelléas. Golaud discovers them. For
> reasons unexplained, Golaud leads Pelléas to an abandoned, stinking well in the

castle basement. Emerging into the sunlight, Pelléas seeks and finds Mélisande. They sit quietly in the shade. Golaud discovers them again and orders Pelléas to leave his wife alone. Golaud questions Yniold, his son by a former wife, about Pelléas and Mélisande. Yniold's childish answers exasperate him. He squeezes the boy's arm, causing him to cry out in pain. Then he has Yniold spy on the suspected pair. His renewed heated questioning frightens the boy.

Pelléas, having been told by his father (a character who never appears) that he looks like one marked for death, makes ready to leave the castle. He asks Mélisande to meet him one last time by the well where she lost her wedding ring. Golaud enters, is furious, insists (against Arkel's entreaties) that Mélisande's eyes conceal her guilt. He seizes her by the hair and throws her down. Taking his sword he leaves. Mélisande laments to Arkel that she has lost her husband's love. Pelléas and Mélisande keep their rendezvous. They confess their love to one another. Golaud bursts in and kills Pelléas with his sword. Mélisande flees with Golaud in pursuit.

Mélisande (who, we only now find out, has recently given birth) has been only superficially wounded by Golaud's sword. She is undergoing what the doctor foresees will be an uneventful recovery in her bedchamber. Golaud, filled with remorse, asks her forgiveness, but also asks to know the truth. She tells him that she and Pelléas were innocent, but he does not believe her and presses her further. She sinks back in exhaustion. To revive her spirits, Arkel shows her infant daughter. Servants appear. Golaud demands to know why. He is desperate to interrogate Mélisande some more, but Arkel bars the way. Mélisande dies. Golaud sobs. Arkel orders him out of the room for breaking the silence.

The superficial (or maybe not so superficial) parallels between this plot and that of *Tristan und Isolde* are hard to miss: lovers in spite of themselves, Pelléas and Mélisande die (the former directly, the latter indirectly) of wounds inflicted by the heroine's rightful husband. Both Wagner's opera and Debussy's could be viewed as mythic or mystical variants of the prosaic (or at least bourgeois) "eternal triangle" motif — variants that subvert the middle-class moral that usually animates the plot: that if forced to choose, one must sacrifice the gratification of one's desires to the greater good of the social order.

But where Wagner had attempted to muzzle morality, or shout it down with a grand and elemental, self-justifying passion, the voice of morality simply speaks a foreign language in Maeterlinck's play and Debussy's opera. Golaud wants definite and rational answers, but nobody understands his questions. Nor can anyone connect Golaud's actions with their consequences: Arkel's last words to Golaud, ordering him out of Mélisande's death chamber, are not peremptory but loving: "Don't stay here Golaud. She needs silence now. Come away, come away. It's terrible, but it wasn't your doing. She was such a quiet little creature . . ." Loving words, and yet mocking all the same. The playwright mocks Golaud's questions with enigmas of his own in the form of recurring motifs, for which we spectators are at a loss to provide explanations. Why wells, dark holes in the ground, in three scenes? Why the crown, glinting in the shadows? Why the ring, which disappears from view? Do they tell us where Mélisande came from after all? Do they tell us why she married Golaud? Or do they simply mock the questions, ours as well as Golaud's? The only answer that "works" within the confines of the drama seems to be that they are symbols, windows on the *au-delà*. They cannot be understood, except as portents of a destiny we cannot shape. Go with the flow, they warn; the need to know is death. We can live if we only don't connect — or rather, if we connect with everything, not just with what we think will satisfy our needs.

Not surprisingly, Debussy saw in all of this an ideal medium for his music — or rather, perhaps, saw his music as an ideal medium for all of this. But how, exactly, did his music provide that medium, that "liquid element" in which the somnambulistic action of the drama could unfold? Recognizing the affinities between *Pelléas* and *Tristan*, but also recognizing the wide gulf that separated the two operas both as drama and as "philosophy," the Polish musicologist Stefan Jarocinski described Debussy's achievement as one of "de-Wagnerizing" opera by "removing the Teutonic pathos and 'will to power.'"[22] On the basis of our previous analyses of Debussy's musical technique we might be tempted to take this observation a step further, and at the same time pinpoint the relationship between Debussy's musical technique and his philosophical or dramaturgical conceptions, by suggesting more concretely that Debussy de-Wagnerized his opera by removing (or "liquidating") the half steps — not every half step, of course, just those that expressed pathos or a "will to power," which is to say the cadential leading tones.

Debussy found the task of composing *Pelléas* exhausting. In fact (just as his hero-worshipped Musorgsky had done in *Boris Godunov*) he wrote the opera twice and never finished another. The first draft took him exactly two years, from August 1893 to August 1895. The apparent aimlessness of the action — or rather, the extreme passivity of all the characters save Golaud — was at first a powerful attraction. "Despite its dream-like atmosphere," he wrote of Maeterlinck's play, "it contains far more humanity than those so-called 'real-life documents'" of *verismo*,[23] the naturalistic melodramas of contemporary Italians like Mascagni and Puccini. In particular, it was bathed in "an evocative language whose sensitivity could be extended into music and into the orchestral ambience." This much was almost a direct paraphrase of Schuré.

But realizing it musically was another story. Debussy's letters, especially those written in 1894, are full of anguish and raillery against what he saw as the limits that his training had placed on his fantasy. "I've spent days trying to capture that 'nothing' that Mélisande is made of," he wrote to one friend.[24] To another he wondered whether there was anything left for a composer to do anymore but recycle clichés: "Impossible to count how often since Gluck people have died to the chord of the [Neapolitan] sixth, and now, from [Massenet's] *Manon* to Isolde, they do it to the diminished seventh! And as for that idiotic thing called a perfect triad, it's only habit, like going to a cafe!"[25] As for old Arkel, he "comes from beyond the grave and has that objective prophetic gentleness of those who are soon to die — all of which has to be expressed with do-re-mi-fa-sol-la-ti-do!!! What a profession!"[26]

Finally, he confided to Ernest Chausson, his closest musical friend after Satie, "I was premature in crying 'success' over *Pelléas et Mélisande*. After a sleepless night (the bringer of truth) I had to admit it wouldn't do at all. It was like the duet by M. So-and-so, or nobody in particular, and worst of all the ghost of old Klingsor, alias R. Wagner, kept appearing in the corner of a bar. So I've torn the whole thing up."[27] The scene to which Debussy was referring was the climactic one, the fourth scene of the fourth act, in which Pelléas and Mélisande exchange nocturnal confessions of love in a garden, and Golaud, intruding on them, kills his rival.

This was, of course, the scene that most closely paralleled the plot of *Tristan und Isolde* (act II), and therefore aroused the strongest anxieties in a composer who had declared that it was "time to be post – Wagner (*après Wagner*) rather than merely in the footsteps of Wagner (*d'après Wagner*)."[28] In view of its dramatic importance and its heavy emotional charge, it is not surprising to learn that this scene was both the first music in Debussy's opera to be sketched, in the summer of 1893, and the last to be completed, in January 1900. In all, it went through three complete rewrites.

Carolyn Abbate has demonstrated the extent to which the revisions of the scene were a conscious effort to exorcise "the ghost of old Klingsor."[29] (Klingsor was the name Wagner gave to the evil sorcerer in the second act of his last opera, *Parsifal*, who is defeated by the pure young title character; by calling Wagner by that name in his letter to Chausson, Debussy was obviously casting both Wagner and himself as characters in what can only too easily remind us of an "Oedipal" drama, a drama of vicarious patricide.) One instance, somewhat trivial but revealing, was the removal of what could be heard as a Tristanesque phrase (Ex. 2-12) at the point where Mélisande, sensing Golaud's approach, sings "Il y a quelqu'un derrière nous" (There is someone behind us). "Symbolically," Abbate comments, "it was Wagner whom Debussy heard standing behind the composition of *Pelléas*," and of course the old man had to go.

EX. 2-12   From the sketches to *Pelléas et Mélisande*, Act IV, scene 4

compare:

Elsewhere, however, despite Debussy's apparent search – and – destroy maneuver, conspicuous references to the *Tristan*-chord were allowed to stay, especially at places where the word *triste* (sad), or even the performance direction *tristement* (sadly), appear (Ex. 2-13). At such places, where despite the fraught dramatic situation Debussy was seemingly unable to resist a fairly sophomoric pun, we seem to have a striking confirmation of Ortega's diagnosis of the modern artist's essentially ironic disposition, creating — at a distance, so to speak — an "artistic art" that insisted upon displaying its artifice, not so much in ostentation as in modesty ("to see to it that the work of art is nothing but a work of art, . . . a thing of no transcending consequence").

The most significant alterations in the scene, however, were the ones that attentuated (or "clouded") the clarity of the tonal relationships. Unlike Wagner's, Debussy's *Tristan*-chords are not harmonically active; like the one in Ex. 2-13, which simply breaks off, they do not form part of any progression to a harmonic goal. Instead,

EX. 2-13   Claude Debussy, *Pelléas et Mélisande*, Mélisande, "Si, si, je suis heureuse . . . ."

(Oh yes, I am happy, but I am sad too…)

they float free of any tether of voice leading, free of "glue," and so does the scene as a whole. One is conscious of Debussy's effort not to impose any abstractly "musical" shape on the scene. Modulations are always unpredictable (hence unpredicted), never telegraphed. The listener is rendered as passive as the characters, borne along by the ill-defined yet incessant harmonic flux, the flux of fate. Still and all, one can discern a tonal plan if one is looking hard enough for it. And while looking for it might not be the best way to approach the opera in the opera house, it is worth doing here, under "laboratory conditions," just so as to appreciate the ways in which Debussy (recalling Mallarmé) "put in the shadows."

EX. 2-14   Claude Debussy, *Pelléas et Mélisande*, Act IV, scene 4, mm. 81–87

EX. 2-14   (*continued*)

Both tonally and dramaturgically, the scene can be broken down into three parts. The first culminates in the declaration of love (Ex. 2-14), surely the most resolutely unrhetorical such declaration in all of opera. The second, which begins with the scene's first explicitly notated key signature (F♯ major), comprises its lyrical core: Pelléas's part slows down to "aria tempo" (halves and quarters rather than quarters, eighths, and sixteenths) as he sings of his love; Mélisande, as ever, is erratic, matter-of-fact, "not all there," and though she reciprocates Pelléas's passion verbally, her music tends to break the mood. (Here Debussy acts as a sort of supreme stage director, controlling the singers' enunciation of Maeterlinck's lines to achieve the characteristically understated interpretation he desires, which may or may not have accorded with the playwright's intent.) The swift third section culminates in the lovers' desperate kiss in expectation of death, and Golaud's attack. Here (Ex. 2-15) even somnambulistic Mélisande manages a fairly long, fairly high note. In this doggedly understated context it comes across as a veritable *Liebestod*!

The entire scene contains only a single strongly articulated authentic cadence, only one spot where a functional "V" and a functional "I" are placed in direct succession. As might be guessed, it leads into the "aria" in F♯ major (Ex. 2-16). But only in a context like this could such a cadence count as "strongly articulated." The dominant is presented in second inversion, with the root C♯ a fleeting melodic presence rather than part of the actual "chord." True, the C♯/D♭ region has had some previous exposure—in one spot it seems to function as tonic, in another as dominant—which could be adduced as support for the cadence in Ex. 2-16. A truly determined analyst might even claim that the whole first part of the scene thus acts as a structural pickup to the second part (and might find further support, as Abbate suggests, in the sketches). But to make such a claim is to value an ounce of light over a pound of shadow. That does not accord very well with the Symbolist scale of values.

A similarly selective reading of the harmonic evidence might seek to connect Pelléas's anxiously asserted and sustained dominant seventh on G at the beginning of Ex. 2-17 with his "very expressive" C major at the end of it, and cast it all as an elaborate preparation for the F-minor cadence at the end. This, too, may accord with Debussy's initial harmonic plan. But to select only these circle-of-fifth moments for conceptual linkage is to ignore (for example) the lengthy pedal point on F♯ (recalling

EX. 2-15   Claude Debussy, *Pelléas et Mélisande*, Act IV, scene 4, mm. 266–271

EX. 2-16   Claude Debussy, *Pelléas et Mélisande*, Act IV, scene 4, mm. 96–98

the scene's tonal focal point) that leads up to the climactic kiss. (And here Debussy may have missed an apparition of "old Klingsor," since the pedal point that prepares the cataclysmic climax of Tristan and Isolde's lovemaking—thwarted in act II but triumphant in act III—was also an F♯.)

Far more salient to the ear and to the interpreting mind are the elaborately liquidated leading tones that dissolve potential dominants wherever (as Mallarmé might have said) lucidity threatens, as where an infusion of functionally undifferentiated whole-tone harmonies neutralizes the key of Pelléas's little aria (Ex. 2-18a). Another such intervention (Ex. 2-18b) turns the leading tone of F♯ into the innocuous third of a D-minor triad. At these points the tension that a German composer would have ratcheted up to the point of purposeful agony is allowed—fatalistically, it might seem—to wither.

Not surprisingly, then, harmonic effects like these rendered *Pelléas* virtually incomprehensible to Richard Strauss ("Richard II," as he was often called), then

EX. 2-17   Claude Debussy, *Pelléas et Mélisande*, Act IV, scene 4, mm. 176–201

EX. 2-17 (continued)

regarded (as we learned in the previous chapter) as Germany's harmonic innovator par excellence. At a performance of Debussy's opera that he attended in 1907 (two years after *Salome*) as the guest of Romain Rolland (1866–1944), the famous French novelist who was also a prolific writer on music, Strauss turned to his host after the first act and said, "Is it like this all the way through?"[30] On being assured that it was, he protested, "But there's nothing in it. No music. It has nothing consecutive. No musical phrases, no development." Spoken like Golaud himself, this. For Strauss, as for all the German maximalists, there could be neither intelligible continuity nor "development," nor even meaningful emotional expression, without semitone connections, or at least powerful expectations based on such connections. Strauss's perplexity was a tribute to Debussy's success at getting rid of the Wagnerian glue, relinquishing the harmonic driver's seat to "fate" rather than the foreordained goals (and the triumphalist esthetics) vouchsafed by the circle of fifths and its half-step surrogates. His quiescence, responsive in a way that German music had not yet become to a new psychological mood, proved far more subversive to traditional practice than Strauss's hyperactivity.

EX. 2-18A   Claude Debussy, *Pelléas et Mélisande*, Act IV, scene 4, mm. 133–135

EX. 2-18B   Claude Debussy, *Pelléas et Mélisande*, Act IV, scene 4, mm. 154–156

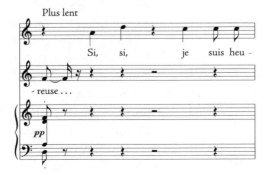

MÉLODIE

Just as Claude Monet was the principal model for the fictional artist Elstir in Marcel Proust's *In Search of Lost Time*, so Gabriel Fauré seems to have been the principal model for Vinteuil, the composer character in the same panoramic novel. The late-blooming Fauré, a pupil of Saint-Saëns both in composition and in organ, was never even slightly involved in countercultural or bohemian activities—from 1896 he was professor of composition at the Paris Conservatory, from 1905 to 1920 its director—but his many settings of "decadent" and Symbolist poetry helped establish a genre of subtly understated art song that the French call *mélodie*. (The actual use of the word seems to originate with Berlioz, who in 1830 published nine settings from the *Irish Melodies* of Thomas Moore under the title "Neuf mélodies," and reused the term a dozen years later in a group of six songs to texts by the Romantic poet Théophile Gautier composed in 1840–41, later orchestrated in 1856 as a cycle entitled *Les nuits d'été* or "Summer Nights.")

Proust himself was especially fond of Fauré's *Le parfum impérissable* ("The imperishable scent;" 1897), a *mélodie* to words by Charles-Marie-René Leconte de Lisle (1818–94), a member of the so-called Parnassians, a group of Parisian poets that took its name from Parnassus, the mountain abode of the Muses in Greek mythology. Their journal, *Le Parnasse contemporain*, was a forum for fastidious "estheticist" or art-for-art's-sake propaganda. In its sensualism, their work prefigured the "decadence" of the next generation. *Le parfum impérissable*, which first appeared in Leconte de Lisle's collection *Poésies barbares*, sums up many of the themes we have already associated with decadence and symbolism: esotericism (here evoked by an exotic locale), refinement (here evoked by the main image, a substance of supreme rarity), and above all the treatment of a sensory impression as the gateway to a spiritual revelation. (Proust's gigantic novel, as its readers never forget, is cast in similar terms, as a flood of emotionally fraught recollection released by the taste of a madeleine, a lemon-flavored pastry.) The poet compares the breaking of a vessel containing a priceless perfume, which then indelibly marks the desert with its scent, to the breaking of a rejected suitor's heart.

FIG. 2-6   Gabriel Fauré with his wife, Marie, playing a reconstructed Babylonian harp (March 1883).

Fauré's tiny song (Ex. 2-19), which transmits the poem to the listener like an urgent, intimate communication to a confidant, manages with harmony to evoke both the permanence of the scent/feeling and the emotional transports to which it gives rise. The deceptively regular returns to the placidly chugging E-major chords of the opening suggest the constant point of reference—one that seems destined to continue forever even after we have "tuned out"—and the modulatory departures, increasingly radical (though never dramatic or "rhetorical"), suggest the emotional leaps. Although the cadences in mm. 9 and 17 (and a final one in m. 31) might seem conventional enough, they are always introduced by five-note (that is, almost complete) whole-tone scales in the voice part that pull the harmony back, gently

EX. 2-19   Gabriel Fauré, *Le parfum impérissable*, Op. 76. no. 1, mm. 1–17

EX. 2-19 *(continued)*

but with mind-boggling speed, from a distant C minor to the predestined key of constancy. It was no doubt that swiftness of modulation, combined with its understated delivery, that induced what Proust, in a fan letter to the composer, called "a dangerous intoxication."[31]

One of the junior Parnassians, Paul Verlaine (1844–96), was Fauré's near-exact contemporary and friend. He went on to become one of the most celebrated of the Symbolists, perhaps as much because of his extraordinary life as for his art. In the title of an essay on several of his contemporaries Verlaine originated the catchphrase *poètes maudits* ("accursed poets"), and lived the role to the hilt. He deserted his wife, and with her the whole bourgeois lifestyle, in order to pursue a homoerotic relationship with his young protégé Arthur Rimbaud (1854–91), then aged sixteen, with whom he led a vagabond existence in Belgium and England. Two years later Verlaine shot and wounded his lover in a drunken fit of jealousy and was imprisoned for two years. Finally he re-embraced the Catholic faith and lived in deliberate poverty, dying prematurely of consumption. (It was during this last, down-and-out phase of his career that he was befriended by the straitlaced Fauré.)

In contrast to the outward turbulence of his life, Verlaine's poetry was famous for its elegance and euphony—in short, its "musicality." His famous treatise in verse, "Art poétique" (1874), begins with a line that became a slogan: *De la musique avant toute chose*, "Music above all!" Composers naturally agreed. Verlaine's verses quickly became, and have remained, the most-set poetry in the French language. Fauré wrote thirteen of his *mélodies* to poems by Verlaine, nine of them collected his first song cycle, *La Bonne Chanson* ("The good song," op. 61, 1892–94), which takes its name from the title of the 1870 collection in which the poems were originally published. It remains Fauré's best-known work.

Verlaine's poetry often evoked the same pseudoarchaism that, as we know, provided French composers with a source of stylistic rejuvenation. The poems in *La Bonne Chanson*, a wedding offering to his bride, were (despite the private and personal sentiments they expressed) of this artificial, highly crafted type. Verlaine even toyed with the idea of calling the set *Vieilles Bonnes Chansons*, "good old songs." The name would certainly have fit *Une sainte en son auréole*, the poem with which Fauré chose to begin his cycle. It is a sort of mock-troubadour song (or *canso*) modeled on seven-hundred-year-old prototypes replete with the imagery of the distant lady ("a saint within her halo, the mistress of the castle in her tower"), direct comparisons with "the noble ladies of yore," and a final reference to her unuttered "Carolingian code name." Fauré's cycle was dedicated to "Madame Sigismond Bardac," alias Emma, his illicit (because married) mistress, who later became the second wife of Claude Debussy. It was a situation redolent of *fins amours* or "courtly love," the idealized knightly worship of a married lady from afar that had provided medieval love songs with their subject matter. Thus the cycle had an intense private meaning for the composer as well; and, like the poet, he too sublimated it in a somewhat affectedly *recherché*, pseudomedieval style that gave his music the same sort of "brand-old" freshness at which Verlaine had aimed. It was a theme to which Fauré continually returned. As late as 1918, he reused the second line of the opening song from *La Bonne Chanson* ("Une châtelaine en sa tour," "The mistress of the castle in her tower") as the title of a little *Fantaisie* for harp, the "troubadour" (or, to be fastidiously correct, the Northern French "trouvère") instrument par excellence.

The piano part in *Une sainte* opens with a thrice-repeated descending pentatonic ("anhemitonic") scale redolent in some contexts of folklore, but here of "good old songs" like troubadour lyrics — or even Gregorian chant, just then undergoing a process of zealous stylistic restoration and revival at the Benedictine abbey of Solesmes, some hundred miles southwest of Paris. French composers were intensely — and somewhat nationalistically — interested in this project, since they regarded the Frankish chant as the earliest French music. (Almost needless to say, they were wrong: the chant was Roman, not French; but as Ernest Renan, the great French historian, famously put it right around this time, "getting its history wrong is part of being a nation.")

Further (and by now familiar) traces of neomedievalism in Fauré's song can be found in vocal cadences that ostentatiously avoid the leading tone, substituting for it a "flat seventh." At the final cadence the voice part descends stepwise to the "final," like most Gregorian chants, while the piano's deceptive cadence in m. 79 surrounds that final with appoggiaturas cunningly drawn from the harmonically neutral whole-tone scale, proceeding from there to a sort of "Lydian" cadence with a raised fourth degree (D natural) that resolves to the fifth of the tonic triad, thus replacing the normal leading-tone progression to the root. The few authentic cadences that survive the winnowing process barely register.

"ESSENTIALLY" (AND INTOLERANTLY) FRENCH

Perhaps more vividly than any other composition of the period, Fauré's exquisite *Requiem*, op. 48, painstakingly composed and revised over a span of twenty-three years (1877–1900), illustrates the characteristics that French musicians then wished to cultivate and propagate as "essentially French" as opposed to what was accordingly to be classified as "essentially German," or stereotypically Italian, or even what was once considered French. A greatly truncated setting of the Requiem Mass, the work does not even contain a Dies Irae, the section that inspired a theatrically thrilling hellfire-and-damnation response from Berlioz in 1837 and again from Verdi in 1874. Instead, as the critic Émile Vuillermoz (at one time a composition pupil of Fauré's) remarked, Fauré's *Requiem* is "a look toward heaven and not toward hell."[32] This attitude is pointedly confirmed at the end of the Requiem by the final section, a setting of the antiphon *In paradisum deducant te Angeli* ("May the Angels lead you into Paradise"), which is not even part of the Requiem Mass as such, but is sung on the way to the gravesite before burial on those occasions when burial immediately follows the service. This comforting representation of angelic harping is also a representation of a state of heavenly bliss, in which nothing remains to be desired. Therefore, the musical representation of desire, from which Germanic "absolute music" (not to mention all of opera) had drawn its sustenance, is virtually suppressed.

The dominant harmony is sounded only twice, and briefly, both times preceded by the iii_6, which considerably attenuates its force by seeming to turn the chord seventh (G) into a mere neighbor to an F$\sharp$ from which it proceeds and to which it returns. Other dominant sevenths are usually kept in check by "common-tone" progressions (as in Ex. 2-20a, where the fifth and seventh over B are transformed innocuously into the third and fifth over D instead of resolving functionally). And, having thus alternated with a harmony "down" a minor third, the tonic D is made to alternate a few measures later (Ex. 2-20b) with the complementary flat mediant harmony (F major), "up" the same minor third, lending D the sort of equilibrium at the center that we have already noted in Debussy, and which imparts the "imperturbable calm" that the American composer Aaron Copland (the pupil of a Fauré pupil, Nadia Boulanger), cited as characteristic both of Fauré's music and of the "French temperament."[33] (But of course that description, and even the effect, was getting to be a cliché; compare Gillmor on Satie above.)

Indeed, Fauré was mythologized even before his death, at the venerable age of seventy-nine, as the Frenchest of the French. Vuillermoz, in an appreciation published in 1922, recalling the Société Nationale de Musique (of which the twenty-six-year-old Fauré, as a protégé of Saint-Saëns, had been a founding member), declared that

EX. 2-20A   Gabriel Fauré, Requiem, *In paradisum*, mm. 17–20

EX. 2-20B   Gabriel Fauré, Requiem, *In paradisum*, mm. 25–29

In the midst of the Wagnerian epidemic, when Saint-Saëns, Franck, Massenet, d'Indy, Chabrier and [Henri] Duparc [1848–1933, a composer of *mélodies*] did not actually succumb, but were all affected by the contagion, he remained refractory toward the virulent romantic microbe, and preserved all his intellectual independence and all his racial sanity. During the epoch when the pupils of César Franck, notwithstanding their demonstrative nationalism, were naively Teutonizing our art, Gabriel Fauré, without professions of faith, without dogmas and without a catechism of industry, was the veritable guardian of our national traditions.[34]

Of course, those "national traditions" (to say nothing of that "racial sanity") were an ad hoc construction—a verbally constructed "discourse," as today's culture critics say, rather than a tangible reality—and as such could always be revised at a moment's notice. Take for example *Ariane et Barbe-bleue* ("Ariadne and Bluebeard"; 1907), the single completed opera by Paul Dukas (1865–1935), the fastidious composer of only a dozen published works, who is celebrated for a single one: *L'apprenti sorcier* or "The Sorcerer's Apprentice" (1897), a symphonic scherzo based on a ballad by Goethe (famously "choreographed" by the Walt Disney studios in the animated film *Fantasia* of 1939). Like *Pelléas et Mélisande*, Dukas's opera was also based directly (without any intervening libretto) on a play by Maurice Maeterlinck, in this case a decidedly "decadent" retelling of a famous folk legend originally committed to literature by the fabulist Charles Perrault in his *Tales of Olden Times* (1697), the original "Mother Goose," considered a national classic by the French.

In Perrault's telling, Bluebeard's seventh wife, Fatima, gives in to curiosity and opens a locked door behind which she discovers the dead bodies of her predecessors. (She is rescued from a like fate by the timely arrival of her brothers.) In Maeterlinck's version, the discarded wives—one of them named Mélisande (so *that's* where she must have been coming from when Golaud discovered her in Debussy's opera!)—are not dead. Indeed, they seem to take pleasure, or at least find security, in their secluded condition. They come to Bluebeard's aid when he is attacked, and finally refuse the freedom offered them in the name of sisterhood by the opener of the door, the tellingly renamed Ariadne (after the Greek mythological heroine who with her famous thread led Theseus out of the darkness of the labyrinth into the light).

Dukas's brilliantly colored score makes much, both in its orchestration and in its tonal relations, of the play's many-sided contrasts of darkness and light. The opera's chief leitmotif is a French (or, more specifically, a Breton) folk song that associates the former wives with "the daughters of Orlamonde," night-bound creatures in search of daylight (Ex. 2-21). But in the play and the opera daylight is rejected—implicitly undoing one of the "master narratives" defining the Teutonic tradition in music from Haydn and Beethoven all the way to Mahler. It would be hard to get more "French" than that.

Dukas, a conservatory classmate and friend of the slightly older Debussy, paid the latter tribute in *Ariane*—not so much by appropriating whole-tone effects that (while very noticeable) were by then nobody's property in particular, but by actually quoting snatches from Debussy's opera whenever the action concerned Mélisande, the character their operas have in common. Debussy was at first flattered and gratified by the homage, as a cordial letter to Dukas attests. But he was sorely baffled when a review by Louis Laloy, a very influential critic of the time, sought to polarize the two operas by contrasting their audiences and their critical followings: the "invertebrate descendants of 'debussyism'" congregating around *Pelléas et Mélisande* (which "must therefore contain unsuspected defects"), vs. the "*Ariane* party" consisting of "those who know how to value the essential qualities of the French spirit and of French art."[35] This invidious comparison must have been motivated at least in part by Dukas's use of a folk song,

EX. 2-21   "Artificially" harmonized folk tune from Paul Dukas, *Ariane et Barbe-Bleue*

Le Chant Soutérrain

Les cinq fil - les d'Or-la-mon- de (La fée noire est mor - te)

Les cinq fil - les d'Or-la-mon- de Ont cher-ché les _ por - tes

a simple, ingenuous (and "modally" diatonic) national artifact to stand out against the artificialities of his personal style, and by the presence in his opera of a "positive heroine" in the person of the light-bearing Ariadne, the would-be liberator. She bore comparison, of course, with Joan of Arc, or with Delacroix's "Liberty leading the people," cherished symbols all. Debussy himself drew the political connection (though without naming Dukas's opera) in a patriotic tirade he published in 1915, while World War I was raging. "Since Rameau," he lamented, way back in the early eighteenth century,

> we have had no purely French tradition. His death severed the thread, Ariadne's thread, that guided us through the labyrinth of the past. Since then, we have failed to cultivate our garden, but on the other hand we have given a warm welcome to any foreign salesman who cared to come our way. We listened to their patter and bought their worthless wares, and when they laughed at our ways we became ashamed of them. We begged forgiveness of the muses of good taste for having been so light and clear, and we intoned a hymn in praise of heaviness. We adopted ways of writing that were quite contrary to our own nature, and excesses of language far from compatible with our own ways of thinking. We tolerated overblown orchestras, tortuous forms, cheap luxury and clashing colors, and we were about to give the seal of approval to even more suspect naturalizations when the sound of gunfire put a sudden stop to it all.[36]

The last sentence is chilling, with its reference to "even more suspect naturalizations." Many commentators have interpreted the phrase as a reference to the Jewishness of Schoenberg (or of Mahler, whom the French loved to jeer as *Malheur*, "misery"), regarded as incompatible with Frenchness. But why, then, the pointed insistence on the loss of Ariadne's assistance, in view of her recent installation at the center of an opera that had been touted in the press (and to Debussy's cost) as a monument to the "essential qualities of the French spirit and of French art"? Was the apparent irony the result of envy or spite . . . or what?

As Anya Suschitzky, a historian of French opera, has pointed out, there were more dangerous, contemporary, and politically volatile resonances within Dukas's opera than those we have noted up to now.[37] In addition to Joan of Arc or Marianne, Maeterlinck's and Dukas's light-bearing Ariadne bore an unmistakable resemblance, as well, to a traditional allegory of "Truth"—a naked woman rising from out of a well and bearing a mirror to catch the sunlight—that had become particularly familiar in fin-de-siècle France owing to its frequent use in press cartoons commenting on the Dreyfus affair, perhaps the most divisive political scandal in the nation's history. (Captain Alfred Dreyfus, the highest-ranked Jewish officer in the French army, had been convicted on trumped-up charges of treason and exiled; his subsequent exoneration was stridently opposed by self-proclaimed "anti-Semites"—so called for the first time.) And in light of that association, a comment Debussy had made three years earlier in a letter to his publisher takes on a familiar and ugly ring: "You're right, *Ariane et Barbe-bleue* is a masterpiece," Debussy wrote, "but it's not a masterpiece of French music."[38] What could this be but a reference to the fact that, like Schoenberg, like Mahler, and like the unjustly defamed and disgraced Captain Dreyfus, the author of *Ariane et Barbe-bleue* was a Jew?

Debussy's remark is all the more troubling in view of his previous resistance to chauvinism, so unusual and refreshing amid the raging nationalistic currents that carried Europe from the aftermath of the Franco-Prussian War to the onset of World War I (and also considering the fact that Emma Bardac, his second wife and the mother of his only child, was of Jewish ancestry). Listing his hates in a letter of 1895, he included (alongside the expected "crowds and universal suffrage") something he called *les phrases tricolores*—"tricolor phrases."[39] The reference, of course, was to the French flag, and the expression could best be translated, perhaps, as "flag-waving."

But by 1912, even Debussy had been swept up in the inexorable current, giving vent like so many others to a rigorous, arbitrarily privileged notion of what made for authentic French music, inevitably implying a similarly rigid and arbitrary, intransigent notion of what made for an authentic Frenchman. Such notions served the cause of national solidarity by negation and exclusion, producing social division rather than cohesion. Must this always be the price of valuing national identity? Must the notion of nation always be racialized?

THE EXOTICIZED SELF

The case of Maurice Ravel (1875–1937), who for at least a dozen years after Debussy's death was widely regarded as the foremost French composer, gives reassurance that a positive response to these questions need not be a foregone conclusion, and that national character can be pursued and achieved without insane appeals to "racial sanity."

Ravel, a pupil of Fauré, wrote in a colorful and sensuous style marked by a deep affinity for Russian music. He, too, was perfectly capable of platitudinous generalization when asked for it. In an interview published in *The Musical Leader*, a British journal, in 1911, Ravel told a reporter that

> The work done in France today is by far more simple than the music by Wagner, his followers, or his greatest disciple, Richard Strauss. It has not the gigantic form of Beethoven and Wagner, but it possesses a sensitiveness which other schools have not. Its great qualities are clearness and order. It is intensely rich in musical matter. There is more musical substance in Debussy's *Après-Midi d'un Faune* than in the wonderfully immense Ninth Symphony by Beethoven. The French composers of today work on small canvases but each stroke of the brush is of vital importance.[40]

But Ravel's remark does not attribute the differences between nations, even when cast invidiously, to biological or spiritual essences, only preferences and practices that can be explained historically or socially rather than "racially." Moreover, when speaking of himself rather than his "school," Ravel blithely contradicted himself, claiming now to "find beauty in all things; the great and the small, the humble and the powerful."

He might have added "all nations." In later interviews, including some that followed the World War, Ravel even admitted to admiring the work of his German contemporaries, albeit with reservations. In one such interview, he called it "curious and a shame that an all but solid wall separates their goals from those of French musicians." Ravel's greater tolerance may have had something to do with his heritage. Born in the Pyrenees to a French father and a Basque mother, he thought of himself as ethnically exotic and was drawn to other manifestations of national or ethnic exoticism, even Jewish ones, which he treated with unusual sympathy. Three of his songs were composed to texts in languages associated with the Jews. This is something one cannot imagine Debussy doing, or even Dukas—for precariously assimilated Jews, as we have already seen, were often reluctant to call attention to, or even to admit, their differences from the surrounding culture.

One of Ravel's *Deux mélodies hebraïques* (1914) was a setting of the kaddish (sanctification), the most hallowed of all Jewish liturgical texts. Its language is Aramaic, the ancient colloquial language of Jews in the Holy Land (hence the language spoken by Jesus). The other song in the 1914 set, and also an earlier "Chanson hébraïque" that formed part of a set of *Chants populaires*

FIG. 2-7 Maurice Ravel, by Achille Ouvre (b. 1872).

(1910), were harmonizations of Yiddish folk songs. These were far more unusual and significant, since they signaled acceptance by a non-Jew not only of the culture of the biblical Hebrews, but also of the recent popular culture of diaspora Jews—the Jews European gentiles encountered in their everyday lives and often despised—as a valid source for serious contemporary art. (Not even all Jewish composers of art music were that tolerant: the most famous of them, Ernest Bloch (1880–1959), was very much a purist on this score, preferring to invent an artificially "biblical," orientalist style of his own rather than draw upon contemporary Yiddish culture.) The 1910 set was written as an invited entry in a folk-song harmonization contest sponsored by a Moscow organization called *Dom pesni* (House of Song). For this purpose the composer was furnished with song melodies, including a Yiddish one that had been collected by the Russian composer and critic Joel Engel in Vilna (now Vilnius, Lithuania), a large town in Russian Poland that had become a center of Jewish culture. The opportunistic circumstances in which the song was composed might seem to minimize its significance, and that of Jewish culture generally, as a source of inspiration for Ravel.

But the 1914 set was composed on Ravel's own initiative, for which purpose Ravel procured a large collection of Jewish folksong arrangements collected and edited by the Russian-Jewish ethnographer Zinoviy (or Süssman) Kisselgof and published the year before in St. Petersburg by the Society for Jewish Folk Music. Unlike his first attempt, Ravel's second Yiddish song—"L'énigme éternelle" ("The eternal riddle") on its French title page; "Alte kasche" ("Old question") in the original—was sufficiently representative of his personal style to draw censure from Abraham Zvi Idelsohn, an authoritative scholarly historian of Jewish music, for disfiguring the melody by harmonizing it "in ultra-modern style, without regard for its scale and the nature of the mode."

Ex. 2-22a contains roughly half of Ravel's setting, while Ex. 2-22b shows the harmonization made by Alexander Zhitomirsky, a member of the St. Petersburg Society, for Kisselgof's collection, which according to Idelsohn represented a "correct" harmonization of the mode and scale in question. Since artistic harmonizations of monophonic folk songs are based on esthetic rather than scholarly considerations, Idelsohn's strictures against the Jewishness of Ravel's setting were no more legitimate or dispassionate than Debussy's against the Frenchness of Dukas. Both were examples of what is now called "identity politics." Both were motivated by intransigence.

EX. 2-22A   Maurice Ravel, *Deux mélodies hébraïques* (1914), no. 2, *L'énigme éternelle*, mm. 1–26

Meanwhile, Ravel's setting of the melody, while as arbitrary as any artistic harmonization of folklore had to be, and dissonant in a manner that no doubt struck the ear of a traditional scholar like Idelsohn as willful, was by no means "without regard for its scale and the nature of the mode." Indeed, the most constant factor in the accompaniment is the distinctive augmented second of the Jewish "Ahavoh rabboh" mode (to adopt Idelsohn's spelling). The augmented second, perpetually oscillating as the lower voice of the piano's "right-hand" staff, seems to illustrate the song's subject: the perpetual imperturbable spinning of the world and its indifference

E X. 2-22A   (continued)

EX. 2-22B   Alexander Zhitomirsky's harmonization in "Ahavoh-rabboh" mode

to mankind's concerns. Together with the piano bass, the same augmented second makes up the ostinato whose brief disruption and reinstatement define the song's ABA form.

Behind the decorative harmonic surface, the song's tonal trajectory is a pristine I–V–I in E minor (with V coming at the midpoint, where Ex. 2-22a ends, the song's most plainly articulated cadence). At the beginning, and at the reprise, Ravel cleverly accommodates the "modal" or "Hebraic" A♯ to the key of E minor by embedding it in a harmonic configuration borrowed from the "octatonic" scale, an eight-note alternation of tones and semitones that can be traced back from Ravel's immediate sources in what was then the latest Russian music, through Liszt, and ultimately to Schubert, all of them composers who at various times Ravel acknowledged as models. This stylistic patrimony somewhat distinguishes Ravel's harmonic idiom from those of his French contemporaries, making it a little more astringent than theirs, a little more dissonant, perhaps a little more accommodating toward semitones, but just as sensuous and luxuriant once a taste for it has been acquired.

The elusive harmonic trajectory of "L'énigme éternelle" can be described as an "octatonic-diatonic interaction," to use a term coined in the 1970s by the American music theorist Pieter van den Toorn.[41] Much of the terminology we now use to describe the style and technique of early-twentieth-century music was coined long after the fact, but so is the terminology we use to describe earlier music; most theoretical generalizations follow practice at a respectful distance, and this has been particularly true in the case of modernist music, which often strove hard on principle to keep its technical bases secret, the better to stay "ahead of its time." Ex. 2-23 shows how the opening chords in Ravel's setting derive from the background scale, and also the well-disguised fact that the two chords are actually a single harmony (one that we will reencounter many times and eventually give a name to) and its inversion.

EX. 2-23   Octatonic analysis of Maurice Ravel's *L'énigme éternelle*

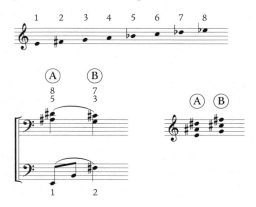

Ravel was surely drawn to the "Ahavoh rabboh" mode, and to this melody in particular, when he noticed the congruence of its first thirteen bars with the notes of the tone-semitone scale, and devised his harmonic accompaniment accordingly. The first diatonic intrusion in the melody is the B in m. 17. Prefigured from the very beginning in the left hand's off-beat eighth note, it will shortly assert itself cadentially (as we have seen), only to be resuppressed from the melody in m. 30 when the original tune (and words) are reprised. Thus the whole setting takes its shape from the tonal (or "modal") interaction of octatonic and diatonic scales. Also noteworthy is the manner in which Ravel altogether suppresses the note A natural from the setting until m. 25 (the tail end of the example), when it is suddenly asserted by the melody (and as the apparent root of Ravel's harmony) to form an effective Far Out Point from which a retransition to the opening harmony becomes especially meaningful. In short, all the most distinctive and seemingly personal (or "original") aspects of the harmonization can be characterized as "deductions" from the borrowed tune, the Hebraic mode, and their perceived harmonic implications.

THE SENSUAL SURFACE

Ravel's eclecticism was more innocent and accommodating than Debussy's probably because it proceeded from a more optimistic, even hedonistic, view of art and its purposes. If Debussy's primary poetic counterpart was Mallarmé, and Fauré's was Verlaine, then Ravel's was surely his friend Henri de Régnier (1864–1936), one of the most prominent younger Symbolists, whose verses abound with the imagery of joyful sensuality. Ravel only set one poem of Régnier's to music, *Les grands vents venus d'outremer* ("The great winds that come from over the sea"; 1907); but on two occasions he used lines by Régnier as epigraphs for instrumental pieces. *Jeux d'eau* ("Fountains"; 1901), dedicated "to my dear master, Gabriel Fauré," is prefaced by a quotation from Régnier's *Fête d'eau* ("Water holiday"), entered in the manuscript in the poet's own hand: *Dieu fluvial riant de l'eau qui le chatouille,* "A river god laughing at the water that is tickling him." And the piano suite *Valses nobles et sentimentales* ("Noble and sentimental waltzes"; 1911), with its title borrowed from Schubert, is headed by a line from one of Régnier's novels in praise of *le plaisir délicieux et toujours nouveau d'une occupation inutile,* "the delightful and ever-renewed pleasure of a useless occupation."

This last could be taken not only as Ravel's artistic credo, but also—to the extent that it was uttered with bravado, in defiance of Germanic importance (or self-importance)—as that of France itself. The very precocious *Jeux d'eau,* written early in the composer's career (just after leaving the Conservatory, in fact), makes the point clearly, but with an ironic fillip. Seemingly all ear-tickling texture and color, and for that reason often looked upon as a programmatic assertion of Frenchness in the face of all that Germany held dear, the piece is actually hung on a frame that turns out to be as pristine a "sonata form" as any German pedagogue could have required. The title is borrowed from Liszt—the third book of pieces in Liszt's series *Années de pèlerinage* ("Years of pilgrimage") contains a famous fountain piece called "Les jeux d'eaux à la Villa d'Este"—and so is the brilliant piano style, slightly "maximalized" by the use of double notes to be played by the thumb, a predilection that the composer could freely indulge within a harmonic idiom that so often treated seconds as stable chord components (in other words, one that treated seventh chords, including inverted ones, as consonant). The form, however, seems to have come right out of a textbook, as comparison with the score will verify.

> Exposition:
> 1st theme m. 1
> 2nd theme m. 19
> Development (mainly of 2nd theme) m. 49
> Recapitulation:
> 1st theme m. 62
> (Cadenza m. 67)
> 2nd theme m. 77

But as usual, the form diagram leaves out what is most interesting; and as usual (for an up-to-date French composer), what is interesting about the music is its soft tonal focus and the ways in which that softness is achieved. As always, dominant chords and leading tones are rare as hens' teeth. The key seems to be unmistakably E major; yet its leading tone, D♯, is most likely to be found (as at the very beginning of the piece) as an ornament to the tonic triad, turning it into a piquant major-seventh chord. The only dominant chord on the first page of the music (Ex. 2-24a), in fact, hence the only cadential confirmation the tonic will ever get, comes on the last eighth-note of m. 6 in the form of a French sixth chord with F in the bass, but with B (presented in the right hand only) arguably functioning as the root. (Typically, however, the chord is filled in by a soft-focus whole-tone scale.)

Much more prominent on the surface of the music are symmetrical "rotations" by major and/or minor thirds. It is necessary to use the clumsy "and/or" in describing the

EX. 2-24A   Maurice Ravel, *Jeux d'eau*, first page

EX. 2-24B   Maurice Ravel, *Jeux d'eau*, mm. 4–5, reduced

(Accidentals apply only to the immediately following note)

phenomenon because the major- and minor-third cycles are often superimposed, as in mm. 4–5 (see Ex. 2-24b). Reducing the second half of m. 4 to four block chords, we may observe a sort of interlocking pair of augmented triads, a construct of major thirds comprising five out of the six notes of the whole-tone scale, transposed four times by descending minor thirds. In conjunction with parallel progressions by whole tones and semitones, these third cycles — /0 4 8 (12)/ for major and /0 3 6 9 (12)/ for minor — will govern much of the short-range harmonic motion. At the short range, circle-of-fifths progressions are a strange special effect.

They remain in effect, however, behind the scenes, and assert their traditional rights over the long-range tonal trajectory, as a comparison of the "second themes" as heard in the exposition and the recapitulation will show. The first time around (Ex. 2-25a), B (=V) dominates the harmonic background (top of the right hand in m. 19, bottom of the left hand in m. 21), but never functions as a triadic chord root for the simple reason that triads have been banished from the scene: the scales in use are pentatonic, and the only intervals sounding as "harmony" are seconds, fourths, and fifths. The melody (left hand in mm. 19–20, right hand in mm. 21–23), while seeming to maintain a sharp tonal focus, in fact cannot come to a cadence in the absence of half steps: none of its notes has clear "priority" over the others. In the recapitulation (Ex. 2-25b), by contrast, the B is first approached by an exceptional circle-of-fifths progression that identifies it unequivocally as a functioning dominant, and, caught by the pedal in m. 77, it anchors the otherwise anhemitonic and ambiguous restatement of the theme that follows like a traditional "organ point." The explicit subdominant in the bass at mm. 80–81 descends so decisively to the tonic that not even the typical withholding of the leading tone on the last quarter of m. 81 can compromise the clarity of the final cadence. (And then, of course, the fugitive D♯, very much in character, reappears as a very stable decoration of the tonic in the last four bars, which take on the character of a coda.)

EX. 2-25A   Maurice Ravel, *Jeux d'eau*, mm. 19–21

EX. 2-25B   Maurice Ravel, *Jeux d'eau*, mm. 75–82

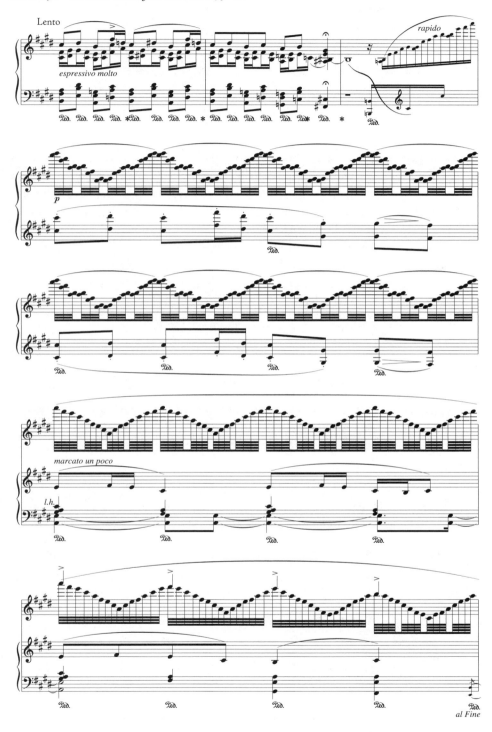

EX. 2-25B (*continued*)

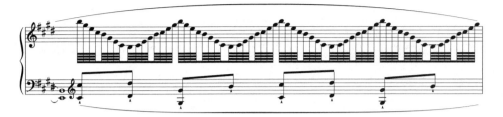

Harmonically the most far-out (or at least the tangiest) moment comes in the "cadenza," as it is somewhat arbitrarily designated in the little form diagram above—more precisely in m. 72 (Ex. 2-26), which contains a long passage in small notes signaling the equivalent of a fermata or "time-out." At this vividly climactic moment, surely meant to invite the listener to visualize the spouting, spurting fountain at full disport, the /o 6/ tritone relationship that elsewhere governs harmonic successions is telescoped into a "simultaneity." Triads on F♯ and C—the former (all on the black keys) consistently confined to the left hand, the latter (on the white keys) to the right—seem to coexist within a six-note "polychord."

EX. 2-26 Maurice Ravel, *Jeux d'eau*, m. 72

There are two ways this chord might be analyzed, both historically and in terms of its functional status. Both involve maximalizations of existing practices. The first, more traditional, explanation would be to regard the harmony as a functional French sixth chord on F♯, the supertonic (II) in E major, in which the two thirds that make up the chord (F♯-A♯ and C-E) have each "sprouted a fifth." This interpretation finds its confirmation at the end of m. 76, when the progression is sorted out into its constituents, the C-major harmony (now sporting a seventh) giving way to the F♯ (now sporting a ninth) within the circle-of-fifths progression already shown in Ex. 2-25b, the F♯ proceeding along the same circle of fifths to the dominant pedal on B.

RUSSIAN FANTASY

The more radical way of interpreting the chord would be to regard it as the product of a symmetrical "interval cycle." The common practice against which this second interpretation needs to be measured is not the "ordinary" tonal practice based on fifths, but a practice that had only arisen in the very latest Russian music, all of it written within a decade or so of *Jeux d'eau*. In his most recent operas, Nikolai Rimsky-Korsakov in particular had been experimenting zealously with cycles of minor thirds as a way of conjuring up supernatural or magical worlds. As he explained in his autobiography, Rimsky-Korsakov had first observed these cycles, and the octatonic scales that could be derived from them, in Liszt's first symphonic poem, the so-called Mountain Symphony.[42] Beginning in the 1890s, Rimsky was himself engaged in a maximalizing quest; he could with considerable justice be called the first Russian modernist.

The reasons for the quest are worth noting. Up to the early 1880s, the dominant genres of Russian opera had been historical dramas and peasant comedies, the former corresponding to the "serious" type of traditional European opera, the latter to the old opera buffa. The assassination of Tsar Alexander II in 1881 brought in its wake the strictest code of censorship the Russian autocracy ever imposed. Historical dramas were virtually banned, and even peasant comedies were regarded as questionable subjects if they involved Ukrainians (who were suspected of separatism). So Russian composers, hitherto virtually obsessed with realism, were forced into an about-face. "Fantastic" subject matter — folk tales and fairy tales — became about the only type the censors regarded as safe. At first by edict, later as a result of a seriously kindled interest in harmonic novelties, the realm of fantasy became Rimsky-Korsakov's virtually exclusive domain.

The harmonic novelties in question were overwhelmingly octatonic: that is, they involved progressions based on the harmonies that could be derived from the 0 3 6 9 "nodes" of the scale, the minor-third cycle that became an octatonic scale when passing tones were added (just as a whole-tone scale resulted from the adding of passing tones to an /0 4 8/ major-third cycle, something one finds as early as Schubert). Ex. 2-27 shows the complex of harmonies that may be drawn from an octatonic scale whose nodes correspond to the /0 3 6 9/ progression Ravel employed in *Jeux d'eau* — that is, the progression that contains the F♯-C tritone axis, and Ex. 2-28 is a scene-setting passage that conjures up the fantastic underwater world of the Sea King in Rimsky-Korsakov's opera *Sadko* (1897).

The notes circled in Ex. 2-28 are the only ones not found in the scale shown in Ex. 2-27. Chromatic passing tones one and all, they contribute to the smoothness of the

EX. 2-27   Triadic harmonies referable to an octatonic collection

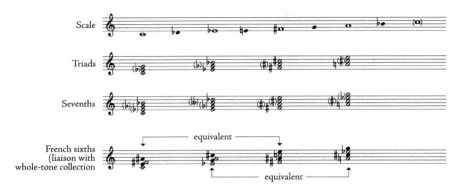

EX. 2-28   Nikolai Rimsky-Korsakov, *Sadko*, Act I, scene 2, mm. 1–23

part writing but do not register as harmonically significant. Thus Rimsky in *Sadko* was actually doing something a bit more radical than Ravel in *Jeux d'eau*, at least from the "structural" point of view: he was mining the octatonic collection for lengthy passages of "seemingly traditional" harmonies that were nevertheless "without tonal motivation," in the words of the music theorist Elliott Antokoletz.[43] What this means is that there is no way, up to m. 19, of deciding which of the constituent harmonic roots in Ex. 2-27 is the tonic. It is only the dominant of C, which is not part of the scale of reference (and which therefore sounds like an agent acting on the harmony from without), that allows a tonic function to emerge. And when it does, it focuses attention on the title character, Sadko, a human intruder on the magical sea world, who is about to sing, and who inhabits the ordinary world of mortals where fifths, not thirds, prevail.

This opposition of "human" music based on fifth relations and "magic" music based on symmetrical cycles of thirds was the harmonic novelty that so attracted and influenced the younger composers of Russia and France alike, beginning with Ravel's generation. The French-Russian affinity will look even stronger in the light of Ex. 2-29, another snatch from the same scene in *Sadko*, where two scales based on symmetrical cycles of thirds (a whole-tone scale in the "soprano," decorated with trills and chromatic neighbors, and an octatonic scale in the "alto") are set in motion over a bass that oscillates between E and its tritone counterpart B♭, the two pitches that (as exhibited in the second part of Ex. 2-29) bisect both scales and furnish the whole progression with a harmonically static axis of symmetry.

The use of dominant-ninth chords for harmony adds to the symmetry in evidence, since the dominant-ninth chord is intervallically (hence inversionally) symmetrical: its constituent intervals form a palindrome (M3-m3-m3-M3) that by definition remains constant whether counted from the bottom or from the top. Although composed by a

EX. 2-29A   Nikolai Rimsky-Korsakov, *Sadko*, Act I, scene 2

EX. 2-29B   The symmetrical scales and their points of intersection

Russian born in the 1840s, this passage could easily slide unnoticed into a composition by a Frenchman born in the 1860s (Debussy) or the 1870s (Ravel). The difference — and it was a crucial one — lay in the degree of calculation involved. The scholarly Russian did these things systematically and "theoretically." The hedonistic "decadent" French did them "by ear." Rimsky thoroughly disapproved. The one time he is known to have attended a concert at which Ravel's music (including *Jeux d'eau*) was played, he was asked his opinion and, "after hemming and hawing for a while"[44] (according to one of his pupils) he said, "As far as the principle of using dissonance with all the rights of consonances is concerned, it's not my cup of tea; although I should hurry right home lest I get used to it and, God forbid, begin to like it.'" So while he may not have wished to like what Ravel was doing, Rimsky grasped it well, just as he grasped the underlying principle that drove maximalism. He took Liszt's innovations further, but drew a line. Ravel overstepped this line, but (as we shall see) drew another. And yet it could be argued that if Ravel went further than Rimsky in his tolerance for dissonance, Rimsky went further than Ravel in his freedom from the circle of fifths. In any case, Rimsky's witticism about "using dissonance with all the rights of consonances" jibes remarkably with a pseudopolitical slogan ("the emancipation of dissonance") that Arnold Schoenberg would soon be touting in earnest. By then, Ravel would no longer be on board. (To him, Schoenberg's stuff was "laboratory music."[45])

But Rimsky's dictum applies well to Ravel's novel idea, that of mixing into pungent "polyharmonies" chords that Rimsky used only in succession. Only once, in a work he did not live to complete, did Rimsky ever try it himself: see Ex. 2-30.

EX. 2-30   Nikolai Rimsky-Korsakov, sketch for *Heaven and Earth* (1908)

Yet here again the younger composer managed to trump the elder at his own game. In *Rapsodie espagnole* for orchestra (1908), another composition with a Lisztian title but Rimskian content, Ravel saturated his music with brilliant orchestral effects he had learned from the Russian composer. The most general influence came, naturally enough, from Rimsky's *Capriccio espagnol* (1887). One very specific device, glissandos of natural harmonics in the strings, came courtesy of Rimsky's *Christmas Eve* suite (1904), given its first French performance in 1907, shortly before Ravel started work on his *Rapsodie*. The most telling appropriation from Rimsky, perhaps, took the form of woodwind cadenzas over fermatas in the strings, borrowed from Rimsky's most popular orchestral work, *Sheherazade* (1888), a symphonic suite (that is, a suite of symphonic poems) based on tales from the *Arabian Nights*.

Rimsky had played a solo clarinet off against repeated pizzicato chords in the strings (Ex. 2-31). The harmonic progression is drawn once again from the repertoire illustrated in Ex. 2-27: dominant sevenths on A, C, and F♯, together with E♭ making up an 0 3 6 9 cycle of minor thirds. Against them, the notes given constant emphasis in the repeated clarinet phrases (E and G), fit in, respectively, as fifth and seventh over A, third and fifth over C, and finally seventh and ninth over F♯. Thus "octatonicism" is reconciled with the older technique, also a Russian favorite, of "common tone" progression.

In Ravel's cadenzas (Ex. 2-32), the harmonies, like those in *Jeux d'eau*, are mixed (or superimposed). In the first, a pair of clarinets noodle arpeggios centering on A over a sustained dominant ninth on E♭: a tritone relationship that fills in the gaps, so to speak, between the C and F♯ in *Jeux d'eau* according to the scheme in Ex. 2-27. In the second, for two bassoons, harmonies built over not two but three roots drawn from a single /0 3 6 9/ matrix are set simultaneously in motion: C♯ (bassoons), B♭ (cellos and basses), and E (violin harmonics).[46] In effect, Ravel has combined the harmonic contents of all three Rimskian cadenzas in Ex. 2-31 into a single (or rather a triple) "polychord."

EX. 2-31   Nikolai Rimsky-Korsakov, *Sheherazade*, II

EX. 2-31 (continued)

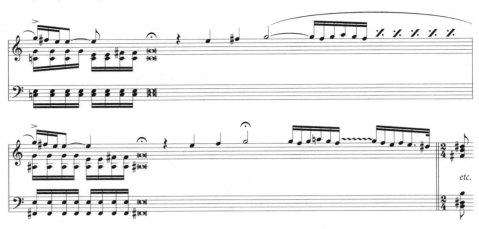

EX. 2-32A   Maurice Ravel, *Rapsodie espagnole*, I, Cadenza at fig. 6

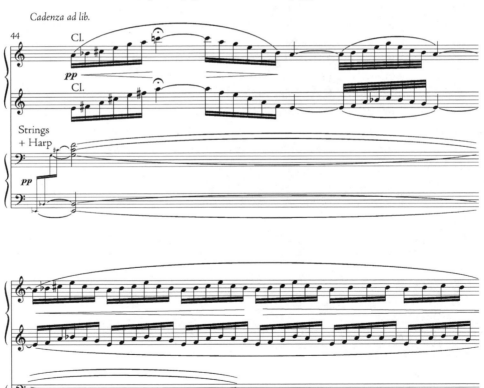

EX. 2-32A   (continued)

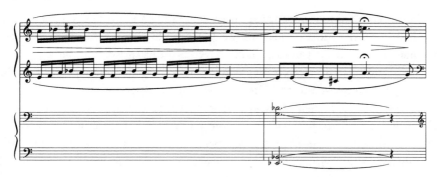

EX. 2-32B   Maurice Ravel, *Rapsodie espagnole*, I, Cadenza at fig. 8

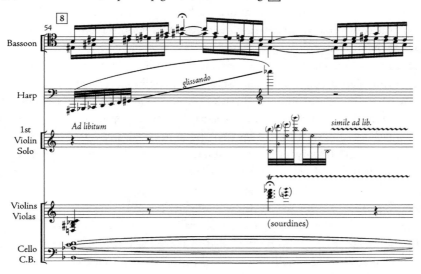

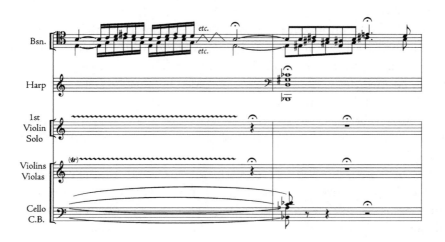

FEMALE COMPETITION

That kind of emulation—outward homage concealing an effort to surpass—has an ancient history in the literate music of the West, and has often seemed to drive that history, insofar as the history of music is conceived as the history of innovative composing techniques. Early instances of creative emulation include the many polyphonic Mass Ordinary cycles composed in the fifteenth century on shared cantus firmus melodies like *L'Homme armé*, with their dizzying feats of contrapuntal virtuosity.

Friendly (or not so friendly) rivalry among composers has surely undergirded many instances of "mutual influence," such as that between Mozart and Haydn, particularly in the domains of string quartet and symphony, which contributed greatly to the so-called emancipation of instrumental music—"absolute music"—in the nineteenth century. Beethoven's semiantagonistic (or at least "agonistic," contestatory) relationship to his immediate predecessors and contemporaries has become proverbial, and, constantly replayed and reenacted by succeeding generations of agonists, created a crisis in the histories of the same genres.

More recent notions, such as historicism and modernism, were similarly saturated with the principles of emulation, contest, and innovation as a measure of strength, to the point where many historians and critics (in particular the literary theorist Harold Bloom[47]), seizing on Sigmund Freud's theory of the "Oedipus complex," the natural rivalry of fathers and sons, have elevated the contest of strength into the essential driving force in the history of the arts. That theory will certainly appear to fit and organize a multitude of facts in the history of twentieth-century music, as we are about to discover them. But is Bloom's theory a diagnosis of romanticism and its more recent metamorphoses, or is it in itself a symptom of them?

One group of critics who would certainly call it a symptom rather than a diagnosis would be feminist critics, who have tended in recent years to read the history of art as driven primarily by the male ego—"machismo," as we often call it now (from the Spanish)—with deleterious effects not only on the fate of women artists, but on the content and quality of art itself. In an article provocatively entitled "Why Have There Been No Great Women Artists?" (1971), the art historian Linda Nochlin subjected the notion of "greatness" to a cultural analysis and concluded that it rested in part on a foundation of fierce self-assertion—behavior deemed unacceptable in a woman, however talented. In this way the question posed by Nochlin's title could become a self-fulfilling tautology: There are no great women artists because women are incapable of [read: socially barred from] greatness—unless, that is, they were willing to be looked upon, and vicariously slaughtered, as "idols of perversity" (to recall the conclusion of chapter 1).

Thus the social costs of artistic success for a woman, amounting to virtual ostracism, were literally prohibitive. "The choice for women," Nochlin wrote, "seems always to be marriage *or* a career, i.e., solitude as the price of success *or* sex and companionship at the price of professional renunciation."[48] This unhappy set of alternatives is well illustrated even by the relatively happy career of Amy Beach (1867–1944), a talented Americn pianist and composer who had to put her performing career "on hold" for the duration of her marriage, and could only reassert herself as a professional after her husband's death.

France, as it happens, was the one country where the institutional means for artistic success became available to women toward the end of the nineteenth century, when the ban on feminine participation in the yearly contests for Rome Prizes was lifted, first in painting, then in music. Nochlin rightly points out that this greater democratization of the artistic and musical academies coincided with (and in a way gave recognition to) a drastic lessening of academic prestige, and a no less drastic weakening of the academies' power to act as gatekeepers regulating access to the arts and professions.

Nevertheless, the removal of barriers to feminine participation did seem to create, as if out of nothing, a cadre of female candidates, showing that there had never been a lack of feminine talent or ambition, only of social outlets for their expression. Women were first allowed to compete for the Prix de Rome in 1903. Over the next decade there were four female finalists for the prize, two of them—Nadia and Lili Boulanger—from a single family. In 1913, the younger of the two Boulanger sisters, the tragically short-lived Lili (1893–1918), became the first woman to win it.

In keeping with a pattern to which Nochlin had already called attention in her essay on women in the visual arts, the Boulanger sisters were the daughters (and granddaughters) of successful composers who had taught at the Paris Conservatory. Their father, who was in his seventies when they were born, had won the Prix de Rome himself in 1835. This created a certain amount of good will toward Nadia when she first entered the competition in 1906; but although she tried four times, and although each time a significant number of jurors judged her work to be the best, she never rose beyond the level of "second runner-up" (*Deuxième second grand prix*), the rank already attained by Hélène Fleury in the 1904 competition. As the music historian Annegret Fauser has observed, this was probably by tacit consent the "glass ceiling" for a woman competitor.[49]

Fauser has speculated that Lili Boulanger's success in 1913 was due in part to a strategy she deliberately adopted in the wake of her sister's failure. In 1908, the consensus had been that the large-limbed and robust elder sister would have won the prize had she not committed a minor infraction of the rules, composing the required fugue for string quartet instead of the customary chorus. Playing as it did into the stereotype

FIG. 2-8   Lili Boulanger.

of the *femme nouvelle*, the aggressive and rebellious "new woman" who threatened traditional family values, Nadia's bold behavior may have inspired a misogynous backlash.

In any case, the slightly built and fair-faced Lili Boulanger presented herself in 1913 not as a *femme nouvelle* but as a *femme fragile*, a tender and submissive maiden, and walked off with the prize. Her enormous talent contributed to her success, no doubt, but as Fauser observes, "Nadia's fate shows that musical talent alone was not sufficient" to overcome prejudice.[50] Lili's prize cantata, the love scene *Faust et Hélène*, set to a prescribed text drawn from Goethe's *Faust*, part 2, was not dangerously original: a salad of near quotations from *Parsifal* and *Siegfried*, it shows that the "default mode" for young French musicians, the style that came with least resistance to a harried prize contestant working on a deadline, was still tinged with Wagnermania, and can seem unintentionally amusing to a listener today. But one thing that it surely is not is fragile. However she chose to present herself to the jury, Lili Boulanger was in her creative work as capable of intensely assertive expression and effect as any male member of her generation. (So which was the disguise and which the "real Lili"—the fragile persona or the assertive music? Or is such a framing of the question, like most dichotomies, a double bind?) In several later works she achieved a much greater individuality without loss of directness. There are no "late" Lili Boulanger works, because she became chronically ill shortly after taking up residence in Rome in accordance with her prize, and died, possibly of malaria, in March 1918, at the age of twenty-four. Her most characteristic compositions are choral: several psalm settings, a *Vieille prière bouddhique* ("Old buddhist prayer"), a war elegy called *Pour les funéerailles d'un soldat* ("For a soldier's funeral"). At the time of her death she was working on an opera based on yet another play by Maurice Maeterlinck, *La princesse Maleine* (previously fancied by both Satie and Debussy).

Lili Boulanger's last completed composition, *Pie Jesu* for mezzo-soprano (or choirboy), string quartet, harp, and organ, was dictated by the composer to her sister Nadia during her final illness. It bears a clearly emulative (are we still prepared to say "macho" or "Oedipal"?) relationship to Fauré's *Requiem*, which contains a similarly scored setting of *Pie Jesu*, the gentle concluding verse of the otherwise omitted *Dies irae* sequence.

Despite the steady atmospheric murmur of semitones in the ostinato accompaniment, the organizing principles of the music are by now familiar from our survey of the French music of the period. The vocal line is "modal" in the fashion of the restored medieval chant. Where the key signature contains one sharp, cadences are made to E, but the leading tone is conspicuously suppressed in "Dorian" fashion (Ex. 2-33a). In the coda, where the key signature changes to three sharps, the vocal cadences on B display an even more literally Dorian character. Here the meter, changing to common time with steady rhythmic activity at the level of the eighth note, reinforces the allusion to Fauré's setting, which moves similarly. The accompaniment, moreover, is progressively purged of its Wagnerian chromaticism, achieving diatonic purity to accompany the concluding "Amen," which Marc Blitzstein, one of the many American composers who studied in the 1920s with Nadia Boulanger, aptly characterized as "the essence of affirmation"[51] (Ex. 2-33b).

EX. 2-33A   Lili Boulanger, *Pie Jesu*, mm. 3–9

EX. 2-33B   Lili Boulanger, *Pie Jesu*, last seven measures

EX. 2-33C   Block representation of last harmony

At the same time the harp part begins to emphasize "pentatonic" fourths and major seconds: its ostinato pattern, reduced to block formation in Ex. 2-33c, shows the way in which a "triad" consisting of a fourth plus a second (or, alternatively, two "stacked" perfect fourths) becomes the normative harmony, replacing the chromatically slithering thirds (normally considered a more consonant interval) heard at the opening. The harmonic change, a triumph of "half-steplessness," signals (or reflects) the triumph of faith over fear that the music is meant to delineate (or inspire). And in view of the common thread linking the many stylistic developments this chapter has traced, it was also a triumph of "gluelessness" and the "essence" of France.

CHAPTER 3

Aristocratic Maximalism

BALLET FROM SIXTEENTH-CENTURY FRANCE TO
NINETEENTH-CENTURY RUSSIA; STRAVINSKY

A MISSING GENRE

It is time to confess to a scandalous omission. An entire genre, with a history extending back as far as the sixteenth century, has been virtually missing from this account of European art music, and it is high time to redress the neglect. The slighted genre is that of theatrical dance and the music written to accompany it — in a word, *ballet*. It is no accident that the word is French. Ballet was French in a much realer, more objective way than any of the Frenchnesses described in the preceding chapter, because it was historically, not merely "essentially" French. It was French, that is, in documented fact, not just by nationalistic assertion.

The European tradition of spectacular professional dancing for theatrical display originated at the court of the French king Henry III, whose Italian-born mother, Catherine de Médicis, sponsored the first *ballets de cour*, courtly entertainments in which poetry, music, stage décor, and dance were all combined in a single dramatic action. The first such grand spectacle, *Circé, ou le Balet comique de la Royne* ("Circe, or the Queen's comic dance spectacle"), was presented at the Petit Bourbon palace on 15 October 1581, under the direction of Balthasar de Beaujoyeulx (ca. 1535–ca. 1587), Catherine's "master of revels." Like Jean-Baptiste Lully, his great successor, and like his royal patroness herself, Beaujoyeulx (born Belgioioso) was a naturalized Italian. The early French ballets incorporated many ingredients imported from Italy, intermixed with local traditions of court pantomime and allegory. They arose around the same time as the Italian court spectacles known as *intermedii*, which were among the immediate forerunners of the nascent opera.

The fantastic success of the early opera is what scotched the growth of the ballet. When transferred from the ballroom floor to the stage under Lully in the seventeenth century, the ballet became only one of the ingredients in the *tragédie lyrique*, the French version of opera, in which the chief dramatic burden, as in opera everywhere, was carried not by dancing but by singing, hence by words. Theatrical dancing thus became an accessory, an element not of dramatic substance but of luxurious ornament, and declined both in creative energy and in prestige.

The French court remained its epicenter. Exquisite solo and ensemble dancing remained an obligatory ornament of the French operatic stage as a reminder of the richness of the court that supported it, and of the power of the French autocracy. It was the courtliest of all the courtly arts. Like the political monolith that sustained it, the French ballet was esteemed throughout Europe as an embodiment of everything aristocratic, and its music was imitated wherever the high aristocratic style was aspired to — most conspicuously at the petty German courts, which maintained orchestras for no other purpose than to perform "Ouvertures," or suites of French dance music (a genre to which J. S. Bach contributed four specimens in the early eighteenth century, and G. P. Telemann dozens).

But the emphasis on dancing as ornament or diversion rather than action, and the limits that impersonal court convention placed on its expressivity, led to dissatisfaction with the way it functioned within — or rather impeded — the developing French opera. Writing about the way in which French composers had to make way for frequent danced divertissements (*fêtes*), Jean-Jacques Rousseau complained in 1761 that "in every act the action is usually cut off at the most exciting moment by a fête: if the prince is happy, one shares his joy and one dances; if he is sad, one wants to cheer him up and one dances."

Rousseau was writing here in the vanguard of romanticism, insisting on naturalness and personal expressivity in place of courtly stylization. Over the course of the eighteenth century, a number of reforms and innovations conspired to undermine the impersonal aristocratic conventions of court dancing and replace them with a new kind of ballet that placed the emphasis on individual characters and their emotional reactions — expressed entirely in supple bodily movements — to an unfolding story line. This kind of ballet, which could be regarded as a self-sufficient "wordless opera," and which was indeed designed to vie with opera for dominance in the realm of music theater, was known as *ballet d'action* or "plot ballet."

In a plot ballet, a scenario, or planned sequence of danced "numbers," took the place of the libretto. The scenarist, who might or might not be the choreographer or ballet master, the designer of the actual danced steps, had a task similar to the librettist's: that of expressing the content of the plot, often a well-known story, in terms of danceable situations. A method of alternating plot-presentation and emotional reflection, reminiscent of the alternating recitatives and arias in opera and clearly modeled on them, became standard. The equivalent of recitative was "pantomime," or gestural mimicry, in which elements of plot were "acted out" in a very stylized way to the accompaniment of loosely structured "mimetic" music. The actual dances, often adapted (like operatic arias) from established ballroom genres, expressed in more general terms the characters' emotional reactions to the events of the plot.

BALLET D'ACTION

The choreographer Jean-Georges Noverre (1727–1810) claimed to be the sole inventor of this type of highly elaborated dance spectacle. And while all such claims to absolute priority can be debunked — Noverre's by dance historians who have identified forerunners of his *ballets d'action* as early as 1702 — Noverre's works were recognized by his contemporaries as an important step toward ballet's "emancipation" from opera (an emancipation ironically achieved by means of emulation). During a stay in London,

Noverre studied the techniques of David Garrick, the famous realistic actor, who returned the compliment by calling Noverre "the Shakespeare of the dance."[1]

Noverre's first great success was *Le jugement de Paris*, a heroic (i.e., mythological) *ballet d'action* produced at Lyon in 1751. The music, now lost, was probably an assemblage of existing pieces by a variety of composers. The first *ballet d'action* composed as a continuous score by a "name" composer was Gluck's *Don Juan* (Vienna, 1761), choreographed by Gaspero Angiolini (1731–1803), Noverre's great rival. The first specialist composer for the new genre was Joseph Starzer (1726–87), an Austrian who worked first at the Russian court in St. Petersburg, later in Vienna with both Noverre and Angiolini, and logged some three dozen ballet scores over the course of his career.

By the end of the eighteenth century, the *ballet d'action* had begun to incorporate subject matter drawn not only from mythology and ancient history but from the full range of literary prototypes on which opera also drew, including scenes from (admittedly idealized) peasant life. Beginning with the work of Charles Louis Didelot at the King's Theater in London (from 1796), ballets were given spectacular stagings that, in their use of flying machines and the like, rivaled the French operas from which the *ballet d'action* had originally spun off. The nascent romantic ballet was poised to present itself, in short, as a full-fledged alternative to opera.

But how viable an alternative to opera? How great a threat to it? For most of the nineteenth century, not very. For one thing, opera (especially when staged in France) often included ballet, sometimes very spectacularly staged, and could boast a more complete representation of the arts in combination. Nor did the ballet divertissements featured in operatic productions encourage spectators to regard the dance as a potential bearer of serious dramatic values. For that there was singing, after all, supplied with words that could specify emotional contexts far more efficiently than the stylized "language" of gesture.

A further blow to the reputation of ballet among serious artists and their audiences was its association with what, in the aftermath of the French Revolution, became identified as outmoded aristocratic taste, and the way in which ballet was sometimes forcibly (and, it could seem, frivolously) interpolated into preexisting scores. The classic instance was the Paris production of Wagner's *Tannhäuser* in 1861, for which Wagner was prevailed upon to supply a short dance divertissement in the first act (called the "Venusberg" music) to depict the title character's dalliance with the goddess Venus on her sacred hill. This, however did not prevent members of the Jockey Club, an association of ballet- (or ballerina-) loving aristocrats, from disrupting performances with catcalls and dog-whistles to protest the absence of a full-scale ballet in the second act, since that meant they had to curtail their dinners if they were to see their girlfriends dance. (Verdi, recalling this fiasco, added an incongruous "Moorish" ballet to *Otello* for the Paris premiere in 1894; it was his very last music for the stage.) Then, too, the relatively lowly status of the composer in its scheme of things discouraged many of the major musical figures of the nineteenth century from becoming involved in ballet. Beethoven, who composed a *ballet d'action* called *Die Geschöpfe des Prometheus* ("The creatures of Prometheus") for the Vienna court theater in 1801, was something of an exception, and he was treated with exceptional deference. More typical was the experience described by Victor Alphonse Duvernoy, an old ballet composer looking back on the conditions of his youth, in a memoir published in 1903:

> In olden days, the scenarist began by finding a choreographer. Between the poet and the dancer a close collaboration was formed. Once the plan of the piece and the dances were arranged, the musician was called in. The ballet-master indicated the rhythms he had laid down, the steps he had arranged, the number of bars which each variation must contain — in short, the music was arranged to fit the dances. And the musician docilely improvised, so to speak, and often in the ballet-master's room, everything that was asked of him. You can guess how alert his pen had to be, and how quick his imagination. No sooner was a scene written or a *pas* [a section of choreography] arranged than they were rehearsed with a violin, a single violin, as the only accompaniment. Even after having servilely done everything the ballet-master had demanded, the composer had to pay attention to the advice of the principal dancers. So he had to have much talent, or at least great facility, to satisfy so many exigences, and, I would add, a certain amount of philosophy.[2]

Only beginning in 1886 was a piano, capable of rendering a semblance of the full score, used at ballet rehearsals for the Paris opera. These were not conditions under which Romantic composers (with rare if notable exceptions) would gladly work, proud as they were of their social emancipation and the vaunted "esthetic autonomy" of their work.

The main exceptions in France were two. Adolphe Adam (1803–56), primarily a composer of comic operas, wrote fourteen full-length *ballets d'action* in two or three acts beginning in 1830, the year of the July revolution when the Paris Opera, including its ballet company, was for the first time removed from the direct control of the royal court and put under private management. One of the results of this change was the installation of the grand historical opera as the reigning operatic genre in Paris, and the relegation of traditionally romantic subject matter — subject matter involving the mysterious "spirit world" — to the province of ballet.

And one of the results of that relegation was the creation of *Giselle* (1841), Adam's masterpiece and the sole survivor in repertory of the Paris Opéra ballets of its day. It is now regarded as the quintessential romantic ballet, familiar to ballet audiences everywhere, making its creator the first "name" composer in history to be remembered chiefly for a ballet. Its scenario, by the romantic poet Théophile Gautier (1811–72), was based on a Slavic legend recounted by Heine in his book *De l'Allemagne* ("From Germany"), according to which nocturnal sprites called wilis (or willies), the ghosts of maidens, lure fickle young men to their death by enticing them into their endless round dance. Adam composed it as a vehicle for Carlotta Grisi (1819–99), "the lightest *sylphide* [airborne creature] of the Opéra,"[3] according to a contemporary press release.

In the first act Giselle, a winsome, wholesome peasant girl, is seduced by Albrecht, a disguised prince; on learning his identity and despairing of his love, she kills herself with his sword. In the second act she is admitted to the company of wilis, but, still loving Albrecht, protects him from her companions' spell and evokes, alas belatedly, his sincere love in return, expressed in a *pas de deux* (a "choreographed number for two," the balletic equivalent of a love duet) in which the two protagonists are personified by instrumental soloists (viola for Albrecht, various woodwinds for Giselle) all accompanied by the harp.

With its moonlit set and a female corps de ballet spectacularly deployed on invisible wires, the second act was an invitation to the composer to come up with comparably rarefied effects of spooky orchestration and harmony, effects reminiscent of Weber's in *Der Freischütz* but wistful ("feminine") rather than menacing or violent in tone (Ex. 3-1). The result was a *ballet d'action* unprecedented in its musical ambition, challenging the supremacy of opera by adopting some of its most sophisticated musical techniques, such as the use of reminiscence motifs, replete with "thematic transforma-

FIG. 3-1   Carlotta Grisi (1819–1899) in *Giselle*, act II (lithograph from a drawing by Challamel). Note the conventions of miming: the ballerina's right arm is in the *J'écoute* ("I'm listening") position.

tion." Ex. 3-2 shows the main reminiscence motif, which first accompanies the meeting of Albrecht and Giselle and last appears at the climax of the act II pas de deux.

EX. 3-1   Adolphe Adam, *Giselle*, Act II, apparition of the wilis

Adam's ballet became a benchmark, defining the style — and the particular ethereal tone — of romantic ballet for the next half-century. After *Giselle*, as Gautier reminisced in a Paris newspaper,

> *Les Filets de Vulcain* and *Flore et Zephyre* [that is, traditional "neoclassical" or mythological subjects of court ballet] were no longer possible. The stage of the Opéra was given over to gnomes [earth spirits], ondines [water spirits], salamanders

EX. 3-2A Adolphe Adam, *Giselle*, Act I, fig. 9

EX. 3-2B Adolphe Adam, *Giselle*, Act II Finale, Valse

[fire spirits], elves, nixes [nymphs], wilis, peris [fairies or air spirits], to all those strange, mysterious folk who lend themselves so wonderfully to the fantasies of the *maître de ballet*. The twelve mansions of marble and gold of the Olympians were relegated to the dust of the scenery store, and artists were commissioned to produce only romantic forests, valleys by the light of that pretty German moon of Heine's ballads. The new type brought in its wake a great abuse of white gauze, tulle and tarlatan, shades dissolved into mist by means of transparent skirts. White was almost the only color used.[4]

The other major musical figure to emerge from the *ballet d'action* in France was Léo Delibes (1836–91), a pupil of Adam, who made his début as a composer of full-length dance spectacles ten years after his teacher's death while working at the Paris Opéra as chorus master. Delibes, who like Adam was primarily a composer of comic operas, went on to write two ballets that have remained repertory staples: *Coppélia* (1870), after a story by E. T. A. Hoffmann that parodies the "Pygmalion" legend (a young girl wins back the love of her sweetheart by impersonating a mechanical doll with which he is infatuated); and *Sylvia* (1876), about a forest nymph in love with a mortal.

By comparison with the romantic ballet of Adam's generation, the music in these scores of Delibes has been called "symphonic"—sometimes (as one might guess) in praise, sometimes in blame, depending on the caller's perspective. In either case, the term ought not to be taken too literally. Sometimes it was merely code for "Germanic." Here it seems to refer to the unusually lengthy mimed episodes in which the freely modulating music follows the action with what might — very loosely! — be termed a process of motivic development, as in Ex. 3-3, from the act I finale in *Coppélia*. The passage accompanies the discovery, by Swanilda, the "young girl" in the summary above, of a key to toymaker Coppélius's shop, and her decision to break in together with her companions to see Coppélia, the mechanical doll.

EX. 3-3   Leo Delibes, *Coppélia*, from the Act I Finale

On leaving her companions, Swanhilda sees something shining on the ground.
Swanilda au moment de se séparer de ses compagnes voit briller quelque chose à terre.

It is a key – the one belonging to Coppelius, who has let it drop.
C'est une clé – c'est celle de Coppélius, qu'il a laissé tomber en se débattant!

Coppelius is far away: why not profit from his absence and visit his mysterious abode?
Coppélius est loin: si l'on profitait de son absence pour visiter cette maison mystérieuse?

They hesitate – but Swanhilda thinks she sees Franz beneath the trees, trying to attract Coppelia's attention.
Elles hésitent – mais Swanilda croit voir sous les arbres, Frantz, cherchant encore à attirer les regards de Coppélia.

She'd like to see her rival…
Elle veut connaitre sa rivale...

EX. 3-3 (continued)

Yet despite the success of his ballets, despite the unprecedented respect his music won for the genre from serious musicians, and despite its popularity in the concert hall owing to the colorful orchestral suites that he cannily fashioned from his scores, Delibes only managed temporarily to buck the French ballet's irrevocable decline in the second half of the century. He had no successors.

The reason was simple: the fortunes of an aristocratic art form rise and fall with that of the aristocracy to whose taste it caters, and the off-again-on-again condition of the French monarchy in the nineteenth century was increasingly parlous and inhospitable to its dependent art-genres. Delibes's ballet career, which began during the "Second Empire" with the monarchy on its last legs, reached its climax in the period of the early "Third Republic." This period, the immediate aftermath of the disastrous defeat by Prussia, was one of fairly puritanical chastening.

"Idle" aristocratic taste for the luxurious and the decorative, already subjected to years of spoofing in Jacques Offenbach's operettas, was widely repudiated in favor of the high spiritual ideals of the Société Nationale de Musique, whose members, at least at first, were unanimously hostile to ballet. Even *Coppélia*, Delibes's masterpiece, with its comic episodes and happy "realistic" ending, bore traces of parody. *Sylvia*, which took its old-fashioned romanticism seriously, was greeted with almost as much mockery as enthusiasm. It was the last of the line. *Ballet d'action*, scarcely a century old, was dead.

OFF TO RUSSIA

Or so it would have been, had it not escaped to Russia. Why Russia? For the same simple reason. In Russia, the strongest autocracy in Europe (and after 1848 the last bastion there of true-blue absolute monarchy), where the theaters remained until 1882 under the direct control of the crown, ballet was fostered to an extent unheard of anywhere else on the continent. By the beginning of the nineteenth century the Russian court was already a magnet for French choreographers, exactly as it had been, during the eighteenth, for Italian opera composers. Didelot served in St. Petersburg for two tours of duty, from 1801 to 1811 and again from 1816 until his death in 1837. He was followed there by Arthur Saint-Léon (1821–70), who retained his connection with the Russian Imperial Theaters even when called back to Paris to stage Delibes's ballets. But the golden age of the Russian "classical" ballet came with the reign of Marius Petipa (1818–1910), widely regarded as the century's greatest choreographer, who headed the company at St. Petersburg's Mariyinsky Theater (called the Kirov in Soviet times) from 1869 until his death.

By the late 1870s, Russia was the only country where one could regularly see "pure" ballet—that is, ballet as a separate entity rather than as an adjunct or appendage to an opera or a play. During his tenure at the Mariyinsky, where he was enthusiastically supported by the imperial family, Petipa created no fewer than forty-six full-evening *ballets d'action* and enjoyed virtually unlimited access to the imperial treasury, so that his productions reached a peak of spectacular grandeur never matched before or since—and completely unavailable to the actual composers of Russia.

For although flourishing in the Russian capitals as nowhere else on earth, and therefore an art of immense national importance for Russia for the prestige it brought the court, the ballet remained a French art, dominated by French artists, and one that admitted Russian practitioners only in subordinate roles. The most important Russian choreographer at this time, Lev Ivanov (1834–1901), never rose above the rank of assistant to Petipa; his chief claim to fame came as choreographer of Chaikovsky's *Nutcracker* (1892), a task that fell to him only because Petipa had taken ill.

And this seemed perfectly natural in a country where until the 1880s French remained the official language of the court (as, a century earlier, it had been in Germany). Nor was composing the music for the imperial Russian ballet a task for Russians. The theater maintained a staff of imported specialists like the Italians Cesare Pugni (1802–70, in Russia from 1851) and Riccardo Drigo (1846–1930, in Russia 1879–1920) or the Austrian Ludwig Minkus (1826–1917, in Russia 1853–86), Petipa's favorite, whose ballets—especially *Don Quixote* (1869) and *La bayadère* (1877)—are still occasionally revived as vehicles for virtuoso ballerinas. The only Maryinsky ballet with a Russian subject or setting was Pugni's *Konyok-gorbunok*, "The Little Humpbacked Horse," (1864, choreography by Saint-Léon), a holiday confection based on a favorite children's story.

Children, in fact, were one of the target audiences for the Mariyinsky ballet, which chiefly performed at matinées—where "the half-empty auditorium contained a special public," according to one wry memoirist, consisting of "a mixture of boys and girls accompanied by their mothers or governesses, and old men with binoculars"—and holiday galas.[5] Russian intellectuals and "serious" artists were not altogether unjustified in thinking ballet an entertainment for snobs and tired businessmen—"the fruits of M.

Petipa's and St. Léon's nonsensical imagination,"[6] as one very serious critic put it in the pages of *Epokha*, an intellectual journal edited by the novelist Fyodor Dostoyevsky. As for Russian composers, largely frozen out of the ballet business anyway, their opinion was well summarized in 1900 by Rimsky-Korsakov, in a letter to a critic who had inquired whether the ballet had matured under Petipa to the point where composers of the front rank might profitably apply themselves to it. "I'm inclined to think not," was the adamant reply:

> And therefore I myself will *never* write such music. *In the first place*, because it is a degenerate art. *In the second place*, because miming is not a full-fledged art form. *In the third place*, balletic miming is extremely elementary and leads to a naïve kind of symbolism. *In the fourth place*, the best thing ballet has to offer — dances — are boring, since the language of dance and the whole vocabulary of movement are extremely skimpy. With the exception of character and national dances (which can also become tiring), there is only the classical, which makes up the greater part. These (that is, classical dances) are beautiful in themselves; but they are all the same, and to stare for a whole evening at one classical dance after another is impossible. *In the fifth place*, there is no need for good music in ballet; the necessary rhythm and melodiousness can be found in the work of any number of able hacks today. *In the sixth place*, in view of its paltry significance in the spectacle, ballet music is usually performed in a sloppy, slapdash manner that would tell sorely on the work of a highly talented composer.[7]

The attitude Rimsky-Korsakov was expressing was to a considerable degree a prejudice, born in part out of professional envy, and in part out of the special high-mindedness (or civic-mindedness) that the traditions of Russian realism had inspired. That prejudice came especially to the fore in an astonishing letter that a young Moscow composer, Sergey Taneyev (1856–1915), had the effrontery to send Chaikovsky, his former Conservatory professor, in 1878, after hearing Chaikovsky's Fourth Symphony. "In my opinion," he wrote,

> the Symphony has one defect to which I shall never be reconciled: in every movement there are phrases that sound like ballet music: the middle section of the Andante, the Trio of the Scherzo, and a kind of march in the Finale. Hearing the Symphony, my inner eye sees involuntarily "our *prima ballerina*," which puts me out of humor and spoils my pleasure in the many beauties of the work.[8]

Chaikovsky protested against Taneyev's assumption that balletic associations must necessarily be a taint: "Do you mean to say that the Trio of my Scherzo is in the style of Minkus or Pugni? It does not, to my mind, deserve such criticism. When the music is good, on the other hand, what difference does it make whether *la Sobiechtchanskaya* [the Moscow prima ballerina] dances to it or not?"[9]

CHAIKOVSKY'S BALLETS

The hidden subtext to this exchange was the fact that "la Sobiechtchanskaya" (that is, Anna Iosifovna Sobeshchanskaya [1842–1918], lead dancer of the Bolshoi Theater in Moscow) had indeed been dancing of late to the music of Chaikovsky, and that was news. (It was in the wake of Chaikovsky's balletic successes that the critic had elicited from Rimsky-Korsakov his irritated condemnation of the genre.) Chaikovsky was the one leading Russian composer to be powerfully attracted to ballet; perhaps more to the point, or at least to the point of this book, he was surely the only major composer of the nineteenth century to be equally known for his symphonies and his ballets — oil and water, as far as most musicians (Taneyev, for one) were concerned — and to be adjudged an outstanding producer of both.

So where Taneyev had feared that Chaikovsky's involvement with ballet would tarnish his reputation as a "symphonist," the historical outcome was just the opposite: the participation of a recognized symphonist like Chaikovsky was among the factors that succeeded (Rimsky-Korsakov notwithstanding) in raising the artistic standing of ballet in late-nineteenth-century Russia, eventually turning it, in a gloriously ironic and unexpected twist, into one of the most prestigious media for early-twentieth-century modernist music. For that to happen, however, ballet had to undergo its own process of "maximalization." Chaikovsky's first ballet, composed in 1875–76 (that is, more or less simultaneously with Delibes's *Sylvia*) and first performed at the Bolshoi Theater in 1877, was called *Lebedinoye ozero* (*Swan Lake*). Both in its scenario (worked out by the composer in collaboration with members of the theater staff) and in its music, it was modeled quite noticeably in several respects on Adam's *Giselle*: enchanted swan-maidens in place of wilis, a tragic mortal lover (Prince Siegfried in place of Prince Albrecht), a moonlit set against which a pas de deux is danced to the accompaniment of obbligato string solos and harp, a wealth of reminiscence motifs.

Like most nonspecialists, Chaikovsky was unprepared for the rigors that the conventions of the genre imposed on composers. Not knowing that "the balletmaster fixes the number of bars in each *pas*, or that the rhythm, the tempo and everything is strictly assigned in advance," he recalled years later with amusement, "I leapt before I looked, began to write, like an opera, a symphony, and it came out such that not one *danseur* or *danseuse* could dance to my music, all the numbers were too long, no one could last them out."[10] Instead of disgusting him (as, we have seen, they disgusted Rimsky-Korsakov), these requirements fascinated Chaikovsky. Once having been through the choreographic mill, he prided himself on his *métier*, his hardboiled professional skill, scorned those who in their ignorance scorned the ballet specialists, and itched to submit again to the ballet discipline, delighted that he was able to come up, like a specialist, with music that sounded spontaneous despite the extreme degree of calculation that had to go into its manufacture.

These attitudes, it is only too obvious, are the very opposite of "Romantic." That, too, was a source of contrarian pleasure to Chaikovsky, whose confessional symphonies have given him an arch-Romantic reputation not only with the public but with critics and historians as well. But in fact no nineteenth-century composer retained a more thoroughly eighteenth-century outlook on his craft than Chaikovsky. It would be wrong to call this paradoxical fact the direct result of his brush with ballet, however. Rather, his involvement with ballet was one contributory factor out of many.

Like an eighteenth-century composer, Chaikovsky was the lucky recipient of patronage: first from a wealthy widow, Nadezhda von Meck, later from the treasury of Tsar Alexander III. Like an eighteenth-century composer, he composed for immediate consumption, often on commission from the imperial theaters. Finally, and most important, his status as a member of the first class to graduate from Russia's first conservatory made him highly conscious of his novel professional status—he was in effect Russia's first full-time "pro" composer—and extremely proud of it.

In all of these ways, it was membership in what could justly be regarded as the last surviving eighteenth-century (hierarchical, aristocratic) society in Europe that shaped Chaikovsky's creative attitudes and made him into not just a successful ballet composer but an avid one. Very sincerely, and of course very unusually for his time, Chaikovsky rated Delibes as a composer far higher than Wagner or Brahms. The reasons, as he expressed them, were that Delibes's music unlike Brahms's or Wagner's (but like Mozart's) remained beautiful (rather than "great") and pleased its hearers (rather than raising them up to its exalted level). Upon witnessing the first Bayreuth *Ring* in 1876, right after finishing *Swan Lake*, Chaikovsky wrote to his brother in disgust, "Formerly, music strove to delight people; now they are tormented and exhausted." Notice that Chaikovsky's reasons for preferring Delibes over Wagner and Brahms were as much social as esthetic ones. That, too, bespoke an antiromantic, "eighteenth-century" attitude.

Stylistically, however, Chaikovsky's music was as "Romantic" as could be, ideally suited to the mysterious moods and magical transformations that suffused the *Swan Lake* scenario. A pair of examples, both based on the evocative "swan theme" that accompanies the first sight of the enchanted maidens, will serve both to point a parallel with Adam's reminiscence technique in *Giselle* and to demonstrate Chaikovsky's more potent powers of transformation, capable of intensifying the dramatic import at the dénouement (the death of Odette, the doomed heroine) to a tragic pitch—or (as ballet purists might object) to fully "operatic" blatancy (Ex. 3-4).

EX. 3-4A Pyotr Ilyich Chaikovsky, *Swan Lake*, beginning of Act II

EX. 3-4A   (continued)

EX. 3-4B   Pyotr Ilyich Chaikovsky, *Swan Lake*, climax of Act IV

By the time Chaikovsky returned to the genre of full-length *ballet d'action* he had achieved world fame. Although he still lived near Moscow, he was now composing on eager commission from the Mariyinsky Theater in St. Petersburg, the imperial capital, working in close collaboration with Petipa and with Ivan Vsevolozhsky (1835–1909), the "Intendant" or imperial theater director himself. A former diplomat, Vsevolozhsky was a powerful bureaucrat, an impresario, an expert ballet scenarist, and a stage designer all in one. In full control of the tsar's unlimited theatrical budget, he created—in the words of the modern choreographer George Balanchine (1904–83), who had his start in the Imperial Theaters School shortly after Vsevolozhsky's time—a Russian "Imperial Style"[11] that surpassed in its lavishness anything previously seen in the nineteenth century, not excluding even the Paris Opéra in its own imperial heyday some sixty years before.

The two ballets Chaikovsky created with Petipa and Vsevolozhsky—*La belle au bois dormant* (*The Sleeping Beauty*, 1889) and *Casse-noisette* (*The Nutcracker*, 1892)—brought the *ballet d'action* to its zenith of development. They are quite different, in fact. *The Sleeping Beauty*, after a famous folk tale found both in the Grimm brothers' collection and earlier in the tales of the French fabulist Charles Perrault, is a *ballet à grand spectacle*, Petipa's specialty—a ballet that mixed a strong plot line with a wealth of exotic divertissement and "apotheoses," spectacular climaxes that summoned a huge and brilliantly costumed corps de ballet onstage.

The shorter and sparer *Nutcracker*, after a tale by E. T. A. Hoffmann, contains some choreography by Petipa, but most of it was the work of Lev Ivanov, who became the first Russian choreographer to create one of the masterpieces of the genre. Nevertheless, *Nutcracker* is of an equally distinctive (and equally French) type, called *ballet-féerie*. The term designates both a ballet that has fantasy creatures—fairies, genies, and the like—in its cast of characters (but *Sleeping Beauty* already had those), and one that aims lavishly for a special marvelous lightness of effect. A *féerie* is a procession of wonders, each there for no other purpose than to be admired: art (or artifice) for art's sake with a vengeance. *Nutcracker*, consequently, has almost no plot. Past the opening scene of a Christmas party at which Clara, a little girl, receives a nutcracker as a gift from her Uncle Drosselmeyer, the whole action consists of dream visions and a final transport to Confiturembourg (Candyland) from which—but this could be scary!—no return is made to round things off.

These culminating ballets of Chaikovsky are masterpieces of what the composer called the *vkusnoye*—the "tasty," or sensuously delectable. Nothing could be further removed from the spiritual or expressive tasks that German composers assigned their art; nor was there (yet) anything much in Chaikovsky's or Petipa's art of the Symbolist ideal of sensuous thrills as a gateway to the *au-delà*, the great suprasensory "beyond." Its special quality is better captured by the less portentous English expression "out of this world." From both the romantic and the symbolist perspectives, such an art was suspiciously hedonistic (another codeword for "aristocratic").

There was of course a long tradition in the nineteenth century for harmonic and timbral exploration, allied with the romantic tendency to value everything unique and exquisite. But in Chaikovsky's "Imperial" ballets, and especially in *Nutcracker*, the recondite harmonies and rarefied timbres have seemingly lost their connection with "expression." Transcending the language of emotion, they have become wonders in their own right — *objets de féerie* — designed to elicit a special "esthetic" emotion found nowhere else but in the experience of art.

That, at any rate, was the theory they prompted. Called "estheticism," it may remind us in some respects of the "impressionism" encountered in chapter 2. It was a powerful stimulus for a brand of maximalistic thought and action in early-twentieth-century art that flourished first, and quite unexpectedly, in Russia. We will get to it presently, but in preparation let us first inspect a couple of *objets de féerie* from Chaikovsky's "Imperial" ballets, both of them famous for their exquisiteness — one timbral, the other harmonic.

A measure of the importance Chaikovsky accorded tone color in his scale of musical values was the urgency — and the secrecy! — that surrounded the great timbral sensation in *Nutcracker*. On a trip to Paris in the late spring of 1891, Chaikovsky discovered "a new orchestral instrument, something between a small piano and a glockenspiel with a divinely marvellous sound,"[12] as the composer put it in a letter to his publisher. "It is called the 'Celesta Mustel,'" he went on, "and it costs 1200 francs. It can be purchased in Paris only at the inventor's shop. I would like to ask you to order this instrument, . . . but I would also ask you not to show it to anybody, for I am afraid that Rimsky-Korsakov and Glazunov will get wind of it and use its unusual effects sooner than I."

This instrument — now it is simply called the celesta — had been invented by Auguste Mustel, a manufacturer of harmoniums and other keyboard instruments, five years before. Chaikovsky's description was basically accurate: it is like a glockenspiel in that the sound it makes is produced by a row of steel bars; and it is like a piano in that the bars (suspended over resonating chambers) are struck not by a mallet but by hammers activated by a keyboard. When the composer heard it he must immediately have thought of Petipa's description of the "voice" of the Sugarplum Fairy in *Nutcracker*: "the sound of the sprays of a fountain."[13] Chaikovsky successfully scooped the competition. (Alexander Glazunov was a prodigy pupil of Rimsky-Korsakov, then all of twenty-five years old, who unlike his stiff-necked teacher had begun flirting with ballet.) The "variation" (solo turn) for the Sugarplum Fairy in the Candyland sequence (Ex. 3-5) was indeed the first important solo ever written for the celesta as an orchestral instrument. The slithery chromatic harmony was of course another touch of *féerie* — something "out of this world."

More dramatic but still exquisite was the fairy music in *The Sleeping Beauty*, especially that assigned to the role of the wicked fairy Carabosse, the villain of the piece. It is derived from a colorful sequential extension of the way in which an augmented sixth chord resolves, observable in embryo as early as Mozart, in which pairs of voices move in contrary motion through an octave or unison. In its most extended version, often called the "omnibus progression" (on the basis of a widely cited but never published study by the American musicologist Victor Fell Yellin), complete ascending or descending chromatic scales can be harmonized by replicating the semitonal motion as a sequence

EX. 3-5   Pyotr Ilyich Chaikovsky, *Nutcracker*, Sugarplum Fairy Variation, mm. 1–12

along a cycle of minor thirds that returns to its starting point, whence it could be repeated ad infinitum (Ex. 3-6).

The "omnibus" is thus a sort of harmonic pinwheel, displaying a dazzling array of "remote" harmonic centers in quick succession but without "going" anywhere. As pure harmonic "color" without functional progression it is the epitome of what Henri de Régnier, quoted by Ravel in chapter 2, called "the delightful and ever-renewed pleasure of a useless occupation"—aristocratic sensuous play at its proudest. Chaikovsky's leitmotivic use of segments from the omnibus progression was the most extensive—and extended—as of its date (Ex. 3-7).

BALLET FINDS ITS THEORIST

Intellectual prestige was finally added to the social and artistic prestige the Russian ballet enjoyed during its opulent phase under Vsevolozhsky when Alexandre Benois (1870–1960), a young student from an old Russian family of Western European extraction long distinguished in St. Petersburg's artistic life, attended the premiere of *The Sleeping Beauty* in 1890, found the experience esthetically overwhelming, and began bruiting it about among his friends, a group of rich young esthetes and dandies who called themselves the "Nevsky Pickwickians" (after Nevsky Prospekt, St. Petersburg's main thoroughfare, which ran parallel to the Neva River).

EX. 3-6 "Omnibus progression"

descending "Omnibus" progression

ascending progression

EX. 3-7A Pyotr Ilyich Chaikovsky, *The Sleeping Beauty*, Carabosse music, no. 1, mm. 1–2

EX. 3-7B Pyotr Ilyich Chaikovsky, *The Sleeping Beauty*, Carabosse music, no. 4 (finale), mm. 37ff

EX. 3-7B (continued)

EX. 3-7C   Pyotr Ilyich Chaikovsky, *The Sleeping Beauty*, Carabosse music, no. 5 (scène), mm. 202–14

"Chaikovsky's music was what I seemed to be waiting for since my earliest childhood,"[14] Benois wrote in his old age, long after becoming a world-famous painter, theatrical designer, and art historian. It embodied "the aristocratic spirit, untouched by any democratic deviations, which reigned in Russia under the scepter of Alexander III; the unique atmosphere of the St. Petersburg Theater School and the traditions that had been pursued in consequence; and finally a rejuvenation of these traditions so that, on this occasion, shaking off the dust of routine, they should appear in all the freshness of something newly-born." As Benois saw it, the Russian Imperial Ballet, that antiquated French entertainment preserved "in a state of mummification," had "continued to live its own life, remote from all disturbances," and in consequence had been saved from the general decline of the art of dance throughout the rest of Europe.

But far more than that, ballet had stood aloof from all the main trends of serious Russian art in the nineteenth century — the trends represented by novelists like Tolstoy or Dostoyevsky, and by composers like Musorgsky or even the Chaikovsky of the operas and symphonies. Precisely because of this, because it was mere purposeless play and divertissement, because it had remained true to seemingly superannuated principles of beauty and stylization, it was far less tainted than opera with the hated residue of realism and was uncompromised by the didactic and social concerns that encumbered modern Russian literature. The Russian ballet, in short, was a kind of *belle au bois dormant* or sleeping beauty in its own right, an outmoded aristocratic toy whose irrelevance to all serious artistic endeavor in Russia was a standing joke until, by a curious quirk of fate, the nature of serious artistic endeavor changed in such a fashion as to make it relevant once more.

It was the Nevsky Pickwickians, grown up into an intrepid estheticist faction known as *Mir iskusstva* ("The world of art"), who planted the awakening kiss. Benois remained their chief theorist, but their chief executive was Sergey Diaghilev (1872–1929), a man of enormous energy and vision who put the group and its magic name on the map, first by organizing *Mir iskusstva* art exhibitions, then by editing a superb arts journal also called *Mir iskusstva*, and finally by assuming the mantle of Vsevolozhsky but on an international scale, becoming, it is no exaggeration to say, the greatest impresario the world has ever seen. His efforts sparked a resurgence of ballet that lasted to the end of the twentieth century and beyond, and, toward the beginning of that century, briefly made ballet one of the major sites of artistic and musical innovation, perhaps the hottest one of all.

But first the enabling theory. Benois expressed it most succinctly

FIG. 3-2   Sergey Diaghilev (1906), by Leon Bakst. The figure in the background is Diaghilev's childhood nanny.

in 1908, in an article called "Colloquy on Ballet" because it was cast in the form of a dialogue between an "Artist," representing the author, and a hypothetical "Balletomane." The latter voices the mindlessly hedonistic view that ballet was just "a fragile, aristocratic amusement" that can have nothing to do with "the serious questions of our day," and whose very existence in the modern world was anachronistic and therefore precarious.[15] To this the artist replies that on the contrary, "the history of ballet is far from over; before it lie even greater prospects, perhaps, than lie before opera or drama." The reason was that ballet was an ideal *Gesamtkunstwerk*, as imagined by Wagner but never realized by him, because he never managed to rid his art of its utilitarian aspect.

And what was that? Words! True art cannot mix with words, precisely because words have fixed, hence earthbound, meaning. Benois's theory of ballet turns out to be the old romantic esthetic of "absolute music" in its maximalistic — or maximally "estheticized" — phase. The Artist continues:

> One thing is clear. After all the temptations of our brains, after all *words*, tedious and confusing, insipid and foolish, murky and bombastic, one wants *silence* and *spectacle* on the stage. Yet it would be wrong to call ballet a dumbshow. Ballet is perhaps the most eloquent of all spectacles, since it permits the two most excellent conductors of thought — music and gesture — to appear in their full expanse and depth, unencumbered by words, which limit and fetter thought, bringing it down from heaven to earth.[16]

The Artist's point is that words, unlike music and movement, are *by nature* utilitarian. They seek to accomplish something specific, and therefore limited. They lead to laughter and tears — to emotions tied to objects and hence unesthetic. "A baby crying for its milk is utilitarian and boring," Benois wrote. "But a smiling baby — that one is holy, surrounded by a divine aureole, full of regal radiance."[17] Ballet's unique capacity was its power to evoke the "esthetic smile," the emotion of pure esthetic delight. That made it supreme among the arts, and certainly among the theatrical arts:

> Even the most abstract and exalted drama is burdened with utilitarianism. In most cases it conceals (sometimes very artfully) a didactic utility, or else at its very climax it reflects our vain concerns, our strivings, our clamberings, our aggressions. In the dramatic theater one either laughs or cries. In ballet, though, the chief meaning is in the smile (and not in laughter or in tears). In the drama the big moment comes when the spectator is most shaken by the depicted sufferings; in comedy it comes when the spectator bursts out laughing; but in ballet it comes when the spectator *smiles*. That is the reason for its existence. The dance is nothing but "a full-length smile," a smile in which the whole body participates.

Opera, according to this theory, is even worse than drama, because it "blasphemously" tries to force music into fusion with the utilitarian medium of words, not to mention the fact that the two media impede each other's comprehensibility (a problem to which most operagoers can indeed attest!) since words make a distracting counterclaim on the faculty of hearing. Was not Wagner's greatest opera, *Tristan und Isolde*, the very one in which the libretto's words mattered the least? So why not get rid of them altogether? Far from a truncated, denatured, or handicapped form of opera (the usual view of *ballet d'action*, even the best of them), Benois now proposed that ballet was the final step in music-theater's liberation from the tyranny of the spoken drama, ultimately in music's liberation from the tyranny of words. Ballet, he insisted, was the artistic wave of the future.

BACK TO FRANCE

And so it became, thanks to Diaghilev. Beginning in 1906, at first with heavy financial backing from the Russian crown, Diaghilev embarked on an epoch-making "export campaign," as Benois rather drily called it, a yearly "Russian season" in Paris, the artistic capital of the world and the political capital of what was, since the accession of Tsar Nikolai II in 1894, Russia's most strategic diplomatic and military ally. Diaghilev's first Parisian presentation was an exhibition of Russian painting from medieval icons to the work of the *Mir iskusstva* circle itself.

The next year, 1907, Diaghilev brought a series of dazzling "historical concerts" in which all the greatest Russian musicians of the day took part: Rimsky-Korsakov, the dean of living Russian composers; Glazunov, his star pupil; the pianist-composers Alexander Scriabin (1872–1915) and Sergey Rachmaninoff (1873–1943), and many others. These concerts were not only historical (that is, presenting works from the full range of Russian musical history) but also historic: they provided a conduit that brought the latest Russian music to French ears like those of Ravel, whose avid absorption of Russian influences we have already observed in chapter 2.

In 1908, Diaghilev brought a legendary production of Musorgsky's *Boris Godunov* (in a version edited by Rimsky-Korsakov) to the stage of the Paris Opéra, which set a never-to-be-surpassed benchmark for luxuriance and spectacle. The next year, 1909, it was a mixed "Russian season" of music theater, now including ballet for the first time. The Russian ballets especially amazed the French, who had considered the ballet to be their national property, but who now saw their version of it thoroughly surpassed. The ballet spectacles, unexpectedly, proved far more successful with the public than the operas. Diaghilev decided to follow Benois's advice, which he had until then resisted, and specialize henceforth in presenting Russian ballets to Parisian audiences.

And yet the French critics had complained that the ballets presented in 1909 did not duplicate the exotic impression created by the Russian operas, and that without an overlay of recognizably Russian style (which meant, for French ears, a folkloristic or "oriental" style) they could not regard the Russian ballet as a truly authentic artistic product. Here indeed was a paradox: the Russian ballet, originally a French import and proud of its stylistic heritage, now had to become stylistically "Russian" so as to justify its exportation back to France. Diaghilev's solution was to commission, expressly for presentation in France in 1910, something without precedent in Russia: a ballet on a Russian folk subject, and with music cast in a conspicuously exotic "Russian" style. He cast about for a composer willing to come up with so weird a thing.

STRAVINSKY

Four composers—all pupils of Rimsky-Korsakov who had possibly inherited his prejudices—refused before Diaghilev found his volunteer: Igor Stravinsky (1882–1971), also a Rimsky-Korsakov pupil, but an ambitious member of a younger generation who had yet to make a name for himself and who therefore had everything to gain from the international exposure Diaghilev promised. In a couple of brightly colored orchestral scherzos the fledgling composer had shown a flair for *féerie*, the chief necessity for a "Miriskusnik" composer—that is, a composer in the spirit of *Mir iskusstva* and its aristocratic, decorative values. Stravinsky was invited to join the team.

For like all ballets, this one would be very much a team effort. As was traditional, the plot and scenario were largely the work of the choreographer, Mikhail Fokine (1880–1942), a brilliant young dancer who had trained under Petipa and Ivanov. The title, *Firebird* (*Zhar-ptitsa*, or *L'oiseau de feu*, as it was called at the Paris premiere), was symbolic: the Firebird, a Slavic mythological creature of gorgeous beauty whose feathers were treasures of incalculable value, had been adopted by the *Mir iskusstva* circle as the trademark of art-for-art's-sake. Fokine patched together a story line from several well-known *skazki* or folk tales, a preposterous farrago as any Russian child could see, but calculated to cater to Parisian preconceptions of what was *du vrai russe*, "truly Russian." It told of how Ivan Tsarevich, the Prince Charming character in Russian fairy tales, with the aid of the Firebird, won the hand of the Princess Nenaglyadnaya-Krasa (Unearthly beauty) by freeing her from a spell cast by the sorcerer Kashchey-Bessmertnïy (Deathless Kashchey).

True to the history of the genre, Stravinsky was only called in when all of this was ready. Here is how Fokine described their traditional, very unequal process of collaboration:

> Stravinsky visited me with his first sketches and basic ideas. He played them for me, I demonstrated the scenes to him. At my request, he broke up his national themes into short phrases corresponding to the separate moments of a scene, separate gestures and poses.
>
> I remember how he brought me a beautiful Russian melody for the entrance of Ivan-Tsarevich. I suggested not presenting the complete melody all at once, but just a hint of it, by means of separate notes, at the moments when Ivan appears at the wall, when he observes the wonders of Kashchey's enchanted garden, and when he leaps over the wall. Stravinsky played, and I interpreted the role of the Tsarevich, the piano substituting for the wall. I climbed over it, jumped down from it, and crawled, fearstruck, looking around—my living room. Stravinsky, watching, accompanied me with patches of the Tsarevich melodies, playing mysterious tremolos as background to depict the garden of the sinister Deathless Kashchey. Later on I played the role of the Princess and hesitantly took the golden apple from the hands of the imaginary Tsarevich. Then I became Kashchey, his evil entourage—and so on. All this found most colorful interpretation in the sounds that came from the piano, flowing freely from the fingers of Stravinsky, who was also carried away with his work.[18]

The music Stravinsky came up with under these conditions fell into two broad categories. One was the folkloric, reserved for the human characters, the Prince and

Princess. The other was the fantastic or *féerique*, associated with the supernatural characters, the Firebird and Kashchey. This dual or bifurcated style had been Rimsky-Korsakov's specialty, brought to what seemed a peak of perfection in his late "fantastic" or fairy-tale operas, of which the last two were composed during Stravinsky's period of apprenticeship. Typically, Rimsky-Korsakov would mine the music for the human characters from his own published collection of 1877, *One Hundred Russian Folk Songs*, and mine the music from the supernatural characters, as we have seen (chapter 2), from the resources of the octatonic (or tone-semitone) scale.

Encouraged by Diaghilev, whose celebrated creative byword was *Étonne-moi!*[19] — "Astonish me!" (i.e., astonish the Parisians) — Stravinsky strove to maximalize the work of his teacher, just as Mahler and Strauss had been maximalizing the work of Wagner. For folk songs, like the one that brings the ballet to its brilliant conclusion, he remained faithful to his teacher's anthology, and in one or two instances, most notably in the "Infernal Dance" for Kashchey's monstrous retinue, he unconsciously plagiarized his teacher's actual compositions. For representing the supernatural, however, he found a way toward unheard-of effects by building directly and deliberately on Rimsky's work.

Just how directly and deliberately can be seen from Stravinsky's starting point, a one-act opera by Rimsky-Korsakov, almost too neatly called *Kashchey the Deathless*, in which Rimsky had taken his own octatonic explorations to their furthest point. In Ex. 3-8, a passage from Rimsky-Korsakov's opera, the harmony is governed by a "stable tritone" like the one governing the bell-ringing progressions in Musorgsky's *Boris Godunov*, and every note is referable to a single octatonic scale as indicated by the numbered degrees.

What attracted Stravinsky's attention was the sequence of thirds in the upper staff of the accompaniment in Ex. 3-8, played by a pair of clarinets in the orchestral original. By the simple expedient of regularly alternating major and minor thirds and further regularizing the progression so that the lower note of each successive third in the series stood a semitone below the upper note of its predecessor, Stravinsky hit upon a sort of universal harmonic solvent: an exhaustive cycle of twenty-four thirds in which no member of the series could recur until all of the others have intervened — an "omnibus progression" indeed! In Ex. 3-9 each "rung" in Stravinsky's exhaustive "ladder of thirds" is given a reference number so that examples of its actual use in the ballet score can be easily compared with the full series.

The ladder's most nearly complete appearance in the score comes in the "Dawn" passage that links the ballet's two scenes (Ex. 3-10); it goes through sixteen progressions. In the example, the harmonies are presented in a notation that emphasizes their derivation from the ladder of thirds. In the actual score, the voice leading is conventional, producing a series of harmonies with what seems to be a bafflingly arbitrary root progression. (Magicians, including harmonic magicians, always do well to conceal their tricks.) The ladder of thirds is set out in Ex. 3-9 beginning with the minor third D/F because that is the interval Stravinsky himself used at the beginning of a musical example that half-explained his procedure (Ex. 3-11) to purchasers of a player-piano roll on which he recorded the score in 1929. As he put it there,

> All that relates to the evil spirit, Kashchey, all that belongs to his kingdom — the enchanted garden, the ogres and monsters of all kinds who are his subjects, and in general all that is magical, mysterious or supernatural — is characterized musically by what one might call a *leit-harmonie*. It is made up of alternating major and minor thirds, so that a minor third is always followed by a major third, and vice versa.[20]

EX. 3-8   Nikolai Rimsky-Korsakov, *Kashchey the Deathless*, scene 2, mm. 171–75

Welcome, long-awaited guest!
Are you going far?

EX. 3-9   Igor Stravinsky, *Firebird*, "ladder of thirds"

Stravinsky's "explanation" actually explains little. Indeed, it rather obfuscates matters by exchanging the positions of the two voices in the second illustrated third. That is one way in which modernists made their reputations: by issuing challenges to analysts, some of which went unmet for decades. But now that Stravinsky's code, as it were, has been broken, some further demonstrations of the ways in which he derived his "magical" harmonies (and melodies) from the ladder of thirds can only enhance our appreciation of the extraordinary ingenuity with which the score of *Firebird* was constructed, even if we now also see how thoroughly rationalized (which means how easily learned and imitated) Stravinsky's maximalizing methods were.

Ex. 3-12a, the very beginning of the ballet, is the passage illustrated in Stravinsky's misleading example. (Now we can see why he spelled the second third the way he did, as F♭-A♭ rather than E-G♯.) Exx. 3-12b through 3-12e are labeled according to notations on the piano roll to show the action they accompany. Ex. 3-12d shows two segments from the ladder of thirds in counterpoint, while 3-12e shows how harmonic progressions can be constructed by juxtaposing segments in block formation. Finally, Ex. 3-12f, the leitmotif of Kashchey's enchanted princesses, constructs "human" (because desire-filled) harmonies, dominant sevenths and *Tristan*-chords, over a pair of rungs from the ladder, as if to illustrate the plight of sentient human beings constrained by a supernatural force.

FIG. 3-3 Piano roll of Igor Stravinsky's *Firebird* ballet, issued by the Aeolian Company, London, in 1929.

Ex. 3-12a also reveals the source of the ballet's main leitmotif, namely the Firebird's. The first four notes of the ostinato melody, consisting of the A♭-F♭ third (the second

EX. 3-10 Igor Stravinsky, *Firebird*, "Dawn"

EX. 3-II   Igor Stravinsky's analytical example from piano roll notes

EX. 3-12A   Igor Stravinsky, *Firebird*, Kashchey music, opening theme

EX. 3-12B   Igor Stravinsky, *Firebird*, Kashchey music, "In the Darkness, Kashchey Watches for Victims"

EX. 3-12C   Igor Stravinsky, *Firebird*, Kashchey music, "Arrival of Kashchey the Deathless"

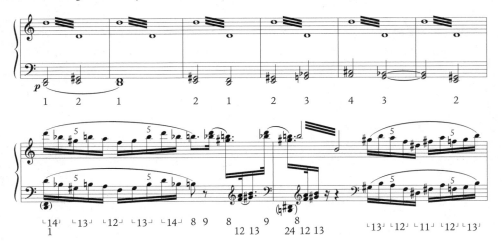

EX. 3-12C   (*continued*)

EX. 3-12D   Igor Stravinsky, *Firebird*, Kashchey music, "Dialogue of Kashchey and Ivan Tsarevich"

EX. 3-12E   Igor Stravinsky, *Firebird*, Kashchey music, "Death of Kashchey"

rung of Stravinsky's ladder), the D (the ladder's bottom, seemingly its generating pitch), and a passing tone to connect the two ladder components, are extracted and subjected to a wealth of separate manipulation to accompany the Firebird's appearances. These manipulations are of an age-old academic sort that every counterpoint student learns: as illustrated in Ex. 3-13 (from a section titled "Apparition de l'Oiseau de feu"), the four-note motif is inverted (I), reversed (R), and reversed in its inverted form (RI).

EX. 3-12F   Igor Stravinsky, *Firebird*, Kashchey music, end

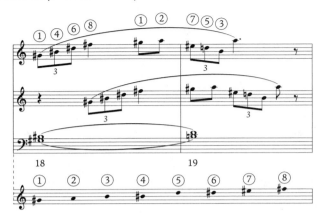

EX. 3-13   Igor Stravinsky, *Firebird*, "Apparition de l'Oiseau de feu"

All of these motivically saturated passages accompany mime, and one of the special features of *Firebird* is its heavy emphasis on mime in addition to virtuoso dancing, as if to dramatize the ballet's similarity (i.e., its superiority) to opera. The dances, musically more conventional, were fashioned into a suite that immediately became a popular concert work. Thus Stravinsky managed in this wildly successful score to appeal both to the broad concert and theater audience and to the composing and critical fraternity, a feat he would duplicate many times over the course of his long career, in the process gaining an eminence (indeed, many would claim, a preeminence) among twentieth-century composers, and a prestige, that would last to the end of his life, more than sixty years later.

What was absolutely unprecedented was that such an eminence and prestige could come to a composer by way of ballet, formerly that most despised of genres. It could never have happened were it not a Russian ballet. The triumph of ballet was thus also the triumph of Russia. Both would enjoy in the twentieth century a hitherto unknown musical distinction, and Stravinsky became the chief protagonist and beneficiary of the intersecting trajectories of conquest that Diaghilev and his "Ballets Russes" had engineered.

PETRUSHKA

Maximalism had been a crucial component of that conquest, and would remain high on the list of Ballets Russes priorities. Successes needed to be topped. And so the next season, 1911, Diaghilev produced a new Stravinsky ballet, in hopes of topping *Firebird*. His hopes were not in vain. Success was even wilder. And although the primary impetus this time had come from Stravinsky, the history of the project and its outcome revealed even more decisively the essentially collaborative nature of the Diaghilev enterprise.

While finishing up the score of *Firebird*, Stravinsky had an idea for a sequel: a primitive sacrificial rite in which a virgin danced herself to exhaustion and death before an idol of Yarilo, the ancient Slavic sun god. The idea was not particularly original: the Russian version of symbolist poetry was rife with images of pre-Christian antiquity (which in Russia had lasted until 988 CE), and there were many attempts to foster, in the words of the poet Vyacheslav Ivanov, a new mythological age. "Poets," another Russian symbolist wryly observed, "wore themselves out trying to roar like wild animals."[21] Neoprimitivism, the quest for a modern style through evocations of prehistory, was the primary engine then driving Russian artistic maximalism. Stravinsky was merely buying in.

Before beginning the new ballet, however, Stravinsky wanted to "refresh himself,"[22] as he put it in his autobiography, by writing a funny concert piece for piano and orchestra that would spoof the antics of a romantic virtuoso. It would take the form of a "combat between the piano and the orchestra," according to an interview Stravinsky later gave a French reporter, in which "a man in evening dress, wearing his hair long, . . . sat himself at the piano and rolled incongruous objects up and down the keyboard, while the orchestra burst out with vehement protests, with sonic fisticuffs."[23] He composed the piece in September 1910.

Afterward, casting about for a title, Stravinsky noticed that some of the searing trumpet blasts he had composed were reminiscent of the kazoo-like instrument that produced the shrill voice of Petrushka (Little Pete), the "Punch" in the Russian "Punch and Judy Show" or fairground puppet theater — a character who, like Stravinsky's mad piano player, was "always in an explosion of revolt." Armed with a cudgel, he would beat up anybody in sight. The skit always ended with his being dragged off to hell by a big black dog. Delighted with the idea, Stravinsky changed the title from "Pièce burlesque" to *Krik Petrushki* ("Petrushka's shriek") and wrote a companion piece based on a few jottings he had already made for the "sacrifice ballet" he had envisioned before starting the concert piece.

These two little pieces for piano and orchestra made for a fascinating contrast. The one that now came first was a madcap puppet dance based on two Russian folk tunes (one from his teacher's anthology, the other from a more recent and "scientific" collection that contained the melodies only, without any artistic embellishment). The second, the original concert piece, was a study in "octatonic maximalism" in which the harmonic language of Rimsky-Korsakov's fantasy operas (exemplified both in Ex. 3-8 from *Kashchey the Deathless* and in Ex. 2-28 from *Sadko*) and already maximalized by Ravel in his *Rapsodie espagnole* (Ex. 2-32) was extended and distorted into a brusquely dissonant idiom of which Rimsky-Korsakov might well have disapproved.

But when Diaghilev, visiting Stravinsky later that fall, heard the two pieces, he was struck not only by the contrast but also by the way both of its elements "maximalized" features of *Firebird* that had proven to be so appealing to his fashionable Paris audience. He immediately envisioned Stravinsky's pieces within a ballet based on the Russian Shrovetide fair, where the puppet theaters flourished. He talked Stravinsky into promising to write the rest of it, and then talked Benois into providing a scenario. In the end, Stravinsky and Benois were *Petrushka*'s parents, but Diaghilev had been the matchmaker.

Benois's ballet combined the puppet-theater and fairground ambience with a love triangle adapted from the old *commedia dell'arte* as revived in the nineteenth century by the French *funambules* or acrobatic mimes: Pierrot (the sad clown) loves Columbine (the ingenue) who loves Arlecchino (the happy clown). Benois recast these roles in terms of the fairground theater: Petrushka himself (transformed from manic Punch into plaintive Pierrot), a ballerina puppet, and an African puppet or "blackamoor."

The two-tiered action unfolds in four scenes. The outer scenes or *tableaux* show the fairground and its revelers, with the first scene culminating in a "Danse russe," namely the first of Stravinsky's piano-and-orchestra pieces, which now accompanies the three puppets dancing before the crowd. The inner tableaux present the love triangle. The second scene, corresponding to the original concert piece, takes place behind the scenes in Petrushka's quarters: the puppet, secretly alive, laments his fate of subjugation to the puppet master and unrequited love.

The third takes place in the blackamoor's quarters, showing the blackamoor and the ballerina happily in love until Petrushka stormily intrudes. At the end of the final tableau, the two male puppets burst out of their quarters into the public square and battle to the death. Many actual Petrushka-plays ended with Petrushka killing a blackamoor; this one ends with the Blackamoor killing Petrushka, so that the title character, like Pierrot, can attract the public's sympathy. The puppet master, summoned by a policeman, shows the crowd that they have been fooled into thinking his wood-and-straw puppets were alive. But at the very end, after the crowd has dispersed, the ghost of Petrushka appears atop the puppet booth and jeers the frightened puppet master. The audience (in the theater, that is) is left not knowing what to think "real."

As in *Firebird*, the plot is a wild mixture of sometimes incongruous objects presented to the French — and accepted by them — as authentically Russian. The music maintains and further maximalizes the fantastic/realistic opposition long traditional in Russian opera, and already maximalized in *Firebird*. Once again the human element (the crowd in the outer tableaux, the puppets appearing before the crowd in the "Danse russe") is represented by diatonic folklore, and the nonhuman (the secret world where the puppets live) by Rimskian chromaticism based on circles of major and minor thirds, that is, symmetrical divisions of the octave by three or four semitones.

But this time the musical contrast, like the poetic contrast it reflects, is treated with a wily irony: the "people" in *Petrushka*, with only negligible exceptions, are represented facelessly by the corps de ballet. Only the puppets have "real" personalities and emotions. The people in *Petrushka* act and move mechanically, like toys. Only the puppets act spontaneously, impulsively — in a word, humanly. Although based on musical echoes of everyday life, the outer ("human") scenes in *Petrushka* are transformed into something far removed from everyday reality by Stravinsky's magic-making orchestration, which at the beginning evokes an all-enveloping accordion (*garmon'* or *garmoshka* in Russian; see Ex. 3-14) and replaces it for the "Danse russe" by a cosmic balalaika. However varied and inventive, the orchestration of the outer tableaux is rarely without some overlay suggestive of street music.

EX. 3-14   Igor Stravinsky, *Petrushka*, opening of first tableau, street-vendors' cries against a steady hum of accordion music

Add to that the extraordinary and unrelieved simplicity of much of the crowd music, quite the boldest and most subversive stroke of all, given the musical climate that reigned during the maximalistic decades we have been investigating. For pages at a time (e.g., the page shown in Ex. 3-15) the Danse russe proceeds with an absolutely unvarying pulse, with nearly flat dynamics, and (almost unbelievably) with nary an accidental nearly half a century after *Tristan und Isolde*.

This strict diatonicism was of course a way of characterizing the vaunted purity of Russia as against the decadence of "Europe" — a surefire means of impressing the French. But still, to achieve such freshness with such simplified means, and with no hint either of monotony or of unsophistication — this was surely Stravinsky's most startling achievement in the "human" tableaux of *Petrushka*. It brought neonationalism — the fashioning of "authentic" modernity out of folk tradition — to what seemed an unsurpassable creative peak.

But now contrast the puppets' secret world, the world of *Petrushka*'s second scene. That scene, the only one to have been written before the "Konzertstück" or concert piece for piano became *Petrushka*, is the only one to be virtually devoid of allusion to folk or popular music of any kind. The sole hint of it comes three measures before the end, in some wheezing concertinalike chords in the muted horns and bassoon, marked "très lointain" (from very far away) — a distant echo from the street, added to the score after the scenario had been planned. The music moves fitfully, impetuously: in 110 bars of music there are sixteen changes of tempo. The volume is in constant flux as well, the harmony intensely chromatic and dissonant. In short, this music, now associated with puppets, is "expressive"—that is, human—with a vengeance. In its ceaseless ebb and flow, its waxing and waning, it analogizes the inner world, the world of passions and feelings with their onsets and abatements.

Although the folk and popular elements in *Petrushka* are abundant, chosen shrewdly and lovingly, and handled with novel resourcefulness and skill, they are so obviously a part of the "outer world," so much a part of what is questioned and derided in this profoundly antirealistic "symbolist" ballet, that there is no cause for wonder that certain representatives of the older traditions of Russian musical nationalism (in particular, and very painfully for Stravinsky, the surviving members of Rimsky-Korsakov's family)

EX. 3-15   Igor Stravinsky, remnants of the piano "Konzertstück" in *Petrushka*, "Danse Russe," fig. 43

EX. 3-15   (continued)

took offense at the work and its creator. But Stravinsky was nothing if not faithful to Rimsky's legacy as he understood it.

This can best be seen precisely where the score is at its most maximalistic, in the novel treatment of harmony and tonality that made the second tableau of *Petrushka* for a while the ne plus ultra—the last word—in modernism. Not a single one of

Stravinsky's apparent innovations lacked a precedent in the music of his teacher and his fellow pupils. Yet there was a difference: past a certain point quantity determines quality; a sufficient difference in degree can amount to a difference in kind. The point that Stravinsky passed, and that Rimsky-Korsakov (and even Ravel in the *Rapsodie espagnole*) had always skirted, was the point at which "octatonicism"—reference to a governing scale of alternating tones and semitones—became not just a color or an exotic accessory to more conventional tonal harmony, but a tonality in its own right.

In "Chez Pétrouchka," the concert piece for piano and orchestra that became the second tableau of Stravinsky's second ballet, an octatonic collection is maintained as a stable point of reference governing the whole span of the composition, whatever the tonal vagaries or digressions along the way. The collection is thus raised structurally to the level of what we ordinarily mean by a "key," governing a hierarchy of pitches and providing a tonal center. It establishes not only a vocabulary of pitches, but also a set of stable structural functions. Hence departures from it and returns to it—on various levels, from that of local "chromaticism" to that of "modulation"—are possible without compromising its role as stable point of reference. The octatonic collection-of-reference is a far more stable referent within "Chez Pétrouchka" than any of the transient diatonic tonalities with which it interacts as the piece unfolds. The composition is thus not only a significant one within its composer's stylistic evolution, but also an important benchmark of early twentieth-century maximalism.

The collection of reference in "Chez Pétrouchka" is the whole-step/half-step scale that includes the C-major and F♯-major triads, which, when superimposed, produce what has become universally known among musicians as the *Petrushka*-chord (see Ex. 3-16). Now just as Wagner's *Tristan*-chord was not the first half-diminished seventh chord in history, neither was the *Petrushka*-chord unprecedented. Ravel had anticipated it in both *Jeux d'eau* and *Rapsodie espagnole* (see Exx. 2-26 and 2-32); Richard Strauss had anticipated it in *Elektra* (1-17b), and even Maximilian Steinberg, a less famous pupil of Rimsky-Korsakov, had used it in a memorial prelude for orchestra in honor of their teacher (and the passage including it had been borrowed from an unpublished sketch by Rimsky-Korsakov himself, shown in Ex. 2-30). There is even a fleeting occurrence of the *Petrushka*-chord near the beginning of *Firebird*.

It is clear, moreover, that Stravinsky conceptualized the chord just as Ravel and Steinberg had done, as a subset of the octatonic collection; for when the chord reappears, along with Petrushka himself, at the end of the third tableau (see Ex. 3-16), it is transposed so that it now mixes the triads of E♭ and A, exhausting the collection of reference by featuring its remaining (complementary) pair of /0 3 6 9/symmetrical "nodes." Thus the C and F♯ triads are not an arbitrarily selected "bitonalism," but rather one of many expressions of an octatonic tonality that pervades the whole composition on many levels. In this sense it was for Stravinsky nothing new.

And yet again there was a significant "maximalizing" difference. In Ravel, Strauss, and Steinberg, the two chords are made to blend into a generalized sonority. Stravinsky makes them stand boldly out from one another. The F♯ is deliberately made to sound

EX. 3-16   Octatonic derivation of the *Petrushka*-chord

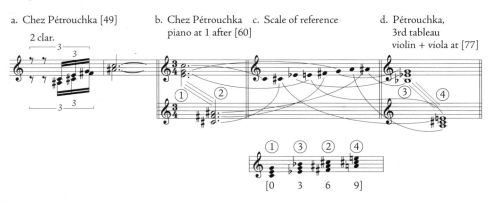

a. Chez Pétrouchka [49]   b. Chez Pétrouchka   c. Scale of reference   d. Pétrouchka,
2 clar.   piano at 1 after [60]   3rd tableau
                                                                                   violin + viola at [77]

[0   3   6   9]

like a foreign element jostling the key (or at least the chord) of C major. This conflict is implied in many ways. In the first place, C major has been cadentially established as the tonic in mm. 1–8 (Ex. 3-17). Not that the cadence that establishes it has been an ordinary one. There is no conventional dominant triad, since almost all the pitches in the passage are selected from the octatonic scale of reference, and no pair of fifth-related chords can be so selected. Instead, C major seems to be selected from among the four potential tonics the scale provides along its /0 3 6 9/nodes: C, E♭, F♯, and A. Indeed, in m. 7, the dominant seventh on E♭ rather ceremoniously defers to C, its defining tones E♭ and D♭ resolving by half steps (that is, as leading tones) to E and C.

Having noted this much, let us look now at the way in which "nonharmonic" tones—that is, tones not referable to the "scale of reference"—are treated. In Ex. 3-17 all such nonreferable tones are circled. They are all resolved to "structural" pitches according to the most ordinary schoolbook techniques, either as passing tones or, in the case of the chord preceding the French sixth in m. 4, as neighbors, complete (D – E♭) or incomplete (G♯ – A, B – C♯). Particularly noteworthy is the B natural on the downbeat of m. 6. Its strong rhythmic placement reinforces its function as an imported leading tone (as it might function, more ordinarily, in the key of C minor). Although its resolution to C is indirect, since its position in a chromatic stepwise descent is alone what justifies its intrusion within an octatonic context, it nevertheless reinforces the contributions of the other half-step resolutions (F♯ – G, D♯ – E) to what is in weak but sufficient effect the tonicization of C in mm. 7–8.

At the passage marked the "Malédictions de Pétrouchka" ("Petrushka's curses"), the *Petrushka*-chord accompanies (or contends with) a piercing melody in the muted trumpets that insists for five measures on a pure C-major arpeggio (Ex. 3-18). Note, too, that during the piano cadenza that leads up to it (Ex. 3-19), the C-major, but not the F♯-major, component of the *Petrushka*-chord is licensed, as it were, to import its dominant into the texture, lending it a truly structural function as against its "opponent's" inert "pedal" quality. Thus it seems clear that Stravinsky regarded the two triadic subsets of the *Petrushka*-chord as independent functional agents, potentially (and at times actually) in conflict. It is fair to speak of the passages in which they contend as being "bitonal," or (as Stravinsky himself always described it) as consisting of "music in two keys" — so long as we bear it in mind that the keys in question were chosen from among the circumscribed and historically validated wares of the time-honored (and specifically Russian) octatonic collection.

EX. 3-17 Igor Stravinsky, *Petrushka*, second tableau ("Chez Pétrouchka"), mm. 1–8

EX. 3-18 Igor Stravinsky, *Petrushka*, "Malédictions de Pétrouchka"

EX. 3-19 Igor Stravinsky, remnants of the piano "Konzertstück" in *Petrushka*, "Chez Pétrouchka," fig. 50

EX. 3-19 (continued)

Finally, this interpretation of the *Petrushka*-chord, as an "active polarity" rather than a passive blend, suits the "poetic concept" and the action of the ballet, where the chord is called upon to accompany outbursts of painful emotion arising out of conflict among the characters. The chord only makes poetic "sense" if we regard the first section of the tableau as being in the key of C. This in no way contradicts the suggestion that the tonality underlying "Chez Pétrouchka" is essentially octatonic rather than conventionally diatonic. For just as a diatonic composition by Ravel or Rimsky-Korsakov might be "flavored" with octatonic condiments, so an octatonic conception may interact with familiar diatonic elements. To see how "deep" octatonicism may be expressed through "surface" diatonicism we need only cast an eye on the end of the tableau: a cadence (Ex. 3-20), just as pronounced as the one in Ex. 3-17, but now establishing F♯ as tonic. Thus the tritone (/0 6/) polarity between C and F♯ not only exists within the work in the local vertical conjunction that has become famous as the *Petrushka*-chord, but is also extended in the temporal dimension to govern the overall tonal trajectory of the music.

EX. 3-20 Igor Stravinsky, *Petrushka*, cadence establishing F-sharp as tonic at end of second tableau

The tritone, moreover, as the midpoint of the octave, is found in every symmetrically apportioned scale. Thus it is a subset of both the octatonic and the whole-tone collections, between which it represents a nexus and a potential modulatory pivot. This dual function of the tritone also finds expression at the surface of the music in the immediate succession of keys that links the C-major opening of the work with its F♯-major conclusion. The Adagietto that follows Ex. 3-18 is centered on D and carries a signature of two sharps, while the music following the Adagietto has E as its center. (For fourteen measures, in fact, the key signature of E minor is explicit.) Thus the sequence of tonal centers forms an ascending octave-bisecting whole-tone progression: C – D – E – F♯. Taking the octatonic collection as a whole as the "tonic" of "Chez Pétrouchka," we can view the interaction between the octatonic and the exclusively whole-tone elements in the sequence of tonal centers as a departure-and-return scheme associated with the "binary form" and its many derivatives since the seventeenth century. The vocabulary has changed, and changed radically; the syntax, however, has remained familiar, enabling that new vocabulary to communicate a coherent and intelligible tonal message.

EX. 3-21   Igor Stravinsky, remnants of the piano "Konzertstück" in *Petrushka*, "Chez Pétrouchka," 4 after fig. 58 ("Petrushka's despair")

For maximum effectiveness, as we have long known, a departure-and-return trajectory needs a Far Out Point. Look now at the climactic moment marked "Petrushka's despair" (Ex. 3-21). The texture consists of a cadenza shared by the first clarinet, the solo piano (by now firmly identified with the title character), and the English horn, over a sustained harmony played first by the trumpets and cornets in B♭, then (when it quiets down) by a quartet of solo cellos.

That harmony is a diminished seventh chord. Comparison with Ex. 3-7 will show how strategically that chord has been selected: it consists precisely of the four "circled" pitches (B, D, F, A♭) that are foreign to the octatonic "collection of reference" that governs the whole composition — or, more specifically, that furnishes it with its point of departure and eventual return. A position of maximum distance from what we might call the tonic matrix — in short, a FOP — has been deliberately assumed.

Not only is this point the extreme point of the tonal trajectory; it is also the most dissonant moment in the piece, hence the most poetically expressive. The clarinet cadenza (notated for an instrument in B♭) consists in the main of arpeggios on another diminished seventh chord (C♯, E, G, B♭) that clashes maximally with the sustained harmony and complements its "foreignness" to the original tonic matrix, since the only pitches now absent from the texture are those of the remaining possible diminished seventh chord: C, E♭, F♯, A. And these, of course, are precisely the roots of the four triads presented in Ex. 3-16 as the potential tonal centers within the governing collection of reference.

The climax of the clarinet part, marked *lamentoso assai* and clearly meant not only as a musical but also as a dramatic climax, at once represents the limit of dissonance and the limit of tonal distance. And even more than that, it is the one moment in the piece that sounds genuinely "atonal" in the sense that its constituent harmonic elements, diminished seventh chords, are harmonies without any single identifiable root. Hence none can function as a tonic in common practice. Despite the novelty of his materials, Stravinsky is deploying them in ways that make long-accepted musical sense. In fact, the novelty of the materials is being exploited to intensify the experience of these common syntactical relationships and make them new again. That is precisely what is meant by maximalism: the radical intensification of means toward traditional expressive ends.

Owing in part to Stravinsky's brilliant success in achieving those expressive ends while at the same time maintaining a proper musical "grotesquerie" in keeping with the

FIG. 3-4 Vaslav Nijinsky in the role of Petrushka.

puppet theme, and in part to the superb performance of the dancer Vaslav Nijinsky (1890–1950) in the title role (especially impressive because male dancing had long been in seemingly irrevocable decline outside of Russia), *Petrushka* was taken seriously — by "serious" artists and critics — as no ballet had ever been taken before. "C'est très à la Dostoevsky"[24] (Just like Dostoyevsky!) was the consensus in the theater. Sarah Bernhardt, the great French tragedienne, said after seeing Nijinsky, "I'm very afraid: I've seen the greatest actor on earth!"[25] Dame Edith Sitwell, an English poet of the avant-garde, who caught the show in London, wrote: "Before the arrival of the Russian ballet in England, the average person had never dreamt that movement could convey a philosophy of life as complete and rounded as any world could be."[26] Echoing Benois, who must have felt a sense of triumph on reading her words, she declared that

> these bright magical movements have, now the intense vitality of the heart of life, now the rigidity of death; *and for speech they have the more universal and larger language of music*, interpreting still more clearly these strange beings whose life is so intense, yet to whom living, seen from the outside, is but a brief and tragic happiness upon the greenest grass, in some unknown flashing summer weather.

Finally, Sitwell found universal meaning in the wordless spectacle she had observed:

> We know that we are watching our own tragedy. Do we not all know that little room at the back of our poor clown's booth — that little room with the hopeful tinsel stars and the badly-painted ancestral portrait of God? Have we not all battered our heads through the flimsy paper walls — only to find blackness? In the dead Petrouchka, we know that it is our own poor wisp of soul that is weeping so pitifully to us from the top of the booth, outside life for ever, with no one to warm him or comfort him, while the bright-colored rags that were the clown's body lie, stabbed to the heart, in the mire of the street — and, with Claudius [the guilty king in Shakespeare's *Hamlet*], we cry out for "Lights, lights, more lights."[27]

THE RITE OF SPRING

With this rapturous reception of *Petrushka* in mind, Stravinsky returned to "The Great Sacrifice," the stone-age ballet he had begun sketching the year before, with a new sense of urgency, knowing what he would now have to top. We can form an idea of what his third ballet would have been like had it been his second — that is, had he composed it right after *Firebird*. As mentioned earlier, the "Danse russe" from the first tableau in *Petrushka* had originally been sketched for "The Great Sacrifice" after Stravinsky had consulted with the man who would eventually write its scenario, the painter and archeologist Nikolai Roerich (1874–1947), a matchless connoisseur of Slavic antiquity.

Stravinsky never left any direct testimony that this was the case, but we can deduce it from the nature of the folk songs on which the "Danse russe" was based. Roerich, who had made a special study (published in 1909) of Russian pagan festivals, told Stravinsky about two of them: Semik, a spring festival of ancestor worship at which wreaths were cast on water to predict the future, and Kupala, the midsummer festival (celebrated in Christian times as St. John's Eve), when images of the sun god Yarilo were burned in effigy, young men leapt over the fire, and then chose brides from among the eligible maidens of the tribe. Together, Stravinsky and Roerich planned the first tableau of "The Great Sacrifice" around these holiday rituals, paying special attention to a passage in an eleventh-century Kievan manuscript called the Primary Chronicle, or "Tale of Bygone Years" (*Povest' vremennïkh let*), in which the Christian monk Nestor the Chronicler had described the wild customs of the surrounding pagan tribes, the "Radimichi, the Vyatichi, and the Severi":

> Living in the forests like the very beasts, there were no marriages among them, but simply games [*igrï*] in between the villages. When the people gathered for games, for dancing, and for all other devilish amusements, the men on these occasions carried off wives for themselves [*umïkakhu zhenï sebe*], and each took any woman with whom he had arrived at an understanding. In fact, they even had two or three wives apiece.[28]

Nestor's very diction (as indicated in the brackets) found its way into the scenario Stravinsky and Roerich worked out, and is now reflected in the titles of the constituent dances. The ceremony here described became the *Igra umïkaniya* ("Game of abduction") in the first tableau. That was the dance that became the "Danse russe" in *Petrushka*. Its main theme was a *khorovod* or ritual dance Stravinsky found in Rimsky-Korsakov's old anthology (Ex. 3-22a). Its title, "Ai, vo polye lipin'ka," means "A Linden Tree Stands in the Field," and the text, slightly paraphrased, runs as follows:

> In the field there stands a linden tree; beneath the linden is a tent; in the tent there stands a table; at the table sits a maiden. She has picked blossoms from the grass; she has plaited a wreath from the garden; it is woven with precious rubies. "Who shall wear the wreath? No old man shall carry off this wreath; my youth shall not be restrained! My sweetheart will carry off this wreath; my youth shall not be restrained!"

It is a matchmaking song about "carrying off the wreath" (=the bride). And the song that formed the middle section of the "Danse russe" (Ex. 3-22b) was even more closely allied with the scenario since it was an *Ivanovskaya*, a song for *Ivanovskaya noch'* or St. John's Eve (=Kupala), with a text that read, "Oh yes, I'm running after a bride!"

In all likelihood, Roerich himself directed Stravinsky (who would probably not have known the ethnographic significance of an Ivanovskaya) to the tune in Ex. 3-22b.

EX. 3-22A   "Ai, vo polye lipin'ka" compared with main tune of "Danse russe"

a.

"Ai, vo pole lipin'ka" as it appears in the L'vov-Pratsch collection (1790)

b.

Petrushka, first tableau: "Danse russe" (transposed to facilitate comparison)

EX. 3-22B *Ivanovskaya* (F. M. Istomin and S. M. Lyapunov, *Pesni russkogo naroda* [1899], p. 167)

Oy da ya— be - zhu,—— be - zhu——— po po zhen - ke,

Oy da do - be - ga - yu— do tsya - so - ven - ki——

But having used it in the "Danse russe," Stravinsky needed fresh tunes when he returned to "The Great Sacrifice" after *Petrushka*. Again Roerich probably came to the rescue, telling Stravinsky that of all the European peoples of the Russian Empire, the Liths and Letts — Lithuanians and Latvians as they are called in modern times — were the most recently Christianized, having remained pagans until 1386, and had performed ritual animal (though not human) sacrifices within living memory. Accordingly, Stravinsky sought out a recently published anthology of Lithuanian wedding songs, from which he adopted several tunes in the first tableau, including the high bassoon melody that opens the whole work, and also the tune given in Ex. 3-23 for use in the *Igra umïkaniya*, the "Game of Abduction" in what became the definitive version of "The Great Sacrifice," performed in Paris in 1913 under the name *Le sacre du printemps*, of which the standard English title, *The Rite of Spring*, is a translation.

EX. 3-23 *Tevuseli manu!* (Anton Juszkiewicz, *Melodje ludowe litewskie* [Cracow, 1900], no. 142)

No. 142

Tè - vu - žė - li ma - nu! Sen - gal - vė - li ma - nu!

Łejs k ma - nę, tė - ve - li į dva - rą stu - žy - ti.

Comparison of this tune with the corresponding section of the new ballet in the composer's arrangement for piano four-hands (Ex. 3-24), and between the new dance and the jolly "Danse russe" that it replaced, shows how determined Stravinsky was to maximalize his achievements in *Petrushka*. The tune is presented only once complete; thereafter it is presented only in fragments, often interrupted by brutally interpolated dissonant chords. Indeed, the whole dance is permeated with the sort of dissonance that had still been a special effect in *Petrushka*: "polychords" consisting of superimposed triads and seventh chords drawn from the /0 3 6 9/nodes of the same octatonic collection employed in "Chez Pétrouchka," namely C, E♭, F♯, and A.

At the very outset of Ex. 3-24, the Primo part is mixing dominant sevenths on C and E♭ against a pounding F♯ in the bass, played by the Secondo. In the last two measures of the example, the Primo continues the dominant seventh of E♭ while the

Secondo arpeggiates triads — very confusingly spelled (perhaps simply to disguise their identity?) — on A and C. A similar arpeggiation in the Secondo part (Ex. 3-25) circulates triads at all four nodes, sounding all the while against "polychordal" mixtures of the same triads in the Primo that are frequently voiced in the maximally dissonant form of "clusters" (scale segments sounded as simultaneous harmony).

EX. 3-24   Igor Stravinsky, *The Rite of Spring* (piano four-hands arrangement), "Ritual of Abduction," mm. 1–10

EX. 3-24 (continued)

EX. 3-25 Igor Stravinsky, *The Rite of Spring* (piano four-hands arrangement), "Ritual of Abduction," mm. 23–28

EX. 3-25   (continued)

Indeed, maximal dissonance was one of Stravinsky's chief means for evoking the pitiless brutality and inhumanity of primitive religion as he imagined it. At the same time he sought validation for his stylistic extravagances in ethnographic authenticity. What is chiefly maximalized in *The Rite*, then, is the neonationalist ideal, the project of wringing stylistic innovation and renewed technical resources from archaic folkloristic models. For this purpose Stravinsky cultivated another manner of treating the octatonic scale, one with fewer precedents in earlier Russian music (though it can be found occasionally in the work of Rimsky-Korsakov and his contemporaries), but which was particularly well suited to the task of harmonizing Russian folk tunes in a maximally dissonant but consistent (and "authentic") fashion.

In addition to the manner of "partitioning" the octatonic collection (or set) already illustrated by the *Petrushka*-chord and the harmonization of the "Game of Abduction" — namely, grouping its constituent tones into four major or minor triads or seventh chords with roots along a cycle of minor thirds — it is also possible to partition the scale (that is, group its constituent tones) into four minor tetrachords with starting pitches arrayed along a similar cycle. (A minor tetrachord consists of the first four notes of the minor scale, its constituent intervals being tone-semitone-tone or TST; see Ex. 3-26.) The reason why this partition of the octatonic scale has a special affinity for Russian folklore is that many Russian folk melodies, especially the ones associated with ancient "calendar songs" that bear the traces of pre-Christian agrarian religious observances (hence especially relevant to the subject of *The Rite of Spring*), are confined precisely to the notes of a minor tetrachord. An especially economical way of giving such a melody a maximalistic harmonization, therefore, would be to accompany it with the tetrachord that forms its octatonic complement — that is, the tetrachord which, when added to the tune's tetrachord, will exhaust the octatonic collection. The two tetrachords that function in this complementary way, like the two constituent triads in a *Petrushka*-chord, have their beginnings or root-notes a tritone apart.

Ex. 3-27a shows an authentic Russian folk song, recorded in the field in the mid-1960s, that belongs to a genre particularly relevant to the action of *The Rite of Spring*: it is a *vesnyanka* (from *vesna*, "spring"), a song that survives from an ancient ritual of "calling

EX. 3-26   Tetrachordal partition of an octatonic scale

in the spring" at winter's end by shouting spells. Like many *vesnyanki*, it is confined in its ambitus to a minor tetrachord. Ex. 3-27b shows a melody of exactly the same structure, hence recognizably (or at least plausibly) a *vesnyanka*, from the section of *The Rite of Spring* called "Ritual Action of the Ancestors." It is harmonized with a vamping bass and a countermelody both drawn from the complementary octatonic tetrachord in the manner just described. It is one of many instances in the ballet of maximalistically harmonized melodies that are either authentic folk artifacts or convincing imitations thereof. By beginning with a piece of folk "reality" and applying a radical new technique to it, Stravinsky sought authenticity and modernity at once.

EX. 3-27A   *Oy vir vir kolodez*, vesnyanka recorded ca. 1965 from the singing of Agrafena Glinkina, Smolensk, Russia

EX. 3-27B   Igor Stravinsky, *The Rite of Spring*, from "Ritual Action of the Ancestors"

EX. 3-27B   (continued)

From the opposition of the "x and y tetrachords," as they are labeled in Ex. 3-27b, Stravinsky educed a three-note harmonic skeleton or "source chord" consisting of the outer notes of the one tetrachord accompanied by the lowest note of its complement, producing an intervallic configuration that can be represented as /o 6 11/. This harmony pervades *The Rite* from beginning to end, giving rise in the process to some of the most famously dissonant chords on its musical surface, like the one that chugs along in ostinato fashion to accompany the "Spring Auguries" in the first tableau, or the first chord in the culminating "Sacrificial Dance" in the second tableau. Ex. 3-28 gives a sampling of them. (In some cases, the inversion of the source chord—/o 5 11/—is used.)

The most maximalistic dances in *The Rite of Spring* are the ones that conclude the two respective tableaux. The "Dance of the Earth" at the end of part I is a montage of ostinatos, one of which is an adaptation of an instrumental dance tune or *naigrïsh* of the kind that, sixty-five years earlier, had furnished the point of departure for Glinka's *Kamarinskaya*, the "acorn from which the oak of Russian music grew," as Chaikovsky had so famously called it.[29] Stravinsky, inevitably conscious of

EX. 3-28A   The *Rite*-chord, "Dance of the Adolescent Girls" (Part I)

EX. 3-28B   The *Rite*-chord, "Sacrificial Dance" (Part II)

EX. 3-28C   The *Rite*-chord, sketch for the "Glorification of the Chosen One" (Part II)

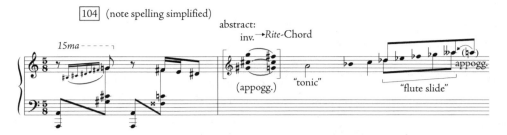

EX. 3-28D   The *Rite*-chord, preparatory measure before "Glorification of the Chosen One"

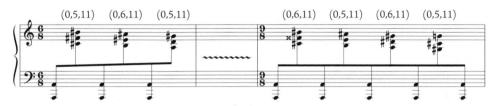

EX. 3-28E   The *Rite*-chord, "Spring Rounds" (Part I)

Middle line, reduced to essential *Rite*-chords:

EX. 3-28F   The *Rite*-chord, "Mystic Circles" (Part II)

this legacy, was resolutely attempting to achieve its *ne plus ultra*. This source melody is shown in Ex. 3-29a as it appears in Stravinsky's sketches for the ballet; directly under it, in Ex. 3-29b, is a hypothetical original version, lacking the whole-tone harmonization; finally, Ex. 3-29c shows an authentic wedding song, adaptable as a *naigrïsh*, for comparison. Another source sketch for the dance is shown in Ex. 3-29d; this one resembles a melody from Rimsky-Korsakov's opera *The Legend of the Invisible City of Kitezh* (Ex. 3-29e).

Between them, these two source melodies provided Stravinsky with all of the material out of which he constructed the "Dance of the Earth"; it is fascinating to trace the process by which it took shape in his sketches. Even the punctuating chord

EX. 3-29A   Source melody for Igor Stravinsky, *The Rite of Spring,* "Dance of the Earth," sketchbook, p. 35

EX. 3-29B   Source melody for Igor Stravinsky, *The Rite of Spring,* "Dance of the Earth," lower line of sketch

EX. 3-29C   Source melody for Igor Stravinsky, *The Rite of Spring,* "Dance of the Earth," Wedding song *Letal golub vorkoval* ("The dove flew, cooing")

Le - tal go - lub vor - ko - val,   le - tal go - lub vor - ko - val,   vor - ko - val, vor - ko - val.

EX. 3-29D   Source melody for Igor Stravinsky, *The Rite of Spring,* "Dance of the Earth," sketchbook, p. 35

EX. 3-29E   Source melody for Igor Stravinsky, *The Rite of Spring,* "Dance of the Earth," Nikolai Rimsky-Korsakov, *Legend of the Invisible City of Kitezh* (1907), Act II

EX. 3-30   Igor Stravinsky, *The Rite of Spring,* "Dance of the Earth," end

EX. 3-30 (*continued*)

that injects a note of unpredictability into the proceedings is a derivation from the first source melody, consisting of a "verticalization" of several of its constituent pitches. What governs the whole is the combination of whole-tone and octatonic elements drawn from scales that have the familiar nodal points C and F♯ in common. By the end of the dance, the timpani is very explicitly directing a harmonic oscillation between these poles. As we found out in the case of the Coronation bells from Musorgsky's *Boris Godunov*, however, a tritone oscillation produces a harmonic stalemate that makes closure difficult. How to end the piece? Stravinsky's first idea for an ending is shown in Fig. 3-5a, a page from his sketchbook. He originally meant to end the dance, and with it the first tableau, with a sustained version of the punctuating chord in full brass, *crescendo al possibile*.

Why did he cancel such a striking idea? Obviously, one can never really know the answer to such a question, but pondering it is instructive. For one thing, the chord might have made too obvious an ending to a section of the ballet the whole

FIG. 3-5A Stravinsky's sketch for the conclusion of *Danse de la terre* (*The Rite of Spring*, end of first tableau).

character of which is one of ceaseless and essentially undifferentiated activity. The blunter ending finally decided upon (Ex. 3-30), just an abrupt and shocking halt, emphasizes in retrospect that very ceaselessness. For another — perhaps more important — thing, the bass note of the sustained chord, an octave G in the tubas, confuses the very clear bipolar tonality of the dance based on oscillation between C and F♯ (the very combination that, in block superimposition, we know as the *Petrushka*-chord).

In any event, the "Dance of the Earth" was a momentous achievement, for it shows how profoundly Stravinsky's musical imagination was stirred by the manipulation of elements abstracted in neonationalist fashion from folk songs, and how thoroughly many of the most pregnantly original of *The Rite*'s technical innovations had their origins in this maximalistic approach to received material. The "Dance of the Earth" is at once one of the most radical sections of *The Rite* — surely the most radical by far in part I — and the dance most rigorously based on folk-derived source melodies.

THE NE PLUS ULTRA

The only dance that exceeds it in its startling maximalism is the one that had to exceed it: the "Sacrificial Dance" at the ballet's end. Like the rest of the ballet it revels in the crashing force of a huge orchestra and a chronically elevated level of dissonance. ("Imagine!" one Russian reviewer exclaimed after the first performance, exaggerating only slightly, "from beginning to end there is not a single pure triad!"[30]) But now Stravinsky added to all of that an equally extreme dislocation of meter in order to convey the lurching, wrenching quality of the dance that will lead the Chosen One to her inevitable death.

This technique of constantly shifting the lengths of measures had been amply prefigured earlier in the ballet, especially past the point at which the sacrificial maiden had been chosen by fate. In the "Glorification of the Chosen One," for example, there is a maddening contest between elements that are absolutely fixed and those that are, so to speak, absolutely variable. The opening $\frac{5}{8}$ measure (given in Ex. 3-28c), with its violent drumbeat in the middle, constitutes the "theme" in the outer sections of the dance. Each of its twenty subsequent appearances is absolutely identical to the first.

What is not uniform is the grouping — that is, the number of identical repetitions that will make up each successive statement of the returning theme (anywhere from one to four) — and also the number of eighth-note beats that will elapse between the statements (anywhere from two to thirty-eight). These intervening beats are "marked" by a vamp of *Rite*-chords as already shown in Ex. 3-28d. The number of these beats being unpredictable, each return to the theme is experienced as a disjuncture, a disruption of an "immobile" uniformity. Momentum is maintained by exploiting this interplay of utter fixity and its opposite, utter mutability. The listener is involved, so to speak, in a harrowing guessing game: When will vamp give way to theme? How many iterations will a given statement of the theme contain? Metaphorically, one is left constantly wondering when one is to be beaten again, and how long the beating will last.

The middle section of the dance, distinguished from the surrounding ones by a key signature of five flats, shifts over to another set of rigidly fixed (or "hypostatized") elements. Three new static ideas, radically differentiated in instrumentation, are intercut. As before, the only variable elements are temporal, "quantitative." But as before, whatever is variable gets varied to the hilt! That simple axiom is the key to Stravinsky's rhythmic innovations in *The Rite*. They are of two distinct types. One is the "immobile," unchanging ostinato or vamp, sometimes quite literally hypnotic, as when the Elders charm the Chosen One to perform her dance of death. That is what their Ritual Action (Ex. 3-27b) is all about, and that is why, except for a brief middle section, the beat-rhythm of that dance is one of the most regular and relentless in the ballet, and the most undifferentiated as to stress.

The other type is the one that was such a novelty — for European art music, that is; in Russian folklore it had been a fixture from time immemorial. This was the rhythm of irregularly spaced downbeats, requiring a correspondingly (and, for "Europe" and for "art," unprecedentedly) varied metric barring in the notation. To demonstrate that the device had precedents in Russian folk song it is only necessary to quote a relevant example from Rimsky-Korsakov's famous anthology. The wedding song "The Bells are Ringing in Yevlashev Village" (Ex. 3-31) is especially convincing because it has a story attached to it. Rimsky transcribed it from the singing of a village woman who worked as a maid for his fellow composer Alexander Borodin. "I struggled till late at night trying to reproduce the song," Rimsky reported in his memoirs. "Rhythmically it was unusually freakish, though it flowed naturally from the mouth of Dunyasha Vinogradova, a native of one of the provincial districts along the Volga."[31] In the end, the meter shifts he adopted have a decidedly "Stravinskian" appearance.

EX. 3-31   *Zvon kolokol v yevlasheve sele* (Nikolai Rimsky-Korsakov, *100 Russian Folk Songs* [1877], no. 72)

Particularly fascinating and innovative (hence influential) was the way in which Stravinsky contrived to have his two rhythmic/metric types — the "passive" ostinato and the active shifting stress — coexist within a single texture. One notable instance comes in the middle section of the Glorification dance. Beneath a variable-downbeat pattern in the violins' and violas' pizzicati, the lower strings, lower winds, and percussion play a rigid figure of four eighth-notes' duration (Ex. 3-32). Neither element is in syncopation with respect to the other, for neither possesses what could be called the defining or dominant rhythm against which the other could be construed as syncopated.

They merely go in and out of phase with one another, fixity and mutability coexisting in concurrent, independent strata.

EX. 3-32   Igor Stravinsky, *The Rite of Spring,* "Glorification," mm. 114–115

Violin I   (5)   (6)   Violin II   (5)   (6)

The most radical — that is, the "maximal" — form of the variable-downbeat technique is one in which the shifting meters are coordinated on the "subtactile" level — that is, by an equalized note-value that is less than the duration of a felt beat, or *tactus*. There was no precedent for this technique even in earlier Russian art music; it was Stravinsky's discovery, his modernist (or neonationalist) breakthrough. And it reaches its zenith, both in terms of complexity of pattern and in terms of fractionated counting value (sixteenths rather than eighths) in the vertiginous "Sacrificial Dance" — the dance "which I could play," as Stravinsky put it in a memoir, "but did not, at first, know how to write."[32]

Also reaching its apogee in the "Sacrificial Dance" was the technique of hypostatization, extreme fixity of musical "objects." More than in any earlier number, the metric processes of the "Sacrificial Dance" are "mosaic," concretized in specific, discrete, and (above all) minuscule musical "tesserae," the variations in the ostensible "metric" patterns actually reflecting permutations of the order in which these tiny fixed elements are juxtaposed. This is the feature called *drobnost'* in Russian — the quality of being not an "organic" whole but a "sum of parts" — raised to the highest power, revealing not just a rhythmic innovation but a novel constructive principle. The literalness of the analogy with tesserae (the tiles in a mosaic) — or "cells," as later analysts (still influenced, it seems, by the "organicist" ideal) have been calling them — is breathtakingly disclosed in Stravinsky's sketchbook, when the composer suddenly takes to representing his fixed musical objects with letters, arranging and rearranging them at will (Fig. 3-5b). And he left the articulation of the irregularly spaced downbeats his sequences of tesserae elicited to the most elemental force of all — to volume alone, as expressed by the bass instruments and percussion, especially the timpani (the octave A's in the Secondo part in Ex. 3-33), which in this dance achieve the status of a terrifying, buffeting force of nature.

THE REACTION

That terror was something that the audience felt — and can still feel, if the orchestra can refrain from showing off the ease with which, nearly a century later, it is now possible to perform Stravinsky's music. The alliance of the music with the stage action and the romantic neoprimitivist ideology that the action embodied makes it possible to continue to speak of Stravinsky's music as "maximalist." Despite its extreme novelty, at least so far as the Paris audience was concerned, its expressive aims were intelligible, indeed familiar.

And yet, as already noted, past a certain point a difference of degree can be — and past another point, can only be — perceived as difference in kind. In *The Rite of Spring* the expressive ends were so fundamentally transformed by the composer's and the

EX. 3-33 Igor Stravinsky, *The Rite of Spring* (piano four-hands arrangement), "Sacrificial Dance"

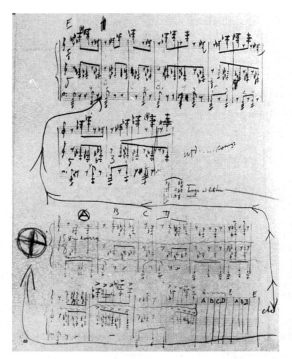

FIG. 3-5B   Stravinsky's sketch for *Danse sacrale* (*The Rite of Spring*, end of second tableau).

choreographer's radicalized expressive means that they could no longer be confidently taken as "traditional" or "accepted." Not only was the audience distracted from the ballet's ancient and time-honored themes by the modernity (to them, the ugliness) of the style with which they were confronted. No less significantly, the composer and the choreographer, by insisting so on the terror of Mother Nature rather than the beauty of human nature, projected a thoroughly alien expressive ambience, alien to all humanistic thought in its brutally dehumanized mien.

The choreographer was Nijinsky, the greatest dancer of the day, but (at the age of twenty-three) still a novice at direction. It was his contribution — now lost, despite strenuous efforts at revival — that, taken as incompetent, was chiefly responsible for the notorious fiasco at the ballet's premiere. The audience's very voluble rejection of the work has become a legend. "The real thing — a big 'Paris' scandal,"[33] critics marveled or scoffed, something to set beside the fiasco of *Tannhäuser* half a century before. And the reasons were similar: the ballet audience expected one thing and got another. Then, it was a short divertissement in the first act, rather than a full-dress second-act operatic ballet. Now, it was prehistoric peasants on stage, instead of sylphides and wilis, stamping on the earth rather than soaring aloft from it. (And, although no reviewer mentioned it, it might also have been a ballet orchestra that contained no harp!) What could be read as maximalism in expressive terms was, in more narrowly balletic terms, read as mere disfigurement. No wonder, as Stravinsky laconically reported in a letter home, "things got as far as fighting."[34] But it was not his music as such that offended, let alone fomented a "riot." It was not even the primary object of the audience's attention that fabled night of 29 May 1913. Many if not most of the reviews failed to deal with Stravinsky's contribution at all beyond naming him as composer; as one of the reviewers candidly admitted, "past the Prelude the crowd simply stopped listening to the music so that they might better amuse themselves with the choreography."[35] When the music was heard again a year later, by itself, in a concert performance under the same conductor (Pierre Monteux) who had officiated at the premiere, the composer enjoyed the greatest triumph of his career.

FIG. 3-6 Drawings by Valentine Hugo (née Gross, 1887–1968) of Maria Piltz as the Chosen One in *Danse sacrale*, coordinated with the accompanying music. The huge, unwelcome contrast between the heavy earthbound steps Nijinsky choreographed for his dancers and the older ballet ideal, exemplified by the winged, ethereal Carlotta Grisi in *Giselle* (Fig. 3-1), was the shock that triggered the famous riot at the premiere of *The Rite of Spring*.

But even among those who hailed the music as a masterpiece were those who perceived a baleful message in the ballet. "Ce ballet est un ballet biologique," declared Jacques Rivière, the editor of the *Nouvelle revue française*, Paris's most sophisticated literary and intellectual journal: "This is a biological ballet."[36] The adjective summons up a variant of neoprimitivism called biologism, one of the bleakest, most antihumanistic of all philosophical visions. Primitivism, the belief that what is least mediated by modern society—children, peasants, "savages," raw emotion, plain speech—is closest to the truth, was compatible with all the noblest aspirations of romanticism. Biologism was something else. Skeptical of all humane ideals, it held life to be no more than the sum of its physical facts and drives: birth, death, procreation, survival. Anything else, it averred, was mere ornament and palliative, a lie. The movements Nijinsky had choreographed for the corps de ballet, the collective, anonymous "body" of dancers, was in Rivière's terrible opinion

> not just the dance of the most primitive man, it is also the dance before there was man. There is something profoundly blind in this dance. There is an enormous question being carried about by all these creatures moving before our eyes. It is in no way distinct from themselves. They carry it about with them without understanding it, like an animal that turns in its cage and never tires of butting its forehead against the bars. They have no other organ than their whole organism, and it is with that that they carry on their search. They go hither and thither and stop; they throw themselves forward like a load, and wait. Nothing precedes them; there is nothing to rejoin, no ideal to regain. Just as the blood within them, without any reason save its pumping, knocks against the walls of their skulls, so they ask for issue and succession. And little by little, by dint of their patience and persistence, a sort of answer comes, that is also nothing other than themselves, which also meshes with their physical being, and which is life.

It was the great thrust of the nineteenth-century science of anthropology to demystify mythology, to demote myths from the status to which post-Wagnerians and Symbolists wished to reelevate them, to that of metaphor for grim biological realities. It was the project of Sir James Frazer, for example, in his encyclopedic study of the myths of the world called *The Golden Bough* (1890), to strip away the anecdotal content of myths and the metaphorical content of rituals to reveal the ruthless rites of propitiation that lay behind them—the very thing that *The Rite of Spring* exposed. It was a threat not only to poetic mythologism but to the sanctity of revealed religion as well, especially Christian religion, for it reduced the Holy Eucharist to a cannibalistic rite no different from those practiced by any number of "savage" tribes. It was all too easy to draw a horrifying parallel between the culminating virgin sacrifice in *The Rite of Spring* and the sacrifice commemorated in every Christian service.

But was that Stravinsky's fault? Or was it just a part of the staging, the part that, once removed from the music, no longer encumbered it? Beginning with that first triumphant performance in 1914, Stravinsky's ballet has been heard far more often in the concert hall (not to mention its countless recordings) than in the ballet pit. Stravinsky himself went on record as saying that that was how he preferred to hear it. In fact, in

1920 he gave an interview to a Paris reporter in which he denied that his music was "programmatic" at all. "Its embryo," he claimed,

> was a theme that came to me while I was finishing *Firebird*. Since this theme and what followed from it were conceived in a stark and brutal manner, I chose as a pretext to develop them the evocation of prehistoric Russia, since I am Russian. But note well that the idea came from the music, not the music from the idea. I have written an architectural work, not an anecdotal one.[37]

There was hardly a word of truth in this, and of course Stravinsky knew it. By 1920, as we will see in a later chapter, he had reasons for wishing to deflect attention from the original subject matter of the ballet and to call attention instead to its form. But can subject matter really be so easily divorced from form, in this or any work of art? Or does the music's reliance on throbbing ostinatos, on arbitrary arrangements of "hypostatized," nonprogressive harmonies and rhythms, and on inscrutable metrical situations that make the future unpredictable and memory useless already inscribe and participate in the great strip-down from culture to nature, from individual reflection to collective action, from psychology to automatism, ultimately from humanism to biologism, that the ballet presents and even seems to celebrate? Is the utter lack of pathos, the withholding of sympathy from the Chosen One, merely an aspect or product of the "anecdotal" content of the work, or is that pitilessness already implicit in the music itself, its form and its technical procedures?

One who felt the music to be complicit in the parlous message and inextricable from it—and hence that there *was* no "music itself"—was Theodor Wiesengrund Adorno (1903–69), an influential German social philosopher whose extensive musical training impelled him to seek evidence of social attitudes in music. He was appalled by *The Rite* because of the way it seemed not only to portray but to perpetrate the annihilation of the ego, the seat of conscious reflection and moral decision. Even the performers, he thought, must submit to this process. The rigorous precision Stravinsky's difficult rhythms required for their coordinated execution ruled out any spontaneous modification of tempo such as conductors employ for purposes of expressivity. The composer constrains—and dehumanizes—his performers just as surely as the primitive tribe constrains the sacrificial maiden, he suggests. The task of realizing Stravinsky's "fluctuations of something always constant and totally static" reduces the conductor (shades of *Petrushka!*) "to puppet-like motions," and conveys to the listeners as well as the ballerina "the immutable rigidity of convulsive blows and shocks for which they are not prepared through any anticipation of anxiety."[38] Adorno wrote these words in 1948, in a book called *The Philosophy of New Music*. *The Rite of Spring* was already thirty-five years old, and accepted everywhere as a twentieth-century classic. By 1948, however, Adorno felt that events had grimly vindicated his reading of the ballet's sinister elevation of an unreflective collective mentality over individual conscience. Those events included the rise of fascism, which Adorno felt to have been prefigured in Stravinsky's dehumanizing music, and the Second World War.

Did Stravinsky's music prefigure fascism? Can any music do such a thing? Does it affect the question to know that between the world wars Stravinsky was indeed a "fascist sympathizer"? What are the implications of such questions for performance and criticism? We seem to be dealing with another "Wagner problem." And just as with Wagner, there would be no problem were the music not a supremely compelling artistic achievement.

CHAPTER 4

Extinguishing the "Petty 'I'" (Transcendentalism, I)

SCRIABIN, MESSIAEN

MAXIMALISM REACHES THE MAX

The "Sacrificial Dance" at the end of Stravinsky's *The Rite of Spring* reaches its dénouement in a massive crunch, denoting a strain the body of the Chosen One can no longer bear. Afterward there is only a tiny coda (reminiscent, perhaps, of the way the "March to the Scaffold" ends in Berlioz's *Symphonie fantastique*) that tracks the concluding mimed action closely: she crumples (flute glissandi); the elders rush up to catch her (sweeping upbeat figure); she collapses in a heap (concluding thump).

That final crunch, the culminating chord in the culminating dance (incompletely represented in piano reduction in Ex. 3-33), consists of eight pitches doubled in many octaves. (When doubling or register are not themselves the issue, one often uses the term "pitch classes,"[1] coined by the American composer Milton Babbitt in the 1940s and popularized in the 1960s, to refer to differently named pitches irrespective of octave position; thus the culminating chord in *The Rite* comprises the pitch classes C D♭ E F F♯ G A B♭.) As usual in Stravinsky, the pitches in question are grouped so that the harmony can be construed as a "polychord" consisting of superimposed C major and F♯ major triads (a *Petrushka*-chord, as we have learned to call it), with an extra A joined to the former by downward extension (to make a seventh chord, or else to produce overlapping A minor and C major triads), and an extra F (or E♯) joined to the latter by upward extension (again to make a seventh chord, or else to produce overlapping F♯ major and B♭[A♯] minor triads; see Ex. 4-1).

EX. 4-1   Culminating harmony in *The Rite of Spring* represented as a maximalized *Petrushka*-chord

Describing the chord in this way is admittedly a mouthful, but it may well reflect Stravinsky's conceptualization of it as a maximalization of his previous octatonic practice. But the process of extension is simultaneously one of transformation, since the chord in question can no longer be referred to the octatonic scale. Thus what can in one sense be described as a difference in degree (whether simply the number of notes heard simultaneously or the amount of crushingly expressive dissonance) can be described in another sense as a difference in kind (transcending the limits of octatonicism to embrace and control a greater chromatic purview). The chord, with its imagined creative history, represents and exemplifies in a nutshell the concept that drove the radical new music of the early twentieth century. It was a ne plus ultra within a ne plus ultra.

But a limit loomed. Eight pitch classes was only four away from complete chromatic saturation — or more to the point, from chromatic exhaustion. Stravinsky never reached the limit. Not to put it past him, it never figured in his expressive designs. But Mahler (unbeknownst to Stravinsky or anyone else at the time) had already come one pitch class closer to the saturation point in his unfinished Tenth Symphony (see Ex. 1-6); and at least four composers were driven to the limit — that is, to the use of "twelve-tone chords" or "aggregate harmonies" — in the period between 1911 and 1915, the years leading up to and immediately following the outbreak of World War I.

It was not a question of mutual influence. The works were not only too widely dispersed geographically for their authors to have been aware of each other's projects, but also, with a single exception, they were all left unfinished like Mahler's Tenth and were never published or even performed during their creators' lifetimes. To describe them as emblematic works of their time might seem a bit paradoxical since their time did not know them. But the idea of reaching limits was indeed something known. It was nothing short of an obsession. Despite their being hidden from contemporary view, then, these unfinished (perhaps unfinishable) works, which will serve as the climactic exhibits, so to speak, of this chapter and the two that follow, will illustrate the predominating obsession of their time in the most concrete and tangible fashion.

And they can serve as emblems in another way as well. What is hidden from view is occluded, or *occult*. By extension, the latter word has acquired a figurative connotation in addition to its literal meaning. It stands for what belongs to the world beyond (hence hidden from) the senses, already identified with the Symbolists' concept of the *au-delà*. And the three great torsos — the *Mysterium* by the Russian composer Alexander Scriabin (1872–1915), the *Universe symphony* by the American composer Charles Ives (1874–1954), and the oratorio *Die Jakobsleiter* by the Austrian composer Arnold Schoenberg (1874–1951) — all concerned matters occult.

They were all grand visionary statements on the borderline between philosophy and religion, a region already broached by Mahler in his grandly visionary Second Symphony, which dealt in its final movements with eschatological matters — matters of literally *ultimate* significance — rarely broached in secular art. These matters were broached more and more insistently in the art of the early twentieth century. They were perhaps the main impulse driving the engine of stylistic maximalism at this crucial time. What better way of exemplifying the way in which music was driven by ideas than with pieces of music that only existed, during their composers' lifetimes, as ideas? (They have all been posthumously, which means speculatively, "realized" by subsequent composer-scholars, and in this way performed and recorded.)

RUSH-TO-THE-PATENT-OFFICE MODERNISM

But first a word about the one composition using aggregate harmonies that was completed and performed — once only — during this phase of maximal maximalism. The composer was the then virtually unknown Alban Berg (1885–1935), formerly a pupil — and still very much a disciple — of Schoenberg. He would win fame in the 1920s as a composer of opera, and we will reencounter him. But the work that concerns us now is a little song cycle called *Fünf Orchesterlieder nach Ansichtskartentexten von Peter Altenberg*, op. 4 ("Five lieder with orchestra on picture-postcard legends by Peter Altenberg"), composed in 1912. The performance, which took place under Schoenberg's direction on 31 March 1913, provoked a reaction similar to the one that would greet the legendary premiere of *The Rite of Spring* two months later.

Altenberg (real name Richard Engländer, 1859–1919) was a popular Viennese writer who specialized in aphoristic "prose poems." The texts Berg set did not literally come from postcards, but from a book of Altenberg's poems (*Altes Neues* [Old News], 1911) in which they were so labeled. Only the two shortest songs from the cycle of five, the second and the third, were on the program Schoenberg conducted. It was the third song, which contained the aggregate harmony, that provoked the most vociferous protests. As one member of the audience later recalled, its

> dissonances and the accumulation of wrong notes produced with all the might of the orchestra became a signal for a storm. A wave of laughter greeted the groans and squeaks of the orchestra, and this increased the singer's nervousness to the point where his voice cracked. The audience tumult grew so great that Schoenberg finally had to interrupt the concert. When, after a while, quiet was restored, Schoenberg, who never left the podium, announced that "those who do not know how to keep quiet can leave the hall." No one followed this invitation, of course, and the song was then repeated, but with the same results except that the laughter and the chaos were much louder, and that this time shouts, hisses and cursing came from the parterre and the galleries, while in the boxes a few fanatics stood brandishing their arms against the uprising hall. At last a commissioner of police appeared on the stage and forbade the continuation of the concert, an occurrence without precedent in the Viennese music world.[2]

The offending song has this poem for a text:

> Über die Grenzen des All blicktest du sinnend hinaus:
> Hattest nie Sorge um Hof und Haus!
> Leben und Traum vom Leben, plötzlich ist alles aus —
> Über die Grenzen des All blickst du noch sinnend hinaus . . . .
> (You gazed pensively over the all-encompassing brink:
> Never a care for home and hearth!
> Life and dreams of living, all of a sudden gone —
> You still gaze pensively over the all-encompassing brink . . . .)

The all-encompassing aggregate harmony, which comes at the beginning in the winds, and again at the end (Ex. 4-2) in string harmonics to accompany the repeated line, is actually a rather obvious example, if an audacious one, of traditional "word painting." The audacity was enough to provoke the public, but its motivation was anything but novel, and far from profound. Although it purports to intensify a typically aspirant, romantic mood, it remains an exercise of wit, and its effect — especially, of course, when analyzed — is comic. To call it that is not necessarily to call it funny, but it

EX. 4-2   Alban Berg, *Altenberg Lieder*, no. 3, end

does imply that the device is an intellectual conceit rather than an expression of feeling or belief. Berg's song thus confronts the age-old dilemma that some three hundred years earlier had midwifed the birth of directly emotional and tragic recitative (hence opera) out of the intellectual conceits of "madrigalism."

The grand eschatological torsos of Scriabin, Ives, and Schoenberg do not put the aggregate harmony to such obviously illustrative, hence potentially trivial, use—and this may be one reason why Schoenberg, to Berg's intense dismay, sharply criticized the *Altenberg Lieder* to his former pupil's face after the notorious concert. As we shall see, Schoenberg regarded the aggregate harmony the way Scriabin and Ives did, as something virtually holy, even taboo, not to be defiled by utilitarian, "madrigalian" use. Berg, having invoked it in an ironic vein, could even be charged with playing into the hands of the philistines who laughed.

But nevertheless his little *Altenberg Lieder* enjoy huge prestige as a landmark in the history of twentieth-century music, a prestige that derives from the way in which that history is often recounted. That telling, and the theory on which it rests, are in themselves a sort of maximalism, in which the neo-Hegelian esthetic values of the New German School, as first enunciated in the mid-nineteenth century, have been universalized and exaggerated. The highest of all values, in this view, is technical innovation, provided that (1) the innovation in question can be viewed as an emancipation, (2) it was "influential" (in other words, that it inspired imitation, or at least turned up in a lot of later music), and (3) it placed the innovator beyond the comprehension of his contemporaries (or beyond all but an initiated elite), so that he might learn, in the words of Milton Babbitt, "how it feels to have the history of music leave you ahead."[3]

These values are nothing if not asocial. When challenged, as we shall learn, they can take more radical, downright antisocial forms. Twentieth-century historiography has also been influenced, like much twentieth-century art making, by the spirit of technological progress, giving rise to a "machine age" esthetic. The American poet William Carlos Williams voiced this view especially forcefully when he maintained that a poem was "a machine made out of words,"[4] and that therefore a great poet was one who showed by his practice how to manufacture a new kind of machine. Much twentieth-century theorizing on music seems to regard it similarly, as a machine made of notes. The attention of composers and critics has thus often been more readily captured by the internal workings of the poetic or musical mechanism than by the expressive work it accomplishes. The resulting esthetic has been aptly characterized by the American scholar Christopher Williams as "techno-essentialist."[5]

Like *The Rite of Spring*, the *Altenberg Lieder* qualify as "historically significant" on all three techno-essentialist counts listed above. The third criterion is met magnificently by the story of its ill-fated first performance, even though Berg (and, it seems, Schoenberg) experienced that event not as a Diaghilevian *succès de scandale* but as a humiliation. The first criterion is met most conspicuously by the aggregate harmony, which admitted a denser dissonance than ever before into musical practice. And the pervasiveness of "patent office modernism," as well as its potential links with nationalism or otherwise parochial biases, are well illustrated by the *Traité de l'harmonie*, a harmony textbook by

Charles Koechlin (1867–1950), a venerable French composer and pedagogue, which appeared in 1928 and contained the news that the earliest twelve-tone chord was actually penned not by the Austrian Berg but by the Frenchman Jean Huré (1877–1930), in an unpublished and unperformed stage work called *La cathédrale*, which was actually written not in 1912, not in 1911, but all the way back in 1910!

The second criterion is met even more conspicuously by the fifth and last song in Berg's Altenberg cycle, a passacaglia that expresses the "chromatic aggregate" not as a harmonic simultaneity (Ex. 4-3a) but as a melodic succession is that repeated as an ostinato (Ex. 4-3b). Such arrangements, placing the twelve pitch classes all in a row, were destined (though nobody foresaw it at the time) to become the basis of one of the century's most widely practiced and propagated compositional methods. The melody in Berg's fifth song has been acclaimed—first by the composer Ernst Krenek (1900–91) in a memorial essay published in 1937, by which time the new method had been established and was gaining many adherents—as history's first "twelve tone row."[6]

EX. 4-3A   Alban Berg, *Altenberg Lieder*, aggregate chord in song no. 3

EX. 4-3B   Alban Berg, *Altenberg Lieder*, twelve-tone theme from no. 5 (passacaglia)

But where *The Rite of Spring*, notwithstanding its stormy premiere, has enjoyed a triumphant career in the concert hall that has lasted from 1914 to the present, the *Altenberg Lieder*, following that lone partial performance (which did not include the fifth song), "fell," to quote Krenek, "like a stone into the abyss of the forgotten from which no one has as yet fetched it." The first complete performance did not take place until 1952; the piano-vocal score was not published until the next year; the full score, not until 1966.

This retarded rediscovery, adding the aura of martyrdom and resurrection to that of its early rejection, has done its bit to enhance the work's prestige even further. But unlike *The Rite of Spring*, Berg's *Altenberg Lieder* did not become a part of history—that is, an entity with a potential relationship to listeners, performers, and composers, available to influence their thoughts and deeds—until two or three decades after the composer's death. To accord it a comparable historical importance because of its hidden relationship to what came later is literally to consign it to the realm of the occult — to mythology rather than history. A great deal of musical historiography in the twentieth century has been mythology of this kind. The tales it has spun are on the record and have been influential. As a part of history in their own right they will need to be dealt with. But they should not be confused with an account of contemporary events.

The foregoing little sermon on history implies no esthetic judgment on the *Altenberg Lieder*. They are properly admired for their intense expressivity — often compared, as we will see, with a style of vividly exaggerated and subjectively distorted painting known as "expressionism" — and for the feats of compositional virtuosity that their expressionistic manner called forth. (Again a parallel with the old Italian madrigal in its "mannerist" phase might be suggestive.) Within the context of their time, however, these songs (like the madrigals of Gesualdo) might be better viewed as eccentric than as pregnant.

FROM EXPRESSION TO REVELATION

And yet the essential motivating metaphor that drove the more potent maximalists of the period to the limit — the aggregate harmony standing for the All, the One, the Universal, the object of all metaphysical and religious striving — was not all that different from the image of the "all-encompassing brink" that inspired Berg. The difference lay in the treatment. Rather than a playful surface ornament as it was with Berg, the aggregate harmony was for Scriabin, Schoenberg, and Ives a symbolic ideal, not to be invoked lightly but to be approached gradually, as the One was to be approached through a properly perseverant spiritual quest, and to be expressed not blatantly but latently, in a properly occult fashion.

For Scriabin, the quest was the work of a lifetime. A piano prodigy, he seemed destined at first for the career of a virtuoso-composer like Liszt or, more precisely, like Chopin, with whom he identified powerfully and on whose very distinctive style he at first attempted to fashion his own, even going so far as to adopt Chopin's characteristic Polish genres like the mazurka, of which he wrote twenty-three between 1889 and 1903. He was drawn even more to that most "poetic" of Chopinesque forms,

FIG. 4-1   Alexander Nikolayevich Scriabin in an engraving from a photograph taken aboard the Volga steamship that carried him on a concert tour through Russia in 1910.

the freestanding aphoristic prelude, of which he composed a complete Chopinesque set of twenty-four (published as op. 11) between 1888 and 1896.

Scriabin continued to write preludes throughout his career, right up to his final work, a set of Four Preludes published in 1914 as his op. 74. As he came ever more explicitly to maintain, short but striking preludes were in their immediacy akin to spiritual disclosures and could function as prophecy. From an art of the sensuously — at times erotically — beautiful, Scriabin's music developed by degrees (each with its clearly identifiable technical preoccupations) into an art of sublime — at times mystical — revelation.

We can take the measure of this transition by comparing a prelude from the middle of Scriabin's career — op. 48, no. 4 in C major (1905; Ex. 4-4) — with a selection from that final group, op. 74. The highly emotional tone of the earlier piece is achieved by methods we have come to associate with Wagner (perhaps by way of Schumann). The primary method is the maintenance throughout of a sense of harmonic tension that is relieved only by the final cadence. Indeed, the last chord of the piece is practically the only pure, unadulterated triad to be found in it. Almost all of the other harmonies, while clearly "triadic" in concept and function, have been altered, either by the use of additives like sevenths and ninths, or by the chromatic tweaking of their constituent pitches so that they become "tendency tones."

The very first chord is an especially telling instance. It is only in retrospect that we can confidently identify it as a tonic harmony. The added B♭, turning its quality into that of a dominant-seventh chord, gives it the implied function "V of IV"; and its short-term resolution to a chord rooted on F confirms that local diagnosis. The raising of its fifth degree to G♯ adds to its implicit short-range function, since now that tone too seeks resolution, in A. But the F chord to which the first chord resolves is no more stable than the first chord had been: it too has been given a seventh that demands resolution, and its fifth has been lowered a semitone (to C♭, spelled B). Its quality, therefore, has been altered to that of a "French sixth," a chord that normally resolves as a ♭VI to a dominant. And so it does — but "deceptively," to the dominant of C rather than the expected dominant of A.

The dominant of A arrives in m. 8, exactly as the dominant of the home key had arrived in m. 4, to round off a pair of parallel periods that together make up the first half of the prelude. It is evident that the novelty of Scriabin's idiom applies only to its harmonic dimension; rhythmically and in its phrase structure (i.e., its form) it remains simple — and in its high rhetorical keyboard style, for all its virtuosity, it remains conventional. As Schoenberg would later put it, "if comprehensibility is made difficult in one respect, it must be made easier in some other respect."[7] Scriabin, like Schoenberg somewhat later, seems to have been attempting to "reduce difficulties by providing a familiar type of unfolding."

But after the cadence on the E-major chord in m. 8 (the only other "pure triad" in the piece and therefore, despite its short duration, a major point of articulation), something happens that is indeed unconventional — though far from unprecedented in our experience — in terms of "normal" tonal practice. What sounds at the very end of

EX. 4-4   Alexander Scriabin, Prelude in C major, Op. 48, no. 4

m. 8 like an A in the bass, the implicit goal of the E major harmony, is made to function very differently, as suggested by its respelling as B♭♭. Impelled by accompanying tones that form with it a French sixth chord, it is directed down to A♭, a root note that in direct juxtaposition with E (and recalling the initial C) suggests that the overall tonal trajectory of the prelude will be based on a symmetrically apportioned cycle of major thirds rather than the locally operating circle of fifths.

The period from m. 9, where A♭ intrudes, to m. 16, where the dominant of C is regained, is based on a modulating sequence progression. In that sense it functions like a development section, and identifies the return of the opening harmony at m. 17 as a thematic recapitulation. This is indeed a "familiar type of unfolding," sanctioned by more than a century of common practice as "sonata form," here applied on a microscopic level. And its familiarity helps us accept the cycle of thirds as harmonically normative. The two halves of a binary form express not the usual I–V, V–I trajectory, but a complementary symmetrical progression: tonic up to mediant (I → III) followed by flat submediant up to tonic: I–III, ♭VI–I. The three points of departure and arrival that articulate the form—I, III, ♭VI—occupy evenly spaced positions along the chromatic scale:/0 4 8/, familiar to us not from common or "classical" practice but from the alternative practice branching off from Schubert to Liszt, thence to Rimsky-Korsakov, Debussy, Ravel, and, most lately, Stravinsky.

One other harmonic idiosyncrasy is conspicuous in this prelude, and that is Scriabin's propensity for approaching V by way of ♭II, expressed not as a "Neapolitan sixth" but in root position. That is something probably picked up from Chopin (e.g., Chopin's Prelude in C minor, op. 28, no. 20; see Ex. 4-5), but Scriabin turned what was in Chopin a rarity into a basic modus operandi. The progression bracketed in Ex. 4-5 and labeled "tritone link" shows up in Ex. 4-4 in mm. 1–2, 5–6, and—climactically—over a two-measure general pause in mm. 19–22. The term "tritone link" (*tritonovoye zveno*) was coined by Varvara Pavlovna Dernova in a dissertation on Scriabin written in 1948 but only published twenty years later, by which time Scriabin had been dead for more than fifty years.[8] It was the first important breakthrough in analyzing Scriabin's until-then enigmatic and refractory harmonic style; like many a modernist, Scriabin kept his methods a secret, the better to stun listeners with their effect.

EX. 4-5   Frédéric Chopin, Prelude in C minor, Op. 28, no. 20, end

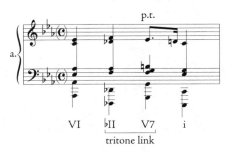

VI   ♭II   V7   i

tritone link

Just how enigmatic Scriabin's idiom eventually became can be seen at a glance in Ex. 4-6, which contains the first and last of the Four Preludes, op. 74. The extravagant expressive markings in French—*Douloureux, déchirant* (excruciatingly anguished) in the first, *Lent, vague, indécis* (slow, indefinite, uncertain) in the last—may seem at first reminiscent of Debussy; but Debussy's art, while it cultivated the *vague* and *indécis*, perhaps, avoided the *déchirant* at all costs. Rather, they point to a common bond in Symbolism, which in Russia achieved an aura of maximalized religious ecstasy that it never approached in France.

Alone among musicians, Scriabin actively participated in "mystical symbolist" circles, attending the meetings of the Moscow Religious Philosophical Society, a forum for avant-garde poetry and theology alike, beginning in 1898. By 1905, he had discovered theosophy, an esoteric mystical doctrine that sought to reconcile Christianity with the

EX. 4-6A   Alexander Scriabin, Prelude, Op. 74, no. 1

EX. 4-6B   Alexander Scriabin, Prelude, Op. 74, no. 4

transcendentalist religions of South Asia, particularly Hinduism and Buddhism, which saw as the purpose of life the achievement of a transcendent enlightenment that would free the soul from the shackling temporality of human desire and allow it to join the eternal unity of the Godhead.

In the strong form with which Scriabin was affiliated, theosophy was a Russian maximalist movement. It was spearheaded and disseminated by a society founded in New York in 1875 by Helena Petrovna Blavatsky (1831–91), a Russian aristocratic émigré. Mystic symbolists and theosophists considered art a medium of gnostic revelation — that is, the direct imparting of divine knowledge unmediated by the imperfect and limited human intellect. Within their circles Scriabin was hailed as a prophet, because his artistic medium was the least trammeled by specific representational meaning, had the least paraphrasable content, and was therefore the most inherently "theurgic" of all the arts — the most capable, that is, of becoming an instrument of theurgy, the channeling of divine influence on human affairs.

In the amicably envious judgment of Vyacheslav Ivanov (1866–1949), the leading mystical-symbolist poet and one of the composer's closest friends, Scriabin was a greater artist than any poet could ever be because of the superiority of his medium. "Where we [poets] monotonously blab the meager word 'sadness,'" Ivanov wrote, "music overflows with thousands of particular shades of sadness, each so ineffably novel that no two of them can be called the same feeling."[9] Music, therefore, "the unmediated pilot of our spiritual depths," is at once the most sensitive of the arts and the most inherently prophetic, "the womb in which the Spirit of the Age is incubated."[10] Scriabin, for his part, consciously modified his style so as to enable his music to serve the spiritualistic purposes his religious and philosophical beliefs demanded. That meant, among other things, making it inscrutable, resistant to analysis. For this reason he has often been attacked as a charlatan, and just as often defended against himself by nonbelievers who nevertheless regard him, in the words of the American music theorist James M. Baker, as "a master of the craft of musical composition."[11] But Ivanov's exaggerated remarks can easily be read as just another maximalization (and a particularly Russian one) of the old German romantic notion of "absolute music." They also accord perfectly with the antiliterary esthetics of Alexandre Benois that (as we saw in the previous chapter) midwifed the rebirth of ballet in Russia. So we should not be surprised to find that Scriabin's late, "inscrutable" idiom has a lot in common with the maximalistic techniques that Stravinsky adopted, just as deliberately and almost simultaneously, in *The Rite of Spring*.

To begin with, in Scriabin's preludes we again confront the total avoidance of "pure triads," even at the ends of pieces. What to make of that? Of the preludes in op. 74, the last (Ex. 4-6b) ends with the most easily described harmony: seemingly a superimposition of the major and minor triads on A. We may then note that the piece begins with the same harmony, this time with the "disagreeing" thirds located at the extremities, as if the chord were inverted. This is a clue that the harmonic idiom of the music, however unusual, is internally consistent. Another indication: we may as yet be at a loss to account for the final cadential approach to the "A major/minor" chord, by way of a tritone, and yet we have already seen that Scriabin's music makes considerable use of "tritone links." The final chord of the first prelude (Ex. 4-6a), unnameable in terms of the common practice, is also approached via a tritone leap in the bass. Such observations give prima facie evidence that the music is following as-yet-undiscovered yet binding rules.

The mere avoidance of pure triads does not in itself demonstrate any real similarity between the idiom of Scriabin's preludes and that of Stravinsky's *Rite*. An arbitrary list of their "common absences" could be infinitely extended. But there are positive affinities as well. For one thing, the bass notes of the chords and arpeggios that inform the left-hand part in Ex. 4-6a — B♯ (=C) in the pickup; A alternating with B♯ in mm. 1–2, followed by F♯ (=G♭) alternating with C in mm. 2–4 — suggest a pattern that is completed on the downbeat of m. 5 and recurs, significantly transposed, in mm. 9–15. We have certainly seen this pattern in Stravinsky, and even earlier. For another thing, the music in Ex. 4-6b falls briefly (mm. 13–16) into a regular sequential period. Allowing for some idiosyncrasies in the note-spelling, the "soprano" voice here outlines some ordinary triads, otherwise a great rarity in these compositions. How are they related?4-6a—B

All of the foregoing observations are of a single phenomenon: reliance on symmetrical interval cycles — that is, cycles of intervals that evenly divide the twelve pitches of the chromatic scale — as governors of the tonal trajectory. The bass pitches in the first prelude describe a cycle of minor thirds (0 3 6 9); the sequential triads in the last prelude describe a cycle of major thirds (0 4 8). Both, but particularly the minor-third cycle, featured prominently in Stravinsky because of the affinity between the minor-third cycle and the octatonic scale. And now look at Ex. 4-7, the end of the third prelude from Op. 74: rarely is the octatonic scale displayed so pristinely on the surface of any music.

EX. 4-7 Alexander Scriabin, Prelude, Op. 74, no. 3, last four measures

As a subset of the octatonic, the /0 6/ tritone relationship was the basis for the harmony in "Chez Pétrouchka" (the second tableau of Stravinsky's second ballet), and the source of the famous *Petrushka*-chord. In like fashion, the prelude sampled in Ex. 4-7 consists of two halves, the second of which is a literal transposition of the first by a tritone; owing to the properties of the octatonic scale, the two halves have identical (or "invariant") pitch content. As for the /0 4 8/ cycle, while not especially prominent in the Stravinsky compositions that we have examined, it was at the heart of Debussy's tonal procedures in *Nuages*, which Stravinsky knew and admired well enough to plagiarize (unconsciously) in the prelude to his early opera *The Nightingale*. Earlier, the cycle (and also its decorated version, the whole tone scale, /0 2 4 6 8 10/, so pervasive in Debussy) had been foreshadowed in our experience in works of Liszt and Schubert, as the /0 3

6 9/ cycle had been foreshadowed in Rimsky-Korsakov and Liszt. It is evident that Scriabin, even at his most purposefully inscrutable, had a considerable patrimony.

But Scriabin maximalized it the furthest, and in ways that bore directly on his theurgic purposes. For one thing, he mined more radical harmonic constructs directly out of the octatonic collection. The choralelike final cadence in the last prelude, right up to its enigmatic "major-minor" conclusion, is a case in point. It is all educed from a single octatonic scale, as shown in Ex. 4-8 (and note the rigorous voice leading in the right hand through a cycle of minor thirds, mirrored at first by the left in contrary motion).

EX. 4-8   Octatonic derivation of final cadence in Alexander Scriabin, Prelude, Op. 74, no. 4

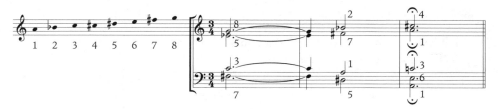

Most significant by far is Scriabin's habit, taken to an extreme in the third prelude from op. 74, of saturating the musical surface with tritones, and then transposing the whole "globally" around a tritone axis. (Compare mm. 1–4 and 9–12 in Ex. 4-6a.) The harmonic stasis, brought about by the tritone's invariance properties (since the tritone, when transposed a tritone, merely inverts or "maps into" itself) produces a trajectory that contains *movement*, so to speak, but accomplishes no *motion*. We have marched in place.

Moreover, whatever goes for melodic tritones will also apply to harmonic tritones, and especially to chords composed of multiple tritones, like diminished sevenths or French sixths. And the French sixth, it will emerge on closer inspection, is indeed the basic referential harmony in these preludes, having taken over the function performed in more traditional tonalities by the major or minor triad.

The final chord in Ex. 4-6a is an especially characteristic Scriabin sonority: a French sixth (F♯ B♯ A♯ E) filled out or garnished by two additives: a G that may be referred along with the French sixth chord to an octatonic scale, and a D that may be referred along with the same French sixth chord to a whole-tone scale (which it nearly exhausts). The French sixth, then, functions here as a kind of "nexus chord" or pivot, linking two different symmetrical scale constructions that have usurped the place of the more traditional major and minor scales, providing a point of intersection between them on which the final chord is poised, as if balanced on a cusp (see Ex. 4-9).

EXTINGUISHING THE "I"

Now what has all of this to do with the theurgic aims of mystic symbolism or theosophy? We may quote the answer to this question directly from Vyacheslav Ivanov, who in a

EX. 4-9   Alexander Scriabin, Prelude, Op. 74, no. 1, final chord compared with its referential scales

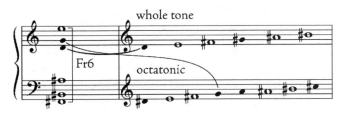

lecture of 1919 enumerated the theurgic effects of Scriabin's music, which if regarded as the composer's ends provide the explanation of his means, as we have been describing them. "Scriabin has expressed in music the most profound ideas of the present day," Ivanov declared, defining them as follows:

1. The vision of surmounting the boundaries of the personal, individual, petty "I"—a musical transcendentalism.
2. The vision of universal, communal mingling of all humanity in a single "I"—or the macrocosmic universalism of musical consciousness.
3. The vision of a violent breakthrough into the expanse of a free new plane of being—universal transformation.[12]

The idea of art as world transformation is the essential Wagnerian ideal. Scriabin was the single Russian composer to accept from Wagner the Orphic mission. We have already defined the Wagnerian resonance in Scriabin in "purely musical" terms when we noted Scriabin's strong insistence on the dominant function. Most of his chords are dominant in color and tendency. In the Prelude, op. 48, no. 4, the chords were mainly dominant sevenths with additives; by the time of op. 74, the chords were mainly French sixths with additives. But the French sixth chord can be viewed as an "altered" dominant seventh, the alteration consisting of the flatting of the fifth degree. If the fifth degree is omitted from the French sixth, the remainder comprises an "incomplete" but fully functional dominant seventh, consisting of a defining root and a tritone in need of resolution.

With any given root, the tritone has only one option for resolving: the seventh must descend a semitone and the third (the functional leading tone) must ascend a semitone. That dual necessity is what gives the chord such a restless will of its own, which when exploited as Wagner did in *Tristan und Isolde* can channel the desires of the listening multitudes. But that desire is a highly egoistic desire; it heightens a listener's awareness of his or her "personal, individual, petty 'I,'" as Ivanov would say, and its selfish needs. Yet the primary selfish need, as Wagner so compellingly if paradoxically emphasized in *Tristan*, is the ego's need for satiation—the extinguishing of desire, which can only come from union with the other: already a transcendence.

Scriabin found a way of representing satiation without resolution, thus quelling the ego's need and achieving its dissolution; and we have already observed the mechanism by which this remarkable effect of quiescence is achieved. It is harmonic invariance based on the tritone. Because the tritone exactly bisects the octave, and therefore replicates itself when transposed by itself, its two tones, while needing resolution as we have seen, are of ambiguous tendency. The way in which a tritone will seek its resolution will depend on external stimuli—that is, the notes that accompany it. When accompanied by a dominant-seventh root, its pitches are defined as leading tone and seventh respectively. The leading tone, as we know, seeks resolution by ascent, the seventh by descent. Yet by changing the defining root we can cause an exchange of the two functions: what had been the leading tone tending upward becomes the seventh tending downward, and vice versa (Ex. 4-10).

EX. 4-10   Alternative cadential harmonizations of the tritone

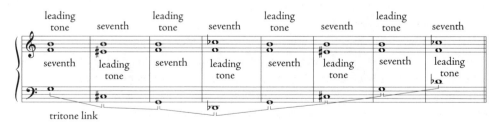

The two roots that accomplish this transformation must of course themselves lie a tritone apart. The direct progression formed by these two chords—chords sharing a tritone in common, their roots lying a tritone apart—was anticipated as early as Liszt and was memorably employed by Musorgsky to simulate coronation bells in *Boris Godunov*. It is the essential Scriabin progression. When turned into an oscillation along the "tritone link," the bass progression continually contradicts and recontradicts the resolution tendencies in the harmonic tritone (see Ex. 4-11). This easy reciprocity of function negates the harmony's "functionality," turning it qualitatively from an active tendency (as in Wagner) into a latent or passive one. Although there is continual root activity, there is no functional progression—marching in place again.

EX. 4-11   Alexander Scriabin's "tritone link"

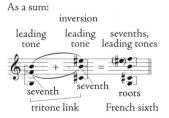

Playing over Ex. 4-11, we seem to examine or experience a single "floating" harmony from a dual perspective, something the Russian music theorist Boleslav Yavorsky (Scriabin's younger contemporary) compared with moving from two-dimensional to three-dimensional space — which in turn is something Scriabin himself hinted at in a remark reported to Varvara Dernova, the discoverer of the tritone link, by Georgiy Rimsky-Korsakov, a grandson of the famous composer and a composer himself: "You have to be able to walk around a chord."[13] Until one of the root notes exemplified in Ex. 4-11 leaves the tritone treadmill and proceeds along the circle of fifths (or, in a pinch, by a semitone as if resolving an augmented sixth), the eventual destination of the tritone is in doubt, and one can even forget that the tritone *has* a destination. A quality of hovering, of time-forgetful stasis, altered consciousness, or even trance, can be induced. The "personal, individual, petty 'I'" is lulled; consciousness is made available for something larger.

Scriabin's whole stylistic evolution can be viewed as the gradual extinguishing of the desiring subject, the "petty 'I,'" so as to make possible a theurgic, world- (or at least consciousness-) transforming transcendence. We have seen the end result in the miniatures of op. 74. We can trace the process through which the composer arrived at their enigmatically attenuated style by sampling some of his larger pieces, which at their largest are truly grandiose. For Scriabin's output spectacularly encompassed both romantic extremes of expression — that of intimate aphoristic disclosure, and that of swollen public oration — and maximalized them both.

APPROACHING THE ULTIMATE

Scriabin wrote ten piano sonatas in addition to his many miniatures, but they were not his biggest pieces. In fact, as his career went on they became smaller: the Fourth Sonata (1904) has two movements, like Beethoven's op. 111, but in reversed order so that it ends with a vertiginous *prestissimo volando* (flying at great speed). From then on, they were all single-movement works like Liszt's Sonata in B minor; and from the Sixth Sonata on, as the whole-tone and octatonic collections took over the normative functions formerly exercised by major and minor tonalities, Scriabin dispensed with the use of key signatures or designations.

Scriabin's public orations were his five symphonies, a genre in which he parted company with his erstwhile model, Chopin, and joined the ranks of symphonic maximalists such as Mahler and Strauss. (Both German names deserve to be invoked, since although Scriabin called them symphonies, the last two were single-movement programmatic works that could just as well have been called tone poems.) The First Symphony (1900), like Mahler's Second, apes Beethoven's Ninth in the use of vocal soloists and chorus for an oratorio-like finale. But Scriabin found his true symphonic métier when he dispensed with words and began finding musical analogues for the new ideas about art's significance that he picked up from his contacts among the mystical Symbolists and, later, from theosophy. The place to begin is the motto opening of the Third Symphony, subtitled *Le divin poème* ("The divine poem"), Scriabin's one multimovement programmatic composition. The use of the motto and the key, C minor, are transparent gestures of tribute to Beethoven's Fifth, the most famous symphony in the world.

But his starting point was as much Wagner as Beethoven, as we can infer directly from the motto theme, which he modeled (how consciously one can never tell) on the opening of the *Tristan* Prelude. In both cases an unaccompanied preparatory melody lasting one measure leads into a startlingly dissonant chromatic chord containing a tritone, urgently demanding an unspecified resolution. Scriabin's chord is the more radical of the two, in keeping with the emulative spirit of maximalism, since it is an ad hoc harmonic structure with no common-practice standing at all.

Where the famous *Tristan*-chord could be classified, if desired, either as homologous (similarly structured) to a half-diminished seventh chord, or (more functionally) as a French sixth with one of its intervals unconventionally altered by contraction, Scriabin's chord may be viewed as a German sixth, homologous to the dominant seventh, with one of its intervals unconventionally altered by expansion, adding to its dissonance and intensifying the affect of egoistic self-assertion (Ex. 4-12).

The most striking parallel between the two openings is the specific way in which the first chord is prepared. Wagner leaps up from the tonic note to the sixth degree, which in the minor mode is a half step above the fifth, and passes through the fifth to a complementary half step below — that is, to the chromatically inflected fourth degree,

EX. 4-12A   Alexander Scriabin, *The Divine Poem*, I, mm. 1–15 (figuration and arpeggiation omitted)

EX. 4-12B   The "Scriabin sixth" and German sixth compared

the "altered" note that gives the *Tristan*-chord its name-worthy color. Scriabin's opening exactly inverts Wagner's procedure. The melody (assuming Db, as at the beginning one must, to be the tonic) leaps down to the chromatically inflected fourth degree and proceeds through the fifth to a complementary half step above—that is, to the sixth degree, which, the mode being major, must also be chromatically inflected to preserve the half-step relationship.

The first resolution of Scriabin's "ad hoc" chord is to an unsullied consonant triad, enhancing the promise of what the symphony's program note calls "joyous and intoxicated affirmation," to be wholly attained (as in the old Beethovenian scenario) in the C-major last movement, when the hero—personified by the solo trumpet—at last comes fully into his own. The trumpet had played the peremptory "summons" motif (the dotted rising sixth) in the third and the sixth measures of the opening as shown in Ex. 4-12. "The free, powerful man-god appears to triumph," according to the program, which, although actually penned by Tatyana Schloezer, the composer's common-law wife (much as Liszt's writings, including programs, were often the work of his mistress, the princess Sayn-Wittgenstein), transmits the composer's intentions well enough to have had his endorsement. "But," the program continues, "it is only the intellect which affirms the divine Ego, while the individual will, still too weak, is tempted to sink into Pantheism," that is, into hedonistic passivity and indolence.

How could such an abstract program be musically represented? Just as in the *Tristan* Prelude, the first phrase of Scriabin's motto theme is seconded by a sequential repetition. But unlike the second phrase of the *Tristan* Prelude, the repetition is no mere intensifying reiteration. It does not terminate in another affirmative cadence, as it might well have done (see Ex. 4-12), but dissolves in a tritone link that palpably weakens its thrust. It is followed, in perhaps all too craftsmanly a fashion, by a second tritone link calculated to prepare the main key of the first movement, thus to launch a conventional sonata form that is interrupted, in a manner reminiscent of Chaikovsky's Fourth Symphony or Franck's Symphony in D minor, by periodic recollections of the opening motto.

These reminiscences must surely have been written, or at least improvised, before the actual opening passage was composed, for they demonstrate the genesis of the "ad hoc chord"—a chord that the composer continued to exploit as a basic component of his harmonic vocabulary, and that has accordingly earned the nickname "Scriabin sixth." The first reminiscence (Ex. 4-13) takes place in Eb major, the classically mandated key of the second theme in a C-minor sonata movement. The local tonic is held out in the treble instruments while the bass proclaims the motto in the new key. At the moment when the theme reaches the fifth note, the inflected lower neighbor tone or appoggiatura to the fifth degree, the trumpet-hero joins in to sound the complementary inflection above. The two voices, trumpet and bass, proceed in contrary motion through the fifth and on to the opposite or reciprocal inflection, thus producing the "Scriabin sixth."

EX. 4-13   Alexander Scriabin, *The Divine Poem*, I, fig. [1]

(chiasmus)

It is a symmetrical, simultaneous exchange of functions (known technically as a *chiasmus*, "cross" in Greek), comparable to the functional exchange involving the two tendency tones over the tritone link, illustrated in Ex. 4-11. It gave Scriabin an idea with enormous consequences. In the music following *The Divine Poem*, simultaneously sounding (rather than successive or progressive) symmetrical relations became the primary means for embellishing or prolonging the dominant function, and this is what led Scriabin to his special domain of quiescently "invariant" harmonic space.

Maximally prolonged "Wagnerian" dominants were long a Scriabin specialty. Even the little Prelude, op. 48, no.4 (Ex. 4-4), is Wagnerian in this sense, built over a dominant that is first sounded in m. 2, sustained through an /0 4 8/ vagary that moves by way of a symmetrical circle of major thirds from III to ♭VI, and not fully resolved until the end of the piece: *Tristan* in a nutshell. The obvious next step, once Scriabin had begun superimposing rather than juxtaposing symmetrically related harmonies, was to combine the two members of the tritone link in Ex. 4-11 into a composite dominant that could be "walked around."

The immediate product of the operation, the Scriabin "double dominant," was a chord homologous to a French sixth, as demonstrated at the beginning of Ex. 4-14. But that was just the beginning. As the example shows, the French sixth is one of only two chords in common practice (the other being the diminished seventh chord) that contain two tritones, the one corresponding to the sustained tendency tones in Ex. 4-11, the other to the complementary roots along the tritone link. Chords consisting of two tritones have exactly the same properties of invariance as a single tritone, but twice as many of them. That is, they are inversionally invariant on two axes of symmetry and transpositionally invariant at two intervals. Such chords were ideally suited for enhancing and furthering—in a word, maximalizing—Scriabin's developing methods of dominant embellishment and prolongation.4-14

Of the two possible double-tritone chords, only the French sixth suited the composer's present purposes, not only because of its Wagnerian associations but also because it was generically related to the "Scriabin sixth," and could even be combined with it to achieve a further maximalized dominant sonority. The two chords had three tones out of four in common. Put together, as the next step in Ex. 4-14, their total of five tones would immediately have suggested to Scriabin, heir along with Stravinsky to the special traditions of Russian "fantastic harmony" going back to Glinka, that with the addition of a single remaining tone he would have a chord that expressed the dominant function by encompassing all the members of the whole-tone scale.

EX. 4-14 Whole-tone scale as expanded dominant

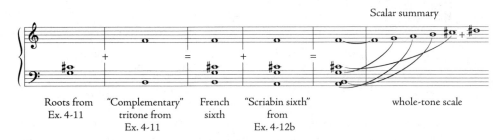

| Roots from Ex. 4-11 | "Complementary" tritone from Ex. 4-11 | French sixth | "Scriabin sixth" from Ex. 4-12b | whole-tone scale |

Invariance potential of whole-tone scale:

first trichord   second trichord   three tritones

This was a momentous discovery. A chord containing the entire whole-tone scale contains three tritones, thus maximizing further the potential for harmonic (that is, inversional and transpositional) invariance. Like the complete twelve-tone aggregate, of which it is, so to speak, a fifty-percent sample, the whole-tone aggregate has the property of stasis: every possible position of the chord is intervallically, hence functionally, identical to every other one. No matter which of its members is in the bass, no matter by which of its constituent intervals it is transposed, the pitch and interval content of the chord never varies. It could be endlessly "walked around"—that is, mined for a great variety of symmetrical constituents (the tritone itself, the augmented triad, the French sixth, the "incomplete" dominant ninth, plus a few, like the "Scriabin sixth," without any common-practice classification) that offered infinite possibilities for motion without functional harmonic progression or resolution.

Best of all, it could be resolved at will to a functional tonic merely by allowing any of its constituent tones to proceed by half step (i.e., as a leading tone) or by fifth (i.e., as a root). And all of these possibilities are in effect doubled by the fact that there are two whole-tone scales—that is, two complementary samplings of the twelve pitches of the chromatic scale, one corresponding to the even-numbered tones counted from any given starting point or "zero pitch", the other to the odd—between which progressions could freely take place without resolving harmonic tension.

ECSTASY, AND AFTER

This description of the potential behavior of the six-tone extended dominant chord has been no mere theoretical exercise. It is a description of the actual behavior of Scriabin's Symphony no. 4, op. 54, subtitled *Le poème de l'extase* ("The poem of ecstasy"), his most famous composition. It is very much a sequel to the *Divine Poem*, again casting the solo trumpet as "Nietzschean" superhuman protagonist, to the point where the symphony becomes a virtual concerto, requiring a credit to the performer. Its surface Tristanisms are too conspicuous to be missed by anyone who knows Wagner.

But the main *Tristan* affinity is profoundly structural and all-encompassing. Like Wagner's opera, Scriabin's symphony consists in the most general terms of a single fundamental gesture, an agonizingly prolonged "structural upbeat" that at the very last moment achieves cataclysmic consummatory resolution. That colossal consummatory gesture is the ultimate reality, the "noumenon" that underlies all sensory and cognitive experience, for which sexual union (as in *Tristan*), the creative act, childbirth or death as subjectively perceived, even the subjective notion of the beginning or the end of time, can be conceptual or "phenomenal" metaphors.

The music is thus laden with a profusion of powerful but apparently contradictory meanings — triumph and annihilation; procreation and spontaneous cosmic genesis; birth and death — that can best be clarified from the perspective of mystical symbolism, as in Vyacheslav Ivanov's "threefold vision" of Scriabin's accomplishment (quoted above), which encompasses both the transcendence of the individual person and the breakthrough to a new plane of being. The extinction or dissolution of the individual ego — the "petty 'I'" — is ideally prefigured in the six-tone dominant chord, for its component tones constitute a symmetrical scale whose intervals are all equal and whose degrees, therefore, are all equidistant, structurally undifferentiated, and hence not subject to functional classification. If one cannot differentiate degrees or identify their functions, one can no longer identify *with* the fluctuations of harmonic tension or respond to them emotionally. One's ego is stilled.

The functional relationships in the *Poème de l'extase* are thus reduced to a single essential dualism: an almost infinitely extended, graded, and variegated dominant that in its ceaseless flux and nuance is almost palpably sensuous, and a crushingly asserted tonic, tantalizingly glimpsed and tasted in advance, but for the most part withheld. Indeed the dualism is more than just a harmonic functional relationship. It is the interaction between two planes of consciousness.

The one, represented by the whole-tone scale, begins inchoate, undifferentiated, selfless, but — as the trumpet's increasing prominence and the ever longer, more insistent dominant pedals announce — coalesces and concentrates itself into an overwhelming manifestation of desire. The other, represented by the diatonic scale, suggests Ivanov's breakthrough to universal consciousness. Since we are constantly reminded that the whole-tone, functionally undifferentiated harmonies are in fact elaborations and prolongations of a single primal function — the dominant function, the most directed harmonic tension of all — the reconstitution of the ego at the same time presages the transcendence of desire. The ecstatic climax at the end of the symphony is in fact the dawn of satiety and quiescence, as Scriabin's later compositions would bear out.

The opening of the *Poème de l'extase* is given in harmonic abstract in Ex. 4-15. (The point of the abstract will emerge most clearly if it is followed while listening to a recorded performance.) The music recapitulates some of the cadential gestures encountered at the beginning of the *Divine Poem* (Ex. 4-12). A series of unusual chromatic chords, each a subset of a whole-tone scale, are quietly resolved by semitone to the C-major triad, thus establishing C major as tonic, thereby foreshadowing and planting expectation of the ultimate breakthrough. The first such resolution, shown in the first "measure" of the abstract, is complete and unambiguous. The second, in the second "measure," leaves a dissonant seventh sounding; tension is not fully discharged, and it will continue to accumulate until the final shattering gesture of consummation.

A third cadential gesture now begins, which lasts until the end of the abstract. Its tension is augmented by the first full simultaneous presentation of the whole-tone collection (as shown in the box in Ex. 4-15), to which notes from the complementary collection are then added, creating a real sense of clash. The first of these clashing tones is A. It begins in the flute but is immediately taken up by the trumpet making its bow

EX. 4-15   Alexander Scriabin, *Le poème de l'extase*, Op. 54, harmonic abstract of beginning

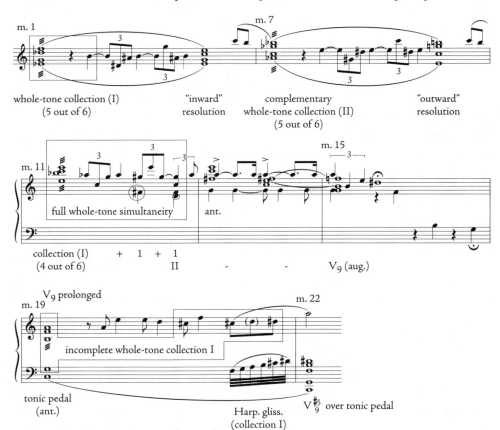

as protagonist. It is sustained through a crescendo, which is another way of building tension, while the bass instruments force the issue by sounding G, the traditional dominant of C major. Under this pressure, the notes of the one whole-tone scale give way to those of the other scale in a fashion that approximates a traditional dominant preparation. At the height of the crescendo, the trumpet, after a pair of attention-grabbing leaps, makes the final approach to the dominant, dramatically resolving E to D♯, which functions in this context as the augmented fifth of a dominant-ninth chord on G, another chord that consists of five of the six notes of a whole-tone scale. The pressure toward resolution has by now grown intolerable.

It is resolved, however, in only one voice, albeit the most important one. The bass resolves dominant G to tonic C along the circle of fifths, but the tones of the augmented dominant ninth remain suspended over the tonic. The trumpet's D♯ returns in the cellos at the downbeat of m. 22 (the end of Ex. 4-15), having been introduced by a full whole-tone scale, sounded by a harp glissando. The clarinet, at the same time, makes a dramatic leap to a high A, the ninth of the ninth chord. We are left, so to speak, with a mixed color — augmented dominant ninth over tonic anticipation (or rather, eventually, a tonic pedal) — arising out of a mixed function, one of those finely graded sensuous nuances for which the *Poème de l'extase* is famous. The mixture produces a sense of disorientation in the listener, and will be exploited for that purpose throughout the composition, becoming one of its most characteristic harmonies. It could even be called the *Extase*-chord, as indeed Scriabin seems to have recognized when he used it, a short time later, to end a piano piece called *Désir* ("Desire;" Ex. 4-16).

EX. 4-16   Alexander Scriabin, *Désir*, Op. 57, no. 1, final chord

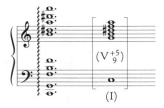

Let us take a walk around this chord. Like so many Scriabin harmonies, it contains a French sixth — the top four notes if the dominant-ninth component of the chord is laid out in close spacing as it is at the end of Ex. 4-16 — which to Scriabin was the invariant harmony par excellence when inverted or transposed. Taking our cue from its presence, let us invert the chord and transpose its members. The obvious axis for such an inversion is the top note, A, the note strategically spotlit by the clarinet's leap at the end of Ex. 4-15. Ex. 4-17 shows what happens when we perform the operation.

Scriabin never used the fascinating chord thus arrived at in the *Poème de l'extase*. Yet he must have performed the operations shown in Ex. 4-17 at some point, for the chord formed by inverting the *Extase*-chord is the most famous Scriabin chord of all, the one christened the "Chord of Prometheus" by the composer's disciple Leonid Sabaneyeff in a famous article (translated by the painter Wassily Kandinsky and edited by Arnold

EX. 4-17   Manipulations of the *Extase* chord

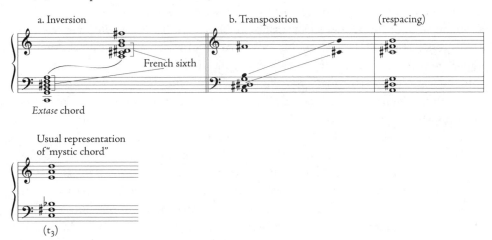

Schoenberg) published in Berlin in 1912[14] and known in the English-speaking world since around 1916 as the "mystic chord" (so renamed by Arthur Eaglefield Hull, Scriabin's first English biographer).[15] Sabaneyeff and Hull pitched the chord up a third from the pitch shown in Ex. 4-17, presumably so as to represent it as if "in C" (i.e., neutrally as to "key"), but the pitch level shown in the example is in fact the one employed at the very outset of Scriabin's Fifth Symphony, subtitled *Prométhée: Le poème de feu* ("Prometheus: The poem of fire"), op. 60 (1910), where it sounds steadily throughout the main thematic exposition (Ex. 4-18).

Scriabin had his own name for the chord. At an early rehearsal of *Prométhée*, his friend and fellow pianist-composer Sergey Rachmaninoff (1873–1943), stunned at the sound of it, asked "What are you using here?" Scriabin answered, "The chord of the pleroma."[16]

The *pleroma*, a Christian gnostic term derived from the Greek for "plenitude," was the all-encompassing hierarchy of the divine realm, located entirely outside the physical universe, at immeasurable distance from man's terrestrial abode, totally alien and essentially "other" to the phenomenal world and whatever belongs to it. Scriabin would have encountered the word in Mme Blavatsky's compendium *The Secret Doctrine* (1888), the theosophists' bible, where it is associated with Promethean concepts like "Spiritual Fire" and "Astral Light" and with angelic androgyny (unisexism). What we know as the "mystic chord," then, was designed by the composer to afford instant apprehension of — that is, to *reveal*, in the biblical sense — what was in essence beyond the mind of man to conceptualize.

Its magical stillness was a mystical or gnostic intimation of a hidden otherness, a world and its fullness wholly above and beyond rational or emotional cognition. In terms that poets as far back as Baudelaire had prized above everything else, Scriabin had created in the "chord of the pleroma" a genuine musical *symbol*: something that establishes a nexus between external phenomenal reality (what Ivanov called *realia*) and the higher noumenal reality that Ivanov called *realiora*, the "more real."[17] In the words of Simon Morrison, a historian of Russian musical maximalism, Scriabin's harmony established "a relationship between the mobile, temporal world of perceptible phenomena" in which we actually hear the chord as a sound, "and the immobile, non-temporal world of essences."[18]

But what produced this uncanny stasis? It arose out of the same conditions we have already observed in the

FIG. 4-2   Autograph page from *Prométhée* (1910).

final harmony of the Prelude, op. 74, no. 1 (Ex. 4-6a), where, as in the "mystic chord," a French sixth chord, which contains two tritones, acts as a nexus between the whole-tone scale, which contains three, and the octatonic scale, which contains four. Unlike Debussy's music, where the whole-tone scale interacts with the diatonic, or Stravinsky's music, where the octatonic scale interacts with the diatonic, Scriabin's late music inhabits a realm from which the diatonic scale, with its functionally differentiated degrees and its strong drive to resolution, has been virtually eliminated.

Its presence may be felt at times behind the scenes, directing some vestigial harmonic progressions along the old circle of fifths, but for the most part we have proceeded, according to Vyacheslav Ivanov's famous formula, *a realibus ad realiora*, ("from the real to the more real"): from the phenomenal world of human senses and desires, long and effectively represented by the functions of diatonic harmony, to the world of spiritual revelation, the world of the pleroma, represented by a unique musical idiom in which there is a strong sense of harmonic fluctuation and root movement—walking, indeed

EX. 4-18   Alexander Scriabin, *Prométhée*, abstract of beginning

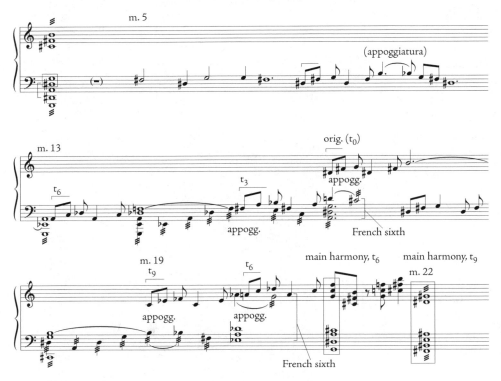

darting, around and between chords and scales—but in which any sense of harmonic direction and potential closure has been weakened to the point of virtual extinction.

ATONALITY?

The chief harmonic ingredient, the French sixth chord, remains recognizably a modified dominant chord in intervallic structure, but there is no longer any dominant function to perform. Where there is no dominant function, of course, there can be no complementary tonic function either. Hence the widespread view that Scriabin's visionary achievement was the breakthrough into "atonality," a concept (or at least a term) that he never knew, but one that excellently fulfills the old Hegelian promise of progress toward emancipation. What makes the view questionable for Scriabin was his continued reliance on the circles of thirds—major in the case of the whole-tone scale, minor in the case of the octatonic—that provide the symmetrical scales with a harmonic background that Scriabin continued to exploit for the sake of tonal coherence.

What Scriabin sought, then, and what he to a large extent achieved, was not atonality at all but a new (he might have said "higher") kind of tonality, one that modulated by thirds rather than fifths through what might be called a musical hyperspace—space bent back into circles by the use of the closed /0 4 8/ and /0 3 6 9/ axes of transposition. Like traditional tonal harmony, and very much opposed in concept to atonality, Scriabin's harmony was at all times firmly *directed*, subject to rules — its own rules, but consistent ones — of voice leading that made its progressions intelligible as such.

In *Prométhée*, for example, even the small amount of it visible in Ex. 4-18, almost all motivic and harmonic transpositions are by minor thirds or multiples thereof (designated t3, t6, and t9 in Ex. 4-18). That preference indicates a preference for the octatonic over the whole-tone as primary frame of reference, and this is confirmed by the melody, in which the B natural from the main harmony is leapt to and then inflected through a slur to B♭, as if resolving an appoggiatura. If looked upon that way, the inflection resolves the "mystic chord" to a chord that is wholly referable to the octatonic scale (Ex. 4-19).

E X. 4-19   The "mystic chord" with top note resolved

The chord thus arrived at, as a matter of fact, would function in Scriabin's Seventh Sonata ("The White Mass"), op. 64 (1911), as a basic point of reference, much as the "mystic chord" had functioned in "Prométhée." As the object of a resolution, the whole octatonic collection could be said to have assumed the role of tonic, much the way it had functioned in "Chez Pétrouchka". The difference, of course, and what makes Scriabin at this point the more committed maximalist, was that he emphasized not the familiar triadic material that can be mined from the octatonic collection, but "unclassified" harmonies of a kind that had come to the fore in "Chez Pétrouchka" only once, at the Far Out Point.

Scriabin thus seems to hover constantly at Stravinsky's FOP. The only exception comes at the very end of *Prométhée*, where a climactic resolution is made to the F♯ major triad, perhaps on an analogy with the blazing climax of the *Poème del'extase*. But resolving the "mystic chord" to an ordinary triad does not come this time as the fulfillment of a mounting agony of desire. Without a traditional harmonic function to fulfill, the chord is unexpected. It can seem arbitrary and even a bit anachronistic.

A much better illustration of Scriabin's unerring sense of harmonic direction, even in the period of his so-called atonality, is *Vers la flamme* ("Toward the flame"), op. 72 (1914), a work that incorporates a sense of direction into its very title. It comes from the last full year of Scriabin's composing career, and represents his style and technique at their most advanced. Yet even in a piece just as shy of "pure triads" as *The Rite of Spring*, Scriabin contrived to maintain a sense of forward momentum and eventual cadence and completion, in keeping with the implications of the title.

Like the much longer *Poème de l'extase*, the whole piece can be interpreted as a single consummatory gesture — what Ivanov, describing the spiritual qualities Scriabin's music conveyed, called *poriv*, a word that literally means "gust" (as of wind, etc.) but can also mean "transport," in the sense of a sudden access of rapture crowning a spiritual ascent. Its general effect can be instantly grasped by comparing the beginning, marked pianissimo and *sombre* (dark), with the fortissimo conclusion with the right hand approaching the very top of the keyboard. These are the two aspects of the piece's starkly concentrated dynamic unfolding: from soft to loud and low to high.

At both ends of the piece, however, the bass note is the same, a recurrence that one expects in tonal music, and that contradicts the notion of atonality. Further, one notes that the chord built over E at the beginning (Ex. 4-20a) is held unchanging but for surface figuration for four measures, and the one at the end (Ex. 4-20b) is held, in block form and in a final arpeggio, for nine. These observations point to what is most constant and characteristic in the piece: a very slow harmonic rhythm accompanying

EX. 4-20A   Alexander Scriabin, *Vers la flamme*, Op. 72, mm. 1–11

EX. 4-20B   Alexander Scriabin, *Vers la flamme*, Op. 72, mm. 129–end

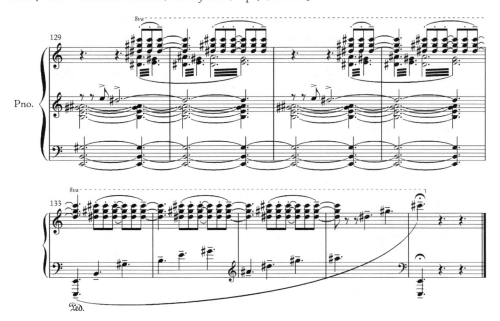

a frenetically active and variegated surface. With the rate of harmonic progression so slow, every chord change registers as a large event. Plotting the changes is easy, and very revealing.4-20a

The first change, as shown in Ex. 4-20a, tells all. The opening chord, almost predictably a French sixth, moves after four measures to another French sixth a minor third away. After another six measures the process is repeated, placing the same chord now at a tritone's remove from the opening, at which distance, as we know, the French sixth chord is invariant. The only differences in pitch content between m. 1 and m. 11 are to be found in the surface embellishment (here, in the appoggiaturas applied to the main chord: A♯ and C♯ in m. 1, A natural and C♯ in m. 11). Armed with these observations, we can more or less predict the harmonic events to come in terms of departure and return, just as we can in traditional tonal music. The specialness of the music, as in traditional tonal music, will lie in the specific strategies through which the composer realizes the foreordained plan.

Having observed the beginnings of a harmonic plan involving rotations around an /0 3 6 9/ axis of minor thirds beginning on E, we may make the prediction that the harmonic basis of the piece will consist of a matrix of chords, probably of "altered dominant" quality, with roots on E, G, B♭, and D♭C♯: call that the primary cycle. In *Vers la flamme*, as in "Chez Pétrouchka," the whole matrix (or "complexe sonore," as Stravinsky once termed it) will stand as tonic. For a dominant—a contrasting but closely related complex—Scriabin will shift, at times, to the /0 4 8/ axis of major thirds (E, C, A♭): call that the secondary cycle.

The whole first section of the piece, up to m. 40, is built around a rotation ascending through three of the four members of the primary cycle. The final progression, to C♯D♭, is withheld, however; in its place we get a sort of deceptive cadence to B minor (practically the only "pure triad" in the piece) that appears first in m. 19 and reappears four times thereafter, its highest voice doubled at the third to produce a seventh chord. (Beginning at m. 27 this chord is briefly promoted to full "structural" status, empowered to import its own /0 3 6 9/cycle; but after only one progression, to D in m. 30, the feint is dropped.) At m. 41—where according to the expression marks emotion is kindled in the form of "a veiled joy"—E is reestablished as root (Ex. 4-20c). The chord quality this time is of another altered dominant, the "dominant minor ninth," alternating with something that might be called the "*Tristan* ninth"; and the harmonic path shifts over to the secondary cycle. Confining our field of vision momentarily to the "oompah" oscillations in the bass, we note the members of the /0 4 8/cycle passing in review: E at m. 41, C at m. 47, A♭ at m. 55, where Ex. 4-20c breaks off. Full circle is achieved at 64, whereupon the /0 3 6 9/primary cycle is reasserted, this time reaching the point withheld in the opening section. The first sounding of a harmony rooted on D♭ in m. 74 is an exhilarating moment, an apex; it palpably conveys the achievement of a new stage in our ascent.

Once E is regained in m. 77, the harmonic rhythm slows to a virtual crawl, but the surface is agitated into rapid oscillations that play on age-old conventions of fire imagery. The primary cycle is maintained to the end with only a single departure:

EX. 4-20C Alexander Scriabin, *Vers la flamme*, Op. 72, mm. 41–55

the abruptly intruding chords rooted on D in mm. 97 and 101 (Ex. 4-20d), which in this context have the character of a Far Out Point, intensifying the sense of return when the opening thematic material is recapitulated transcendentally in m. 107. The most noticeable difference between this spot (Ex. 4-20e) and the beginning of the piece

EX. 4-20D   Alexander Scriabin, *Vers la flamme*, Op. 72, mm. 97–103

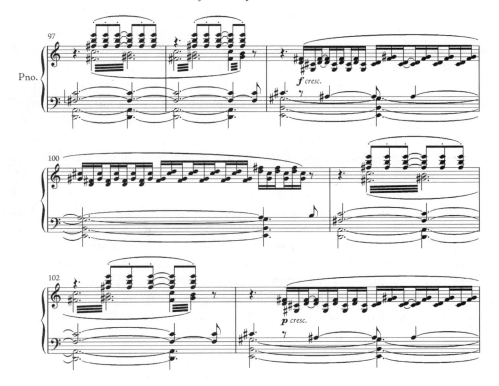

EX. 4-20E   Alexander Scriabin, *Vers la flamme*, Op. 72, mm. 108–111

is the contrast in loudness and register. More subtle, but also more telling, is the transformation of the French sixths from the opening into dominant sevenths. The perfect fifths in the bass give these chords a solidity that reinforces the sense of arrival and approaching climax. What is perhaps most remarkable is the way our ears have been conditioned by all the harmonic rotations that have gone before not to expect any "tonal" resolutions. The dominant sevenths here have all the stability of a tonic.

But as members of a symmetrically disposed *complexe sonore* they are all functionally equivalent. How can one of them be further promoted to the status of first (that is, last) among equals? Its sheer statistical predominance might suggest E as the best candidate for selection (and we have already observed that E provides the final bass note). But Scriabin actually found a better way to signify the completion of his spiritual *poriv*. Like the first section, the final one withholds the last member of the/0 3 6 9/cycle. There is a distinct sense of stalling at 6 (i.e., B♭, the tritone antipode) in mm. 117–124. Lasting eight measures, it is the composition's longest-sustained single harmony. After the stall, the return to E can seem a fallback, one reiterated in mm. 127–129 when B♭ again fails to pierce the implicit barrier.

All the greater, then, is the sense of breakthrough at the very top of the final arpeggio, already shown in Ex. 4-20b, when at last C♯, the very note withheld as a harmonic root, provides the melodic capstone. What gives the sense of finality here is not a gesture of reinforced return, as in a traditionally tonal composition, but a gesture of pattern-completion. As traditional tonal styles gave way to various maximalized idioms during the fraught decades of the early twentieth century, pattern-completion emerged as an effective alternative way of creating tonal expectations and achieving tonal fulfillments. *Vers la flamme* was a benchmark in this process.

THE FINAL BURST

Ivanov regarded this effect of *poriv*—sudden elevation, transporting burst—as an explicitly religious gesture. He related it on the one hand to the *Sursum corda*, the "heart-lift" at the Elevation of the Latin Mass—on which, as both he and Scriabin knew very well, Liszt had composed one of his most harmonically adventurous pieces—and on the other, to Scriabin's constant striving to transcend the human plane. The result of Scriabin's final attempted breakthrough to the *realiora*, the superhuman superreal, may be glimpsed in the sketches he left at the time of his death for the *Acte préalable,* or "Preparatory Act," that reflected something of the *Mysterium*, an unrealized (and unrealizable) project that would have been Scriabin's ultimate musical and religious testament.

The *Mysterium* was to have brought the Wagnerian concept of *Gesamtkunstwerk* to its unsurpassable maximum: indeed, as originally conceived, Scriabin's work was to have been the *opus ultimum* of all time, literally the last word in art. For starters, it would have combined both of the meanings the Wagnerian term conveyed: Wagner's original notion, of a collective or communal creation, plus the later one, not attributable to Wagner but exemplified by his works, of combining all artistic media in a single coordinated expressive or symbolic act.

The composer, who had long been dabbling in symbolist poetry (including a verse counterpart to the *Poème de l'extase* which he had finally decided to suppress), drafted a text for the work that summarized theosophical doctrine concerning the origin and destiny of the cosmos. To this music would be added, along with stage spectacle, choreography, and even aromatic effects to engage the powerfully suggestive sense of smell. The concept began, literally, as a "Mystery Play," a representation of religious teachings in the form of a Wagnerian opera along the lines of *Parsifal* (or, even more to the point, the opera Wagner did not live to write, which would have depicted the life of the Buddha).

As he worked, however, the composer began to imagine something far more grandiose: not a mere artwork but an all-encompassing ritual enactment, lasting seven days and seven nights, in which there were to be no spectators, only participants; which would be performed once only, in a specially constructed temple in India; and which would so transform the consciousness of the participants as to give them — and with them, the entire world — access to a higher plane of consciousness transcending humanly imagined time and space. It would literally bring human history to an end.

The reader may be feeling relieved that Scriabin did not live to realize this plan: he died of blood poisoning, the result of a poorly treated boil on his lip, shortly after his forty-third birthday. But as much as two years before his death the composer had conceded that he, being after all only human, could not accomplish such a world-transforming goal. He was, in other words, and despite the insinuations of his many detractors, far from crazy (inasmuch as he was able to recognize his erstwhile delusions and scrap them); but the experience left him literally, and very sadly, disillusioned about the nature and value of art.

Instead of the *Mysterium*, then, he settled on a more modest project, which he called the *Acte préalable*, a "preparatory act" that would at least impart to its hearers something of the euphoric grandeur of the symbolist ideal. This is the work for which actual musical sketches exist. Intended no longer as an achievement of a state of spiritual transcendence but rather as a speculative representation of such a state, the sketches for the "Preparatory Act" reveal the final, literally unexceedable stages of the composer's stylistic and technical evolution.

We already know something of them, since the enigmatic preludes from op. 74 were actually incorporated into these sketches. Among the other things they contained was a series of aggregate harmonies — "ultimate" chords each containing all twelve pitch classes. Yet how can there be a "series" of such chords? In any structurally or functionally meaningful sense there can be only one. And that is precisely what gave the aggregate harmony its poetic significance: What better means could there be for musically representing the *vselenskoye* (as it is called in Russian), the universal or All-in-One in its literal plenitude? A twelve-note chord can be neither transposed nor inverted. It is everywhere, and everything, at once.

Yet (as Berg's third "Altenberg Lied" already showed) even a twelve-note chord can be varied in color and in "voicing," that is, the registral disposition of its individual components. And here we may note genuine connections between Scriabin's twelve-note chords and the harmonic explorations we have already traced. The eight distinct aggregates that can be deciphered from his *Mysterium* sketches are not undifferentiated clusters of semitones, but are laid out registrally in ways that emphasize and combine older invariant structures. In one of them, triads are built systematically on C, E♭, F♯ and A, the nodes of an /0 3 6 9/ "primary cycle" of minor thirds as we called it in *Vers la flamme*. And then to these triads, which together exhaust an octatonic scale, major sevenths (B, D, E♯ and G♯, respectively) are added to supply the four tones missing for full chromatic representation (Ex. 4-21a).

Another aggregate (Ex. 4-21b) places two French sixth chords, equivalent to the content of an octatonic scale, in distinct registers that would no doubt have been further distinguished in timbre when orchestrated. The four remaining tones of the chromatic scale, which (as we may recall from "Chez Pétrouchka") are equivalent to a diminished seventh chord, are placed atop the French sixths, in a third contrasting register. The twelve notes of the full chromatic scale have been in effect partitioned into three separate inversionally and transpositionally invariant harmonies, each containing two inversionally and transpositionally invariant tritones for a "universal," all-encompassing total of six.

E X. 4-21A   Aggregate harmony from Alexander Scriabin's sketches for the *Acte préalable*

E X. 4-21B   Aggregate harmony from Alexander Scriabin's sketches for the *Acte préalable*

Since it is harmonic progression that had always articulated the structural rhythm of music, which is to say its sense of directed unfolding in time, a music based on universal invariant harmonies became quite literally timeless, as well as emotionally quiescent. The two qualities, invariance and timelessness, insofar as we are equipped to interpret musical messages, are in fact aspects of a single quality of quiescence, expressed respectively in two musical dimensions, the "vertical" and the "horizontal." Interpreting these chords in light of Scriabin's development — or, as he had once hoped and assumed, hearing them in the context of the enacted *Mysterium* — we seem to experience an eschatological revelation: a *gnosis* (occult knowledge) that only music may impart: the full collapse of time and space and the dissolution of the ego (Ivanov's "petty 'I' ").

It was a dissolution at which the composer deliberately aimed, as we learn from a memoir by Boris de Schloezer, an eminent music critic who, as Tatyana Schloezer's brother, was Scriabin's brother-in-(common)-law. Far from the solipsist of the *Poème de l'extase* or the Promethean protagonist of the *Poème du feu*, the author of the *Mysterium* "no longer dwelt on his own role; what was uniquely important to him was the act itself, and he was willing to be dissolved in it."[19] But that dissolution presaged the end of Scriabin's composing career. He reached the impasse, it is now thought, before his untimely death prevented his ever overcoming it. In a manner that made him all the more an object of worship to the mystical symbolists who surrounded him, Scriabin renounced the *Mysterium* in favor of the "Preparatory Act," and then renounced the "Preparatory Act" in favor of silence. As Simon Morrison has put it, Scriabin

> was not in the end defeated in his plans — he triumphed — but they exacted a high cost: writer's block and compositional paralysis. He did not fail: no artist could accomplish what he attempted to accomplish. Rather, he transcended artistry. His vision [in the words of the mystical-symbolist poet Valeriy Bryusov] dissolved in the "mighty bonfire" of a "holy sacrifice."[20]

It was Scriabin who faced first, and perhaps most starkly, the maximalist's dilemma: the fulfillment of his aims spelled the end of his — or any — art.

A MAXIMALIST AGAINST THE TIDE

Scriabin has often been viewed by historians as a dead end, not only because of this dilemma but because of the more mundane historical fact that he had few identifiable heirs. As we will learn in later chapters, there would be a sharp antimetaphysical turn — sometimes called "positivist," sometimes "materialist," most often "classicist" as it related to the arts — in the decades following World War I. In the aftermath of a real apocalypse — a real end-of-the-world experience — apocalyptic thought began to look like the opposite of avant-garde.

In Russia, Scriabin's luxuriant musical style was much imitated for a while. By 1931, however, only sixteen years after Scriabin's death, Dmitry Shostakovich, the leader of the younger generation of what by then were called Soviet composers (educated after the Russian Revolution of 1917), frankly called him "our bitterest musical enemy."[21] In part this may have been because Soviet education was militantly antireligious. But Shostakovich put it this way: "Scriabin's music tends to an unhealthy eroticism; also to mysticism and passivity and escape from the realities of life." Attention everywhere — not just in the atheistic Soviet Union but (as we shall see) in Western

Europe and America as well—was increasingly focused on the real world and its exigencies, which entailed a substantial loss of faith even in "ordinary" romanticism, let alone its maximal, religiously transcendent phases.

The only Russian composers who maintained a Scriabinistic stance well into the later twentieth century were a couple of religiously minded émigrés who lived most of their lives in France: Nikolai Obouhov (or Obukhov, 1892–1954) and Ivan Wyschnegradsky (1893–1979). Obouhov found his own way to what he called "total harmonies" or aggregates, but his motivation was similar to Scriabin's. His *Berceuse d'un bienheureux* ("Beatific lullaby"), composed in Russia in 1918 but published in Paris in 1921, begins with three widely spaced aggregates partitioned like Scriabin's into identifiable layers. They serve to illustrate the Biblical aphorism, "Blessed are the poor in Spirit, for theirs is the Kingdom of Heaven" (Ex. 4-22). Wyschnegradsky actually managed to continue Scriabin's maximalism past

EX. 4-22   Nikolai Obouhov, *Berceuse d'un bienheureux*, beginning

the seeming limit imposed by the aggregate, by joining a small but hardy contingent of composers who split the musical atom, so to speak, dividing the semitone into smaller "microtonal" intervals. This provided a greater spectrum of available pitches for musical use, but (like much maximalist music) would raise serious problems of perception. We will face them in due course.

FIG. 4-3 Olivier Messiaen; Paris, 1983.

Obouhov and Wyschnegradsky were marginal figures, regarded as eccentrics out of step with the majority of their fellow composers, whose numbers gave them the power (and the right?) to define the musical "mainstream." But there was one resolute maximalist who managed, despite everything, to acquire a major reputation and maintain it throughout the period of positivist or classicist "retreat" with which he was completely out of sympathy, and even exert a considerable influence, though not without controversy. Despite the chronological discrepancy, then, the proper context to begin investigating and evaluating his music is the present chapter rather than one more contemporaneous with his work.

Our unregenerate maximalist is Olivier Messiaen (1908–92), a French composer whose Scriabinish affinities, like Obouhov's and Wyschnegradsky's, were a matter not merely of stylistic or technical means, but of spiritual ends. Indeed his technique as such, which (unlike many modernists) he loved to describe, often in phenomenal detail, was not directly modeled on Scriabin's. Though demonstrably among them, Scriabin was only one of a great number of highly disparate sources that Messiaen combined into his remarkably eclectic modus operandi. But the spiritual vision that drove him, and the purposes he wished his music to serve, were so like Scriabin's as practically to assure that they ended up in what might be called the same esthetic space.

Yet perhaps the word "esthetic" is misleading, since it refers to beauty. Rather, Messiaen wrote, "let us have a *true* music," italicizing the word himself;

> that is to say, spiritual, a music which may be an act of faith; a music which may touch upon all subjects without ceasing to touch upon God; an original music, in short, whose language may open a few doors, take down some as yet distant stars.[22]

The words, for all their religious euphoria, come from the preface to Messiaen's *Technique de mon langage musical* ("Technique of my musical language," 1944), one of the most systematic expositions any composer has ever given to the mechanisms of his art. And past the preface, the treatise is true to its title. It resolutely ignores all meaning and treats "language" alone—or as Messiaen put it, "technique and not sentiment," abstracted and broken down in extraordinarily schoolmasterly fashion into its rhythmic, melodic, and harmonic dimensions.

Any seeming paradox or contradiction is dispelled when one considers the nature of the truth that Messiaen designed his art to convey. It is neither a personal doctrine nor an occult one, but rather "the theological truths of the Catholic faith,"[23] as dogmatically set forth in scripture. Messiaen was an extreme rarity among leading twentieth-century composers (indeed, among composers since the advent of romanticism) in being a working church musician. For more than forty years, beginning in 1930, he served as regular Sunday organist at the Église de la Sainte-Trinité (Church of the Holy Trinity), one of the largest churches in Paris.

Messiaen wrote many of his most important works for La Trinité's huge Cavaillé-Coll organ, and was without question the most important organist-composer of the twentieth century, as César Franck, who also served as organist for many years at a Parisian church, and who also wrote a highly spiritualized brand of modern music, had been in the nineteenth. For a further parallel, both Messiaen and Franck were famous and much-sought-after teachers of composition, whose pupils and disciples formed an elite group of modernists who universalized their master's teaching and made it an important "mainstream" influence.

But Franck, whose career ended shortly before the great wave of maximalism broke, was never drawn to such radically novel means as Messiaen proposed, nor did he ever systematize his practices so thoroughly into a teachable method. It was the latter that made Messiaen such a potent force in the technique of contemporary music even among those who held his esthetic principles in disrepute. He managed to transform theological dogma into musical dogma, and that is why Messiaen always objected to being called a mystic. Rather than a mystic he was a *scholastic*, in the medieval sense of the term. Like Saint Thomas Aquinas, he sought to embody the mysteries of faith in a rational and transmissible discourse. No wonder his self-analysis was so "schoolmasterly," and so influential. What were means for him became ends for many.

As already observed, Messiaen's treatise very rigorously analyzes his maximalistic techniques into their rhythmic and melodic-harmonic domains. And yet the remarkable thing is how much the pitch and durational aspects of his innovative "language" had in common. The chief innovation with respect to pitch was the use of what Messiaen called "modes of limited transposition," and the chief durational innovation was a preference for what he called "nonretrogradable rhythms." Both of these impressively named devices depend on a single quality, one that has already figured frequently in our encounters with musical maximalism, and especially in Scriabin. That quality is invariance: more specifically, invariance achieved by means of symmetry.

"THE CHARM OF IMPOSSIBILITIES"

Messiaen named and described his "modes of limited transposition" for the first time in 1935 in the preface to *La nativité du Seigneur* ("The nativity of our lord"), a book of nine "meditations" for organ on passages from sacred texts, to be played during the celebration of Mass. Only the name that Messiaen gave his "modes" was new. The concept had been familiar as such for almost a century, ever since Liszt had made his first systematic experiments with symmetrical cycles of thirds and scales derived from them. Messiaen had in good scholastic fashion merely carried the process of systematization, begun by Liszt and already maximalized by Scriabin, to the point of theoretical exhaustion.

"Of limited transposition" was Messiaen's term for invariance; it refers to the property certain pitch configurations have of replicating themselves when transposed by certain intervals. The one we have most recently been concerned with, thanks to Scriabin, has been the French sixth chord, which retains its pitches when transposed by a tritone. We also know that the French sixth chord can be embedded in two scales that share its properties of invariance: the whole-tone scale, which retains its pitches when transposed by any of its constituent intervals (thus being, except for the untransposable chromatic scale, the mode of most stringently limited transposition), and the octatonic scale, which retains its pitches when transposed by every alternating interval in its makeup (that is, by the minor third, the tritone, or the major sixth). These scales being the most firmly established modes of limited transposition, they are naturally enough the first and the second mode in Messiaen's classification, and the ones most frequently used by far, even by him.

Messiaen, with his scholarly bent, was well aware of the historical precedents for the use of these scales. Any French musician would have associated the whole-tone scale with Debussy (and with Dukas, Messiaen's teacher); but Messiaen also knew, as did few others at the time, that the octatonic scale was the special predilection of Russian composers — Rimsky-Korsakov, Scriabin, Stravinsky — and of Ravel, whose Russian affinities were common knowledge but rarely described so cogently in terms of actual technique. It is clear that Messiaen was an unusually perceptive music analyst, which not only enabled him to rationalize and describe his own techniques with remarkable detachment, but also gave him, in the words of grateful former students, clairvoyant insight into the half-formed methods they were groping toward in their own compositions. They thus acquired from Messiaen technical facility without it necessarily entailing dependence on his own methods.

Ex. 4-23 shows Messiaen's seven modes of limited transposition as ingeniously arranged by the British music analyst Anthony Pople into a chart that indicates their interrelationships: to wit, that mode 1 is included in modes 3 and 6; mode five in modes 6 and 4; and modes 2, 4, and 6 (hence 1 and 5 as well) in mode 7, the largest of the lot.[24] The reason why modes 1 and 2 are the most useful modes of limited transposition is simply that they are the most limited. Mode 1 can be transposed only once without replicating itself and mode 2 can be transposed only twice. Mode 3, which could be likened to a whole-tone scale with every other interval broken into two half steps, can be transposed without invariance three times. The rest have only one transposition (inevitably it is the tritone) at which replication takes place, leaving five or more available transpositions. As Messiaen puts it, the more limited a mode's potential for transposition the more "strangely charming" it is, since it is "at once in the atmosphere of several tonalities, *yet not polytonal*, the composer being free to give predominance to one of the tonalities or to leave the tonal impression unsettled."[25]

EX. 4-23 The modes of limited transposition

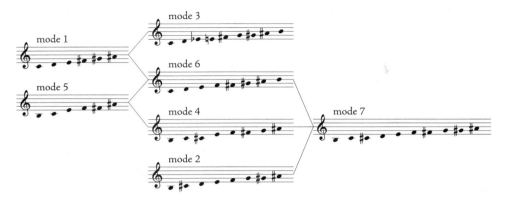

Example 4-24 shows a passage from another organ work of Messiaen's — *Les corps glorieux* ("Glorious bodies", 1939), a set of "seven brief glimpses of resurrected life" — in which the modes of limited transposition are deployed in Messiaen's most typical manner. It is the beginning of the second piece in the set, *Les eaux de la grâce* ("Waters of grace"), which carries an epigraph from the Apocalypse or Book of Revelation at the end of the New Testament: "The Lamb [i.e., Christ], who is at the heart of the throne, will be their shepherd and will guide them to the springs of the water of life." Like most organ music, the piece is notated on three staves: one for each hand at the keyboards, the third for the feet at the pedals. The three levels thus distinguished are rigorously differentiated by mode. Easiest to spot is the whole-tone scale (that is, "mode 1") in the pedal part. Less obvious is the confinement of the right hand part to mode 2, what up to now we have called the octatonic scale. Partly it is the orthography — the note-spelling — that occludes it. Comparison with Ex. 4-23 will show that Messiaen has adhered strictly to the mode 2 orthography given

FIG. 4-4 Magister Lambertus, illumination from *Liber floridus* (Flemish, fifteenth century) showing the three trumpets of the Apocalypse: (1) hail, fire, and blood; (2) the mountain hurled into the sea; (3) the flaming star.

there, using only sharps to represent the "black keys." Thus the status of the first chord in the right-hand part as a familiar B♭-major triad may not be immediately apparent. But in fact all the chords in the right hand are major triads (or to be really fastidious, homologous to major triads), with roots—G, B♭, C♯, E—that lie along a familiar symmetrical track, the /0 3 6 9/ circle of minor thirds.

EX. 4-24   Olivier Messiaen, *Les corps glorieux*, no. 2 (*Les eaux de la grace*), mm. 1–8

The left-hand line belongs to mode 7, the ten-note collection, which at this particular transposition consists of the other two modes combined. As must necessarily be the case, the two notes not present in the scale (C and F♯) lie a tritone apart. The C is withheld for the duration of the piece; the F♯ makes an occasional appearance (in mm. 4, 6, and 8 within the confines of Ex. 4-24), but its inconspicuous rhythmic placement and its conjunct melodic behavior identify it as a "nonharmonic" tone, apparently allowed in for the same reason nonharmonic tones are used in ordinary tonal harmony, for the sake of smooth voice leading.

There are four points of intersection — F, G, B, and D♭C♯ — between the mode 1 and mode 2 scales. One of these, G, is the root of the sustained chord that finishes each phrase in the right hand. Does that make G the tonic of the piece? It would be hard to justify such a conclusion, given the fact that the note G never coincides in the pedal part with the right-hand concluding chords. Instead, at these points there is a perhaps equally decisive cadential descent in the pedal to A. And the middle voice — the mediator, so to speak — emphasizes on every downbeat major thirds that correspond to every apparent root in the right-hand part *except* the G.

So no clear sense of pitch priority emerges from the texture. Instead there are three clearly defined but functionally inchoate tonal planes — polymodality, so to speak, in place of polytonality. The modal overload, plus the apparent carelessness of dissonance in Messiaen's contrapuntal scheme, are two aspects of his maximalism (over Scriabin, let us say). In fact both aspects are more "maximal" than the look of the score conveys, for Messiaen employs the organ "registration" (the actual deployment of the organ pipes in relation to the keys and pedals, as regulated by hand levers, or "stops") to complicate both the texture and the pitch content of the sounding music.

The pedal part is "registered" to sound an octave higher than played, so that the fast-moving left-hand part is the true bass. But that very part is so registered (by a stop called "Nazard et Tierce") as to produce full triads on every note, the fifth and the third sounding softly in a register two octaves higher than that of the written note. "The general quality," in the aptly metaphorical words of John Milsom, a British scholar, "is of a bright triadic halo hovering over each notated pitch."[26] All of this, perhaps needless to say, will be quite disorienting to anyone attempting to follow a performance of the piece from the score, and even to the player. And the "halos" produce an ineffable harmonic smudge that seems to contradict all the meticulous modal planning we have been considering. Recalling Scriabin, it is hard not to see these effects of disorientation and "analytical frustration" as part of the very point of the music.

Nor are such effects confined to the pitch domain. Another characteristic Messiaenic touch is the way he keeps the meter of the music as indefinite as its tonal orientation. Not only the number of beats per measure, but also the length of the beats themselves, is unpredictably variable. The variable lengths come about by the interpolation, in every other bar, of an extra sixteenth-note that lengthens one of the eighth-note pulses to a dotted eighth. This device — Messiaen calls it simply the "added value" — is one of the principal topics addressed in *Technique de mon langage musical*. He attributes it, perhaps significantly, to the music (or at least to the music theory) of India, a land that exerted a crucial influence, though not technically a musical one, on Scriabin as well.

Also Indian in origin, Messiaen assures his readers, is the other technical device with which his name is chiefly associated, that of "nonretrogradable rhythm." The term means nothing more than a rhythmic palindrome: an arrangement of note values that reads the same both forward and backward. One arranges such a thing most easily by working outward from a midpoint. Messiaen called the midpoint the "free value" or the "central common value." Functionally speaking, of course, it is an axis of symmetry. Ex. 4-25, taken from *Technique de mon langage musical*, consists of a lengthy melody in which each measure is cast as a rhythmic palindrome. The first and last measures have identical (nonretrogradable) rhythms as well, and the third and fourth measures from the end are rhythmically identical, adding extra (or, more precisely, inner) dimensions of self-reversability to the symmetry of the whole.

EX. 4-25   Olivier Messiaen, *Technique de mon langage musical*, example 33

Putting the two axes of symmetry together, the harmonic axis represented by the modes of limited transposition and the temporal axis represented by the nonretrogradable rhythms, allows the coordination of the vertical (spatial) and horizontal (temporal) dimensions in dual representation of invariance = constancy = immutability = eternity. That is the time-transcending truth that religion reveals through music, its handmaiden, in Messiaen's esthetic universe. And that, Messiaen explicitly informs the reader, is the source of his mysterious hold on the listener. "Let us think now of the hearer of our modal and rhythmic music," he writes, in a passage to which Scriabin might gladly have subscribed:

> He will not have time at the concert to inspect the nontranspositions and the nonretrogradations, and, at that moment, these questions will not interest him further; to be charmed will be his only desire. And that is precisely what will happen; in spite of himself he will submit to the strange charm of impossibilities: a certain effect of tonal ubiquity in the nontransposition, a certain unity of movement (where beginning and end are confused because identical) in the nonretrogradation, all things which will lead him progressively to that sort of *theological rainbow* which the musical language, of which we seek edification and theory, attempts to be.[27]

SO OLD IT'S NEW

In language that seems as if borrowed from the Russian mystical symbolists who inspired (and were inspired by) Scriabin, Messiaen writes that one of his primary aims in composing as he does is "l'atrophie du moi"—the atrophy, or wasting away, of the "I," the petty self. It will not be difficult to discover in his musical methods (to quote the English composer Wilfrid Mellers, one of Messiaen's most sympathetic critics) the means toward the "complete reversal of the will-domination of post-Renaissance Europe."[28] One aspect of this reversal was simply and literally the revival of pre-Renaissance practices long since considered obsolete by musicians caught up in the flux of history.

Many of the rhythmic techniques Messiaen describes in his self-analyzing treatise of 1944—canons by augmentation, by diminution, by "the addition of the dot"—were common during the ars nova of the fourteenth and fifteenth centuries, the heyday of "mensural notation," as was the idea of organizing musical structures around what Messiaen called "rhythmic pedals," durational plans that could be mentally conceptualized but not followed perceptually (that is, sensorially) during performance. Messiaen, who claimed to have been ignorant of it at the time, had in effect revived the concept of the isorhythmic motet, and for the same purpose the original medieval practice had served: to represent (and in some small measure render present to human understanding) the divine eternal harmony of the cosmos, a harmony that expressed itself precisely in the coordinated movement of heavenly bodies in seemingly independent orbits.

Rhythmic pedals (*talea* in Latin, *tala* in Sanskrit) were the chief medieval means for representing cosmic harmony. And at the same time they provided a genuine meeting point between time-honored European (in fact, French) and Indian musical practices. But Messiaen also revived the other aspect of medieval isorhythm, namely the abstractly conceived melodic ostinato or *color*. Ex. 4-25 embodies a hidden sequence of 16 pitches that is repeated four times (or almost, since the last repetition ends two notes short of completion). One discovers it with delighted surprise.

But of course it was never hidden at all. It was right on the surface, but too big—that is, too *great*—for immediate detection. Like the truths of astronomy and many other scientific truths (as well, needless to say, as religious truths), it is the sort of fact that reflective intellect reveals sooner than the senses. Putting such a thing into an artwork is an implicit warning against assuming that true knowledge can only be gained empirically. The highest truths, Messiaen's music implies, are revealed truths. Theology was truth. Anything beyond that, Messiaen implied along with countless theologians, was mere history. Take that, Hegel, and all who followed.

And yet while the truths may be transcendent, the means of representation (the work, after all, of mortals) are inevitably historical, the product of the fleeting moment. Messiaen's music does not sound like a medieval motet. His ear, like the ears he addresses, has been otherwise conditioned. His "musical language" confronted and accommodated the musical styles of its time in an openly omnivorous and opportunistic spirit, even as it sought to extend them in the spirit of maximalism. And that is why his work has been so useful as a model to many composers who not only failed to share his religious commitments, but were hopelessly caught up in "patent-office maximalism," something Messiaen outwardly decried as the rat-race of historicism, and yet something in which he was willy-nilly a participant, and a very successful one at that.

A kind of summa or compendium of the practices cataloged in *Technique de mon langage musical* was the *Quatuor pour la fin du temps* ("Quartet for the end of time," 1940–41), for violin, clarinet, cello, and piano, written during Messiaen's brief confinement in a stalag (German prisoner-of-war-camp) in the early stages of World War II, and first performed there by the composer and the three other camp inmates for whom it was written. The title, of course, is another reference to the Apocalypse, Messiaen's eternal subject, and the work is prefaced by another epigraph from the Book of Revelation (10:5–6):

> Then the angel that I saw standing on the sea and the land raised his right hand to heaven and swore by Him who lives for ever and ever, who created heaven and earth and the sea and everything in them: "There shall be no more time; when the seventh angel shall sound his trumpet, the hidden purpose of God will have been fulfilled, as he promised to his servants the prophets."

Ex. 4-25 above, though taken from Messiaen's 1944 treatise, was in fact a quotation from the Quartet's dénouement: the sixth movement, a thunderous monody for all four instruments in unison called "Danse de la fureur, pour les sept trompettes" ("Dance of fury, for the seven trumpets"), a sort of speculative transcription of the apocalyptic angelic call. We have already observed some of its "timeless" qualities. The Quartet's first movement, "Liturgie de cristal" is an evocation of prophecy. The piano part is organized isorhythmically throughout: that is, its pitch and rhythmic contents are organized in two independent repeating cycles. The rhythmic cycle, a pattern of seventeen durations, is taken (indirectly) from a thirteenth-century Sanskrit treatise by the Hindustani musician Sharngadeva, whose table of talas Messiaen found reprinted in a standard French reference source, Lavignac's *Encyclopédie de la musique et dictionnaire du conservatoire*.

The pitch cycle consists of a series of twenty-nine chords that overlaps the rhythmic cycle just as the color of an isorhythmic motet overlapped its *talea*. Ex. 4-26 contains enough of the piece to permit the identification of both cycles. It was surely no accident that Messiaen selected for his pitch cycle another prime number to go with Sharngadeva's seventeen, since that insured that the beginnings of the patterns would coincide neither with one another nor with any recurrent downbeat (at least until the 493rd repetition, unlikely to occur within the confines of a given piece). Their hidden conjunction, impossible to detect by ear, was already an intimation of eternity. The sounding piece is merely a sample of its infinite expanse.

Above the isorhythmic piano part, the cello contributes a line, played entirely in ethereal artificial harmonics ("flageolets," or flute tones, in French), that takes the form of a five-note melodic ostinato organized into patterns that display the "charm of impossibilities" in two dimensions. Its pitches are confined to the first mode of limited transposition (a.k.a. the whole-tone scale), and its durations are cast in a recurring series

EX. 4-26   Olivier Messiaen, *Quatuor pour la fin du temps*, I ("Liturgie de cristal"), mm. 1–12

*Glissando bref; id. aux passages similaires.

EX. 4-26   (continued)

that is palindromic (or "nonretrogradable") along two axes of symmetry (that is, from two midpoints), as shown in Ex. 4-27.

This, too, may be corroborated in Ex. 4-26 by noting the reversed recurrence of note values in the cello around the dotted quarter at the beginning of m. 9. The remaining parts, for clarinet (heard alone at the outset) and violin, are marked "comme un oiseau" (like a bird), and imitate actual birdsong: according to the preface to the score, the clarinet is a blackbird, the violin a nightingale, two birds that sing at dawn, thus adding another level of metaphor to the musical message. (Ornithological life-drawing would become an obsession for Messiaen in the 1950s, culminating in a massive cycle of piano compositions called *Catalogue d'oiseaux*, "Catalog of birds.") These parts participate less than the others in Messiaen's games of symmetry and invariance. The notes of the violin part may be referred to "mode 7," the largest (ten-note) scale of limited transposition, but with a pitch collection that big, "referability" may be a happenstance. The clarinet part partakes of the full chromatic gamut — the ultimate mode of limited transposition, it may be tautologically argued, since it cannot be transposed at all; but Messiaen did not so regard it.

Yet these "free" parts, constrained not by systematic theory but by nature, are the most obvious symbols of revelation, for birds have been thought of as prophets, or as direct emanations from the Godhead, since ancient times and in many cultures. Recall

EX. 4-27   Analysis of Olivier Messiaen's rhythmic palindromes

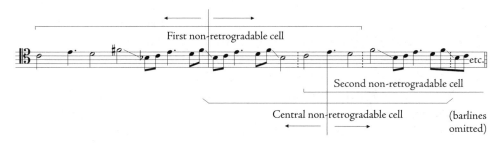

the dove that whispered the divine chant to Pope Gregory the Great according to the tradition that arose in conjunction with the earliest musical notations. Recall Wagner's Forest Bird who revealed the secrets of the gods to Siegfried, or Schumann's Prophet Bird, both of them figments of German folklore. Russian folklore has its ornithological prophets as well, as we know from Stravinsky's *Firebird*, and Hans Christian Andersen wrote a fairy tale that casts the nightingale in the role of Orpheus, the divine musician. Messiaen's apocalyptic birds have a distinguished Romantic lineage.

THE *SUMMA SUMMARUM*

To see Messiaen's musical cosmology maximalized to the very limit one must look to his gigantic *Turangalîla-symphonie*, a ten-movement, seventy-five-minute blockbuster for a 107-piece orchestra, composed in 1946–48 and first performed by the Boston Symphony Orchestra under a young conductor named Leonard Bernstein in 1949. The orchestra is not only huge but unprecedentedly variegated as well. There are parts for fifteen different percussion instruments requiring eight players, and a "continuo" of six keyboard instruments including tubular bells and glockenspiel. (If keyboard-operated models for these are not available, the minimum number of players goes up to 109.)

The remaining keyboard instruments are a celesta, a vibraphone (an American invention consisting of a xylophone with metal bars and an electric-motor-driven mechanism to produce a controlled variation in amplitude that sounds like vibrato), a piano prominent enough to require a virtuoso soloist with feature billing (for the first forty or so performances it was the composer's second wife, Yvonne Loriod), and an ondes martenot ("Martenot Waves"). This last, invented in 1927 by Maurice Martenot, a musically trained engineer (who called it the *ondes musicales*), was one of the earliest and most successful electronic instruments, producing its sound by means of an electric oscillator. It, too, is treated in *Turangalîla* like a concerto soloist. (For the first dozen or so performances, the player was the inventor's sister Ginette.)

According to Messiaen, who devised it, the title is a composite of two Sanskrit words: *turanga*, meaning the measurement of time by movement, and *lîla*, meaning the play of the divine will on the cosmos (and, by poetic extension, the force of love). In their conjunction the two words are as protean (and, ultimately, as unfathomable) in meaning as *Liebe + Tod = Liebestod* in Wagner's *Tristan und Isolde*, which Messiaen acknowledged to be the symphony's inspiration. "*Turangalîla* signifies, at one and the same time, a love song, a hymn to joy, time, movement, rhythm, life and death," the composer wrote, seemingly leaving room for any desired interpretation of his words. Yet one thing does emerge with clarity: where *Tristan und Isolde* had shown time and movement to be powerfully unidirectional, to the point where it virtually defined the "Western" outlook on the nature of music for a hundred years, Messiaen's concept of time, like Scriabin's, while ostensibly Wagnerian in inspiration, was cyclic and ultimately quiescent, as the *Turangalîla-symphonie* so massively demonstrates.

Three of the movements in the symphony bear the name "Turangalîla" in their own right: they are the work's quintessential "time and motion studies." The seventh movement, *Turangalîla 2*, an orgy of cycles and palindromes, is the densest of all, and in that sense the most maximalistic. Its many discrete components and subsections, juxtaposed like the tiles in a mosaic, can be classified into several recurring groups. What follows is a very selective description of some of the main events and relationships, keyed to the rehearsal figures in the score so that they may be verified there by interested readers.

- The opening piano cadenza, clearly recognizable (on the basis of Ex. 4-26) as birdsong, is full of rhythmic palindromes. Taking the sixteenth-note rest in the second measure (an "added value") as the midpoint, and ignoring grace notes, the first of them (for example) can be traced by moving forward to the end of m. 3 and back to the third eighth note of m. 1. The birdsong cadenza continues with accompaniment at fig. 3, and returns briefly by itself at fig. 9 with the same nonretrogradable rhythm as at the beginning. The very end of the movement reproduces the end of the opening cadenza.

- The section beginning at fig. 1 is identifiable by the chromatic scale descending in the ondes martenot and ascending in contrary motion in the cluster of low trombones. This simple contrary motion seems to rotate the idea of a rhythmic — temporal, "horizontal" palindrome by 45 degrees, so that it becomes spatial ("vertical"). At fig. 6 the scales are again set in motion with reversed trajectories: this could be interpreted either as an inversion ("vertical" reversal) or a retrograde ("horizontal" reversal) of the section at fig. 1. Another reversed recurrence comes at the end (fig. 12), resulting in a repetition or recapitulation of the music at 1, but harmonically enhanced. (The ondes martenot line, for example, is doubled by the violins in parallel diminished-seventh chords: chords, that is, which sample every other pitch of the second mode of limited transposition and therefore share its invariance properties.)

- At fig. 2, the unpitched percussion contribute a little bazaar of rhythmic palindromes. The easiest one to spot is the one between the woodblock (second line in the score) and the bass drum (sixth line), because it fits exactly into the time allotted. Counting the sixteenths within each notated value, the woodblock series is **12 14 1 2 7 8 16** (played twice) and the bass drum is precisely the reverse. The triangle (top line) has the series **15 13 3 4** (played three times plus one note) and the maracas (fourth line) have precisely the reverse (played three times plus three notes). The "small Turkish cymbal" (third line) has the series **5 6 9 11 10** (played three times, the last not quite complete) and the "Chinese cymbal" (fifth line) has precisely the reverse. Notice that every value from 1 sixteenth to 16 sixteenths is represented once in the scheme. That is what Messiaen called the "gamme chromatique de durées" (chromatic scale of durations).

- At fig. 7 the chromatic scale of durations is played in consecutive ascending order by the triangle, and backward (or in consecutive descending order) by the bass drum, doubled (on the attacks) by the string basses, who reinforce the notion of *gamme chromatique* by simultaneously executing a chromatic scale in the ordinary meaning of the term. At the same time the piano is playing a repeating series of three chords in the right hand, and another in the left in a rhythmic canon with the right at the time interval of a quarter note. Comparison with Ex. 4-26 will reveal that the rhythms so treated make up the very same pattern of seventeen durations from Sharngadeva's treatise already used in the *Quatuor pour la fin du temps* (nor do these two exhaust its appearances in Messiaen's work).

And that is not all. The upper strings and a group of winds (clarinets, bassoons, and horns) are simultaneously engaged in another isorhythmic game. The strings have a pair of chords that are first heard on the first and last sixteenths of the first measure. The second chord always comes on the last sixteenth of alternating measures; but the first chord advances along the chromatic scale of durations: at 7 it is on the first sixteenth, at 7 + 2 it is on the second, at 7 + 4 it is on the third, and so on. The second wind chord is always on the downbeat, while the first advances by chromatic durations, beginning with the second sixteenth at 7, the third at 7 + 2, and so forth, so that the string chords always function as pickups to the wind chords. In the third measure before 9, where the advancing wind chord and the advancing string chord coincide on the last sixteenth, the two chords plus the high piccolo note together produce . . . yes, an aggregate harmony.

How much of this is actually meant to be "heard"? How much is mere "notation"? The bass drum part at fig. 2 is obviously notation, not sound. (The sound of a single drumbeat lasting two measures cannot even be imagined.) But this was nothing new. Similarly overloaded medieval polytextual motets suggest the answer to the question with which this paragraph began. As the singing eagle said to Dante, in the latter's *Paradiso*, "As are my notes to thee who canst not follow, such is the Eternal Judgement to you mortals." Where ultimate truth is to be revealed, the senses must be overcome, the mind boggled.

Containing Multitudes (Transcendentalism, II)

IVES, RUGGLES, CRAWFORD; MICROTONALITY

In every work of genius we recognize our own rejected thoughts: they come back to us with a certain alienated majesty. Great works of art have no more affecting lesson for us than this. They teach us to abide by our spontaneous impression with good-humored inflexibility then most when the whole cry of voices is on the other side. Else, tomorrow a stranger will say with masterly good sense precisely what we have thought and felt all the time, and we shall be forced to take with shame our own opinion from another.[1]

— RALPH WALDO EMERSON, "SELF-RELIANCE" (1841)

We live in succession, in division, in parts, in particles. Meantime within man is the soul of the whole; the wise silence; the universal beauty, to which every part and particle is equally related; the eternal ONE.[2]

— EMERSON, "THE OVER-SOUL" (1841)

Music is essentially the manly art.[3]

— WILLIAM LYON PHELPS, *MUSIC* (1930)

MAXIMALISM, AMERICAN STYLE

The two epigraphs from the *Essays* of Ralph Waldo Emerson (1803–82) may seem to be in contradiction. One places a proud and (it might be thought) typically American emphasis on individualism; the other places an equally strong premium on collectivity. Yet Emerson's essay on "Self-Reliance" is also the source of his most famous maxim: "A foolish consistency is the hobgoblin of little minds, adored by little statesmen and philosophers and divines."[4] The great American poet and preacher would surely have chimed in gladly with Walt Whitman's celebrated lines (in "Song of Myself" from *Leaves of Grass*, published somewhat later) proclaiming, on America's behalf, "Do I contradict myself?/Very well then I contradict myself, (I am large, I contain multitudes.)" And indeed, from a particular philosophical perspective Emerson's two insights may be easily reconciled — or, to speak philosophically, "synthesized." That standpoint can be found in a distinctively American strain of idealist thought that historians of philosophy now call New England transcendentalism (or "Transcendentalism," unqualified and with a capital T, to use the name its proponents, like Emerson, preferred). Flourishing in and around the town of

Concord, Massachusetts, between the 1830s and the 1850s, the movement is often cited as the first indigenously American "school" of philosophy.

That may be an exaggeration. For one thing, its roots are overwhelmingly German (Emerson's "Over-Soul," for one thing, being a direct translation of Hegel's *Überseele*). For another, it may not have been sufficiently systematic to qualify as a real "school of thought." As Michael Moran, a historian of Transcendentalism, has noted of its devotees, "although nearly all had made some attempt to read the German philosophers, very few had persevered to the point of mastering them."[5] Instead, they imbibed their philosophy from Romantic poetry, both by Germans like Goethe and by English nature poets like Wordsworth and Coleridge, who had imbibed Germanic idealism before them.

It was from these poets, predominantly, that Emerson derived the chief tenets of his philosophy. Still, he gave Immanuel Kant the (perhaps undeserved) credit for his biggest idea, first put forth in a Boston lecture of 1842. A Transcendentalist, he told his audience, believes in "a very important class of ideas, or imperative forms, which did not come by experience, but through which experience was acquired; that these were intuitions of the mind itself."[6] Transcendentalists, therefore, and simply, were people who had embraced a "tendency to respect their intuitions," whether or not such intuitions could be supported by observation or rational argument.

The chief intuition, paraphrased by Octavius B. Frothingham in his Emerson-authorized history of the movement (1876), was "the immanence of divinity in instinct," which made possible "the transference of supernatural attributes to the natural constitution of mankind."[7] In short, by trusting their individual instincts (or, as Emerson said, "respecting their intuitions"), people could gain direct access to the all-encompassing wisdom of God. Here was the link between the individual and the collective. The only requirement, of course, was that instinct or intuition be truly that, rather than one's conventional schooling in disguise. And this was, for most people, a very difficult requirement indeed.

This call to unlearn one's learning was given its most memorable literary expression in *Walden; or Life in the Woods* (1854), the philosophical memoirs of Emerson's disciple Henry David Thoreau (1817–62). It put New England transcendentalism in touch with a long line of inspirational "gnostic" or "primitivist" thinking. It was not so much a system of thought, then, as it was (to quote Frothingham) "an enthusiasm, a wave of sentiment, a breath of mind that caught up such as were prepared to receive it, elated them, transported them, and passed on."[8] Transcendentalism enters our narrative at this point — quite some time after the movement, properly so called, had ended — because it inspired Charles Ives (1874–1954), a New England composer, with both the vision and the self-reliance to become the one American whose music fully embodied the maximalistic spirit that was seizing his European counterparts in the first decades of the twentieth century.

No descriptive phrase could better capture Ives's expressive purposes than Frothingham's. He meant his music to provide a rush of sentiment and enthusiasm — some of it transcendental, much of it nostalgic — that would catch up such as were prepared to receive it and elate them. And to accomplish this, Ives was prepared to go to stylistic extremes that forced (or enabled) him to renounce his conventional schooling and follow his "instincts" to a degree that few other composers had the fortitude (or saw the need) to match. Yet because his vision was in so many ways a nostalgic one, Ives is a rare instance of a composer who, although the very model of a musical maximalist, cannot really be called a modernist.

TWO AMERICAN CAREERS

His principles, extravagantly idealistic both in the philosophical and in the ordinary meaning of the word, as well as the social and material conditions in which he grew up, mandated that Ives practice his musical vocation nonprofessionally. In this, his career somewhat resembled those of the Russian composers of his parents' generation. He was born in Danbury, Connecticut, into the family of George Ives (1845–94), the town bandmaster, who had served as the youngest Union bandleader during the American Civil War. From the age of fourteen, Charles Ives began following in his father's footsteps as a town musician, serving as Sunday organist in local churches before going off to New Haven, Connecticut, in 1894, for undergraduate studies at Yale University.

In later life Charles Ives tended to idealize the memory of his father both in words and in musical deed: his compositions often nostalgically evoked the nineteenth-century band music his father performed, as well as the congregational hymns he often accompanied in his youth. And he gave his father, an enthusiastic musical tinkerer if an unsuccessful composer, most of the credit for arousing in him an appetite for musical adventure. But George Ives's musical profession did not earn him much in the way of income or social respect, and he ended up, to his son's shame, as the family black sheep.

That may have been one of the factors that eventually dissuaded Charles Ives, despite strong inclinations and many indications of talent, from pursuing a musical career.

He studied at Yale with Horatio Parker (1863–1919), then a dashing young composer (only eleven years older than Ives) who had trained in Munich under the then-famous organist and composer Joseph Rheinberger, and who was widely regarded at the time as the white hope of American music. Parker's career was modeled on his own teacher's. It was the very career that Charles Ives had modestly embarked upon in Danbury, but Parker practiced it at the highest possible level of prestige. After returning from Munich, Parker was appointed to successive positions as organist and choirmaster in various New York

FIG. 5-1   Charles Ives, Yale graduation photo (1898).

FIG. 5-2 Horatio Parker, Ives's composition teacher at Yale.

parishes: first in Brooklyn, next in Harlem (then a fashionable neighborhood), finally at the Church of the Holy Trinity, one of the city's most affluent congregations. In 1892 he was appointed by Dvořák to the distinguished faculty of the National Conservatory of Music.

In 1893, the year before Ives came to study with him, Parker produced (at the age of thirty) his magnum opus, the oratorio *Hora novissima*, set to verses from a famous sacred poem by the twelfth-century Benedictine abbot Bernard of Cluny. It made him famous. It was the first American work to be performed at the august Three Choirs Festival in England, a performance that brought with it an honorary doctorate in music from the University of Cambridge. It secured for Parker not only his appointment as Battell Professor of the Theory of Music at Yale (beginning in 1894, Ives's freshman year), but also the organist-choirmaster's post at Boston's Trinity Church. When Ives met him, Horatio Parker was at the very zenith of American musical success. He had won high eminence and a comfortable, socially respectable position by doing the work that Ives had begun to do. He was a natural role model for his pupil.

With Parker, Ives went through a thorough training that culminated in the writing of a traditional symphony (à la Dvořák), now known as his First Symphony, as a graduation piece. All during his college years he maintained his Sunday church employment, now in New Haven, a larger town than Danbury. Upon leaving Yale in 1898, he continued to seek professional employment in the socially respectable domain of sacred music, finally securing the post of organist and choirmaster at New York's Central Presbyterian Church, a prominent place of worship with an affluent congregation, where Ives worked from 1900 to 1902.

This was a fairly high-prestige job; and it is clear that until his late twenties, Ives was aiming at a career in Horatio Parker's footsteps. The impression is more than confirmed by Ives's first important bid for public recognition as a composer: *The Celestial Country*, a cantata for soloists, chorus, and instrumental accompaniment, on which he embarked the year after graduating from Parker's class, and which he performed with his choir at Central Presbyterian Church on 18 April 1902 — a performance to which critics were invited, and about which notices were published in the *Musical Courier*, the leading American professional periodical, and the *New York Times*, the country's newspaper of record. Ives proudly identified himself to the reporters as Parker's former pupil.

And not surprisingly, his debut work was modeled, in every dimension and particular, on Parker's *Hora novissima*. Even the text, a long hymn by Henry Alford (1810–71), the dean of Canterbury Cathedral, was chosen because Ives was under the mistaken impression that it was a translation of verses from the same poem by Bernard of Cluny on which his teacher had based his most successful work. The most unusual number in *The Celestial Country*—a quartet for the four soloists in a meter that alternated bars of $\frac{4}{4}$ with bars of $\frac{3}{4}$ (Ex. 5-1), singled out for admiring comment by Ives's early (posthumous) biographers after his later maximalist experiments had become legendary—turns out to have been the number most clearly derivative from Parker. The middle section of the bass aria in *Hora novissima* displays the same rhythmic quirk, made even more "radical" by the occasional interpolation of measures in $\frac{5}{4}$ meter (Ex. 5-2). (Ives copied the $\frac{5}{4}$ interpolations elsewhere in *The Celestial Country*.)

EX. 5-1 Charles Ives, *The Celestial Country*, no. 3, mm. 50–57

EX. 5-1 (continued)

EX. 5-2 Horatio Parker, *Hora novissima*, no. 3, mm. 33–47

EX. 5-2 (continued)

Dan - da fi - de-li-bus   Est i - bi ci - vi-bus,

A distinctively harmonized descending chromatic scale, which recurs in *The Celestial Country* as a sort of leitmotif, also has a conspicuous counterpart in *Hora novissima* (Ex. 5-3). Perhaps significantly, however, Ives's attempts at contrapuntal virtuosity (like the stretto between soprano and tenor at the beginning of Ex. 5-3a) fall considerably short of Parker's impressive feats of craft, like the canon by augmentation that crowns *Hora novissima*'s first choral fugue (Ex. 5-4). It may have been the recognition that he had fallen short of his model that impelled Ives to take the unexpected step of resigning his post at Central Presbyterian a week after the performance and renouncing a professional career in music. Or it may have been the faint praise that his work received in the press, the *Times* reporting that it "has the elementary merit of being scholarly and well made" and the *Courier* that it "shows undoubted earnestness of study."

EX. 5-3A   Charles Ives, *The Celestial Country*, no. 7, mm. 107–115

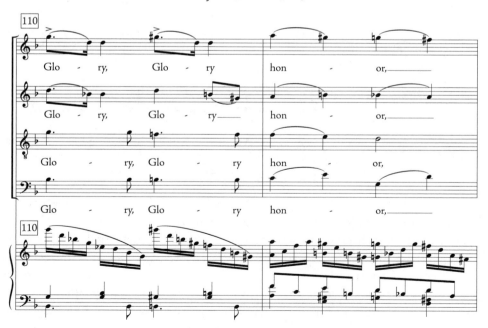

Glo - ry, Glo - ry   hon - or,

Glo - ry, Glo - ry   hon - or,

Glo - ry, Glo - ry   hon - or,

Glo - ry, Glo - ry   hon - or,

EX. 5-3A *(continued)*

Whatever the reasons, the 1902 performance *The Celestial Country* was the last public performance an Ives work would receive for more than twenty years. His Second Symphony, on which he worked concurrently with the cantata, and which is now regarded as his first really characteristic work, would not be played until 1951. The twenty years of his creative seclusion, moreover, were the very years during which Ives composed the amazing maximalist scores on which his legendary reputation now rests. That combination of circumstances has given rise to a great deal of interesting speculation about the meaning of his work and its relationship to his environment.

EX. 5-3B   Horatio Parker, *Hora novissima*, no. 1, mm. 138–146

Some of that speculation, inevitably, has been psychological. Ives's beloved father died suddenly during the first year of Ives's study with Parker, leading (in the opinion of the psychoanalyst Stuart Feder, who wrote a full-scale psychobiography of the composer called *Charles Ives, My Father's Song*) to a sorely ambivalent attitude toward the professional success Parker represented, and which his father never achieved. To

EX. 5-4 Horatio Parker, *Hora novissima*, no. 4, mm. 128–134

succeed on Parker's "high art" terms, Feder argued, would now feel to Ives like a betrayal of his father, the "failed village bandmaster."

Ives's autobiographical *Memos*, dictated to a secretary in old age and posthumously published, are full of gushing, somewhat guilt-ridden praise for George Ives and grudging, somewhat sarcastic comment on Parker's teaching. Some of it, particularly the remark that "Parker was a bright man, a good technician but perfectly willing to be limited by what Rheinberger had taught him,"[9] has led to the conjecture that Ives's rebellion had a nationalistic or patriotic basis. He withdrew from professional activity, according to some of his early biographers, because (like Glinka, with whom superficial parallels were easily drawn) he found no support in the professional world of "art" music for genuinely indigenous art.

Feder made a different interpretation, a more convincing one. Ives, in his view, was in a double bind. "Even if the performance had been [more] successful in Parker's terms," he writes,

> Ives would have viewed it as giving in — submitting to Parker and giving up an individuality which he valued and cultivated and had shared with his father. Equally important, success in music, especially the prospect of earning as comfortable a living as Parker did, would declare Charlie once and for all superior to George.[10]

Under these terms, success in music would have been as intolerable as failure. The only recourse was to "give up music" altogether. Yet there was a peculiarly American dimension to Ives's dilemma after all, because, according to historians of the period, it was a dilemma that an American would have felt then much more acutely than a European. To Feder's psychoanalytical interpretation we may add that of the social historian Frank R. Rossiter, who sees Ives as succumbing "to enormous pressures that his society and culture brought to bear upon him, pressures that insisted he be a 'good American' in his attitude toward music."[11] These powerful pressures had to do with gender identification and role-playing. In Rossiter's blunt assessment, the dominant American view during what historians now call the Progressive Era (or, less approvingly, the "gilded age") was that "classical music was for sissies and women."[12] It was no place for an American man, especially one with Ives's family background.

FIG. 5-3 Charles Ives in Battery Park, New York, ca. 1917.

The place for an American man was business, and it was there that Ives took refuge from his musical conflicts. Most of the men in his family were in business or in a "respectable profession" like law or medicine. One of them, a cousin of his father's, was working as a medical examiner for the Mutual Insurance Company, and got Ives a job there as an actuary after college. Ives held on to this "day job" as a fallback during the years in which he was setting his sights on a musical career. Having given up that ambition, he made insurance his career, moving out into the field as a sales agent. In 1906, he and another Mutual agent named Julian Myrick started their own firm. Within a short time Ives & Myrick was the most successful insurance agency in the country. His sacrifice of the one career and success in the other has made of Ives a potent but ambiguous symbol. "Ives, from one point of view, chose integrity over compromise," the American composer David Schiff has written, adding that "he also chose to become a millionaire rather than an artist."

SEXUAL—AND STYLISTIC—POLITICS

But did he stop being an artist? His business career gave Ives the courage to write music (and write it in quantity) of a kind that fully expressed his idealistic commitments. Yet here, too, a certain amount of gender role-playing seems to have been a factor. His fear of the effeminacy associated in America with classical music fed his maximalistic inclinations, since to his mind a conspicuously "strong" and dissonant style was an assertion of masculinity. The abundant Ives apocrypha is full of stories attesting to this sort of blustery machismo, including one in which he rebuked a protesting member of the audience at a modern music concert by shouting, "Stop being such a goddamn sissy! Why can't you stand up before fine strong music like this and use your ears like a man?"[13] The *Memos*, too, abound in raillery against "old ladies of both sexes" who patronized "nice" music.[14] (Here, as Rossiter points out, Ives the wealthy but conflicted businessman was rebelling against his own social class.) And as the *Memos* reveal, at least one of Ives's most stylistically radical scores—the Second String Quartet, composed, like most of the music that followed Ives's professional withdrawal, over a lengthy span of years (1907-13)—originated in protest against the feminine connotations of its genre. After attending recitals by the Boston-based Kneisel Quartet, one of the most prestigious chamber groups then playing in America, Ives recalled,

> It used to come over me . . . that music had been, and still was, too much of an emasculated art. Too much of what was easy and usual to play and to hear was called beautiful, etc.—the same old even-vibration, Sybaritic apron-strings, keeping music too much tied to the old ladies. The string quartet music got more and more weak, trite, and effeminate. After one of those Kneisel Quartet concerts in the old Mendelssohn Hall, I started a string quartet score, half mad, half in fun, and half to try out, practise, and have some fun with making those men fiddlers get up and do something like men.[15]

The quartet's three movements, according to the *Memos*, were originally called "I. Four Men have Discussions, Conversations, II. Arguments and Fight, III. Contemplation." (In the published score the titles were replaced by a general note: "String Quartet for four men who converse, discuss, argue (in re 'politics'), fight, shake hands, shut up, then walk up the mountainside to view the firmament.") The second movement, actually the first to be composed (1907–11), is the one that most concretely embodies the attitudes and anxieties expressed in the *Memos*. The implied scenario that it enacts is probably clear enough from the sounds of the music, but it is vividly spelled out in some oft-quoted marginalia found in Ives's manuscript score.

The second violin is cast there as one "Rollo Finck." The first name is that of the hero in a series of boys' books Ives knew from his childhood, a paragon of good behavior. The surname is that of Henry Theophilus Finck (1854–1926), the influential music critic of the New York *Evening Post*. Rollo is thus the epitome of the good little "feminized" musician against whose smug, limited values Ives spent his years of creative seclusion protesting. In no other work is the programmatic import of his maximalized idiom so explicitly set forth.

EX. 5-5A   Charles Ives, String Quartet no. 2, II, mm. 31–42

EX. 5-5B Charles Ives, String Quartet no. 2, II, mm. 65–69

Rollo starts out by interrupting the proceedings with some sentimental cadenzas (Ex. 5-5a). The first two are marked "Andante emasculata"; the third time, marked "Largo sweetota," he briefly gets the rest of the quartet to join him before being swatted down as before (in one case with the marking "Allegro con fisto"). The first little cadenza carries the additional notation, "alla rubato ELMAN (pretty tone, ladies)," in sarcastic allusion to the Russian-born violin prodigy Mischa Elman (1891–1967), who had just made his sensational New York debut at the time when Ives was composing the quartet, and whose "most glorious attribute" (according to *The New Grove Dictionary of Music and Musicians*) was "his rich, sensuous and infinitely expressive tone, which became legendary."[16] Ives had little use for it. "My God," he once exclaimed in print, "what has sound got to do with music!"[17] At various points Rollo simply drops out of the doings. "Tut, tut," Ives notes in the margin, and "Too hard to play — so it just *can't* be good music, Rollo." On returning after one such absence, Rollo plays doggedly on the beat while the rest of the quartet is enjoying a riot of hemiolas and syncopations (Ex. 5-5b). "Beat time, Rollo!" reads the marginal note. Over one last florid but not too difficult passage for the second violin Ives writes "Join in again, Professor, all in the key of C. You can do that nice and pretty." Motivated so obviously by anxiety and resentment, the humor here has not worn well. In an age when social equality is taken more seriously (and more literally) than it was in Ives's day, when misogyny

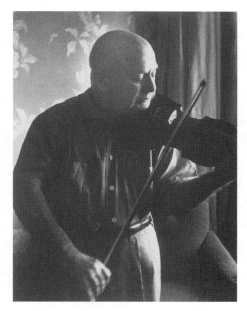

FIG. 5-4   Mischa Elman.

and homophobia have become openly identified and debated social issues, and when the sexual politics informing, say, Strauss's *Salome* or Stravinsky's *The Rite of Spring* are no longer thought irrelevant to their critical evaluation, the masculinist aspect of Ives's maximalism has come in for some reproach. While few have been inclined to go as far as Lawrence Kramer, Ives's severest critic, who reads the second movement of the Second Quartet quite simply as "gay-bashing,"[18] the value of his stylistic adventures, in light of what is now often regarded as their questionable social motivation, is no longer taken quite so readily for granted as it once was.

And yet their motivation was no single thing, and the stylistic dichotomy between the "strongly" dissonant (replete with "polytonal" chords and even "clusters" of semitones) and the "nice" can be read, like all dichotomies, in various ways depending on the context. In "Nov. 2, 1920" (sometimes called "An Election"), a song to a meditative prose text by the composer expressing his disgust at the repudiation of Woodrow Wilson's visionary internationalist policies in the presidential election of 1920, in favor of small-minded "normalcy" (as the successful Republican candidate, Warren G. Harding, famously called it[19]), the stylistic dichotomy symbolizes the "difficult" politics of idealism vs. the "easy" politics of expediency (Ex. 5-6; note in particular the setting of the words "Now you're safe, that's the easy way!").

Yet while what is "easy" is stigmatized in the song, what is "popular" is not. Ives viewed popular music not as commercial but as "populist" — music expressing "the voice of the people" — and loved to quote it symbolically. He sets the words "over there" to a snatch from George M. Cohan's rousing World War I morale song of the same name, and he reminds Americans of their patriotic duty in the song's final measures with an equally brief snatch from the national anthem. Allusions like these to popular and patriotic songs are chiefly responsible for Ives's reputation as an "Americanist" (or American regionalist) composer.

But his repertory of allusions actually ranged much further and wider than that. As this very song confirms, Ives was an "internationalist" rather than an "isolationist," and his musical idiom was by no means confined to American sources. Indeed, the

EX. 5-6   Charles Ives, "Nov. 2, 1920" (a.k.a. "An Election"), mm. 12–17

EX. 5-6 *(continued)*

most "American" thing about "Nov. 2, 1920" is not the source of its quotations, or even its style, but the fact that Ives saw fit to use his art to engage in political debate in the spirit of American participatory democracy. The "Note" appended to the score even seems to equate the song, in its intended effect, with an actual political pamphlet Ives had written in favor of a Constitutional amendment that would substitute direct popular referendums for many of the functions and duties performed by the Congress, especially in the conduct of foreign policy.

And yet that very "Note" falls back on gender stereotyping when Ives complains that "the voice of the people sounding through the mouth of the [political] parties, becomes somewhat emasculated," and the song makes sneering reference to "all the old women, male and female, [who] had their day today." It may also be pertinent to recall that the election of 1920 was the first to take place after the passage of the Nineteenth Amendment, which guaranteed women's suffrage, and it was widely felt (not only by sore losers) that the women's vote had helped the handsome Harding win the office he would later disgrace with scandal.

But lest it be thought that Ives's idealism was always tinged with its opposite, and that consonant traditional harmony was only present in his music to be mocked as effeminate, consider the song from "Paracelsus," to a text by Robert Browning, in which the dichotomy seems to work precisely the other way round in the expression of a "purer" (that is, less overtly political) strain of transcendentalism. Philippus Aureolus Bombast von Hohenheim, known as Paracelsus (1493–1541), was a Swiss alchemist and physician who made important contributions to the use of chemical agents in the treatment of disease. Browning's dramatic poem (1835) is a meditation on pride, in which the brilliant Paracelsus is portrayed as having ultimately failed to do the good that was within his grasp to accomplish because of a lack of empathy toward his less gifted fellow men. The lines Ives set are uttered by Paracelsus in response to the altruistic example of the poet Aprile, who has revealed to him his error in pursuing power to the exclusion of love.

Here the complex and "difficult" idiom — expressed in an introductory piano solo in as overloaded a texture as the mind can conceive or the hand perform — is associated with the futile quest for power (Ex. 5-7a). The lucid and consonant final page (Ex. 5-7b), with its cadence on an unalloyed D major triad that is presented completely without

EX. 5-7A Charles Ives, "From 'Paracelsus,'" mm. 1–6

EX. 5-7B Charles Ives, "From 'Paracelsus,'" *Andante molto*, end

EX. 5-7B *(continued)*

irony, represents the superior force of love, showing the way to the simplicity of a higher truth. The form of the song — progressive clarification, approaching the sublime resolution of all conflict and variety — is as characteristic of Ives as any other.

Sometimes called Ives's "epiphany" form, it illustrates two important aspects of his maximalism. First, the dissonant and "modern" is not necessarily given preference over the traditional and consonant. Unlike that of many European maximalists, Ives's idiom is not driven by an ideal of evolutionary stylistic progress. It obeys no mandate of history. Rather, in a manner that is often compared with American ideals of democratic pluralism, all styles coexist in Ives's music, each with its own expressive and symbolic tasks to perform. And second, it is only for the sake of expression and representation that style is developed, never for its own sake. As Ives liked to put it, it is "substance" that determines (and is therefore prior to) "manner."[20] Thus, when the substance or expressive purpose demanded it, Ives was prepared to compose in a relatively traditional manner or style — a "Parker" style, so to speak — at any time throughout his career. His mature music therefore shows little in the way of stylistic "evolution," which is one reason why it fits the modernist template so poorly.

Indeed, he despised a great deal of modern music (especially by Debussy, Ravel, and Stravinsky) that seemed to him to be more concerned with manner — style for its own sake — than with substance. We may deduce from this, perhaps, that his idea of substance, or the proper expressive content for music, was essentially (and conventionally) Germanic. That is, it continued to value "human content," the representation of emotion and spirituality above all, and passionately to resist the tendency identified in chapter 2 as "dehumanization."

TERMS OF RECEPTION

"From 'Paracelsus'" bears the date 1921, nearly the latest date an Ives score can bear; for in that year his composing career, save only a few exceptional efforts, came effectively to an end. The reason usually given for his creative cessation is a severe heart attack suffered in September 1918, which left him in precarious health for the remaining 35 years of his life. In semiretirement from business, Ives began putting his manuscripts in order and prepared two items — the Second Piano Sonata and *114 Songs* — for private publication. They were issued, respectively, in 1920 and 1922. A few other compositions were published, by subscription only, in the *New Music Quarterly* series edited by Henry Cowell (1897–1965), a California composer devoted to the cause of disseminating what he called "ultramodern music." And one, an "Orchestral Set" called *Three Places in New England*, was issued by a commercial firm in 1935. Except for a campaign song for the Republican candidate, William McKinley, in the election of 1896, it was the only conventionally published Ives score to see print before World War II. Very gradually, performers began discovering his music and introducing it to audiences, in most cases long after it was written.

As Robert Crunden, a historian of the Progressive Age who has written perceptively about Ives and his strangely misshapen career, has put it, "prizes and publicity finally poured in as ill health made their enjoyment difficult."[21] Describing Ives's life, with rueful irony, in terms of the conventional format associated with great composers since Beethoven, Crunden observes "three phases," which he calls "youthful normality, creative vigor in both music and business, and then decline amidst growing fame." But as Crunden also suggests, the most telling of Ives's "periods" has been the fourth — his posthumous reception, which turned him retrospectively, and at the cost of considerable distortion, into a modernist giant.

The height of Ives's prestige and (somewhat later) his popularity actually crosscut Crunden's third and fourth phases, lasting from 1939 roughly until his birth centenary in 1974. During this period he was honored as a (or even as *the*) founding father of American music — its first original master, its Great Emancipator, and the author of its Declaration of Independence from Europe (or, as the conductor Leonard Bernstein put it at the time of the Second Symphony premiere in 1951, "our Washington, Lincoln and Jefferson of music"). The event that triggered the boom was the first public performance of the complete Second Piano Sonata, subtitled *Concord, Mass., 1840–60*, by the pianist John Kirkpatrick, in a New York recital that took place on 20 January 1939.

Actually it was not so much the performance itself that did the triggering as it was a remarkable review that it elicited from a seasoned and influential critic. Lawrence Gilman (1878–1939), the chief music reviewer for the *New York Herald Tribune* since 1923, head program annotator for the New York Philharmonic-Symphony Orchestra, and author of half a dozen widely read books on modern music beginning with Wagner, greeted Kirkpatrick's performance with a delirium of praise. In words that have been reprinted more frequently, perhaps, than any others in the annals of American music criticism, Gilman pronounced Ives's Sonata to be "exceptionally great music — it is, indeed, the greatest music composed by an American, and the most deeply and essentially American in impulse and implication."[22] Kirkpatrick's performance, he added, "was that of a poet and a master, an unobtrusive minister of genius."

Gilman's extraordinary sympathy for the work was the result of a deeper sympathy with Ives's purposes, which in the case of the Second Piano Sonata was more than ever the translation into music of the spiritual essence and effect of transcendentalist philosophy. No less than Ives's music, Gilman's criticism — to quote Wayne Shirley, a music bibliographer and historian of American music — was "rooted in the tradition that holds that music is ideally a vehicle for the expression of philosophical ideas."[23] Gilman provided his readers with a valuable key to those ideas as embodied in Ives's music.

But Gilman's review also contained a negative, defensively chauvinistic component that played a major role in the subsequent distortion of Ives's legacy. Referring acerbically to "the two distinguished composers" — probably the old visitor Dvořák and the more recent Swiss immigrant Ernest Bloch (1880–1959) — "who are sometimes said to have produced the best music written in America," Gilman dismissed them with the simple observation that they "cannot be called Americans at all: they were born in Europe, and their music is about as 'American' in quality as the Mediterranean or the Quai d'Orsay," while "Charles Ives is as unchallengeably American as the Yale Fence," and therefore musically authentic in a way that a Dvořák or a Bloch could never be. Nor did Gilman stop even there. He capped his eulogy by calling attention to the fact that

> Before he was twenty-five, [Ives] had begun those audacious experiments in the organization of sound and the development of scales and counterpoint and rhythms which, for those who have studied their outcome in his later works, make the typical utterances of Schönberg sound like Haydn sonatas. And we are to bear in mind that when Ives was evolving this incredible ultra-modernism of the American nineties, Schönberg, then in his early twenties, had not yet ventured even upon the adolescent Wagnerism of his 'Verklärte Nacht'; and the youthful Stravinsky was playing marbles in Oranienbaum.

Wittingly or not, Gilman had set the terms of Ives's assimilation not to the esthetics of transcendentalism or any other expressive tendency, but to that of modernism, the neo-Hegelian historiographical legacy of the New German School, which chiefly values artists in proportion to their technical and formal innovations. It was not the best vantage point from which to view Ives (or, some might argue, any artist). It made for trouble, and his serious devaluing, later; for it turned the Ives boom into a bubble that might easily be pricked. If the Great Emancipator were merely the Great Anticipator (as a skeptical joke of the period had it), then the basis of his reputation would stop being what his work accomplished (in the present) and become simply a matter of when it was written (in the past). Ives became vulnerable to musicological (or pseudomusicological) attack.

The first attacker was Elliott Carter (b. 1908), a famous composer who had known Ives as a boy and whose attitudes toward his former mentor were, as often happens, full of filial conflicts (or "Oedipal" ones, to speak the language of pop psychology). During the Ives centennial year Carter sounded the most jarringly dissonant note when he reminisced to an interviewer about

> a visit on a late afternoon to his house on East 74th Street [in Manhattan], when I was directed to a little top-floor room where Ives sat at a little upright piano with score pages strewn around on the floor and on tables — this must have been around 1929. He was working on, I think, *Three Places in New England*, getting the score ready for performance. A new score was being derived from the older one to which he was adding and changing, turning octaves into sevenths and ninths, and adding dissonant notes. Since then, I have often wondered at exactly what date a lot of the music written early in his life received its last shot of dissonance and polyrhythm. In this case he showed me quite simply how he was improving the score. I got the impression that he might have frequently jacked up the level of dissonance of many works as his tastes changed. While the question no longer seems important, one could wonder whether he was as early a precursor of "modern" music as is sometimes made out. A study of the manuscripts would probably make this clear.[24]

But Carter certainly knew that the terms of Ives's reception, and the way in which his achievement was by then described in all the history books, made the question not only supremely important but also very threatening to the composer's reputation. The sly invitation implied in the last sentence was quickly taken up by a number of scholars — in particular Maynard Solomon, a musicologist with an interest in psychoanalysis who had already published a psychobiography of Beethoven and would later write one about Mozart. The article that ensued from his investigation, "Charles Ives: Some Questions of Veracity," quickly became a cause célèbre following its publication in 1987.

Relying to a large extent on the work of other scholars, Solomon presented evidence that Ives had deliberately altered some of his manuscripts so as to mislead researchers into accepting earlier dates for some of his works than were in fact the case. Solomon interpreted the composer's alleged mendacity as an effort generally to protect his precious reputation as an isolated "original" (in keeping with the transcendentalist individualism expressed in the first epigraph at the top of this chapter), and specifically to enhance his idolized father's role (rather than that of any European contemporary) in the formation of his radical style.

And yet the appearance of image-polishing seemed to cast a troubling reflection on Ives's personal integrity, and Solomon did suggest that Ives himself had been caught up, following Gilman's celebrated review, in the modernist (or "historicist") tendency to "confuse the patent-office with the Pantheon, to regard the invention of a new technique as the most significant measure of creativity."[25] Solomon warned that "it cannot be sufficiently stressed that the value of Ives's music is wholly independent of issues of priority and modernism."[26] But like Carter's, his disclaimer rang false. To attribute Ives's actions to "an obsessive concern over issues of priority,"[27] without acknowledging the obvious fact that his own research had been similarly motivated, made the article look like a vendetta. It led to a huge dispute among Ives specialists, tinged with a hostility that belied everyone's claim to be dispassionately (or "objectively") seeking the truth.

The row over dating seemed especially unfortunate since the arguments of both sides, whether upholding it or impugning it, were focused on Ives's reputation as a modernist — a label that, as Crunden and other historians have convincingly argued, is the wrong one to apply. For a while, musicology seemed unable to cope with the idea that a composer could be a radical maximalist without being a modernist — that is, without a primary commitment to technical innovation, and without challenging (let alone revolting against) contemporary social norms.

Ives's esthetic outlook is far better understood when its connection with the European — and particularly the German — past is acknowledged. Like the transcendentalism to which he professed allegiance, his artistic aims and commitments were neither as radical nor as indigenously American as often claimed. And his radical techniques mostly celebrated the very opposite of progress: their purpose, paradoxically, was to evoke — nostalgically, unironically — a vanished (or imaginary) rural or small-town America. To put Ives's fundamental expressive concerns in a proper focus, two works in particular (or movements from them) will need a close-up look: the *Concord* Sonata, the subject of Lawrence Gilman's excited praise, and *Three Places in New England*, the subject of Elliott Carter's equivocal memoir.

MANNER AND SUBSTANCE

At the very least, the obsession with dating (even to the extent that Ives himself, in his postcomposing phase, may have abetted it) was fundamentally un-Ivesian, since it was wholly concerned with "manner" (the way something was said), rather than "substance" (the something itself). To understand the "something" we need to know what composers Ives took as expressive examples. The answer to this question may be surprising, since Ives's models of substance were none of them composers who shared Ives's interest in a radical manner. Rather, they were composers who expressed orthodox spiritual values, and did so in a way that by the early twentieth century was deemed distinctly old-fashioned, if not downright unfashionable.

In the epilogue to *Essays before a Sonata*, a little book he published and distributed alongside the *Concord* Sonata in order to explain its "substance," Ives indulged in some reminiscences of his own changing tastes:

> A man remembers, when he was a boy of about fifteen years, hearing his music-teacher (and father), who had just returned from a performance of *Siegfried*, say with a look of anxious surprise that somehow or other he felt ashamed of enjoying the music as he did, for beneath it all he was conscious of an undercurrent of make-believe — the bravery was make-believe, the love was make-believe, the passion, the virtue, all make-believe, as was the dragon; P. T. Barnum would have been brave enough to have gone out and captured a live one! But that same boy at twenty-five was listening to Wagner with enthusiasm — his reality was real enough to inspire a devotion. The "Preislied" [Prize-Song from *Die Meistersinger*], for instance, stirred him deeply. But when he became middle-aged — and long before the Hohenzollern hog-marched into Belgium [that is, before World War I made everything German unfashionable in America] — this music had become cloying, the melodies threadbare — a sense of something commonplace — yes — of make-believe, came. These feelings were

fought against for association's sake and because of gratitude for bygone pleasures, but the former beauty and nobility were not there, and in their place stood irritating intervals of descending fourths and fifths. Those once transcendent progressions, luxuriant suggestions of Debussy chords of the ninth, eleventh, etc., were becoming slimy. An unearned exultation—a sentimentality deadening something within—hides around in the music. Wagner seems less and less to measure up to the substance and reality of César Franck, Brahms, d'Indy, or even Elgar (with all his tiresomeness); the wholesomeness, manliness, humility, and deep spiritual, possibly religious, feeling of these men seem missing and not made up for by his (Wagner's) manner and eloquence, even if greater than theirs (which is very doubtful).[28]

The strictures against Wagner and Debussy are familiar: they express Ives's usual, very conservative (or at least very unmodernist) resistance to decadence and sensuality, along with the (typically American? typically Yankee?) fear of effeminacy that we have noted before. But the list of antidotes, with the exception of Brahms, can seem a bit bizarre. A taste for Franck, d'Indy, and Elgar was by the 1920s, when Ives enumerated them, as dated as a taste for Rossini would have been in the heyday of Wagnerism. Their religiosity and "uplift" were among the things discredited, as we shall see, by the "Hohenzollern hog-march"—the imperialist war to which Ives himself makes reference—at least as far as a younger generation was concerned. Ives's maximalism, at least as expressed in the *Concord* Sonata, begins to seem an attempt to give new life—or at least some artificial life-support—to an esthetic stance that had become in modernist eyes tarnished if not altogether outmoded, but one that Ives continued to cherish for its once-unsullied idealism.

Franck appears to have been Ives's unlikely special favorite. That may have been partly due to his organist's background; Ives kept a reproduction of Jeanne Rongier's portrait of Franck seated at the organ tacked to the inside door of his music studio. In any case, Elliott Carter has reported that Ives's "main love" was for "Bach, Brahms and Franck, for he found in them spiritual elevation and nobility, which, like many a critic of his generation, he felt contemporary music had simplified away."[29] If, following this lead, we take Franck (rather than the more obvious Liszt) to have been Ives's particular model in the *Concord* Sonata, his attempt at a sort of antimodernist spiritual revival turns out to have been surprisingly specific.

Franck's Symphony in D minor had a decisive impact on American composers, particularly on the "Boston school" of which Horatio Parker, Ives's Yale professor, was a latter-day member. In its "aspiring" quality and its emphasis on the "moral obligations of the artist"[30] (to quote Edward Burlingame Hill, Parker's Harvard counterpart), the Franck Symphony was the most Germanic of French symphonies, and the greatest of all standard-bearers for the supremacy of "substance" over "manner." Like all nineteenth-century symphonies in D minor (and many others besides), it was haunted by the lofty spirit of Beethoven's Ninth; but it also mined Beethoven's last quartet for an emblematic motive that audibly haunted the work and carried its spiritual message from first movement to last.

Ives made a similar appropriation from Beethoven in the *Concord* Sonata: the first four notes of the Fifth Symphony, perhaps the most famous (and at once the most heavily fraught and the most hackneyed) single motive in all of music by the time Ives chose it to pervade his work and carry its spiritual message through all the movements. Each of Ives's movements bore the name of a Transcendentalist writer (or family of writers) associated with Concord — Emerson, Hawthorne, "the Alcotts," Thoreau — and attempted to represent or interpret the gist of that writer's message. Most of the *Essays before a Sonata* (the title of which was already an evocation of Emerson) was devoted to describing the way in which, Ives felt, his music embodied their ideas. The overriding message that united them all, the essence of New England transcendentalism, was symbolized in the Beethoven motive, to which Ives devoted a special explanation in the chapter on Emerson:

> There is an "oracle" at the beginning of the *Fifth Symphony*; in those four notes lies one of Beethoven's greatest messages. We would place its translation above the relentlessness of fate knocking at the door [as Beethoven himself once described it to an interviewer], above the greater human message of destiny and strive to bring it towards the spiritual message of Emerson's revelations, even to the "common heart" of Concord — the soul of humanity knocking at the door of the divine mysteries, radiant in the faith that it *will* be opened — and the human become the divine![31]

From the "Paracelsus"-like opening page of "Emerson" (Ex. 5-8) to the quiescent closing pages of "Thoreau" with their pastoral flute obbligato (Ex. 5-9), the Fifth Symphony motif suffuses and unifies the otherwise sprawling *Concord* Sonata. "Emerson," itself (according to *Essays before a Sonata*) the portrait of an oracle, abounds especially with Beethoven's call, sometimes presented as a major third, sometimes minor. The accented repeated notes, first in the right hand then in the left, in the opening bars mark its first appearances; thereafter, one easily uncovers at least a hundred more. The optional flute solo at the end of "Thoreau" — an evocation of Thoreau's description of his own nocturnal flute-playing by the side of Walden Pond — places the Fifth Symphony idea in the context of a long melody that sums up many of the sonata's themes. In the *Essays before a Sonata* Ives associated it with "human faith." Its beginning is first prefigured on the second page of "Emerson," in the middle voice over a Fifth Symphony bass. The final dying-away at the end of "Thoreau" is a variation on the Fifth Symphony motif that suggests a quiet ecstasy of affirmation by replacing the falling third by a fourth repeated note — utter unity or "wholeness" (Emerson's "the ONE") is attained.

EX. 5-8   Charles Ives, "Concord" Sonata, I ("Emerson"), beginning

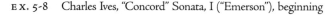

EX. 5-8 (continued)

On the first page of "The Alcotts" (Ex. 5-10), a domestic portrait in a distinctly tamer style than the rest, the Fifth Symphony motif is presented in yet another context, that of indigenous American hymnody. As the Ives scholar J. Peter Burkholder has shown, Ives conflates the Beethoven gambit with the openings of two well-known tunes from the Protestant hymnal—Simeon B. Marsh's *Martyn* (or *Jesus, Lover of My Soul*) and *The Missionary Chant* (*Ye Christian Heralds*) by Charles Zeuner (Ex. 5-11)—as if to depict the divine presence that informs the homely devotions of the famous New England literary family (or any sincere religious exercise).[32]

There is an uncanny resonance between Ives's "Transcendental" reinterpretation of Beethoven and the uplifting interpretations of Franck's Symphony that ran rampant with the spread of "music appreciation," especially in America. A major source of such morally edifying art interpretation was the English critic Matthew Arnold, and, as it

EX. 5-9   Charles Ives, "Concord" Sonata, end of IV ("Thoreau")

EX. 5-9   (continued)

*Small notes in piano played only if flute is not used.

happens, one of Ives's other professors at Yale, William Lyon Phelps (1865–1943), with whom Ives studied English and American literature, was one of America's leading "Arnoldians," and a specialist in the poetry of Robert Browning (the author of "Paracelsus"), to whom Ives dedicated an overture. As Burkholder has emphasized, Ives nurtured a special regard for "Billy" Phelps for the rest of his life, corresponded with him in later years, and even sent him a copy of *Essays before a Sonata*, which Phelps enthusiastically (if somewhat cursorily) reviewed in the *Yale Alumni Weekly*. "Some of the roots of the 'Concord' Sonata," Burkholder has argued, "reach back to Phelps's course, where Ives must have studied Emerson, Thoreau, Hawthorne, and the Alcotts in depth."[33] Some of Ives's mature ideas about music may also owe something to Phelps's example. Phelps collected his thoughts on the subject — many of them adapted straight from the poetry of Browning — in a little volume published in 1930. The third epigraph at the head of this chapter, as wishfully Ivesian a thought as ever uttered, comes from it. So does this:

> The paradox is that Music, the most universal of languages, knowing no boundary lines, should have been monopolized by the Germans . . . . If one collected all the music in the world written by men who were not Germans, put it together, and multiplied it by ten, the product would not equal in value the music written

EX. 5-10   Charles Ives, "Concord" Sonata, beginning of III ("The Alcotts")

by Germans alone. In the Music Hall facing the lake on Michigan Avenue in Chicago, the committee placed on the façade the names of what they considered to be the five greatest composers in all history. They are Bach, Mozart, Beethoven, Wagner, Schubert — all Germans. And the first names on a substitute list would also be Germans.[34]

EX. 5-11A   Simeon B. Marsh, *Martyn*

EX. 5-11B   Charles Zeuner, *The Missionary Chant*

And this:

> When we see the Sistine Madonna, or read *Hamlet*, we admire the extraordinary power of Raphael, of Shakespeare. But when we hear the Ninth Symphony, *we are listening to the voice of God.* Beethoven was more passive than active, the channel through which flowed the Divine Will.[35]

These conventionally Romantic and conventionally Germanocentric ideas were Ives's, too, despite his predilections for regionalisms à la Dvořák. Like Dvořák, Ives

FIG. 5-5A Matthew Arnold (1822–1888), ca. 1844.

FIG. 5-5B William Lyon Phelps, Ives's English teacher, with a volume of Browning open before him.

believed in the ennobling force of the "beautiful forms of art," that is to say the forms and techniques of Germanic instrumental music and of the composers who wrote it, whether or not of German birth. In no sense was he a rebel, whether in the name of America or in any other cause, against the reverent Europeanized esthetics, or even against the tastes, of his elders; he wanted, rather, to give them a more emphatic, more personalized, more ideal (and yes, perhaps a more "masculine") expression, and that prompted a certain blustery uncouthness of manner. But the substance remained exactly what it had been before. That is certainly maximalism. But just as certainly it is not modernism.

NOSTALGIA

The other side of the coin, where Ives's maximalism was concerned, could not have stood in greater superficial contrast to the visionary transcendentalist side. It consisted of wildly humorous scherzos — or, perhaps better, "scherzoids" (since they do not always follow the "classical" scherzo-and-trio form) — of a hearty, heavy, unsubtle (and again, one cannot help noticing, Germanic) kind reminiscent of Beethoven. The Ivesian difference was that his scherzoids were usually programmatic, and the programmatic content was almost invariably nostalgic, evoking the composer's idealized, even fictionalized, New England boyhood. Again, nothing could be less modernist than these affectionate pictures of carefree youth in a socially homogeneous and harmonious, preindustrial and pretechnological setting, in which all stylistic excesses were justified in the name of fun, or in that of "realism"—presenting things "just as they [never] were."

Like the American literary realism with which they may so easily be compared, these pictures were projections of what American cultural historians like Richard Hofstadter call the "agrarian myth"[36]—America's own neoprimitivist fable, proclaiming the moral superiority of the unspoiled, abundant country over the polluted, corrupt and disgusting modern city. In these pieces, as Ives's biographer Jan Swafford points out, "Ives painted Danbury as the idyllic country village it had not been since his father's boyhood, if then."[37] Even when not concerned with his Danbury boyhood, Ives's scherzoids were nostalgic and resolutely innocent in their humor, and it was that innocence—that studied naivety—that guaranteed the authenticity of the radical stylistic means. Ives's own description of a piece he may never actually have written—*A Yale-Princeton Game*, sketched (according to the *Memos*) in 1898 and subtitled "Two Minutes in Sound for Two Halfs Within Bounds"—shows this connection, and the implicit guarantee, to have been entirely conscious and deliberate:

> To try to reflect a football game in sounds would cause anybody to try many combinations etc.—for instance, picturing the old wedge play (close formation)—what is more natural than starting with all hugging together in the whole chromatic scale, and gradually pushing together down to one note at the end. The suspense and excitement of spectators—strings going up and down, off and on open-string tremolos. Cheers ("Brek e Koax" [the obscene noise made by the title characters in Aristophanes's comedy *The Frogs*] etc.)—running plays (trumpets going all over, dodging, etc. etc.)—natural and fun to do and listen to—hard to play. But doing things like this (half horsing) would suggest and get one used to technical processes that could be developed in something more serious later, and quite naturally.[38]

A whole worldview (call it "realist" or call it "primitivist") is implied by Ives's obsessive insistence on using the word "natural" to describe musical experiments that ran counter to every learned (or "common") practice and convention. Also implied is the answer to the eternal question that Ives propounded at the very outset of the prologue to his *Essays before a Sonata*:

> How far is anyone justified, be he an authority or a layman, in expressing or trying to express in terms of music (in sounds, if you like) the value of anything, material, moral, intellectual, or spiritual, which is usually expressed in terms other than music?[39]

Whether the thing expressed is as lofty as Emerson's Over-soul or as earthy as a football game, the justification is found precisely in the liberation that it may prompt from the tyranny of common practice.

The most famous and in many ways most characteristic of Ives's "scherzoids" is "Putnam's Camp," the second of his *Three Places in New England*. The place in question is a historic site near the composer's birthplace, a field that served as campgrounds to the troops under the command of Israel Putnam, the Revolutionary War general who was Connecticut's most illustrious military hero. The composition in this case is in a form approximating the traditional scherzo-and-trio (or march-and-trio), in keeping both with the military theme and with the scenario related in Ives's program note:

> Near Redding Center, Conn., is a small park preserved as a Revolutionary Memorial; for here General Israel Putnam's soldiers had their winter quarters in 1778–1779. Long rows of stone camp fire-places still remain to stir a child's imagination. The hardships which the soldiers endured and the agitation of a few hot-heads to break camp and march to the Hartford Assembly for relief, is a part of Redding history.
>
> Once upon a "4th of July," some time ago, so the story goes, a child went there on a picnic, held under the auspices of the First Church and the Village Cornet Band. Wandering away from the rest of the children past the camp ground into the woods, he hopes to catch a glimpse of some of the old soldiers. As he rests on the hillside of laurel and hickories, the tunes of the band and the songs of the children grow fainter and fainter;—when—"mirabile dictu"—over the trees on the crest of the hill he sees a tall woman standing. She reminds him of a picture he has of the Goddess of Liberty,—but the face is sorrowful—she is pleading with the soldiers not to forget their "cause" and the great sacrifices they have made for it. But they march out of camp with fife and drum to a popular tune of the day. Suddenly a new national note is heard. Putnam is coming over the hills from the center,—the soldiers turn back and cheer. The little boy awakes, he hears the children's songs and runs down past the monument to "listen to the band" and join in the games and dances.
>
> The repertoire of national airs at that time was meagre. Most of them were of English origin. It is a curious fact that a tune very popular with the American soldiers was "The British Grenadiers." A captain in one of Putnam's regiments put it to words, which were sung for the first time in 1779 at a patriotic meeting in the Congregational Church in Redding Center; the text is both ardent and interesting.[40]

The last paragraph, evidently, is meant as a testimony to the "authenticity" of Ives's music, for the whole composition could be described, only slightly stretching a point, as a fantasy or takeoff on "The British Grenadiers" (Ex. 5-12). The tune appears almost complete, but (being part of a dream) surrealistically distorted, in the flute (=fife) part at mm. 91–97 (Ex. 5-13a). Its first fragmentary occurrence, also in the flute part (echoed by oboe and clarinet), is at mm. 14–16 (Ex. 5-13b), and it is more or less continuously present (migrating from winds to brass to strings) between m. 126 and m. 155. Thus it is the only tune that appears in all three sections of the piece.

EX. 5-12 March: *The British Grenadiers*

EX. 5-13A   Charles Ives, "Putnam's Camp" (*Three Places in New England*, II), mm. 91 ff.

EX. 5-13B   Charles Ives, "Putnam's Camp" (*Three Places in New England*, II), mm. 14 ff.

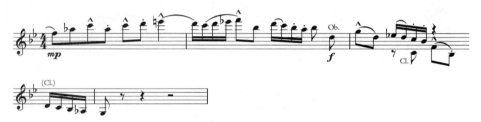

Wherever it pops up, however, it has plenty of company. In the outer sections it mainly accompanies, as a countermelody, the tune of Ives's "Country Band March," an early composition that was largely cannibalized in "Putnam's Camp," but which turns up piecemeal in many of his larger works (including "Hawthorne" in the *Concord Sonata* and the "Comedy" movement of the Fourth Symphony). The concern for period authenticity that led to the use of "The British Grenadiers" did not prevent Ives from quoting anachronistically when he felt like it. Marches by John Philip Sousa (1854–1932) make occasional appearances against the "Country Band March," including a pair in very unequal tandem at m. 27 (Ex. 5-14): the famous "Semper Fidelis" (1888) in the trombone and tuba against "Liberty Bell" (1893) in the first violas (!), where it hardly stands a chance of being heard. At the same time, to complete the collage, a snatch from Stephen Foster's "Massa's in de Cold, Cold Ground" (1852) sounds forth gaily in the flute.

To attempt a full catalog of allusions in "Putnam's Camp" would be fruitless, since some of them are so brief or so altered in the telling as to be ambiguous: is that really the Civil War song "Marchin through Georgia" in the flute at m. 147? Others stick out, as Ives meant them to, like sore thumbs: in mm. 34–35 the trumpet, flute, and first violins collaborate (or try to) in "Yankee Doodle," each instrument entering in a different key. (Here Mozart had anticipated Ives by more than a century but with similar intent in his *Musical Joke*, K. 522 [1787], subtitled "The Village Musicians.") A better joke is the very end of the piece, with the bass instruments starting up "The Star-Spangled Banner," only to be drowned out by the roar of the final chord, topped with a snatch of "Reveille" in the trumpet.

The middle section, or dream sequence, contains one of Ives's most celebrated effects. Most of it is based on another early Ives composition, called *Overture "1776."* The whole-tone (or whole-tone-scale-plus-C-sharp) chord in m. 64 with its appoggiatura — a spot that Swafford very aptly relates to the words *mirabile dictu* (wondrous to relate) in the program — marks the splice between the two early pieces. (The splice back to the "Country Band March" comes at m. 120, and the raucous coda is borrowed once again from *1776.*)

EX. 5-14   Charles Ives, "Putnam's Camp," (*Three Places in New England,* II), mm. 27–30 in full score.

EX. 5-14 (*continued*)

The pleadings of the "Goddess of Liberty" are set off against the threatened mutiny by pitting two groups of instruments against one another at two different tempos (Ex. 5-15). They are calibrated in a proportion of 4:3, so that a half note at the new tempo, articulated by the piano and snare drum together halfway through m. 68, equals a dotted quarter of the *Andante animato* established in m. 65. The relationship of the two speeds is made particularly clear by giving the piano and drum the same familiar parade march rhythm (known as the "street cadence") that the orchestral basses have already been playing at the old tempo, so that the effect is one of two superimposed marches.

Irritated by a critic's remark that the full-orchestra rhythm at m. 124 (Ex. 5-16) had been borrowed from Stravinsky (most likely the "Sacred Dance" from *The Rite of Spring*, which the notation in sixteenth notes offset by rests superficially resembles), Ives went out of his way to explain his technical procedure, somewhat elliptically, in

EX. 5-15   Charles Ives, "Putnam's Camp," (*Three Places in New England*, II), fig. $\boxed{\text{H}}$

EX. 5-15   (*continued*)

the *Memos*. In reality, he points out, the measure simply brings back the rhythm of the faster group from the middle section (he calls it the "piano-drum part"), notated in terms of the prevailing beat—an effect that looks strange on paper, owing to the unusual subdivision of the beat, but that is easily performed:

> The two rhythms going together (in the piano-drum part) are nothing but a beat or pulse on the first of four 16th-notes, and one on the first of three 16th-notes. Say, if a band is marching at 120 = ♩ = ♪♪♪♪, the next fastest marching (keeping

EX. 5-16   Charles Ives, "Putnam's Camp," (*Three Places in New England*, II), 2 before fig. N

the ♪ insert spot unit the same) will be stepping to three 16ths or [figure], and if two bands feel like marching on these accents,

one is: [musical notation]
the other: [musical notation]

Then, for three 4/4 measures, if the top band stops playing, the second one is playing off-accents. In the third measure, it is simply:

[musical notation]
 1   2   3   4

It will be the measure cited above [m. 124]. It doesn't take much musical intelligence to see that (or to do that, for that matter). In putting these two rhythms together, the 16th-notes don't have to be struck all the while. They will be played in various phrases, omitted in others. The more they are in, the more variants will occur, etc. I'll bet 1000 people have thought of this, perhaps played this — yet, because they don't know what it is, they say it is meaningless [when they see it], or influenced by Orcus from Australia [i.e., Stravinsky]![41]

This passage from the *Memos*, with its reference to two hypothetical bands, may have been the source of one of the most durable of all Ivesian legends. The version that follows is from *Charles Ives and His Music* (1955), by the husband-and-wife team of Henry and Sidney Cowell, the first book-length study of the composer. "The germ," the Cowells wrote,

> of Ives's complicated concept of polyphony seems to lie in an experience he had as a boy, when his father invited a neighboring band to parade with its team at a baseball game in Danbury, while at the same time the local band made its appearance in support of the Danbury team. The parade was arranged to pass along the main street as usual, but the two bands started at opposite ends of town and were assigned pieces in different meters and keys. As they approached each other the dissonances were acute, and each man played louder and louder so that his rivals would not put him off. A few players wavered, but both bands held together and got past each other successfully, the sounds of their cheerful discord fading out in the distance. Ives has reproduced this collision of musical events in several ways: From it, for example, he developed the idea of combining groups of players (sections of the orchestra) to create simultaneous masses of sound that move in different rhythms, meters, and keys. Thus his polytonality may be polyharmonic, each harmonic unit being treated like a single contrapuntal voice (as the bands played two separate tunes, each with its own harmonic setting); and it may also be polyrhythmic.[42]

Whether it originated with the composer or it was mere biographical embroidery, and despite its having been canonized by decades of repetition, this famous anecdote is pretty obviously a tall tale, concocted for the same reason that prompted Ives to assure a sympathetic critic that his radical ways "came not only from folk music he was brought up with but to a very great extent from the life 'around & in him.'"[43] For a progressive and a populist like Ives, his strange music would be unacceptably esoteric and "elite" were it not validated by his everyday experience, of which it formed a nostalgic record. It was this conviction that impelled Ives to incorporate so much of the ambient music of America — a music that included hymns and ragtime, but also Bach and Wagner — into his most maximalistic works. Life was his subject, and America was his life. Once again, obsession with technical novelty — "modernism" — had little to do with it.

And neither did "nationalism," as the term is often understood musically. Ives went out of his way to make this clear in the *Essays before a Sonata*, where he condemned the mere "stylistic" cultivation of local or vernacular color as a typical "over-influence by and over-insistence upon manner"[44] — the very bane of modern music. He reacted angrily to one H. K. Moderwell, who had written of ragtime in a magazine article that it was "the perfect expression of the American city," where "you feel in its jerk and rattle a personality different from that of any European capital," making it "the one true American music." Ives, who helped himself abundantly to both real and imitation ragtime in many of his scherzoids, countered that no music could be so described. Ragtime, he asserted, "is one of the many true, natural, and, nowadays, conventional means of expression." It had, he allowed, "its possibilities; but it does not 'represent the American nation' any more than some fine old senators represent it."

REACHING—AND TRANSCENDING—THE LIMIT

Like most romantics in the tacitly (or passively) German tradition, Ives believed that the highest musical expression transcended all particulars, but that particulars could be an avenue toward that transcendence. The quest for universal transcendence was, for Ives, as effective a spur to stylistic maximalism as the race to the patent office was for others. So it comes as no surprise that Ives's most maximalistic conception was also his most transcendent: nothing short of a "Universe in Tones."

Between 1911 and 1915, Ives accumulated sketches for a symphony with that ambitious name, inspired by the elation he had felt one autumn day while looking out over Keene Valley in the Adirondacks. It would be "a striving," as he put it in the margins of one of the sketch pages, trying desperately to capture his ineffable conception in words,

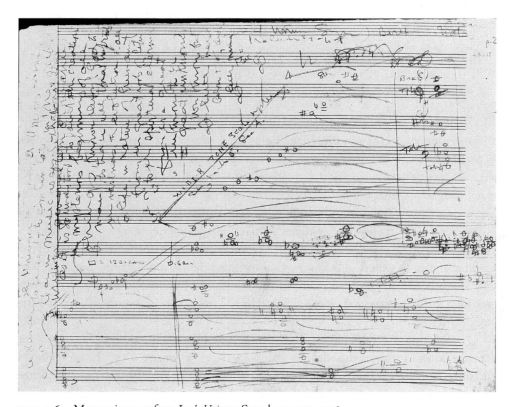

FIG. 5-6   Manuscript page from Ives's *Universe* Symphony, 1911–1916.

to present and to contemplate in tones rather than in music as such, that is — not exactly written in the general term or meaning as it is so understood — to paint the creation, the mysterious beginnings of all things, known through God to man, to trace with tonal imprints the vastness, the evolution of all life, in nature of humanity, from the great roots of life to the spiritual eternities, from the great unknown to the great unknown.[45]

He never came close to finishing it. All that remained of the project at the time of his death forty years later was a sheaf of verbal descriptions, plans, jottings of chords, scales, rhythms, occasional themelets, but little clue as to continuity. Stuart Feder, Ives's psychobiographer, has suggested that the work was never meant to be completed — that its conceptual grandiosity was a compensation for the composer's waning powers of invention. In 1932, aged fifty-eight but creatively enfeebled, Ives dashed off a poignant memo in which he tried to describe the progress he had made and the work that still remained to do, so that "in case I don't get to finishing this, somebody might like to try to work out the idea, and the sketch that I've already done would make more sense to anybody looking at it with this explanation."[46]

At least two performing versions of Ives's "Universe" (or *Universe Symphony*) have been made by posthumous accomplices (Larry Austin and Johnny Reinhard, both of them composers), much as the "Prefatory Act" to Scriabin's *Mysterium*, described in the previous chapter, has been speculatively "completed" by the Russian composer Alexander Nemtin. But given the state of the materials Ives left behind, these arrangements cannot really be called completions or realizations. Ives's "Universe" is only a concept. But what a concept! According to the *Memos*, it was to be literally the Story of Everything — or, in Emersonian terms, the revelation of THE ONE. There would be three orchestras, the first consisting of nothing but percussion and representing "the pulse of the universe's life beat." The other two would divide the remaining instruments into high and low groups. And there would be three overlapping movements, to be played without pause or significant variation in tempo: "I. (Past) Formation of the waters and mountains. II. (Present) Earth, evolution in nature and humanity. III. (Future) Heaven, the rise of all to the spiritual."

This does indeed resonate with Scriabin's *Mysterium* — and with a whole antecedent line of European symphonic transcendentalism: the line of "Weltanschauungsmusik" that began with the "Representation of Chaos" at the beginning of Haydn's *Creation*, reached successive milestones with Beethoven's Ninth, Wagner's *Ring*, and Mahler's "Song of the Earth" (completed just as Ives was starting his "Universe" sketches), and culminated in the "maximal maximalism" of Scriabin, and now Ives. As if in uncanny sympathy with the Russian composer's final project (of which he could have known nothing), Ives reached tonal saturation with aggregate chords that marked, for harmonic maximalism, the end of the line.

But the uncanniness is only seeming: both Scriabin's project and Ives's were epitomes of mystical philosophies (in Ives's case Emersonian, in Scriabin's theosophical). For both of them the aggregate harmony logically symbolized "epitome" itself. Ives's aggregate chord, built up from low C in the sketch depicted in Fig. 5-6, superimposes perfect fourths and tritones — or, in other words, extends to exhaustion the process of which Stravinsky's three-note *Rite*-chord (as defined in chapter 3) was the beginning.

Since a tritone equals a perfect fourth plus a semitone, the series amounts to a circle of fourths (=fifths) alternating (or added to) a "circle of semitones" (=the chromatic scale), synthesizing the two intervallic circles that exhaust the full chromatic spectrum, producing (after Scriabin's) a second philosophy-driven saturation of musical space. Significantly enough, Ives had previously used the same all-encompassing alternation of fourths (or fifths) and tritones in the outer voices of his Psalm 24 ("The Earth is the Lord's"), possibly composed as early as 1894, to express the earth's "fullness". But what marked the unexceedable limit for Scriabin prompted a new fundamental departure in Ives, who thus showed himself to be, of the two, the more committed maximalist. It set him off in pursuit of *microtones*.

Usually, though by Ivesian standards overnarrowly, microtones are defined as pitch differences smaller than a semitone, the interval that has functioned in official music theory since the days of the Franks and their "Gregorian" chant, at the dawn of recorded musical history in the West, as the inviolable musical atom, the smallest pitch discrimination that is treated as meaningful in ordinary musical discourse. Once the twelve-tone, equal-tempered chromatic scale had become the standard, the commonest way of conceptually splitting this atom was to imagine it divided evenly by two, into "quarter tones." One of the earliest experimenters in quarter tones, Ives claimed, was none other than his father George, who (according to an unconfirmable and perhaps apocryphal account in the *Memos*) rigged up various microtonal contraptions — one of them a box of violin strings with weights attached — to overcome the limitations of arbitrary theory and "enjoy an original relation to the universe," as Emerson put it in his essay on self-reliance.

As Ives observed, we hear microtones whenever we listen to "nonmusical" sounds, for they exist in unlimited unordered profusion in the untheorized world of nature. A music that incorporated microtones would thus be, in the pantheistic transcendentalist view, a more natural and "universal" music than one circumscribed by stingy official theory. Only such a music would truly give access to the transcendental greening experience at which all of Ives's music ultimately aimed. Thus, Ives's "Universe in Tones" would of necessity unfold through a chorus of transcendentally unified microtonal tunings:

> some perfectly tuned correct scales, some well-tempered little scales, a scale of overtones with the divisions as near as determinable by acousticon [an imaginary measuring device], scales of smaller division than a semitone, scales of uneven division greater than a whole tone, scales with no octave for several octaves,[47]

as he put it in his somewhat bewildering memo of 1932. But all of these scales would be tuned to the same fundamental pitch, the A at the rock bottom of the piano keyboard, which would thus assume the holy Emersonian status of THE ONE.

Missing, of course, was any description of the technical means by which these state-of-nature scales would be produced, for such means did not exist in 1932, which is another reason to accept Feder's idea that the *Universe Symphony* was never meant to be realized in performance but rather to exist only as a work of inspiring "conceptual art." Whether he knew it or not, Ives was placing himself in a long tradition of speculative musical thought, one that might even be characterized as Western music's oldest and most distinguished maximalistic strain.

The earliest "microtonalist" in the modern history of Western art music was Nicola Vicentino (1511–ca. 1576), the Italian humanist musician who invented a keyboard instrument, the *arcigravicembalo*, with a 53-tone scale that could reproduce the pitches of the "enharmonic genus" described by various ancient Greek theorists. The purpose of the invention was to reproduce the miraculous effects of *ethos* (emotional and moral influence) that ancient Greek texts attributed to the music of the time.

Ever since the sixteenth century, there have been musicians dedicated to "just intonation"—natural tunings thought to be more capable of producing true emotional catharsis than the corrupted temperaments of modern music, which were invented to satisfy "merely musical" criteria of beauty. In the seventeenth century their ranks included the Dutch scientist and musical amateur Christiaan Huygens (1629–95), who theorized a 31-tone octave; in the eighteenth the French acoustician Joseph Sauveur (1653–1716), who published the first theoretical account of the overtone series (the harmonies of natural resonance) in 1701; and in the nineteenth the English organist Robert Holford Macdowall Bosanquet (1841–1912), who in 1875 built a harmonium tuned according to Vicentino's specifications. The leading speculative theorist along these lines in the twentieth century was Joseph Yasser (1893–1981), a Russian-American organist and scholar who proposed a division of the octave into nineteen equal intervals.

New composition according to just-intonation principles had to await the advent of twentieth-century maximalism. Just intonation's most distinctive twentieth-century exponent was Harry Partch (1901–74), a "neohumanistic" musical dramatist whose adaptations of Greek myths were accompanied by a large instrumentarium of his own invention, tuned to a 43-interval octave. He once described himself rather acerbically as a "musician seduced into carpentry,"[48] and in so doing pinpointed the gravest problem experimenters with nonstandard tunings have always faced: that of practical hardware. Nevertheless, the just-intonation line lasted throughout the twentieth century, pursued by Eivind Groven (1901–77) in Norway, and by Ben Johnston (b. 1926) and La Monte Young (b. 1935) in the United States, among others.

The omnivorous microtonal apparatus Ives envisaged for his "Universe in Tones" seems to incorporate just-intonation components along with everything else imaginable. But in terms of practical composition, Ives belonged to the other microtonal "school," the one that split the intervals of the artificially equal-tempered chromatic scale into smaller, equally "artificial" (because equal-tempered) units. It lacked the ancient pedigree and the "greening" impulse, and can be understood only in terms of contemporary maximalism, the late-late-romantic drive to expand the expressive—or just the technical—resources at a composer's disposal.

Its pre-Ivesian history was very short. Probably the earliest experimenter in the field was Julián Carrillo (1875–1965), a Mexican composer who around 1895 began research into what he called the "sonido trece" (thirteenth sound) system, involving successive splits of the semitone into quarters, eighths, and sixteenths of a tone. His first practical compositions using the system did not appear until 1922, after he had found solutions to the many attendant problems of notation and instrument-construction.

In 1906, Ferruccio Busoni (1866–1924), a very famous Italian pianist and composer living in Germany, published a pamphlet, *Entwurf einer neuen Ästhetik der Tonkunst*, ("Sketch for a New Esthetic of Music"), in which he theorized the possibility of something really new: music based on a tripartite rather than a binary division of the tone (third-tones rather than semitones). He made no move at all toward implementation. The first composers to do so were the exact contemporaries Alois Hába (1893–1973), a Czech, and Ivan Wyschnegradsky (1893–1979), a Russian émigré living in Paris, both of whom experimented with sixth- and twelfth-tones that would permit the combination of Busoni's third tones with Carrillo's quarter tones. Like Carrillo, they began publishing their work in the 1920s.

Thus Ives's *Three Quarter-Tone Pieces* for two pianos tuned a quarter tone apart may be viewed with seemingly equal justice as Ives's ultimate nostalgic tribute to his father and to the homespun Yankee-tinker esthetic he loved to affect, or as the one time Ives was acting as a full-fledged member of the current avant-garde, contributing to what was at the time a modest high-tech vogue. Although based to some typically indeterminable extent on old sketches, the pieces were among Ives's latest. They were composed or completed in 1923–24 at the instigation of E. Robert Schmitz (1889–1949), a French-American pianist who ran a concert organization called the Franco-American Musical Society, which sponsored a New York performance of the second and third pieces in February 1925. Except for a single performance of a violin sonata the year before, this was Ives's first noteworthy public hearing since *The Celestial Country* in 1902.

ACCEPTING BOUNDARIES

And yet these pieces, while technically (or at least technologically) "advanced," were not composed in anything like an avant-garde spirit. Nowhere is there the sense, manifest in both the writings and the compositions of Hába or Carrillo, of reinventing music theory and performing practice from the ground up. There is no impulse to cast out the common practice or to replace it. Rather, there is a sense, in the outer movements, of expressively extending the common practice, and, in the "scherzoid" middle movement, of parodying it.

While Ives's solution to the hardware problem was eminently practical in that (unlike the work of all the composers named in the foregoing background sketch) it did not require the invention of any new instruments, there was one utopian feature that has been modified whenever the pieces have been publicly performed. The score presupposes that the first piano is tuned a quarter-tone sharp. Since no reputable piano tuner will agree to put so much extra stress on the instrument's mechanism, in practice the second piano is tuned flat.

As to the esthetic or perceptual problems that attend the use of microtones, there is not only the evidence of the score, but also an article that Ives wrote for Schmitz's house organ, the *Franco-American Music Society Bulletin* in the issue of 25 March 1925, which appeared shortly after the partial premiere of his pieces. In it, Ives starts right out by disavowing the sort of radical individualism associated with modernism, in favor of a socially mediated or "communitarian" esthetic that was more in keeping with New England idealist thinking associated not only with Emerson but also with Wendell Phillips (1811–84), a leading Bostonian abolitionist and social reformer whom Ives quotes. "To go to extremes in anything," Ives wrote with pointed irony,

> is an old-fashioned habit growing more and more useless as more and more premises of truth come before man, though to hold that music is built on unmovable, definitely known laws of tone which rule so as to limit music in all of its manifestations is better — but not much — than brushing everything aside except ecstatic ebullitions and a cigarette. Instead, why not go with Wendell Phillips (who won't join a radical party or a conservative one) and assume that "everybody knows more than anybody."[49]

Next Ives cites the standard treatise on acoustics (*On the Sensations of Tone* [*Die Lehre von den Tonempfindungen*], 1877) by Hermann Ludwig Ferdinand von Helmholtz (1821–94), in which the great German physicist tried to give equal recognition to both the physical (natural) and social sources of musical theory and practice: "*The system of scales, modes, and harmonic tissues,*" Ives quotes (italicizing every word for emphasis),

> *does not rest solely upon unalterable natural laws, but is at least partly also the result of aesthetical principles, which have already changed, and will still further change, with the progressive development of humanity.*

The prospect facing all who would enlarge the practice of music along microtonal lines, Ives implies, is to find a truly meaningful basis for it that neither claims the spurious authority of nature nor relies wholly on the spirit of arbitrary arrogant innovation, but that seeks to forge a new consensus between composer and listener.

The task, then, is "the assimilation of quarter-tones with what we have now."[50] The method Ives proposes is one he claims to have adopted from his father, who "after working for some time became sure that some quarter-tone chords must be learned before quarter-tone melodies would make much sense and become natural to the ear, and so for the voice." There follows the only technical discussion of Ivesian harmony the composer ever furnished; and inasmuch as it is corroborated by the score, it is worth quoting as a gauge of his intentions.

> Chords of four or more notes, as I hear it, seem to be a more natural basis than triads. A triad using quarter-tones, it seems to me, leans toward the sound or sounds that the diatonic ear expects after hearing the notes which must form some diatonic interval, say the fifth C–G. Thus the third note, a tone halfway between E and D sharp, enters as a kind of weak compromise to the sound expected — in other words, a chord out of tune. While if another note is added which will make a quarter-tone interval with either of the two notes, C–G, which make the diatonic interval, we have a balanced chord which, if listened to without prejudice, leans neither way, and which seems to establish an identity of its own.[51]

After acknowledging the necessity of retaining perfect octaves and fifths even in quarter-tone music (for they are "such unrelenting masters in the realm of the physical nature of sounds"), Ives proceeds to some practical examples. Imagining a piano with two keyboards, like a harpsichord, in which the upper one is tuned a quarter tone sharp, Ives starts out with the "out of tune triad" he had considered and rejected as a basis, and then suggests the addition of an "upper" A sharp. "If listened to several times in succession," the resulting chord

> gathers a kind of character of its own — neither major, minor, nor even diminished. A chord of these intervals, it seems to me, may form a satisfactory and reasonable basis for a fundamental chord. It has two perfect fifths, three major thirds a quarter-tone flat, with an augmented second a quarter-tone flat completing the octave. It gives a feeling of finality and supports reasonably well a simple quarter-tone melody. By quarter-tone melody I mean a succession of notes fairly evenly divided between notes in both pianos or keyboards. If the diatonic notes [that is, the normally-tuned ones on the lower keyboard] are taken as a general basis for a melody, using the quarter-tones only as passing notes, suspensions, etc., the result is not difficult for the ear to get.

The chord just described, together with the kind of melody that is proposed (or supposed) to go with it, make up the basic or "normative" material of the first of Ives's *Three Pieces*. It first appears in m. 18 (Ex. 5-17a), exactly as Ives described it in his article (except that the sharps have been respelled as flats). This primary quarter-tone consonance retains the perfect intervals of conventional tonal practice, and substitutes for the imperfect consonances tones that exactly split the difference between their major and minor variants. The way the E♭–B♭ fifth in the first piano alternates with a D–A fifth suggests, moreover, that Ives was seeking within the quarter-tone domain for an equivalent to the major-minor opposition: an alternation between thirds and sevenths a quarter tone greater than minor ones and thirds and sevenths a quarter tone less. The dotted lines connecting notes between the parts in mm. 26–28 identify the notes in piano I as "using the quarter-tones as passing notes," according to the prescription for intelligibility formulated in the article.

EX. 5-17A   Charles Ives, *Three Quarter-Tone Pieces*, first piece, mm. 18–28

EX. 5-17A *(continued)*

The second movement is despite the unusual circumstances a typically nostalgic scherzoid replete with hymn-tune reminiscences ("Bringing in the Sheaves" among others), but more consistently in ragtime style, the quarter tones here parodying the sort of piano — in bars or "houses of ill repute" — on which ragtime was often, if not usually, played. The "normative consonance" makes a triumphant appearance to harmonize what sounds like a snatch from "The Battle Cry of Freedom." The funny (or fun-filled) aspect of the piece extends to its inordinate difficulty of execution, the pianists being required to execute quick "chromatic" runs of quarter tones that amount in practice to almost impractically rapid hockets (Ex. 5-17b).

EX. 5-17B   Charles Ives, *Three Quarter-Tone Pieces*, second piece, mm. 53–56

According to the *Memos*, the third piece was a reworking of an old quarter-tone "chorale" for strings that the composer variously dated 1903–1914 or 1913–1914 in different work lists. The earlier dating may have been one of those backdated bids for patent-office priority that have bedeviled Ives scholarship, for there is good internal evidence that the piece was written at least during, and probably after, the Great War. The chorale as such occupies only the first three systems, and consists mainly of showing ways in which the "normative consonance" (this time spelled the way it is described in the *Memos*) may be quitted and approached with smooth quarter-tone voice leading. The final phrase experiments with the application of a dominant to the quarter-tone

EX. 5-17C   Charles Ives, *Three Quarter-Tone Pieces*, third piece, end

tonic, but it is not clear how seriously: the effect may be read as a parody of wheezy church harmoniums to complement the preceding barroom piano.

Beginning in m. 16, chorale gives way to passacaglia over a quarter-tone adaptation of the ancient *passus duriusculus*, or chromatic descent from the tonic to the lower fifth. What will prove to be the main theme of the piece begins hazily to emerge in triplets. The final page (Ex. 5-17c) is peroration: the theme returns in quarter tones, signaled by the dotted lines connecting the melody notes; at the pickup to m. 53 the theme begins again, now confined to the second piano and proceeding in semitones, only to begin yet again at the pickup to m. 55 in its original diatonic form, by which time all listeners will presumably have recognized it as "America" ("My country, 'tis of thee"). At the culminating point (m. 56), the American hymn is trumped by the climactic line ("Aux armes, citoyens!") from "La Marseillaise", the French national anthem. The linkage of the two may have been no more than a graceful nod to Schmitz's Franco-American Music Society. But the effect is serious, even moving, and the intended significance may have been greater. The same juxtaposition of national hymns is found at the climax of one of Ives's most fervent songs, an April 1917 setting of John McCrae's famous poem "In Flanders Fields," a tribute to the Allied war dead—not a subject about which Ives was inclined to joke (Ex. 5-18). The ending of the Third Quarter-Tone Piece may have been intended, and can certainly be read, as a transcendental moment to transform (and perhaps embarrass) the irreverent humor that preceded it—another instance of timeless elevated substance channeled or transmuted through a new manner.

EX. 5-18   Charles Ives, *In Flanders Fields*, end

The visionary aspect of Ives's maximalism is the crucial one. It both impelled his radicalism and limited it, lest manner impede substance. Conceived as a medium of vital transcendental communication, Ives's maximalism sought maximum compromise with the common practice—or rather, with the expectable expectations of listeners. He sought extension, rather than replacement, of the commonly accepted norms and aims of music, and his utopianism was tempered by acceptance of natural constraints, whether "physical" or "human."

Ives appealed to physical nature when, imagining a possible "fundamental chord" consisting of C and E on his lower keyboard vs. G and A♯B♭ on the upper, he finally rejected it on acoustical grounds: It "has no fifth—that inexorable thing—a part of the natural laws which apparently no aesthetic principle has yet beaten out."[52] The best Ives could offer on behalf of such a chord was the hope that "some day, perhaps, an Edison, a Dempsey, or an Einstein will or will not suppress [the supremacy of the fifth] with a blow from a new natural law." But, he implies, that day is not today.

As to human nature, he appeals both to "natural" conservatism and to what a European would probably call typically American pragmatism when he comments that, "quarter-tones or no quarter-tones, why tonality as such should be thrown out for good I can't see," although, he is quick to add, "why it should be always present, I can't see."[53] The matter is to be adjudicated not by appeals to history or trips to the patent office, but "on what one is trying to do, and on the state of mind, the time of day or other accidents of life."

Ironically enough, Ives's caution—or his emphasis on the easily apprehended "substance" of the music rather than on its peculiar manner—actually stood in the way of reception at the 1925 premiere. Olin Downes, then just starting what would be a thirty-year tenure as chief music critic of the *New York Times*, dismissed the quarter-tone pieces by "Charles St. Ives" (as he carelessly transcribed the name from his program) as "having been thought in the customary tonal and semi-tonal [?] medium," so that "the result was simply that the music sounded a good deal out of tune."[54] The critic claimed to be receptive to microtonality, but only provided the music "had a quality far more native to small divisions of tones than those heard last night."

MORE PATENT-OFFICE MODERNISM

Such a music was Julián Carrillo's. Compared with Ives's apparent caution, his stance with regard to microtonality was uncompromising indeed. It required an enormous investment in hardware, a new system of notation, and the pitiless sacrifice of the common practice toward which Ives showed such solicitude. It was the stance of true modernism, against which Ives's more moderate posture can be viewed in relief.

Carrillo's best known composition is the *Preludio a Colón* ("Prelude to Columbus"). It was composed in 1922, published (in 1944) in Henry Cowell's *New Music Quarterly*, which had already served as showcase for Ives's most radical music, and was even recorded in the 1940s by an ensemble called the Ensemble of the 13th Tone in Havana. It is scored for a chamber sextet consisting of a flute that has been adapted to produce quarter tones; a violin that (or rather a violinist who) is asked to play in quarter tones;

a soprano who is asked to sing them (wordlessly); a harp that mainly plays pedal glissandos, some of them microtonal; a guitar with frets adapted to produce quarter tones; and an *octavina* (or *guitarrón*), a large bass guitar mainly used in Mexican urban popular music (*mariachi*) ensembles, with a long fingerboard fitted with frets that can produce eighth tones.

The very first sentence of Carrillo's preface to the published score proclaims his music's claim to fame: "This 'Preludio a Colón' is the first composition in the world written in 16th tones." He proceeds immediately to an explanation of the notation, which substitutes numbers for the conventional notes on a staff, since the latter cannot show intervals smaller than the semitone (and is in any case designed with diatonic modes in mind). By letting zero equal C and dividing the tone by sixteen, it is possible to fix any pitch down to the sixteenth part of a tone. If C is zero, then D is 16 (0 + 16), and E (the tonic pitch of the *Preludio*) is 32 (0 + 16 + 16). Continuing by whole tones, F♯ will be 48 (32 + 16), F natural will be 40 (32 + 8 or 48 − 8), the quarter tone between E and F will be 36 (32 + 4 or 40 − 4), and the eighth tones on either side of the quarter tone will be 34 and 38. In other words, increments of 2 represent eighth tones, increments of 4 represent quarter tones, and so on. (Although the proud first sentence advertises sixteenth tones, they are apparently only theoretically available; pitch increments by 1 do not occur in the score.)

Why do the musical results seem so trivial? One could answer, Ivesianly, that the manner has utterly swamped the substance; but that presumptuously presupposes knowledge of the purported substance. Or one might notice how often the melodic lines are confined to ascending and descending scales and arpeggios. Having replaced a familiar musical idiom with an exotic one, avoiding compromise with common practice yet (apparently) unwilling to impose any arbitrary constraint on the novel material, the composer (evidently) contents himself with displaying its properties, affording the audience what amounts to an extended ear-training session.

Thus the piece opens (Ex. 5-19) with the octavina demonstrating a scale of eighth tones that (it seems) deliberately falls one-eighth short of a semitone, then proceeds to a demonstration by the violin of descending scale of quarter tones decorated with neighbors. Next, the guitar and octavina demonstrate an ascending and descending scale (or is it an arpeggio?) that proceeds by increments of 20, producing intervals of $\frac{5}{4}$ tone. Much later in the piece (16 measures from the end), the same pair of instruments performs a scale that proceeds by increments of 12, producing intervals of $\frac{3}{4}$ tone. This would seem to have interesting possibilities, since the interval in question is half of a minor third, which is half of a tritone, which is half of an octave. The resulting scale, which divides the octave into eight equal intervals, might be described as "equal-tempered octatonic," a term that resonates with a lot of the French and Russian music written over the preceding several decades.

Nothing is done with it, however, except to repeat it a few bars later with doublings at the major and minor third. Seven bars before the end, the flute and guitar play scales in contrary motion that alternate increments of 20 and 12; that is, they proceed by alternating the two unusual intervals ($\frac{5}{4}$ tone and $\frac{3}{4}$ tone) within an unequally divided

EX. 5-19   Julián Carrillo, *Preludio a Colón*

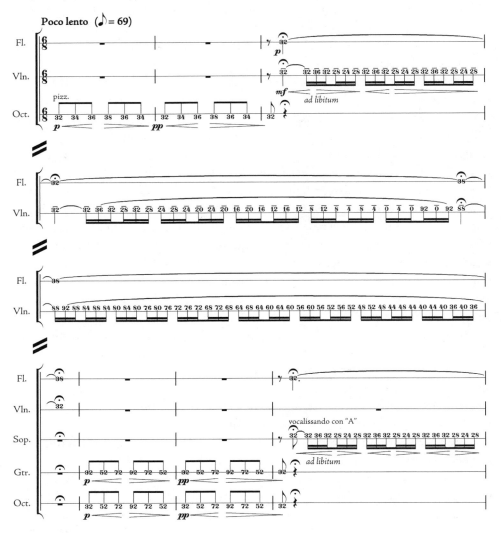

major third. Carrillo seems to be feeling his way toward a new harmonic idiom, and taking his listeners with him step by step. But the composition as such, like a great deal of modernist or maximalist music that lacks (or shuns) a clear imaginal or expressive content, seems to devolve into a technical exercise, of interest only to the extent that the hearer is interested in the technique being exercised.

The situation obviously recalls Ortega y Gasset's description, quoted in chapter 2, of modernist art as "art for artists." One wonders whether the composer would have regarded as valid the benevolently intended reaction of one critic, reviewing the recording of the piece, who praised it not as a composition but as a collection of "weird and intriguing sounds, not unlike those one hears from insect life in a field on a hot summer afternoon."[55] One suspects, rather, that the composer would have regarded as valid only a critique of his music that addressed its technical premises. It would be difficult to imagine an attitude toward musical innovation further removed from that of Ives. But if Carrillo's *Preludio a Colón* is the first unequivocal instance of Ortega's "art for artists" that we have encountered, it will surely not be the last.

TRANSCENDENTALISM VS. FUTURISM

Partly in connection with Henry Cowell and his *New Music Quarterly*, a recognizable school of American maximalists or "ultramoderns" — Carl Ruggles (1876–1971), Wallingford Riegger (1885–1961), John J. Becker (1886–1961), Dane Rudhyar (1895–1985), Ruth Crawford (or Ruth Crawford Seeger, 1901–1953), and Cowell himself — briefly came into view, seemingly ranged around Ives. If Ives seemed to dominate the

FIG. 5-7A Ruth Crawford Seeger (photograph by Fernand de Gueldre).

group in terms of publications, it was partly because he was bankrolling the venture with his business fortune and Cowell was showing his gratitude. Nevertheless, the school was a coherent one. Its members shared both a technical orientation and an expressive purpose, which like Ives's own may be jointly summed up as transcendental maximalism. All, that is, employed radical means toward spiritual ends.

Two of the group, Rudhyar and Crawford, were like Scriabin drawn to theosophy, and used their music to convey its occult concepts. Rudhyar (or Daniel Chennevière, as he was known in his native France before he emigrated to America in 1916), was a practicing astrologer. Crawford, the piano pupil of Djane Lavoie Herz (1888–1982), a Scriabin disciple who had known the Russian composer in Brussels at the height of his involvement with theosophy,

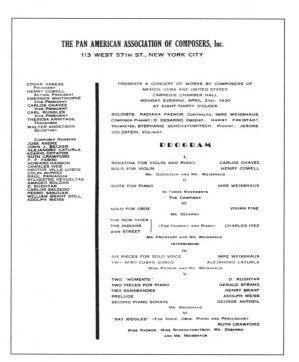

FIG. 5-7B Program for a concert of the Pan American Association of Composers, 21 April 1930.

was described at the beginning of her career as a member of "the Rudhyar-Scriabine faction."[56] In 1928 Cowell published a set of preludes by Crawford in the *New Music Quarterly*. The sixth, composed in 1927, is marked *Andante mystico* and dedicated "with deep love and gratitude to Djane, my inspiration." The impulse to aggregate-completion, the ever-present sign of spiritualist maximalism, is especially clear in this piece: the two-measure right-hand ostinato presents nine (out of twelve) pitch classes, and the root and fifth of the F♯ minor triad arpeggiated in the left hand supply the tenth and eleventh tones. The remaining pitch class, D, is saved for the ninth measure, when the bass note shifts to G, to provide the crowning touch (Ex. 5-20).

The unusual pedaling, deploying all three pedals so that the sostenuto pedal sustains the sound whenever the damper pedal is cleared, insures that the twelve-tone aggregate, or something close to it, is maintained as a resonance throughout. This effort

EX. 5-20   Ruth Crawford, Prelude no. 6 (Andante mystico), beginning

EX. 5-20   *(continued)*

*Accidentals affect only individual notes before which they occur.

to sustain the aggregate sonority apparently follows a precept of Rudhyar's that finally makes explicit what we have long observed to be an implicit maximalist principle linking musical practice with the transcendentalist or theosophical conception of "the ONE." This link is precisely what Rudhyar intends by the strange term "syntonistic," when writing that

> whereas in the classical tonal music, each distinct harmony had to keep its resonance separate, in this "syntonistic" music there is in theory but one harmony, that of the whole body of Sound or of Nature, and therefore chords must be made usually to blend their resonances.[57]

Although she never experimented with microtonality as a composer, some of Crawford's letters describe her enthusiasm on hearing Carrillo's work, which she found "very fascinating and moving," and (possibly owing to her theosophical predilections) likened to something "extremely oriental, Hindu in effect."[58]

Ruggles also made aggregate-completion an explicit basis of his composing practice. The best-known example is the opening theme from the orchestral fantasia *Sun-treader*, published by Cowell in 1934, Ruggles's largest work (its astrally elated title borrowed, like much in Ives, from the poetry of Robert Browning). The theme (Ex. 5-21) consists of two widely arching phrases separated by a sixteenth rest. The first presents all the pitch classes except C♯/D♭ (with the opening A♭–A climactically repeated in reverse), and the second presents all but B, with D♭, the pitch withheld from the first phrase, now forming the very pinnacle of the melodic arc. The brackets display the many embeddings (or "imbrications," to use current music-theory language) of the tritone-plus-fourth motif we have already noted several times as endemic to maximalistic music in many countries. Like Ives in the *Universe* (and Stravinsky in *The Rite*, as well as several other composers we will be meeting shortly), Ruggles used it as a basic constructive element.

As for Cowell himself, his earliest (and most radical) music was written for performance at the Temple of the People, a theosophical colony, which the young composer joined in 1916, located in Halcyon, a California coastal town somewhat to the north of Santa Barbara. The community patriarch, John Varian, installed a giant harp in his home to represent the mythical harp of life on which the Celtic gods had played.

EX. 5-21   Carl Ruggles, *Sun-treader*, opening theme

FIG. 5-8   Henry Cowell.

The notion of that cosmic music, and the Irish myths that Varian retold in his poems, inspired in Cowell, the precocious son of an Irish immigrant, the work that made his early fame.

Cowell took a more direct approach to aggregates, producing them by laying palms, fists, and forearms on the piano keyboard. The results, called "elbow music"[59] by detractors, and "concordances of many close-lying notes" or "secundal harmonies" by their more pretentious admirers, became celebrated as "tone clusters," the term Cowell devised for them in 1921. The playing technique as such, which Cowell probably discovered the way countless other children discover it, went perhaps a decade further back. Cowell notated it for the first time in *Adventures in Harmony*, a "novelette" for piano written (or written down) in 1913, when the composer was fifteen or sixteen, at the request of his piano teacher, who was a devoted member of the Halcyon temple.

The first piece Cowell composed after he joined the temple himself was *The Tides of Manaunaun*, first played in the summer of 1917 as part of the music to accompany a Halcyon pageant called *The Building of Banba*, a dramatization of the Irish creation myth. The "story according to John Varian," printed above the music when it was published in 1922, recounts that

> Manaunaun was the god of motion, and long before the creation, he sent forth tremendous tides, which swept to and fro through the universe, and rhythmically moved the particles and materials of which the gods were later to make the suns and worlds.

The music consists of a jiglike tune in the natural minor mode (hence identifiably "Irish"), accompanied by forearm clusters spanning two octaves.

The split-level effect, one hand confined to traditional modes and scales, the other to clusters, was dictated by the motivating poetic idea, which Cowell and Varian represented in many variants. Another Halcyon tone-cluster piece, *Voice of Lir*, portrayed the father of the gods, whose commands for creating the universe were only half understood since he had only half a tongue. Therefore, according to Varian's legend, "for everything that has been created there is an unexpressed and concealed counterpart." This simple dichotomy between the precisely formed and the inchoate was a "natural" for depiction in the usual Cowellesque way, playing simple folk tunes against clusters. Cowell's apparent nonchalance with regard to stylistic discrepancy, and his indifference to (or at least his unironic acceptance of) the seeming mélange of "advanced" and "regressive" techniques, is another indication, like those we have encountered in Ives, that maximalism (especially, perhaps, when practiced by Americans) could stand entirely apart from the aesthetic of modernism.

But there was another side to Cowell. Another poetic idea motivated another kind of cluster music, the "futurist" kind, stimulated by a short trip to New York in the fall of 1916, where he met another notorious maximalist of the day, the phenomenally long-lived Leo Ornstein (1893–2002). Ornstein, an immigrant from Russia, made music that celebrated — or at least was obsessed with — speed, aggression, and the mechanization of modern life. He gave sensational piano recitals at which he assaulted audiences (to their great delight) with modestly clustery pieces bearing titles like *Suicide in an Airplane* (1913, Ex. 5-22b) and *Wild Men's Dance* (1915, Ex. 5-22a). These pieces were as of then the most spectacular musical responses to the call put out by the *futuristi*, a boisterous group of Italian artists headed by the poet Emilio Marinetti (1876–1944) and the painter Luigi Russolo (1885–1947), for an "Art of Noises" that would replace all conventional music as the appropriate sonic representation of the machine age.

A title like *Wild Men's Dance* (later amended to *Danse sauvage*) might sound more like primitivism than futurism, but as the composer and Cowell scholar Michael Hicks has observed, "in musical terms, futurism and primitivism are the same,"[60] quoting as clincher Ornstein's own avowal that he used clusters in his futuristic compositions to "project the dark brooding quality" that for him characterized "prehistoric man." Cowell provided another confirmation when he changed the title of one of his compositions from the futuristic *Dash* to the primitivistic *Tiger*.

In a spirit of friendly competition with Ornstein, Cowell produced *Dynamic Motion* (1916, Ex. 5-23), which at first he announced to audiences as an evocation of the New York subway. It brought him publicity — "at the finish," one reviewer reported in 1922, "three women lay in a dead faint in the aisle and no less than ten men had refreshed themselves [illegally, Prohibition being then in force] from the left hip"[61] — and eventual patronage, which enabled him to launch his important publishing activities. But for Cowell, futurism was a passing fling. His predilection, like Ives's, was more for the pastoral and spiritual mode than the urban, materialist one. As his career went

EX. 5-22A   Leo Ornstein, *Danse sauvage*

EX. 5-22B   Leo Ornstein, *Suicide in an Airplane*

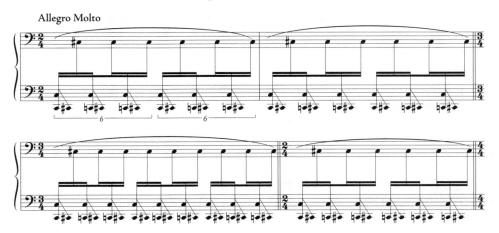

EX. 5-22B   (*continued*)

on, he retreated considerably from his maximalist phase, seeking (as he put it to a reporter in 1955) "an amalgamation of the techniques introduced from about 1908 to about 1930, combined with the familiar elements, producing a literature with more substance, but less individual distinctions."[62] By then he was far from alone, as we shall see.

EX. 5-23   Henry Cowell, *Dynamic Motion*, mm. 1–18

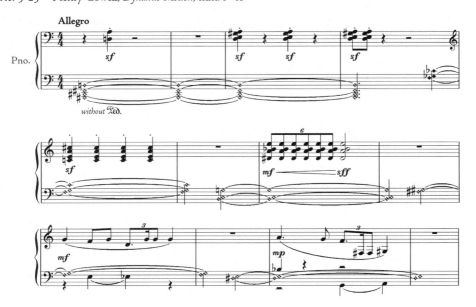

EX. 5-23   (continued)

But his "retreat" was already in full swing by the 1920s, for which reason Cowell is often taken less than seriously by historians in the romantic-modernist tradition. Only his cluster pieces are treated as "historic," and even then the "futuristic" ones are given preference over the "Celtic" ones, despite the evidence that this weighting reverses Cowell's own scale of values. He has been overridden, or overruled, by "history" — which is to say, by historians. Having an inkling that this would be the case, Cowell began backdating his early compositions very much the way Ives has been accused of doing, assigning *The Tides of Manaunaun*, for example, to 1912, which gave him a clear year's priority over Ornstein, and ensured his place in the history books.

Yet was it a retreat? Was the up-to-dateness of *Dynamic Motion* clearly superior, artistically, to what may seem the quaintness of *The Tides of Manaunaun*? As early as 1933 the critic Nicolas Slonimsky called Cowell's Celtic pieces "audaciously conservative."[63] It was an apt characterization, and one that would go on describing Cowell until his death thirty-two years later. The clever contradiction in terms betrays many ambivalences; and so did Cowell's own behavior, as when he told his interviewer that "substance" (that Ivesian word!) does not depend on "individual distinctions," but at the same time rewrote his autobiography so as to polish his innovative image.

But then the very same ambivalence haunted the very outset of this chapter, with its contradictory quotations from Emerson. It had a long history in America, where — as Hicks has noted, echoing an insight voiced a century and a half earlier by Alexis de Tocqueville in *De la démocratie en Amérique* (*Democracy in America*, 1835) — there has always been felt a contradictory yet "insatiable need to be both an individual and a conformist, self-sufficient yet bound to the canons of civilization."[64] But it was also an ambivalence, born of modernism and its conflicting demands, that would presently be felt throughout the world of art.

CHAPTER 6

Inner Occurrences (Transcendentalism, III)

SCHOENBERG, WEBERN, AND EXPRESSIONISM; ATONALITY

Art is the cry of distress uttered by those who experience at first hand the fate of mankind. Who are not reconciled to it, but come to grips with it . . . . Who do not turn their eyes away, to shield themselves from emotions, but open them wide, so as to tackle what must be tackled. Who do, however, often close their eyes, in order to perceive things incommunicable by the senses, to envision within themselves the process that only seems to be in the world outside. The world revolves within — inside them: what bursts out is merely the echo — the work of art.[1]

— ARNOLD SCHOENBERG (1910)

REJECTING SUCCESS

I the middle of chapter 1 we stole a glance at a tiny song, *Erwartung* ("Anticipation"), by Arnold Schoenberg, composed in 1899 (Ex. 1-9). Its purpose there was to illustrate *Jugendstil*, "decadent" sensuality at its prettiest. It also illustrated the device of "the smallest link" — the use of half-step neighbors to create "color chords" that had no theoretical "textbook" standing as harmonic entities, but that were justified by the logic of voice leading. Compared with the gigantic symphonies of Mahler or the bloated one-act operas of Strauss, its immediate companions in that chapter, the song seemed modest in the extreme. There was little in it to suggest that its composer would eventually take transcendental maximalism to its furthest, most threatening extreme, or that as a pedagogue he would play an unparalleled role in its dissemination.

Schoenberg's whole career was fraught with ironies, contradictions, and ambiguities, beginning with the paradox that one of the outstanding academic music theorists and composition teachers of the twentieth century was himself self-taught. By the time he wrote *Erwartung* the Vienna-born

FIG. 6-1 Arnold Schoenberg, by Egon Schiele.

Schoenberg had had little musical instruction beyond the violin lessons, starting at age eight, that were typically thrust on middle-class Jewish boys. Later he taught himself cello and played in amateur quartets and orchestras. His early composing consisted of imitating the violin duos he was assigned as a child, and arranging pieces to play with his companions. He had some informal instruction in harmony from one of his playing partners, but when it came to composing in "classical" forms, he had to look them up in an encyclopedia.

In 1895, Schoenberg, then working as a bank clerk, showed some of his early efforts to Alexander von Zemlinsky (1871–1942), a young conservatory-trained composer who was conducting one of the amateur orchestras in which Schoenberg played. Zemlinsky gave his friend a few lessons in counterpoint and some general advice, and that was the extent of Schoenberg's "formal" training. A string quartet that Schoenberg wrote while consulting with Zemlinsky (who later became his brother-in-law) was accepted for performance in 1897. With that, lessons came to an end. Zemlinsky having declared him an equal, from then on Schoenberg lived the life of a professional, albeit usually unemployed, composer.

He earned his living over the next several years by conducting amateur choruses and orchestrating operettas (never having had any official instruction at all in conducting or orchestration), and in his spare time composed two works that are now recognized as masterpieces. One was *Verklärte Nacht*, op. 4 ("Transfigured night," 1899), a tone poem scored, unusually, not for orchestra but for string sextet, as if Schoenberg were deliberately casting himself as heir to both the "New German" tradition of programmatic composition in the spirit of Liszt, Wagner, and Strauss, and the "Classical" chamber-music tradition of Brahms.

Its program followed the plot of a narrative poem by Richard Dehmel, the same poet who wrote the text of the song *Erwartung*. Vienna's leading "decadent," Dehmel enjoyed a reputation for daring subject matter and *Verklärte Nacht* was no exception. It tells of a magnanimous man who forgives the woman he loves illicitly for becoming pregnant by her lawfully wedded but unloved husband. In Schoenberg's musical interpretation, the man's promise to accept the child as his transforms the anguished mood of the tone poem's D-minor beginning into a radiant D major that gleams with the starlight of natural and artificial harmonics.

Though certainly up-to-date, the music of *Verklärte Nacht* was in no way ahead of its time. Nevertheless, it achieved a scandalous reputation when the very conservative Wiener Tonkünstlerverein (Vienna Musicians' Club), which had sponsored the performance of his early quartet, rejected the tone poem for containing what its jury considered to be a compositional error (Ex. 6-1): a chord that might arguably be analyzed as a dominant-ninth chord in "fourth inversion" (ninth in the bass), but which—like the "color chord" in the song *Erwartung*—is better justified as the product of voice leading by semitones in all voices in contrary motion.

At least Schoenberg claimed that the score was rejected for this reason, in an essay he wrote almost half a century later (from which the example, asterisk and all, was taken).[2] It seems at least as likely that it was rejected because of its risqué subject matter.

EX. 6-1   Offending passage from Arnold Schoenberg, *Verklärte Nacht*

But whatever the reason for it, this experience seems to have equipped Schoenberg with the resentment and the sense of alienation that a modernist giant needs. From then on, in a transformation that dated almost precisely from the turn of the century, it became a point of pride and principle with Schoenberg and his pupils (like Berg, whose early aggregate harmony was discussed in chapter 4) always to be pushing the envelope of stylistic and technical innovation.

Even so, like any "maximalist's," Schoenberg's expressive aims remained those of his forebears, and were readily recognizable as such even when his stylistic and technical means were self-consciously advanced. That is why the other masterpiece of his early years, a vast cantata called *Gurrelieder* ("Songs of Gurre") for five solo voices, a speaker, three male choruses, a double (eight-part) mixed chorus, and an orchestra containing four flutes, four piccolos, five oboes, seven clarinets, three bassoons, two contrabassoons, ten horns, seven trumpets, seven trombones, four harps, twelve percussionists, and strings to match, was such a great success when it was finally performed.

Based on a volume of poems by the Danish romantic writer Jens Peter Jacobsen that purported to retell a set of Nordic myths like the ones in Wagner's *Ring* (but in a "decadent" erotic manner reminiscent of *Tristan und Isolde*), the work was composed over the course of a single year (March 1900–March 1901). The orchestration took much longer. Schoenberg worked on it until 1903, when, despairing of ever getting the work performed, he turned to other projects. He did not return to it until 1910, by which time his reputation had grown to the point where a performance could be secured. He completed the scoring in 1911, and the work was finally heard the next year.

It was received with amazement and delight by a public already used to Mahler and Strauss. The self-taught composer exhibited astounding mastery of every branch of compositional technique, not excluding counterpoint (for the gigantic final chorus is cast as a double canon). Having put himself so thoroughly through the mill, he now appeared to many as virtually the miller-in-chief. One who thought so was Richard Strauss, who had exerted his influence on Schoenberg's behalf after seeing the first orchestrated excerpts from *Gurrelieder* as early as 1901. He secured a government stipend to see the younger man through the task of scoring the colossal work, and then got Schoenberg his first teaching job (the first of many) at a private conservatory in Berlin.

But by 1912, Schoenberg's style had undergone a remarkable metamorphosis, and he no longer thought *Gurrelieder* a representative (or a particularly valuable) composition. He famously refused to acknowledge the audience's applause, preferring alienation to acclaim. He offended his erstwhile benefactor Strauss as well, publicly chiding him for failing to make a comparable stylistic advance. His intransigent stance became a modernist paradigm. Combined with his awesome technical command and his increasingly prestigious teaching posts, it invested Schoenberg with a moral authority that made him influential out of all proportion to the frequency with which his music was ever performed.

EXPRESSION BECOMES AN "ISM"

The problem with *Gurrelieder*, so far as Schoenberg was concerned, was not merely its public appeal but its very public ("extrovert") orientation. Mythic pageantry was certainly a viable and time-honored manifestation of romanticism, but Schoenberg's artistic isolation had wed him to an older and, he thought, truer romantic attitude. Indeed, Schoenberg's was an updated and intensified version of the original German romantic attitude, the one associated musically with Beethoven (as interpreted by critics such as E. T. A. Hoffmann), and with the "Schubert circle."

These early romantics saw the highest, most serious purpose of art in expressing and achieving a unique human subjectivity, the quality they described as *Innigkeit*, "inwardness." Only through artistic creation — or, failing that, through artistic empathy — does one truly become a person, according to this very pure romantic view. But only an art that is uniquely personal can be the vehicle through which true personhood — a truly "inner" expressive freedom or "autonomy" — is achieved and communicated. Such art was by nature very difficult both to create and to understand, since it demanded the resolute avoidance of traits that made artworks (and their creators) seem similar to one another rather than different and unique. In a word, it demanded the rejection of conventions.

The task that confronted artists who returned to this goal a hundred years after Beethoven and Schubert was more difficult yet, since the stylistic departures that distinguished the work of the early romantics had long since become conventional. Even the music that had seemed to mark the furthest extreme of originality and personal idiosyncrasy at the beginning of the century — Mahler's and Strauss's — had become socially accepted and (in Schoenberg's view) conventional by 1911, when the composer wrote to the painter Wassily Kandinsky, then a close friend, a famous letter that reads today like a public manifesto: "One must express *oneself*! Express oneself *directly*! Not one's taste or one's upbringing, or one's intelligence, knowledge, or skill. Not all these *acquired* characteristics, but that which is *inborn, instinctive*."[3]

As Schoenberg came to see it, all that *Gurrelieder* had displayed, with its gaudy orchestration and ostentatious counterpoint, was taste, intelligence, knowledge, and skill. Worse, the emotions so stunningly portrayed — the amorous ecstasy, the blasphemous rage, the ghostly horror, the glorious elation — were not Schoenberg's but those of Jacobsen's characters. They were "anyone's" emotions, and they were expressed in terms that anyone could have learned from models in Wagner and Strauss. Nor were the oratorio's plot and action, being external to the emotions, a valid subject for art, which to be authentic must henceforth concern itself, Schoenberg now decreed, with "the representation of inner occurrences"[4] alone.

Schoenberg first used this phrase in a lecture he delivered in 1928, to account for the unprecedented turns his art had taken since the time of his early and (he now thought) spurious success. It was his definition of "expressionism," a term that over the course of a decade or so had become fairly common as a describer of contemporary German art, and that is now part of the standard art historian's vocabulary. It is less often used in connection with music; but when it is, it is invariably applied to Schoenberg. As long as he accepted it himself, however belatedly, it seems fair to adopt it here, especially as his outburst to Kandinsky, quoted above, was perhaps the best capsule summary ever made of expressionist aims.

ART AND THE UNCONSCIOUS

It seems an even better one, and even more exactly suggests the difference between expressionism and the earlier ("Hoffmannesque") romantic concept from which it grew, when the sentence that immediately precedes it is reinstated. "Art," declared Schoenberg to Kandinsky, "belongs to the *unconscious*!"[5] He was using, as we would now say, a "buzzword." Expressionism, especially as preached and practiced in Schoenberg's Vienna, cannot be fully understood apart from the psychoanalytical movement that sprang up at the same time and in the same place. Both movements had the same compelling if paradoxical aim: to explore the human unconscious, in the one case through scientific inquiry, in the other through art.

But how can one consciously do that? According to Sigmund Freud (1856–1939), the founder of psychoanalysis, the "inner occurrences" that conditioned human subjectivity, and therefore provided the most authentic subject matter for expressionist art, were governed by emotions, drives, and wishes of which the human subject was unaware, often because they were socially unacceptable and therefore repressed from consciousness. Thus the expressionist artist's subversive task was to portray something—or rather, the results of something—that was hidden not only from others but even from the one doing the portraying.

As Schoenberg put it in a program note accompanying one of his most radical expressionist works, *Five Orchestral Pieces*, op. 16 (1909; first performed in London in 1912), "the music seeks to express all that swells in us subconsciously like a dream."[6] Even before one asks how one is to make such subject matter intelligible or communicable, and even before one shudders at the thought of the nightmares such art might communicate, one has to ask how such a subject matter can even be apprehended by the artist's own conscious creative faculty. How can one express what is unknowable?

That is the expressionist version of the old romantic conundrum of "absolute music"—music that describes the indescribable and expresses the inexpressible—updated for the psychoanalytical age. Absolute music achieved this feat, in Hoffmann's inimitable phrase, by becoming the "secret Sanskrit of the soul." Schoenberg faced an even harder task. Sanskrit, the ancient liturgical language of the Hindus, a dead and distant tongue that for Hoffmann symbolized everything esoteric, was after all a "natural language," a real medium of communication. To realize the demands of expressionism without compromise would entail the old philosophers' riddle of

FIG. 6-2   Sigmund Freud's study at his house in Maresfield Gardens, London, 1938–1939.

a "private language," a manifest contradiction in terms. Or was it? Could one, truly recording one's "inner occurrences" and doing full justice to their uniqueness, utter anything but nonsense? Can something truly and totally unique ever be communicated?

It would be better to leave these inevitable paradoxes to one side for now. We will have to return to them — repeatedly — because Schoenberg's work posed with particular urgency and clarity the cursed question of intelligibility, alias "comprehensibility" (to use the word he himself preferred) or "accessibility" (to use more recent critical language). It is a question that has always dogged modernist art, and in the wake of Schoenberg's influence the question achieved the dimensions of a crisis. But first we must trace the process through which Schoenberg — courageously? quixotically? — attempted to meet the impossibly contradictory demands that art and history, as he envisioned them, were making not only on him, but on all artists who aspired to authenticity.

"EMANCIPATION OF DISSONANCE"

In later life, Schoenberg liked to say that the musical explorations that made him notorious were thrust upon him against his will. Generalizing from what he perceived to be his own experience, he made bold to assert that "Art is born of 'I must,' not 'I can.' "[7] There was a certain pomposity to the claim. It smacked of Hegel's "world-historical" figure, the unconscious or unwilling servant of history's grand design. But there was a kernel of biographical truth in it as well. It is a fact that a period of severe psychological disturbance immediately preceded Schoenberg's most radically maximalist phase. In 1906–1907 he suffered a major depression, one of several such periods that made his creative output sporadic. (The catalogue of no other comparably productive composer includes so many unfinished works.) His wife, neglected, deserted him and their two small children for a lover, the expressionist painter Richard Gerstl, who committed suicide when she returned to Schoenberg (the composer having also seriously if briefly contemplated taking his own life).

This turbulent episode has often been singled out as the catalyst of Schoenberg's new and radical idiom. While it may be doubted whether the composer's emotional and marital upheavals could in themselves have furnished him with musical ideas, let alone a theory of art, the extremity and the sheer violence of the style that emerged — for many, its most compelling aspects — may well have been conditioned by the extremity and violence of the emotions for which Schoenberg now sought an expressive or confessional outlet. The specific means through which Schoenberg sought to realize these ends, however, were conditioned by his knowledge and experience as a musician.

With Schoenberg, equally important and influential as a composer and as a music theorist and pedagogue, we have a unique opportunity to compare theory with practice, particularly at this early phase of his career when he incorporated his most radical artistic ideas directly into his theoretical writings. The most important of these was the *Harmonielehre* ("Textbook of harmony"), which appeared in 1911 as the distillation of nine years of teaching experience, during which time his pupils had included Alban Berg (1885–1935) and Anton von Webern (1883–1945), who as composers would join Schoenberg in his quests and are now regarded as forming, with him, what amounts to an expressionist "school" (sometimes referred to as the "Second Viennese School" by those who have sought to put them in a direct line of succession from the "school" of Haydn, Mozart, and Beethoven).

The *Harmonielehre* is a basic course. It begins like any other harmony textbook with elementary instruction on major and minor scales, triads and inversions, progressions, modulations, and the like. Its final section, however, deals with what was at the time avowedly experimental material; and this concluding portion begins, very significantly, with a brief chapter, "Consonance and Dissonance," in which that most categorical harmonic distinction is boldly relativized. The first two sentences in this chapter declare the expressionist bias of the whole book: "Art in its most primitive state is a simple imitation of nature. But it quickly becomes imitation of nature in the wider sense of this idea, that is, not merely imitation of outer but also of inner nature."[8] Schoenberg's discussion of consonance and dissonance is actually a veiled description of his own recent music, cast artfully (and perhaps ironically recalling the Wagnerian slogans of old) as a speculation on what the future may have in store. The difference, he asserts, is only a matter of degree, not of kind. Consonance and dissonance are no more opposites than two and ten are opposites, as the frequency numbers (i.e., the measurable ratios of the overtone series) indeed show; and the expressions "consonance" and "dissonance," insofar as they signify an antithesis, are false. It all simply depends on the growing ability of the analyzing ear to familiarize itself with the remote overtones, thereby expanding the conception of what is euphonious, suitable for art, so that it embraces the whole natural phenomenon.

What today is remote can tomorrow be close at hand; it is all a matter of whether one can get closer. And the evolution of music has followed this course: it has drawn into the stock of artistic resources more and more of the harmonic possibilities inherent in the tone.

So if I continue to use the expressions "consonance" and "dissonance," even though they are unwarranted, I do so because there are signs that the evolution of harmony will, in a short time, prove the inadequacy of this classification.[9]

Dissonances, Schoenberg proposes, are simply "the more remote consonances." It is a first step toward liberating musical thinking from convention — "from one's taste or one's upbringing, or one's intelligence, knowledge, or skill," as Schoenberg put it to Kandinsky the same year that the *Harmonielehre* was published — and opening it up to "that which is *inborn, instinctive*."

Schoenberg called the logical conclusion (and the practical result) toward which such thinking aimed the "emancipation of dissonance."[10] The term has excellent political "vibes," especially when one considers that it is the composer, rather than "dissonance" itself, that is liberated by such a turn. As far as dissonance itself is concerned, it is not so much liberated as conceptually erased. (What are the implications of such erasure for listening? Is the listener liberated along with the composer? Let us repress these questions for now, on Freud's assurance that what is repressed must inevitably return.) As the concluding chapters of the *Harmonielehre* confirm, the first result of the "emancipation of dissonance" is the composer's absolution from the obligation to resolve complex harmonies into simpler ones.

THEORY AND PRACTICE

So much for the theory. To observe it in practice, we can return to the harmonic progression we encountered at the beginning of the song *Erwartung*. Such progressions, in which "color chords" arise from the use of multiple neighbor tones, occur time and again in Schoenberg's early songs. The one in Ex. 6-2 comes from *Der Wanderer* ("The wanderer"), op. 6, no. 8, a Nietzsche setting that dates from 1905. In the context of E-flat major, the unusual chord achieves both its intelligibility and its poetic effect from its easily apprehended relationship to the tonic triad.

EX. 6-2   Arnold Schoenberg, *Der Wanderer*, Op. 6, no. 8, mm. 9–11

Six years later, in the *Harmonielehre*, Schoenberg suggests that such chords no longer need justification by voice leading. In a passage that is famous for its sardonic wit, he cites some strong dissonances in one of Bach's motets that conservative musicians (he calls them "aestheticians," upholders of beauty) would surely decry in a modern composition, and a celebrated example from Mozart's G-minor Symphony (Ex. 6-3). He notes that in all cases they are products of "non-harmonic tones" on their way to resolution; but he takes special satisfaction in pointing out that Mozart's chord (almost exactly like the ones cited in Ex. 6-2 from Schoenberg's own music), which functions as an "incomplete neighbor" (that is, an appoggiatura), lacks a preparation.

EX. 6-3   Arnold Schoenberg, *Harmonielehre*, examples 232 and 233

Casting himself in solidarity with Mozart, Schoenberg speculates on what prompted such licenses. Mozart emerges in Schoenberg's description as something of an expressionist himself, creating "according to the laws of *his* nature" despite the protests of the uncreative upholders of convention. But more significant, perhaps, is Schoenberg's assertion that a continual evolution in musical style led from Mozart's innovations to his own, making them not only predictable but inevitable — which is another way of saying that they were necessary. Whereas even in Mozart "such harmonies have been used almost exclusively where they can be explained as passing tones and the like," for the composer of the present, "they are henceforth just chords"; and he adds, even more ominously, that "they are only superficially annexed to the old system, for they are judged according to a different principle, according to their origin, and are not referred to roots."[11]

Why ominously? Because if such chords are no longer dependent for their understanding and use on their relationship to functional harmonies (i.e., harmonies with roots), and if they can succeed one another with all the freedoms of consonances, then the whole system of functions, undergirding what at least since the seventeenth century had provided music with its "tonality," becomes moot. And indeed, one of the closing chapters in the *Harmonielehre* — significantly, it is the first chapter in which Schoenberg cites his own works as examples — bears the title *Über schwebende und aufgehobene Tonalität* ("On Fluctuating and Suspended Tonality").

The former, fluctuating tonality, is a key that is suggested though never fully established through a cadence, and is therefore inherently unstable. The prime example, unsurprisingly, is the Prelude to Wagner's *Tristan und Isolde*. Suspended tonality, for which Schoenberg cites precedents in "classical development sections," is a situation in which no key at all is forecast. Rather than harmony, what holds such music together will be the coherence of the thematic material: its motivic consistency "creates the opportunity for such harmonic looseness through its characteristic figurations."[12]

ATONALITY?

These are the conditions under which music becomes, in a word that has become standard terminology over Schoenberg's objections, "atonal." Schoenberg objected to the word because its connotations were purely negative: merely to say what something is not is a far cry from saying what it is. He preferred to call his music "pantonal," suggesting a single transcendent, all-encompassing tonality rather than the mere avoidance of custom, but the term failed to catch on. Other candidates that have been proposed over the years — "contextual," "motivic" — have fared even less well. Like "Gregorian chant" and "English horn," "atonal music" is one of those historically sanctioned misnomers we have to live with. Resigning ourselves to it, however, should not dull our perception of its inadequacy or its disadvantages.

The greatest disadvantage has been the creation of a spurious and very misleading antonym — "tonal music" — that has arisen in the wake of the polemics surrounding "atonality." The term never existed (because it never had any reason to exist) during the "common practice" period it ostensibly describes. Its crude lumping effect has all too often discouraged precise distinctions and clear conceptualization.

For one thing, the polemical question "tonal vs. atonal" often intrudes needlessly into discussions of consonance vs. dissonance, or of chromatic vs. diatonic, and confuses the issues. The definition of tonality rests neither on levels of consonance nor on degrees of chromaticism, but on the functional differentiation of scale degrees. If high chromaticism is taken as a sign of atonality, then the Prelude to *Tristan und Isolde* might be regarded as an example (or, perhaps, a harbinger) of atonality, when in fact few compositions depend more clearly or crucially on functional distinction between the dominant (in this case endlessly prolonged) and the tonic (in this case excruciatingly withheld).

Similarly, if high dissonance is taken as a sign of atonality, then the "horror fanfares" in the finale of Beethoven's Ninth Symphony might be regarded as an example or a harbinger of atonality, when in fact their whole effect depends on our recognizing an actual collision between the tonic and the diminished seventh on its leading tone (a common substitute for the dominant that preserves and even intensifies its functional tendency). In fact, both Wagner's composition and Beethoven's (indeed, Wagner and Beethoven themselves) have been advanced as harbingers of atonality by those intent on giving Schoenberg's practices a historical justification. Such a tendentious exploitation of the term is already evidence of its deleterious potential: calling Beethoven or Wagner "atonal" hardly enhances our understanding of them, or even of Schoenberg.

But now consider a composition based entirely on the whole-tone scale (as Ex. 2-8, Debussy's "Voiles", comes close to being). As long as it remains within the confines of the scale it will contain no chromaticism, and its dissonance can only be relatively mild, since minor seconds, major sevenths, and even perfect fourths are excluded from its vocabulary. And yet (as we learned in chapter 2) the whole-tone scale, which contains neither perfect intervals nor semitones, and in which all the steps are equal, can assign no functional differentiation to its degrees and support no traditionally functional cadences. Thus traditional tonal relations can be effectively challenged without any chromaticism or dissonance, while a high level of chromaticism and dissonance can actually serve to enhance our awareness of tonal functions.

Everything depends on how chromaticism, or dissonance, or any other musical characteristic, is handled. And that signals another danger. Terms like "tonal" and "atonal" are often mistakenly thought to refer to inherent qualities of music rather than compositional practices, and (as in the case of consonance and dissonance) to place in categorical opposition what is better viewed on a continuum. Can we actually draw a categorical line between "tonal" and "atonal" and pinpoint its crossing with precision? Do we know what we mean when we say that one piece (or even one composer) is more or less "tonal" than another? Are we stating a fact or making an interpretation?

As our present discussion of Schoenberg's music continues, and in chapters to come, it should become evident that in music, as in so many other arenas, a priori insistence on black-and-white distinctions is intellectually counterproductive. It hinders observation, desensitizes the mind to nuances and ambiguities, and reduces analysis to crude pigeonholing, lowering rather than enhancing its cognitive benefit. Experience teaches us that life is lived (and art is created) in infinite shades of gray.

So to understand what Schoenberg meant when he spoke of his breakthrough into a "pantonal" idiom, one where tonality is permanently fluctuating (or permanently suspended), we need to evaluate the relevant musical procedures and their results, but we also need to inquire further as to the reasons why Schoenberg—both as a musician and, more generally, as an artist—felt the need for just these procedures. Only in this way will we end up with a precise and positive concept and avoid the intellectual black hole into which empty negative categories like "atonality" can beckon us.

"CONTEXTUALITY"

One strategy might be to observe a single motivic entity operating in Schoenberg's music both in a context where it has differentiated degree functions and in one where it does not. A clue toward finding such a motive comes from a composition by Berg, a *Kammerkonzert* ("Chamber concerto") for violin, piano, and thirteen wind instruments, which he composed in 1923–1925 and offered to Schoenberg as a belated fiftieth-birthday present. It opens with a five-bar motto in which Berg, using the German pitch-letter associations familiar from the famous BACH cipher (B♭–A–C–B), encoded Schoenberg's name, Webern's name, and his own name as musical themes played respectively by the piano, the violin, and a French horn from the accompanying band (Ex. 6-4):

ArnolD SCHönBErG = A – D – Eb – C – B – B♭ – E – G;

Anton wEBErn = A – E – B♭ – E;

AlBAn BErG = A – Bb – A – B♭ – E – G

EX. 6-4   Alban Berg, motto from the *Kammerkonzert*

Berg's compliment to his teacher, as he pointed out in a letter, hinged on the fact that the notes in the names of Webern and Berg are all included in that of Schoenberg (a feature that the later musical development would make conspicuous).[13] But he was not the first in the Schoenberg circle to use the pitch-letter code to construct thematic material. Schoenberg himself had long made a habit of it. And what is more, he often used his own name for the purpose, as if signing his work. Indeed, he may have got the idea in the first place from being an enthusiastic amateur painter. Alternatively (or simultaneously), the cipher of his name may have symbolically or superstitiously embodied for Schoenberg the essence of his singular identity, the "inborn, instinctive self" which (as we know from his letter to Kandinsky) he regarded as the true subject matter of any artist's — any *true* artist's — art.

Varieties of the motif with which Berg began his Chamber Concerto can be found in many of Schoenberg's early works. Since most of the time he used only the six tones derived from his surname — Eb ("Es" in German), C, B ("h" in German), B♭, E, G — this particular group of notes is often informally called the "Eschbeg set" in the voluminous analytical literature that has grown up around his work. Perhaps its earliest occurrence (Ex. 6-5) was sighted by the music analyst Allen Forte in one of the songs from Schoenberg's op. 6 (the set from which Ex. 6-2 above is also drawn).[14] It is the beginning of the third item in the opus, *Mädchenlied* ("The maiden's song") to a poem by Paul Remer, composed in October 1905.

In this early instance, every note in the Eschbeg set can be assigned a function within the signature key of E minor, which is why Eb and B♭ are spelled D♯ and A♯. That, plus the fact that this is the earliest known occurrence of the set, plus the presence in the passage of a single note that is foreign to the set (the F♯ in the right hand on the second beat of m. 1), might seem to weaken the argument that Schoenberg was employing his signature set as a pitch source "with premeditation" (to use the precise vocabulary of criminal law). On the other hand, the frequency with which the set occurs from this point forward in Schoenberg's work has been cited by some as sufficient evidence of his premeditation, even the first time.

EX. 6-5   Arnold Schoenberg, *Mädchenlied*, Op. 6, no. 3, beginning

But there is no need to insist upon or argue the point. Even if we concede that this early occurrence was coincidental (or, to take the middle ground, that his early unpremeditated use of the set might, on reflection, have prompted Schoenberg's later premeditated usages), the passage still affords us the comparison we seek between functional and nonfunctional — or if you must, "tonal" and "atonal" — deployments of the same group of tones, so that we may discover the particular ("positive") properties of "atonal" syntax.

For the nonfunctional counterpart we can turn to one of Schoenberg's most famous compositions, the last movement of his Second String Quartet, op. 10 (1907–1908), the work with which his "expressionist" style is often said to begin. As he had previously done in *Verklärte Nacht*, he transferred to the chamber medium devices more often found in contemporary orchestral music. Following the example of Mahler, who had ended his Second Symphony with two movements in which the instrumental ensemble suddenly accompanies the singing of a text, Schoenberg added a soprano solo to the concluding movements of the Second Quartet, singing poems by Stefan George (1868–1933), Germany's leading avant-garde poet.

The slow movement, a theme and variations in a very chromatic but still functioning G♭ major, incorporates a setting of "Litanei," a quasi-religious poem about renunciation. It ends with a prayer, "Kill my longings, close my wounds, take my love away and grant me Thy peace!" The quartet's finale could be understood as the answer to the prayer. It is a setting of a much longer poem called "Entrückung," a highly poetic noun of George's invention that comes from the verb *entrücken*, which simply means "to remove" or "to carry off." The new noun might be translated as "transport" or "rapture" or (most literally) "swept-awayness." Both the poem's title and its famous opening line, "I feel the air of another planet," have become emblems of the musical departure Schoenberg intended his setting both to symbolize and to enact.

As shown in Ex. 6-6 (given in Alban Berg's transcription for voice and piano) 'Entrückung' begins with some word-painting involving both an explicit external gesture and an esoteric "inner" meaning to which, after our discussion of the Eschbeg set, we can gain privileged access. Schoenberg described the outer side of it in a program note he wrote to accompany a recording issued in 1949. The arching "arabesques" (curving lines) that are passed up from cello to viola to the violins, representing "the

EX. 6-6   Arnold Schoenberg, Quartet no. 2, IV (*Entrückung*), arr. Berg, m. 1

departure from earth to another planet," suggest the experience of "becoming relieved from gravitation — passing through clouds into thinner and thinner air."[15]

TONAL OR ATONAL?

That much is fairly obvious. What the composer withheld from this description, possibly because it would have required too technical an explanation for a record sleeve, is the really crucial matter: each one in the initial series of arabesques, minus its first and last notes, is a transposition of the Eschbeg set, Schoenberg's musical signature, leaving no doubt as to exactly whose consciousness is being buffeted through space, and focusing attention not merely on the buffeting but on the consciousness itself, that is, the "inward," subjective experience.

The exactness of the transpositions — as it happens, through an ascending circle of fifths — shows the composer treating this crucial musical configuration far more explicitly as a *motif*, a discrete and basic melodic shape, than he had done previously. Ex. 6-7 shows the untransposed Eschbeg set, economically represented so that its constituent pitches ascend within the narrowest possible intervallic confines. (Forte calls this manner of representing a pitch-class set the "best normal order"; it is very useful for making comparisons.) The four transpositions at the start of *Entrückung*, all similarly displayed, follow the original set.

EX. 6-7   Transposition of the "Eschbeg" set in Arnold Schoenberg, Quartet no. 2, IV (*Entrückung*)

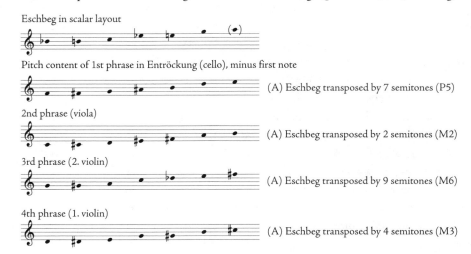

EX. 6-8   Arnold Schoenberg, Quartet no. 2, IV (*Entrückung*), arr. Berg, mm. 21–26

The interval of transposition between the pitch level of original Eschbeg set and that of the first arabesque is the same—a perfect fifth (=seven semitones, hence t7)—as the interval separating the arabesques from one another: additional evidence that the original set was the conceptual point of departure (and implying that the "transport" begins already some way off the ground). The notes that sandwich the Eschbeg set at the extremities of each arabesque are also motivically significant. As indicated in parentheses at the end of each line of Ex. 6-7, the final note of each arabesque, transposed to the pitch level of the original set, supplies the note corresponding to the composer's first initial, A, making the signature more complete ("A. Sch[ön]be[r]g"). And the beginning notes of each arabesque, defining the ascent by fifths, together comprise a transposition of the opening phrase in the voice part (*Ich fühle Duft . . .*, Ex. 6-8), calculated so that if the two four-note groups are laid side by side, an unbroken series of ascending fifths is the result, suggesting a direct continuation by the voice of the spiritual ascent announced by the strings:

$$(\text{Strings}) \,|\, (\text{Voice})$$
$$\text{G}\sharp\text{A}\flat - \text{D}\sharp\text{E}\flat - \text{B}\flat - \text{F} - | - \text{C} - \text{G} - \text{D} - \text{A}$$

In the third measure, the four-note group to the left of the vertical line, consisting of the respective opening pitches of the four string arabesques, is turned into an explicit motive in the "left hand" staff of Berg's keyboard transcription (Ex. 6-9). It is sequentially repeated there three times (the last sequential repetition falling one note short—note well which note!—of completion). Three measures later it is back for another sequential treatment, in diminution and "permuted" (that is, with its pitches presented in a different order: E♭–A♭–(E♭)–F–B♭ instead of F–E♭–A♭–B♭). In m. 9 (left-hand staff) it is transposed for the first time to the pitches-/C–G–D–A/- on which the voice will eventually make its entrance (Ex. 6-10).

Is the music "atonal"? Ex. 6-10 seems to say no. The cello's G and C pizzicati under the sustained D–A fifth in the viola in m. 9 are expanded into sustained bass fifths (G–D in m. 13 and C–G at the end of m. 15) that fairly scream "Cadence!" But the very necessity of "screaming" in this context underscores the arbitrariness of the

EX. 6-9   Arnold Schoenberg, Quartet no. 2, IV (*Entrückung*), arr. Berg, mm. 3–6

EX. 6-10   Arnold Schoenberg, Quartet no. 2, IV (*Entrückung*), arr. Berg, mm. 9–15

EX. 6-10   (*continued*)

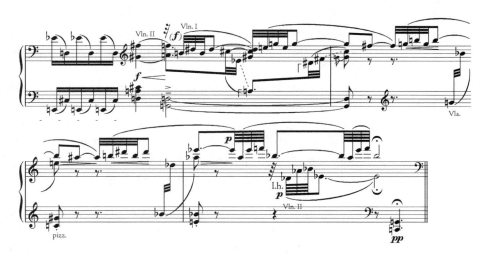

cadential gesture. The big V–I in C, like the "big Five-Ones" in Mahler's Second, seem to be little more than a "terminating convenience"[16] (to borrow a term from the music analyst Pieter van den Toorn), rather than a true functional "outcome" of the music that preceded it.

Elsewhere, despite the ample use of the circle of fifths (a "tonal" mainstay if ever there was one), the sense of tonal function (or of tonal "attraction") is attenuated to what seems the vanishing point. For one thing, the circles of fifths tend to go in the "wrong" direction—not the centripetal "V–I" direction but the other way, centrifugally, as if perpetually seeking the next dominant. For another thing, the circle is "real," as the language of fugue writing would put it, rather than "tonal." That is, all the fifths are perfect, so that the implied complete circle is closed not after a diatonic seven progressions but a full chromatic twelve. For a third, until m. 13 no tone is allowed to assume the function of a dominant root. The B♯ that might have functioned as a leading tone over the initial G♯ in Ex. 6-6 is withheld from the first arabesque. Not until the crest of the second arabesque does it appear (spelled as C); and, as a note-count will verify, it is the twelfth pitch class out of twelve to arrive, so that there is little chance of the ear's connecting it with the initial G♯ in any harmonically functional manner.

Finally, and this is particularly interesting, when the C finally arrives toward the end of the second arabesque in Ex. 6-6, the ear has likely been conditioned by the first arabesque to interpret the note as an appoggiatura rather than a potentially functional "harmonic tone." How is that possible in a harmonically "functionless" context? Simply by the rhythm and contour of the melodic writing, which apes the shape of an appoggiatura—a leap from upbeat to downbeat, landing on a tone that moves by step in the direction opposite to the leap.

The music that formed the immediate historical background to Schoenberg's expressionistic idiom was particularly rich in expressive appoggiaturas (or *Seufzer*, "sighs"—look back at Ex. 1-7, from the Adagio in Mahler's Tenth!), and it is clear that

Schoenberg intended such associations to remain in force. His radical style very effect-ively demonstrates the extent to which melodic shapes may continue to suggest local, quite conventional harmonic implications even in the absence of explicit harmonic func-tions — or rather, it demonstrates the extent to which our listening is always laden with unconsciously learned (or "picked-up") theory that the canny composer (who has also picked it up) is free to exploit. The question "tonal or atonal?" is thus not only a question about composing methods. It is also a question about listening habits and strategies.

The voice part, too, is riddled with appoggiaturas — even more conventionally expressive in the presence of a text. Measures 38, 39, and 40 all contain "sigh" figures to enhance the emotional impact of the poet's rueful appeal to "thou radiant, beloved specter, caller-forth of all my anguish" (Ex. 6-11a). There is an ineluctable sense that the A♯, C♯, and F resolve respectively to A, C, and E as dissonance resolves to consonance, even in the absence of any confirmation from the actual harmony. And then, in mm. 54–55 (Ex. 6-11b), all at once there is confirmation. The resolution of D to C♯ establishes a dominant chord just as it would in Mahler or Strauss: it is as if Schoenberg were twisting a dial to bring the key of F♯ in and out of focus.

EX. 6-11A   Arnold Schoenberg, Quartet no. 2, IV (*Entrückung*), arr. Berg, mm. 38–40

EX. 6-11B   Arnold Schoenberg, Quartet no. 2, IV (*Entrückung*), arr. Berg, mm. 51–55

The coda, which begins with the voice repeating its opening motive in agreement with a shimmering F♯ major triad (Ex. 6-12), is kept pretty well in focus by the use of tonic and dominant pedals. The movement, in its implied progression from tonal indefiniteness to regained definition, demonstrates the location of "tonality" and "atonality" on a contextual continuum, and the impossibility of drawing a categorical line between them. Even when there is no obvious return to "functionality," Schoenberg's expressionistic music often ends with unmistakable cadential gestures, usually involving half-step progressions that continue, just as they had been doing in Mahler and Strauss, to provide (on a "local" if not a "global" level) a sense of tonal motion and closure.

EX. 6-12   Arnold Schoenberg, Quartet no. 2, IV (*Entrückung*), arr. Berg, mm. 100–105

A LITTLE "SET THEORY"

For a final demonstration we can turn to the first of Schoenberg's *Sechs kleine Klavierstücke*, op. 19 ("Six little pieces for piano," 1911), a set of tiny, aphoristic piano pieces in an idiom that finally seems purged of all "tonal reference" (Ex. 6-13). No single pitch emerges from the texture with sufficient frequency to suggest itself as a candidate tonic; fifth relations are not salient; major or minor triads are not in evidence, nor are dominant-seventh chords. It would appear that the whole conventional vocabulary of music has been suppressed in favor of a private language.

And yet even if a familiar vocabulary is missing, there still remain vestiges of a familiar syntax. There are significantly recurring harmonies: both in the middle of m. 3 and on the downbeat of m. 5 are chords that could be cumbersomely described (in "tonal" terms) as a minor seventh chord without a fifth and with a major seventh along with the minor seventh. In m. 5 the four notes are F – A♭ – E♭ – E while the corresponding notes in m. 3 are C – E♭ – B♭ – B (the last note being the first in the right-hand melodic figure that enters after a sixteenth rest). The same harmony, expressed as an arpeggio or melodic succession, is also heard at the very beginning of the piece in the left hand.

EX. 6-13   Arnold Schoenberg, *Sechs kleine Klavierstücke*, Op. 19, no. 1

EX. 6-13 (continued)

A similar example comes in the middle of m. 2, where we find a distinctive chord — a tritone atop a perfect fourth — that we have already encountered in Stravinsky's *The Rite of Spring*, where it was so prevalent that we ended up calling it the *Rite*-chord. Its appearance in m. 2 is prefigured as the harmonic sum, so to speak, of the last three notes in m. 1 (the F♯, interestingly, being the upward resolution of a downward-leaping appoggiatura). As an arpeggio, it reappears at the beginning of m. 8 in inverted form, the tritone now below the perfect fourth rather than above. Note, too, that the right-hand triplet at the beginning of m. 5 consists of the same intervals compressed into the "best normal order": flip the E♭ and D into a seventh, put the A in the middle, and the result is another *Rite*-chord.

For a third example, compare the three-note chord in the left hand in m. 1 with the long-sustained chord in the right hand that lasts from the downbeat of m. 15 virtually to the end of the piece. It may not be immediately apparent that the one is the intervallic inversion of the other, but putting both chords into "best normal order" will make their relationship clear. The closest possible spacing of the notes in the first chord is B – D♯ – E, a major third beneath a semitone; a similar operation at measure 15 produces D♯ – E – G♯, a semitone beneath a major third. And once we have noticed this much, we can notice the many transposed occurrences of the same harmony (or "intervallic set"): the first arpeggiated right-hand chord in m. 7, the three right-hand thirty-second notes in m. 8 (B♭ – D – A) that follow the arpeggiated *Rite*-chord we have already noted, and so on.

One could go on noting correspondences like these almost indefinitely. Sometimes they resemble traditional contrapuntal devices: in m. 2, for example, the right hand melody (or rather its descending component) is mirrored in diminution by the thirty-seconds in the left hand. At other times they are purely harmonic: at the end of m. 5 (left hand) and in m. 7 (right hand) an augmented triad is the second chord in a pair, suggesting a cadential approach. Elsewhere (m. 3, left hand; last measure, both hands) multiple neighbors suggest cadences, just as they had done in early songs like *Erwartung* and *Der Wanderer*, now even in the absence of a tonic. One might even go so far as to suggest that the use of multiple neighbors lends the final chord in the piece the de facto status of a tonic even though it is not (as Schoenberg often put it) a "codified" harmony.

Contextual relationships like these arise, to use Schoenberg's own expression, from "working with the tones of a motive"[17] — that is, a group of notes with a distinctive intervallic profile. But the relationships we have been tracing, while numerous and cumulatively impressive, are not the whole story, or even the most significant part of it. The story as it stands shows Schoenberg working, even in a piece of only seventeen measures' duration, with a great many scattered motives. What justifies such a procedure if we assume (as anyone coming out of the intellectual and artistic traditions in which Schoenberg's style developed would have had to assume) that a piece of music should be "all of a piece"? Is there any principle by which all the scattered observations we have been making can be related?

For an answer, look once again at the chord in the middle of m. 3 (C – E♭ – B♭ – B), one of the first musical events we noted in taking the piece apart. If we refer it to Ex. 6-5, from Schoenberg's *Mädchenlied*, op. 6, no. 3 (a "tonal" song in E minor), we may note, to our possible surprise, that all of its tones are found there. And that means (if we recall the significance of Ex. 6-5 in the argument of this chapter) that all its tones belong to the "Eschbeg set," Schoenberg's musical signature. They are, in fact, the first four notes of the set with their order rearranged (as 2 – 1 – 4 – 3). And if we continue to survey the right-hand melody in m. 3, we encounter all the remaining tones, even including the A that provides the composer's first initial, so that the set assumes its complete "A. Schbeg" form.

The implications of this observation are far-reaching. To begin with, all of the relationships we have traced to the chord in m. 3 — the chord in m. 5, the left-hand melodic phrase at the very outset — are likewise traceable (through transposition) to the "A. Schbeg" (or "Aschbeg") set. And that also means that any other group of tones that can be derived as a transposed or untransposed subset from the "Aschbeg" set are related (or at least "relatable") to all the other ones. That includes virtually all the musical configurations we have noted. They are all related to one another, if the "Aschbeg" set is regarded as the nexus.

To demonstrate this we have to put the "A. Schbeg" set in its "best normal order." In the order of Schoenberg's name the constituent tones are A – E♭ – C – B – B♭ – E – G. The closest possible spacing of these tones is G – A – B♭ – B – C – E♭ – E. If we call G "zero" and count by semitones, the Aschbeg set looks like this: /0 2 3 4 5 8 9/. Now we are ready to compare the other pitch configurations we have noted to the Aschbeg set. The fourth-tritone configuration, noted in m. 1, m. 2, and m. 8 (among other occurrences) reduces to /0 1 6/. This configuration can be "mapped" onto the numerical form of the Aschbeg set by adding 2 to each of its members: /2 3 8/. Each of the resulting numbers can be found in the Aschbeg set.

This can easily be put in more familiar musical terms. All that the numbers really mean is that if you start on the A (= 2), you can construct a fourth-tritone chord out of the notes of the Aschbeg set: A – B♭ – E♭, which if spaced B♭ – E♭ – A is an exact transposition of the chord in m. 3. Similarly, the third + semitone configuration that we traced in m. 1 (left hand) and m. 15 (right hand), when placed in best normal order (/0 1 5/), can be mapped onto the Aschbeg set by adding 3: /3 4 8/ (the numbers corresponding to B♭ – B – Eb, a transposition of the D♯ – E – G♯ in m. 15).

Did Schoenberg do all this "math"? Of course not. He needed only to have the Aschbeg set in mind as his starting point, select subsets from it, and transpose them as he wished. It is we who need the math to demonstrate (or at least plausibly propose) the first premise, namely that Schoenberg had the Aschbeg set in mind as his starting point. There are other ways of showing (or proposing) this as well. The piece actually begins with a very slightly modified Aschbeg set, consisting of the first two notes in the right hand and the left-hand part up to the three-note chord we have already analyzed from another perspective. The sum of all these pitches is "Aschbeg" minus the B♭, and with a G♯ in its place. The G♯ is not really as much of a deviation as it may seem. Its enharmonic equivalent, A♭, is "As" in German: the first two letters of Aschbeg.

There are at least two more complete Aschbegs embedded in the music of op. 19, no. 1. The left-hand part of m. 7, plus the pickup at the end of m. 6 and the first right hand note in m. 8, amounts to Aschbeg transposed down a semitone. The most hidden or "occult" occurrence of the set is found in m. 5. It needs to be illustrated with an example, since it crosscuts three of the polyphonic voices delineated in Schoenberg's notation. It should be emphasized, though, lest anyone suspect it to be fortuitous, that the pitches involved are all contiguous (see Ex. 6-14).

EX. 6-14   "Aschbeg" set in Arnold Schoenberg, *Sechs kleine Klavierstücke*, Op. 19, no. 1, m. 5

GRUNDGESTALT

Never before have we devoted so much space to analyzing so little music. It was a necessary extravagance, matching the extravagant intricacy of the composition. That intricacy was mandated by Schoenberg's famously contradictory aims, according to which a spontaneous impression had to be undergirded by a very deliberate, even cerebral, process of control. On the one hand, Schoenberg aimed to compose "expressionistically," as if by primitive instinct, avoiding all trace of established or uncritically accepted routine; and on the other, he felt a strong obligation to compose "responsibly," unifying his composition "organically," according to the standards set by the masters he revered. The result was an "athematic" music, as Schoenberg called it, in which there were no obvious tunes — and no obvious "received" formal design — on the musical surface, but in which there was a teeming "subcutaneous" profusion of complex motivic work.

What unified the composition was no longer a theme in the traditional sense but what Schoenberg called the *Grundgestalt* or "basic shape": a motivic complex that could serve as a source or quarry for everything that happened in the composition (or at least everything that happened in the pitch dimension). All melodic shapes, all harmonies, all contrapuntal textures were to be derived from it by the composer — and therefore, at least theoretically, deducible through analysis, which thus constitutes a test of the composer's success (or, even more strongly, of his ethics).

PSYCHOLOGICAL REALISM

So there we have some more questions to be repressed for the time being, while we delve further into Schoenberg's repulsive yet fascinating psychological terrain. The word "repulsive" here is not an esthetic judgment but (as the epigraph atop this chapter already suggests) a statement of fact. The use of art — sometimes didactically, sometimes voyeuristically — to explore what was ugly or obnoxious was another long-standing project that expressionism brought to a head; and it should come as no surprise that Schoenberg's most extreme essay in the expressionist vein should have been a portrait of a sexually obsessed madwoman to set alongside counterparts in Wagner and Strauss and vastly outstrip them.

In creating it, Schoenberg brought musical expressionism to its Far Out Point — which in effect meant bringing German romanticism itself to its final shriek. Considering that for a century or more art had been defined as inherently romantic, and music as the most essentially romantic of the arts, the magnitude of Schoenberg's achievement — or at least of his attempt — has to be regarded as "historic." It is what won for Schoenberg his devoted disciples and his enormous authority, and also what insured that his name would remain a lightning rod for controversy second only to Wagner's.

Schoenberg's madwoman was the protagonist of a twenty-five-minute "mono-drama" — a one-act opera with a single character — that he composed, at white heat, between 27 August and 12 September 1909. Like the early song through which we first encountered Schoenberg's name (and very likely in tribute to it) the opera was called *Erwartung*, "Expectancy." But whereas the early song, in keeping with the fashion of its time, described an expectation (and gave a foretaste) of sensual pleasure, the new opera, subtitled *Angsttraum*, or "Nightmare," depicted a prolonged foreboding of psychic horror, the kind of maximalized emotional tension without hope of relief for which only "emancipated dissonance" — dissonance with no possibility of resolution — seemed capable of providing an adequate symbolic medium.

Like the exiled Wagner some sixty years before, Schoenberg achieved this aggressive technical and expressive breakthrough in creative isolation, not to say seclusion. Like *The Ring*, *Erwartung* had to wait many years for its first performance, which took place in Prague (by then no longer in Austria but the capital of Czechoslovakia) in 1924 — all of which further enhanced Schoenberg's prophetic aura and gave the music, when finally heard, the force of revelation to its devotees.

The weird libretto was of a sort no established writer of the time would have agreed to write. It was composed at Schoenberg's request by a family friend of the Zemlinskys named Marie Pappenheim (1882–1966), an avocational poet who had recently come to Vienna from Pressburg (now Bratislava in Slovakia) to study medicine, eventually becoming a well-known dermatologist. The disjointed, often ungrammatical monologue she came up with has often been compared with the sort of emotionally overwrought running babble an "analysand" or patient in psychoanalysis might utter from the couch in "free association."

That was surely no coincidence. Marie Pappenheim's brother, the psychiatrist Martin Pappenheim, was an early follower of Freud, and her cousin Bertha Pappenheim was the notorious "Anna O.," arguably the first analysand. A patient of Josef Breuer, Freud's mentor and early collaborator, Bertha Pappenheim underwent a celebrated but later bitterly contested cure from hysteria by means of hypnosis and "recovered memory." Whether true memories or merely fantasies and hallucinations produced through hypnotic and autohypnotic suggestion, the therapeutic results of Bertha Pappenheim's "talking cure," when written up by her therapist in "The Case of Anna O.," were a medical and literary sensation. It was the ongoing (indeed, still-raging) controversy over the reliability of hypnotically induced results that led Freud to modify the method so as to replace hypnosis with the fully conscious talk therapy known as free association.

But it was precisely the ambiguity of psychic phenomena, the impossibility of distinguishing with certainty between recalled (or even lived) experience and fantasy, the very pitfall that compromised the "Case of Anna O." scientifically, that Marie Pappenheim now sought to exploit artistically in the libretto she fashioned for Schoenberg. Its dramatic situation is simplicity itself; the ramifications to which it leads are unfathomable. A woman (nameless, like most characters in expressionist drama) finds herself at the edge of a wood, anxiously looking for her lover. At the end of the opera she stumbles on his corpse and immediately begins a jealous rant that leaves us wondering whether she has murdered him.

The whole drama consists of her "inner occurrences," as Schoenberg would say, a compound of immediate sensation, memory, fantasy, and hallucination. At the end, as in contemporary literary experiments with the "stream of consciousness," we are left to wonder whether what we have witnessed is "real," a dream, or a psychotic symptom. (In keeping with this irreality and uncertainty the Metropolitan Opera in New York once staged *Erwartung* with a set that contained, in addition to the phantasmagorical moonlit forest, a grand piano to suggest that perhaps the distraught protagonist had never left her parlor—or else perhaps that, stumbling through the real forest, she imagines herself all the while at home.)

Like the other fin-de-siècle madwomen we have met, Schoenberg's "Frau" symbolized, in her violent loss of emotional control, the imagined consequences of the stresses to which modern civilization subjects its members, and also the displaced response of men threatened by the emancipation of the weaker sex. Thus, like most fin-de-siècle art (and like psychoanalysis, for that matter), it expressed a crucial ambivalence, using a radically innovative approach, and a vocabulary of extreme modernity, in order to critique, or even indict, the modern world.

The indictment was much stronger than before. Previous manifestations of the madwoman theme, whether in the operas of Strauss or the ballets of Stravinsky, had camouflaged it with the exotic trappings of antiquity (classical, biblical, primitive), enhancing its voyeuristic allure and distancing it from its uncomfortable contemporary relevance. Schoenberg and Pappenheim gave it a raw, unvarnished treatment that laid its social and psychological message bare. Neither Stravinsky's Chosen One nor Strauss's title characters have any interior life. They are not "subjects." We see them act, we witness their drives and compulsions, but we are not privy to their reflections. (Indeed, it would have contradicted the whole primitivist assumption to allow the Chosen One to have any such thing as a reflection.) Schoenberg's madwoman is nothing but reflection; we are left unsure whether indeed she has an external life to match her inner turmoil. Her intense subjectivity coupled with her namelessness allows her to represent both an autonomous contemporary psyche in all its unfathomable complexity, and an archetypal Every(wo)man. Through the prism of Schoenberg's opera, *Salome* and *The Rite of Spring* themselves assume a clearer focus as cultural symptoms.

Indeed, Schoenberg made the parallels between his opera and its German antecedents inescapable. Where the woman imagines kissing her dead lover, Schoenberg forces the listener to recall Strauss's necrophiliac Salome (Ex. 6-15). And when she lets out the one word—"Help!"—that she unambiguously speaks (or shrieks) aloud rather than to herself, Schoenberg literally quotes a similar frenzied moment from the part of Kundry, the madwoman in Wagner's *Parsifal* and the progenitor of the whole fin-de-siècle line (Ex. 6-16).

EX. 6-15A   Richard Strauss, *Salome*, mm. 319–320

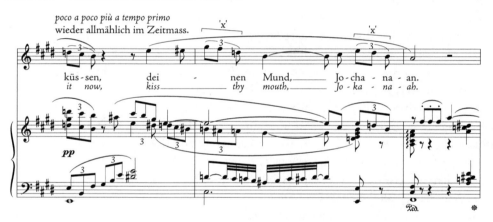

EX. 6-15B   Arnold Schoenberg, *Erwartung*, mm. 263–264

The scenario consists of four scenes separated by little orchestral interludes during which the singer leaves and re-enters the stage. They are chiefly distinguished from one another, again in a manner typical of expressionist theater, by lighting effects. The first scene is bathed in moonlight; the second takes place in "blackest darkness." The third has a split stage (one side dark, the other moonlit), and the last is illuminated

EX. 6-16A   Arnold Schoenberg, *Erwartung*, mm. 190–195

EX. 6-16B   Richard Wagner, *Parsifal*, Act II, "Lachte!"

EX. 6-16B   *(continued)*

in multicolored light. They can be taken as representations of states of consciousness (Freud's conscious "ego" vs. the unconscious "id"). It is during the "black" second scene that the woman has a presentiment of the grisly end, mistaking a log in her path for the dead body she will find (although she is not yet consciously aware of the presentiment). All of this, moreover, can be taken as a metaphor of music itself—or at least of Schoenberg's music, if we remember his avowal to Kandinsky that art must express the instinctive and the inborn, the part of ourselves that is wholly unconscious and uncorrupted by convention.

But how "unconscious" is the music that represents this instinctive or reflex state? Webern, Schoenberg's devoted pupil and spokesman, insisted that, as a representation of unconscious and irrational thought, *Erwartung* contained no thematic repetitions or developments—that is, nothing of musical "logic." Both in its flow of pitches and rhythms and in its coloring, the work represented, in Webern's view

> an uninterrupted succession of sounds never before heard; there is no measure of this score that fails to display a completely new sound-picture, and so this music flows onward, giving expression to the most hidden and slightest impulses of the emotions.[18]

This description has set the tone for many others, and for ever more extravagant claims, such as the music theorist Robert Morgan's contention that the speed with which Schoenberg composed *Erwartung* suggests that the opera in all its complexity of design "surfaced directly—without intervention of conscious control—from the composer's innermost subliminal thought processes," and that the music therefore "almost completely defies rational musical analysis."[19]

These remarks exemplify the hyperbole that has always surrounded Schoenberg's achievement, itself a testimony to its benchmark-setting maximalism. And yet a close look at virtually any measure of the score will tell another story—the story already implied by our analysis of the tiny piano piece, op. 19, no. 1, but projected on a vast scale. What made it possible for Schoenberg to compose his opera so quickly, as that close look will immediately disclose, was an extremely high degree of melodic and harmonic consistency. The material out of which *Erwartung* was assembled, though often tendentiously characterized by the composer and his disciples as a sea of possibilities even more limitless than Wagner's, turns out to have been in fact quite limited, as effective composing always demands. In other words, the composer created his own rules but then followed them scrupulously.

ATONAL TRIADS

To demonstrate this, we need only take a melodic and harmonic inventory of the opening measures (Ex. 6-17) and spot-check the rest. And our inventory will start right off with something familiar. The very first harmony in the score, consisting of the three notes played before the first bar (a melodic quarter-note upbeat in the bassoon and an accompanying fourth that comes in on the last sixteenth), turns out to be an inversion of the same *Rite*-chord we have already spotted in the little piano piece, and which can be sighted in any number of early Schoenberg scores. (Transpose the accompanying fourth up an octave, as in Ex. 6-18a, so that it is above the bassoon's G♯ rather than below it, and the more familiar voicing of fourth + tritone will appear.)

The harmony is just as pervasive in *Erwartung* as it had been in *The Rite*. It is Schoenberg's basic harmonic building block, in fact, providing his music with a sonic norm much as the triad had always done in "common-practice" harmony. So from now on it will make some sense to call it the "atonal triad," not only because of its prevalence but also in reference to its structure. Just as the triad is a superimposition of thirds, so this chord is a superimposition of fourths; and just as triads may superimpose thirds of the same kind or of different kinds, so can "fourth-chords." When the thirds in a triad are of different kinds, moreover, the harmony can be inverted: the difference between the major and minor triads in common practice is defined according to whether the major third is below or above the minor third. Similarly, atonal triads like Schoenberg's can be inverted according to whether the augmented fourth is below or above the perfect fourth. And just as ordinary triads can be extended by "stacking" more thirds atop the basic pair to make seventh and ninth chords, and so forth, so the atonal triad may be extended by stacking alternating perfect and augmented fourths above the basic pair. We have already seen this happen (and seen it extended to the maximum) in the sketches for Ives's *Universe Symphony* (Fig. 5-6).

All of these potential features (many of which Schoenberg later codified in his *Harmonielehre*) are immediately actualized in *Erwartung*. The left-hand component of the downbeat chord that immediately follows the initial harmony is an atonal triad with the augmented fourth on the bottom—a "major" atonal triad, if you will. But the melodic B that the chord accompanies can be construed as an extension of the chord according to the principles just described: it stands a tritone above the top note of the atonal triad, producing a four-note harmony that alternates augmented and perfect fourths. And now note that that flute figure that comes in immediately afterward continues the alternation with an E a fourth above the B, and a B♭ a tritone above the E. (The E♭ at the end of the flute figure, preceded by a sort of "leading tone," could be added to the configuration if desired. And the choice of A for the bass of the next

EX. 6-17   Arnold Schoenberg, *Erwartung*, Op. 17, mm. 1–7

chord can now be rationalized as well: it too is an extension of the same series of fourths and tritones.) Thus we are observing the interpenetration of the horizontal and vertical dimensions that the "emancipation of dissonance" made possible; but we are also observing the extreme normative limitation that Schoenberg is voluntarily placing on his "emancipated" harmonic and melodic materials. The harmony of *Erwartung*, to a remarkable degree, consists of chords alternating fourths and tritones, ranging all the way from the basic three-note unit we are now calling the "atonal triad" to extensions of six notes or more. The series of chords in the second measure offers immediate confirmation of this generalization. In transcribing them for piano, Schoenberg had to prune them radically; they are spelled out in full in Ex. 6-18b. Particularly telling is the way the melodic D is suspended over a harmonic shift that embeds it in two successive extended atonal triads. Atop the first it stands at the distance of a perfect fourth, and above the second the distance expands to a tritone; in context, the effect is analogous to that of a modal mixture.

The pervasiveness of the atonal triad and its extensions can be corroborated in almost any bar of *Erwartung*. It supports many if not most of the important vocal entrances, starting with the first: the harmony at the first sung note is an inversion similar to the one noted at the very beginning. It is sorted out in Ex. 6-18c, where the voice's C♯ appears as the "tenor." The relationship is confirmed and clarified at the next harmony, where the voice straightforwardly plays bass extension to an atonal triad represented in the piano's right-hand part. By contrast (or complement), at the next important voice entrance (m. 7) it plays "soprano extension" to an atonal triad represented in the left-hand part.

EX. 6-18A   Atonal triads and extensions in Arnold Schoenberg, *Erwartung*

EX. 6-18B   Atonal triads and extensions in Arnold Schoenberg, *Erwartung*

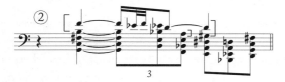

EX. 6-18C   Atonal triads and extensions in Arnold Schoenberg, *Erwartung*

The ultimate extension of the atonal triad, as we have already learned from Ives, is the aggregate harmony, the full chromatic gamut sounded as a chord. This famously happens at the pianissimo ending of *Erwartung*, where a series of chromatically ascending six-note extensions is met by a chromatically descending series. The two lines become a fuzzy stretto, with different groups of instruments moving at different rates of speed, so that ultimately a sonically saturating glissando effect is achieved, only to be suddenly cut off, sans ritardando and sans crescendo, at curtain's fall.

This striking effect has supported many interpretations. The most obvious one is dramatic, or rather representational: a musical rendering of being emotionally engulfed, or even, perhaps, of fainting dead away. Another, equally convincing, interpretation (which in no way contradicts the first) is technical. It was memorably described by the pianist and critic Charles Rosen in a short handbook on Schoenberg. "The saturation of musical space," Rosen suggested, "is Schoenberg's substitute for the tonic chord of the traditional musical language."[20] By characterizing "the saturation of chromatic space" as "a fixed point toward which the music moves, as a point of rest and resolution," Rosen ascribed to it a "closure" function (which, of course, is what he meant by calling it a substitute tonic in the first place). The idea had profound implications for Schoenberg and his notion of "pantonality," and we will come back to it.

CROSSING THE CUSP

But first we need to investigate the other pervasive motif in *Erwartung*, which first appears as the three notes (C♯–A♯–D) that initiate the lyrical oboe line in mm. 1–2, and reappears in transposition as the last three notes of the same phrase (E–C♯–B♯). The two notes that come in between, G and D♯, replicate the same motif when combined with the E that follows them, thus producing a pair of overlapping (or "imbricated") statements (Ex. 6-19a). This motif consists of a semitone and a minor third enclosed within a major third. Its "best normal order" is /0 1 4/, with the semitone beneath the minor third. But like the atonal triad, it can appear in the score with either interval on top (or to put it more formally, it has an inversional equivalent). And it can be varied (or distorted) in other ways as well.

In one guise or another, then, this motif inhabits virtually every measure of the score. At the end of m. 4, for example, it is found both at the end of the voice part and also as the nervous staccato ostinato running beneath. Stretched out as if on a rack, its intervals expanded to sevenths and tenths, it comes at the end of m. 6 (F–D–C♯). A comparison of the staccato bass chords in m. 1 and the bass arpeggio in m. 3 will show a version of it (A–C–C♯) crossing the cusp between harmony and melody, and it is followed in m. 3 by a transposition (G♯–B–C) that maintains a common tone (Ex. 6-19b). All of these procedures become standard means of composerly navigation

EX. 6-19A   Melodic motif in Arnold Schoenberg, *Erwartung*

EX. 6-19B   Melodic motif in Arnold Schoenberg, *Erwartung*

EX. 6-19C   Melodic motif in Arnold Schoenberg, *Erwartung*

as the music unfolds. Particularly telling are the settings, like the one at mm. 301–302 (Ex. 6-19c), where the motif and its inversion are both multiply embedded in a single melodic line (sometimes even further reinforced by the accompaniment).

In 1967 Herbert Buchanan, a doctoral candidate in musicology at Rutgers University, published a short article, "A Key to Schoenberg's *Erwartung* (Op. 17)," that took nearly everyone by surprise.[21] He had discovered that the closing measures of the opera contained a quotation, encompassing both text and music, lengthy and literal enough to be obvious to anyone alerted to its presence (and in fact almost immediately repeated), from an early song of Schoenberg's: *Am Wegrand* ("By the roadside"), op. 6, no. 6 (1905). (The relationship had previously been noted in a footnote to Theodor Wiesengrund Adorno's book *Philosophy of New Music* (*Philosophie der neuen Musik*, 1949), but as Adorno's work was as yet untranslated and little known in the American academy, Buchanan may well have found it independently.) What was surprising about the discovery was not only the fact that it seemed to contradict the opera's reputation for "athematicism," but also the fact that the song in question, although it was composed only four years earlier than the opera, was quite conventional (or "tonal") in harmonic design. Even in its operatic recycling, the passage in question can be analyzed perfectly straightforwardly in D minor (Ex. 6-20).

EX. 6-20A   Arnold Schoenberg, *Am Wegrand*, mm. 3–4

EX. 6-20B   Arnold Schoenberg, *Am Wegrand*, mm. 22–24

EX. 6-20C   Arnold Schoenberg, *Erwartung*, mm. 411–412

As the example shows, the quotation from the song in the opera is not exact. Rather it is a conflation of two spots. The opening voice melody in Ex. 6-20a is transferred to the orchestral bass in Ex. 6-20c, and the voice countermelody in Ex. 6-20b is transferred to the orchestra in Ex. 6-20c and accompanied in the operatic voice part by a modified transposition of itself that descends in alternating semitones and minor thirds, so that it consists almost entirely of imbricated /0 1 4/ motifs or inversions thereof (Ex. 6-21a).

Meanwhile, the middle voice or harmonic filler in the orchestra part is also saturated with /0 1 4/ motifs. The first beat contains the motif labeled "b" in Ex. 6-21a (D–F–C♯); the second contains a new motif "f" (F–F♯–A), a transposed permutation of "b"; between the second and third beats motif "b" reappears, as does motif "f" in the fourth beat (Ex. 6-21b). And finally, the orchestral bass, which as we know is a direct quotation from *Am Wegrand*, a song in D minor, contains a four-note group in which the /0 1 4/ motif and its inversion are imbricated (Ex. 6-21c).

Thus motif b/b′ in Ex. 6-21c, which on its original occurrence in *Am Wegrand* had been invested with tonal functions (another way of saying that its constituent pitches were identifiable as degrees 7♯–1–2–3 in D minor) has been abstracted to serve, throughout *Erwartung*, as a basic melodic shape or *Grundgestalt* with only contextual harmonic significance. Its progress from the one (functional or "tonal") status to the

EX. 6-21A   /0 1 4/ motif in Arnold Schoenberg, *Erwartung*, m. 411, voice part

EX. 6-21B   /0 1 4/ motif in Arnold Schoenberg, *Erwartung*, m. 411, figuration

EX. 6-21C   /0 1 4/ motif in Arnold Schoenberg, *Erwartung*, m. 411, bass

other (contextual or "atonal") one might seem to symbolize Schoenberg's progress, as he then conceived it (or at least as he later described it), over the hump from his "tonal" to his "pantonal" period. That could well have been his reason for interpolating the quotation from the older song. The unanswerable question, already broached, is whether he consciously mined a tonal piece for a motif to abstract and as it were "denature," or whether memories of *Am Wegrand* were stirred when Schoenberg found himself playing so extensively with the tones (or, more precisely, with the intervallic relationships) of one of its characteristic motifs.

MUSICAL SPACE

But now the repressed questions must be faced. Why was it desirable to denature tonality? Why was emancipation of the dissonance a necessary step? Unrelieved dissonance suited certain dreadful or turbulent moods, all right, of a kind then favored by many artists, especially German ones. But other moods — joy, serenity, contentment, anything "positive" — were seemingly put off limits. Were they no longer suitable for artistic representation? Did they merely reflect a "false consciousness" that it was the duty of true artists ("who do not turn their eyes away," in the words of our epigraph) to unmask? And why was motivic saturation so desirable, especially when (as we have seen) its exacting compositional requirements could seem to contradict the "instinctive" creative freedom Schoenberg proclaimed?

As long as we view Schoenberg solely as an "expressionist," a dealer in emotions, these questions will continue to disturb us. But there was another, equally potent and equally distinguished component in Schoenberg's Romantic legacy that he consciously

FIG. 6-3 Wassily Kandinsky and Schoenberg with their wives, Nina and Gertrud, at Pörtschach on the Wörthersee, 1927.

sought to maximalize: the legacy of the Sublime. Alongside his fascination with "inner [that is, psychic] occurrences" was an equally strong interest in spiritual transcendence and the possibilities of representing it in art. From a rationalist perspective the two impulses — psychological realism vs. occult revelation — can seem to be in contradiction. From a more accommodating perspective that regards psychic phenomena as emanations from a spiritual source (or as "microcosmic" reflections of the "macrocosm"), they can be viewed as complementary. It is when we adopt this complementary perspective that Schoenberg's musical innovations (or rather, his motivations toward them) become coherent.

Significantly, the most unambiguous expressions of Schoenberg's interest in the occult are found in his correspondence with Kandinsky, the early abstract painter, who justified his own artistic radicalism in terms of his religious strivings, and who summarized his theories in a book entitled *Über das Geistige in der Kunst* (*On the Spiritual in Art*), published in 1912. In a letter to Kandinsky dating from the same year, Schoenberg proclaimed "a *unity of musical space demanding an absolute and unitary perception*"[22] (his italics) to be his creative ideal. And he associated this aim with a book that both he and Kandinsky worshipped at the time, Honoré de Balzac's philosophical novel *Séraphîta* (1835), "perhaps the most glorious work in existence," as the musician gushed to the artist.

The long central chapter in *Séraphîta* is an imaginary (and fanciful rather than historically accurate) exposition of the teachings of the occult philosopher Emanuel Swedenborg (1688–1772), as related to Wilfrid, a man of thirty, and Minna, a girl of seventeen, by an androgynous ethereal being with whom both are in love and who in the last chapter ascends to an angelic state. The two lovers, who are left to share

FIG. 6-4 Emanuel Swedenborg.

the love they bore for the angel, are privileged to witness the assumption and are vouchsafed a vision of heaven:

> Wilfrid and Minna now understood some of the mysterious words of the being who on earth had appeared to them under the form which was intelligible to each — Séraphîtus to one, Séraphîta to the other — seeing that here all was homogeneous. Light gave birth to melody, and melody to light; colors were both light and melody; motion was number endowed by the Word; in short, everything was at once sonorous, diaphanous, and mobile; so that, everything existing in everything else, extension knew no limits, and the angels could traverse it everywhere to the utmost depths of the infinite.[23]

This vision is what inspired Schoenberg toward his integrated musical space. Many details in Balzac's heavenly depiction found echo in Schoenberg's musical theorizing. Where in Balzac's heaven "colors were both light and melody," Schoenberg's *Harmonielehre* contained a famous speculation on the possibility of composing "tone-color melodies" (*Klangfarbenmelodien*) that would add another dimension of integration to his utopian musical universe, with timbre playing a role normally assigned to pitch.[24] The closest he came to realizing it was in the third of the *Five Orchestral Pieces*, called "Farben" (colors), where very slowly changing harmonies shimmer with dovetailed instrumental voicings that cause the timbres of sustained tones to shift subtly before one's ears. (In private, Schoenberg habitually referred to his famous color-piece as "Morning by a Lake"; in 1949, he finally added the title to the score.) But it was not just a vision that Schoenberg wanted to transmit. He also wanted to convey an experience — Wilfrid and Minna's experience in ascending to Séraphîta's abode, where "everything existed in everything else." As we already know from his quartet setting of Stefan George's *Entrückung*, Schoenberg regarded his musical breakthroughs in spiritual terms — very much as an "ascent to a higher and better order,"[25] as he put it in a letter to Nicolas Slonimsky, another Russian correspondent. He viewed "pantonality" very much as Balzac presented Séraphîtus/Séraphîta. Surmounting the major/minor dichotomy, voiding all distinctions between particular keys, was for him an achievement comparable to embodying androgyny or double gender. Pantonal music, like Balzac's angel, was a perfected being. To Webern he confided that pantonality, like androgyny, "has given rise to a higher race!"[26]

Like Scriabin's, then, and like Mahler's and Ives's, Schoenberg's was a *Weltanschauungsmusik*, a music that embodied a spiritual "worldview" or universal existential revelation. And it was this in addition to being a music of primal unconscious emotional expression and a music of unprecedented motivic integration. Indeed, as we are about to see, it was the spiritual Weltanschauung that provided the conceptual link between the emotional expression, which depended on the emancipation of dissonance, and the motivic integration, which the same emancipation made possible. One of the most overdetermined musical visions at a time of many visionary extremes, Schoenberg's was the most complex and far-reaching maximalism of them all, and by far the most lastingly influential.

Thus the most important (or at least the most fundamental) thing that the emancipation of dissonance vouchsafed was not the expression of catastrophic emotions, though that was a spectacular by-product, but the achievement of a fully integrated musical space, in which the "horizontal" and "vertical" dimensions were at last made equivalent, and (to recall Balzac), everything musical could exist in everything else. Only by emancipating the dissonance, Schoenberg argued, could musical practice become fully adequate to the musical imagination. "Every musical configuration," he wrote,

> every movement of tones has to be comprehended primarily as a mutual relation of sounds, of oscillatory vibrations, appearing at different places and times. To the imaginative and creative faculty, relations in the material sphere are as independent from directions or planes as material objects are, in their sphere, to our perceptive faculties. Just as our mind always recognizes, for instance, a knife, a bottle, or a watch, regardless of its position, and can reproduce it in the imagination in every possible position, even so a musical creator's mind can operate subconsciously with a row of tones, regardless of their direction, regardless of the way in which a mirror might show the mutual relations, which remain a given quality.[27]

In other words, as long as composition was constrained by rules of consonance and dissonance, or by harmonic functions, "horizontal" ideas like melodies could not always be "vertically" represented, as chords. And a harmonic progression would no longer mean the same thing (whether "syntactically" or "semantically") if it were played in reverse, or if all or some of its intervals were inverted. Imagine a G-major triad followed by a C-major triad. In the context of the key of C major this can mean "the end." But if reversed it can mean anything but that. And if inverted, so that the G-major triad were a C-minor triad, and the C-major triad an F-minor triad, it would all of a sudden (in the same tonal context) lose its syntactical significance altogether and pick up instead a terrific freight of emotion.

If the voice leading were strictly reproduced, moreover, the inversion would be a syntactic anomaly. And if, perchance the G-major chord were a dominant seventh, and the inversions (instead of reproducing the original voice leading) took the respective chord roots as their axis, the result would be a syntactic absurdity (Ex. 6-22).

EX. 6-22   A "tonal" cadence inverted

These trivial examples, or a slightly less trivial one once published by the music theorist Joseph Schillinger, who both reversed and inverted the opening phrase of Bach's F-major keyboard invention (Ex. 6-23) will suffice to establish that in "tonal" music, musical space is neither reversible nor invertible without distortion or loss of meaning.

But as our analyses both of *Erwartung* and of op. 19, no. 1 have already demonstrated, thanks to the emancipation of dissonance in Schoenberg's expressionist music the horizontal and the vertical are indeed interchangeable and inversions are functionally equivalent. Musical space has been unified, or equalized in every dimension, so that musical objects and ideas (i.e., motifs and their derivatives) can now be "reproduced," just as the mind can imagine them, "in every possible position, . . . regardless of their direction."

EX. 6-23   Joseph Schillinger's inversion of the subject of Bach's F-major Invention

"BRAHMINISM" REVISITED

It is certainly possible to view this as a "purely" musical advance, without justification on expressionist or spiritual grounds. In that case it would be a maximalization of the sort of contrapuntally saturated textures we have found in Brahms (particularly in his chamber music), textures that had already become an object of virtual fetish worship on the part of "Brahmin" critics and music lovers. Motivic saturation could also be seen as a historical advance from the point of view of the New German School, recalling their insistence that the general tendency in music history was toward the integration of form and content, with Wagner's "endless melody," a musical texture in which everything was "thematic" (that is, based on meaning-bearing leitmotifs) setting the standard. Once again

FIG. 6-5   Alban Berg and Anton Webern, spring 1912.

Schoenberg could be seen as the synthesizer of the Brahms-Wagner antithesis, which gave him a special importance within a historical narrative based on "dialectics." (But see the epilogue to this chapter for a critique of this historical claim.)

One of the first to argue in this way on Schoenberg's behalf was his pupil Alban Berg, in an article called "Why Is Schoenberg's Music So Difficult to Understand?" Like the Chamber Concerto it was a fiftieth-birthday offering to his teacher, first published in a "Festschrift" or celebratory volume devoted to Schoenberg in 1924. The article consists mainly of an analysis of Schoenberg's "official" First Quartet (op. 7), not the one performed under Zemlinsky's auspices in 1897, but one composed in 1905, in which Schoenberg asserted that he had achieved "a direction much more my own."[28]

Berg, undoubtedly on Schoenberg's authority, associated this new direction with the quartet's unprecedented level of motivic saturation. There was "hardly any" material in the quartet, he claimed, even in its accompanimental figuration, its ornamental details and textural "fillers," that cannot be traced to its germinating motifs. Having quoted the first ten measures of the quartet, Berg noted that he had in fact supplied the reader with the whole hour-long quartet *in nuce* (in a nutshell). That made the music more difficult to understand than any other contemporary music because comprehending its luxuriance required more cognitive work from the listener. And, Berg provocatively averred, it also made the music better than any other contemporary music. Such "unheard-of excess" of motivic richness, unifying the music in all its "harmonic, polyphonic and contrapuntal domains," had not previously existed "since Bach."[29] But the claims did not stop there. The emancipation of dissonance, Berg implied, made it possible to eliminate that "hardly any" and produce a music in which literally every note, whether melodic or harmonic, was "thematic." If the manner of the First Quartet was better than what had been before, then the manner of the Second Quartet was better yet, and so on into the music contemporaneous with Berg's essay. The "progress" claim, coupled with the more-than-implied "Brahmin" snobbery of the title, made Berg's essay immediately controversial, and the controversy has not subsided to this day.

The reason controversy has never subsided had to do not only with the brashness of the rhetoric, but also with the sheer impressiveness of the technical achievement, which made Schoenberg's music such an influence on other composers and music theorists even as audiences continued to find it difficult and, in the opinion of many "laymen," unrewarding. It is certainly not the aim of a book like this to resolve controversy, nor is there room for the kind of close analysis it would require of an hour-long composition fully to sustain Berg's thesis. And yet the only evidence given thus far of the remarkable motivic consistency made possible by "emancipating the dissonance" has been a two-page piano piece lasting perhaps a minute, and a very general description of an opera that, like any opera, can claim coherence on the basis of its plot and text even without considering the music in detail.

As a parenthesis, then, let us replicate Berg's experiment, so to speak, with one of Schoenberg's emblematic expressionist compositions: "Vorgefühle" ("Premonitions"), the first of the *Five Orchestral Pieces*, op. 16, composed with characteristic speed in May

1909, shortly before *Erwartung*. Specifically, let us consider the whole piece in the light of Ex. 6-24, a reduction of its first three measures, which (we may propose) foreshadows the whole piece *in nuce*, as study of the full score will confirm.

EX. 6-24   Reduction of Arnold Schoenberg's *Vorgefühle*, mm. 1–3

Such a detailed comparison will indeed show that literally every note in the orchestral piece, "in all its harmonic, polyphonic, and contrapuntal domains," can be referred to Ex. 6-24, which could therefore be asserted as the composition's *Grundgestalt*. But Ex. 6-24 already betrays numerous motivic interrelationships. The first three sixteenth-notes in the running bass, to begin with, are an arpeggiation of the "atonal triad" at the downbeat of m. 2, which in terms of sounding duration counts as the main harmony in Ex. 6-24. Its "best normal order" is /0 1 6/.

The next three notes in the bass are an arpeggiation of the second chord in m. 1, which is a transposition of the chord that is held by the bassoons, and then the trombones, through the whole second half of the piece. Its constituent intervals could be represented in best normal order as /0 4 5/ (or, transposed up a semitone, as /1 5 6/. And the final chord in Ex. 6-24, the only one that contains four notes, is the sum of the two already tabulated: its constituent intervals could be represented as /0 1 5 6/. Not only that, but it too is explicitly arpeggiated in the running bass (the last two notes in m. 2 and the first two in m. 3).

The remaining two chords (the first in the piece and the one between the two repeated atonal triads in m. 2) are both presented as neighbors to the longer-sustained harmonies, proceeding to them in a way that should by now look habitual with Schoenberg, by semitones in contrary motion. Remarkably enough, these two chords, obviously "ornamental" in duration and function as implied by voice leading, are the only traditionally consonant harmonies in evidence. The one in the middle of m. 2, though wearing an enharmonic disguise, is actually an E-major triad. Thus the structural functions of consonance and dissonance seem to have been effectively (and perhaps parodistically) reversed. The one remaining harmony that will be found to play an important role in the composition, an augmented triad, may be found in the conjectural *Grundgestalt* as given in Ex. 6-24 by connecting (or collecting) the rhythmically prominent notes in the top voice: F, A, C♯. Thus local or contextual pitch "hierarchies" (ad hoc assignments of relative importance) continue to play a role in determining the syntax of the music.

MAXING OUT

And yet Berg's article, written long after the fact, was an anachronistic measure of Schoenberg's achievement. By 1924, as we shall see, "purely musical" values were staging a strong comeback; but in the heyday of early twentieth-century maximalism, they could never have sustained the kind of claims Schoenberg himself was making for his "pantonality." The reason why the spiritual or spiritualist element has taken a back seat in discussions of Schoenberg to the seemingly contradictory discourses of "expressionism" and "pure music" (between which it had originally provided the necessary mediating link) has partly to do with changing fashions: occult matters greatly declined, and abstract or "structural" matters greatly surged after World War I as standards for validating or evaluating art. But it also has to do with Schoenberg's notoriously spasmodic artistic production. The masterwork that would have given supreme expression to his spiritual concerns remained unfinished, and is little known.

Late in 1912, Schoenberg was seized with the idea of composing an operatic trilogy on the subject of Balzac's *Séraphîta*, the philosophical novel that so excited his imagination. Again he turned to Marie Pappenheim for the libretto. Alternatively, and concurrently, he planned a vast choral symphony in emulation of Mahler's Eighth (the "Symphony of a Thousand"), which was itself a maximalization of Beethoven's Ninth. The earliest surviving sketch for the symphony, dated 27 December 1912, is a recitative labeled "seraphita." The culminating movement, for which the text was finished in January 1915, would have been a counterpart to the mystical final chapters of Balzac's novel, which contained the vision of heaven.

This text contained several plain or covert paraphrases from Balzac, of which one—the Archangel Gabriel's opening speech, "Whether right, left, forward or backwards, up or down, one has to go on without asking what lies before or behind"—resonates as well with Schoenberg's description to Kandinsky of his "absolute and unitary" musical space, the original stimulus for the emancipation of the dissonance. We know its musical setting not from the symphony finale, which Schoenberg never wrote, but from the sketches of a work that eventually took its place in his creative agenda: *Die Jakobsleiter* ("Jacob's ladder"), another grandiose oratorio that would have been something to set beside *Gurrelieder*, and which he started to compose in 1917.

The music leading up to Gabriel's Balzac-inspired opening line is given in Ex. 6-25a. It begins with an ostinato derived from a six-note "row of tones," as Schoenberg put it, that alternated half steps and whole steps from a starting point on C♯. (This strict alternation of tones and semitones makes Schoenberg's row a segment of what we now call the octatonic scale, of course, but there is no evidence that he conceived it that way.) To achieve the heavenly unity he sought, Schoenberg intended to base all the themes in the oratorio on this "row," which (whether by coincidence or design) begins with the same D-minor scale-segment (C♯–D–E–F) that he had previously mined from *Am Wegrand* for use in *Erwartung*. (It comes back in the second half of *Die Jakobsleiter* to represent the voice of "the liberated soul.")

The maneuver that made the opening of *Die Jakobsleiter* demonstrably a musical representation of Balzac's heaven was the immediate combination of the ostinato drawn from the octatonic segment with the complementary hexachord (F♯, A, B♭, B, C, E♭)—that is, the remaining six tones necessary to complete the aggregate. Like the octatonic hexachord from which Schoenberg derived the opening ostinato, this hexachord is also invariant when inverted, and can therefore represent or actually display the equivalency of "up and down, right or left, forward or backward."

Schoenberg demonstrated these properties by presenting the second hexachord as a pair of the /0 1 4/ motifs so familiar from *Erwartung*, the one quite conspicuously the inversion of the other (Ex. 6-25b). They are sounded piecemeal but then sustained in the winds while the strings continue to sound the first hexachord as an ostinato running beneath.

As soon as the two wind chords have been completed in the higher register and are being sustained there, the string ostinato running beneath accelerates into a rhythmic diminution, which is then treated as a stretto. That is, different instruments enter in counterpoint with different orderings of the six tones of the hexachord, so calculated that after six such entries all six constituent tones are continuously present in the texture. Chalk up another aggregate simultaneity to go with Scriabin's and Ives's!

Just as in the *Acte préalable* (the ultimate exhibit in chapter 4) or the *Universe* symphony (the ultimate exhibit in chapter 5), we now have a completely saturated and completely symmetrical—which is to say a completely unitary, completely invariant, and functionally quiescent—musical space. And like its companions, Schoenberg's construction exists and was motivated not simply as a technical feat but as a metaphor for a spiritual vision, a Weltanschauung. Or rather, to put it at once more boldly and more truly in terms of its conception, like Scriabin and Ives, Schoenberg was using his music here as a medium of occult revelation—a representation or even an enactment of an "ascent to a higher and better order."

When the origin of atonality in a transrational, uncanny discourse is recognized, and its nature as a medium of occult revelation is grasped, both its heritage and its reason for being are clarified. It emerges as the outcome of a hundred years of romantic striving for sublime utterance. *Die Jakobsleiter*, with its religiously symbolic aggregate harmony, stands along with the grandiose torsos of Scriabin and Ives at the end of the line that began with Haydn's "Chaos" and Beethoven's Ninth. *Erwartung*, with its culminating aggregate symbolizing emotional overload, had already pressed to a seemingly unsurpassable limit the capacity of music to underscore and intensify dramatic catharsis—the purging power of terror. No wonder Schoenberg had to give up his attempt to surpass the unsurpassable. His failure to complete *Die Jakobsleiter*, like Scriabin's to complete the *Mysterium* or Ives the *Universe*, was emblematic of a predicament in European culture. Maximalism had maxed out.

Unless, that is, it went in the other direction.

AT THE OPPOSITE EXTREME

The idea of the "aggregate" or full chromatic gamut as symbolizing closure, or (more practically) as providing the opportunity for it, is curiously corroborated at the opposite end of the temporal and expressive scale by a number of pieces of extraordinary—indeed

EX. 6-25A   Arnold Schoenberg, *Die Jakobsleiter*, mm. 1–8

↑Aggregate harmony from this point

EX. 6-25B   Complementary hexachord and derivative harmonies

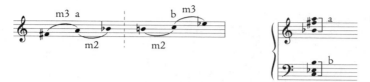

unprecedented—brevity. Among the most curious yet (backhandedly) characteristic products of the maximalist impulse, they bore a relationship to Beethoven's Bagatelles (or Schubert's *Moments musicaux*) comparable to the relationship that *Gurrelieder* or *Die Jakobsleiter* bore to the Ninth Symphony. They provided an arena in which Schoenberg, and even more enthusiastically and committedly his pupil Webern, could strive for the maximum in compression—"every glance a poem, every sigh a novel," as Schoenberg put it in a preface he contributed to the first edition of Webern's *Bagatelles* for string quartet, composed in 1911–1913 but only published in 1924. Even at the tiny end, determined extremism of this kind is a mark of the maximalist impulse.

Ex. 6-26 contains three such pieces, composed for increasingly elaborate performing media. The first is the sixth and last of Schoenberg's *Kleine Klavierstücke*, op. 19, composed in June 1911, and conveying (as the composer remarked one day) the emotion he felt at Mahler's funeral in May. It is nine measures long. Next comes the fifth of Webern's six *Bagatelles*, op. 9, composed a year or two later. It goes on for twelve measures; but as they are half the length of Schoenberg's measures, the piece is actually shorter. Finally comes the fourth of Webern's *Five Pieces for Orchestra*, op. 10, which lasts only six measures at a faster tempo, and is the shortest of all. (Webern exceeded its brevity only once, in a five-measure piece for cello and piano composed in 1914.)

These microscopic pieces all share a principle of structure (if such a word may be used to describe something so short). Webern put it best, or at least most vividly, in a memoir about the writing of the *Bagatelles*:

> I had the feeling here that when all twelve notes had gone by, the piece was over . . . . In my sketch-book I wrote out the chromatic scale and crossed off individual notes. Why? Because I had convinced myself: this note has been there already. It sounds grotesque, incomprehensible, and it was unbelievably difficult. The inner ear decided quite rightly that the man who wrote out the chromatic scale and crossed off individual notes *was no fool*.[30]

Webern exaggerated slightly. No piece, whether by him or by Schoenberg, was ever over after a single round through the twelve pitch classes. But the three pieces chosen for Ex. 6-26 come close.

If, adopting the method Webern described, one wrote out the notes of the chromatic scale and crossed them off as they occur, one would note the gradual accumulation of the twelve in Schoenberg's piano piece (Ex. 6-26a). The pair of chords that open it, and which together comprise a hexachord (half the chromatic gamut), form a ground that lasts until m. 6, against which the remaining pitches are gradually set off—D♯ and E

EX. 6-26A   Arnold Schoenberg, *Kleine Klavierstücke*, Op. 19, no. 6

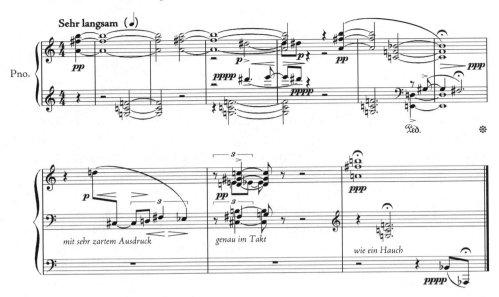

as an expressive "sigh" figure in m. 3, B♭ as an extension of the fourths in the second "ground chord" in m. 5, immediately followed by D and G♯.

The twelfth and last pitch, C♯, comes in m. 7, after the ground chords have cleared. The single line of which it is a part, marked "with very tender expression," has the character of a recitative, perhaps. In any case it is a transition to the last pair of bars, in which all twelve pitches are quickly "recapitulated," and which ends with a final sounding of the ground chords. They are clearly a coda. So despite its brevity, the piece has a clearly delineated, and by no means untraditional, formal structure; and that structure is articulated by means of the gradual introduction and exhaustion of the chromatic gamut, just as Webern implied.

The profusion of expression marks corroborates the impression of traditional "romantic" expressivity. In Webern's *Bagatelle* (Ex. 6-26b) they are even more profuse. Every note carries detailed performance directions, and an extraordinary range of tone colors (pizzicato, tremolando, *sul ponticello*) is employed, recalling Schoenberg's call for *Klangfarbenmelodien*. Crossing off the pitches, we note the first "exhaustion" with the first violin's A in m. 7. Starting the next count with the next note, G, we note the next closure in the whispered pizzicati in m. 11 (again A, one of the two notes plucked together, can be called the last pitch), followed by a rest. The remainder, again, is coda; and again the pitches are "recapitulated" faster than they had been "exposed."

Perhaps the most remarkable feature of this miniature is its tonal organization, reminiscent in microcosm of others we have seen. The opening measure fairly proclaims its symmetry. The ascending second in the second violin scrapes the insides of the major third sustained by the viola and cello. To continue the implied contraction would mean a convergence on D, the very note that appears in the first violin in m. 2. Reversing our perspective now, moving out from the axis D to C♯/D♯ and thence to C/E, we have

EX. 6-26B   Anton Webern, *Sechs Bagatellen* Op. 9, no. 5

reason to expect B/F to follow—and these are exactly the new pitches introduced by the first violin and viola on the downbeat of m. 3. And our next expectation, for B♭/G♭, is immediately fulfilled by the next pair of new pitches, played as a double stop by the first violin at the end of m. 4 and then sustained.

Only three pitches remain, and they are supplied in mm. 6–7. True, they are not introduced in precisely the order that our outward symmetrical expansion would imply: A♭ comes before, not after A. But we have good corroborating evidence of Webern's symmetrical conceptual layout at the very end, when D, the note identified in the first two bars as the axis pitch, returns to close the piece. It is the "tone center" in the newly literal sense we have already encountered in Strauss and Debussy, and will encounter again, maximalized, in the work of the Hungarian composer Béla Bartók, Webern's contemporary.

Finally, the "orchestral" piece (Ex. 6-26c): as if to compensate for its profusion of colors, it is the most austerely economical with pitches. The reason for putting the word "orchestral" in quotes has to do with Webern's use of solo strings rather than sections, so that the piece is actually scored like chamber music, for nine instruments "one on a part." Crossing off our pitches as before, we note the first completion in the trumpet's "concert

B" (notated as C♯ for a trumpet in B♭) in m. 2. For the first time since we have been counting, by the way, the twelve pitches have been introduced without any repetitions.

EX. 6-26C   Anton Webern, *Fünf Stücke* Op. 10, no. 4

The second count begins with the second "concert A" in the clarinet in m. 2 (again notated for an instrument in B♭, thus as B). Again the pitches accumulate without any redundancies (and with the clarinet's trill in m. 5 supplying both the eighth and the ninth pitches). Only the last phrase, in the solo violin (to be played "as if exhaling"), which supplies the twelfth pitch (B♭), indulges in the luxury of a few redundant tones. Its first note, A♭, had already been played (as G♯) by the trombone; its last three pitches, more poetically, could be understood as starting another go-round that trails off into silence.

Given such extreme parsimony, the three notes contributed by the snare drum are somewhat enigmatic. Since they neither reinforce the beat, like a traditional percussion part, nor coincide with the attacks of any other part, they have to be understood as another melodic phrase in counterpoint with the rest. An even more vivid instance of *Klangfarbenmelodie* takes place in the second piece from the set, in which a tiny triangle tremolo takes over directly from a phrase played by the solo first violin in artificial harmonics, *tremolando*. One clearly has the sense that a single melodic line, in a single approximate "color," has passed from the range of definite pitch into that of indefinite.

It often happens that hostile reviewers seem to sense the implications of radical novelties better than those who affect a more tolerant, less committed stance. Lawrence Gilman, whose important review of Ives's *Concord* Sonata helped make the history of that piece, performed a similar service in the case of Webern's *Five Pieces for Orchestra*. Reviewing the New York premiere in 1926 and perhaps thinking to make fun, he nevertheless captured its claustrophobic expressive intensity better than any contemporaneous writer. Unlike most of his fellow reviewers, Gilman knew romanticism when he heard it, however attenuated. "Men of our generation," he began,

> aim, in such extreme cases as that of Webern, at a pursuit of the infinitesimal, which may strike the unsympathetic as a tonal glorification of the amoeba. There is undeniably a touch of the protozoic: scarcely perceptible tonal wraiths, mere wisps and shreds of sound, fugitive astral vapors, though once or twice there are briefly vehement outbursts, as of a gnat enraged. The Lilliputian Fourth Piece is typical of the set. It opens with an atonal solo for the mandolin; the trumpet speaks as briefly and atonally; the trombone drops a tearful minor ninth. (The amoeba weeps.)[31]

THE IVORY TOWER

After three quarters of a century one can appreciate the intelligence that informed Gilman's sally. (Most contemporary critics failed to detect any expressivity in atonal music; they heard in it nothing but an outrageous and inexplicable—and therefore insulting—style.) At the time, Schoenberg and his pupils did not recognize good will from any critical corner. Their embattled (or "alienated") posture—another maximalized inheritance from romanticism, though not often recognized as such—was widely imitated by modernists who otherwise had little in common with them. "The customer is always wrong" became an implicit motto.

What made the Viennese version of alienation so influential was Schoenberg's, and his disciples', willingness to act upon it. Immediately upon the end of the First World War, in November 1918, they organized a sort of concert bureau. They called it the *Verein für musikalische Privataufführungen*, or Society for Private Musical Performances. It was subsidized by subscriptions, by the contributions of its members, and by occasional donations from wealthy or aristocratic patrons. Its offerings were not advertised in the papers, and critics were never invited. Indeed, anyone buying tickets was treated with automatic suspicion. One had to promise never to write about the performances for publication. Nor were subscribers informed of the programs in advance (so as to insure "equal attendance at every meeting"). Even applause was forbidden, as if in church.

Not only the public but the performers, too, were watchdogged. The Society's Statement of Aims, written by Berg with Schoenberg's approval, included the proviso that

> performers will be chosen preferably from among the younger and less well known artists, who place themselves at the Society's disposal out of interest in the cause; artists of high-priced reputation will be used only so far as the music demands and permits; and moreover that kind of virtuosity will be shunned which makes of the work to be performed not the end in itself but merely a means to an end which is not the Society's, namely, the display of irrelevant virtuosity and individuality, and the attainment of a purely personal success. Such things will be rendered automatically impossible by the exclusion (already mentioned) of all demonstrations of applause, disapproval, and thanks. The only success that an artist can have here is that (which should be most important to him) of having made the work, and therewith its composer, intelligible.[32]

Such an idealistic statement does contrast baldly with the commercialism (and "commodification") that had by the early twentieth century become pervasive in the economy of all the arts, and that has only mushroomed since. The benefits of self-subsidy, moreover, were tangible: the performances given by Schoenberg's Society before its tiny coterie audience, thanks to its mandated insistence on adequate rehearsal, were legendary in their accuracy; especially difficult pieces were often repeated within programs, and in successive programs as many as six times.

Such a venture could only be short-lived. The Society's first concert took place in December 1918; by the end of 1921 it had fallen victim to the rampant inflation that plagued the economies of war-torn Europe. Within that short period, though, it managed to present 117 concerts at which 154 contemporary compositions by a wide variety of composers were given a total of 353 performances. And Schoenberg, though he ran the Society dictatorially and earned for that reason some ill will, seems to have been genuinely altruistic in his motives. He did not allow any performances of his own music until the second season, and devoted so much time to the enterprise that he completed no work of his own during the whole period of the Society's existence.

Still, none of the Society's seemingly revolutionary aspects — the resolute shunning of publicity, the intransigent pecking order that placed the composer at the top of a social hierarchy, the pious atmosphere — were really new. As already noted, they were all implicit in the aesthetics of romanticism, and had been explicit in music criticism ever since Liszt, writing about John Field in the 1850s, saw fit to praise the pianist's "indifference to the public," whom he "enchanted . . . without knowing it or wishing it."[33] Field, wrote Liszt, "was his own chief audience." All that Schoenberg's Society for Private Performance did was to institutionalize that circumstance and enforce it with a code of etiquette.

The irony of the situation, of course, was that the idealism expressed by Liszt and maximalized by Schoenberg, as a reaction to the commercialization of art, was the product of that very commercialization. But commercialization has gone much further since Schoenberg's day. (For one thing, Schoenberg knew sound recording, the ultimate musical commodifier, only in its relative infancy, and did not take a stand on its potential for affecting the history of music in the twentieth century for good or ill. Needless to say, it will be a major theme in our own assessment of that history.)

The other major, far-reaching implication of the Society's aims and practices was an outgrowth of the neo-Hegelian esthetics first advanced (also in the 1850s) by the New German School, according to which art was valued not with reference to its consumers but only with reference to its own autonomous history. The public was at best irrelevant to this history, at worst a brake on it. Art needed protection from people. It needed the sanctuary that Schoenberg's Society provided for it. (More recently, that sanctuary has been sought in institutions of higher learning.) This has proven to be Schoenberg's most controversial legacy. Does the public have any legitimate claim on artists? Are artists entitled to social support without any requirement of a reciprocal social responsibility? Has society a right to expect from the artists it supports work of social value? Does protection from the public help or hinder the development of art? Does there come a point when a stocktaking becomes possible — or necessary? And if so, who decides that it is time to perform it, and who then gets to actually do it?

Most disquieting of all for the twentieth century, the great century of democracy and totalitarianism alike, is Schoenberg's most central precept, which he enunciated explicitly in an essay of 1946, composed in America, where for ten years he had been living as a refugee from totalitarian persecution: "If it is art it is not for everybody; if it is for everybody it is not art."[34] Can such a proposition be defended in a democracy? If not, is there something wrong with art? Or with democracy?

EPILOGUE: HOW MYTHS BECOME HISTORY

SCHOENBERG'S BRAHMS

Recall the quotation, toward the end of Schoenberg's "atonal" monodrama *Erwartung*, of the opening phrase from *Am Wegrand*, a song in D minor (Ex. 6-20). Although it had originated in a "tonal" context, the phrase contained a motif (or a pair of inversionally equivalent motifs) that had been serving in the opera as a *Grundgestalt*, a fundamental musical idea or "basic shape" that gave coherence to the harmonically nonfunctional ("atonal") musical texture. There is no reason to suppose that the D-minor melody had been the actual source for the intervallic motif as it appears in the opera. More likely the association occurred to Schoenberg in the course of work, in response to the poetic idea or dramatic situation that the song and the opera had in common: waiting anxiously and fruitlessly for a desired person to appear.

Nevertheless, the notion of a motif crossing over or "progressing" from a tonal to an atonal context attracted Schoenberg, because it represented his stylistic transition to atonality — the "emancipation of dissonance," as he preferred to call it — not as an arbitrary revolution against previous musical norms but as a methodological extension. As such, it could be described as a logical, or in terms of "dialectical" history even an inevitable, outgrowth from "common practice."

As reflective and self-aware as any modernist, and preoccupied to the point of obsession with his place in history, Schoenberg never resolved his ambivalence on this score. At times, he represented his technical innovations as a virtual starting-over-from-scratch, even a musical bath in Lethe, the mythical river of forgetfulness. His strongest statement of this kind came in a program note he wrote late in 1909 or early in 1910 for the first performance of his *Das Buch der hängenden Gärten* ("Book of the hanging gardens"), op. 15, a song cycle set, like the ending movements of the Second String Quartet, to poems by Stefan George. In these songs, for the first time, Schoenberg unflinchingly maintained his "fluctuating" or "suspended" tonality, and his fully "emancipated" treatment of dissonance, right up to the double bar, withholding all tonal closure. At once aggressive and defensive, the note asserts:

> With the *George-Lieder*, I have succeeded for the first time in approaching an expressive and formal ideal which has haunted me for years. Up until now, I lacked the strength and self-assurance to realize it. But now that I have started definitely upon this road, I am aware that *I have burst the bonds of a bygone aesthetic*; and, although I am striving towards a goal which seems certain to me, I foresee the opposition which I shall have to overcome; I feel the heat of the animosity which even the least temperamental will generate, and I fear that some who have believed in me up till now will not admit the necessity of this evolution.[35]

But even as he proclaimed his radicalism, Schoenberg's ambivalence showed through. He simultaneously characterized his achievement as a break (a "bursting of the bonds") and as an evolution. In later writings, evolution definitely gained the upper hand over break in Schoenberg's self-evaluation, and he emerges ever more consistently in his own telling as a maximalist rather than a revolutionary, even as a sort of conservative, finding precedents for almost all of his stylistic departures in Wagner's "roving harmony" and in what he called Brahms's "developing variation" technique.

Of the two, the Wagner connection was the one more easily perceived and conceded by the composer's contemporaries, especially those who knew the *Gurrelieder*, Schoenberg's epic (that is, "Wagnerian") cantata. Even Schoenberg's expressionist music had an obvious affinity to Wagner's music, consisting as it did of a formally free (or ad hoc) web of motifs. But Wagnerian leitmotifs were heterogeneous and referential, whereas Schoenberg dealt in nonreferential (or rather, self-referential) motifs that were ideally related, in the spirit of romantic "organicism," to a single basic shape (what Emerson called THE ONE). That is why Schoenberg especially prized his descent from Brahms, in whose techniques of *thematische Arbeit* ("working-out of themes") he came to see the source of his own *Grundgestalt* idea.

But of course, or perhaps even needless to say, the Brahms from whom Schoenberg descended was Schoenberg's Brahms — a Brahms very compellingly (and influentially) reimagined in terms of the characteristics that linked their styles. Unlike his Wagnerian heritage, which he accepted as self-evident, Schoenberg very actively propounded his descent from Brahms. This gives us another opportunity to compare theory with practice. On one occasion, for example, asked in a radio talk to explain his own methods, Schoenberg responded by citing and analyzing the first theme from Brahms's

F-major Cello Sonata, op. 99, a late work (composed in 1886) that Schoenberg, a cellist himself, had known when it was new and thought difficult to understand (Ex. 6-27).

E X. 6-27   Johannes Brahms, Cello Sonata no. 2, Op. 99, first theme, as cited by Schoenberg

Schoenberg emphasized the way Brahms built up the theme by gradually expanding on the initial two-note group: first by reversing its contour and contracting it to a semitone; next by disjunctly linking two versions of the falling pair, the first expanded to a whole tone, and the second (evened out to vary the rhythm) expanded to a minor third, the sum of a semitone and a whole tone; next by linking two versions of the first (ascending) pair conjunctly (so that the middle note does double duty), and expanding the interval from a fourth to a sixth (the previous third, inverted); then ascending further (the interval between the two three-note groups inverting the already-repeated ascending fourth) and varying it with a fifth in place of the sixth; and finally, summarizing everything in a five-note phrase that ascends through a fourth, a sixth, and another fourth, then falls by a fifth (an inverted fourth), with the two longest notes, F and G, representing the falling seconds from before in an expanded inversion encompassing a ninth (which is also the largest interval previously achieved, in the fourth phrase).

We could retell this story even more "Schoenbergianly," perhaps, by putting it in reverse. Then it would more closely resemble the painstaking analysis given above of the little piano piece, op. 19, no. 1 (Ex. 6-13). Thus, if we take the concluding five-note phrase as a *Grundgestalt*, we could then systematically derive every previous (and succeeding) thematic event from it. The fact that in this case Schoenberg's practice seems to resemble his theory in reverse is significant; for his self-constructed link to Brahms was a classic case of reverse (or double-reverse) historical narration, reversing into forward motion a lineage that had originally been traced retrospectively.

The most celebrated instance of this rhetorical ploy was another radio talk, given to mark the centenary of Brahms's birth in 1933 and significantly titled "Brahms the Progressive." In it, Schoenberg illustrated "developing variation" (the building up of larger musical entities from the endlessly varied repetition of smaller ones) by subjecting two themes of Brahms to a really atomistic analysis. First he showed how the theme from the slow movement of Brahms's String Quartet in A minor, op. 51, no. 2, could be derived from the tiniest particle, a two-note scalar descent labeled "a" in the diagram he drew up when revising the talk for publication in 1947 (Ex. 6-28). Again, the closest equivalent of the Schoenbergian *Grundgestalt* is not so much the two-note atom, but something a bit more characteristic—say perhaps the four–note "molecule" labeled "e" in the diagram. As the accompanying legend shows, "e" rather than "a" functions in context as a nexus set, relating all the others including the last.

EX. 6-28   Arnold Schoenberg's diagram of Brahms's Op. 51, no. 2 theme

Schoenberg's most famous Brahms analysis is the second one in "Brahms the Progressive." It concerns *O Tod* (O Death!), from Brahms's biblical cycle *Four Serious Songs*, op. 121 (1896), his last important composition. Its very telling analytical diagram is shown in Ex. 6-29; what it "tells" is how much more important the idea of motivic saturation was to Schoenberg, in analyzing Brahms, than were the guiding principles of voice leading and harmony that were likely paramount in Brahms's mind, as they would have been in the mind of any "tonal" composer.

Note, for example, the apparent violence Schoenberg must do to the bass line in mm. 8–10 (reversing notes at will and selecting arbitrarily from the newly ordered result) in order to reproduce his motif "e," a pair of descending thirds outlining a seventh. Even more subtly and significantly revealing are the rising thirds labeled "b" in mm. 2–5. It is doubtful whether Brahms could have considered the quarter-eighth pair labeled "b" in m. 5, where the second note is a dissonant appoggiatura, to be the motivic

EX. 6-29   Arnold Schoenberg, analysis of "O Tod" from *Brahms the Progressive*

EX. 6-29 *(continued)*

equivalent of the similarly labeled pairs of half notes that precede it, where all the tones are "chord tones." Did Schoenberg really think that harmonic considerations — matters of consonance and dissonance — were no longer relevant to motivic identity in Brahms? Had Brahms already emancipated the dissonance?

Surely not, nor is it likely that Schoenberg really thought he had. Indeed, the emancipation of the dissonance was the one aspect of his own practice for which Schoenberg never claimed an explicit precedent in earlier music. But in a sense the claim he made in "Brahms the Progressive" was even bolder, and certainly more controversial. Calling Brahms a progressive was nothing if not polemical, since Brahms himself opposed the idea of musical progress that was proclaimed in his own day by the "young Hegelians" of the New German School. Calling him a progressive was Schoenberg's way of saying that Brahms, like any other great composer, served history's design willy-nilly.

What was progressive about Brahms, then, was the fact that he was in Schoenberg's view a Schoenberg-in-training or a Schoenberg-in-waiting, whose motivic webs foreshadowed Schoenberg's own in density. And to imply this much was further to imply that the emancipation of dissonance, Schoenberg's great "bursting of the bonds," was in a larger sense no break at all but rather the unique and necessary culmination of all previous musically progressive practice, realizing a historical tendency that Schoenberg was the first to identify and formulate explicitly, but which many historians, in thrall to his charisma, have since endorsed.

ONTOGENY BECOMES PHYLOGENY

So compelling was the force of Schoenberg's musical example, for a time, that it prompted a widespread revision of music history in which Schoenberg's backward narrative bridge from himself to Brahms was not only "reversed into forward motion" but also generalized so that it became not the story of two composers or of a specific musical technique called developing variation, but the story of "Western music" itself. To recall high-school biology class, an "ontogeny," the individual development of a single member or representative of a type or species (here, Schoenberg) had been generalized into a "phylogeny," the historical development of the species itself.

Perhaps the first such generalizer was Schoenberg's pupil Berg, who in "Why Is Schoenberg's Music So Difficult to Understand?" drew a straight developmental line from Schoenberg back to Bach (but represented it as a line extending from Bach forward to Schoenberg). The most influential generalizer, however, was Schoenberg's other outstanding pupil, Webern, a trained musicologist as well as a composer and conductor, who embodied the new historical line both in words and in musical deed.

In a set of lectures given in 1933 (the same year as "Brahms the Progressive") and later published as *The Path to the New Music*, Webern asserted that "for the last quarter of a century major and minor have no longer existed, only most people still do not know it."[36] When originally uttered aloud, that remark could only have sounded like a partisan pronouncement. But over the years the idea of the *collapse of traditional tonality*[37] around 1907 or 1908 (the years that circumscribe the composing of Schoenberg's Second Quartet) has been turned into a "fact," indeed a standard cliché of music historiography.

The phrase in italics comes from a textbook published in 1991. The event in question, tonality's "collapse," had by then been long accepted by historians as an empirical fact. And yet it — obviously — never took place. To believe that it did is to commit an error that often attends the very beginning of the narrative of "Western music," namely the assumption that the rise of literacy put an end to "orality." Similarly, the "rise" of polyphony (another famous nonevent) is often thought to have put an end to "monophony" but didn't, any more than the "rise" of instrumental music put an end to vocal. Innovations add to the range of options available within an existing or traditional practice. They augment it, but (except in the utilitarian realm of technology) do not normally supplant it.

So it was with Schoenbergian "atonality." Since his time it has been an option, and a line of development that for a while commanded wide assent among modernist composers. But "tonal" music has obviously continued, both in oral and in literate practice, and still accounts for the vast preponderance of the music composed and performed in Europe and America. To claim that all of this music is based on premises that have long since "collapsed" is of course to stigmatize it. That is a rhetorical, rather than a historical, allegation. One name for it is propaganda.

Another is myth. The bald assertion of tonality's collapse or demise around 1908 is one of the myths of modernism, akin to Virginia Woolf's famous sentence (in "Mr. Bennett and Mrs. Brown," an essay published in 1924) that "on or about April 1910 human nature changed." Both statements, which plainly (and deliberately) contradict ordinary experience, are examples of "hidden history," in which the inexplicable is explained by reference to the occult, and in which ordinary experience is tainted as evidence of limited capacity (a technique well described by Hans Christian Andersen in his tale, "The Emperor's New Clothes").

To give the myth of tonality's collapse more historical credence, another myth was invented. It, too, went through a process of progressive generalization. A textbook of 1960 put it this way: "The whole course of late Romantic music, especially in Germany, tended toward atonality."[38] Many historians have since reconsidered the one-sidedness of such a description, even of Wagner, whose *Tristan und Isolde* is invariably cited as the "crisis" or precipitating work. Nevertheless, by 1991, the process of generalization had gone on apace. The textbook from which the myth of tonality's collapse was quoted continued in this fashion:

> Yet traditional tonality did not collapse all at once. The entire nineteenth century — arguably even the common-practice period as a whole — had witnessed a progressive weakening of its constructive force, along with corresponding shifts in compositional esthetic. Any effort to understand twentieth-century music must consider its relationship to these earlier developments out of which it grew, in part as their extension, in part as a set of new departures.[39]

These efforts have proceeded by compounding the myths just described — the hidden crisis, the "progressive weakening" — with the one cited earlier, the generalization of Schoenberg's retrospective claim of kinship with Brahms. The product of all this mythmaking has been an artificially sequent narrative that masquerades a particular result as a general necessity. In more specialized studies, the story is narrated in greater detail, but it retains its "synecdochic" character (that is, its substitution of parts for wholes). One of its most sophisticated formulations came in an extended study by the music theorist Joseph Straus called *Remaking the Past: Musical Modernism and the Influence of the Tonal Tradition*, a book that amounted to a sustained gloss on "Brahms the Progressive." The late nineteenth century is characterized there

> as a period in which motivic association, a secondary and dependent determinant of structure in the classical and early romantic eras, was elevated into a central and independent organizing principle. Recent scholarship on late romantic music (particularly that of Wagner, Brahms, Liszt, and Mahler) has concentrated more and more on what [the music analyst] Allen Forte calls "the primal importance of the motive." In the music of this period, motivic structure waxes as tonal structure wanes.[40]

The particular version of the historiographical myth to which Straus makes reference by invoking Allen Forte is the one that (in Straus's words) traces "the growing importance of contextual motivic relations and their increasing independence from a tonal framework" in the music of the late nineteenth century. He calls this asserted process of development "motivicization," and claims that it was an aspect of common composerly practice in the period we have been calling "maximalist." To all of this commentary, one can make the same basic objection as one can make to Schoenberg's own analysis of Brahms's *O Tod*. The crucial "independence from a tonal framework" is a function not of the music analyzed — Wagner's, Brahms's, Liszt's, or Mahler's — but of the analytical technique that is brought to bear upon it.

As Schoenberg's purpose in anachronistically analyzing Brahms's music was the justification of his own, so the vast historiographical and analytical literature that has grown up in the wake of "Brahms the Progressive" has had the purpose and effect of turning Schoenberg's particular innovations into the general history of twentieth-century music, so that "each opus" of his, in the words of the conductor Robert Craft, "is a turning point in music itself."[41] They were that because in the retrospective view of his devotees, Schoenberg was uniquely responsive (and responsible) to what the German philosopher Theodor Wiesengrund Adorno, in a book of 1949, finally called "the tendency of the musical material itself" and the historical obligations it imposed.[42] Webern, in his lectures of 1933, had already charged musicians who failed to recognize these obligations with "utter dilettantism."[43]

"MOTIVICIZATION" IN PRACTICE

That characteristic resort to browbeating was surely the least attractive product of modernist mythography. There were much more attractive ones. Webern gave a fascinating practical demonstration of how historiographical ideas can be translated into composerly procedures, when in 1934–1935 he transcribed for orchestra the six-part ricercar from Bach's *Musical Offering*. The most characteristic feature of the orchestration, and at the same time one of its more enigmatic traits, is the way Webern cut up (or, as music analysts would say, "segmented") the famous "royal" theme given Bach by Frederick the Great as a subject for improvisation. On its every appearance, the 8-measure theme is divided into seven timbrally differentiated parts, numbered for reference in Ex. 6-30.

EX. 6-30   Theme from Bach's Six-part Ricercar as segmented by Anton Webern

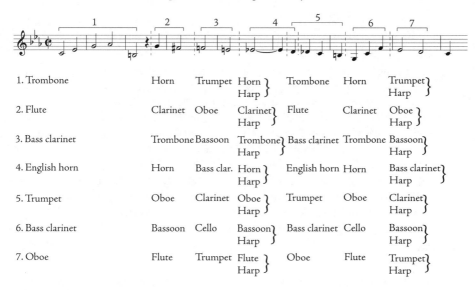

At first blush we are apt to notice nothing more than the seemingly arbitrary shifts of timbre. We may be inclined to write it off as another attempt at *Klangfarbenmelodie*, "tone-color melody," or attribute it to Webern's penchant for what was sometimes called

his "pointillism," with reference to the French postimpressionist painterly technique of applying color in little daubs that contrast close up but blend when viewed from afar. When all the voices get going in Webern's scoring, and with all the countersubjects given a treatment just as pointillistic as the subject gets, the kaleidoscopic effect is indeed entrancing.

But a closer look reveals something else as well. The colors do not only contrast; they also recur in a consistent pattern whenever the theme is sounded. Thus segments 1 and 5 are assigned to the same instrument on every appearance of the theme (first the muted trombone, then the flute, then the bass clarinet, then the English horn, and so on), as are segments 2 and 6 (first the muted horn, then clarinet, muted trombone, "open" horn, etc.). The constant use of the harp as a doubling instrument in segments 4 and 7 consistently associates them with one another, as well as with segment 2, which uses the color the harp doubles in segment 4, and segment 3, which uses the color doubled by the harp in segment 7. (Sharp-eyed readers will notice that the assignment of the cello to motif 6 and bassoon to motive 7 in the sixth line of Ex. 6-30 reverses the established pattern. The example is accurate: the apparent "error" was Webern's.)

If we now notice that the two segments doubled by the harp (4 and 7) are identical in pitch content (E♭ descending to D), we have made an association between color and motif—the first of many. This observation turns out to coincide with Webern's compositional strategy, as we learn in a letter he sent the conductor Hermann Scherchen, who was preparing the first performance in 1938. "My instrumentation attempts to reveal the motivic coherence" of the ricercar, he wrote.[44] Knowing this much prompts an analytical strategy. Replacing the word "segment" with "motif," then, we may survey Webern's achievement thus:

- The next logical step is to observe that the two motifs associated by harp-doubling with the two identical ones, namely 2 and 3, also consist (like motives 4 and 7) of descending semitones.
- Turning our attention next to all the motifs that share the color doubled by the harp in segment 4—namely segments 2, 4, and 6—we notice a pair of subtle interrelationships. First, motifs 4 + 6 reproduce motifs 6 + 7 in reverse order. Second, motifs 2 and 4 connect over an augmented second, which is the inversion of the diminished seventh at the end of motif 1, surely the most characteristic interval in the theme.
- Not only that, but the contents of motifs 2 (G + F♯) and 4 (E♭ + D) can be replicated within motif 1 at a transposition of a fourth (or fifth, depending on direction): C, B, A♭, G; and now remember that the second entry (or "answer") in a fugue or ricercar is at that very transposition, so that the next time motif 1 is heard, it will use the pitches of motifs 2 and 4.
- And of course anything said about motifs 2 + 4 can also be said about motifs 2 + 7.
- Meanwhile, motifs 3 + 7 (associated by color) equal motifs 3 + 4 (associated by contiguity), and also equal motifs 2 + 3 at a transposition of a second. Putting this another way, one can say that motif 3 is to motif 2 what motif 4 (or 7) is to motif 3. And is it a coincidence that motifs 3 + 2, or 4 + 3 are transpositions of the famous B-A-C-H cipher?

- And by the same token, motif 5, which covers four descending half steps, equals motifs 2 + 3 + 4(= 7).
- Finally, motif 1, the longest of the motifs and the most characteristic, being the famous *Kopfmotiv* or head motif of the royal theme, summarizes all the intervallic relationships we have noted in the others. Its extremes, C and B, encompassing a descending semitone, reproduce the contiguous contents of motifs 2, 3, 4, 5, and 7; and its third and fourth notes (G + A♭) invert the same interval. Its final interval inverts the nexus of motifs 2 and 4 (associated by color). Its second and fifth notes coincide with the odd interval (a diminished fourth) that defines the contour of motifs 4 + 5, which fill the interval in by a scalewise chromatic descent; and the consonant fifth that stands at the extremities of the opening key-defining triad is inverted and sequentially repeated in motif 6.

Since everything that happens later can be derived from it, motif 1 can be defined as the *Grundgestalt* of the ricercar, and all the succeeding motifs—indeed the whole ricercar—can be viewed as its "developing variations." Our heads may be swimming at this point the way they were on concluding the analysis of Ex. 6-13, the first tiny piano piece from Schoenberg's op. 19. And no wonder, for by dint of his atomistic rescoring of the ricercar Webern has managed to cast Bach, as Schoenberg had already cast Brahms, as a Schoenberg-in-training. Even more to the point, not a few decades but a full two centuries of music history have been cast as prelude to the emancipation of dissonance, which finally freed from all irrelevant constraints the kind of motivic writing Webern has elevated to a primary compositional objective of Bach's, and an immanent feature of his music (which it took Webern's interpretation fully to "reveal").

And yet it should be clear by now that what we have witnessed has been less a revelation than a revision of Bach's priorities, and that the historical precedent that Webern has cited was in fact of his own ingenious devising. It should also be obvious that refuting the historical claims made by composers or arrangers does not amount (in itself, anyway) to a refutation, or even so much as a comment, on the artistic value of the work they have produced. As listeners, we are perfectly free to welcome Webern's commitment to pseudohistorical fiction (to put it as bluntly as possible) if we take pleasure in the artistic result.

As historians, we are obliged to be more wary. But we are also obliged to take note of the fiction, since once it was adopted it made real history. Like the dicta of the old New German School, of which it was in its way a maximalization, this strain of tendentious twentieth-century music historiography became in its own right a significant and influential aspect of twentieth-century musical thought. As many of the chapters that follow will attest, it has had a decided impact on the histories of composition, performance, and audience reception, none of which can be fully understood without reference to it.

Mere refutation, then, can never suffice to dispel a mythology. Attention must be paid. The myths must be accounted for, above all as sociological phenomena with ramifications leading beyond music, and beyond esthetics, into matters of general philosophy, history, and politics.

Social Validation

BARTÓK, JANÁČEK

WHAT IS HUNGARIAN?

O f all the non-Germanic nations within the polyglot Hapsburg Empire, the Hungarians — or Magyars, to name them in their own exotic tongue of proud Central Asian descent — were the most successful in maintaining a distinct political, linguistic, and cultural identity during the eighteenth and nineteenth centuries. They had a history of independence, and an indigenous dynastic aristocracy — recall the Eszterházy family, Haydn's employers — whose hereditary rights the Austrian rulers were for the most part careful to respect. In return for that respect they earned loyalty. For many Magyars, Austrian suzerainty meant liberation and protection from the Turks. It also promised the reunification, even the enlargement, of the old Hungarian kingdom, a process that was completed in 1711.

The Austrian emperor was at first only nominally the king of the Magyars, who maintained their traditional social administration, centered on large and politically autonomous baronial counties and estates like Eszterháza. Ironically enough, real political strife with the Austrians only began with the reformist reign of Joseph II (r. 1765–90), often regarded as the most liberal of the Hapsburg emperors; for among Joseph's reforms was the centralization of the imperial government, which threatened the autonomy of the Hungarian counties. (Among other things, the proposed reforms would have made German the only legal language in the empire.) The solution sought by the Hungarian nobles was a constitution that would guarantee their rights as citizens. Thus Hungarian nationalism was joined in an especially conspicuous way with political liberalism — or at least what passed for liberalism within a basically feudal context.

Matters flared briefly into armed conflict in 1849. Lajos (or Louis) Kossuth (1802–94), a zealous politician unsatisfied with the parliamentary government granted by the Austrians the previous year (in which he was the finance minister), declared a Magyar republic with himself

FIG. 7-1   Lajos Kossuth, by Francis d'Avignon.

as president. He was beset with rebellions from the large German, Slavic, and Romanian minorities, who felt secure under Austrian imperial rule and feared repression at the hands of Magyar nationalists. These uprisings, plus the intervention of Russia on the side of its sister empire, forced Kossuth into exile—and into legend as a martyr to the cause of freedom. He lived on for more than forty years, mainly in England and Italy. A fiery orator, he made several lucrative speaking trips to the United States, where he was billed as the Hungarian Patrick Henry or Nathan Hale. Shortly before his death he was given amnesty, which he refused. Nevertheless, his body was returned to Budapest and given a heroic burial.

For a while after Kossuth's attempted revolution, Hungary suffered reprisals and was ruled like an occupied territory. That only made nationalistic aspirations seethe. A compromise—the great *Ausgleich*, or settlement—was reached after the Austrian crown suffered a military defeat at the hands of the Prussians in 1866, and needed to regain the loyalty of its minorities. Hungary was granted its own constitution, its own parliament, its own legal code in its own language, its own currency and postal system, and what is more, political dominance over many of the other non-German parts of the empire, including Slovakia, the Balkan regions of Slovenia and Croatia, Transylvania (a partly Romanian- speaking district in the Carpathians) and Ruthenia (where the local population spoke Ukrainian). All of these territories and more were now administered not from Vienna but from Budapest.

The emperor Franz Joseph I, already in the nineteenth year of his reign, came to Budapest to be separately crowned King of Hungary in 1867, and his empire officially became "Austria-Hungary." His title became "Seine kaiserliche und königliche Majestät" ("His imperial and royal majesty") in specific recognition of Hungary's nearly coequal status, and "k.u.k." became the official designation of all the centralized institutions that remained, notably the armed forces. Yet although it was widely heralded as a victory for the Hungarian nation, the *Ausgleich* once again mainly served the political and economic interests of the nobility and the *haute bourgeoisie* ("urban elite class").

As long as Austria-Hungary lasted, the voting population of the Hungarian sector never exceeded six percent, and the proportion of titled aristocrats to the total population was the highest in Europe. The *Ausgleich* did not still bourgeois nationalism; indeed, Hungarian nationalism became a complicated and contentious thing, with many classes within a rigidly stratified society claiming to be the "true" Hungarian nation. Self-avowed nationalist politics covered the whole political spectrum from aristocratic reaction to revolutionary socialism.

Like its political counterpart, cultural nationalism and its reflections in the arts burgeoned and fermented as the turn of century approached, and reached in the early decades of the new century a maximalist phase that looked like a modernist revolution. In music, the change was especially pronounced: a new model of "Hungarianness," entailing a new source in folklore and a new musical style, was advanced, and correlated with other, more cosmopolitan manifestations of modernist style. In no other country did modernism so successfully ally itself with domestic (as opposed to exotic) nationalism. The qualification is necessary because we have encountered a seemingly similar alliance in Russian music like Stravinsky's. But that was an alliance of expedience, made strictly for export purposes, and addressed a foreign audience. The new Hungarian product arose in response to needs at home, and had far less to do with the merchandising of exoticism.

The old Hungarian nobility had long "possessed" (i.e., patronized and cultivated) a distinctive music, the so-called *magyar nóta* ("Hungarian tune"), which in educated Hungarian circles was regarded as a stylistic emblem of the national identity. It was also recognized abroad by composers, at first chiefly Viennese, who occasionally imitated it for effect, and by their audiences, who relished it as the *style hongrois* ("Hungarian style"). It was also known, especially abroad, as the "Gypsy style," because outside of Hungary (and in Hungarian urban centers as well) it was known mainly through performances by Gypsy violinists, whose distinctive playing style—heavily inflected with emotionally laden sforzandos, glissandos, and rubatos—was an integral part of the experience.

Ex. 7-1 begins with an actual *magyar nóta*, written down in a manner that tries to convey something of its performance style and published as a piano solo in 1832. (Only the right-hand part, containing the melody, is given.) Like most published *magyar nótak*, it has two linked parts, slow (*lassú*) and fast (*friss*). Next comes a little garland of Viennese imitations (of either the *lassú* or the *friss*), beginning with a pair of extracts from the earliest famous one, the "Rondo all'ongarese" ("Rondo in Hungarian style") that caps a piano trio by Haydn, first published in 1795.

From these examples, many (though not all) of the characteristics of the *style hongrois* can be deduced: dotted rhythms, syncopations, augmented seconds, distinctive cadence patterns, and so forth. Apart from the cadence patterns, perhaps, none of these characteristics were uniquely the property of the *style hongrois*. Like most stylistic "signifiers," it was not a single trait but a pliable cluster. That gave it great flexibility: two

EX. 7-1A *Magyar nóta* and *style hongrois*, Ignác Ruzitska, *Búcsuzó és friss magyar* (Farewell and Fast Hungarian)

EX. 7-1A (continued)

EX. 7-1B *Magyar nóta* and *style hongrois*, Franz Joseph Haydn, *Rondo all'ongarese*, the last minore (piano right hand)

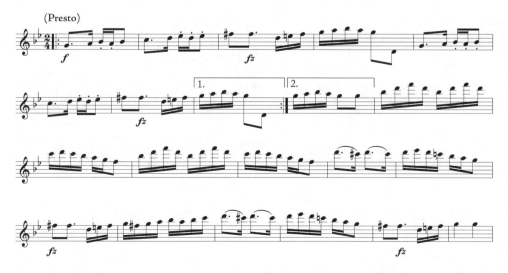

EX. 7-IC *Magyar nóta* and *style hongrois*, Franz Schubert, "Great" Symphony in C, II, mm. 160–166 (oboe)

EX. 7-ID *Magyar nóta* and *style hongrois*, Johannes Brahms, Hungarian Dance no. 5 (1869), mm. 33–48 (Primo right hand)

melodies could be equally obvious exemplifications of the Hungarian cluster without necessarily having any specific traits in common.

Of course there was also a native Hungarian "school" of composers who employed the *magyar nóta* style in works cast in the larger vocal and instrumental forms of European art music. One was Mihály Mosonyi (1815–70), who was given the name Michael Brand at birth, but who translated it into its Hungarian equivalent as an act of patriotism. He composed two symphonies, a piano concerto, a large number of chamber and piano works, and three operas, all with the avowed purpose of "creating, alongside the German, Italian, and French currents in music, a fourth world-famous style, the Hungarian,"[1] but he never gained the sort of international reputation that would have realized such an ambition.

By common consent the "national composer" of Hungary during the nineteenth century was Franz (or Ferenc) Erkel (1810–93), an opera specialist, whose "historical dramatic opera" *Bánk bán* (1861) occupied a hallowed place in Hungarian culture analogous to that of Glinka's *A Life for the Tsar* in Russia. The patriotic play by József Katona on which it was based, written in 1815, was twice banned by the Austrian censors for the way it used a thirteenth-century revolt against foreign infiltration as an allegory of contemporary Hungarian resistance to the Hapsburgs. Ex. 7-2 shows the climax of a tragic duet between the title character (heroic tenor), and his doomed wife Melinda. The *magyar nóta* idiom here assumes a high dramatic posture, in which the dominating musical figures are descending dotted sequences typical of Gypsy violin music, and "noble" short-long rhythms derived from the distinctive accentual patterns of the Hungarian language.

EX. 7-2   Franz Erkel, *Bánk bán*, Act II, scene 1, duet

Inevitably, though, the greatest figure associated with the *style hongrois* in the nineteenth century, and its chief ambassador to the world at large, was Franz Liszt. Although he was surely the most cosmopolitan of all musicians, and the adopted standard bearer for the New German School with its universalist agenda, Liszt was nevertheless of Hungarian birth, and eager to take creative (and commercial) advantage of the fact. Most of his compositions in the *style hongrois* were virtuoso vehicles — nineteen Hungarian Rhapsodies, a *Hungarian Fantasia* with orchestra, and the like — in which he translated the Gypsy violin idiom, just as he had the Paganini idiom, into perfect keyboardese (replete with tremolo effects to evoke the accompanying *cimbalom* or Hungarian dulcimer).

Later in life, Liszt occasionally used the idiom more "seriously," as in a set of *Hungarian Historical Portraits* for piano (composed between 1870 and 1885) dedicated to seven Hungarian patriots (including Mosonyi, but not the still-banned Kossuth), or the grandiose *Hungarian Coronation Mass* for soloists, chorus, and orchestra, expressly composed for the separate crowning of Franz Joseph in 1867. The Hungarian coloring in the Mass is most pronounced precisely at the most solemn moment, the Benedictus, where (following the exalted example of Beethoven's *Missa Solemnis*) Liszt entrusted a wordless prayer (already heard in the Offertory) to the solo violin (Ex. 7-3).

Previously, Liszt had written (or had his companion, Princess Sayn-Wittgenstein write) a substantial book, *Des bohémiens et de leur musique en Hongrie* (1859, published in English as *The Gipsy in Music*), in which he characterized the *style hongrois* as "a great movement" in art, on an expressive and formal par with all other European musics. This was one of the classic statements for music of Johann Gottfried von Herder's early Romantic ideal — or the old Herderian ambivalence which insisted on assigning equal value both to the specific idiosyncrasies and to the common humanity of all particular cultures. The purpose of writing the book was to explicate an exotic idiom that European audiences might find baffling, and at the same time to celebrate and demonstrate its universal validity. The chief merit of the music, and for a romantic there could be no higher one, was its immediacy and authenticity of expression. "In the very act of passing the bow across the violin-strings," Liszt enthused, "a natural inspiration suggested itself; and, without any search for them, there came rhythms, cadences, modulations, melodies and tonal discourses." The Gypsy violinist "revealed that golden ray of interior light proper to himself, which otherwise the world would never have known or suspected." Hungary's role, in Liszt's view, was nurturing rather than creative; but that was enough to make the Gypsy idiom truly Hungarian.

> The Gypsy art can never be separated from Hungary, whose arms it must forever bear on seal and banner. To Hungary it owes a life passed entirely within its limits and in its atmosphere. To Hungary also the attainment of its virility and maturity are due, dependent as these were upon appreciation of its noble elements. It has also Hungary to thank for supply of its greatest needs — comprehension and sympathy. The haughtiness of its rhythms, their imposing dignity and sudden cries, remindful of those of a startled steed at sound of the trumpet — all from the very first, went straight to the Hungarian heart.[2]

EX. 7-3   Franz Liszt, *Hungarian Coronation Mass*, violin solo from Benedictus

Jonathan Bellman, a historian of the *style hongrois*, has pointed out that by attributing the actual origin of the *magyar nóta* to the Gypsies, rather than just its propagation through performance, Liszt committed an offensive error in Hungarian eyes. As Bellman put it, "Hungary only understood the rhythms, in Liszt's view—it did not produce them."[3] And yet the Hungarian language, in which every word (even foreign ones) are pronounced with a strong accent on the first syllable, seems the obvious source of those "haughty rhythms" Liszt celebrated. Liszt, who was brought up speaking German and who made French, the international tongue of European aristocracy and diplomacy, the vehicle of his mature career, was never fluent in the vernacular of the country of his birth and may not have been equipped to appreciate its relationship to the music he described. But he got the part about haughtiness right; for that is the aristocratic posture par excellence, and as we know, the *magyar nóta* was most actively patronized and promoted by the Hungarian gentry or small-landowner class.

A CHANGE OF COURSE

We do not need to adjudicate this old controversy about the origins of the *magyar nóta*. What is significant to us is the tension its lurking presence contributed to the new, maximalizing phase of Hungarian musical nationalism, the chief protagonist of which, Béla Bartók (1881–1945), was the most famous Hungarian-speaking composer Hungary ever produced. Bartók began his career in the self-conscious image of Liszt, as a virtuoso pianist committed both to Hungarian nationalism and to the advancement of all the most "progressive" ideas in the music of his time. Both aspects of Bartók's creative agenda were equally pertinent to his eventual preeminence among Hungarian musicians.

The work that brought him his first celebrity was a symphonic poem, *Kossuth*, composed in 1903 and first performed the next year. Its self-evident patriotic associations were enhanced, at the time of its premiere, by renewed tensions between Hungarians and Austrians, sparked by Hungarian demands that their language be used equally with German within the "k.u.k." army, and that Hungarians be given equal opportunity to command. The

FIG. 7-2 Bartók collecting songs from Slovak peasants in 1907.

composition embodies a kind of narrative of the 1848–1849 revolution, in which the Austrians are represented by a grotesque distortion of Haydn's famous imperial anthem ("Gott, erhalte Franz den Kaiser"), and Kossuth (by extension, the Hungarians) by a melody in the noblest *magyar nóta* style (Ex. 7-4).

EX. 7-4   Béla Bartók, *Kossuth*, opening theme

A list of the self-evident Hungarian characteristics of this theme would begin with the "haughty" accompanying rhythms, and go on to include dotted pairs on every downbeat (some of them ornamented by breaking the short note into two thirty-seconds as notated), the use of the raised fourth degree (D♯), the "crowded" upbeats (four sixteenths, quintuplets, eventually sextolets as well), and so on. But as the Hungarian-born Bartók scholar Judit Frigyesi has emphasized, equally important is the fact that Bartók has fashioned an "endless," motivically evolving melody out of these materials, of a kind that is never found in popular music, but only in the most advanced "post-Wagnerian" symphonic compositions like the tone poems of Strauss and the early symphonies of Mahler.[4]

There are indeed many specific resonances in *Kossuth* with Strauss's *Ein Heldenleben* ("A hero's life," 1898) and the first movement of Mahler's Second Symphony, which (as we may recall from chapter 1) represented a *Todtenfeier*, a heroic funeral. The appropriateness of these resonances for glorifying a Hungarian national hero is obvious, and so the "progressive" aspect of Bartók's achievement was a full partner in its nationalistic agenda. In the view of Hungarian modernists, their country's coming of age as a musical nation demanded both its possessing the particularity of a national style and its meeting the universal standard of modernity.

The problem was that by the end of the nineteenth century, the *style hongrois*, in Bellman's words, "was ubiquitous as entertainment music," and "through familiarity had lost much of its quality of strangeness."[5] Both its commonness and its associations with café genres could only devalue it in the eyes (and ears) of modernists. As long as musical nationalism implied the use of the *magyar nóta* idiom, or what Bartók described as "popular art music," it could only impede the development of a universally viable Hungarian modernist music. As Frigyesi puts it, there seemed to be a barrier between "national" and "serious" music.[6] The contradiction gave rise to a dilemma.

The solution that Bartók hit upon, together with his fellow composer-nationalist and frequent collaborator Zoltán Kodály (1882–1967), might at first seem paradoxical. They strove for universal viability by seeking a more authentic "Hungarianness." Kodály, who had a rural upbringing, had long been aware that the peasant music of the Hungarian countryside was of an altogether different style and character from the *magyar nóta*. He began to study it seriously, published his first articles about it in 1904, began making collecting expeditions in 1905, and in 1906 earned a Ph.D. in literature with a dissertation on the stanzaic structure of Hungarian folksong. Meanwhile, partly as a result of a chance encounter with a peasant singer, partly in emulation of Kodály's activities, Bartók also began transcribing peasant songs.

In 1906, the two composers issued an epoch-making anthology, *Magyar népdalok* ("Hungarian folksongs"), consisting of twenty transcriptions with piano accompaniment, the first ten arranged by Bartók, the rest by Kodály. The preface, signed by both but written by Kodály, expressed the hope that, once provided with access to them, the Hungarian public "might get to like" authentic folksongs.[7] "If only these primordial expressions of the spirit of our people would meet with even half the affection they deserve!" the editors exclaimed. But these "primordial expressions" of Hungarianness were something even Bartók had only encountered in adulthood. They were not his "native music." Even for him they were an acquired taste.

FIG. 7-3   Bartók and Kodály with the Waldbauer-Kerpely Quartet, March 1910 (photograph by Aladár Székely).

And so the preface ended on a pessimistic note: "The overwhelming majority of Hungarians are not yet Hungarian enough, no longer naive enough and not yet cultured enough to let these songs touch their hearts." And indeed, the anthology sold only 150 copies in twelve years. The epoch that it marked was slow in coming, reforming the editors themselves, and other members of the nation's musical elite, long before it did the general public. Throughout his life Kodály grumbled that in Hungary those who were cultured were not Hungarian and those who were Hungarian were not cultured. What might have been a racist complaint in other contexts was in this case a particularly forthright statement of the dilemma facing Hungarian modernists, who wanted equally to be national on the peasant model and to be sophisticated, which implied urbanity. It was a dilemma that pervaded every aspect of their creative lives, and would haunt their legacies.

As always, reform proved to be a two-way street. Bartók summed up the import of the new folk idiom he and Kodály had discovered, in sharp and somewhat sneering contrast to the older *style hongrois*, in a memoir dating from 1918:

> Its expressive power is amazing, and at the same time it is devoid of all sentimentality and superfluous ornaments. It is simple, sometimes primitive but never frivolous. The more valuable part was in the old ecclesiastical or old Greek modes, or based on more primitive pentatonic scales, and the melodies were full of the freest and most varied rhythmic phrases and changes of tempi, played both *rubato* and *giusto* [in strict time].[8]

But in their zeal, Bartók and Kodály considerably exaggerated the simplicity of the music in the course of arranging it for publication, so that it would conform to their modernist aesthetic ideals. In 1938, when they could afford a less polemical approach (and when Bartók had the use of a low-speed phonograph that made them easier to transcribe), they reissued the collection with the "superfluous ornaments" they had originally suppressed reinstated (see Ex. 7-5). Also typically exaggerated or mistaken was Bartók's assumption that the unusual diatonic structure of the peasant melodies represented survivals of medieval or even ancient Greek modes. There is no need to assume such historical connections between diatonic scales, simply because they do not conform to those of the major/minor key system.

But these inaccuracies and equivocations were born of the composers' wish to justify a change in their own composing style. Creative fervor temporarily gained the upper hand over scholarly scruples. As Bartók put it in a slightly later (1921) version of the same memoir,

> The outcome of these studies was of decisive influence upon my work, because it liberated me from the tyrannical rule of the major and minor keys .... It became clear to me that the old modes, which had been forgotten in our music, had lost nothing of their vigor. Their new employment made new rhythmic combinations possible. This new way of using the diatonic scale brought freedom from the rigid use of the major and minor keys, and eventually led to a new conception of the chromatic scale, every tone of which came to be considered of equal value and could be used freely and independently.[9]

So the primary value of the rediscovery of the old was the possibility it created of achieving the new, yet without any loss in national specificity (which alone could guarantee "authenticity"). The simple peasant music, precisely because it was little known and previously uncultivated by composers of "art music," offered modernists greater scope for creative appropriation than the ornate and highly stylized *magyar nóta*, which had its own tradition in art music, and which therefore carried a heavy baggage of associations, including some (to urban commercial genres, to the reactionary nobility, etc.) that nationalists of Bartók and Kodály's generation had to reject.

Exhilarated by his breakthrough, Bartók eagerly began to theorize about the proper relationship between "peasant music" and "modern music," eventually arriving at a three-tiered prescription that he published in a Budapest music magazine in 1931. Excerpted and laid out in tabular form, Bartók's schema looks like this:

1. We may, for instance, take over a peasant melody unchanged or only slightly varied, write an accompaniment to it and possibly some opening and concluding phrases. This kind of work would show a certain analogy with Bach's treatment of chorales. Two main types can be distinguished among works of this character:

   a. In one case accompaniment, introductory and concluding phrases are of secondary importance, and they only serve as an ornamental setting for the precious stone: the peasant melody.

EX. 7-5   Two versions of no. 1 from Bartók/Kodály, *Magyar népdalok*

b. It is the other way round in the second case: the melody only serves as a "motto" while that which is built around it is of real importance. In any case it is of the greatest importance that the musical qualities of the setting should be derived from the musical qualities of the melody.

2. Another method by which peasant music becomes transmuted into modern music is the following: the composer does not make use of a real peasant melody but invents his own imitation of such melodies. There is no real difference between this method and the one described first.

3. There is yet a third way in which the influence of peasant music can be traced in a composer's work. Neither peasant melodies nor imitations of peasant melodies can be found in his music, but it is pervaded by the atmosphere of peasant music. In this case we may say, he has completely absorbed the idiom of peasant music which has become his musical mother tongue. He masters it as completely as a poet masters his mother tongue.[10]

The last, and obviously most important (because most creative) manner of assimilation is — perhaps deliberately — the most vaguely expressed, since the greatest vagueness imposes the fewest limits. It seems clear, though, that what Bartók is describing is related to what, with reference to Stravinsky in chapter 3, was termed "neonationalism," the adoption from folklore not of thematic material but of style characteristics, abstractly conceived. Bartók's reference to the "mother tongue" is significant, precisely since he recognizes that urban composers like himself do not learn the idiom of peasant music from their mothers but must master it through deliberate application, as an adult learns a foreign language. So the "Hungary" that this music, composed according to Bartók's precepts, represents is no real Hungary but an idealized Hungary constructed by combining rural (or "primitive") raw material with the most sophisticated, urbane techniques of elaboration and development: the Hungary of the liberal utopian imagination.

And just because it was liberal, and because it was utopian, Bartók's musical nationalism, unlike any we have seen before, was pluralistic and all-embracing in a manner recalling the eighteenth-century philosophy of Herder, the original romantic nationalist. Bartók studied, and in his creative work assimilated, the folk music not only of the Magyars, but of all the peoples who inhabited "greater Hungary" — Romanians, Slovaks, Bulgars, Croats, and Serbs — and even ethnically remoter peoples like the Turks (distantly related linguistically to the Magyars) or the Arabs of North Africa (coreligionists to the Turks), both of whose musics Bartók researched on location, and about which he published treatises. He was reviled for the catholicity of his musical range by narrower nationalists; and eventually Bartók felt impelled to leave a Hungary that had allied itself politically with the German Nazis, the most virulently narrow nationalists of all. He may be justly viewed as the last of the Herderians, in contrast to the — sadly — more typical twentieth-century nationalists who had betrayed Herder's pluralistic legacy.

A PRECARIOUS SYMBIOSIS

Bartók almost immediately began incorporating the melodies of peasant songs into his original compositions, alongside modernist explorations of a kind familiar to us from the work of other composers. The two lines of development were kept in a kind of symbiosis thanks to what could be called Bartók's neonationalist credo, his insistence "that the musical qualities of the setting" — that is, the original composition — "should be derived from the musical qualities of the melody." His unique synthesis was the result of an unerring eye for musical qualities latent in the folk material that could be brought into conformity with the modernistic concepts that attracted him.

He was, in short, as committed a modernist and a maximalist as any of the composers whose work we have been tracing in the last few chapters, but he felt a need unfelt by the others to justify his stylistic predilections to his social conscience. Grounding in folklore provided a social validation for his art, just as it did for German artists a hundred years before, who remade their art in the spirit of Herder's romanticism. Bartók and the rather less maximalistically inclined Kodály were the only European modernists who remained faithful to this strain of romanticism at a time when it was the complementary strain — the egoistical strain that justified its ways solely on grounds of fidelity to one's own unique subjective self — that captured the imaginations of the Germans.

Bartók never openly opposed his social conscience to Schoenberg's arbitrary "instinct," but there are passages in his writings that allude to social matters under cover of "nature." In the romantic view an "authorless" folksong was the product of impersonal nature rather than human subjectivity: hence the implicit superiority of the new Hungarian music. In an article of 1928, written at the request of E. Robert Schmitz and his Pro Musica Society in New York (already encountered in chapter 5, under the name "Franco-American Musical Society," as the sponsors of Charles Ives's quarter-tone music), Bartók undertook to answer the questions, first, "whether contemporary music of Hungary and the contemporary music of other countries have any points in common," and second, "whether contemporary Hungarian music differs from that of other countries."[11] After tracing in some detail the process, which we will trace below, whereby novel harmonies and tonalities could be milked from the "musical qualities of the melody," Bartók summed up by conceding that "many other (foreign) composers, who do not lean upon folk music, have met with similar results at about the same time — only in an intuitive or speculative way, which, evidently, is a procedure equally justifiable." But, having already injected a slightly ironic tone with the word "evidently," Bartók played his trump card. "The difference," he added immediately, "is that we created through Nature."

And several paragraphs later, Bartók allowed himself to spell out the implicit negative critique just a bit:

> One point, in particular, I must again stress: our peasant music, naturally, is invariably tonal, if not always in the sense that the inflexible major and minor system is tonal. (An 'atonal' folk music, in my opinion, is unthinkable.) Since we

depend upon a tonal basis of this kind in our creative work, it is quite self-evident that our works are quite pronouncedly tonal in type.[12]

So there it was at last, a social prescription: unless modern art music, however maximalistic, rested on a "natural" basis, by which Bartók meant something that would now be more likely called a social basis, its style would be "unthinkable." Composers and their audiences had to speak a common language, and that language had to be determined by "nature" — that is, a social consensus that subsumed the individual. The same assumptions encompassed and motivated aspects of Bartók's professional activity that set it sharply at odds, both esthetically and ethically, with the work of his Viennese contemporaries. He wrote, for example, a wealth of pedagogical piano music designed to train musicians from childhood in the idiom of contemporary music; and here he was especially careful to keep the nexus between peasant music and modern music clear. Kodály's pedagogical work was even more extensive than Bartók's; many regard it as his most important achievement.

The idea of Schoenberg, Berg, or Webern writing music for training children, or incorporating folklore into their work except as an ironic invocation of "innocence," is as unthinkable as was the idea of an "atonal folk music." Bartók and Kodály, in keeping with the traditions of the Hungarian urban intelligentsia from which they had emerged, maintained, alongside their modernist nationalism, a sense of social mission that was regarded elsewhere as inimical to stylistic progress. Most twentieth-century artists were impelled (or compelled) to choose between these goals. Even Kodály did, eventually. Only Bartók, among the century's universally recognized maximalists, attempted to fuse them. That makes him, for historians, a uniquely interesting "phenomenon."

The crucible in which Bartók tried in most concentrated fashion to work out his maximalized peasant-song idiom was a set of fourteen innocently titled Bagatelles for piano (op. 6), composed in May 1908. The set contains everything from straightforward harmonized folk song to modernistic experiment; but within its confines (and with a sidelong glance or two at other works) it is possible to show the relationship between the one extreme and the other with special clarity. Simplest by far, apparently, is Bagatelle no. 4 (Ex. 7-6a), nothing more or less than a song Bartók himself had recorded on a phonographic cylinder from the singing of a peasant the year before (Ex. 7-6b), harmonized in a sort of "impressionist" style. The words show it to be a sort of cowboy's lament:

> I was a cowherd,
> I slept by my cows;
> I awoke one night,
> Not one beast was in its stall.

To designate this setting as "impressionist" in style is to call attention to the prevalence of seventh chords in the harmonization, often moving in parallel à la Debussy. Bartók may well have thought of his setting that way, since 1907, the year in which he collected the song on which he based his bagatelle, was also the year in which he discovered the piano music of Debussy—a discovery that Bartók compared, in terms of its impact on his development, to his discovery of peasant song itself.

Just as salient to the analytical eye is the resolute diatonic purity of the setting (apart from the deliberately jarring chromaticism at the ends of the third and fourth phrases). There are no leading tones in evidence, as there were even in Bartók's 1906

EX. 7-6A   Béla Bartók, Bagatelle, Op. 6, no. 4

*Régi magyar népdal a Dunántulról.

*Old Hungarian Folksong from the district west of the Danube: "When I was a cowhand I fell asleep near the cattle. I awoke about midnight. Not one cow was left."

EX. 7-6B   Song model for Béla Bartók, Bagatelle, Op. 6, no. 4

folk-song harmonizations. That means that there can be no real dominant chord, since the dominant of D minor, by definition, is an A-major triad. Instead, we have a harmonization not in the conventional minor but in an unaltered "Aeolian mode" or natural minor. In that mode all the primary chords are minor (i, iv, v) and the secondary chords are major (III, VI, VII) or diminished (ii°).

This means that in the second phrase, for example, which is a reharmonization of the first with added sevenths, all the primary harmonies are "minor-minor" seventh chords (/0 3 7 10/). What is, at least in retrospect, the most characteristically Bartókian aspect of that harmony is the fact that its constituent intervals, counting from the top or bottom, are a palindrome — m3, M3, m3 — which means that to count from the top is the same as counting from the bottom. The chord is inversionally symmetrical. And Bartók enhances the inversional symmetry of his harmonization even further when he can — in m. 4, for example, where he adds a ninth to the VII chord (on C) so that its intervals, too, become palindromic: M3, m3, m3, M3.

Between the minor-minor seventh chord and the dominant ninth we may observe in passing an important distinction between two types of symmetry: those with an odd number of elements in which there is a single axis (like the M3 in the minor-minor seventh) as opposed to those with an even number of elements in which there is a double axis (like the m3/m3 pair in the dominant ninth). We will return to this point later, for it will assume enormous importance for Bartók as he maximizes the style we are in the process of discovering. Another little point that will become bigger concerns the one chromatic touch in Bagatelle no. 4: the G♯ and F♯ that decorate the cadences in mm. 8 and 12. Together they are a kind of double chromatic neighbor encircling the fourth degree of the scale, so that instead of proceeding from the fifth degree to the third through two whole steps (T–T) we proceed by an alternation of semitones and whole tones (S–T–S). That, too, is a symmetrical arrangement of intervals, indeed a "symmetricalized" one.

Like its predecessor, Bagatelle no. 5 (Ex. 7-7a) is based on a folk song that Bartók collected himself, this time one of Slovak origin (that is, from the northernmost province of what was then "Greater Hungary"). Ex. 7-7b shows the original tune as Bartók transcribed it, in a collection that remained unpublished until 1970. (The words are sadder than Bartók's quick setting might immediately suggest: "Hey, before our door the jilted lad plants a wild rose.") Once again the harmonization insists (even more emphatically than in the previous bagatelle) on the intervallically symmetrical minor-minor seventh chord as primary consonance.

But this time the melody, too, is cast in a mode (the "Dorian") that is intervallically symmetrical. It is the only diatonic mode that retains all its intervals when inverted. (See Ex. 7-8a; the other diatonic modes are related by inversion as follows: major inverts to Phrygian, minor to Mixolydian, Lydian to "Locrian.") And as Bartók apparently discovered (or at least demonstrated in his music) earlier than Stravinsky, the Dorian mode, conceived as a pair of symmetrical T–S–T tetrachords placed a whole step apart, can interact easily with the octatonic scale, conceived as a pair of similar tetrachords placed a half step apart (see Ex. 7-8b; either tetrachord can be held in common while the other is transposed).

EX. 7-7A   Béla Bartók, Bagatelle, Op. 6, no. 5, mm. 1–19

*Tót népdal Gömör megyéböl.

*Slovakian Folksong from the province of Gömör: "Hey, at our doorstep the smart boy is planting a white rose."

EX. 7-7B   Song model for Béla Bartók, Bagatelle, Op. 6, no. 5

EX. 7-8A Dorian inversional symmetry

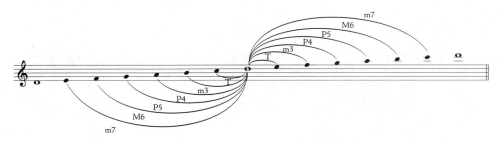

EX. 7-8B Dorian/octatonic interaction

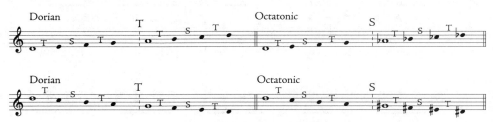

Bagatelles 4 and 5 both conform to the method labeled "1a" in the extract given above from Bartók's essay on the relationship between peasant music and modern music. The original tune in both cases occupies the foreground, the composer's additions, however imaginative and suggestive, being merely the "ornamental setting for the precious stone." Before proceeding with the Bagatelles into more abstractly stylized territory, we can savor the difference between the ornamental style labeled "1a" and its counterpart, "1b" (in which "the melody only serves as a 'motto' while that which is built around it is of real importance"), by comparing Bagatelle no. 4 (Ex. 7-6a) with a piece written a year later, the second in a set of *Four Dirges* for piano, which Bartók published (as op. 9A) in 1912 (Ex. 7-9a).

It is not immediately evident that the dirge is based on the same folk melody as the bagatelle, but Ex. 7-9b, which reconstructs their relationship, will make it clear. The dirge melody is constructed by omitting all tones from the folk tune that do not conform strictly to a pentatonic scale, and making up for their absence with neighbors and internal repetitions. In addition, even rhythms have been made uneven to enhance the prevalence of "noble" Hungarian short-long patterns. The tune, in short, has been rendered folkier than the folk; or rather, it has been recast to conform to a set of theoretical abstractions, the first step in "utopianizing" folklore and rendering it fit for modernist use.

Thereafter the tune is developed in various ways: through enharmonic modulations, by altering its intervals, and (most interestingly) by allowing its predominant structural interval to multiply. That interval is the perfect fourth, which begins the melody and also (in the dirge) brings its first and last phrases to an end. Beginning in m. 31 a variant of the melody is played (Ex. 7-9c) that begins as if splicing the beginning and ending fourths together (mm. 31 – 32) and repeating the same little symmetrical stack of fourths a couple of measures later (m. 34).

This is one simple instance of one of Bartók's most pervasive neonationalist techniques: mining his tunes for harmonic symmetries and exploiting them in both the horizontal and the vertical dimension. The technique led him to many of the same harmonies we have seen in the "atonal" (or pantonal) works of Schoenberg and his pupils, but in the case of Bartók it is often possible to trace the novel harmonies back

EX. 7-9A   Béla Bartók, *Four Dirges*, Op. 9a (1912), no. 2, mm. 1–29

EX. 7-9B   Béla Bartók, *Four Dirges*, Op. 9a (1912), no. 2, mm. 1–14, compared with folk tune in Ex. 7-6b

EX. 7-9C   Béla Bartók, *Four Dirges*, Op. 9a (1912), no. 2, mm. 31–37

to a specific folk-melodic source, showing the process to have been less speculative than empirical. In the middle of Bagatelle no. 7 (Ex. 7-10), there is a long melodic passage consisting of the same superimposed perfect fourths we have just observed in Dirge no. 2, a harmony about which Schoenberg speculated in a famous passage from his *Harmonielehre*, and used with striking effect in his *Chamber Symphony*, op. 9 (1906). But Bartók's stacks of fourths encompass exactly five notes, which if compressed into "best normal order" (as defined in chapter 6) would coincide exactly with the pentatonic ("black key") scale, the scale to which (according to Bartók) all the oldest Hungarian peasant songs conformed.

EX. 7-10   Béla Bartók, Bagatelle, Op. 6, no. 7, mm. 49–70

The fourth-melodies, especially when accompanied as they are in Dirge no. 2 and Bagatelle no. 7 by dissonant harmonies (often involving a "white key/black key" opposition), are among Bartók's most elemental modernistic abstractions from folklore. The next stage of abstraction for Bartók, as it was also for Schoenberg, was the "verticalization" of melodic formations, precisely as happens in Bagatelle no. 11 (Ex. 7-11a), where the fourths now occur not as successions but as vertical piles. The immediate juxtaposition of fourth chords at the tritone, as happens in mm. 14–15, introduces another sort of symmetry to the mix, one that will recall the alternations of perfect fourths and tritones that we have already observed in the work of Schoenberg, Stravinsky, and Ives. With Bartók the essential harmonic unit is not the three-note "atonal triad" or "*Rite*-chord" as it was with Schoenberg or Stravinsky. Rather, it takes the form of a four-note unit consisting of two fourths at the tritone, as happens melodically at the very climax of Bagatelle no. 11 (Ex. 7-11b).

EX. 7-11A   Béla Bartók, Bagatelle, Op. 6, no. 11, mm. 1–18

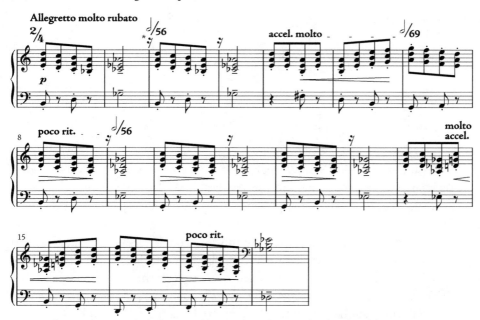

*A pause between the measures, the duration of the pause being determined by the value of the rest.

For its harmonic extension (or "verticalization"), see Ex. 7-11c, the coda of Bagatelle no. 8. The harmonies suspended there over the tonic pedal look like pairs of tritones at the minor ninth (=semitone); but that is the inversion of the "four-note unit" at the climax of Bagatelle no. 11 (Ex. 7-12). In either case, the harmony can be described as the atonal triad plus its inversion, analogous to an ordinary triad expanded to include both the major and the minor third. As we will see, it is the "Bartók chord" par excellence. For reasons that will emerge later, it is often called the "Z-tetrachord" by analysts.

EX. 7-11B   Béla Bartók, Bagatelle, Op. 6, no. 11, mm. 55–60

EX. 7-11C   Béla Bartók, Bagatelle, Op. 6, no. 8, end

EX. 7-12   "Z-tetrachords" in Béla Bartók, Bagatelles, Op. 6, nos. 8 and 11

For the ultimate in Bartókian symmetry, at least as expressed within the *Fourteen Bagatelles*, consider the second item in the set (Ex. 7-13). Bagatelle no. 2 was a recital favorite of the composer, who often played it as an encore and recorded it more than once. The catchy opening is a demonstration of "axial symmetry," wherein every interval is invertible around the same "axis pitch," in this case A. The opening dyad, A♭B♭, is A ± one semitone. The third BG, with which the left-hand melody begins, is A ± two semitones. The next interval in the left hand, CG♭, is A ± three semitones, and so it goes: D♭F = A ± 4 and DF♭ = A ± 5. The whole complex, reminiscent of a similar array that governed the harmony of *Salome* by Richard Strauss, Bartók's early hero (see chapter 1), is summed up in Ex. 7-14. Not that Bartók was the only composer to "inherit" the technique from Strauss: we have already spotted it, in more rudimentary form, in Webern's fourth Bagatelle for string quartet (Ex. 6-26b).

But in the fifth measure of Ex. 7-13 comes an interesting deviation. As Ex. 7-14 shows (and as we may remember from *Salome*), any axis pitch—that is, the point where two chromatic scales in contrary motion intersect at the unison or octave—will have a counterpart at the tritone (that is, the other place where the scales will so intersect). That point is reached at the end of the Bagatelle's fourth measure with the high E♭ in the left hand, to be followed (we can only expect) by another E♭ an octave below to

EX. 7-13   Béla Bartók, Bagatelle, Op. 6, no. 2

EX. 7-13 (*continued*)

complete the pattern. Instead, Bartók writes E♭. The unexpected note might either be viewed as a "wrong note" joke or as a sort of deceptive cadence. Either way, an unstated (or unreached) goal is acknowledged.

But this is momentous. Implying a goal in advance is something that in our experience only "tonal" harmony, with its preassigned functions and directed motion, can do. Bartók's axial symmetry has managed to do the same: it has identified E♭ with a function that can be either fulfilled or evaded. And of course the axis itself, the A about which there has been so much to say, has been similarly implied rather than sounded outright. And yet its ruling presence is felt "behind the scenes" just the way an implied tonic (like the A major or minor triad that is forecast but never sounded through the whole Prelude to Wagner's *Tristan und Isolde*) can rule in absentia in tonal music. Axial symmetry, then, can be construed (or deployed) as an alternate form of functional tonality that takes the chromatic scale rather than the circle of fifths as its basis.

EX. 7-14   Axial symmetry in Béla Bartók, Bagatelle, Op. 6, no. 2

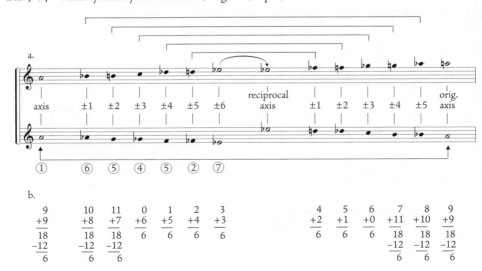

And just as harmonic functions can furnish a form-defining trajectory for tonal music (most basically, the binary form with its movement from tonic to dominant and back by way of a Far Out Point), so can the reciprocal axes in a symmetrical array. That is precisely how Bartók's Bagatelle no. 2 is laid out. The cadence on E♭, evaded in m. 5, is finally made (in a conventional "tonal" way) in mm. 7–8. The section thus inaugurated plays with another symmetrical formation that encompasses both A and E♭: namely the /0 3 6 9/ circle of minor thirds with which Bartók had been familiar since encountering it in the music of Liszt. All the triadic roots in mm. 8–12—E♭, C, and F♯—are drawn from it. Only one member, A, is withheld; and that, of course, is to forecast it as the final goal of the bagatelle's tonal trajectory.

The approach could not be neater. Beginning in m. 17 the music begins to stutter on the dyad ED, which is eventually played (mm. 18–21) as a pulsing harmonic interval like the A♭B♭ pair at the outset. And just as the original dyad initiated a regular expansion to approach the E♭ pole, so the ED dyad and its consequences point us back toward A—an A that, whimsically, is never allowed to materialize (except disguised as B♭♭ resolving to A♭). An evasive action similar to the one in mm. 5–6 is employed in mm. 20–23 to skirt the A and prepare a return, instead, of the A♭B♭ dyad from which the piece had taken off. The coda reproduces the first 6 measures with registers adjusted, and the D♭ from mm. 5–6, which makes consonances with both A♭ and B♭, is allowed to end the piece as a specious tonic—a sort of "tonal" pun.

A BIT OF THEORY

As in the case of Schoenberg, whose creative methods were later explained by analysts using concepts (like the rudimentary "set theory" we explored in chapter 6) that the composer never knew or needed, so Bartók's symmetrical structures were rationalized long after his death according to "paradigms" or models with which he was probably unfamiliar as such. The fact that analytical methods are sometimes anachronistic does not necessarily lessen their appropriateness or their explanatory potential (or else we would have long since stopped using Roman numerals to label chord functions in Bach or Mozart). As explained with reference to Schoenberg, we often need them in order to infer and then demonstrate to our own satisfaction the premises on which the composer was relying a priori.

A case in point is a handy method devised by the composer George Perle (b. 1915) to represent symmetrical arrays like the one Bartók employed in the second Bagatelle, and more importantly, to compare them. It may already have occurred to the reader that, with its "pluses and minuses" arranged around a stationary center, axial symmetry à la Bartók or Strauss or Webern is a "zero-sum game." That is, whatever is added on one side is taken away on the other, so that the "sum"—in this case A (or E♭)—does not change. If that sum could be represented numerically, there would be a means of classifying axes, of measuring progressions from one to another, and (most important, analytically) of assigning any interval or chord one may chance to encounter to its potential place within a symmetrical array.

The trick is done by numbering the pitch classes from an arbitrary starting point on C (like the "fixed doh" of French-style *solfège,* or sight-singing technique), thus,

$$C = 0$$
$$C\sharp D\flat = 1$$
$$D = 2$$
$$D\sharp E\flat = 3$$
$$E = 4$$
$$F = 5$$
$$F\sharp G\flat = 6$$
$$G = 7$$
$$G\sharp A\flat = 8$$
$$A = 9$$
$$A\sharp B\flat = 10$$
$$B = 11$$

and then calculating the sums of the two chromatic scales whose intersections define the symmetrical array. That is what is done in Ex. 7-14b. The array in Ex. 7-14a begins with one of the points of intersection: 2 As. A being nine semitones above C, the sum of two As is $9 + 9$, or 18. But since we are dealing with idealized pitch classes rather than actual pitches, we need to conceptualize everything within a single ideal octave; hence 12 is subtracted from all sums 12 or above, since 11 defines the limit of an octave, after which "zero" comes again. Thus the index number or "sum" of our two As is 6. And so is the index number for the reciprocal point of intersection, the two Ebs ($3 + 3$), around which the same series of dyads take their place but in the opposite order.

As Perle's method represents them, all axes (points of intersection between chromatic scales in contrary motion) have the same index numbers as their reciprocals. In other words, whereas with individual pitches we assume "octave equivalency," in the case of axes we assume "tritone equivalency," thus:

TABLE 7.1

AXIS PAIR	INDEX NUMBER	SUMS
C–F$\sharp$G$\flat$	0	$0 + 0$ or ($6 + 6 - 12$)
C$\sharp$D$\flat$–G	2	$1 + 1$ or ($7 + 7 - 12$)
D–G$\sharp$A$\flat$	4	$2 + 2$ or ($8 + 8 - 12$)
D$\sharp$E$\flat$–A	6	$3 + 3$ or ($9 + 9 - 12$)
E–A$\sharp$B$\flat$	8	$4 + 4$ or ($10 + 10 - 12$)
F–B	10	$5 + 5$ or ($11 + 11 - 12$)

The odd index numbers belong to arrays in which the chromatic scales in contrary motion cross without actually intersecting on unisons or octaves. Whereas the intervals in an intersecting array like the one in Ex. 7-14 are limited to the intervals that contain an even number of semitones, namely M2/m7, M3/m6, and aug4/dim5 in addition to the octave/unison (o), the intervals in a nonintersecting array, like the one in Ex. 7-15, will have the complementary set — m2/M7, m3/M6, P4/P5 — in which all the intervals contain an odd number of semitones. As noted above, a symmetrical array can have either a single or a dual axis, depending on whether it contains an odd or even number of members. Thus the array of dual axes and their tritone reciprocals (taking the minor second as the axis since it is closest to the unison) will look like this:

TABLE 7.2

AXIS PAIR	INDEX NUMBER	SUMS
C/C♯D♭—F♯G♭/G	1	$0 + 1$ or $(6 + 7 - 12)$
C♯D♭/D—G/G♯A♭	3	$1 + 2$ or $(7 + 8 - 12)$
D/D♯E♭—G♯A♭/A	5	$2 + 3$ or $(8 + 9 - 12)$
D♯E♭/E—A/A♯B♭	7	$3 + 4$ or $(9 + 10 - 12)$
E/F—A♯B♭/B	9	$4 + 5$ or $(10 + 11 - 12)$
F/F♯G♭—B/C	11	$5 + 6$ or $(11 + 0)$

EX. 7-15   A representative "odd" array (sum 7)

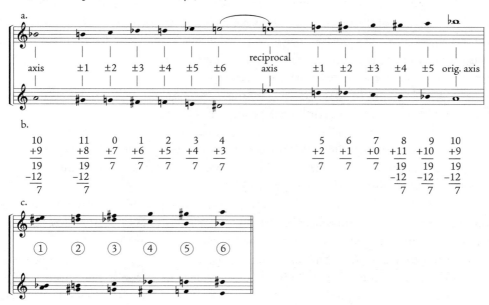

SYMMETRICAL FUGUE, SYMMETRICAL SONATA

To show how thoroughly (and literally) the relationships mapped out in these charts and diagrams could function as an alternative tonal system (easily grasped by the ear without the help of charts or diagrams), we can look ahead to two of Bartók's best-known works, composed considerably later in his career. Once their basic outlines were established in the music he composed around 1908, his methods served him faithfully to the end, making his style a remarkably consistent one over the whole course of his creative life.

We will start with the later of the two, *Music for Strings, Percussion, and Celesta*, composed in 1936 on commission from Paul Sacher (1906–99), a Swiss conductor who had married into a wealthy industrial family and paid many famous composers to write music suitable for the organization he led, the Basel Chamber Orchestra. We will start with it because its first movement, remarkably, projects the selfsame tonal trajectory as Bagatelle no. 2 of 1908, but over a far longer span of time and with far from whimsical effect.

Music for Strings, Percussion, and Celesta is a four-movement composition comparable in that respect to a traditional symphony. Its movements, however, possibly in keeping with the fact that it was commissioned by a chamber orchestra whose main business at first was performing an eighteenth-century repertoire, are in a slow-fast-slow-fast sequence more reminiscent of an old Italian concerto grosso. The fast movements are distinctly "neonationalist" in style, being cast in a modernistic idiom obviously based on folklore. The third movement is typical of a genre Bartók called "night music"—not, however, in the sense of the eighteenth-century convivial *notturno* or serenade, which was aristocratic party music; nor in that of the Chopinesque nocturne, which was a dreamy mood piece; but in the sense of a night spent camping outdoors, in proximity to enigmatic, indefinable sounds of nature.

The night music in *Music for Strings, Percussion, and Celesta* is particularly noted for its pioneering use of the timpani glissando, a technique made possible only a few years earlier when improved models of pedal timpani became available. (Bartók's first use of this uncanny effect, possibly the first by anyone, was in his *Cantata profana* of 1930, a setting of a folk legend in verse, where it accompanies a magical transformation.) In Ex. 7-16a, which reproduces the first page of the score, the timpani glissandos are cast in dialogue with another typical Bartók night sound, a nattering diminution-augmentation or accelerando-ritardando effect on a single note, here played by the xylophone. (The first partial use of this effect in Bartók's music, indeed his first "night piece," is found—not surprisingly—in that same remarkable set of *Bagatelles*, op. 6, the crucible of Bartók's maximalistic style; see Ex. 7-16b.)

Against this background, the violas enter with a melody that in its chromaticism is obviously no folk tune, but which nevertheless bears traces of "Hungarianness" in its rhythm, its tiny accented note-values on the beat aping the short tonic stress patterns of Magyar speech as if placing a human "figure" against a landscape. Accompanying the viola melody is a sustained tremolo in the lower strings that sounds the tritone C/F♯ as a pedal that will last until m. 16. Although we must again tantalizingly postpone pursuit of its ramifications, it is worth noting one more fact: the pedal tritone, plus the xylophone pitch (F) and the pitches of the timpani glissandos (B/F♯)—in other words, all the pitches that accompany the "Hungarian" melody—together form what has already been cryptically identified as a "Z-tetrachord." Now compare Ex. 7-16c,

EX. 7-16A Béla Bartók, *Music for Strings, Percussion and Celesta*, III, mm. 1–10

drawn from a later passage in the third movement, where the rustling night sounds (represented by a murmured cacophony of simultaneous arpeggios or glissandos from celesta, harp, and piano) reach their peak. The pedal, now in the double basses and timpani, has moved to a doubled E♭, while the glissandos pit black-key pentatonic scales, of which E♭ is a member, against various scales from which it stands out: white-key pentatonic, whole-tone, white-key glissandos. Without implying that Debussy would

EX. 7-16B Béla Bartók, Bagatelle, Op. 6, no. 12, mm. 1–8

*A gradual acceleration, in which there is no definite number of notes (and similarly in subsequent measures with the same figuration).

EX. 7-16C Béla Bartók, *Music for Strings, Percussion and Celesta*, III, 1 after letter B

have necessarily recognized or sanctioned it, the texture here could be aptly characterized as maximalized "impressionism."

Putting the pedals together—C/F♯ + E♭—and noting that they make up a diminished triad, we might be tempted to relate the harmony here to the /0 3 6 9/ circle of minor thirds that is so familiar by now from its use by Liszt, Ravel, and Stravinsky, all composers with whose works Bartók was enthusiastically familiar, and that we have already observed in Bagatelle no. 2. But where Liszt, Ravel, and Stravinsky would most likely have integrated the circle of thirds with its octatonic scalar extension (a technique to which Bartók was certainly no stranger), we now have another, uniquely Bartókian context with which to ally it — namely, the "sum 6" symmetrical array already displayed in Ex. 7-14, where E♭ is one of the axes along with A, and where the C/F♯G♭ pair is situated right between the axes on both sides.

Excellent evidence that this was Bartók's own way of conceptualizing the harmonic symmetry that his pedals expressed can be found in the notation of the glissandi in Ex. 7-16c, especially the upward-sweeping white-key glissandos in the piano part. Ex. 7-14 was introduced in conjunction with the Bagatelle no. 2 and used the note-spellings found there, including F♭ in place of the more usual E, presumably so that the expansion from F♭/D to the axis octave E♭ could be represented as a pair of leading-tone resolutions, as in a traditional augmented sixth chord. The F♭–D spelling is retained in Ex. 7-16c.

But anyone encountering that passage in the context of a performance of *Music for Strings, Percussion, and Celesta,* or a sequential perusal of the score, would have had even better evidence that Bartók conceptualized its tonality in terms of the "sum 6" array in Ex. 7-14; for the implications of that array are worked out both systematically and startlingly over the course of the first movement. Perhaps in response to the concerto grosso idea (also reflected in the occasional *concertante* writing for keyboard instruments and string soloists in the fast movements), Bartók cast the movement as a fugue. Here is how he described it, in his own dry and halting English, in the preface to a revised edition of the score, published after he had already taken wartime refuge in America:

> On certain principles fairly strictly executed form of a fugue, i.e. the 2nd entry appears one fifth higher, the 4th again one fifth higher than the 2nd, the 6th, 8th and so forth again a fifth higher than the preceding one. The 3rd, 5th, 7th, etc. on the other hand enter each a fifth lower. After the remotest key — E flat — has been reached (the climax of the movement) the following entries render the theme in contrary movement until the fundamental key — A — is reached again, after which a short Coda follows.[13]

For the sake (he evidently thought) of clarity, Bartók's description emphasizes the procedural similarity between his fugue and the familiar textbook rules of fugue writing. A traditional fugue begins with "an entry one fifth higher," and so does Bartók's. But his fugue keeps on mounting higher — and plunging lower — by fifths, as may be seen in Ex. 7-17a, which shows the start of the process: violas starting on axis-pitch A, the third and fourth violins entering at the fifth above (E), the cellos at the fifth below (D), the second violins another fifth above (B). A "maximalized fugue," then? Yes, but to leave it at that would do scant justice to the plan. To take it all in at once, and also see its relationship to the other music of Bartók that we have looked at, we need a diagram (Diagram 7-1 shown following Ex. 7-17a). Numbers in parentheses in Diagram 7-1 refer to the measures in which each entry of the subject takes place; numbers in brackets show the relationship of each vertical pair to the axis pitch as in Ex. 7-14.

EX. 7-17A   Béla Bartók, *Music for Strings, Percussion and Celesta*, I, mm. 1–15

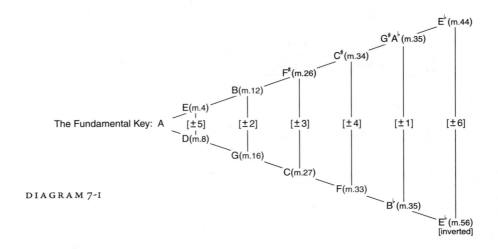

DIAGRAM 7-I

By pairing the entries at the upper fifth with those at the lower fifth, as in the diagram, we can see that Bartók's "fugal" procedure is in reality another way of projecting the same "sum 6" symmetrical matrix from which Bagatelle no. 2 had been derived, but doing it in a grand way that covers an imposing span of time and invokes a long and distinguished fugue-writing heritage that it, in effect, caps. Each of the pairs in the diagram above has its counterpart in Ex. 7-14.

The crucial theoretical point that Bartók's fugue thus demonstrates is the way in which the circle of fifths can be mapped onto the chromatic scale (the "circle of semitones"), the only other interval cycle to exhaust all the pitch classes, so as to traverse the same progression from an axis pitch to its reciprocal. The achievement of E♭ (Ex. 7-17b), which takes place in both the ascending and descending "voices" as conceptualized in the diagram, provides the same tangible sense of climax as the continually foreshadowed but evaded E♭s had done in the bagatelle. That sense of climax or completion conditions the same out-and-back tonal trajectory, utterly different yet wholly analogous to the out-and-back trajectories of tonal music. The much-truncated coda, which begins with the upbeat to the fourth measure of Ex. 7-17b in the cellos and basses with the subject in inversion, spells out the idea of axial symmetry in as many ways as Bartók could think of. At the very end (Ex. 7-17c), in a summary that manages to be both grave and witty, the two violin parts play the second phrase of the subject, covering exactly the range between the primary axis (A) and its reciprocal (E♭), in note-against-note counterpoint with its inversion. It is almost as if they were actually performing a slightly abbreviated version of Ex. 7-14 itself.

A NEW TONAL SYSTEM?

Among Bartók's most impressive achievements were his six string quartets, all of them very elaborate major works, and all very different from one another. They were composed between 1908 and 1939, a period that encompassed virtually his entire mature career in Europe. Bartók's intense cultivation of the genre, one of the emblems of the European "classical" tradition, attests to his concerns both for synthesizing the

EX. 7-17B   Béla Bartók, *Music for Strings, Percussion and Celesta*, I, mm. 56–64

EX. 7-17C   Béla Bartók, *Music for Strings, Percussion and Celesta*, I, mm. 86–88

particularly national with the universal, and for conceiving the universal in terms of tradition and advancement in equal measure.

The Fourth String Quartet (1928), completed six years earlier than *Music for Strings, Percussion, and Celesta*, is often looked upon as the culmination or far out point of Bartók's maximalistic explorations. It brings his preoccupation with symmetry to a peak that encompasses two musical dimensions: both the "vertical" dimension of harmony, as in the works we have already considered, and the "horizontal" dimension of form as it unfolds in time. In it he deployed for the first time the all-encompassing symmetry of "bridge form," as he called it, meaning the casting of the constituent sections in a movement (like the nocturnal slow movement of the *Music for Strings, Percussion, and Celesta*) or even the constituent movements in a full-length "classical" composition like a string quartet, in the form of a palindrome.

Like several of the works that followed it (including the Fifth Quartet, the Second Piano Concerto, and the Concerto for Orchestra composed in America), the Fourth Quartet contains five movements, in which a unique central movement is flanked fore and aft by neighbors of similar character, while the outer movements draw on a common fund of thematic or motivic material. But when representing the form schematically (as in his preface to the Fourth Quartet), Bartók did not designate the sections simply as ABCBA as one might label the sections of a rondo, but rather ABCB′A′, to denote his concern that there be a dynamic forward momentum as well as a sense of return, as in the classical sonata form. To quote László Somfai, the leading Hungarian Bartók scholar, despite all its "quasi-geometrical symmetry," Bartók's bridge form "is not static: it does not return to its origins but progresses towards a cathartic outcome,"[14] which of course implies a drama.

In the Fifth Quartet and the Second Concerto, the middle movement is a wild scherzo flanked by slow movements (the first lyrical, the other stunned and immobile). In the Fourth Quartet (as in the Concerto for Orchestra) the arrangement is just the opposite: the central movement is an almost motionless "night music". In the Quartet this central movement is replete with a Hungarian speech-song intoned by the cello that first alternates, then joins, with nature sounds (prominently including bird calls) against a backdrop of impassively sustained harmonies. The flanking movements in the Fourth Quartet and the Concerto for Orchestra are scherzos. In the Quartet each scherzo is a coloristic tour de force as their performance directions declare: *Prestissimo, con sordino* in the fore position, *Allegretto pizzicato* in the aft. (Here Bartók first used the technique of snapping the string against the fingerboard—designated with ♀—that all string players now call the "Bartók pizz," although it had been anticipated as early as 1673 by the Austrian violinist composer Franz von Biber to imitate cannon-fire in a *Battalia* for strings.)

The relationship between the outer movements in the Quartet is most vividly grasped by taking a peek at their respective last pages, which are self-evidently similar (Ex. 7-18). The concluding phrases, marked *pesante* (weighty), are virtually identical. The last movement, however, is no mere reprise of the first. The similar conclusions are reached by differing trajectories; and even on the last pages a closer look reveals telling contrasts of detail. All the motifs on the last page of the quartet (Ex. 7-18b) are diatonic, while those at the end of the first movement (Ex. 7-18a) begin as segments of the chromatic scale and approach the diatonic conclusion only at the very end. The chromatic segments may be found in the finale, too, and dominate its middle, so that the final movement makes a longer, more systematic and decisive approach to a diatonic conclusion that the first movement only briefly foreshadows. Thus even at this preliminary, fairly superficial stage we may discern a sense of ongoing motivic development and resolution linking the outer movements.

But the shared material that unites them actually lies, so to speak, beneath the motivic threshold. A very quick spot survey of the finale will prepare us for a close analysis of the first movement, the longest and most elaborate of the five. (The possibly misleading fact that there are more than twice as many measures in the finale should be balanced against its faster tempo, its two-beat rather than four-beat measure length,

EX. 7-18A   Béla Bartók, Quartet no. 4, I, end

EX. 7-18A *(continued)*

EX. 7-18B Béla Bartók, Quartet no. 4, V, end

EX. 7-18B (*continued*)

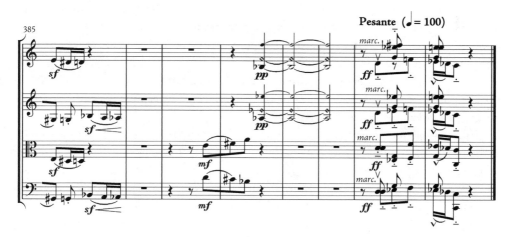

and its much lower density of detail.) The finale's very first harmony (Ex. 7-19a) can be our starting point. It contains a thrice-doubled C and a G that is duplicated even more amply (six times in all; though like the C it is sounded in only three octaves). This strongly reinforced fifth is obviously being projected as a "normative" sonority, analogous to a tonic. And indeed there is no measure that does not contain it somewhere until m. 57. But its absence is fleeting. It reasserts itself dramatically in m. 75, and is thereafter again omnipresent for a while, but in conjunction with its counterpart at the tritone, the fifth F♯/C♯. That already rings a Bartókian bell (and a Stravinskian one as well, if we recall *Petrushka* from chapter 3).

EX. 7-19A   Béla Bartók, Quartet no. 4, V, m. 1

EX. 7-19B   Béla Bartók, Quartet no. 4, V, m. 11

But let us return to Ex. 7-19a and take note of the two "foreign" pitches, F♯ and D♭. They are the equivalent of the F♯/C♯ just described, but their unusual spelling on their first appearance alerts us that something unusual yet strangely familiar may be afoot. A sharped note tends upward, a flatted one downward; so again we may have a case of neighbors scraping, as it were, the insides of an interval. This assumption is confirmed in a long passage beginning in m. 11 (Ex. 7-19b), in which the cello adds both neighbors simultaneously (the note-spelling now looking especially bizarre) to the viola's normative fifth in the same register.

In Ex. 7-19c, moreover, which begins at m. 31, the neighbor harmony is transferred to the inner voices, while the outer ones play a theme that consists of the fifth and its neighbors strung out as a sort of arpeggio (identified, when sighted in the Bagatelles, as the "Z-tetrachord,"), in which semitones alternate with fourths (or, as Bartók sometimes insists in his spelling, with augmented thirds). In m. 37 another variant appears, in which the lower G is replaced by a G♯ and the tune approaches a "Hungarian" pentatonic mode. At the pickup to m. 48 yet another variant appears, this time accompanying the normative fifth (now weirdly spelled with a B♯) and the neighbor tones (spelled with an ordinary C♯ in place of the weird D♭). The changed spellings suggest a reversal of the

EX. 7-19C   Béla Bartók, Quartet no. 4, V, mm. 31–53

EX. 7-19C (continued)

EX. 7-19C   (*continued*)

perspective. Now it is the original normative interval, spelled as the augmented third G/B♯, that is playing the role of double neighbor to a newly normative F♯/C♯.

So C(B♯)/G and F♯/C♯(D♭) are in a kind of harmonic stalemate. That much, as the reference to *Petrushka* reminds us, is nothing new. We've seen it before in Ravel, too, and it even arises occasionally in the work of Rimsky-Korsakov, since it arises "naturally" out of octatonic relationships based on the /0 3 6 9/ circle of minor thirds. (When C/G is at "0," F♯/C♯ will be at "6".) Indeed, Bartók confirms this common heritage at m. 44, when A and E (at "9") take over briefly as the normative fifth, providing a halfway house between C/G and F♯/C♯. Indeed, almost the entire pitch content of the first section of the movement can be referred to the same octatonic scale that provided the basic tonality in the second tableau of *Petrushka* — namely, the one that can be constructed out of triads on C, E♭, F♯, and A, and that can be represented in numbers (with C as "zero") as /0 1 3 4 6 7 9 10/.

Of the "missing" pitches /2 5 8 11/ (=D, F, G♯A♭, B), only the G♯A♭ figures prominently in the music we are surveying, first as a complementary neighbor to G in Ex. 7-19b, and later, in a single melodic appearance (m. 38), as the result of a transposition. The rest appear before m. 90 only as embellishments to the accompanying ostinato rhythm: the F in the cello as a neighbor to E at m. 44; the D only as part of a folk-primitivistic slashing-the-open-strings effect in the viola (also at m. 44). The B never appears at all, which makes its sudden prominence, beginning in the viola part at m. 90, such an event (Ex. 7-19d). Marking a sudden modulation, just as in traditional "tonal" music, it serves to articulate an important formal division.

But something else is happening as well. The superimposed fifths (or "Z-tetrachord") C/G + C♯D♭/F♯, whether appearing as an ostinato harmony or as a melodic phrase, are "overdetermined" in this music. It is a subset of the octatonic scale, as it would be in Stravinsky or Ravel, but the alternating use of each constituent fifth as a neighbor scraping the insides of its counterpart recalls the thoroughgoing symmetrical arrays that are uniquely Bartók's. If we were to continue the pattern implied by the progression from C/G to D♭/F♯ (that is, adding a semitone to the bottom and

EX. 7-19D   Béla Bartók, Quartet no. 4, V, mm. 90–101

subtracting one from the top), the next interval to appear would be D/F, followed by D♯/E, an axis pair.

But we've been there before: it is all laid out in Ex. 7-15, our "representative 'odd' array" expressing "sum 7." Notice now how our two "Z-related" fifths function within the array: as "contiguities," or immediate successions on either side of the reciprocal axis — first "forward," so to speak, with C/G before D♭/F♯, then "backward." Another way of expressing the relationship would be to note that they exchange places on opposite sides of the reciprocal axis. The C/G and D♭/F♯ are in second place (±2) following each axis pair respectively, and the D♭/F♯ and C/G are in third place (±3).

There is yet a third way of viewing their relationship. Turn back to p.393 and look at Ex. 7-15c, which has not been discussed or even mentioned up to now. It simply shows the two halves of Ex. 7-15a superimposed. The familiar Z-tetrachord now comes as a discrete harmony in positions 3 and 4 (its two forms being related, so to speak, by inversion: two fourths superimposed at the tritone vs. two fifths). But the same harmony also comes at the ends, as the sum of the two axis pairs (again expressed in inversion: two semitones superimposed at the tritone vs. two major sevenths). The remaining harmony, at positions 2 and 5, is a diminished seventh chord that sums up the /0 3 6 9/ symmetry associated with the octatonic scale. For a final demonstration of the "overdetermination" of Bartókian symmetry, note that the Z-tetrachords at positions 1+3 (or 4+6, their inversions) sum up the contents of the octatonic scale laid out a few paragraphs above, and the chord at positions 2 and 4 is the complementary collection of "missing" pitches.

From this we may draw one final "theoretical" conclusion (or rather, make one more a priori generalization) before going back to the music. Just as two different Z-tetrachords appear in Ex. 7-15c, a summary of the harmonic relations of a single "odd" (or dual-axis) symmetrical array, so any one Z-tetrachord will appear in two such arrays. And just as the two Z-tetrachords within a single array stand at the distance of a minor third (easiest to see in Ex. 7-15c if position 1 is compared with position 4, or 3 with 6), so the two arrays between which a single Z-tetrachord can function as a pivot or bridge will have "sum" numbers that differ by 6 (representing the tritone).

Thus, in Ex. 7-20 (following a demonstration first published by the Bartók scholar Elliott Antokoletz[15]), each of the Z-tetrachords in Ex. 7-15c is written out four times, in permutations that show how it may be laid out around four different dual axes of symmetry, each located at a distance of a minor third from its neighbors. The index or "sum" number of each axis semitone is entered so as to confirm the observations made in the previous paragraph, which link Bartók's symmetrical scheme with the transposition routines already associated with "octatonicism" in the works of Stravinsky, Ravel, and Rimsky-Korsakov, and, behind them all, Bartók's revered compatriot Franz Liszt. An even simpler demonstration of that association is the bare fact that the sum of the two Z-tetrachords in question, or any two found in the same symmetrical array, is the octatonic scale itself (see Ex. 7-20c).

But now it is time, once and for all, to ask why they are called "Z" tetrachords. The answer to that question, along with a peek at Bartók's maximalism at its far out point, will emerge from a brief but comprehensive stab at analyzing the first movement of the Fourth Quartet. The very first measure (see Ex. 7-22) contains the telltale clue (as if we needed one by now) that the movement is based on a symmetrical array. A glance at the two violin parts, moving out from a semitone or "compound semitone" (minor ninth) to an augmented second, tell us that, and also specify the semitone E/F as one of the axes. Ex. 7-21a shows the whole array, set out in two tiers like Ex. 7-15c.

The first phrase in Ex. 7-22 (mm. 1–2) is constructed almost entirely out of the intervallic relationships presented in Ex. 7-21a. Besides the semitone E/F and the augmented second E♭/F♯ in the violins (positions 1 and 2 in the top staff of the array), there is the sixth C/A in the cello (position 5) and the concluding simultaneity B/B♭

EX. 7-20   Permutations of the Z-tetrachord

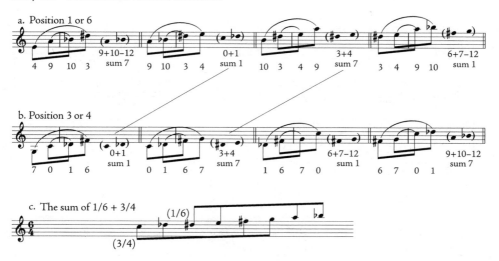

EX. 7-21   Symmetrical arrays for Béla Bartók, Quartet no. 4, I

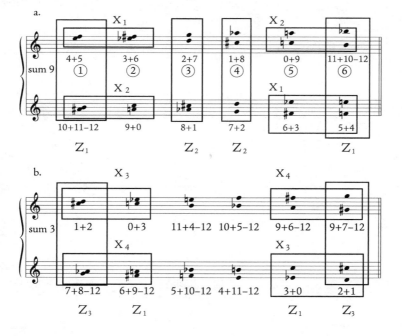

in the second violin and cello (position 6). Position 3 (the fourth G/D) also comes as a simultaneity in m. 2 (cello and first violin). The second phrase (mm. 3–4) replays it all on the lower staff of Ex. 7-21a, beginning with the two violins on A/C (position 2) and B/B♭ (position 1), and then the viola entry on A♭ against the first fiddle's C♯. The viola then proceeds to A/C (position 2) expressed as a sixth, to mirror the cello's sixth in m. 1.

At the pickup to the fifth measure, the cello repeats the last three notes played by the first violin, but in typically reversed order, asserting a "horizontal" axis of symmetry

EX. 7-22   Béla Bartók, Quartet no. 4, I, mm. 1–22

EX. 7-22 (*continued*)

to go with the vertical ones we have been investigating. Its descending third is then imitated by the other three instruments, each entering a semitone above the last and holding the final note so that a maximally dissonant cluster, which sets the tense or angrily agitated tone that will persist throughout the movement, is built up and tied over the bar.

That cluster, however, is no "mere" cluster. It is one of the most important motives in the movement, so important that it was christened "X" or "the X set" by George Perle in a very influential article, "Symmetrical Formations in the String Quartets of Béla Bartók," published in 1955.[16] That article, one of the first to unlock the secrets of Bartók's symmetrical arrays, made the X-set famous along with its counterpart the

Y-set, which follows immediately on the second eighth of m. 6. As the "X-set" was a four-note cluster encompassing three semitones, so the "Y-set" was an equally elemental particle, a cluster of three whole tones. Since both sets contained four notes, they are now more commonly known as the X and Y tetrachords.

Both, obviously, are intervallically (hence inversionally) symmetrical. The middle semitone of the X-tetrachord is its dual axis of symmetry; the whole-tone cluster has an unplayed single axis between its middle pair of notes. Thus, as Ex. 7-23 shows, the axis of symmetry for the first X-tetrachord in the quartet (m. 5) is C♯/D, while the axis for the first Y-tetrachord (m. 6) is C♯/D♭. And as the cello part in m. 7 shows, the characteristic motif whose progress from chromatic to diatonic is in effect the story of the quartet, originates as a rhythmicized "horizontalization" of the X-tetrachord, initially played for maximum dissonance against an accompanying Y-tetrachord. But the Y-tetrachord is just as frequently "horizontalized." Many of the longer melodic phrases in the movement can be parsed into alternating X's and Y's (see Ex. 7-23c).

The passage in mm. 7–11 of Ex. 7-22 pits the two symmetrical hexachords one against the other with increasing speed, while in mm. 11–12 the quartet pairs off into two duos at the octave, demonstrating the symmetry of the X-tetrachord by playing it against its inversion from a common starting point at C♯/D♭, the axis of the Y-tetrachord. But of course these inversionally equivalent motives are also palindromic, having a pitch succession that is the same reading front to back or back to front. Just as in Schoenberg's atonal utopia, in Bartók's symmetricalized musical space there is "no absolute up or down, right or left." Bartók, too, has "emancipated the dissonance," and with similar effect. But his musical utopia is not "pantonal." There are definite normative harmonies, which can be departed from, returned to, progressed between, and embellished; and so, despite everything, a sense of pitch hierarchy is maintained.

And there is a sense of closure at m. 13, brought about in a way that recalls the ending of Schoenberg's *Erwartung*: a cluster covering the tritone B♭–E, which amounts to two conjunct X-tetrachords interlocking on their common point of origin, C♯/D♭, and filling in the space of the original Y-tetrachord (see Ex. 7-23d). That space is exactly half of the total available musical space, leaving the other half in reserve for "complementation," thus allowing for further harmonic movement.

The air having been cleared by the cluster chord and the following two-beat rest, the music at m. 14 has the effect of a new theme. It is none other than what we have already encountered as the main theme of the last movement, the one that, together with its transpositions, exhausts an octatonic scale. So it does here. Note well the outer limits of the theme at its two transpositions: in the second violin, beginning at the pickup to m. 16, the limits are defined as the tritone C♯/G; in the first violin, beginning at m. 17, the limits are the tritone G♯/D.

The same limits are described "inside out" (i.e., D/A♭) by the viola, beginning at the pickup to m. 19. On repetition, the viola connects the A♭ to a high D♭ that comes down via a G, thus combining in one line the two tritones expressed by the two violin parts. The first violin takes a cue from this at mm. 20–21, with a line that turns the viola's tritones inside out again, combining the tritone G♯/D going up

EX. 7-23   X- and Y-tetrachords

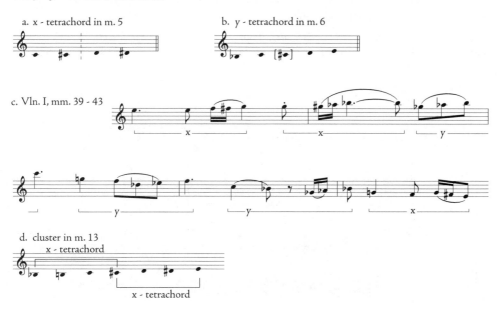

a. x - tetrachord in m. 5

b. y - tetrachord in m. 6

c. Vln. I, mm. 39 - 43

d. cluster in m. 13

x - tetrachord

x - tetrachord

with the tritone G/C♯ coming down. In m. 22, the first violin plays a variant that is entirely confined to the two tritones (compare mm. 31 – 34 in Ex. 7-19c from the last movement).

But this configuration, of course, is none other than our "Z-tetrachord," and now we have an inkling into the origin of the term. It was coined by Leo Treitler, an eminent music historian who was then a graduate student in composition at Princeton University, in an article of 1959, "Harmonic Procedure in the *Fourth Quartet* of Bela Bartók."[17] Treitler demonstrated the functional equivalence of this harmony, which (as we have already noted) is inversionally symmetrical at multiple axes, with the "X" and "Y" tetrachords already named by Perle. This cumulative process of discovery, in which the work of various scholars contributed toward the elucidation of Bartók's symmetrical arrays and the tonal system to which they gave rise, was one of the notable detective stories of twentieth-century musicology.

Once discovered as a discrete harmony, the Z-tetrachord revealed fascinating properties. As a look back at Ex. 7-21 will confirm, the Z-tetrachord that Bartók gradually introduces over the span of mm. 18 – 22 in the first movement of the quartet is deeply embedded in the structure of the "sum 9" array, where it is labeled "Z_2." It is the sum of the intervals in positions 3 and 4, whether one reads the top staff, the bottom staff, or the two staves as a simultaneity. It is, in effect, the inversional-cum-palindromic fulcrum or balance-point of the array. And the X-tetrachord is just as deeply embedded in the array: it is the sum of the intervals in positions 1 and 2, as well as positions 5 and 6 in any one staff. And the content of the tetrachord as it is first displayed as a harmony (m. 5) corresponds exactly to the intervals in positions 1 and 2 on the upper staff of the "sum 3" array (Ex. 7-21b).

Now that we know the story of the tetrachords' christening, and are armed accordingly with some insight into their shared properties, we can appreciate what happens in the long passage beginning in m. 48 (Ex. 7-24a), characterized by dogged sequences of mirror writing and by one of the most widely imitated aspects of Bartók's

EX. 7-24A   Béla Bartók, Quartet no. 4, I, mm. 48–57

EX. 7-24A *(continued)*

EX. 7-24B Béla Bartók, Quartet no. 4, I, mm. 75–82

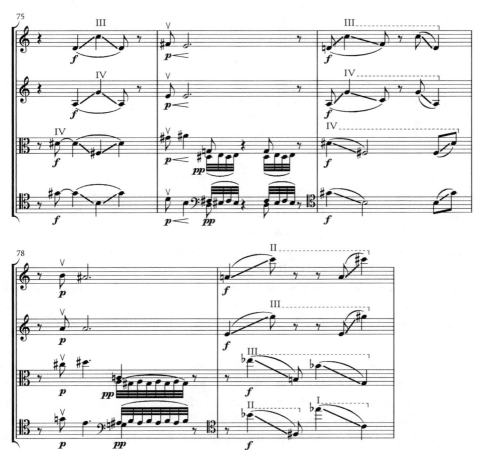

maximalistic quartet manner: grinding glissandos in contrary motion. The latter take over in m. 75 and drive the movement to a peak of harmonic tension. Every harmony from m. 75 to m. 93 (see Ex. 7-24b for its beginning) consists of one of the three symmetrical tetrachords. As Treitler noted in his article of 1959 (building on an observation that Perle had published four years previously), "the z-group is related to the y as the latter is to the x; i.e., the y expands to the z [as the x expands cadentially to the y]." But when Z proceeds to Z, the relationship can be described as "octatonic complementation": the two will always be found in complementary positions in a symmetrical array, their sum being an octatonic scale (see Ex. 7-25, an analytical reduction of Ex. 7-24b).

EX. 7-25   Béla Bartok, Quartet no. 4, I, octatonic complementation ("Z to Z progressions") in mm. 75–82.

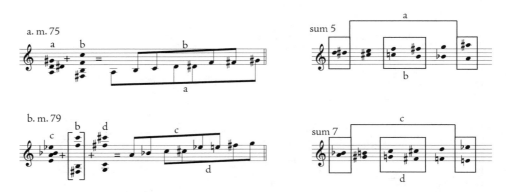

Beginning at m. 83, the "horizontalized" version of the X-tetrachord begins insinuating itself into the chordal texture, leading to a conspicuous reprise ten bars later of the movement's opening phrases, juxtaposed with horizontalized X-tetrachords and mirror glissandos of even greater compass than before (Ex. 7-26). One recognizes in this section the return of many of the opening gestures, including the modified reintroduction of the Z-tetrachord. (See Ex. 7-27 for an illustration of the process, in which some extra notes are interpolated that can be referred equally to the octatonic or to the "folk" pentatonic scale.) It is surely no accident that the Z-tetrachord in violin II now corresponds to the sum of the axes in Ex. 7-21b.

RETREAT?

The movement, in fine, breaks down into a four-part scheme: mm. 1–49, mm. 50–93, mm. 93–126, mm. 126–160. All of the observations we have been making—the "bithematic" structure of the first section; its thematic correspondences with the third; the seeming dissection of the music into its elementary particles in the second; the integration of elements from the second section within the otherwise "recapitulatory" third; the significantly modified tonal scheme of the third; to which we may now add the quickened tempo and percussive address of the last—conspire to produce an impression of a symmetrically reinterpreted "sonata form" as the composers of

EX. 7-26   Béla Bartók, Quartet no. 4, I, mm. 93–104

EX. 7-27   Béla Bartók, Quartet no. 4, I, re-introduction of Z-tetrachords after reprise (mm. 112–114)

the nineteenth century had inherited it from Beethoven, replete with exposition, development, recapitulation, and coda.

That format does not correspond exactly to any modern historian's description of sonata form. Such a description, based on a historical investigation of its origins and genealogy in the eighteenth century, must emphasize the sonata's descent from the earlier binary form (which means interpreting it chiefly in harmonic or "tonal" terms). But the conservatory textbooks of the nineteenth century interpreted the form, based chiefly on its thematic content, as "ternary" or "ternary plus coda." This was the model Bartók inherited, learned, and adapted.

All of this raises some important and interesting historical questions — or are they merely "historiographical" ones? In keeping with the "modernist" spirit as defined in chapter 1, a spirit that unquestionably drove much of the musical thought of the early twentieth century, our discussion of Bartók has emphasized his most maximalistic devices, and these at their peak period of concentration. This peak period, it has probably been noticed already, came significantly later with Bartók than it had with Schoenberg, who was an older composer than Bartók, or with Stravinsky, who was his almost exact contemporary. And that partially explains the curious fact that Bartók's most maximalistic phase simultaneously entailed a reaffirmation of fidelity to "timeless" musical standards, as exemplified by the fugue and the sonata, genres that the early twentieth-century maximalists since Mahler had made a point of ignoring. (And even Mahler had made a point of modifying his deployment of sonata form in accordance with the post-Wagnerian precept that "content must create its own form.").

As we are about to discover, the turn back toward the timeless or the "classic" was perhaps the dominant esthetic swerve of the so-called "interwar" decades, the 1920s and 1930s, a period in the history of twentieth-century music that is often christened "neoclassical." To a certain extent it was characterized by its protagonists (and to a much larger extent by their critics or detractors) as a retreat or even a regression: a pullback from the brink or abyss — or, from the detractors' point of view, from responsibility to one's historical obligation.

One would hesitate to apply such a term to so aggressively, even recalcitrantly discordant a work as the first movement of Bartók's Fourth Quartet, let alone a work so intricately realized on premises so novel as to require the combined efforts of a generation of scholars to crack its code. It hardly seems to be shrinking back from anything. And if it evokes a form that textbooks purvey as a sort of exemplary musical behavior, it does so in a way that implicitly challenges the form to embrace a novel, almost feral dynamism. One would be hard put to deny its composer's commitment to the technical advancement of his art, even at the risk of its comprehensibility to a nonprofessional audience.

And yet if we compare the Fourth Quartet of 1928 with the *Music for Strings, Percussion, and Celesta* of 1936, we might be tempted to question that commitment after all. And as we shall see later, were we to compare the works Bartók composed in America during his last five years of life with those of his maximalistic peak, we might be even more inclined to wonder at his creative path, if our model of composerly responsibility is founded on notions of progress and technical advancement.

Bartók, it seems, could not have believed in those "progressive" notions to compose the way he did in the last decade or so of his career — but in that case, how is one to explain his maximalistic phase? Is it fair to describe the move away from it as a retreat, or is that a necessarily (and therefore superfluously) prejudicial term? Can one move forward in time yet backward in "history"? These paradoxes and contradictions indeed became a crux — a problematical moment — in the history of twentieth-century music. The way in which historians, critics, and composers have dealt with it provides another example — actually, a whole heap of examples — of historiography's impact on history. From this point on, that crux and its impact will be one of our predominating themes.

THE OLDEST TWENTIETH-CENTURY COMPOSER?

Here is how Theodor Wiesengrund Adorno (1903–69), the musical philosopher whom we met in chapter 6 as an advocate of Schoenberg and his pupils, managed to "salvage for history" a composer he admired, but one whose music failed to keep up with the pace of Viennese innovation. Perhaps significantly, the composer in question, Leoš Janáček (1854–1928) was, like Bartók, a member of one of the outlying non-Germanic populations within the old empire of which Vienna was the center and capital. "Where the evolutionary direction of Western music failed to be realized fully," wrote Adorno,

> as in some of the rural regions of southeastern Europe, tonal material could be used, until quite recently, without shame. One thinks of the magnificent art of Janáček: all its folkloristic tendencies clearly must be counted part of the most progressive dimension of European art music. The legitimation of such music from the periphery is based ultimately on the fact that a coherent and selective technical canon emerges from it. Truly exotic music, the material of which, even though it is familiar, is organized in a totally different way from that of the West, has a power of alienation which places it in the company of the avant-garde and not that of nationalistic reaction.[18]

Although Adorno was arguing from a position that he identified as "progressive," it is painfully easy now to perceive the smug ethnocentric bias that informs it — and it becomes even easier if we switch the terms around. What is permitted to Janáček (or Bartók, whose music is discussed nearby) would be thought unworthy of a German, Adorno implies, for the task of German music is to represent "the West" (and even "humanity") in general terms. Moreover, the authenticity of Janáček's "magnificent art," which Adorno quite wrongly assumed to have been the product of a rural or agrarian society, is measured entirely in terms of its appeal to urban Germans, for whom it is exotic (and therefore "alienated"), rather than in terms of its appeal to the composer's compatriots, the group to whom it was actually directed in the first place, the educated and urban strata of Czech society. Germany, or rather the German-speaking urban centers with their emotionally self-absorbed upper-middle class, remained for Adorno the measure of all things. That in itself was evidence of its (and his) emotional self-absorption.

Meanwhile, the very definition of alienation—the loss or renunciation of fellow-feeling in the wake of emotional stress or social injustice—proclaims its irrelevance to artists like Janáček, the object of Adorno's ostensible praise, who saw right through it. "Not everyone understands a fellow man," Janáček told a London audience in 1926:

> Once an educated German said to me: "What, you grow out of folk song? That is a sign of a lack of culture!" As if a man on whom the sun shines, on whom the moon pours out its light, as if all that surrounds us was not a part of our culture. I turned away and let the German be.[19]

But of course this statement, too, must be unpacked. The man who made it was at the age of seventy-one just beginning to enjoy "world" celebrity after half a century of strictly regional (and not even "national") fame. That is one of the reasons why Janáček had such a strangely shaped career, one that made him by a fairly wide margin the oldest composer who is customarily (and rightly) treated as a representative "twentieth-century" figure, alongside contemporaries young enough to be his children or even his grandchildren. He was older than Mahler or Richard Strauss, but his music is more often (and more tellingly) compared with that of Debussy, Stravinsky, or Bartók. Part of the reason for that was its determined anti-Germanism.

The attitude toward culture (and nature) with which Janáček countered the cosmopolitanism of "educated German" taste was (like Bartók's) akin to the relativistic attitudes first put forth by Herder, an educated German, a century and a half before to counter the cosmopolitan universalism of Enlightened France. But like everyone else who has figured in the last several chapters, Janáček participated in the suddenly quickened tempo of stylistic change that seized European composers around the turn of century. That made him a modernist. And he applied his radically renovated technique to an intensified or radicalized pursuit of traditionally accepted expressive tasks, which made him a maximalist. The remarkable difference was that he accomplished all of this at a singularly advanced age.

One of the major factors contributing to what may seem his retarded development was indeed the place of his birth, but not for the kind of reason that would typically occur to an "educated German" like Adorno. Janáček was a Moravian—a member, that is, of what was even within Czech-speaking society a slighted minority. Moravia, the central farming area of what became Czechoslovakia in 1918, is bounded on the west by the more urbanized Bohemia, and on the east by "Magyarized" Slovakia. (Since the division of 1993, Moravia has been the eastern portion of the Czech Republic.) Brno (called Brünn in German), Moravia's industrial center and its one large town, was under Austrian rule even more a Germanized city than Prague, the Bohemian (later the Czech) capital. It was officially a German-speaking city before 1918, and a predominantly German-speaking one even after, as long as Janáček was alive.

Janáček, born into the Czech-speaking family of a village schoolmaster, was sent for his education to a monastery in Brno, and after more advanced studies in Prague, Leipzig, and Vienna, he returned there and settled down to a lifelong career as music teacher and choral conductor in the Moravian capital. In 1881 he founded the Brno Organ School under the auspices of the Society for the Promotion of Church Music in Moravia, served as its director for thirty-eight years, and continued on the staff until his seventieth birthday. He was Brno's most prominent musician, but as of his sixtieth birthday, in 1914, he was almost completely unknown outside of that city. Even in neighboring Bohemia he was thought of as an insignificant provincial, a "hick." That is what retarded his career. The earliest work of Janáček's that is now a world repertory item, the opera *Její pastorkyňa* ("Her stepdaughter", known outside the Czech lands by the name of its title character, *Jenůfa*), composed between 1895 and 1903, could not get a hearing in Prague until 1916, twelve years after its Brno premiere, when the composer was sixty-two. When it finally did reach the Czech capital it made such a sensation that it was immediately picked up (in German translation) by the Vienna Opera, and made its way in short order as far as America, where it was staged (in 1924) by the Metropolitan Opera in New York.

Its chief appeal to early audiences was less its folkish exoticism (by then an old story) than its effectively shocking treatment of a violent plot, very much in the naturalistic spirit of the "verismo" operas of Mascagni and especially Puccini (Janáček's close contemporary). In act I a jealous lover slashes the title character's face; in act II her stepmother kills her illegitimate child. Act III contains the novel and emotionally potent turn that made the opera so successful: the crime is discovered, the stepmother condemned, but both she and the lover receive forgiveness from the title character, who marries the man, now sincerely contrite, who had slashed her, acting not in the spirit of martyrdom but in that of mature empathy and Christian reconciliation.

The opera, as a result, cannot easily be read as a social criticism (and might today merit some feminist criticism on its own account). Ultimately it did not threaten the traditionally patriarchal values of its audience, and it was further aided in its foreign conquests by the presence in the title role of a fashionable singer, Maria Jeritza (1887–1982), a great Vienna favorite who, as it happened, was a native of Brno. By 1924 she was "the Metropolitan's most glamorous and beautiful star"[20] (according to *The New Grove Dictionary of Opera*), and Janáček's opera was staged there as her novelty vehicle. It did not immediately hold the stage outside of Central Europe.

But its international success, however fleeting in the short run, stimulated its formerly pent-up composer into a frenzy of creativity. In the twelve years that remained to him after the Prague premiere of *Jenůfa*, Janáček wrote five more operas: *Výlet pana Broučka do XV. stoleti* (Mr. Brouček's Excursion to the 15th Century, 1917), a patriotic comedy after a fantasy novel by Svatopluk Čech, composed to greet the impending proclamation of independent Czechoslovakia; *Káťa Kabanová* (1921), another realistic tragedy after the classic play *The Storm* by the Russian dramatist Alexander Ostrovsky;

Příhody Lišky Bystroušky ("The adventures of little foxy sharp-ears", usually translated "The cunning little vixen," 1923), after a series of whimsical captioned drawings published in a Prague newspaper; *Věc Makropoulos* ("The Makropoulos affair", 1925) after a surrealistic play by Karel Čapek, whose futuristic satire *R. U. R.* was the source of the word "robot," one of the few international borrowings from a Slavic language; and *Z mrtvého domu* ("From the house of the dead", 1928), after a grim novel of prison life by Fyodor Dostoyevsky.

In addition to these operas, between the ages of sixty-two and seventy-four Janáček wrote a large concert setting of the Slavonic Liturgy, *Glagolská mše* ("Glagolitic mass", 1926); a major song cycle, *Zápisník zmizelého* ("The Diary of One Who Disappeared", 1919); several orchestral works including a *Sinfonietta* (1926) composed for an outdoor national sports rally; a dozen chamber works including two string quartets and two chamber concertos for piano (one of them, *Capriccio* for piano left-hand, flute, and brass sextet, written for a one-armed veteran of the First World War). It seemed virtually a life's work crammed into a dozen years, testifying to a revived and rejuvenated creative vitality without precedent or counterpart in the work of any other composer. (In a unique case like this one looks for as many biographical explanations as possible: another that is often cited in connection with Janáček's late explosion of creativity is an invigorating infatuation with a much younger woman who seems not to have reciprocated his passion, but served passively as a stimulant to the composer's fantasy life.)

This amazingly varied body of late work was united by the composer's newly maximalized style — more evidence, perhaps, of Janáček's access of self-confidence in the aftermath of belated success. His maximalism, typically, was what attracted to Janáček the interest of historians; but it was differently motivated from the other maximalisms we have noted, and had different consequences. Uniquely, it never took an abstract turn. Unlike any of the other maximalists (save Ives) whose music we have examined in detail, Janáček never tried to generalize his new methods into a rationalized compositional technique. Indeed he decried such efforts as leading to music that "depends on just notes and ignores man and his surroundings," or music that "seeks only an acoustic quality."[21] This put Janáček at odds even with Bartók, who was very much driven, at a certain point in his career, to generalize his socially validated innovations into a systematic technique. The act of generalization, Janáček believed, was inimical to social validation, precisely because it put social reception at risk. Of all the latter-day Herderians, he was surely the most orthodox in his insistence that his music be accessible to the population on whose natural artifacts it drew.

And that is why Janáček is generally classified as a folklorist. He never disavowed the category. In his youth he made the same kind of expeditions into the field that Bartók would later make. With an older collaborator named František Bartoš (1837–1906) he published large collections ("Bouquets") of Moravian folk songs with piano accompaniment in the 1890s. One of the most abundant genres in his catalogue of works is that of folksongs arranged for male chorus, which he produced in quantity for his own choirs to sing. As late as 1926 he observed that "if I grow at all, it is only out of folk music . . . ."[22]

But it is nevertheless something of a misnomer, for it applies only to the earlier portion of his career, and wholly fails to account for his maximalist phase, the very period that Adorno was so eager to ascribe to Janáček's "progressive folkloristic tendencies." The list of late operas given above, unlike a comparable list covering the first four decades of Janáček's career, is not confined to Czech subject matter to which collected folklore might have been appropriately applied. Two are adaptations from Russian literature and have Russian settings, and *The Makropoulos Affair*, while nominally set in Prague, concerns an international opera diva, who knows but renounces the secret of eternal life (a "universal" subject if ever there was one), and her very urbane circle of acquaintances.

The subjects of these operas did not grow out of folklore at all, and neither did the music that provides their ambience. That music grew out of a natural element that Janáček valued even more than folklore as a wellspring for art. To complete now the sentence of which the first half was quoted two paragraphs earlier, Janáček declared in 1926 that he grew out of "folk music, *and out of human speech*," the most basic expressive element of all, which (in Janáček's passionately held view) underlies all folklore, as well as all cultivated art.

SPEECH-TUNELETS

Janáček's veneration of speech as thought-and-feeling-made-incarnate gets down beneath the level even of Herder's original argument about human linguistic diversity, and in fact somewhat contradicts it. The thoughts and feelings to which language gives access are the common emotional fund of humanity. What is linguistically diverse is the means of expression, which inevitably influences the thing expressed but is not tantamount to it. That is why Janáček felt he could express and intensify through a music based on Czech speech the thoughts and feelings of Russian merchants and prisoners, or an international opera diva of French birth, and through that music communicate universal feelings to international audiences. But full expressive intensity in any language could only be achieved through maximum (that is, maximalized) particularity—in Janáček's case a music more closely based on the rhythms and intonations of the Czech language than any previous music had ever been based on any language.

Janáček planted the seed of his maximalist style around 1897 when he began jotting down what he called *nápěvky mluvy*—literally "speech-tunelets"[23] (as translated by Michael Beckerman), better known in English as speech melodies—in notebooks. It seems significant that the beginnings of his interest in notating speech melodies should have roughly coincided with the end of his folksong collecting activity. The one effectively replaced the other as essential bearer, for Janáček, of musical truth. Folk song was the highly stylized and already generalized product of what at the level of speech was fully specific and particular.

The melodic curves and rhythms of speech, though dictated to a large extent by the conventions of language, were also influenced by spontaneous emotion, and by a person's individual identity. They were, in Janáček's words, "windows into a person's soul."[24] He obsessively jotted down whatever distinctive speech he heard around him

as a potential model for his music — even, notoriously, the last words of his dying daughter — and advocated the method for others as well. It was "objective" and "scientific" evidence for what most composers tried to capture vaguely and subjectively. Janáček began carrying around stopwatches and even more exact time-measuring devices like "Hipp's chronoscope," which gave readings of very short durations. His obsessive behavior gave him a local reputation for eccentricity that caricaturists were quick to capitalize on (see Fig. 7-4).

In a series of published articles Janáček demonstrated with examples what he thought of as his most significant discovery, the fact that speech melodies revealed subliminal thoughts and emotions unexpressed by the words alone. Some of these articles took the form of interviews in which the words of Janáček's interlocutor were furnished with musical notations. One such musically recorded conversation took place, at Janáček's request, with Bedřich Smetana's daughter, whom he interviewed in 1924, her father's centennial year. Janáček asked her to recall something her father had said, in hopes that it would disclose a distinctive speech pattern that might help account for the greatness (as well as the Czechness) of Smetana's music. The only phrase she could come up with after forty years was a remark her father had made while leafing through the score of one of his operas: "All this will be appreciated eventually" (Ex. 7-28).

EX. 7-28   Bedřich Smetana's speech melody as recalled by his daughter and notated by Leoš Janáček

"The register of the Maestro's speech would probably have been an octave lower," Janáček remarked, but assured the reader that "the rhythm of the evenly pulsing beat and the melodic flow would be authentic," and then added, in triumphant italics: *This is probably how Bedřich Smetana used to speak.*"[25] And yet, as Janáček knew better than anyone, Smetana's was not typical Czech speech. Its evenly pulsing beat was evidence of Smetana's having learned Czech as an adult, after his basic speech pattern had been formed on German. Native Czech speech is rhythmically distinctive in a manner that it became Janáček's obsession to capture; and that is what chiefly gave his later music its maximalist edge. This was the fundamental musical "discovery" that made a modernist of him.

Actually, of course, it was no discovery at all, just as it was no "discovery" to observe that a speaker's tone of voice can contradict the uttered words. Anyone sensitive to irony (indeed, anyone who has been caught in a lie) knows that much; and anyone who speaks the Czech language knows its two most distinctive rhythmic/dynamic properties (both of which it shares with Hungarian). According to the first, a word in Czech can have only one accent, and it all but invariably comes at the beginning. The second is a strongly marked distinction between short and long syllables that is independent of the stress pattern. The Czech diacritic resembling the French "acute accent" is placed over long syllables. When the syllable so marked is not the first syllable, stress and length fail to coincide; the word is "syncopated" in a manner that anyone learning Czech as an adult finds difficult at first to grasp and imitate.

A good illustration is the name Janáček itself. Faithfully rendered in musical notation (as in Ex. 7-29, which reproduces an example from John Tyrrell's history of Czech opera[26]), it looks (particularly in $\frac{3}{4}$ time) like something out of a late score by Janáček himself. The reason why it looks typically Janáčekian is that before him composers did not set the Czech language with such fastidious attention to its rhythms, whether it was because (like Smetana) they spoke — and heard — the language imperfectly, or because (like Dvořák) they set verse librettos that imposed on the words a "foreign" rhythm.

EX. 7-29 "Janáček" as a speech tunelet

Ja - ná - ček   or   Ja - ná - ček

Janáček, too, began his operatic career setting that kind of libretto. After 1916, however, when the success of *Jenůfa* gave him the courage of his musical convictions, he insisted on a laconic prose style that would not interfere with the natural rhythms of the language — and that meant writing his librettos himself, so loath were most professional writers to sacrifice the elegance of imported verse forms. To illustrate the fanatical care with prosody that arose out of Janáček's conviction that "objectively" rendered speech patterns were an infallible register of human subjectivity, and to gauge the impact of that "scientific" purism on his later music, John Tyrrell set up an ingenious musicological experiment, contrasting the text setting in two versions of the composer's earliest opera, *Šárka* (1887–88), the first dating from long before the "discovery" of speech melodies, the other from 1918, at the beginning of the composer's maximalist adventure.[27] Ex. 7-30 shows two of Tyrrell's most revealing specimens:

In Ex. 7-30a, the word "Přemysle" is contracted into a triplet so that its last syllable will not fall on a downbeat and thus pick up an unwanted musical stress. Even more striking is the elongation of the second syllable in "velký," so that it lasts seven times as long as the accented first syllable. In the earlier setting, only the accent had been faithful

EX. 7-30 Comparative settings from Janáček's *Šárka*

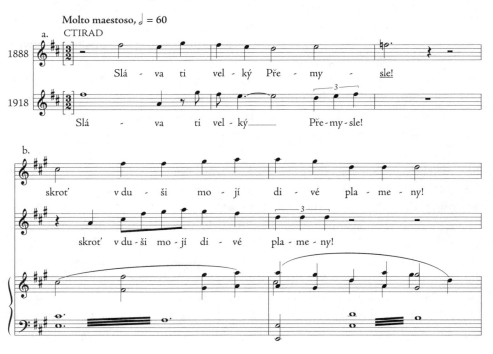

to the word's normal pronunciation, not the relative length of the syllables, which is the more distinctively Czech index of fidelity. The result of both changes is to make the line remarkably varied, and at the same time remarkably asymmetric, in rhythm. Symmetry is even more graphically violated in Ex. 7-30b.

There was only one previous composer who used rhythms as finicky as these in operatic music, and for a similar reason. That was Musorgsky, the radical Russian "realist" whose lifetime overlapped somewhat with Janáček's, and whose music was surely known to the Czech composer. (*Boris Godunov* was a repertory opera in Czech theaters beginning in 1910.) Janáček's interest in Russian culture and his familiarity with it are attested, as we have seen, by the literary sources of two of his late operas. Such a "Pan-Slavic" interest, it is worth adding, was common among Czech patriots who resented Austrian rule.

Yet it would be rash to assume that Musorgsky was a decisive "influence" on Janáček, and not only because Janáček denied it. Composers are rarely forthcoming or trustworthy on this question; but the fact that Janáček publicly claimed in 1903 that *Jenůfa* was the first opera ever written to a prose libretto strongly suggests that he was unfamiliar as of that date even with *Boris Godunov*, which has a lengthy and famous comic scene set quite conspicuously (and groundbreakingly) to prose. (For what it is worth, Janáček is not known to have attended a performance of Musorgsky's opera until 1923.)

Traces of Janáček's interest in speech melody extend further back than his maximalist years, and the most distinctive aspect of his prosody — namely, the fastidious syncopations arising out of the noncoincidence of stress and length in Czech — can have no counterpart or precedent in Musorgsky because the feature has no counterpart in Russian. Most of all, Janáček's use of speech rhythms became far more pervasive in his music than in Musorgsky's, and led to a far more radical (and a far more general) recasting of his style. If Musorgsky was an influence on Janáček, then, Janáček was all the more impressively a maximalist.

So profound and formative was Janáček's dependence on Czech speech rhythms that it remained evident in his music even when there was no speech. It pervaded his instrumental music, too, and the instrumental component of his operas, informing every musical level with the dramatic significance of speech. That is perhaps the operas' greatest distinction. But to appreciate it in context a preliminary instrumental example may be useful. Ex. 7-31 comes from is a little piano piece, *Listek odvanuty* ("A blown-away leaf"), originally composed for harmonium in 1901 and eventually published in a set called *On an Overgrown Path* (*Po zarostlém chodníčku*) in 1911. Ostensibly a folkloristic piece, it is really a study in long unstressed "syllables." To accommodate them the basic

EX. 7-31   Leoš Janáček, *A Blown-away Leaf* (from *On an Overgrown Path*, no. 2), mm. 1–17

duple meter of the melody in the second strain is distended to $\frac{5}{8}$; the final eighth is never played, however, just "waited out."

A MUSICO-DRAMATIC LABORATORY

Rhythms like these pervade Janáček's later operas, in vocal and instrumental parts alike. Indeed, the orchestral part, which provides the essential continuity in these declamatory works, consists largely of ostinatos drawn from key vocal phrases (along with leitmotifs of a more conventional kind). It is sometimes wrongly assumed that these ostinatos are drawn directly from life, by way of the composer's speech-tunelet notebooks. Rather, they are drawn from the librettos, as mediated by the composer's own imagined speech. *Kat'a Kabanová*, the first opera wholly conceived after *Jenůfa*'s Prague premiere, was the great laboratory of Janáček's maximalist technique.

The title character, Katerina Kabanová (Katya for short), is a merchant wife in a Volga town, who takes a lover during her husband's absence on a business trip, confesses in shame, and, hounded by her vindictive mother-in-law, kills herself in despair. The concluding portion of the last scene contains the lovers' last meeting, the suicide, and its aftermath. It is fairly self-contained, but knowledge of the origins of two of its themes is needed for a full grasp of its musical and dramatic properties, and their relationship to speech melody.

The first (Ex. 7-32a) is the opera's main leitmotif, first heard at the very beginning of the overture. It consists simply of eight thwacks on the kettledrum, four on the dominant and four on the tonic. Although its aural effect is "duple-metered," it is always notated in triplets so that when it appears in counterpoint with other thematic material it sounds as though it is moving at a slower tempo than the rest. This rhythmic effect enables it to intervene portentously at fraught moments of the drama to sound an "implacable" note of doom. It is especially prone to appear whenever Katya's music soars lyrically aloft, to quash it. At the beginning of act III it is finally given an "objective" referent in the thunder accompanying the storm that gave Ostrovsky's original play its title.

EX. 7-32A   Leoš Janáček, *Kát'a Kabanová*, motifs, timpani motif

The other motif is one that is developed at the beginning of the final scene from another idea planted early on. The first Allegro theme in the overture gives a preview of the music that accompanies the husband's departure on his business trip in act I (Ex. 7-32b). On the surface it is merry traveling music, set for flutes and oboes, accompanied by the characteristic sound of Russian sleigh bells. Closer inspection or longer acquaintance reveals the hidden resonance of the menacing timpani motif at its beginning (marked "X"). And as the opera unfolds, the myriad repetitions of the group marked "Y" invest that group, too, with a dramatic significance that accords with its resemblance (surely no accident) to the beginning of the Dies Irae, the old funeral chant that had carried a grisly baggage of associations through the whole nineteenth century, ever since Berlioz had quoted it in the *Symphonie fantastique*.

EX. 7-32B   Leoš Janáček, *Káťa Kabanová*, motifs, Allegro theme

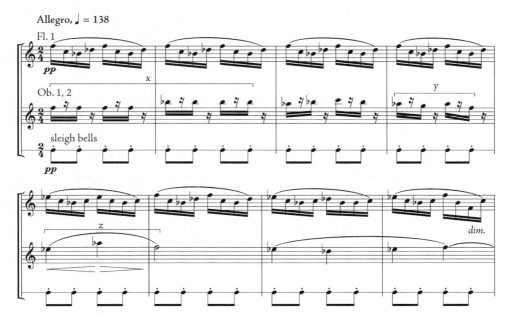

At the beginning of the final scene, the husband and a servant rush on stage in pursuit of Katya, who has already confessed her sin and fled. They shout her name to a speech-tunelet that reverberates in the orchestra at three levels of diminution (Ex. 7-32c). The tunelet is then immediately subjected to an expressive chromatic transformation that becomes the next orchestral ostinato (Ex. 7-32d).

EX. 7-32C   Leoš Janáček, *Káťa Kabanová*, motifs, "Katérino!" with its accompaniment

EX. 7-32D   Leoš Janáček, *Kát'a Kabanová*, motifs, chromatic transformation and ensuing ostinato

Another example is found in the last measure of Ex. 7-32d, when the oboe immediately picks up the speech tunelet "Bude zle!" ("There'll be trouble," or "You'll be sorry"). As an instrumental motif, the phrase haunts the music that follows; but it had already appeared in the orchestra at the very beginning of the scene, in advance of (and disguising!) its derivation from a speech-tunelet (Ex. 7-32e). Thus speech pervades the music even before it is heard as speech, and relates dramaturgically to the more "purely" melodic aspects of the music as well.

Turning now to the concluding scene and following the musical-dramatic development in the process of its unfolding, we may observe similar transformations of speech-tunelets into orchestral motifs at every turn. One happens almost immediately (Ex. 7-33a), when Katya's obsessive "At' vidím cokoli, at' slyším cokoli" ("All I see around me, all I hear around me"), reverberates in the orchestra as if illustrating the thought. But the most impressive and dramatically significant instance occurs at the Moderato that immediately follows, where the tunelet arising out of Katya's wishful line, "Snad, kdybych s ním mohla žít" ("Ah, if only I could

EX. 7-32E   Leoš Janáček, *Kát'a Kabanová*, motifs, Curtain (*Opona/Vorhang*) Music

live with him") is immediately echoed in a phrase that, gently rocking in alternation with its descending counterpart, accompanies the whole last meeting of the lovers (Ex. 7-33b).

Although the resemblance is patent, neither the pitch sequence nor the rhythm of the tunelet is exactly paralleled by the ostinato. The rhythm has been adjusted, possibly, to recall in its regular long-short-short-long pattern the rhythmic palindromes (or "mirror-rhythm,"[28] as Tyrrell calls it) of Moravian folk songs. If so, it must have been an unconscious impulse that guided the composer's fancy, since Moravian folklore would seem to have little to contribute to the expressive ambience of an opera set in Russia. To identify Janáček's music with it here creates a "problem." Taking a closer look at the words to which the original tunelet is set in Ex. 7-33a, however, we notice

EX. 7-33A   Leoš Janáček, *Kát'a Kabanová*, Act III, scene 2, obsessive reverberations of speech tunelet

EX. 7-33A   (continued)

EX. 7-33B   Leoš Janáček, *Kát'a Kabanová*, Act III, scene 2, transformation of speech tunelet into love music

EX. 7-33B (continued)

that the last vowel in the triplet (*s ním*) carries the mark of lengthening, so that when pronounced idiomatically by a Czech singer, its rhythm would already approach that of the orchestral ostinato. It is likely that Janáček notated the orchestral part differently from the vocal so as to indicate to the instrumentalists something of the rhythm the singer would produce "instinctively." All the closer, then, are the implicit bonds between the music at all its levels and the contours and rhythms of Czech speech. Speech, with all its attendant and automatic emotional expression, pervades the ambient music in which the characters live and breathe.

As Boris, her lover, prepares to take his final leave of her, Katya begins to hallucinate, hearing an offstage chorus that sings to an unearthly vowel that Janáček directs be "somewhere between U and O," representing "the sighing of the Volga" into which she will soon be hurling herself (Ex. 7-34a). The pentatonic motive thus introduced, which shares many intervals with the complex of motives quoted in Ex. 7-32, participates along with them at the opera's grisly climax, where all of these motivic relationships reach an epitome (Ex. 7-34b). The last human voice is the mother-in-law's, icily dismissing the horrified onlookers with thanks for their attention. Her music is based on Ex. 7-32b, with an extra emphasis on the "Y" motif, associated with the Dies Irae. Following that, a stormy little orchestral fantasy brings the opera to a close, bluntly juxtaposing the "X" and "Y" motives against the "Volga sigh," while the ostinato repetitions of "Y" ineluctably recall the obsessive repetitions of Katya's name at the beginning of the scene (Ex. 7-32c).

Katerina's final page of music (Ex. 7-35), beginning where she hearkens dementedly to the singing of birds, seems suddenly, and startlingly, to resemble a traditional mad scene in the romantic vein of Donizetti. Like Lucia di Lammermoor, Katya withdraws right before the dénouement into a fantasy world represented by the dulcet music of an accompanying flute. But no sooner is the comparison made than it turns

EX. 7-34A   Leoš Janáček, *Kát'a Kabanová*, Act III, scene 2, "Sighing of the Volga"

EX. 7-34B   Leoš Janáček, *Kát'a Kabanová*, Act III, scene 2, end

EX. 7-34B (continued)

EX. 7-34B   (*continued*)

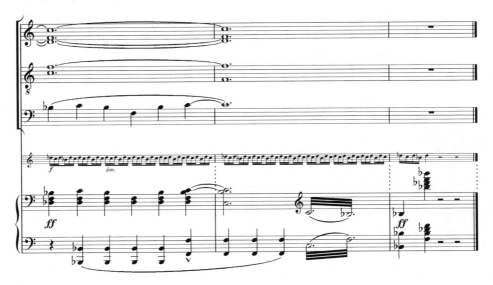

ironic. The romantic mad scene in bel canto operas was always their most ornately "musical" moment. Dementia was depicted, and its fascination conveyed, through lavish ornamentation and roulades.

Meanwhile, it would be difficult to imagine music more starkly denuded than the mad scene in Janáček's opera. The vocal writing is straight syllabic declamation, as sedulously modeled on speech as ever. The bird song consists of a typical ostinato phrase, repeated like an obsession but never embellished or even varied, except to distend it by the use of dissonant skips. It is accompanied by a harsh percussive tattoo drawn from the notes of the Volga's "sigh." This demonstratively stripped-down, barren sonority is the nub of Janáček's maximalism. What is maximalized is laconicism, "plain speech" deliberately void of "poetry" in the name of "unvarnished truth" — the realist or naturalist strain in nineteenth-century literature and literature-influenced music brought to a peak (or perhaps one should say a nadir). All during his astonishingly fertile final decade, Janáček was becoming increasingly obsessed with spareness, and with a bluffness of expression that was virtually without precedent.

He began ruling his own staves rather than using manufactured music paper for his orchestral scores lest he be seduced by all those empty bars to pad his orchestration. He began deliberately flouting schoolroom rules of voice leading (rules that, unlike Musorgsky perhaps, he knew as well as any composer) to lend his music a rough-hewn or "primitive" texture. The climactic love music quoted in Ex. 7-33b is a vivid case in point: even at this tender moment the music must borrow a bit of honest clumsiness from the deliberately unprepared $^6_4$ chord with which it begins, and from the deliberately skewed intervals (augmented second against augmented fourth in contrary motion) with which it proceeds.

In *From the House of the Dead,* his last opera and almost his last work, Janáček brought artlessness to an extreme in his depiction of sensibilities hardened and distorted

EX. 7-35 Leoš Janáček, *Kát'a Kabanová*, Act III, scene 2, Katerina's suicide

EX. 7-35 *(continued)*

FIG. 7-5 Janáček, page of the autograph manuscript for *From the House of the Dead.*

by prison life. In Ex. 7-36a, a $^4_2$ chord is approached by leap in similar motion, and proceeds, again in inelegant similar motion, to another voicing of the same dissonant harmony. Ex. 7-36b is an ostinato that accompanies one prisoner's rueful narration of the brutal crime for which he was sentenced. An unprepared $^4_2$ chord ascends in similar motion to the next harmony without resolving its dissonance, and descends, also in similar motion and without resolution, to a $^6_4$ chord that is supposed to mark the cadence (not to be confused, of course, with a "cadential $^6_4$"). On its repetition the ostinato is accompanied by an ersatz "tonic pedal" on E♭ that jars wretchedly with the soprano E.

EX. 7-36A   Leoš Janáček, *From the House of the Dead*, Act III, 6 before fig. [15]

EX. 7-36B   Leoš Janáček, *From the House of the Dead*, Act III, ostinato at fig. [26]

Both in Ex. 7-36b and at various points in the final scene from *Kát'a Kabanová*, the harmony is tinged with whole-tone effects. Janáček was attracted to Debussy's music and studied *Pelléas et Mélisande*, which as an essay in prose-setting especially interested him. Nevertheless, his whole-tone usages seem more indebted, yet again, to Russian music, where, in the wake of Glinka's *Ruslan and Ludmila* the whole-tone scale was usually associated, as it is in Janáček, with evil or horror. Rather than cooling the emotional temperature, as whole-tone harmony did for Debussy, it remained for Janáček, as it had been for the Russians, an emotional stimulant.

RESEARCH VS. COMMUNICATION

But then so was everything in Janáček. His music, however novel its ways and means, always avidly sought popular appeal, and the composer measured his success in terms of his popularity. His role model, he was unabashed to admit, was Puccini. (Indeed, few commentators have failed to notice that the title character's first entrance in act I of *Kát'a Kabanová*, not yet singing but accompanied by her soaring leitmotif, directly parallels the analogous moment in *Madama Butterfly*.) Despite Adorno's wishful attempt at "co-opting" him, alienation simply was not this composer's bag. He was as enthusiastic a communitarian as a modernist could be. As a result, his historical prestige has suffered. Many twentieth-century histories of twentieth-century music omit him altogether, or write him off in spite of everything as an insignificant regionalist. Janáček made his comeback into history during the 1950s, when he was rediscovered (first in England) not in the classroom but in the opera house, largely thanks to the efforts of Charles Mackerras (b. 1925), a conductor who had studied in Prague with Václav Talich (1883–1961), Czechoslovakia's outstanding orchestra director.

Prestige attaches itself more readily to the esoteric than to the popular. It has been the lonely modernist's chief consolation, and it has been as avidly sought by some as social acceptance has been sought by others. One cannot imagine Janáček setting up a Society for Private Performances or writing a fawning letter to a potential aristocratic patron lauding "the fairest, alas bygone, days of art when a prince stood as a protector before an artist, showing the rabble that art, a matter for princes, is beyond the judgement of common people."[29] That is what Schoenberg wrote, in 1924, to Prince Egon Fürstenberg, the bankroller of a contemporary music festival in the South German town of Donaueschingen. The attitude it encapsulates is the one to which the term "elite" — or, more balefully, "elitist" — is now often applied. It regards art as both the product of elite circumstances and the creator of elite occasions.

The dichotomy between the elitist model epitomized by Schoenberg and the populist model epitomized (practically alone among modernists) by Janáček has been perhaps the most contentious issue in twentieth-century music and musical politics. Few composers have been as single-mindedly committed to an extreme position as have these two. Most have been ambivalent, susceptible to both pulls. Bartók was one. The thrust of this chapter has perhaps too easily suggested a grouping of Bartók with Janáček against the Vienna Schoenberg circle, the one group associated with the spirit of particularism as against the other's universalism, or with the provinces as against the capital, or with the cause of vulnerable national minorities as against the tyranny of the powerful cosmopolitan majority. The ivory tower might seem the "natural" prerogative of one group, social validation the "natural" requirement of the second.

But Bartók was torn, like all educated Magyars, both between the universal and the particular and between the elite and the popular. He could be contrasted with Janáček as easily as with Schoenberg, depending on the vantage point from which we choose to view him. Like Janáček but unlike Schoenberg, he sought inspiration in folklore. But like Schoenberg and unlike Janáček, he felt the urge to generalize and systematize his innovations. Like Janáček but unlike Schoenberg, he claimed simplicity as a virtue. But like Schoenberg and unlike Janáček, he saw virtue as well in abstraction, which led him, at times, to write music not easily followed by nonprofessional audiences. His music, too, creates elite occasions, and he knew it. He once discouraged a correspondent from performing some of his more difficult works "in places where the level of music is like that of the provincial towns of Hungary," since they "will merely deter listeners who do not have the necessary level of preparation."[30] He was well aware that he was appropriating from "simple" people the basis for an art that excluded them, and at times it troubled his conscience. For all his fascination with symmetry, this was an asymmetry he could not reconcile.

Placing Bartók and Janáček in opposition usefully shifts the ground of contention a little from its usual terrain. A composition like Bartók's Fourth Quartet, with its systematically worked out symmetrical schemes and not always obviously expressive (therefore "alienating") dissonance, implicitly upholds a model of composition driven as much by "research" as by the urge to communicate. The research model implies further an emphasis on the making of the artwork rather than on its effect, and, ultimately, an emphasis on the rights of the autonomous creative individual rather than those of the receiving community. Observing all of this in Bartók, we are observing it within the "camp" identified, in broadest and crudest terms, as the "socially committed" one. And that should suffice to show how uselessly broad and crude such terms can be.

CHAPTER 8

Pathos Is Banned

STRAVINSKY AND NEOCLASSICISM

THE "REAL" TWENTIETH CENTURY BEGINS

O n the evening of 18 October 1923, Aaron Copland, an American then finishing up a two-year stint as a composition student in Paris and about to turn twenty-three, happened in on a concert at which the latest work by Igor Stravinsky was to have its premiere. For thirteen years, since the unveiling of the *Firebird* ballet, and especially since the scandalous opening night of *The Rite of Spring* in 1913, Stravinsky's name had been synonymous with "savage" Russian (read: semi-Asiatic) maximalism at its most exotic, obstreperous, even orgiastic. It had been only four months since the first performance of a new ballet, *Svadebka* ("The peasant wedding," presented in Paris as *Les noces villageoises*), seemingly a starker, lither version of *The Rite*, in which the dancers were accompanied by vocal soloists and a chorus singing, sometimes shouting, fierce or bawdy ritual songs whose texts had been collected by folklorists, accompanied by a clangorous "orchestra" consisting of nothing but four pianos and a monster assemblage of percussion.

Like everyone else present that October night in Paris, Copland was in for a shock. Almost twenty years later, still marveling at it, he recalled "the general feeling of mystification that followed the initial hearing", of the new work, an octet for winds (flute, clarinet, and pairs of bassoons, trumpets, and trombones). "Here was Stravinsky," he wrote,

> having created a neoprimitive style all his own, based on native Russian sources — a style that everyone agreed was the most original in modern music — now suddenly, without any seeming explanation, making an about-face and presenting a piece to the public that bore no conceivable resemblance to the individual style with which he had hitherto been identified. Everyone was asking why Stravinsky should have exchanged his Russian heritage for what looked very much like a mess of eighteenth century mannerisms. The whole thing seemed like a bad joke that left an unpleasant aftereffect and gained Stravinsky the unanimous disapproval of the press.[1]

And yet, looking back in 1941, Copland could report an even bigger surprise:

> No one could possibly have foreseen, first, that Stravinsky was to persist in this new manner of his or, second, that the *Octet* was destined to influence composers all over the world in bringing the latent objectivity of modern music to full consciousness by frankly adopting the ideals, forms, and textures of the preromantic era.[2]

F I G. 8-1   Stravinsky, *Svadebka* (*Les Noces*), Royal Ballet, London.

Indeed Copland, although he did not know it yet, was seeing his own future. Stravinsky's Octet seemed to usher in a new creative period, not only for Stravinsky but for European and Euro-American "art music" generally. It is commonly called Stravinsky's neoclassical phase; and though like most catchphrases it will require a lot of qualification and amendment, it contains enough truth to make it useful. Moreover, as Copland could already see in 1941, and as we can see much more easily now, while Stravinsky's huge prestige made his sudden recourse to "eighteenth-century mannerisms" a more newsworthy event than anybody else's could have been at the time, the move as such was far from unprecedented, either within Stravinsky's own work or in the wider world of music. The musical manifestations, meanwhile, were symptoms in turn of a pronounced general swerve in the arts that reflected a yet greater one in the wider world of expressive culture.

The history of twentieth-century music as something esthetically distinct from that of the nineteenth century begins not at the fin de siècle, then, but here, in the 1920s. As with anything so big and brusque and sweeping, we will have to funnel in on it, returning to Stravinsky's Octet, and to some other bearers of the new esthetic wind, only after we have taken some account of the wider cultural terrain. Copland's evaluation of the Octet can serve as our guide to the issues, though. He associates the new manner with "objectivity," and with the deliberate adoption of a "preromantic" stance, announced externally by the unexpected resurrection of "eighteenth-century mannerisms." In the

Octet, in short, three separate (or at least separable) tendencies in the culture of the early twentieth century suddenly came together in a "crux"—a compelling cluster or knot. Our first task will be to unpack it.

PASTICHE AS METAPHOR

The feature of the Octet that most forcibly impressed early listeners (especially composer-listeners) like Copland—namely the "pastiche" element that impressed him as a "mess of eighteenth-century mannerisms"—was actually its least distinctive or necessary aspect, however useful it was as an attention-grabber, and however durable it has proved as a superficial mark of "neoclassicism." The deliberate imitation or revival of "ancient" or obsolete musical styles for specific emblematic or expressive purposes has a history that goes back at least as far as the Renaissance. Opera was born out of one such revival, associated with the northern Italian academies of the late sixteenth century.

An even more literal attempt to revive ancient music was *musique mesurée à l'antique*, a music rhythmicized according to the meters of ancient Greek poetry, through which musicians who shared the aims of the French poet Jean-Antoine de Baïf (1532–89), or who belonged to his Académie de Poésie et Musique, tried to duplicate the feats of what the Greeks called *ethos*, the direct influence of music on morals and behavior. Ex. 8-1, by Claude Le Jeune (d. 1600), set to a *vers mesuré* by Baïf himself, not only imitates the Greek quantitative meter but also adopts the "chromatic tetrachord" (half step, half step, minor third) as described by the theorist Aristoxenus in the fourth century BCE.

The result may not be authentic Greek music; in fact, with its triadic harmony and conventional "Renaissance" counterpoint, we can be sure that it bears no stylistic resemblance at all to any ancient original. But, like Stravinsky's Octet as described by Copland (which neither he nor anyone else ever confused with actual eighteenth-century music), it also bore scant resemblance to the styles listeners at the time regarded as normal for contemporary music. A listener unaware of Le Jeune's expressive or "ethical" purpose would have been in the same predicament Copland was in when confronting Stravinsky's Octet. It would have produced (indeed, was in part designed to produce) mystification.

By the late eighteenth century, composers had a sufficiently historical or "modern" sense of changing musical fashion to enjoy stylistic pastiche as a form of exoticism. Mozart may have been the earliest composer to write what might be called "epicurean" or "gourmet" parodies of outmoded styles, notably those of Bach and Handel, whose music he discovered late in life at the Viennese salon of Baron van Swieten: yet another reason for attributing to Mozart the earliest truly "modern" (or even modernist) musical sensibility. Whereas Haydn discovered Handel as the national composer of England during his visit of 1795, and imitated his grandiose oratorio style in *The Creation* (Die Schöpfung) and *The Seasons* (Die Jahreszeiten) for purposes of religious edification, Mozart composed a keyboard suite in the style of Handel (K. 399) as early as 1782, for no other purpose than sensory delectation—aural "deliciousness." Mozart also wrote imitation "Baroque" music for ritual use, especially in his Masonic cantatas and his Requiem, and echoed it parodistically in the last act of *The Magic Flute*,

EX. 8-1   Claude Le Jeune, *Qu'est devenue ce bel oeil* (Le printemps, no. XXX)

EX. 8-2   W. A. Mozart, Gigue for piano, K. 574

which contains a little chorale setting that mimics the style of Bach's then very little known church cantatas. One of his best known pastiches is a Gigue, K. 574 (Ex. 8-2), that (to keep up the culinary metaphor) adds a maximum of chromatic spice to the Bach-Handel recipe.

"Delicious" neoclassicism begins with Mozart, then, and continues thereafter in an unbroken, albeit minor, stream. Simply as pastiche, Stravinsky's Octet was part of that stream. And if pastiche were all that it was, it would never have had the major influence that Copland rightly attributed to it, no matter how formidable the composer's prestige. For "delicious" pastiche or stylistic parody was by then a part of every concertgoer's experience. In certain contexts, imitation eighteenth-century music had even become something of a nineteenth-century specialty.

The chief context, easily guessed, was the theater, where the setting could call for it. One of the most popular *morceaux de concert* (concert pieces — "morsels" — extracted from operas or ballets) in the late-nineteenth-century orchestral repertory was the entr'acte or curtain music before the second act of *Mignon*, an opéra comique by Ambroise Thomas (1811 – 96), the very respectable director of the Paris Conservatory. An adaptation of a novel by Goethe (*Wilhelm Meisters Lehrjahre* or "The Education of Wilhelm Meister") that is set in the late eighteenth century, the opera concerns the adventures, mainly amorous, of a stage-struck youth who falls in with a troupe of traveling players.

The entr'acte (Ex. 8-3) is in the form of a gavotte, a sprightly court dance of the seventeenth or early eighteenth century with a distinctive upbeat figure, known to nineteenth-century musicians primarily thanks to its presence in many of Bach's instrumental suites. Thomas's gavotte precedes, and sets the tone for, a boudoir scene that was considered very risqué. After the entr'acte had become popular in its own right, Thomas interpolated into the scene a "rondo-gavotte" (*Me voici dans son boudoir / Et je sens mon coeur battre d'espoir*, or "Here I am in her boudoir, and I feel my heart beating with hope") based on its familiar strains. The character who sings it, moreover, was recast from a tenor to a boyish contralto "in trousers" to make the part, the situation, and the music seem even sexier by virtue of androgyny.

EX. 8-3   Ambroise Thomas, *Mignon*, Entr'acte to Act II, mm. 9 – 25

"Delicious" here takes on a new connotation, now covering any sort of sensual delight. And "the eighteenth century," invoked by countless nineteenth-century writers and playwrights as a time at once of sybaritic innocence and of aristocratic guile, became a sort of fairyland or sexual playground, no different in principle from the romantically imagined "Orient." That sexualized eighteenth century found a new metaphorical referent in "period" music harmonized and orchestrated as flavorsomely as possible, not at all for the sake of stylistic authenticity, but for the sake of that metaphorical resonance with sensuality.

This strain of fake eighteenth-century music as soft-core nineteenth-century pornography reached its maximalist phase in a pair of operas by Richard Strauss and Hugo von Hofmannsthal. They followed directly on the same team's *Elektra* and are often viewed by historians as an unfortunate stylistic retreat from the composer's far out point. In the first of them, *Der Rosenkavalier* ("The cavalier of the rose", 1911), the curtain goes up on a pair of naked women in bed (one of them a "boy," but without his trousers). The title of the second, *Ariadne auf Naxos* ("Ariadne on the Isle of Naxos", 1912, rev. 1916), deliberately evokes one of the most distinguished libretto traditions of the old mythological *opera seria*, one that went all the way back to Monteverdi and included works by Handel, Galuppi, Sarti, and Riccardo Broschi, the brother of Farinelli, the great castrato.

Strauss's *Ariadne* began life as a musical play-within-a-play to cap a revival of *Le bourgeois gentilhomme*, Molière's farce about a rich status-seeker's pretensions to aristocratic manners. The deflation of an *opera seria* by a troupe of masked comedians was a metaphor for the social incongruity of Molière's comic situation. In its final, fully operatic form, Strauss's work is still an opera about operas and all their esthetic and (sometimes scandalous) social subtexts, rather than a straight dramatization of its ostensible subject.

Its prologue features some backstage amorous byplay involving the pretty coloratura soprano from the comedy troupe and the ostensible composer of the *opera seria* who is cast, by now predictably, as a delicious boy-toy in trousers. So Strauss's "neoclassical" operas turn out not to have been such a retreat after all. Their social and sexual conceits are even more "avant-garde" than the ones in Strauss's earlier, stylistically sensational operas (in which upsetters of social or sexual proprieties are duly punished), and the eighteenth-century stylistic veneer is an integral part of their "decadence," masking or excusing an otherwise socially unacceptable (if aristocratic) "libertinage." Meanwhile, the nineteenth-century eighteenth-century pastiche had ridden the coattails of *morceaux de concert* like Thomas's, or of operatic and ballet suites and divertissements, to an independent status as nineteenth-century instrumental music. The independent keyboard or orchestral suite, unattached to a theatrical source or prototype, became its main vehicle. Originally modeled on the Bach keyboard and (especially) orchestral suites, some of which were published for the first time in the Bach-Gesellschaft (Bach Society) edition beginning in Bach's centennial year of 1850, the genre spread far and wide and even had its specialist composers.

One of the earliest such pieces was a Suite for piano, op. 38 (1855), by the Russian piano virtuoso Anton Rubinstein. It had ten movements: Prelude, Minuet, Gigue, Sarabande, Gavotte, Passacaille, Allemande, Courante, Passepied, Bourrée. But even if the Bach keyboard suites were Rubinstein's obvious model, what he actually produced was not an imitation Bach keyboard suite. For one thing, it was an encyclopedic compendium that did not follow its Prelude with the normal sequence of dances that Rubinstein knew perfectly well from the actual suites of Bach. And for another, much more important, thing, the cultivation of an "olden style" had always prompted, *and was meant to prompt*, a great deal of chromatic or quasi-"modal" harmonic *piquanterie* that was as plainly anachronistic to its practitioners as it is to us now, just as the "folk" or "oriental" styles of the time were knowing, sophisticated inventions whose credentials did not at all depend on their authenticity. In all cases it was the pretext for modern harmonic, melodic, and (in the case of orchestral music) timbral invention that justified pastiche and cinched its popularity with audiences.

The earliest specialist composers of orchestral suites were Germans: the long-lived Franz Lachner (1803–90), who in his youth had been a friend of Schubert's, and Joachim Raff (1822–82), who had been a pupil and disciple of Liszt (and had his earliest experience with the orchestra as the ghost-orchestrator of Liszt's early symphonic poems). Between them, Lachner and Raff wrote eleven orchestral suites between 1861 and 1881. Next in line was the Frenchman Jules Massenet (1842–1912), who in his more usual guise of opera composer wrote an Ariadne opera packed even fuller of eighteenth-century parodies than Thomas's *Mignon*. Between 1865 and 1881 Massenet composed seven *suites caractéristiques* for orchestra, less concerned with the archaic sort of "stylization" than with the exotic (*Scènes hongroises*, 1871; *Scènes napolitaines*, 1876; *Scènes alsaciennes*, 1881). He did write at least one conspicuous bit of fake old music, however: a curiously titled *Sarabande du XVIe siècle* ("A sarabande of the sixteenth century"), somewhat overshooting the mark, in 1875.

In that same year Pyotr Chaikovsky, Rubinstein's most famous pupil and a composer with whom Stravinsky would later avidly claim kinship, wrote the first of his four orchestral suites. It contains two "neobaroque" movements: an opening *Introduzione e fuga* avowedly "in Lachner's manner"[3] (five of Lachner's seven suites having fugues, not usually regarded as much of a nineteenth-century genre, as either first movement or finale), and a concluding Gavotte (Ex. 8-4), recognizable as such from its kinship with Thomas's famous rondo-gavotte, even if it does not have the characteristic two-quarter pickup that was the actual eighteenth-century gavotte's most distinctive feature. It ends with a blazing reprise of the fugue subject from the first movement, a mixture of genres that could never have occurred in the eighteenth century, but which epitomizes the "culinary" aspect of nineteenth-century pastiche, for which stylistic or generic traits were so many "ingredients" for subtle blends and striking juxtapositions.

Chaikovsky's Fourth Suite, op. 61 (1887), brought things full circle. Subtitled *Mozartiana*, it consisted of orchestrations of four items by Mozart (one of them, the sacred chorus *Ave verum corpus*, K. 618, mediated through Liszt's keyboard transcription). The opening movement is none other than the Gigue for piano, quoted in Ex. 8-2, which was already a pastiche. Chaikovsky's orchestral treatment, which matched the *piquanterie* of Mozart's own harmonization, was a compliment from one master chef to another, and a commemoration of a Mozart (rather different from the one normally worshipped by the romantics) who shared Chaikovsky's taste and gift for delectable, often retrospective parody.

In its way, Chaikovsky's *Mozartiana* was a harbinger of the so-called silver age of Russian culture, a massive resurgence of aristocratic taste that began in the 1890s and lasted until the 1917 revolution. It valued above all what was fantastic, decorative, and life-(or lifestyle-)enhancing in art, rather than what was personally expressive or "sincere" or "true to life" (those ideals being the vulgar hallmarks of the bourgeoisie). For all of this, too, an assumed eighteenth-century style (what Russian artists then

EX. 8-4   Pyotr Ilyich Chaikovsky, Gavotte from Suite no. 1, mm. 35–54

EX. 8-4   (*continued*)

called the "Versailles" style) was the prime esthetic metaphor. Russia was its natural home because Russia, as the last surviving autocratic or "absolutist" empire in Europe, was in effect the last great eighteenth-century state. The Russian silver age was in effect the last great flowering of European court art.

Chaikovsky's major contributions to the Versailles style (or "Imperial" style, as cultural historians call it now) were his next-to-last opera and his next-to-last ballet, both performed for the first time in 1890. The opera, *Pikovaya dama* ("The queen of spades"), was a fantastic, surrealistic retelling of a famous ghost story by Pushkin, in which the setting was deliberately pushed back to the eighteenth century to enable the composer to write a pastiche divertissement. (One of its ingredients, a Sarabande in a deliberately "incorrect" four-quarter time, combined both metaphors—the delectable and the disquietingly unreal—in a single ironic gesture.) The ballet, *Spyashchaya krasavitsa* ("The sleeping beauty"), was based on a "Mother Goose" tale by the French fabulist Charles Perrault (1628–1703), an authentic "Versailles" author, and set a standard for opulence and sensuous beauty that Sergey Diaghilev, the Russian impresario who first presented Stravinsky to an astonished Paris, strove all his life to equal.

CRACKING(JOKES) UNDER STRESS

Again we have come full circle, back to Stravinsky, whose pastiche Octet took Aaron Copland, and many others, by surprise in 1923. Placed against the background of early-twentieth-century maximalism, the surprise was genuine. But given the background we have just traced, it might almost seem predictable. What made it so influential just then? Or to ask the question another, possibly more suggestive way, what made it so timely? The answer lies in a tension that had been dogging maximalist or modernist art from the beginning—that is, ever since those terms have been appropriate describers of artistic aims or artistic products.

Our definition of maximalist art has emphasized the continuation of traditional aims by radically intensified means. Our definition of modernism has emphasized "high self-regard and self-consciousness" (to quote from chapter 1), and *"urbanity in every* meaning of the word from 'citified' to 'sophisticated' to 'artificial' to 'mannered.'" From the very beginning, it was obvious that the stance described by modernism was very much at variance with the "traditional" aims of art, if by tradition we mean the romantic tradition, which valued spirituality, sincerity, naturalness, spontaneity, and a host of other qualities that cannot stand the presence of irony (as anything as self-aware as modernism must imply).

This is a tension that maximalist artists had to bear. Some bore it more gracefully than others. Some, notably the French composers of Satie's and Debussy's generation, more willingly sacrificed romantic values, to the extent that their art has been described as "dehumanized." (And recall that among the works that demonstrated their dehumanizing commitment to modernism in chapter 2 were already a couple of pastiche sarabandes!) Others tried tenaciously to have it both ways: to be fully modern, but also fully spontaneous and spiritual and self-expressive. Most conspicuous among these, of course, were artists in the German tradition like Mahler—but even more so the artists, like Schoenberg and Webern, to whom the epithet "expressionist" is applied. That tension or divided consciousness was among the things that drove their art—which, as we have seen, took maximalism to the max—to its extremes.

And yet the irony inherent in modernism could not always be denied or repressed, and in at least one work of Schoenberg's it gained the upper hand. Not by accident, perhaps, that one work, *Pierrot lunaire* ("Moonstruck Pierrot", 1912), became the one work of Schoenberg's maximalist phase to achieve real popularity despite—or more likely because of—its apparent atypicality within his output. Its absence from the discussion of Schoenberg in chapter 6, which placed sole emphasis on the sincerely self-expressive and spiritualist aspects of his work, has surely been a glaring one for anyone who knows it. Now it is time to make good the omission, as the tension between the modern and the romantic approaches its crisis.

The lengthy subtitle of *Pierrot lunaire*, Schoenberg's op. 21, is worth quoting, for it is as succinct a description of this very eccentric piece as one is likely to come up with: "Thrice seven poems from Albert Giraud's *Pierrot lunaire* (translated by Otto Erich Hartleben), for a speaking voice, piano, flute (alternating piccolo), clarinet (alternating bass clarinet), violin (alternating viola) and cello." The source was a then-famous collection (published in 1884) of fifty little poems by a Belgian poet whose real surname was Kayenbergh, all of which concern the antics of the title character, Pierrot. The proverbial whiteface clown whose persona as ever-hopeful but always disappointed lover originated as one of the masked roles in the old *commedia dell'arte*, Pierrot became a key figure of romantic pathos thanks to the legendary portrayals of the role by the great Parisian mime Jean-Baptiste-Gaspard Deburau (1796–1846).

Giraud made a show of going back to a preromantic source by casting his Pierrot poems as "rondels," adapting to his purpose one of the stiffly stylized late-medieval "fixed forms." Every one of Giraud's poems has thirteen lines divided 4 + 4 + 5, of which the first and second come back as the seventh and eighth, and the first comes back again as the last. The use of this strict archaic format, as well as the focus on a masked character and his erratic doings, already recall the esthetics of ironic

FIG. 8-2   *Pierrot Lunaire* ensemble at the first performance, 16 October 1912: left to right, K. Essberger, clarinet and bass clarinet; Jakob Malinak, violin and viola; Schoenberg; Albertine Zehme, *Sprechstimme*; Eduard Steuermann, piano; Hans Kindler, cello; H. W. de Vries, flute and piccolo.

pastiche as briefly surveyed earlier in this chapter. Giraud's poems inhabited an odd, rather remote corner of the symbolist domain that crosscut the funny-peculiar and the funny-haha.

Schoenberg greatly increased Giraud's already considerable ironic distance by resorting to the weird device of melodrama — dramatic recitation to musical accompaniment — rather than conventional singing for his Pierrot settings. This, too, was an eighteenth-century pastiche of a sort, for that was the century in which the melodrama was invented and chiefly flourished. (The earliest use of the device on record is by the Austrian composer Johann Ernst Eberlin in 1753; the first "classic" of the genre is *Pygmalion* by Jean-Jacques Rousseau, probably written in 1762.) Like many minor genres, melodrama had a specialist composer: Georg Benda (1722–95), a member of a famous Bohemian family of musicians, who worked mainly in Prussia. His first and best-known melodrama (*Ariadne auf Naxos*, as it happens) was first performed in 1775 and imitated by many composers, including Mozart.

Many German romantic operas, including standard repertory items like *Fidelio* and *Der Freischütz*, made occasional use of melodrama, so that it maintained a presence in German theaters, and especially in Vienna, long after its vogue had passed. At the very end of the nineteenth century, the period that formed the immediate background to *Pierrot lunaire*, there was a sudden flare-up of interest in it. In 1897, at his publisher's request (thus as a frankly commercial venture), Richard Strauss made a melodrama setting of—or rather, wrote a piano accompaniment to—*Enoch Arden*, a long, sentimental narrative poem by Alfred, Lord Tennyson. But several literary-minded composers, mainly German and Czech, took a more serious view of the genre's possibilities, seeing in it a means for insuring maximum realism and verbal clarity despite the presence of music.

As was typical of Germans, they saw their use of melodrama as the fulfillment of history's mandate. "Our modern opera is taking a path that *must* lead to the melodrama,"[4] wrote one of its new enthusiasts, Engelbert Humperdinck (1854–1921). "With the dominant endeavors of our time, which no one can avoid, to bring reality to the stage, one must find a form that is suitable to this trend, and in my opinion the melodrama is that form." Humperdinck is best known not for his melodramas but for his first opera, *Hänsel und Gretel* (1893), a work for children based on the famous Grimm fairytale, in which folksongs are given a very skillful Wagnerian treatment. Ever since its premiere it has been a perennial Christmas favorite in many countries. It could be that it was his willed infatuation with melodrama that prevented Humperdinck's later stage works from achieving comparable popularity.

In any case, Humperdinck's melodramas are the ones that stood closest to Schoenberg's, because he was the first to control (or at least try to control) the speaker's part by the use of a relatively full musical notation that specified both rhythm (exactly) and pitch (approximately). Previously, the words of a melodrama were simply entered above the musical staff. In eighteenth-century works (and also in Strauss's *Enoch Arden*), the recitation and the music tended to alternate, as in an "accompanied" recitative, so that there were few problems of coordination. Where the speaker recited along with continuous music, the usual objective was nothing more than to arrive at the end of the passage together. Ex. 8-5, from Humperdinck's opera *Die Königskinder* ("The king's children", 1910), shows his new method: what looks like an ordinary folklike tune, of a kind that abounds in *Hänsel und Gretel*, is notated with little *x*s in place of note-heads, turning the notes so marked into what Humperdinck called *Sprechnoten* ("speaking-notes").

EX. 8-5   Engelbert Humperdinck, *Die Königskinder*, from Act I

im Brun - nen - spie - gel sah ich mich ein

As the composer explained, the *Sprechnoten* "are used for the purpose of indicating the rhythm and inflection of intensified speech (the melody of the spoken verse) and for placing these passages in agreement with the accompanying music." As usually interpreted in performance, the notation directs the singer (or speaker) to aim for the notated pitch according to the notated rhythm, but immediately to begin sliding toward the next pitch, as one's voice does in normal speech. Schoenberg probably picked up the idea directly from Humperdinck; there are little passages of melodrama in Schoenberg's

Gurrelieder (on which he began work in March 1900), notated precisely according to Humperdinck's method.

In *Pierrot lunaire* the practice is characteristically (that is, "expressionistically") maximalized. Schoenberg transferred the *x*s from the note-heads to the stems, so that he could apply the technique to half notes and dotted halves. That unnatural slowing down of the tempo of the speaking voice (*Sprechstimme*), the bizarre expansion of its range by the use of enormous melodic skips, and the extreme chromaticism that replaced Humperdinck's (or the early Schoenberg's) folksiness, greatly changed the effect of the melodrama. It now connoted a kind of dementia, "tales told by an idiot, signifying nothing," expressionism ironically mocking itself.

This perception was greatly enhanced by the accompanying chamber ensemble, modeled incongruously (but in fact very shrewdly) on the sound of a cabaret orchestra. It turned the whole sensation of *Pierrot lunaire* into one of a deranged nightclub act at the furthest (hence most ironic) remove from the churchy ivory tower environment Schoenberg's advanced music otherwise inhabited. Early performances, conducted by the composer, featured Albertine Zehme, the actress who commissioned the work and to whom it is dedicated, who declaimed the poems alone onstage under a spotlight, dressed not as Pierrot but as Columbine, the garishly beckoning *femme fatale* figure in the old masked comedy, and with the orchestra concealed behind a screen. Audiences found it titillating, and after a remarkable initial Berlin "run" to full houses, Schoenberg found himself with a relatively lucrative road show on his hands. He and Frau Zehme toured the piece for more than a decade.

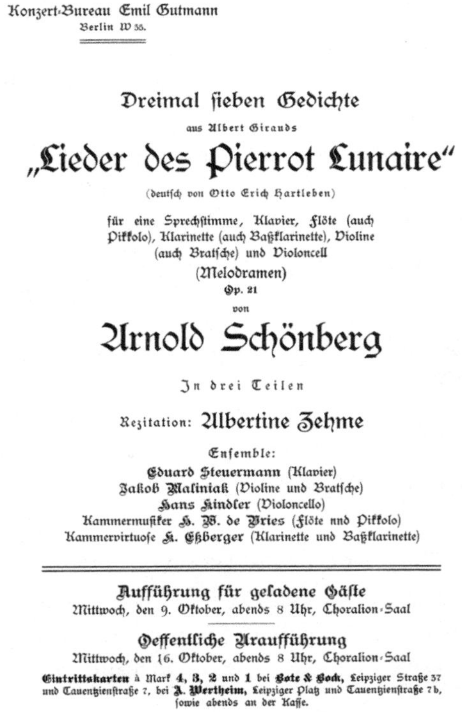
Konzert-Bureau Emil Gutmann
Berlin W 35.

Dreimal sieben Gedichte
aus Albert Girauds
„Lieder des Pierrot Lunaire"
(deutsch von Otto Erich Hartleben)
für eine Sprechstimme, Klavier, Flöte (auch Pikkolo), Klarinette (auch Baßklarinette), Violine (auch Bratsche) und Violoncell
(Melodramen)
Op. 21
von
Arnold Schönberg

In drei Teilen

Rezitation: Albertine Zehme

Ensemble:
Eduard Steuermann (Klavier)
Jakob Maliniak (Violine und Bratsche)
Hans Kindler (Violoncello)
Kammermusiker H. W. de Vries (Flöte nnd Pikkolo)
Kammervirtuose K. Eßberger (Klarinette und Baßklarinette)

Aufführung für geladene Gäste
Mittwoch, den 9. Oktober, abends 8 Uhr, Choralion-Saal

Oeffentliche Uraufführung
Mittwoch, den 16. Oktober, abends 8 Uhr, Choralion-Saal
Eintrittskarten à Mark 4, 3, 2 und 1 bei Bote & Bock, Leipziger Straße 37 und Tauentzienstraße 7, bei A. Wertheim, Leipziger Platz und Tauentzienstraße 7b, sowie abends an der Kasse.

FIG. 8-3 *Pierrot Lunaire*, poster for the preview (by invitation) and the public premiere.

Its popularity caused the composer's reverent disciples some consternation. One of them, Egon Wellesz, declared himself "suspicious of people who know only *Pierrot lunaire*, and admire Schoenberg on the strength of this one work," and even a little suspicious of the single advanced composition by Schoenberg "that may have a certain effect on even an unpracticed hearer."[5] No fair enjoying dessert without eating your peas! And pay no attention to the jokes, Wellesz seems to be insisting in particular. By and large the grim literature that has grown up around the embattled figure of Schoenberg and his works has followed this advice. But the jokes are plentiful, they are often pretty good, and they constitute what was surely the timeliest and culturally most significant aspect of the score. That unanticipated popularity, suspicious or no, has something important to tell historians.

Ex. 8-6 shows the first quatrain of *Mondestrunken* ("Moondrunk"), the first in the set of twenty-one melodramas and one of Schoenberg's most famous compositions, at least in terms of the frequency with which it has been described and analyzed in print. It sets the scene for all the hallucinatory verses to come, showing the "poet" Pierrot swilling "the wine that through the eyes is drunk," that is, the moonlight that makes him rave. In the unrhymed singing translation given below, the refrain lines are set in italics to show how they return not only here but in every one of Giraud's rondels. On each recurrence their meaning is somewhat altered by the context.

> *The wine that through the eyes is drunk,*
> *at night the moon pours down in torrents,*
> until a spring-flood overflows
> the silent far horizon.
>
> Desires, shuddering and sweet,
> are swimming through the flood unnumbered!
> *The wine that through the eyes is drunk,*
> *at night the moon pours down in torrents.*
>
> The poet, whom devotion drives,
> grows tipsy on the sacred liquor,
> to heaven turning his enraptured gaze
> and reeling, sucks and slurps
> *the wine that through the eyes is drunk.*

The music is very easy to analyze, since its all-important *Grundgestalt*—the intervallic shape or "cell" that provides the melodic and harmonic raw material—is presented at the very outset in the form of an ostinato in the piano part. It may be very easily traced throughout the piece, sometimes literally repeated, sometimes varied through interpolations (piano right hand in mm. 5–6), intervallic alteration (piano right hand in m. 16) or sequences. Chords to which it directly gives rise are easily spotted (e.g., piano in m. 10).

The reason why the derivation of chords from ostinato tune is so easy is that the first five notes of the ostinato are drawn from a single whole-tone scale, to which the first note plucked on the violin also belongs, thus completing it. We may recall from the previous chapter that completion, whether of a limited set like the whole-tone scale or of the whole chromatic "aggregate," was an important criterion of coherence for Schoenberg in composing his "pantonal music." The ubiquitous "atonal triad" makes its anticipated appearances in the harmony (beginning with the piano in m. 7, second beat), and is also subtly prefigured in the ostinato. The ostinato's last two notes, C♯ and G, can either of them combine with the initial G♯ and the D that falls on the second strong beat to make atonal triads (D–G♯–C♯ or G♯–D–G).

That much is straightforward. But as soon as the voice part is reckoned into the analysis, perplexity and ambiguity prevail. Counting both the piano and the violin parts, the opening ostinato contains nine different pitches, leaving three to complete the aggregate. All three are introduced by the voice part; two of them, A and B, are the first notes the voice "sings," while the remaining note, F, is given a prominent rhythmic placement (at the beginning of m. 6), and is the longest note the voice has "sung." Schoenberg, characteristically, is making something of a production out of the first aggregate-completion.

But the importance attached to the specific pitches A, B, and F is flatly contradicted by the *Sprechstimme* technique, especially considering that Frau Zehme, for whom the settings were written, was notoriously unconcerned with the niceties of pitch, and especially considering that Schoenberg claimed later that despite his fastidious notation, he neither expected nor wanted any greater exactness from the speaker. This may be confirmed by listening to a recording Schoenberg made of *Pierrot lunaire*, with a different singer, in 1940. Corroboration of another sort can be found in a later melodrama, *Ode to Napoleon Bonaparte*, for speaker, piano, and string quartet, composed in 1942. Here Schoenberg contented himself with a much cruder notation for the speaker, in which only a single staff line is used, and the notes are placed either on it, above it, or below it, to denote rough high, middle and low registers. In the preface to the score, Schoenberg claimed that this notation would have sufficed for *Pierrot* as well, and that he should have used it then to avoid misconceptions about his intention.

Thus a seemingly important feature of the tonal organization as represented by the score turns out to be entirely chimerical when it comes to actual sound. Schoenberg, so often meanly accused of writing mere *Papiermusik* ("on-paper music") or *Augenmusik* ("music for the eyes," not the ears), here does it on purpose and, it would seem, in jest. A much more thoroughgoing irony of this kind, and a much funnier one (in a bewildering sort of way), is found in *Der Mondfleck* ("The moonspot"), no. 18 in the cycle of twenty-one:

> *A snowy fleck of shining moonlight*
> *on the back side of his smart new frock coat,*
> so sets forth Pierrot one balmy evening,
> in pursuit of fortune and adventure.
>
> Sudden — something's wrong with his appearance,
> he looks round and round and then he finds it
> *— a snowy fleck of shining moonlight*
> *on the back side of his smart new frock coat.*
>
> Hang it! thinks he: a speck of plaster!
> Wipes and wipes, but it won't vanish!
> On he goes, his pleasure poisoned,
> rubs and rubs till almost morning at
> *a snowy fleck of shining moonlight.*

EX. 8-6   Arnold Schoenberg, *Pierrot lunaire*, no. 1, *Mondestrunken*, mm. 1–18

EX. 8-6 (*continued*)

Now here (Ex. 8-7) is an analyst's delight: a strict canon at the octave between the violin and the cello, a freer canon (or perhaps a sort of fugue) at the twelfth between the clarinet and the piccolo, and in the piano part a harmonized version of the clarinet-piccolo canon, in doubled note-values (that is, at half the tempo), with the parts inverted, and with a third voice entering in the middle of the texture an octave below the first entry of the subject, so that the orthodox tonal relations of a fugue (E answers B answers E, or I – V – I) are scrupulously maintained. *Not only that*, but (as shown in Ex. 8-7) in the middle of m. 10 the string and wind parts reverse direction, producing a perfect melodic and rhythmic palindrome, while the piano continues to develop its fugue!

It is enough to boggle the mind, and it has elicited a lot of awestruck hyperbole, like Charles Rosen's announcement that *Der Mondfleck* "is one of the most elaborately worked out canons since the end of the fifteenth century."[6] But how elaborately "worked out" is a canon or a fugue that is written in a style that recognizes no distinction between consonance and dissonance, so that harmonically speaking, literally anything goes? The essence of counterpoint has always been its "dissonance treatment." That, and that alone, is where the skill is required and displayed. What makes Bach's *Musical Offering* or *Art of Fugue* the astonishing tours de force that they are is not just the complexity of the texture, but the fact that that complexity is achieved within such exacting constraints. Take away the constraints and you have rendered the tour de force entirely pointless.

But of course Schoenberg knew that perfectly well — much better than his humorless admirers. Look again at the text: it is all about frenzied but pointless activity. That is a perfect description of an elaborate contrapuntal texture with "emancipated dissonance." Or to put it the other way around, an elaborate contrapuntal texture with emancipated dissonance is a perfect metaphor for the urgent but ineffectual efforts Pierrot is making. (Notice, too, some traditionally comic word painting: the instrumental parts go into reverse just when the text describes Pierrot "looking round and round.") From a bogus masterpiece of counterpoint, *Der Mondfleck* becomes a genuine masterpiece of self-mocking irony. (Once, to a pupil, Schoenberg cracked that "now that I've emancipated dissonance, anybody can be a composer.") Most pertinent of all, perhaps, to the discussion with which this chapter began is the fact that this most ironically distanced item in *Pierrot lunaire* is the very one that musically (as well as textually) parodies archaic forms. Once again pastiche has served as metaphor for an ironic modernist sensibility. From the unlikeliest of quarters, it seems, namely the "expressionist" camp, we have confirmation of Ortega y Gasset's diagnosis of modern art (first quoted in chapter 2) as "play and nothing else," and therefore as "invariably waggish" or jesting, because its primary concern is with style, the "how" rather than the "what" of art. And that, Ortega suggests, is why modern art "avoids living forms" but instead, making an end run around the immediate past, claims kinship with the imagined eighteenth century. "The imperative of unmitigated realism that dominated the artistic sensibility of the last century," Ortega wrote, including all art that aspires to direct communication of feeling,

> must be put down as a freak in aesthetic evolution. It thus appears that the new inspiration, extravagant though it seems, is merely returning, at least in one point,

EX. 8-7   Arnold Schoenberg, *Pierrot lunaire*, no. 18, *Der Mondfleck*, mm. 9–11

to the royal road of art. For this road is called "will to style." But to stylize means to deform reality, to derealize; style involves dehumanization. And vice versa, there is no other means of stylizing except by dehumanizing. Whereas realism, exhorting the artist faithfully to follow reality, exhorts him to abandon style. An enthuasiast of realist painting, groping for the suggestive word, will declare that it has "character." And character, not style, is distinctive of nineteenth-century art in all its media. The eighteenth century, on the other hand, which had so little character, was a past master of style.[7]

BREAKING WITH TRADITION

Ortega was writing in 1925, two years after Stravinsky brought forth his Octet, when the big change in sensibility that he was describing was (or seemed) a fait accompli. In 1912, it did not yet look that way. *Pierrot lunaire*, as the quotation above from Wellesz already implied, seemed an exceptional work within Schoenberg's output, even a somewhat deviant one. It had been commissioned from an outside party, after all; it did not arise "spontaneously" out of his own artistic imagination. And, at the time, its commitment to irony was not as obvious as it may appear today.

Stravinsky, who attended one of its "first run" performances as Schoenberg's guest, had mixed feelings about *Pierrot*. On the one hand he admired the instrumental writing enormously, and even imitated it a bit in his next work (three songs on Japanese poems accompanied by a small chamber ensemble with piano like the one in *Pierrot*.) But on the other hand he thought it esthetically outmoded, comparing its wallowing in the macabre with what he called the "Beardsley cult,"[8] implying that Schoenberg was still under the influence of the paintings and drawings of the British "decadent" artist Aubrey Beardsley (1872–98), whose most famous work was a set of gruesome illustrations to Wilde's *Salomé*, on which Strauss based his most overtly "decadent" opera (see Fig. 1-6).

What as of 1912 was a widely resisted "call" — that modern artists give unambiguous preference to irony over sincerity — had by 1925 become the order of the day, to resist which could seem downright backward. This was a much more significant rupture than the one created by maximalism, which however it impressed audiences with its radical means, nevertheless remained faithful to its (and their) immediate esthetic heritage. The ironic break meant — for the first time — the rejection of the immediate past, a true break with tradition. Artists were now against something as well as for something. The break created divisions and dissension among artists as well as between artists and audience. If we insist on maintaining the fiction that a new century is a new age, then the triumph of the "ban on all pathos," as Ortega called it, was the true beginning of the twentieth century for art.

One of the clearest and most eloquent spokesmen for the ban was the English poet and critic Thomas Ernest (or T. E.) Hulme (1883–1917). In a series of articles published near the end of his short life, he articulated better than anyone else what the new movement was against, and why. In one, called "Romanticism and Classicism," he put things in bluntly political terms: "It was romanticism that made the revolution; they who hate the revolution hate romanticism."[9] In another, "Modern Art and Its Philosophy," he brought up matters of religion. Romanticism, he argued, was the culminating phase of humanism, the fatal hubris "which is the opposite of the doctrine of original sin: the belief that man as a part of nature was after all something satisfactory." He went on:

> The change which Copernicus is supposed to have brought about is the exact contrary of the fact. Before Copernicus, man was not the center of the world; after Copernicus he was. You get a change from a certain profundity and intensity to that flat and insipid optimism which, passing through its first stage of decay in Rousseau, has finally culminated in the state of slush in which we have the misfortune to live.[10]

In place of the decadent moral flabbiness Hulme saw in romanticism, which valued exactly what seemed to him least valuable in humanity (namely, its transient and irrational feelings), he called for a return to "the dry hardness which you get in the classics."[11] And one way of recapturing that was to emulate classical "stylization," as Stravinsky seemed to do in his Octet. Even before he wrote that work, in fact, Stravinsky had been co-opted (as we would now say) by the increasingly antiromantic factions that were springing up in England and France, and made their involuntary standard bearer.

Perhaps the first to do this was the French critic Jacques Rivière (1886–1925), the editor of *La nouvelle revue française*, an artistically avant-garde but politically conservative and aggressively nationalistic literary forum. In his reviews of Stravinsky's early ballets, Rivière promoted the composer from the status of mere musician to that of exemplary artist for France, where neoclassical sentiments merged inextricably with nationalistic ones. When everyone else was exclaiming at the orgiastic dissonance of *The Rite of Spring*, marveling at Stravinsky's *âme slave* ("Slavic soul") and the sublime terror his music evoked, Rivière called *The Rite* "the first masterpiece we may stack up against those of impressionism," for the following reasons:

> The great novelty of *The Rite of Spring* is its renunciation of "sauce." Here is a work that is absolutely pure. Nothing is blurred, nothing is mitigated by shadows; no veils and no poetic sweeteners; not a trace of atmosphere. The work is whole and tough, its parts remain quite raw; they are served up without digestive aids; everything is crisp, intact, clear and crude. Never have we heard a music so magnificently limited. If Stravinsky has chosen those instruments that do not sigh, that say no more than they say, whose timbres are without expression and are like isolated words, it is because he wants to enunciate everything directly, explicitly, and concretely. His voice becomes the object's proxy, consuming it, replacing it; instead of evoking it, he utters it. Thus Stravinsky, with unmatched flair and accomplishment, is bringing about in music the same revolution that is taking place more humbly and tortuously in literature: he has passed from the sung to the said, from invocation to statement, from poetry to reportage.[12]

What Rivière called for in these prescient articles of 1913, without yet actually naming it, was a new sort of neoclassicism that had little or nothing to do with the fairyland type the romantics had enjoyed. Rather than a "delicious" or a "culinary" pastiche, Rivière called for a "denuded" or "stripped-down style" (*style dépouillé*) of unprecedented plainness. The first critic who seriously applied the word "neoclassical" to a work of Stravinsky (or anyone else, for that matter) had this sort of "dry hardness" in mind, rather than a gratifying stylistic soufflé.

That critic, Boris de Schloezer (1881–1969), was like Stravinsky a Russian exile in Paris. The article in which he used the word was published in 1923, the year of the Octet, but nine months before its first performance. It concerned a different work, Stravinsky's *Symphonies d'instruments à vent* ("Symphonies [or concords] of wind instruments"), a memorial to Debussy that had created a big stir in 1920 when its amazingly "stripped down" concluding section, arranged for piano, had been published in the appendix to a Debussy commemorative issue of a French music magazine (Ex. 8-8). What made the *Symphonies* "neoclassical" for Schloezer, thence for many others, was the assumption that it was

> only a system of sounds, which follow one another and group themselves according to purely musical affinities; the thought of the artist places itself only in the musical plan without ever setting foot in the domain of psychology. Emotions, feelings, desires, aspirations — this is the terrain from which he had pushed his work. The art of Stravinsky is nevertheless strongly expressive; he moves us profoundly and his perception is never formularized; but there is one specific emotion, a musical emotion. This art does not pursue feeling or emotion; but it attains grace infallibly by its force and by its perfection.[13]

These words were arguably irrelevant to the poetic conception of the *Symphonies d'instruments à vent* as a memorial piece or *tombeau* for Debussy that demonstrably mimics the liturgical contents of a Russian Orthodox *panikhida* or funeral service, just as Rivière's description of *The Rite* was arguably irrelevant to *its* original concept. Nevertheless, these writings about Stravinsky are of great historical moment, not only for what they tell us about the reception of Stravinsky's music, but because they had an enormous impact on the composer himself. They "influenced" him decisively toward his own brand of neoclassicism, of which the Octet was probably the first fully conscious manifestation. Stravinsky immediately became an ardent propagandist for the new esthetic, giving it an especially strong expression in some famous fighting words uttered in the heat of esthetic battle during the 1920s and 1930s. In his autobiography, *Chronicles of My Life* (1936), he summed it all up by saying that "music is, by its very nature, essentially powerless to *express* anything at all, whether a feeling, an attitude of mind, a psychological mood, a phenomenon of nature, etc.," and went on to claim that

> expression has never been an inherent property of music. That is by no means the purpose of its existence. If, as is nearly always the case, music appears to express something, this is only an illusion and not a reality. It is simply an additional attribute which, by tacit and inveterate agreement, we have lent it, thrust upon it, as a label, a convention — in short, an aspect unconsciously or by force of habit, we have come to confuse with its essential being.[14]

Three years later, lecturing at Harvard University, Stravinsky inveighed against Wagner and his *Gesamtkunstwerk* or "total work of art." The Wagnerian system, he railed, despite all the claims made for it as the bearer of music's historic destiny, "far from having raised the level of musical culture, has never ceased to undermine it and

EX. 8-8 Igor Stravinsky, *Symphonies d'instruments à vent*, final section as published in *Revue Musicale*

finally to debase it in the most paradoxical fashion."[15] And that is because Wagner, more than any other romantic composer, had yoked music, "a purely sensual delight," to "the murky inanities of the Art-Religion."

Stravinsky's first pronouncements of this kind came almost immediately after Schloezer's article about his *Symphonies*, and almost certainly in response to it. In a program note that accompanied performances of the *Symphonies* in the late 1920s and 1930s, Stravinsky described it as entirely formalist and transcendent — that is, without "extramusical" content of any kind. It was, he wrote, no more and no less than an arrangement of "tonal masses, sculptured in marble, to be regarded objectively by the ear."[16] Like any number of other modern artists, Stravinsky had been brought round, over the decade between 1913 (*The Rite of Spring*) and 1923 (the Octet) to a view of art that completely sacrificed sincerity to irony. Rivière and Schloezer had helped him get there. We are always influenced by those who praise us, especially when the praise is so intelligent, so hyperbolic — and so timely. Stravinsky did what was necessary to keep that praise coming.

THE END OF THE "LONG NINETEENTH CENTURY"

But nobody's words are ever as eloquent as events, and over that crucial decade events had completely transformed the world that European and American artists knew. The First World War, known simply as "The Great War" until there was a Second, was one of the most horrific watersheds in European history. It put a dismal end to what many historians in its wake have called "the long nineteenth century," which had begun with another watershed event, the French Revolution, which Hulme, and modern neoclassicists in general, so abhorred. What had united the long nineteenth century were its optimism and its faith in progress, and these were the Great War's first and most permanent casualties.

To call it a "world" war is of course a Eurocentric conceit, although its territory spread wider than that of any previous war, with battles fought in parts of Asia and Africa as well as Europe, and with the United States belatedly joining in (marking America's first participation in a war fought on foreign soil). But a "great" war it surely was, indeed the greatest ever, if greatness is measured in terms of awful numbers. It smashed four empires: the ancient Austrian one, the recent German one, the far-flung Ottoman Turkish one, and the huge but contiguous Russian one (which however would soon be reconstituted as the Soviet Union). It was the first war to be fought not only on land and sea, but also in the air. It was the first war to witness the use of machine guns, tanks, aerial bombing, and poison gas. It was the first modern war to include episodes of genocide (particularly of Armenians at the hands of the Turks in 1915 on suspicion of conspiring with the Russians).

But even the "legitimate" military carnage was on a scale never before imaginable. Of the four most heavily engaged belligerents, the British lost a million men (out of an adult male population of some twenty million), the Russians and French 1,700,000 each, and the Germans and Austrians more than three million combined. The total war dead approached nine million. Measured against the puny proximate cause of the war — Austria's avenging the assassination of the emperor's nephew and heir by a Serbian nationalist — and the benefits it secured (despite all the rhetoric, none at all), these futile losses produced a desperate and irreparable disillusionment. "This is not war," an Indian soldier conscripted to fight with the British wrote home after being wounded, "it is the ending of the world."[17] Another writer, even more chillingly, compared it to "the guillotining of a world."[18]

The worst episode, the Battle of the Somme (July to November 1916), where 70,000 British soldiers were killed (20,000 in a single day) and 170,000 wounded, "marked the end," in the words of John Keegan, the war's most eminent historian, "of an age of vital optimism in British life that has never been recovered."[19] That despond was by no means confined to the British; they, after all, were on the winning side. Last to lose their optimism, of course, were the politicians and generals who managed the struggle. As another historian, Tony Judt, comments, they "were in a war they had not expected and did not understand; but the insouciant enthusiasm with which they sent hundreds of thousands of young men to their death retains its power to shock and nauseate a century later."[20]

The wave of shock and nausea produced by the Great War reverberated keenly but for the most part indirectly in the arts, chiefly in the form of irony, black humor, and cynicism. Indeed, irony has been the one indispensable ingredient in practically all European art ever since — and a lot of American art as well, although America's late entrance in the Great War, its relatively light losses (some 114,000), and the prestige its soldiers and its president Wilson were accorded in the aftermath, spared its population and its artists the immediate slough of despond and allowed the persistence of an optimism that registered particularly, as we will see, in the 1920s.

The triumph of Ortega's "ban on all pathos" is only understandable in the context of the encompassing disillusionment of Europe. It cast a retrospective pall over all the seriously spiritual and exalted art the previous century had produced. All rhetoric of hope and glory now seemed a lie. "The plunge of civilization into this abyss of blood and darkness," wrote Henry James,

> is a thing that so gives away the whole long age during which we have supposed the world to be, with whatever abatement, gradually bettering, that to have to take it all now for what the treacherous years were all the while really making for and *meaning* is too tragic for any words.[21]

The only thing to do was laugh, or at least scoff. "The more revolting it was, the more we shouted with laughter," wrote the war correspondent Sir Philip Gibbs in a book of 1920 pointedly titled *Now It Can Be Told*. That laughter was

> the laughter of mortals at the trick that had been played on them by an ironical fate. They had been taught to believe that the whole object of life was to reach out to beauty and love, and that mankind, in its progress to perfection, had killed the beast instinct, cruelty, blood-lust, the primitive, savage law of survival by tooth and claw and club and ax. All poetry, all religion had preached this gospel and this promise. Now that ideal was broken like a china vase dashed to the ground. The

contrast between That and This was devastating. The wartime humor of the soul roared with mirth at the sight of all that dignity and elegance despoiled.[22]

Even after the sardonic laughter had died down, dignity and elegance, beauty and love, and especially progress to perfection remained under suspicion. They were now regarded, one and all, as lies. Hence the preference, keenly if as yet wishfully noted by Rivière in Stravinsky even before the war, for the matter-of-factly said over the rhapsodically sung, for fact over feeling, for reportage over "poetry." As Ernest Hemingway put it in *A Farewell to Arms* (1929), "abstract words such as glory, honor, courage, or hallow were obscene beside the concrete names of villages, the numbers of roads, the names of rivers, the numbers of regiments and the dates."[23] Surveying the language of poetry before and after the Great War, the literary critic Paul Fussell noted the unlamented demise of "high" diction, the kind in which —

A friend is a *comrade*
Friendship is *comradeship, fellowship*
A horse is a *steed*, or *charger*
The enemy is *the foe*, or *the host*
Danger is *peril*
To conquer is to *vanquish*
To attack is to *assail*
To be earnestly brave is to be *gallant*
To be cheerfully brave is to be *plucky*
To be stolidly brave is to be *staunch*
Bravery considered after the fact is *valor*
The dead on the battlefield are *the fallen*[24]

— and so on, in favor of the plain and "ugly" language of poets who can no longer muster belief in what Hemingway derided as the "abstract words." (Fussell names T. S. Eliot's *Waste Land* of 1922, "with its rats' alleys, dull canals, and dead men who have lost their bones.") The point holds true, maybe truer even, if one compares the grandiose work of the musical maximalists we know — Strauss, Mahler, Scriabin, Schoenberg, Stravinsky, and perhaps especially Ives (who like other Americans carried prewar optimism into the postwar world, or tried to) — with the modernist music we shall be encountering from here on. The maximalists went into a profound eclipse: Mahler was banished from the active repertory (except in a few places particularly associated with him, like Vienna, New York, and Amsterdam) until the 1960s, when Ives, too, was rediscovered (or rather, wholly discovered for the first time). Scriabin has yet to make a full comeback. The contrast can best be observed, perhaps, in the work of composers like Stravinsky and Schoenberg, whose prime creative years straddled the divide. They became the harbingers of the great disillusion.

VITAL VS. GEOMETRICAL

But there was yet another factor that produced the triumph of irony—Ortega's "dehumanization"—in modern art. Our best entrée to it will come through the visual arts rather than literature; and once again T. E. Hulme (who—now it can be told—perished in the trenches at Passchendaele in 1917, one of England's unlucky million) can be our guide. In accounting for the death of naturalism in twentieth-century art (a death he enthusiastically hastened to abet), Hulme invoked a pair of terms that had first been introduced into art history by the German scholar Wilhelm Worringer in a book called *Abstraktion und Einfühlung* ("Abstraction and empathy", 1908).

The terms are "vital" (whence "vitalism") and "geometrical." Worringer had posited them as the poles of an ever-swinging pendulum. The sentimental "slush" that had seeped into art (and politics) over the course of the long nineteenth century, Hulme argued, was due to an excess of vitalism, the view of art that equated its beauty with its power to evoke a pleasurable empathy. Any work of art that a vitalist finds beautiful can only be

> an objectification of our own pleasure in activity, and our own vitality. The worth of a line or form consists in the value of the life which it contains for us. Putting the matter more simply we may say that in this art there is always a feeling of liking for, and pleasure in, the forms and movements to be found in nature.[25]

But when we lose our capacity to exult in the world and our place in the order of things—or in other words, when we lose our optimism—we shall incline toward the "geometrical" art, the kind which, Hulme clairvoyantly predicted, was going to gain ascendancy in the twentieth century. It was art that "most obviously exhibits no delight in nature and no striving after vitality. Its forms are always what can be described as stiff and lifeless."[26] Hulme associated such art with the "tendency to abstraction"—not the kind of fuzzy grandiloquent "abstractions" that Hemingway derided as false sentiment, but just the opposite, the kind of abstraction associated with geometrical archetypes: something realer than the real, superhumanly real. For "dehumanization," make no mistake, aimed higher, not lower, than the human.

"What is the nature of this tendency?"[27] Hulme asked, rhetorically. "What is the condition of mind of the people whose art is governed by it?" His beautifully lucid answer, in "Modern Art and Its Philosophy," is indispensable to any understanding of the music that followed, and repudiated, the long nineteenth century. "While a naturalistic art," Hulme wrote,

> is the result of a happy pantheistic relation between man and the outside world, the tendency to abstraction, on the contrary, occurs in races whose attitude to the outside world is the exact contrary of this.
>
> In art this state of mind results in a desire to create a certain abstract geometrical shape, which, being durable and permanent, shall be a refuge from the flux and impermanence of outside nature. The need which art satisfies here, is not the delight in the forms of nature, which is a characteristic of all vital arts, but the exact contrary. In the reproduction of natural objects there is an attempt to purify them of their characteristically living qualities in order to make them necessary

and immovable. The changing is translated into something fixed and necessary. This leads to rigid lines and dead crystalline form, for pure geometrical regularity gives a certain pleasure to men troubled by the obscurity of outside appearance. The geometrical line is something absolutely distinct from the messiness, the confusion, and the accidental details of existing things.

That messiness and confusion were most apparent in music when it came to the expression of irrational subjective feeling, the very thing that romantic artists gloried in. So subjective expression (and freedom of expression) became the bête noire, the hated "black beast" of postwar esthetics, as already hinted in several extracts from the writings of the postwar Stravinsky. Hostility to the arbitrariness and unpredictability to which subjective expression gives rise, and the refuge that artists (and others) sought in the Necessary and the Immovable can be observed not only in music composition but also, possibly even more vividly, in musical performance.

A great change in the performance style of all European classical music, regardless of age or origin, followed the Great War. The ban on pathos was translated directly into a ban on two practices that symbolized pathos in musical performance: *tempo rubato* (spontaneous, unnotated variation in tempo) and similarly unnotated fluctuations in dynamics. Play with variable tempo and dynamics and you are playing "romantically." That is how all music was played up until the 1920s, as early phonograph recordings testify. No music is played like that any more, not even romantic music. All music is played "as written," within a hierarchical chain of command (composer to editor to performer, with an additional step when a conductor is employed) that takes all initiative away from the person actually producing the sounds.

Stravinsky can again be our witness. In his Harvard lectures of 1939, he drew a radical distinction between two kinds of performance, which he called "execution" and "interpretation." Between them, he warned, "there exists a difference in make-up that is of an ethical rather than of an esthetic order."[28] Execution is "the strict putting into effect of an explicit will that contains nothing beyond what it specifically commands." Interpretation is the expressive input from the performer that goes beyond what the text explicitly prescribes, and it is "at the root of all the errors, all the sins, all the misunderstandings that interpose themselves between the musical work and the listener and prevent a faithful transmission of its message." Stravinsky heaps scorn on what in 1939 was not yet quite as bygone a performance style as it has since become:

> The sin against the spirit of the work always begins with a sin against its letter and leads to the endless follies which an ever-flourishing literature in the worst taste [that is, "vitalist" music criticism] does its best to sanction. Thus it follows that a *crescendo*, as we all know, is always accompanied by a speeding up of movement, while a slowing down never fails to accompany a *diminuendo*. The superfluous is refined upon; a *piano, piano pianissimo* is delicately sought after; great pride is taken in perfecting useless nuances — a concern that usually goes hand in hand with inaccurate rhythm.[29]

The literalness on which Stravinsky is insisting, and (taking the long view a book like this encourages) which represents the ultimate triumph of the literate tradition over the oral (which is where pupils learn to make unnotated nuances by imitating their teachers), is the most durable and tangible result of the postwar triumph of dehumanization. In place of seemingly arbitrary decisions symbolizing the influence of emotion (which are not really arbitrary, of course, but which are maintained by oral tradition) one "takes refuge," as Hulme would say, in what is Necessary and Immovable, namely the written text, which thus becomes even more of a sacrosanct and timeless monument than ever. What is written, in its relative permanence, becomes Holy Writ.

SOME MORE TROUBLING POLITICS

The authoritarian control thus vested in the text (and behind the text, in the composer) has obvious political parallels, and there is no evading its relationship to the rise of totalitarianism in postwar Europe. That relationship was not a direct or causal one. Neither brought about the other, nor does an antiromantic compositional style or performance practice necessarily commit a musician to totalitarian politics. To cite a famous counterexample, one of the most influential literalists among twentieth-century performers, the conductor Arturo Toscanini (1867–1957), who so famously exhorted the musicians he led to play *Com'è scritto* ("Just as written"), was famous for his opposition to the Italian dictator Benito Mussolini, and later to the German dictator Adolf Hitler. Conversely, some totalitarian regimes, notably the Soviet dictatorship in Russia, would support the production of "vitalist" or neoromantic music as a palliative influence on the population.

And yet T. E. Hulme did state it as a general axiom that "they who hate the revolution hate romanticism"; and the general level of correlation between "neoclassical" esthetics and totalitarian politics is high enough to suggest that both were, at least in considerable part, responses to a common stimulus in the destructive chaos of the Great War and its immediate aftermath. Ortega y Gasset, the great theorist of dehumanization, was also one of the architects of Spanish fascism and a sworn enemy of democracy. His most famous book, *The Revolt of the Masses* (1929), argued that an intellectual minority must always be in a position to exercise control over the uneducated majority so as to preserve civil order. Merely to note this much, of course, would be to imply guilt by association, a tactic as unreliable as it is unfair. But Ortega himself drew the connection between his esthetics and his politics in the very essay from which all our previous quotes from him have come.

Modern art is hated, he argued in "The Dehumanization of Art," because it is socially divisive. But where a humanitarian like Tolstoy would curse it for that reason, Ortega blesses it:

> Through its mere presence, the art of the young compels the average citizen to realize that he is just this — the average citizen, a creature incapable of receiving the sacrament of art, blind and deaf to pure beauty. But such a thing cannot be done after a hundred years of adulation of the masses and apotheosis of the people. Accustomed to ruling supreme, the masses feel that the new art, which is the art of a privileged aristocracy of finer senses, endangers their rights as men. Whenever the new Muses present themselves, the masses bristle.

For a century and a half the masses have claimed to be the whole of society. Stravinsky's music or the plays of [Luigi] Pirandello [1867–1936, another apostle of the new irony] have the sociological effect of compelling the people to recognize itself for what it is: a component among others of the social structure, inert matter of the historical process, a secondary factor in the cosmos of spiritual life. On the other hand, the new art also helps the elite to recognize themselves and one another in the drab mass of society and to learn their mission which consists in being few and holding their own against the many.

A time must come in which society, from politics to art, reorganizes itself into two orders or ranks: the illustrious and the vulgar. That chaotic, shapeless, and undifferentiated state without discipline and social structure in which Europe has lived these hundred and fifty years cannot go on. Behind all contemporary life lurks the provoking and profound injustice of the assumption that men are actually equal. Each move among men so obviously reveals the opposite that each move results in a painful clash.

If this subject were broached in politics the passions aroused would run too high to make oneself understood. Fortunately the unity of spirit within a historical epoch allows us to point out serenely and with perfect clarity in the germinating art of our time the same symptoms and signals of a moral revision that in politics present themselves obscured by low passions.[30]

These are fighting words on behalf of the most barefaced elitism we've encountered yet—an elitism that, many would argue, has been thoroughly discredited by the subsequent historical record—a record that includes previously unimaginable atrocities carried out by powerful elites against the powerless. The question that remains unresolved is whether art that was once so promoted can be divorced from the politics and subsequently enjoyed in a "purely" esthetic way, or whether (as Ortega actually implies) art is always, or inevitably, the "stalking horse"—the benign cover or concealment—of politics.

Those who would argue that art, inhabiting a realm of its own, is politically neutral and innocent, must contend with Stravinsky's assertion that questions of musical performance are "of an ethical, rather than of an esthetic order." For ethics, unlike esthetics, is not so easily detached from politics—that is, from the actual or symbolic ordering of society. And given that much, can one fully separate Stravinsky the musician from the man who gave the following statement to a reporter from a Rome newspaper, right before an audience with *Il Duce* ("The Leader") himself in 1930?

I don't believe that anyone venerates Mussolini more than I. To me, he is the *one man who counts* nowadays in the whole world. I have traveled a great deal: I know many exalted personages, and my artist's mind does not shrink from political and social issues. Well, after having seen so many events and so many more or less representative men, I have an overpowering urge to render homage to your Duce. He is the savior of Italy and—let us hope—the world.[31]

Many extenuating circumstances could be mentioned: Stravinsky, a Russian aristocrat by birth, had been uprooted and disinherited by the Bolshevik revolution and (like Schoenberg, as quoted in the previous chapter) sought the protection of a prince who now, through no fault of Stravinsky's, suffers history's contempt for deeds as yet undreamt of when Stravinsky gave his interview. Does Stravinsky now deserve to share in that contempt? Are artists who enjoyed the patronage of this century's bloodsoaked dictators stained with the blood that soaked them? If so, what about the tyrants of the past and the artists whom they patronized? Shall we hold Louis XIV's misdeeds against Lully? Louis XV's against Rameau? Is Michelangelo answerable to the Lutherans for the policies of the popes who commissioned his idolatrous images?

But of course Stravinsky could have chased or chosen other patrons, and his enthusiasm for Mussolini's authoritarian politics seems to have been at the time sincere. Does that mean, as embarrassed biographers sometimes write, that he was politically "naive"? Or is naïveté simply the name we give retrospectively to the backing of losers? One writer has "excused" Stravinsky for his attraction to Mussolini (which led him, in other press interviews, to profess personal loyalty to the Duce and even call himself a fascist[32]) by suggesting that anybody might have been "bamboozled" by the sort of flattering attention Mussolini paid the composer. But of course by the 1920s Stravinsky was the most famous composer alive; flattering attention was paid him everywhere.

In back of all these questions is the most troubling and durable one of all: how is artistic excellence, which always comes at a high price, to be reconciled with ideals of political and social equality? Who is to pay for "the art of the few," when the few who used to pay are no longer able to do so, and when the many wield unprecedented political and economic power? Many have argued that "high art" has been living, since the First World War, on borrowed time. It is not hard to find evidence to back this argument up, and we will certainly be sifting it in the chapters to come (along with counterarguments and counterevidence).

If the argument is true, though, then it follows that the art, specifically the musical works, that will henceforth supply the subject matter of this book are engaged in a holding or rearguard action against an inexorable historical tide that can only be reversed if the progress of democracy is reversed. Putting it this way puts the cultural authenticity of "classical music" sorely in question (especially if democracy is regarded as unquestionable). Whatever the answers may be, and of course we will sample many, the question has been in the back of every thinking musician's mind since the 1920s.

AND NOW THE MUSIC

Turning at long last to Stravinsky's Octet, the work that started this tortuous discussion of sinister subtexts and convoluted circumstances on its way, we may be relieved — or dismayed — to find that, taken on its own terms, it is such an innocently diverting little piece. But of course to say that much is already a joke — or at least an exercise, like everything else in this chapter, in irony.

For nothing ever comes "on its own terms," and nothing can be taken that way. History provides everything with a context. And nothing, therefore, can ever be truly innocent (of history, that is). Copland's bewildered reaction to the piece — not the sort of reaction one normally has to an innocent diversion — has already established that much for us. What bewildered him was not "the music itself" but the context in which he heard it: a concert at which a Stravinsky premiere (i.e., if past performance was anything to go by, a scandal) was about to take place. Hearing an innocent little

EX. 8-9   Igor Stravinsky, *Octet for Winds* in Arthur Lourié's piano transcription, I, mm. 1–4

diversion rather than the expected shock was of course a shock; and as Copland tells us, it led to a press scandal after all.

Or again—"on its own terms" the Octet's opening gesture, a trill in the two bassoons—Ex. 8-9, given like all the other citations from the Octet in piano reduction to avoid possible confusion about pitch on account of the transposing clarinet and trumpet parts—is courtly, decorous, charming. But those terms again depend on context: what is courtly, decorous, and charming in a work signed "Mozart" is brash and polemical in a work signed "Stravinsky" (at least the first time). So music can be listened to "on its own terms" only by listeners who are ignorant of historical contexts. Ignorance is bliss, one may retort. But even then, the context provided by ignorance is not neutral or transparent, since my ignorance is conditioned by my interests and predilections, or by their absence, and will differ from yours. "Listening to music 'on its own terms,'" then, can never be written without the use of "scare quotes"—the quotation marks that turn whatever is inside them into its opposite, or that at least put the statement and its negation on equal terms. The name of that game, of course, is irony. Listeners play it too.

The three movements of the Octet have time-honored Italian titles (Sinfonia, Tema con variazioni, Finale), more mock decorum masking a somewhat anxious commitment to the Necessary and the Immovable in the face of the world's disarray. "Sinfonia," to a historian, connotes an opera overture, the "cradle of sonata form." And sonata form is the form this music takes, for the first time in Stravinsky's work since his graduation piece, a conventional symphony (opus 1, also—coincidentally?—in Eb major) that he wrote under Rimsky-Korsakov's direction in 1905–07 just to prove that he could. Here again Stravinsky is proving that he can, or that he (and we) still can, even after those explosive prewar ballets; and, going further, asserting that he not only can but must—and so must you. "He declares that he is creating a new epoch with this," wrote a fellow Russian émigré, Serge Prokofieff, to a friend back home, "and that this is the only way to write nowadays."[33] Prokofieff was skeptical; to him Stravinsky's neoclassical music sounded like "Bach with smallpox."[34]

Jealous rival though he was, Prokofieff was on to something. Stravinsky once described his pastiche procedure in works like the Octet as a revival of "the constructive principles" of "eighteenth-century classicism."[35] But perhaps it would be a truer description to call it a revival of certain aspects of the phonology and morphology of eighteenth-century music, as a linguist might say (phonology being a vocabulary of usable sounds and morphology the combination of sounds into distinctive and characteristic patterns), but with constructive principles that bear the mark of Stravinsky's older neoprimitivist style, with its static ostinatos, its stable dissonances, and its abrupt disjunctures. Thus the opening trills say "eighteenth century" without actually sounding like eighteenth-century music, because the harmony and voice leading in which they are embedded would have been impossible in the eighteenth century.

The kind of stuttering melody that follows the bassoon trill in the flute (Ex. 8-10) is also characteristically Stravinskian rather than "classical," but the figuration that takes over in the same instrumental part toward the end of the example again says "eighteenth century," and more particularly, "Bach." Melodies that move between two distinct and discrete registers, implying a sort of harmonically-driven counterpoint, are familiar to twentieth-century musicians primarily from Bach's sonatas and suites for solo violin or cello. The conditions that gave rise to them are of course absent in Stravinsky's music. His flute melody is not there to supply its own "bass" and imply a harmonic progression. But even if it does not perform harmonic functions, it has a function to perform as a stylistic marker (or "morpheme").

EX. 8-10   Igor Stravinsky, *Octet for Winds* in Arthur Lourié's piano transcription, I, mm. 5–32

EX. 8-10 *(continued)*

The Allegro moderato that furnishes the body of the first movement is so cut-and-dried a "sonata form" as to be a virtual self-parody: first theme in trumpet II (Ex. 8-11a); second theme in trumpet I (Ex. 8-11b); a development (Ex. 8-11c) in which the anapestic rhythms from the accompaniment to the second theme come to the fore for a workout; and then, right on schedule, a recap (Ex. 8-11d) in which the anapests accompany the main theme. Those anapestic (short-short-long) rhythms in sixteenths and eighths also shout "Bach" to anyone who knows the Third Brandenburg Concerto, but the fragmented texture in which they disport themselves here is anything but Bachian.

The Tema con variazioni begins (Ex. 8-12) with a little in-joke to reward those in the know about Stravinsky's harmonic idiom and its sources (in 1923, almost nobody beyond the circle of Rimsky-Korsakov's surviving pupils). The "classically" regular eight-measure theme, played *ben cantabile* ("singing nicely") at the outset by flute and clarinet at the double octave, is one of Stravinsky's longest "octatonic" melodies — that is, melodies drawn exclusively from a scale of alternating half steps and whole steps, in this case A – B♭ – C – C♯ – D♯ – E – F♯ – G. As we have observed many times, the octatonic scale reproduces itself when transposed by a minor third; so the repetition of the melody by the second trumpet beginning on E rather than C♯ involves no modulation. Rather, the transposition supplies the D♯ that completes the representation of the octatonic scale.

Of course no such scale was ever employed during the eighteenth century; again Stravinsky's "neoclassical" style shows itself to be no pastiche but an ironic mixture of styles in which everything is used with equal self-consciousness and nothing can be taken stylistically for granted. The ironic mixture in this case is especially obvious

EX. 8-11A   Igor Stravinsky, *Octet for Winds* in Arthur Lourié's piano transcription, I, mm. 42–48

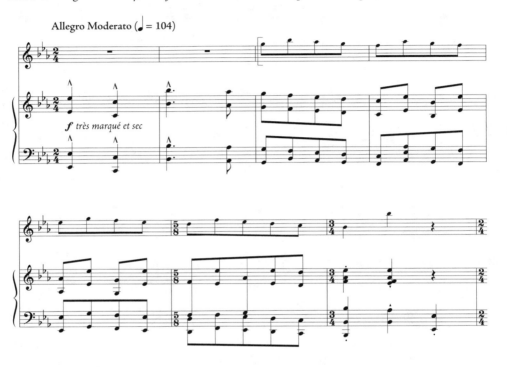

EX. 8-11B   Igor Stravinsky, *Octet for Winds* in Arthur Lourié's piano transcription, I, mm. 71–74

EX. 8-11C   Igor Stravinsky, *Octet for Winds* in Arthur Lourié's piano transcription, I, mm. 88–91

(and especially ironic) because the "pure" octatonic melody is accompanied in a straightforwardly recognizable D minor, a diatonic scale based on a tonic note that is not even present in the octatonic scale it is accompanying. Another joke, less arcane at the time, was ending the theme, on the last beat before the double bar, with a chord in

EX. 8-11D   Igor Stravinsky, *Octet for Winds* in Arthur Lourié's piano transcription, I, mm. 137–151

EX. 8-12   Igor Stravinsky, *Octet for Winds* in Arthur Lourié's piano transcription, II ("Tema con variazioni"), mm. 1–14

EX. 8-12   (*continued*)

attacca
subita

the "normally" unstable second inversion (or $^6_4$ position); the prank is repeated at the very end of the Octet, to show once and for all that it is only phonology and morphology that have been borrowed from obsolete styles, not grammar or syntax or any other "constructive principle."

EX. 8-13   Igor Stravinsky, *Octet for Winds* in Arthur Lourié's piano transcription, II, variation B, final cadence

attacca subita

Thereafter it is fairly unpretentious fun and games, very much in the untroubled spirit of the divertimento, the aristocratic party music of the eighteenth-century. What is marked "Var. A" is really a linking device (Stravinsky called it the "ribbons of scales variation") that comes as a refrain to connect the more elaborate "character" variations—that is, variations in the manner of recognizable genres. Variation B mimics a march, an inevitable choice for an ensemble dominated by brass. Its deadpan or "throwaway" final cadence (Ex. 8-13) must have especially unsettled early audiences who expected to have their ears clobbered by the composer of *The Rite of Spring*. Variation C is a waltz that metamorphoses smartly into Variation D, a polka, without the mediating link. The ribbons of scales return, however, to introduce the last variation (Ex. 8-14), which takes the small intervals of the theme and inverts them into large ones that give rise to more "Bachy" or "Baroquey" disjunct melodies already noted at the beginning of the Sinfonia.

The Finale (Ex. 8-15) seems at first the most candidly "pastiched" movement of all, what with its walking bass, its resolutely contrapuntal manner, and even a couple of specific references to the Bach musicians knew best in the 1920s (that is, the Bach you practiced at the keyboard—see the first bassoon in mm. 20–22, which brings the

EX. 8-14 Igor Stravinsky, *Octet for Winds* in Arthur Lourié's piano transcription, II, variation E (fugato), mm. 1–7

first C-minor fugue from the *Well-Tempered Clavier* to mind). It is also the movement, however, that most ostentatiously refuses the syntactical norms of eighteenth-century (i.e., "tonal") music. The C-major scale in the second bassoon that marches up a tenth and down again for thirty-two measures at the outset is as inert an ostinato as anything in *The Rite*, and takes little notice of its contrapuntal partners. (Compare the two bassoons at the outset and at mm. 11–12: the same ingredients differently aligned but equally indifferent as to the placement of the dissonances.)

This earnest contrapuntal start is thereafter continually mocked and subverted. The first time the whole texture, chugging in the woodwinds, is made the accompaniment to an incongruously lyrical line in the brass. The last time (Ex. 8-16), the energetic Bachian anapests from the first movement, having built up toward what seems an inevitable climax, suddenly give way to the smooth, "cool," and unmistakable syncopated rhythms of American dance music, vintage 1923. The surprise had been telegraphed slightly, when the bass instruments (at the beginning of the example) assumed the "3 + 3 + 2" pattern endemic to Latin American dance genres like the Afro-Cuban rumba or the Brazilian maxixe. That rhythm, and its derivations, dominates the rest of the movement, finally in ironic counterpoint with a "Bachian" two-register tune, slowed down in the second trumpet to end the piece.

This was not Stravinsky's first appropriation of American popular music, nor was he alone. He had included a "ragtime" in a little suite to accompany a dancing princess in *Histoire du soldat* ("The soldier's tale", 1918), a play with music based on a Russian folk tale, updated and translated into French, which he wrote in collaboration with a Swiss writer to make some quick money. Some indication of what such music meant to Stravinsky, and to many other Europeans, at the time may be gained from another *Ragtime*, this one scored for an ensemble of eleven instruments, that he completed (or

EX. 8-15 Igor Stravinsky, *Octet for Winds* in Arthur Lourié's piano transcription, III (Finale), mm. 1–33

EX. 8-15   (*continued*)

said so afterward) on the very morning of the Armistice that ended the Great War, 11 November 1918.

The American military presence in Europe from 1917, which turned the tide of the conflict and allowed it to end, made everything American wildly popular for a time. The going metaphor was borrowed from a familiar military hospital scene: New World giving Old a blood transfusion. America was young and vigorous. Its blood was healthy. Its exciting, novel, rhythmically infectious popular music was a symbol of that peculiarly determined postwar insouciance and dogged buoyancy. The use of popular music — traditionally ephemeral, humble, happy-making — fit perfectly with the new irony as well, teasing the inflated solemnity and the gaseous piety with which high art had been surrounded, and music most of all, in the prewar decades.

Strangely enough, it fit in perfectly with Stravinsky's Bachy style, too, as the ending of the Octet shows, and as can be readily explained "theoretically." The characteristic "baroque" rhythms — the walking basses, the energetic anapests — all involve eighths and sixteenths, values below the level of the *tactus* or "felt" beat (traditionally represented by the quarter note). They are, therefore, "subtactile" pulses. Ragtime and dance-music syncopations, too (what Stravinsky and other Europeans loosely called "jazz"), relied on a well-articulated subtactile pulse — that is, the little rhythmic subdivisions to which the accented long notes were shifted in the syncopated "jazz" style.

What is more, the rhythmic innovations of Stravinsky's "Russian" period — that is, the period of his maximalistic folk ballets — were based on equalized subtactile pulses as well. (Recall the shifting meters of the "Danse sacrale" in *The Rite*, which have nothing in common but the constant underlying sixteenth-note pulse that is often unexpressed on the lurching rhythmic surface.) It is this common rhythmic feature that allowed Stravinsky to draw, with facetious "objectivity," on such a wide assortment of seemingly unrelated idioms and yet have it all come out sounding "like Stravinsky."

PLUS SOME FAMOUS WORDS ABOUT IT

That self-evident mood of facetiousness that makes the Octet so charming, once the initial shock has worn off, gave Stravinsky another avenue for ironic play. He accompanied its appearance with a mock-forbidding manifesto, "Some Ideas about My Octuor" (using the French word for octet), which he published in a London arts magazine in January 1924. (It was the first of many such publicity pieces with which Stravinsky sought to manage the reception of his work.) Originally, this spectacularly

EX. 8-16   Igor Stravinsky, *Octet for Winds* in Arthur Lourié's piano transcription, III, end

humorless little essay must have been meant as a joke at his readers' expense, such as many French composers were then playing in accordance with the reigning postwar mood of debunkery. Stravinsky maintained the deadpan better than they, with the result that his peremptory words were taken seriously (at least by those unfamiliar with the music). Eventually Stravinsky seems to have taken them seriously himself.

Serious or no, it is an excellent gloss on the whole strange notion of "objectivity" in art that carried so much weight with composers burned by the big lies of romanticism. It begins right off with the announcement, "My Octuor is a musical object."[36] And it proceeds from there to define a stance that a French contemporary, Charles Koechlin, writing in 1926, called "an art that wishes to be plain, brisk, non-descriptive, and even non-expressive"[37] — and therefore the only truly novel or modern movement in music. Here are a few of Stravinsky's barked-out points, every sentence a paragraph unto itself, slightly edited to compensate for his (or his translator's) faulty English, and numbered for ready reference:

1. My Octuor is not an "emotive" work but a musical composition based on objective elements which are sufficient in themselves.

2. I have excluded from this work all sorts of nuances, which I have replaced by the play of volumes.

3. I have excluded all nuances between the *forte* and the *piano*; I have left only the forte and the piano.

4. The play of these volumes is one of the two active elements on which I have based the action of my musical text, the other element being the tempos [Stravinsky has "movements"] in their reciprocal connection.

5. This play of tempos and volumes that puts into action the musical text constitutes the impelling force of the composition and determines its form.

6. I admit the commercial exploitation of a musical composition, but I do not admit its emotive exploitation. To the author belongs the emotive exploitation of his ideas, the result of which is the composition; to the executant belongs the presentation of that composition in the way designated to him by its own form.

7. Form, in my music, derives from counterpoint. I consider counterpoint as the only means through which the attention of the composer is concentrated on purely musical questions. Its elements also lend themselves perfectly to an architectural construction.

8. This sort of music has no other aim than to be sufficient in itself. In general, I consider that music is only able to solve musical problems; and nothing else, neither the literary nor the picturesque, can be in music of any real interest. The play of the musical elements is the thing.[38]

The whole antiromantic platform passes in review. Plank 1 pronounces the ban on pathos. Planks 7 and 8 declare the formalist agenda: music is architecture in time and nothing else. Plank 6 is especially arch in its refusal to honor the romantic insistence that art and artists be "disinterested," devoid of any ulterior motives (but especially commercial ones). Stravinsky was only one of many artists who were reclaiming their etymological identities as artisans or artificers — skilled makers and doers, and professionals — as opposed to dreamers, reformers, philosophers, priests, politicians, or saints.

But plank 6 had another aim as well. In conjunction with planks 2 – 5, which describe the volumes and tempos of the composition in absolute terms of contrasted being that preclude all "becoming" or nuance, it ties the performer's hands and proclaims the inviolability of the text. (Actually it does even more than that, explicitly equating "text" and "work" for the first time and declaring the act of performance superfluous and even maleficent: in several other planks Stravinsky equates performance with "deformation.") Plank 3 exaggerates the case somewhat. The text of the Octet has its share of crescendos and descrescendos. But more characteristic of it are markings like "*p* subito" or "sempre *p*" or "staccato e *mf* sempre." And there are frequent streams of constant note values (as in a lot of baroque music, it is true) that enforce uniformity of tempo, since there are no differences to exaggerate.

The ultimate point in the direction of inelastic (and inexpressive) uniformity was reached in the works for piano that Stravinsky wrote in the 1920s for his own use as performer. That side career was undertaken out of necessity. Stravinsky had not only been deprived of his family inheritance by the Russian revolution, he was also deprived of the income from his most popular works because of his nationality: Russia did not sign international copyright agreements until the 1970s. The pieces he wrote for his own performance appearances were among the most severe and uncompromising of his early neoclassical pieces, partly because his piano playing, while competent, was not of a sort to compete with flamboyant virtuosos like his fellow émigré Serge Rachmaninoff (1873–1943), or even with Prokofieff. He therefore sought to make a virtue of nonflamboyance (or, to put it positively, of seriousness and assiduousness). The success he had with audiences, as we know because Rachmaninoff and Prokofieff grumbled about it in their letters, shows that he shrewdly calculated the allure of elitism. Whatever Stravinsky did was "chic." Stravinsky wrote himself three such vehicles in quick succession: a three-movement Concerto for piano and wind band (1923–1924), a three-movement Sonata (or to be Gallicly exact, a *Sonate*, 1924), and a four-movement suite called *Sérénade en la* ("Serenade in A", 1925). The exclusion of strings from the accompaniment to the Concerto was characteristic of Stravinsky at this time. Strings were too "humanoid" and "expressive" for his taste (especially as they were played then, with lots of throbbing vibrato and lots of *portamento* or sliding pitch). "Wind instruments seem to me to be more apt to render a certain rigidity of the form I had in mind than other instruments," Stravinsky wrote in "Some Ideas about My Octuor," especially the strings, "which are less cold and more vague."[39] The *Sonate* is distinguished by its expression markings — or rather, its lack of them. The first and last movements are headed, simply, $\quarternote = 112$, as cold and precise and expressively noncommittal as one could wish.

The *Sérénade* is a little less austere than that. Its movements have titles that give at least some indication of character, and the overall title, like "divertimento," recalls an aristocratic eighteenth-century entertainment genre. The suite was composed on commission from a record company that thought Stravinsky's reputation bankable (and the composer, who had made a point of "admit[ting] the commercial exploitation of a musical composition," readily acquiesced). The contract specified that the final product would be a set of two 10-inch 78 RPM discs, played by the composer, with one movement on each side, thereby imposing a time limit of three minutes per movement.

The third movement, "Rondoletto" (Ex. 8-17), again takes the absence of expression (or at least the absence of expression markings) to an extreme. Like the outer movements of the *Sonate* it carries only a numerical metronomic indication of tempo. Even more noteworthy is the absence of any dynamic marking. The whole composition implicitly unfolds at a single level of volume—the default level, or the level at which one plays without giving any particular thought to the matter (sometimes called "mezzo-fortissimo" by "studio hacks" who make their living sight-reading commercial jingles). The only exceptions are sforzandos, used as cadential punctuation, and a single "subito meno *f*." Also spectacularly unvaried is the rhythmic motion, a nearly unrelieved stream

EX. 8-17   Igor Stravinsky, *Sérénade en la*, "Rondoletto," mm. 1–27

EX. 8-17 *(continued)*

of sixteenth notes (the only relief being those same cadential chords marked *sforzando*, and there are only two). Not even at the end of the piece does Stravinsky leave the modification of the tempo to the "deformer." He "composes in" the ritardando as a series of gear shifts, from sixteenths to triplet eighths, thence to ordinary eighths and finally to quarters and halves.

That is "rigidity of form" and "dehumanization" with a vengeance. Indeed, Stravinsky was greatly attracted to the pianola, or player piano, which could perform with a mechanized rigidity beyond human capability (further identifying "dehumanization" with the superhuman, not the sub). He spent many hours transcribing his early works for the instrument, finally writing a piece for it directly (*Étude for pianola*, 1917); and he did his best, as his own piano performances from the period attest, to turn himself into a walking pianola. It would appear, then, that a memento of *futurismo*, the maximalist worship of the Machine Age, lingered — ironically! — in Stravinsky's "neoclassicism," further compromising its ostensibly retrospective character. It was meant to be — and certainly did become, for a while — the music of the future.

CHAPTER 9

Lost — or Rejected — Illusions

PROKOFIEFF; SATIE AGAIN; BERG'S *WOZZECK*; *NEUE SACHLICHKEIT*, *ZEITOPER*, *GEBRAUCHSMUSIK* (HINDEMITH, KRENEK, WEILL); KORNGOLD, RACHMANINOFF, AND A NEW *STILE ANTICO*

BREACHING THE FOURTH WALL

ynical modernism born of postwar disillusion was nowhere more pervasive than in theater, hitherto preeminently the art of illusion. "Illusionist," in fact, was the name derisively given by the hardened modernists of the twenties to the traditional theater, which thought of itself as realistic. There was no contradiction, really. Precisely to the extent that it strove to convince spectators that the staged and scripted action they were witnessing was real, the realistic theater obviously traded in illusion. Not that anybody was ever really convinced, of course; but audiences were eager to play along with conventions, whether of romanticism or of realism, for the sake of the emotional payoff they received in return for their "willing suspension of disbelief, which constitutes poetic faith."[1] (The famous quoted phrase is by the English Romantic poet Samuel Taylor Coleridge.)

One of the main conventions on which theatrical illusions of reality depended was the imaginary "fourth wall" that separated the audience from the players, who were never allowed to see through it. All illusion of reality would be destroyed the moment the players showed any awareness of the audience's presence, let alone addressed it directly. The only traditional genres in which the fourth wall could be breached were farce and satire, which made the least pretense to realism, and even occasionally mocked it. But what was an exceptional "special effect" in traditional theater became ubiquitous, as an aspect of irony, after the Great War, when artists became compulsorily self-conscious, and art had to advertise itself as art as a pledge of good faith.

The playwright most often cited as the protagonist of this move was Luigi Pirandello, already named for us by Ortega in a passage quoted in the previous chapter. As its very title suggests, Pirandello's play *Sei personaggi in cerca d'autore* ("Six characters in search of an author," 1921), challenges every convention of the illusionist theater, at times by ironically exaggerating them. The characters, refugees from an unfinished play, invade a rehearsal of a different play and, flagrantly breaching the fourth wall, confront the author, the actors, and the director with the request that they resolve the horrifying drama of betrayal and incest, murder and suicide in which they have become involved.

By thus insisting (or pretending to insist) that there are levels of reality within the theatrical illusion, Pirandello blurs the line between theatrical illusion and lived reality and directly exhorts the audience to ponder what he has done. And by portraying (or pretending to portray) the characters as independent agents (and therefore human), the whole "realistic" theatrical enterprise, the conventions on which it is based, and all parties to them from author to audience, are implicitly accused of voyeurism, taking pleasure in the misery of others. Like Stravinsky, but somewhat earlier, Pirandello unmasked the esthetic illusion to expose its ethical infractions. He used art to indict art and mock its audience for complacently believing in the "vitalist" fallacy.

But Pirandello had forerunners, and one of them was a composer. Serge Prokofieff (1891–1953), whom we met in the previous chapter as one of the "neoclassical" Stravinsky's skeptical younger colleagues, actually anticipated Stravinsky in stylistic pastiche, and anticipated Pirandello in the ironizing game. As often happens, there was more of personal rivalry than of principled opposition in Prokofieff's demurrers to Stravinsky. In the summer of 1917, between the two big political upheavals that shook Russia during that turbulent year (first the February revolution that toppled the tsar, then the October coup d'état that put the Soviet government in place), Prokofieff sought escape by going to a country house where there was no piano on which to experiment, and both as a lark and as an exercise to discipline his ear, writing a symphony "in the style of Haydn."

Needless to say, it was no such thing. Rather it was a "culinary" romp of a kind that, as we saw in the previous chapter, composers had turned out all through the nineteenth century (and particularly in Russia). Its "eighteenth-century" was the usual imaginary one, pasteurized and homogenized: Prokofieff's third movement, for example, was not a minuet, as in any Haydn symphony, but an anachronistic gavotte (Ex. 9-1). In view of the quirky harmonic progression that breaks every rule of eighteenth-century voice leading, moreover, it is obvious that Prokofieff was prompted to write his gavotte less by the example of Bach than by the example of Ambroise Thomas or Chaikovsky, as displayed in Exx. 8-3 and 8-4.

The "neoclassicism" of Prokofieff's "Classical Symphony," then, was not really modernist—another reminder that stylistic "retrospectivism" as such was neither a necessary component of neoclassicism or, when present, a sufficient one. It can amount, as in Prokofieff's "Classical Symphony," to nothing more than ingratiating nostalgia. Prokofieff's next major work, however, though it was not stylistically retrospective at all, was a milestone in the postwar "neoclassical" project. And although it took the form of a genuinely funny comic opera called *Lyubov' k tryom apel'sinam* ("The love for three oranges"), it was found (like Pirandello's comedies) to be anything but ingratiating by its early audiences. "They found mockery and challenges and grotesques in my *Oranges*," the composer wrote, compounding irony with irony, "while all I had done was write a merry show."[2]

EX. 9-1   Serge Prokofieff, "Classical Symphony," III (Gavotte), in the composer's piano arrangement

ART AS PLAYTHING

Prokofieff wrote his merry show in New York, having joined the great wave of emigration that followed the revolutions of 1917, a disastrous "brain drain" for Russia that cost

it a number of leading composers, including (besides Stravinsky and Prokofieff) the towering figure of Sergei Rachmaninoff (1873–1943) who in addition to being the most prominent Russian composer of his generation was a world-renowned piano virtuoso and an outstanding conductor as well. (The transliterated spellings Prokofieff and Rachmaninoff are those that the composers themselves adopted for professional use abroad.)

Prokofieff left Russia by traveling east, so as to avoid the battlefields of World War I. He sailed from Vladivostok, a Siberian port on the Pacific, and made his way to New York by way of Yokohama, Japan, and San Francisco. He had a draft scenario for the new opera with him on board ship, given him by the famous theatrical director

FIG. 9-1   Serge Prokofieff, by Pyotr Konchalovsky (1876–1956).

Vsevolod Meyerhold (1874–1940), with whom he had planned to collaborate. By the time he reached his American destination he had elaborated the libretto into its final form. Having signed a contract with an American impresario, he wrote the opera (in Russian) in 1919 in New York, for performance in 1921 in Chicago (in French).

Prokofieff's libretto was an adaptation of a draft by Meyerhold that was an adaptation of a commedia dell'arte scenario (that is, a blueprint for improvisation by a troupe of masked players) by Carlo Gozzi (1720–1806), a Venetian "gentleman" playwright, that was itself an adaptation of a pair of fairy tales that were published in Naples in 1634. With every telling the work became further encrusted with theatrical artifice and esthetic doctrine, so that by the time Prokofieff was through with it, *The Love for Three Oranges* was the epitome of "art about art," almost more Pirandellian than Pirandello.

The story, stemming from the old Neapolitan tales, was silly simplicity itself. An old king, to cure his son's melancholia, oils the pavement in front of the palace in hopes that somebody will take a tumble and make the prince laugh. The victim turns out to be the dread witch Fata Morgana, who takes revenge by casting a spell on the prince, causing him to fall in love with three oranges, which he must seek though it take him to the ends of the earth. Inside the last of them, he finds the beautiful princess who becomes his bride. (The other oranges also contained fairy princesses, who shriveled up and died when the prince did not give them water in time.)

The *fiaba* or theatricalized fable that Gozzi fashioned on the basis of this story was already a polemical work — the sort of tract or pamphlet in the guise of art that became suddenly popular again in the aftermath of the Great War. Gozzi's aristocratic taste had been offended by the vulgarized theater of his day, as exemplified by modern playwrights who turned out sham tragedies, "in which you find characters hurling themselves from windows or turrets without breaking their necks, and similar miracles"[3] (here we might substitute the bloated musical harangues of Mahler or Scriabin), or equally sham comedies of manners that "titillate under pretext of moral instruction" (and here we might substitute the gaudy operas of Strauss).

The quotes are from a wholly superfluous but exceptionally detailed scene in Gozzi's otherwise rough scenario, which he called the *contrasto in terzo*: a "quarrel trio" in which three characters, one of them the author's obvious stand-in, for no good reason declare and debate their preferences in drama. When Meyerhold fleshed out Gozzi's scenario for some performances in St. Petersburg in 1914, he seized upon the "quarrel trio" and expanded it to the point where it became, both temporally and spatially, the frame of the entire play.

The spatial frame consisted of twin turrets on opposite sides of the stage, housing a collection of clowns representing a bunch of "esthetes" noisily advocating contradictory convictions about what drama ought to be. They form the onstage audience for the theater-within-a-theater in which the action takes place. This much was already a standard practice, if an unusual one, in the traditional theater when ironic distancing was called for: recall the players in *Hamlet*, or, more recently, the puppet show in Stravinsky's *Petrushka*. But Meyerhold took it so much further than any previous dramatist as to turn the difference into one not just of degree but of kind: many theater historians regard his *Love for Three Oranges* as the very cradle of modernist theater.

Meyerhold's action began with a parade in which the actors portraying the esthetes — divided into camps of "Realistic Comedians" and "High Tragedians" — entered dueling with quills. The fight was broken up by a trio of "cranks" or eccentrics. One, restraining the Comedians, shouts: "We are fed up with your wares, contemptible farce-mongers, these four- and five-act comedies without any content at all, but with the inevitable pistol shot at the end!"[4] Another, holding off the Tragedians, thunders: "We are bored to death with plays that have such a load of dreary philosophy and such a dearth of healthy laughter, to say nothing of stagecraft!" The third, pointing through the fourth wall at the audience (the real one, that is, sitting in the dark), said, "Look — they are waiting there for some actors who can show them the real thing!" The battle, thus joined, continued in an undertone, and with frequent eruptions, throughout the play. The constant comment from the onstage "audience," and its strenuous exhortations to the actors, completely destroying any sense of theatrical illusion, furnished the play's temporal frame.

Meyerhold's *Love for Three Oranges*, then, was perhaps the earliest application, at least in such an overwhelming dose, of the illusion-destroying "art as art" gimmickry that would within a couple of decades become a modernist cliché. What makes it historically so significant is the clarity of its descent from an eighteenth-century aristocratic model, thus connecting two important strands in what would become the heritage of postwar "neoclassicism." Even if Prokofieff had never set it, Meyerhold's response to Gozzi would have been a prime document of the nascent modernist manner and its sources. But since Prokofieff did set it, it becomes an indispensable link in the history of twentieth-century opera as well.

Prokofieff's opera is a "document" in its own right, since Prokofieff seized upon Meyerhold's distancing ideas and expanded them as much as Meyerhold had expanded Gozzi's. To Meyerhold's Comedians, Tragedians, and Cranks (the latter's number upped to ten), Prokofieff added a couple of opera-specific groups of his own devising: "Lyricists," forever demanding "romantic love, moons, tender kisses," and "Empty Heads," bent on "entertaining nonsense, witty double entendres, fine costumes." In this way Prokofieff thought to cover every possible sort of hackneyed operatic situation and the sort of taste that demanded it.

The running gag in Prokofieff's *Love for Three Oranges* is the way in which the Comedians, Tragedians, Lyricists, and Empty Heads butt in whenever the action approaches one of their pet stereotypes to egg it on; but of course in so doing they unerringly puncture whatever mood it is that they are trying to abet. The Cranks, eager to foil all factions (but particularly the Tragedians), do more than that. They actually intervene in the plot — Pirandello-fashion, we may be tempted to say, but before Pirandello — to change its course. The audience in the theater, like Pirandello's audience, is both entertained and given lots to ponder.

The third scene of act III, in which the Prince opens the magic fruit and finds the princesses, would by rights have been the big "pathos scene" in the opera. It has love, it has death, and it bids fair to supply all the attendant emotions in abundance. But the onstage spectators quash everything. The three princesses come out of their oranges dying of thirst, each begging for water more insistently — exactly a major second's worth more insistently — than the last: see Ex. 9-2. Between the appearance of the second princess and that of the third, a passing platoon of soldiers carries off the two corpses most unsentimentally. When the third princess is about to die of thirst, and the Tragedians are licking their chops at the prospect, the Cranks fetch from their turret a bucket of water, deposit it at center stage, and save Princess Ninetta's life (Ex. 9-3). No tragedy.

The Prince now sings at relative length of his love for the Princess: his little solo, forty measures in all, is actually the longest "aria" in the whole stingy opera. When the Princess begins to respond, the Lyricists smell a love duet in the making and shout "At

EX. 9-2A Serge Prokofieff, *Love for Three Oranges*, Act III, scene 3, fig. 384 (the first princess begs for water)

Give me something to drink! Right away, or else I'll die of thirst, of cruel thirst, of mortal thirst!

last! Something romantic, sentimental!" The Cranks hiss at them to shut up. Their fight distracts the lovers from their singing. No love duet. These interferences by the "audience" on stage carry to the audience in the hall a message that Ortega, that happy theorist of "dehumanization," would have gladly endorsed: For better or worse, the meddling Cranks affirm, the play is literally their plaything—and art is ours. That is the affable side of disillusion. Art is fun again. Expect no more from it.

A NEW ATTITUDE TOWARD THE "CLASSICS"?

Unlike so many modernist classics, then, *The Love for Three Oranges* is easy to enjoy once the shock of its novelty has worn off. It was one of the harbingers of that revolution in taste, begotten (it is true) of misery, that cultivated hygienic belly laughs to replace the neurasthenic wheezing of prewar "decadence," a therapeutic against late, late romanticism's gangrenous grandiosity. From this standpoint the emblematic moment, just as it

EX. 9-2B   Serge Prokofieff, *Love for Three Oranges*, Act III, scene 3, fig. 391 (the second princess begs for water)

Nicolette: Give me something to drink! Right away, or else...
Linette: Just a drop! My eyes grow dim...

was for Gozzi, is the scene of the hypochondriac Prince's cure in act II. At the sight of Fata Morgana's knobby knees and withered behind, the Prince goes into gales of laughter, represented in the music by a little set piece over an ostinato (Ex. 9-4a), and with the Prince's "ha-ha-ha-HA" an inevitable parody of the opening unison in . . . need it be named?

The new debunking spirit was perhaps most vivid when the objects debunked were the untouchable icons of the past. Beethoven's Fifth came in for ribbing from many sides. Stravinsky quoted its last movement in a little *Souvenir d'un marche boche* ("Souvenir of a 'Kraut' March") that he contributed to a lavish art book that was sold in 1915 to raise money for Belgian war relief (Ex. 9-4b). In a ballet called *El sombrero de tres picos* ("The three-cornered hat"), produced by Diaghilev's Ballets Russes in 1919, the Spanish composer Manuel de Falla (1876–1946) poked more fun at it (Ex. 9-4c) when a bunch of asinine gendarmes come knocking peremptorily and "fatefully" at someone's door.

But as early as 1913, Erik Satie had already spoofed the Fifth's colossal coda in a cute little piano piece with a ridiculously serious subject: "de Podophthalma," the last of a suite of three *Embryons desséchées* ("Dried embryos"), music purporting to give a scientific description of marine life (Ex. 9-4d; it depicts crayfish hunting for food and incorporates the French equivalent of "A-Hunting We Will Go" in addition to the Beethoven reference). A deliberate study in pompous triviality, it passes a wicked judgment on the romantic taste for big statements in art.

EX. 9-2C   Serge Prokofieff, *Love for Three Oranges*, Act III, scene 3, fig. 415 (Ninetta, the third princess, begs for water)

Give me something to drink! Right away, or else I'll die of thirst

EX. 9-3 Serge Prokofieff, *Love for Three Oranges*, Act III, scene 3, fig. 418 (Princess Ninetta gets her drink)

Les Ridicules (ténore) apportent de la tour un seau d'eau et, l'ayant placé au milieu de la scéne, retournent dans la tour.

"Hey! Listen, have you got some water?" "Seems we do." "Well, let her have it. Let her wet her whistle"

(Stage direction:) The cranks (tenors) bring a bucket of water out of their tower and place it center stage. Then they go back into the tower.

EX. 9-4A Caricature of Beethoven's Fifth, Serge Prokofieff, *Love for Three Oranges*, Act I, scene 1

EX. 9-4B Caricature of Beethoven's Fifth, Igor Stravinsky, *Souvenir d'un marche boche*

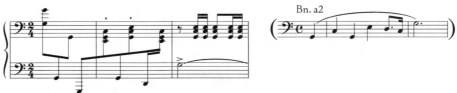

EX. 9-4C Caricature of Beethoven's Fifth, Manuel da Falla, *El sombrero de tres picos*

EX. 9-4C (*continued*)

EX. 9-4D Caricature of Beethoven's Fifth, Erik Satie, "De podophthalma" (from *Embryons desséchées*, no. 3)

Of course to a card-carrying Frenchman like Satie, or a Russian in wartime like Stravinsky, Beethoven's Germanness was both bait and butt. But the mood spread widely after the war, when disgust at Germany translated into disgust at artistic pretensions to weight and significance, especially in music (the "German" art par excellence, at least in its weightier manifestations). Part of the postwar cult of irony, certainly on the part of "Allied" (or, in Falla's case, "neutral") composers, was de-Germanification. Wagner, banned in many Allied countries during the war, did not come back immediately; and when he did, it was no longer with the sense that he bore the banner of the universal tradition in music, but very much as a German.

"HOW" VS. "WHAT"

Yet in the final analysis, *The Love for Three Oranges*, being a farce that can be read as satire, came by its irony the old-fashioned way, as did all the little spoofs quoted in Ex. 9-4. Their frostiness and cynicism had a long history in musical comedy. And Prokofieff's ingratiating music, while modern enough and (when needed) grotesque, is audience-friendly in a manner that comedy traditionally demands. In the guise of an orchestral suite it has been a repertory piece since the time of the premiere. For all the artifice expended on it by three successive adapters, moreover, the opera makes a fairly unpretentious impression, as a farce must. Coming in 1919 (or in 1921, to give it the date of its first performance) it might well have proven an isolated experiment in "farcical maximalism" rather than a bellwether.

It was only when devices of ironic distance comparable to those in *The Love for Three Oranges* began to show up in operas with serious or tragic or pretentious subjects, or operas by German composers who still took Beethovenesque notions of musical greatness at face value, that a "sea change" in the cultural atmosphere was incontestable. Such subjects would have received a very different sort of treatment from musical dramatists who traded unself-consciously in empathy and sincerity — or rather, who could still trade unself-consciously in the sort of illusions of empathy and sincerity that artists in the romantic tradition were trained to administer.

Alban Berg's opera *Wozzeck*, conceived in 1914 and composed between 1919 and 1922, is now widely regarded as the most serious and significant opera to emerge from the postwar decade. Despite its arcane harmonic idiom ("atonality" à la Schoenberg, the composer's teacher) and its great difficulty for performers, the opera became an immediate international hit after its Berlin premiere in December 1925, with seventeen productions in Germany and ten abroad by 1933, when performances were temporarily halted by the Nazi regime. By now it is a staple of the operatic repertory everywhere. (The last bastion of resistance, New York's Metropolitan Opera, fell before it in 1958.) Productions of it are not newsmakers; they are expected, and accepted, the world over.

Any attempt to account for the "unaccountable" success of this "difficult" "atonal" composition must of course begin where it began, with the story. Berg based the opera on *Woyzeck*, a brutal naturalistic play by Georg Büchner (1813 – 37), a short-lived and for a long time very obscure German writer who had been rediscovered by the expressionists. Inspired by a notorious crime story as reported in the newspapers, the play depicted

FIG. 9-2 *Wozzeck*, autograph score page from Act I, scene 4 (Passacaglia): Wozzeck and the Doctor.

the mental and moral degeneration of a miserable, much-despised soldier, who, crazed by jealousy and despair, murders his mistress. One sees the passive and dullwitted title character abused by all with whom he comes in contact—by his captain, who treats him as a personal servant; by a doctor, who employs him as a guinea pig for dietary experiments; by a conceited drum major who seduces his mistress Marie and beats him up into the bargain; and by Marie herself, who taunts him over his humiliation—until even this human block of wood is provoked to crude and tragic action.

Left unfinished at Büchner's death, *Woyzeck* was speculatively pieced together from a sheaf of unfinished variants that even left the ending in doubt, by an editor who misspelled the title as *Wozzeck* thanks to the author's difficult handwriting. It was first published in 1879 and first performed in Munich in 1913. The first Vienna performance, which Berg attended, took place the next year. Berg excerpted fifteen of its twenty-seven brief scenes and set them practically verbatim, the way Debussy set Maeterlinck's *Pelléas et Mélisande*. Thus rendered even more compact and concentrated than the original play, Berg's opera traded brazenly in the kind of shocking violence made popular by the operas of the verismo school. The abject title character, moreover, and the world as seen through his increasingly demented eyes, were a natural for expressionistic — that is, luridly subjective — depiction.

Unlike the laconic original, which made a studied attempt at deadpan reportage, Berg's musical treatment was highly manipulative: "operatic" in the fullest (indeed, potentially derogatory) sense of the word, replete with authorial interventions in the form of orchestral interludes that commented on the action — in the Wagnerian manner, one might say, or like a Greek chorus — by the use of leitmotifs. Berg saw himself as exposing a social problem — that of society's ill treatment of *wir arme Leut*, "us poor folk" as Wozzeck calls his kind in the first scene, a phrase that reverberates thereafter as a verbal leitmotif. Not only did Berg give it a musical counterpart which could function much more freely in the opera's texture than a catchphrase can ever do in a play, but he bent every effort to acting as his title character's defense attorney, as he frankly put it in an essay on the opera, justifying his crime through "an appeal to humanity through its representatives, the audience."[5]

The opera's classic status testifies to the composer's success in accomplishing these goals — not that they are at all unusual goals for an opera composer. What was exceedingly unusual was the way in which Berg went about the task, which only seemed to place gratuitous obstacles in his path. For the relationship between the humanizing music and the horrific subject is not at all direct. It is mediated through a huge and potentially distracting — or at least distancing — barrage of composerly virtuosity.

Some of that virtuosity was of a familiar kind — brilliantly colored orchestration, mimicry of many kinds of "ambient" music (folksongs, marches, waltzes, all reflected through an "atonal" distorting mirror), intricate motivic work and leitmotivic trans-formations. Wagner and Strauss, too, were ostentatious musical manipulators, and Wagner's operatic reforms succeeded at least in part because he was able to turn his project into a staggeringly impressive composerly tour de force. But the Wagnerian or Straussian virtuosity, however allied it may have been with "symphonic" techniques, was self-avowedly "liberatory." It aimed at the destruction of "rounded" or discrete musical forms and the enabling of a new time-scale based on whole acts, freeing the composer to react without "purely musical" mediation to the shape of the drama.

Berg's opera, in stark contrast, invokes a whole panoply of discrete ("closed") musical forms and genres; and what is more, the forms and genres were those of instrumental music, seemingly alien and irrelevant to opera, some of them just as obsolescent as the ones Stravinsky was reviving in his piano and chamber music. The first scene of the opera, for example, in which Wozzeck is shown shaving the Captain and putting up with the latter's self-absorbed and insensitive maunderings, is cast in the form of a grotesque orchestral suite, as follows:

mm. 1–29: "Präludium"
30–50: "Pavane"
51–64: "Cadenza" (solo viola)
65–108: "Gigue"
109–114: "Cadenza" (contrabassoon)
115–136: "Gavotte" (mm. 127–132 "Double I"; mm. 133–136 "Double II")
136–153: "Air"
153–171: "Reprise" (Präludium in reverse)

It has been pointed out time and again that, so far as the listener in the opera house is concerned, all of this information is altogether arcane and immaterial. One could go further and show that the designations do not even fit. A pavane was a sixteenth-century dance in duple meter and with three repeated strains. (Obsolete even in Bach's day, it was the sort of esoteric item only musicologists were likely to know about in Berg's day, except for a modish piano piece by Ravel that might conceivably have been Berg's "source.") Berg's duple meter is disguised by triplets and is not consistently maintained. Instead of three strains there is something like a loose ternary form. The gigue and the gavotte, while conforming a little more to their prototypes, are still unrecognizable except to an analyst of the score who has been alerted to their presence. (The "doubles" of the gavotte, for example, do go through successive rhythmic diminutions—first to triplets, then to sixteenths and thirty-seconds—but without having recognized the gavotte one cannot know that the faster rhythms represent doubles, or even variations.) If we accept that these references to baroque dances are in-jokes, then we are back to Ortega's ironically "jesting" art, quite at odds with the cathartic social tragedy that brought *Wozzeck* success in the opera house. Of course, the opening scene *is* largely satiric (at the expense of the idiotic Captain, who fancies himself a philosopher). But it has one very serious moment, Wozzeck's speech about "us poor folk" (Ex. 9-5), and that moment is not exempted from the in-joke, being designated "Air" in apparent reference to Bach's famously lyrical Air from the D-major orchestral suite with which it shares its $\frac{3}{2}$ time

EX. 9-5   Alban Berg, *Wozzeck*, Act I, scene 1, "Air" ("Wir arme Leut")

EX. 9-5 (continued)

Poor folk like us! Money you see, Captain, sir, money! Somebody who has no money! Well, just let him try bringing his own kind into the world in a good moral way!

signature, and which was known separately to millions as the "Air on the G String," after a famously sentimental concert transcription by the German violinist August Wilhelmj.

But if Wozzeck's "Air" is part of the ironic or distanced substratum that haunts the scene, his actual music is treated virtually without irony, and has two moments of special poignancy. One is the setting of the first three words, which, as we know, became one of the opera's chief leitmotifs. Characteristically for a composer in Schoenberg's orbit, Berg treats the leitmotif (according to the principles of "emancipated dissonance") both as a melody and as a harmony, the latter being the sum of all its notes played as a piquant and memorable "seventh chord" (minor triad plus major seventh) of a kind that never occurs in diatonic practice, hence has no classified status in "tonal" music (Ex. 9-6).

The other special moment comes slightly earlier, at the join between the first and second doubles of the "Gavotte" (Ex. 9-7). The Captain has reproached Wozzeck for having a child out of wedlock, and therefore unbaptized. Wozzeck reminds the Captain of Jesus's charity, quoting his words from the Bible, "Suffer the little children to come unto Me." The whole passage is set off at a slower tempo than the rest, which becomes *Noch langsamer* ("even slower") at the biblical quote, followed by a veritable spotlight of a *Molto rit.* at the end of the measure. The harmony comes to rest, at the last beat, on a dominant-seventh chord that is prepared (through an augmented sixth) as if it were the actual dominant of C minor, and the violins corroborate its status with a throbbing, extended G — an unequivocally "tonal" moment of repose to coincide with, and underscore, a rare moment of unfeigned human warmth.

Both the musical effect and the attendant mood are broken by the next words from the infuriatingly obtuse Captain, accompanied by the usual busily "motivic" atonal web. But that atonal web has now been characterized, through contrast, as representing the inhumane, uncaring world that "Wir arme Leut" are forced to inhabit, as it is perceived by the opera's tortured protagonist. Berg has turned his irony on his own "normal" musical language, which is now paradoxically branded as abnormal or subnormal in its distance from true human feeling. This brief ironic byplay, contrasting the "tonal" with

EX. 9-6   Alban Berg, *Wozzeck*, "Wir arme Leut" leitmotif

EX. 9-7   Alban Berg, *Wozzeck*, Act I, scene 1, "Quasi Gavotte," transition from "Double I" to "Double II"

"...even if nobody says Amen before he was made. The Lord spake: 'Suffer the little children to come unto me!'"
"What is He saying there? What kind of weird answer is that?"

the "atonal," is redeemed at the other end of the opera with a wrenching cathartic force that must account for much of the opera's success with audiences who could not care less about gavottes, let alone "atonality."

That cathartic moment depends for its effect on the audience's enduring the ugliness of the central dramatic intrigue, Marie's infidelity with the Drum Major. It is developed over the whole course of act II, the five scenes of which are cast, according to Berg's arcanely jesting scheme, as a five-movement symphony:

> Scene 1: "Sonata," in which Marie, preening herself after her night with the Drum Major, nevertheless accepts money from Wozzeck to care for their child, and experiences a moment of bad conscience; Scene 2: "Fantasia and fugue," in which the Captain and the Doctor, taunting Wozzeck, plant the first inkling in his mind that Marie has been unfaithful; Scene 3: "Largo," in which Wozzeck confronts Marie, who is cold and defiant; Scene 4: "Scherzo," in which Wozzeck sees Marie dancing in the arms of the Drum Major; Scene 5: "Introduction and Rondo," in which the Drum Major beats Wozzeck and gloats over him.

Having experienced the ultimate humiliation, the formerly passive Wozzeck is now ready for the retaliatory action that is displayed in act III. The relationship of the music to the action is still mediated through a scrim of ingenious technical studies, but no longer does the composer invoke arcane or "classic" genres. Rather, each scene is designated an "Invention," concerned with some elemental musical particle. Their "abstract" musical procedures are vivid and readily apprehended along with the drama. Where in the earlier acts there had been harsh raillery and satire, there is nothing now but a headlong dash to catastrophe.

- Scene 1, in which Marie reads from the Bible and repents, is called an "Invention on a Theme," and takes the form of a theme, six brief variations, and a concluding "fugue" (actually just a fugal exposition), all of them duly marked off in the score, but just as easily followed by ear. The last two variations, in which Marie reads with mounting emotion, "lapse" into the key of F minor, repeating the effect already encountered in Wozzeck's colloquy with the Captain, whereby tonal harmony underscores the moments of particular emotional warmth, as if to convey its pressure.
- Scene 2, the most famous tour de force in the opera, is called an "Invention on a Note," and depicts the murder, by the side of a lake. It is haunted from beginning to end by the note B, sometimes (as at the beginning) held out as a bass pedal; sometimes reiterated in a high register in a weird tone-color like string flageolets (artificial harmonics) or xylophone; or sometimes sustained in a tremolo. At the climactic moment (Ex. 9-8), when the moon rises blood-red and Wozzeck comes after Marie with a knife, the B is simultaneously sustained by the strings as a pedal in six octaves, pervading the whole range of the orchestra, and also beaten as a tattoo by the kettledrum that crescendos to the moment of the lethal deed and decrescendos to the end of the scene. Twice the note is prominently sung: first by Wozzeck, unaccompanied by the orchestra, to the word "Nothing," when the nervous Marie asks what's on his mind; then by Marie, screaming "Help!" as Wozzeck plunges the dagger into her throat. (This moment will resonate with the same cry in Schoenberg's *Erwartung*—Ex. 6-16—in the memory of anyone who has heard it.) The

entr'acte following this scene consists of two unison Bs played by the orchestra in deafening crescendos (Ex. 9-9), leading into

- Scene 3, in which Wozzeck's deed is suspected by the denizens of a tavern to which he has repaired. It is called "Invention on a Rhythm," and consists of myriad repetitions of the eight-note rhythm first heard in the thundering bass drum during the entr'acte and then hacked out as the curtain goes up on "an out-of-tune upright piano on stage," as the score specifies. The rhythm is derived from the start of Wozzeck's shout at the climax of scene 2, *Ich nicht, Marie! und kein Andrer auch nicht!* ("Not I, Marie, and no one else either," in Ex. 9-8). Probably the most arcanely "irrelevant" and inaudible musical jest in the score is the fact that the series of instrumental entrances that take place during, and contribute to, the first big crescendo in the entr'acte are spaced out according to this rhythm, something that can be discovered only by analyzing the score. As the scene progresses, the rhythm is set against itself at many different rates of speed over a basso ostinato that also consists of repetitions of it, all symbolizing Wozzeck's mounting fear and guilt.

EX. 9-8   Alban Berg, *Wozzeck*, Act III, scene 2, the murder

E X. 9-8 (continued)

("What did you say?")
"–Nothing....."
"Look how red the moon has risen!"
"Like bloody steel!"
"Why are you shivering? What do you want?"
"Not me, Marie! And no one else either!"
"Help."

EX. 9-9   Alban Berg, *Wozzeck*, Act III, Entr'acte between scenes 2 and 3

- Scene 4 is an "Invention on a Six-Note Chord." The chord that pervades it would once again have felt right at home in *Erwartung*: it can be construed as consisting of an "atonal triad" plus a stack of perfect fourths (Ex. 9-10). The reference may well have been intentional, since Wozzeck is depicted in this scene as gripped, like the mad protagonist of Schoenberg's "monodrama," by anxious forebodings. He returns to the scene of the crime, where he has left incriminating evidence behind. He finds the murder weapon and throws it into the lake, but, fearing it is too near the shore, wades out and drowns. (This climactic event was contributed by the editor who prepared Büchner's unfinished play for posthumous publication; it could not have been Büchner's intention, because it departs from the historical events to which the playwright was otherwise faithful, and Büchner has his Woyzeck reappear in a later scene.) The Doctor and the Captain happen by, hear ominous sounds arising from the lake, and flee. The sounds made by the waters closing in on Wozzeck are another reminiscence of *Erwartung*: they consist of overlapping chromatic scales at different tempos, like the final "dissolve" in Schoenberg's opera.

EX. 9-10   "Leitharmony" in Alban Berg, *Wozzeck*, Act III, scene 4

"Thematic chord" in Act III, sc. 4

- Scene 5, designated "Invention on an Eighth-Note Motion" depicts Wozzeck's and Marie's little son on his hobbyhorse, uncomprehending when cruelly taunted by a group of children with his mother's death (Ex. 9-11). It is cast in $\frac{12}{8}$ meter, and the eighth notes, which represent the children at play, never let up. The harmony at the end of the scene (and the opera) is poignant: the eighth-note ostinato begins to oscillate between two chords that together contain five notes of a whole-tone scale. The remaining note, G, is played by the strings together with its fifth, D, which is not part of the whole-tone scale, but by consonantly supporting the G gives it the weight of a tonic root whose third, B, is found within the whole-tone ostinato — thus bringing the whole wretched and violent action to rest on what is to all intents and purposes an unconventionally prepared but esthetically conventional, and even placid, tonic triad. That incongruous "unearned" placidity, distilling the perspective of the dopey little boy who is left alone onstage at the end, casts an ironic pall over everything that preceded it.

The ostensibly "abstract" inventions through which Berg shaped the scenes of act III are less overtly ironic, less obviously a jest in their relationship to the starkly naturalistic action, than those of the preceding acts. In every case, the inventive play unfolds through pressing ostinatos that symbolize through analogy the obsessions that now drive the maddened title character. By turns we are bombarded with obsessively repeated pitches, rhythms, and chords as the opera runs its obsessive, bloody course. The famous entr'acte between scenes 2 and 3 — the unison crescendos on the symbolically fraught B — returns us frankly to the world of expressionism, allowing us momentarily to inhabit the mind of the deranged antihero whose head is throbbing with the memory of his crime. And surely no art was ever less ironical than expressionism.

Yet the separation of elements — now pitches, now rhythms, now chords — is even here supremely "artful" and showy. The moment we notice the technical tours de force that constitute the portrayal (and here we can hardly help noticing them) we are put at a distance from the events portrayed in a manner that Ortega y Gasset, in his famous tract of 1925 (the year of *Wozzeck*'s premiere), equated purely and simply, and very approvingly, with the nature of art itself. Despite all the vividly "veristic" and "expressionistic" aspects that Berg inherited from his immediate predecessors, and even

EX. 9-11   Alban Berg, *Wozzeck*, Act III, scene 5, end

EX. 9-11 *(continued)*

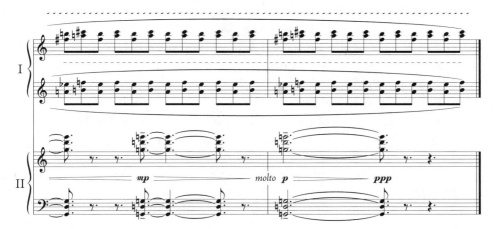

maximalized, there is also, in ironic contradiction, the same refusal (or inability) to make his art "transparent" that characterizes virtually all of postwar modernism, and that completely contradicts the aims of verismo or expressionism—and, behind them, of romanticism.

PUTTING THINGS "IN QUOTES"

The passage in Ortega's essay subtitled "A Few Drops of Phenomenology" (after the branch of philosophy that inquires into the nature of appearances and perception) can help us understand Berg's predicament. Ortega imagines a deathbed scene witnessed by the wife of the dying man, his doctor, a reporter, and a painter.[6] Their various relationships to the event are analyzed in turn. The author's conclusion is that as the four witnesses are each more detached from the event emotionally than the last, they are by the same token increasingly observant of it in all its details. It is that maximum detachment that enables the artist "objectively" to channel the emotions of the lived reality into significant form. That form then becomes, for the artist and those who truly appreciate his art *as* art, the object and the aim of contemplation. And that is irony at its highest and best, no longer to be simply identified with humor. It is the irony that transforms experience into art.

Wozzeck is a monument to that idea—or rather, it reflects the historical moment in which that idea achieved its completest triumph over the earlier, "vitalist" view of art as a mirror reflection or reproduction of lived reality, valuable only to the extent that it transmitted to observers the feelings of a participant. Although dependent for its originating impulse on "lived" reality—in Ortega's case the great man's death, in Berg's the historical crime that had first served Büchner as an inspiration—the artwork becomes a part of objective reality in its own right, with its own independent claim on our attention that arises out of its skillful making. Its effect on us is the product of the artist's manipulation of his materials, not the "content" alone; and while that is of course true of all art, art is now under an obligation to "show its hand" and make its manipulations known.

This applies even—or especially—to the great expressive climax in *Wozzeck*, where Berg made his most direct appeal to empathy. The entr'acte between scenes 4 and 5 of act III has its own place in the composer's list of "inventions." He called it *Invention über eine Tonart*, an "Invention on a Key." It provides a true catharsis after Wozzeck's tragic death—or rather, a catharsis to mark Wozzeck's death as tragic—and as such is notably out of character with Büchner's tight-lipped little play. At once a "slow waltz in the lachrymose tradition of Gustav Mahler" and a "parade of leitmotives"[7] (as one critic, who rather deplored its intrusion, put it), it reaches its searing turning point at the moment shown in Ex. 9-12, where a deafening twelve-tone "aggregate sonority" suddenly gives way to an obsessively reiterated V–I bass progression in D minor, thus bringing the "invention on a key" into conformity with the obsessive-compulsive ostinato technique of the other act III inventions.

This apparently "vitalist" interlude, in which ironic distance seems all at once to vanish, has been a focus of critical controversy. Many have resisted what they have seen as the composer's despotic attempt to force the listener's sympathy. George Perle has objected to the very concept of an "invention on a key" on purely technical grounds: "It is difficult to see what distinctive features are to be inferred from this title that would differentiate the movement from any other tonal composition."[8] Noting that the other inventions are based on what Berg called "unifying principles" (pitches, chords, rhythms, etc.), Perle notes that musical forms based on such principles "may be either 'tonal' or atonal.' The 'unifying principle' implied in the term 'key,' on the other hand, belongs to another level of analytical discourse entirely."

But that is so only if the presence of a key is considered a normal (or a "default") aspect of music; and that, of course, is not the case in *Wozzeck*. The act III interlude is (by several orders of magnitude) the biggest of those "tonal" moments that impinge on the atonal world of this opera at strategic intervals like comments from beyond, or without, thus setting up the biggest, most "global" irony of all: what is normal elsewhere is abnormal here and vice versa. The "normal" language of tonality can only be spoken in *Wozzeck* as a foreign tongue. And the necessary use of so many ironic quotation marks in this paragraph shows how thoroughly inverted or "ironized" the expressive situation has become. Tonality is only available for use here "in quotes," the subject of special treatment in the form of a technical "invention" along with all those hidden "tonal" forms in the first two acts (the symphonies, the fugues, the gigues, and the gavottes) that turn out to be unrecognizable in the absence of tonality.

But as soon as we respond as "normal" listeners to the stimulus of the interlude's tonal catharsis, black and white are radically reversed. All the rest of the opera is now placed "in quotes." The distance of its special world from the "normal" world of music becomes a part of the characterization, a metaphor for Wozzeck's crazed condition. The reason why audiences respond to *Wozzeck* "despite" its atonal language turns out to be the same as the reason why atonal music has become popular in film soundtracks as a representational device. Audiences understand it in both contexts as a metaphor for physical or psychological abnormality; it symbolizes stress, aberration, horror. It consummately conveys the terror in Wozzeck; but to summon pity the

EX. 9-12   Alban Berg, *Wozzeck*, Act III, Entr'acte between scenes 4 and 5 ("Invention on a Key"), climax.

composer had to resort to an "invention on a key." In his very success with the atonal idiom, still unequaled and probably never to be surpassed, Berg exposed its limitations. There could be no greater irony, in all senses of the word. What Berg (or rather, what *Wozzeck*) seemed to be suggesting, unwelcome as the news might be even to Berg himself (to say nothing of his teacher), was that the "emancipation of dissonance" was meaningful only to composers, not to listeners, for whom (no matter at what point the line is drawn or how many harmonies are eventually accepted as "harmonious") dissonance and consonance nevertheless remained, and would always remain, a meaningful (indeed, a meaning-creating) antithesis. Reaction to this uneasy suggestion — that the all-important emancipation of dissonance might be just another of the twentieth century's utopian pipe-dreams — must inform what otherwise seems Stravinsky's insufferably snobbish remark that "what disturbs me about *Wozzeck*, a work that I love, is the level of its appeal to 'ignorant' audiences."[9]

Despite its popularity, then, or even because of it, *Wozzeck* remains a controversial work, both from the standpoint of its historical significance and because of the unresolved tensions between its surface action and its arcane structure. Berg himself was equivocal about the latter problem. In a 1928 talk about the opera he claimed that his recourse to "musical forms more or less ancient" was simply a way of differentiating the different scenes and thus maintaining interest. It was solely his business, he insisted, claiming in conclusion that

> No matter how cognizant any particular individual may be of the musical forms contained in the framework of this opera, of the precision and logic with which everything is worked out and the skill manifested in every detail, from the moment the curtain parts until it closes for the last time, there must be no one in the audience who pays any attention to the various fugues, inventions, suites, sonata movements, variations, and passacaglias — no one who heeds anything but the idea of this opera, which by far transcends the personal destiny of Wozzeck. This I believe to be my achievement.[10]

And yet the published score contradicts this assertion to the extent that "the various fugues, inventions, suites, sonata movements, variations, and passacaglias" are explicitly labeled and even analyzed, so that the reader may be properly impressed with "the precision and logic with which everything is worked out and the skill manifested in every detail." (Act I, scene 4, for example, in the Doctor's office, is the one that contains the passacaglia to which Berg makes reference: every one of its twenty-one variations is labeled for the reader.) It was probably with reference to ostentatious analytical labels like these that the American composer Roger Sessions, writing in 1933, could ridicule "an opera whose remarkable feature when heard is its fidelity to the text, its responsiveness to every changing psychological nuance," but which "proves on examination to be constructed in its various scenes on the external models of classic forms, without, however, the steady and consistent ['tonal'] movement that gives these forms their purpose and their character."

Sessions suspected "the presence of a merely speculative element" in Berg's music,

> tending to be completely dissociated from the impression actually received by the ear and the other faculties which contribute to the direct reception of a musical impression, and to produce what is either a fundamentally inessential *jeu d'esprit* [witticism] of sometimes amazing proportions, or a kind of scaffolding erected as an external substitute for a living and breathing musical line.[11]

Clearly the words of an unreconstructed vitalist, these. But as we have noted many times, it is sometimes the negative critiques that offer the best perceptions into the relationship between an artwork and its time.

While in his indignation Sessions may have exaggerated the extent to which *Wozzeck* could be reduced to a *jeu d'esprit*, he was nevertheless on to something significant about the work and about its time. Berg was fascinated by intellectual games, puzzles, ciphers, and codes of all kinds. (We have already seen an example of this predilection in his Chamber Concerto, in which the themes encode the names of Schoenberg, Berg, and Webern; see Ex. 6-4.) His music is packed with riddles and hidden symbols. Some of it (like numerological symbolism) reflected Berg's personal superstitions; some of it had urgent autobiographical significance (like the coding of his initials and those of a secret lover in the music of his *Lyric Suite* for string quartet). And some of it, to be sure, was simply (merely? purely?) playful.

George Perle, who first decoded the secret love messages in the *Lyric Suite*, also came across a letter to Schoenberg in which Berg wrote out a harmonic curiosity (Ex. 9-13a) that Perle rather grandly christened the "Master Array of Interval Cycles."[12] All it amounts to is a superimposition of note-rows that proceed from a common starting point by uniform intervals of increasing size. At the bottom of the array is the chromatic scale (proceeding by minor seconds); above that is the whole-tone scale (proceeding by major seconds); above that is an arpeggiated diminished seventh chord (proceeding by minor thirds); then an arpeggiated augmented triad (proceeding by major thirds), and so on.

The array has fascinating properties indeed. Once past the initial unison, every chord formed by the superimposition is intervallically symmetrical: first a cluster of semitones, then a whole-tone aggregate, then a diminished seventh chord, then an augmented triad, and so on. And since once the tritone is passed the intervals all recur in their inverted form, the array (when pushed through twelve progressions) becomes a palindrome as well. Berg was in effect stumbling playfully on the same intersection of symmetries that (as we learned in chapter 7) was the object of Bartók's — and, later, Perle's — diligent research.

And once he'd stumbled on it, it went right into *Wozzeck* (Ex. 9-13b), and into one of the most serious scenes at that: Wozzeck's agonized confrontation with Marie in the middle of act II. One cannot say that the presence of this curiosity in any way compromises the seriousness of the scene as far as the listener is concerned; but its presence certainly does confirm Ortega's diagnosis of the modern art of the 1920s as essentially "jesting," even when serious, and therefore ironic. The very fact that Berg took delight in loading his opera with so much hidden brainy baggage — from "ancient forms" to interval arrays to number symbols and more — is an aspect of that jesting, ironic stance, and (more seriously) of the emergent divide between "research" and "communication" as composerly ideals.

The delight that the research aspect of Berg's work has afforded analysts — to the point where many studies of *Wozzeck* have completely ignored the opera's dramatic aspect and concentrated solely on its fascinating "poetics" or making — is another symptom of that irony, and that divide. Modernist music, increasingly, meant one thing to audiences, another to professionals: the "poietic" and the "esthesic" were drifting

EX. 9-13A   Alban Berg's "master array"

EX. 9-13B   Alban Berg, *Wozzeck*, Act II, scene 3, incorporation of the "master array"

apart. Some have regarded this as a liberation, others as a tragedy. The aspect of *Wozzeck* that many find miraculous is the way in which Berg managed, particularly in act III, to yoke poietics and esthesics to a common purpose. The purposes are measurably less common in the earlier acts of the opera, and there are many later modernist works in which there is no discernable connection between the two, even works in which there seems to be no discernable esthesic component at all.

Berg never approached such an extreme. His "research" (except, perhaps, in his Chamber Concerto) never became an end in itself. But the ends to which it was the means were not only communicative. In a commentary on Berg's jeux d'esprit that was far less contentious but no less insightful than Sessions's, the literary critic Herbert Lindenberger, who began his career with a study of Büchner, compared Berg's "form-consciousness" in *Wozzeck* to other manifestations of "classicism" in the art of the 1920s. These included Stravinsky's, of course, but also, as Lindenberger reminds us, the literary work of writers like James Joyce and T. S. Eliot.

He quotes Eliot's defense of Joyce's novel *Ulysses*, in which (as in *Wozzeck*) naturalistic content is presented within, and through, a framework of recondite technical tours de force and jeux d'esprit. That frame, in Joyce's case, was derived from Greek mythology, and in particular from Homer's *Odyssey*. Joyce, like Berg, had been accused of turning art into mere wit; but Eliot suggested that his method was "a way of controlling, of ordering, of giving a shape and a significance to the immense panorama of futility and anarchy which is contemporary history."[13] Lindenberger very reasonably compares Joyce's method as described by Eliot to "the function of the tight musical forms which Berg employs to contain the chaotic and characteristically modern materials that he found in Büchner's play."[14] This comparison brings *Wozzeck* within the purview of another, more famous, dictum of Eliot's: "It is a function of all art to give us some perception of an order in life, by imposing an order upon it."[15] But what Eliot propounds as a universal principle, it is now easy enough to see, was more a symptom of an obsession peculiar to his time, a time when artists in all media, including many (like Schoenberg and Stravinsky) who regarded one another as esthetic antagonists with nothing at all in common, but all reeling together at the futility, the anarchy, the loss of faith, and the havoc wrought by the most needless and destructive of all wars, took refuge together in a consoling order they had purchased by a huge investment in irony.

IRONY AND SOCIAL REALITY

But did that consoling sense of order jibe with Berg's avowed purpose, in *Wozzeck*, of exposing a social problem? Or was it just a palliative? And what is the point of exposing a social problem if not to do something about it? Otherwise, it could again be argued (and it certainly *was* argued), the exposure amounts to no more than voyeurism, no more socially useful than the titillation Puccini's suffering heroines afforded the gawking men in the traditional opera theater. Indeed, such titillation was socially regressive, the argument went, because it was experienced (or rationalized) as pity, vice thus masquerading as virtue.

That is why Joseph Kerman, among others but especially eloquently, refused to be taken in by the famous "tonal" interlude in act III. His were the dismissive comments about it ("lachrymose waltz," "parade of leitmotives") quoted above, and he went on from there to reproach the composer for mistaking pity for self-pity, turning what might have been a call for social action into a voluptuous wallow in self-gratifying sentiment. Kerman, writing in the 1950s, was echoing a common complaint of the 1920s, when stimulating social action through art was one of the chief orders of the day, especially in the new republics of Germany and Austria, and the young Soviet Union, where political and social revolution were the chief facts of recent history.

One Soviet critic, Boris Asafyev, in a book about Stravinsky completed in 1926 and published in 1929, hailed his "neoclassical" phase not as a restoration of the past but as an awakening to contemporary reality. "Contemporary life," he wrote, "demands discipline of the will and a steady concentration of all the faculties from those who wish to be in the mainstream of work and affairs and not be left standing on the bank."[16] And so does contemporary art. In contemporary music, as Asafyev described it, responses to these demands "can be seen in the striving for severity of construction, for clarity of writing, for concentration of the greatest tension within the shortest possible time, for the attainment of the greatest expression with the most economical expenditure of performing forces."

That already sounds like Stravinsky's Octet, which for Asafyev did not mark a return to Bach but on the contrary "asserts the dynamics of life." And no matter how many stylistic allusions such music made to the preromantic "classics," those gestures were always to be read as metaphors for postromantic reality, "the impetuous current of our lives with its springy rhythms, its flying tempi, and its obedience to the pulsations of work." Moreover, Asafyev adds, such music "has not been able to escape the influences of contemporary city streets." Think of the end of Stravinsky's Octet, where Bach morphs unexpectedly but, in retrospect inevitably, into a Charleston, the dance rage of the twenties.

The legacy of romanticism, by contrast, was "hypnotic, sterile, hedonistic." It encouraged passivity, whereas for Asafyev the goal of contemporary music was to bring the virtuosity formerly expended on casting hypnotic spells "out into the world of actuality," which required a style "nearer to the street than to the salon, nearer to the life of public actuality than to that of philosophical seclusion."[17] Such a style exudes "energy, action, and actuality" rather than mere subjective "reflection," which can only lead to paralysis of the will. It is "rooted in the sensations of contemporary life and culture and not merely in personal sentiments and emotions." The reality it presents is a *social*, not an "inner," reality.

The word Asafyev keeps coming back to — "actuality" (*aktual'nost'* in Russian) — was an attempt to render an untranslatable German word, *Sachlichkeit*, of which a literal English translation might be something like "thinginess," since the German root, *Sache*, means "thing." It conveys concreteness, alertness, objectivity, sobriety, hard reality, matter-of-factness as opposed to romantic make-believe. Since 1923, when it was coined by Gustav Hartlaub, the director of a German museum, the phrase *neue Sachlichkeit* ("new actuality") had been an artistic watchword in Germany, the esthetic emblem of the fragile Weimar Republic (so called because its constitution was drafted in the East German town of Weimar in 1919) that was set up to replace the fallen German Empire with an experiment in liberal democracy. It could be taken in retrospect as a "leftist" counterpart to Ortega's "dehumanization."

Until the composer flinched in act III, *Wozzeck* might have qualified as an example of *neue Sachlichkeit*. (Its literary prototype by Büchner, although it preceded the actual concept by about a hundred years, came closer to it.) But postwar Germany did not lack for unflinching composers, who in the spirit of *neue Sachlichkeit* invented a new kind of topical opera called *Zeitoper*, another untranslatable term that might be approximated as "opera of the times," or even "now-opera." A now-opera was an opera about things right now, rather than things eternal. It was not necessarily an opera about current events; indeed, some of the most conspicuous *Zeitopern* were cast as allegories. But the composer who wrote it was acting as a citizen commentator, not a priest of art whose kingdom was not of this world, and the work was valued for its contemporary relevance, not its timeless merit. It was inevitable that *Zeitoper* and *neue Sachlichkeit*, together with the related notion of *Gebrauchsmusik* (music for use rather than contemplation), should have arisen first in postwar Germany.

If, as we have seen, World War I looms as a great divide even in the historiography of the victor nations, how much more a cataclysm did it seem to the losers, for whom it brought immediate political upheaval and economic chaos, the palpable legacy of "decadence." *Gebrauchsmusik* and *neue Sachlichkeit* were not just a reaction to romanticism, but a reaction to all the forces that were seen to have precipitated the war, forces that preeminently included nationalism. Having experienced ruin, German artists, the ostensible heirs of the "mainstream", were more suspicious than anyone else of the lie of transcendence, any promise of immortality, permanence, lasting value. Hence the cult of the perishable, the ephemeral, the transient. Hence, too, the notion of an art that was not only to be used but to be used up. Obsolescence—blithely planned obsolescence, the considered rejection of "masterpiece culture"—was the price of true contemporaneity. The chief standard bearer for all these antiromantic notions was Paul Hindemith (1895–1963), a fabulously gifted all-round musician who was an internationally acclaimed viola soloist as well as Germany's leading composer in the 1920s and 1930s. He had begun his career as the expressionist's expressionist, with a pair of scandalous one-act operas—*Mörder, Hoffnung der Frauen* ("Murderer, the hope of womankind", 1919), which glorified rape, and *Sancta Susanna* ("Saint Susanna", 1922) about sexual hysteria in a convent—that made him famous when they were condemned from Lutheran pulpits and banned in Frankfurt. These operas maintained prewar "maximalist" styles (the first "post-Strauss," the second "post-Debussy"). Another early opera, however, *Das Nusch-Nuschi* (1921), showed signs of postwar irreverence for high artistic values, holding up to ridicule one of the sublimest moments in Wagner's *Tristan und Isolde*. It, too, caused a scandal.

The planned-obsolescence factor first showed itself in Hindemith's instrumental music. The last movement of his *Kammermusik Nr. 1* (Chamber Music No. 1, actually a sort of symphony for chamber orchestra) was titled "Finale: 1921" and quoted a foxtrot popularized that year by a German dance band. The next year's model, the *Suite "1922"* for piano, sported a "Shimmy" and a "Boston," American dances similar to the Charleston. The composer's own title-page cartoon (Fig. 9-3) shows a chance moment on a bustling thoroughfare (compare Asafyev's emphasis on "the street" as inspiration).

Nach einer Originalzeichnung des Komponisten

FIG. 9-3 Title page of Hindemith's *Suite "1922."*

Urbane antimetaphysics of another sort was embodied in the music Hindemith wrote for himself to perform, epitomized in another product of 1922, the Sonata for solo viola, op. 25, no. 1. This was *Spielmusik* ("player's music"), unadulterated by any higher purpose than ... well, than spieling it. The activity of performing it was its content. (Again compare Asafyev's emphasis on "energy, action, actuality.") "I composed the first and fifth movements in a buffet car between Frankfurt and Cologne and then went straight on to the platform and played the sonata,"[18] the notoriously prolific Hindemith boasted in a footnote to his enormous catalogue of works. That was turning matter-of-factness into a high artistic principle, and so was Hindemith's zeal to insulate his music from "tiresome rubato-playing and 'expression'-art"[19] by the use of sloganeering performance directions. The fourth movement of the solo viola sonata (Ex. 9-14), set at a palpably unplayable tempo of $\quarternote = 600 - 640$, carries the rubric "Frantic tempo. Boisterous. Beauty of tone is unimportant."

EX. 9-14   Paul Hindemith, Sonata for solo viola, Op. 25, no. 1, IV

"AMERICANISM" AND MEDIA TECHNOLOGY

The *Zeitoper*, where all of these Weimarish notions intersected and reached their peak, was ushered in, on 10 February 1927, by *Jonny spielt auf* ("Johnny goes to town"). The hit of the decade, if not the century, it made its composer, Ernst Krenek (1900–91), a precocious Czech-born citizen of Austria who had already written four operas, a European celebrity at twenty-six, and financially independent for the rest of his long life. During the next season, 1927–28, *Jonny* had forty-five productions and 421 performances as far west as Antwerp and as far east as Lemberg (now L'viv in Ukraine). By 1929 it had been performed on three continents, and its libretto had been translated into fourteen languages. "Now-opera" deserved its name: it had a prominence in the cultural life of its time matched only by the French and Italian grand operas of the nineteenth century and never equaled since, for opera soon lost its status as mass entertainment. (Krenek went on to write sixteen more operas, of which only one had more than a single production.)

The title character, a Negro jazz musician who wins the girl from a dreamy postromantic German composer and steals a magic life-giving violin from a glamorous virtuoso who perishes under the wheels of a boat-train headed for America, was an obvious allegory of the New World's triumph over the old in the wake of the exhausting war. Its "Americanism" was essentially a call to "lighten up" and live in the present. Many European conservatives were more sensitive to its implied endorsement of racial miscegenation, taking the opera as yet another symptom of what the pessimistic historian

Oswald Spengler, in the title of his 1922 best-seller, called *Der Untergang des Abendlandes* ("The decline of the west"). Its lean, mean textures and speedy, angular music, alert and twitching with new-world rhythms, were a threat to all traditional Germanic values of "inwardness" and "depth." Its emblematic sound is that of mechanically reproduced music (an American invention): onstage record players and radios blaring the "American" dance music associated with the title character. One of the opera's main leitmotifs is a shimmy (Krenek wrongly labeled it a "Blues") called *Leb' wohl, mein Schatz*—roughly, "Bye-bye, baby"—played in breakneck fashion by the orchestra at what Krenek calls a *schnelles Grammophon-Tempo* (quick record-player tempo), leaving absolutely no time for subjective reflection (Ex. 9-15).

An even more ironic clash between the "classical" form of a *Zeitoper* and its ephemeral content pervades Hindemith's *Neues vom Tage* of 1929. The title, literally "News of the Day," is what newsboys shouted on German city streets; the English equivalent would be "Read all about it!" or "Extra! Extra!" Its subject, however, is not the news of any particular day, but the idea of contemporary celebrity, sensation-mongering, publicity, and instant comment—an idea that has only grown more timely as the news media have grown ever quicker and more ubiquitous. A divorcing couple, Eduard and Laura, attract the attention of the press, which follows them everywhere, even into the

EX. 9-15 Ernst Krenek, *Jonny spielt auf,* "Leb' wohl, mein Schatz"

EX. 9-15 (continued)

bathroom. (Act II begins with the presumably naked Laura in an onstage bathtub, singing an aria about the modern miracle of indoor plumbing.) Laura and Eduard hire publicity managers and restage their quarrel nightly for the benefit of a gawking public. In the process they fall in love again, but the public insists on its own satisfaction and they must divorce as promised. The coloratura bathtub aria (Ex. 9-16) is a good example of Hindemith's brand of musical satire, in which traditional operatic forms are held up in a kind of mutually ridiculing tandem with the shallow stuff that passes for contemporary news in an age of burgeoning media.

MUSIC FOR POLITICAL ACTION

The result is a kind of panorama of contemporary mores, mocking to be sure but not indignant: the opera colludes with the butts of its own satire, affording its own public the kind of titillation the libretto ostensibly condemns, and ensuring a good (yes, and lucrative) reception. Was that hypocrisy or just good fun? Here the consternation came not just from the right, as with *Jonny spielt auf*, but from the left as well. For in Weimar Germany there were many who felt that the newly detached and ironic brand of art

EX. 9-16   Paul Hindemith, *Neues vom Tage*, Bathtub Aria

EX. 9-16 (continued)

that went by the name of *neue Sachlichkeit*, well suited as it was to social comment, had to justify its existence by virtue of a worthy social purpose, and that meant more than fun.

"I have just played you some music by Wagner and his followers," wrote Kurt Weill (1900–50), another composer of *Zeitopern*, in a newspaper article published on Christmas Day, 1928, and cast as an imaginary conversation with schoolchildren:

FIG. 9-4   Kurt Weill and Lotte Lenya at Brook House, 1942.

> You saw that it had so many notes in it that I couldn't play them all. You tried to sing along with the melody but that didn't work. You felt that the music was making you sleepy, or even a bit drunk, affecting you like alcohol or some other drug. But you didn't want to go to sleep. You wanted to hear music that you

could understand without explanation, that you could really absorb, and with tunes that you could quickly learn. Apparently you do not know that your parents still go to concerts sometimes. This is a custom that comes from the last century, arising out of social conditions that are no longer relevant to your generation. There are again today great issues that are of concern to everyone, and if music cannot be placed in the service of the general public then it has lost its reason for being.

Write this down! Music is no longer something for the few.[20]

Claiming to have "started from scratch" in an effort to adapt opera to these contemporary demands, Weill names the collaborator with whom he has joined forces, a man already famous for theatrical reform: Bertolt Brecht (1898–1956), who is often named together with Meyerhold and Pirandello as one of the great destroyers of theatrical illusion. Unlike the others, Brecht had an overtly political purpose, to which Weill also subscribed. The "service to the general public" of which Weill spoke was, in his and Brecht's view, public political education or indoctrination as a stimulus to revolutionary political action. To achieve this purpose, music had not only to change its style, renouncing the paralyzing emotional "hypnosis" that Wagner had practiced so well, but also its function within the drama.

Brecht called his theatrical style "epic theater." In place of an illusion of real action, epic theater incorporated narrative, montage (scenes played in counterpoint from various separately lighted areas of the stage), and direct exhortation of the audience in defiance of the fourth wall. Sets and lighting were deliberately nonrealistic, and Brecht even allowed the staging process — the work of stagehands, the moving of props, the backstage assembly areas — to be visible to the audience. The purpose of all of this was frankly didactic: Brecht and his collaborators wanted to engage the audience's fully conscious critical faculties and rationally argue a persuasive political case. That way the audience would not be rendered passive, like a hypnotized subject, attentive only to its own feelings, but rather active, engaged with social problems, and motivated to alleviate them. The urgent purpose of the contemporary theater, these artists felt, was to break the "music trance" associated with romanticism.

The effect of witnessing the stage machinery in action made the artificiality of the drama evident to the spectators, and enabled them to retain their critical faculties. Indeed, seeing how artificial the theater was produced an effect Brecht called *Verfremdung*. It is usually translated as "alienation" or "defamiliarization," but all it really means is that the epic theater makes its action and workings as "strange" (*fremd*) as possible, allowing the audience a distanced perspective that enables them to keep the play and its message distinct, so that they will leave the theater pondering not the former but the latter. Making things look in the theater the way they look in life — that is, familiar — encourages us to take them for granted, to pay them no real attention. (We all know what familiarity breeds.) Making them strange, putting them at an unaccustomed distance, makes us (as Ortega also taught) newly observant and newly impressionable.

It would be no distortion of Brecht's purpose, and no insult to his integrity, to say that his epic theater was an instrument of political propaganda, and that therein lay its justification. "Once the content becomes, technically speaking, an independent component, to which text, music and setting 'adopt attitudes,'" Brecht wrote,

> once illusion is sacrificed to free discussion, and once the spectator, instead of being enabled to have an experience, is forced as it were to cast his vote; then a change has been launched which goes far beyond formal matters and begins for the first time to affect the theater's social function.[21]

The role of music in the epic theater, according to Weill, was similar to that of the newly noticeable stagecraft. Refuting a hundred years of operatic theorizing, or at least turning his back on it, Weill declared that "music cannot further the action of a play or create its background." So much for Verdi, so much for Wagner, so much for all who have sought to make the music of an opera a continuous and flexible ambience for dramatic action or a subliminal intensifier of feeling. Instead, Weill contended, music "achieves its proper value when it interrupts the action at the right moments," in order (as Brecht would say) to adopt an attitude toward the action and influence the spectator's response to it.

The musical interruption thus serves as a jolt, to puncture whatever illusion of reality remains and reengage the full, wide-awake attention of the audience, all the better to monger the message of the play. The musical numbers that accomplish this—Weill liked to call them "songs," borrowing from English (but pronounced "*zonks*" in German)—serve the same purpose that the casting of rules or teachings in rhythm and rhyme had served since time immemorial. The music makes the message memorable. But to be memorable, music must be simple and direct. In practice, this meant imitating the form, and to some extent the style, of popular music.

Weill called this jolt or interruption-effect, borrowing from the Latin, a musical *Gestus*, a word combining the idea of "gesture" with that of "deed." The proper function of music in the theater he called its "gestic character"[22] (*der gestische Charakter der Musik*). He illustrated it in his newspaper talk by suddenly interrupting it and ordering the imaginary class of schoolchildren to "sing No. 16" (Ex. 9-17):

EX. 9-17   Kurt Weill, "No. 16"

And what is this singsong "No. 16?" Weill playfully refrains from identifying it, so that in the context of the article it seems as if he were calling on a congregation to sing out of a hymnal. But most of his readers would have recognized it as one of the numbers from his big hit of the previous summer, *Die Dreigroschenoper* ("The threepenny opera"), even if they didn't know that it happened to be "No. 16" in the printed score. The tune

FIG. 9-5   Brecht and Weill, *Die Dreigroschenoper*
(Oldenburg, 1929): Maria Martinsen as Jenny.

gives a fair idea of the level of simplicity at which Weill aimed, and the words ("Man lives by his wits, but off a head like yours a louse at best could live") give the flavor of the "gestic" interruptions — cynical, even insulting sermonettes about social injustice and the audience's complacent complicity in it. (For the "schoolchildren" he was addressing in the newspaper piece, Weill softened "louse" to "mouse.")

A play in dialogue with musical numbers, *Die Dreigroschenoper* was the second show Weill had produced in collaboration with Brecht. Like *Jonny spielt auf*, it was one of the legendary box-office sensations of the Weimar Republic, with over three hundred performances in a single Berlin theater during the first year of its run. By 1933, the publisher had licensed a total of 133 productions worldwide. Such a play would have been called a Singspiel in the eighteenth century. To that extent, it was an ironized return to an outmoded or preromantic genre like so much of the art of the 1920s. It even had a specific eighteenth-century model, *The Beggar's Opera* (1728) by the English playwright John Gay, a satirical "ballad opera" about London low-life in which the music had consisted of harmonized popular tunes. (Weill quoted one of them for effect, but otherwise wrote a new and original score.) The clever subtitle Weill and Brecht came up with, *Songspiel*, captured both its "classical" resonances and its contemporary relevance. In the original production, the "antioperatic" thrust was maintained by casting cabaret singers and dramatic actors who could more or less carry a tune in the singing roles, rather than operatically trained voices. (One of the actresses was Weill's wife, Lotte Lenya, who supervised a famous New York revival in translation, which ran for 2,611 performances in the mid-1950s.) The original "pit orchestra" consisted of seven cabaret musicians "doubling" on a total of twenty-three instruments. The "gestus" or interruption-effect of the music was enhanced by radically changing the lighting for each song, displaying its title on a screen, and keeping the instrumentalists visible to the audience at all times.

Die Dreigroschenoper makes a fascinating comparison with *Wozzeck*, since both operas had as their stated aim the exposure of a social problem — namely, society's hypocritically "criminalizing" mistreatment of the poor. But where *Wozzeck* adopted a conventional attitude of pity toward its subject, allowed its audience a satisfying (or self-satisfying) catharsis that left it feeling virtuously compassionate, and clothed the drama in a prodigally — even ostentatiously — inventive musical fabric, *Die Dreigroschenoper* maintains a tone of unmitigated anger and sarcasm, challenging its audience's presumption of moral superiority and indicting its complacency, while using music that (as Weill proudly demonstrated in his newspaper article) rejected the advanced musical techniques and idioms of the day as ostentatiously as Berg had embraced them.

The act II finale, which carries the title 'Ballade über die Frage: 'Wovon lebt der Mensch?' ("Ballad about the question, What keeps a man alive?") makes the comparison with *Wozzeck* particularly pointed, since it deals explicitly with the plight of "arme Leute" (poor folk), the quintessential Wozzeckian theme. Where the title character of Berg's opera, though he ends a criminal, is presented as a good man more sinned against than sinning, the main character of *Die Dreigroschenoper*, Macheath (alias Mac the Knife), is the head of a gang of street robbers — a confirmed and dedicated (indeed a professional) felon.

In Gay's opera Macheath's frank villainy is used as a witty foil to expose the hypocritical villainy of polite society. No better way is proposed, and the satire (like most eighteenth-century satire) is of the mildest, friendliest sort. In Brecht's adaptation, Macheath's villainy is decried as the inevitable result of social injustice. It is not humorously endorsed after Gay's fashion, but neither is it sanctimoniously condemned. The message of the play, which Weill's music intervenes to underscore, is that villainy must be eradicated humanely, not by zealous self-righteous punishment, but by attacking its root cause, poverty.

The final ballad in act II takes place just after Macheath has escaped from prison. He had been fingered by a group of whores whom he has continued to patronize although married (to two women at once, it later turns out), and who have been bribed to betray him by one of his fathers-in-law not for any reason of justice but merely so that his daughter can come back home and go on working for her father without pay. The ballad (Ex. 9-18), sung by Macheath together with one of the whores who has turned him in (and who will turn around in the next act and betray him again, for money), describes the dog-eat-dog reality the "arme Leute" must confront, a world in which the idle moralizing of the well-fed has no place.

It is sung in front of the curtain, directly to the audience. Not only does this breach the fourth wall, it amounts to a stepping out of character, as Brecht often prescribed: "the actor must not only sing," he wrote, "but show a man singing."[23] The audience no longer feels it is watching the antics of fictional characters, but rather that it is seeing and hearing two singing actors for whom Brecht and Weill have written a harangue with no other purpose than to defy the audience's right to pass a moral judgment on the action it has observed: "For even honest folk [yes, you!] will act like sinners/Unless they've had their customary dinners!" (as translated for the New York production by the American composer Marc Blitzstein).

RIGHTEOUS RENUNCIATION, OR WHAT?

It is obvious, of course, that the music to which this sardonic number is set, despite Weill's avowals in the newspaper, is not music for twelve-year-olds. It is the work of a sophisticated and highly trained professional, one who had all the technique it

EX. 9-18   Kurt Weill, *Die Dreigroschenoper*, "Zweites Dreigroschenfinale," mm. 18–31

EX. 9-18   (*continued*)

pei - nigt, aus - zieht, an - fällt, ab - würgt und frißt.   Nur da - durch

lebt der Mensch, daß er so gründ - lich ver -

ges - sen kann, daß er ein Mensch doch ist.

would have taken to compose another *Wozzeck,* and in fact one who at first seemed headed in exactly that direction. The son of a well-known synagogue cantor, Weill was a composing prodigy and was given a training of the most elite caliber. At eighteen he enrolled in Engelbert Humperdinck's composition class at the Berlin Conservatory. Two years later, he was accepted into a master class for young composers that was created for Ferruccio Busoni (1866–1924), then the most sought-after composition teacher in Europe, at the Prussian Academy of Arts. He worked with Busoni for three years, absorbing his teacher's ideas about what he called *junge Klassizität* ("young classicism" as antidote to "decadence"), but he was also attracted to the music and teaching of Schoenberg, who reciprocated his esteem to the extent of nominating him for a government stipend.

Weill's early works included a symphony (1921), two string quartets (1919, 1923), a violin concerto (1924, scored like Stravinsky's piano concerto for a wind orchestra), and most characteristically, a *Sinfonia Sacra* (1922) whose three neobaroque movements (Fantasia, Passacaglia, Hymnus) reflected Busoni's neoclassical teachings most directly.

The musical style that Weill employed, however, was very far from that of the early "neoclassicists," resembling instead the "pantonal" style of Schoenberg's expressionist phase. His first opera, *Der Protagonist* (1924) had a libretto by Georg Kaiser, then Germany's leading expressionist playwright, and cemented his early alliance with the Viennese atonalists. The composer with whom the young Weill was most frequently compared, in fact, was Berg.

So the style of *Die Dreigroschenoper* was the result of a deliberate, radical, and very controversial renunciation. Was it a sacrifice to social conscience, or just a commercial sell-out? The work professes the former in no uncertain terms, but its great commercial success suggested the latter to many, especially artists who maintained a traditional commitment to "disinterested" romantic values. Schoenberg, the most adamant of them all, refused even to recognize a distinction between social commitment and commercial compromise, accusing Hindemith, Krenek, and Weill equally of "a lack of conscience" and "a disturbing lack of responsibility."[24] The artist's primary obligation, under romanticism, was not to other people but to art. A social conscience was therefore no conscience at all. Indeed, lack of a proper contempt for the world and its inhabitants was contemptible. The greatest sin of *neue Sachlichkeit*, in Schoenberg's eyes, was its esthetic "nonchalance." Yet even if we decide not to hold his success against the composer, concluding that results do not necessarily reflect on motives and granting Weill and Brecht the benefit of every doubt, a dilemma remains. Can an art dedicated to shocking the middle-class public out of its complacency be said to have succeeded when that very public consumes it with delight? Brecht himself, sensitive both to this point and to the possibility that Weill's contribution was upstaging his own, eventually belittled the music in *Die Dreigroschenoper* and claimed to prefer a revised version in which the actors would improvise minimal melodies of their own: he called this better style of didactic theater music "Misuk" (pronounced mee-ZOOK) as opposed to "Musik" (moo-ZEEK), the normal German word for music, which for him denoted something merely "culinary"[25] — that is, sensuously appealing rather than instructive.

There was no chance of revising *Die Dreigroschenoper* in this way; not only were audiences unlikely to accept it, but Weill's contribution was legally protected, even from Brecht. And yet Weill, too, faced a problem posed by the popularity of his art and the political compromise that implied. Was there a politically effective alternative? If his art were to maintain a "difficult" stylistic exterior, as critics faithful to Schoenberg (like Adorno) insisted that art must do if it was to communicate a difficult social message, but that difficulty dissuaded its potential audience to the point where no one was listening, then has it succeeded any better? Can "serious" art ever be an effective medium for political propaganda or a spur to social action? Or is it doomed by its very nature to be either an esthetic plaything or, worse, an instrument for the maintenance of social hierarchies?

No one could possibly claim now that *Die Dreigroschenoper*, a proven audience favorite thanks to its catchy music, has been an instrument for social change. But Weill and Brecht also experimented with more modest works in a less flamboyantly entertaining style, with a sterner sense of utility (*Gebrauch*), and with unsentimental messages that were at times truly unpalatable by ordinary theatrical standards. Among these more ascetic products of their collaboration were what Brecht called *Lehrstücke* (didactic pieces or "lessons") and *Schulopern* ("school operas").

A *Lehrstück* was a work meant for amateur performance that would discipline the political attitudes of the participants along with their performance skills, and also furnish the eventual spectators with moral and political instruction. The first of them, *Der Lindberghflug* ("Lindbergh's flight", 1929), was produced by Brecht in collaboration with both Weill and Hindemith. (Later Weill reset it alone as a cantata for professional performance.) It was meant, and was probably the first musical work to be meant, primarily for radio performance, making extensive use of sound effects (propellers, wind, murmuring waves, cheering crowds) that depended for their effect on the invisibility of their source.

The work was a determined attempt to divest Lindbergh's famous solo transatlantic flight of its heroic aura—or rather its aura of heroic individualism. Lindbergh (tenor) introduces himself in an aria that could serve as a textbook illustration of *neue Sachlichkeit* matter-of-factness: he gives his name, his age, his nationality, and a list of the equipment he is carrying. The baritone soloist, a "listener" to broadcast flight news, was directed to render his part mechanically, "without identifying his own feelings with those contained in the text, pausing at the end of each line; in other words, in the spirit of an *exercise*." The emphasis was taken away from the man and placed on the event as a scientific or technological breakthrough that depended on many besides the flyer himself. (Indeed, Lindbergh—who had compromised himself on the eve of World War II by expressing admiration for the Nazi regime—actually disappeared from a revised version of the *Lehrstück* that Brecht prepared in 1950 under the title *Der Ozeanflug*, "The ocean flight.")

NEW-MORALITY PLAYS

Together with Hindemith alone, Brecht produced another *Lehrstück* that was first performed under that name alone in 1929 at a new music festival near the German resort town of Baden, but was later published as *Das Badener Lehrstück vom Einverständnis*, "The Baden lesson on acquiescence." It embodies an even more stringent version of the lesson contained in the Lindbergh piece. It is also about a flyer, an unnamed pilot who is injured in a crash. He appeals for help but is persuaded by the chorus that he does not deserve it; rather he is taught to acknowledge the insignificance of his own life within the social scheme, and to accept death.

In *Die Massnahme* ("The measure taken," 1930), a *Lehrstück* written in collaboration with the Communist composer Hanns Eisler (1898–1962), this message is magnified startlingly. A "young comrade," who has responded to a moral dilemma as a feeling individual rather than in accord with Party doctrine, is killed for the good of the cause—but only after his "assent" is demanded and given. Part of what makes *Die Massnahme* so startling to recall is our present awareness of the similarity between the measures it advocates hypothetically and those actually taken several years later at the notorious Moscow "show trials," where many old revolutionaries were forced or (worse) persuaded to confess to capital offenses of which they were in fact innocent. Its text often resorts to straight political exhortation—"Agitprop" or agitational propaganda, as it was called in Communist circles—drawn in part from the writings of social and civic activists including Lenin, the founder of the Soviet state.

Eisler's settings of these texts, for "workers' chorus," were in a rigorously simplified style, mainly unison singing or two-part harmony accompanied by brass and percussion (and piano, whenever the bourgeoisie needed to be mocked). Songs like these, meant in the first place to give the singers a sense of political solidarity, were called "mass songs" (*Massenlieder*) or "battle songs" (*Kampflieder*). At particularly forceful moments, the chorus left off singing altogether and shouted in rhythmic unison. At the first performance, after-hours at one of Berlin's largest concert halls, the composer, who might have conducted, instead practiced what he preached, standing among the choristers in a gesture of working-class solidarity. The title phrase in "Change the World: It Needs It" (*Ändere die Welt, sie braucht es*, Ex. 9-19), with words by Brecht, became a famous Communist slogan in its own right. The text justifies violence in a good cause. The distinctive style of the setting stems from a prevalence of tritones, evidence of the composer's familiarity with the modern music of his day.

EX. 9-19   Hanns Eisler, *Die Massnahme*, "Ändere die Welt, sie braucht es," mm. 19–38

EX. 9-19 (continued)

sin - ke in Schmutz,___ um - ar - me den Schläch - ter, a - ber

tempo *pp*

än - dre die Welt, sie braucht es.

Nevertheless, *Die Massnahme*, submitted for performance at a Berlin New Music Festival, was rejected by a screening committee, of which Hindemith was a member, on grounds of "artistic mediocrity." Yet its perpetrator had renounced a training every bit as elite and prestigious as Weill's, and far more so than Hindemith's. Eisler had been a pupil of Schoenberg, no less, who had once named the political renegade-to-be, together with Webern and Berg, as "the most talented young composers, with the best preparation, whom I have taught." Unlike Weill's, Eisler's idealism was never questioned; he never had a popular hit, and never sought one. Even Weill came, eventually, to despise him—but that is not a story for this chapter.

Possibly the most stylistically significant *Lehrstück* or *Schuloper* (the collaborators used the terms interchangeably) was *Der Jasager* ("The yea-sayer," or "He who says yes," 1930), which Weill and Brecht wrote for performance by schoolchildren, plus a single adult performer—the Teacher, to emphasize even further the didactic nature of the piece. Its first performance was given under prestigious government sponsorship, underwritten by Berlin's Central Institute for Education and Instruction and acted by the pupils of the Berlin Academy of Church and School Music: this was the closest to official recognition that the idea of modernist, ostensibly left-wing *Gebrauchsmusik* ever achieved in Weimar Germany. Thereafter, the little school opera had almost as many productions in its modest domain as *Die Dreigroschenoper* had on Germany's glamour stages. Adopted by the German Ministry of Education as a curricular offering, it was produced in more than three hundred German schools by 1932.

Like the plot of *Die Dreigroschenoper*, the plot of *Der Jasager* was borrowed from an archaic source, in this case an exotic one as well: a fifteenth-century Japanese Noh play (or ceremonial drama) that tells of a boy who, to obtain medicine for his sick mother, accompanies a group of students over a dangerous mountain pass, but falling ill, bows to custom and allows himself to be hurled into the valley so as not to stay the progress of the group. Like the original *Lehrstück*, and like *Die Massnahme* (if not so blatantly topical as these), it is another study in "Einverständnis" or acquiescence for the sake of the common good, didactically proclaimed by the chorus that both opens and closes the show (Ex. 9-20a).

Unlike the brazen score of *Die Dreigroschenoper*, with its flashy gestures toward contemporary popular music, and unlike Eisler's raucous *Massenlieder*, Weill's music for *Der Jasager* is quietly serious and almost ascetically spare. In this it seems to be vying

EX. 9-20A   Kurt Weill, *Der Jasager*, no. 1 (chorus)

EX. 9-20A *(continued)*

with the "stripped down" or denuded style—the *style dépouillé*—that French critics were hailing in the "neoclassical" works of Stravinsky. But where Stravinsky's asceticism was an asceticism of chic, and an explicit rejection of "content," Weill's asceticism served the needs of the grave and semiritualistic text—the overriding *Gebrauch* or use-value to which his art was subservient.

In an essay on *Der Jasager* that he published in a Berlin arts magazine, Weill came close (almost as close as Stravinsky or Schoenberg, to say nothing of Brecht) to asserting his ideas prescriptively, as an obligation on all composers. He glossed the term *Schuloper* in three ways: first, as a school for composers of opera, teaching them a new foundation for musical theater; second, as a schooling for performers, teaching them "simplicity and naturalness"[26]; and third, as instruction on how art may be placed at the service of social institutions, rather than being a selfish end in itself. Only then did he take up the matter of the play's moral teaching and the way in which the music enhanced its persuasiveness.

The climactic scene, in which the boy does the thing for which he is named (Ex. 9-20b), is a study in purposeful restraint: climax by vast understatement. Rarely have so few notes been called upon to do more expressive work. The expression, moreover, however histrionically it is curbed, is of the traditional "romantic" type. Although one of the reasons for restraint was the *neue Sachlichkeit* precept that persuasion must be rational rather than emotional and acquiescence freely considered rather than coerced, the very presence of music says and does otherwise. Stephen Hinton, a historian of "Weimar" musical culture, has pointed out that the chorus that narrates and reflects upon the child's sacrificial death modulates to the traditional lamenting key of D minor, the very key on which Berg wrote his cathartic "invention" at the climax of *Wozzeck*, and that in this radically stripped-down context, its stark dissonances carry a payload of "immense human grief."[27] What the music seems to convey is less a celebration of submission to the demands of a collective or corporate body than a resigned recognition that such a sacrifice is sometimes necessary, and that one must be taught to know when that is the case.

EX. 9-20B   Kurt Weill, *Der Jasager*, no. 10 (concluding scene)

EX. 9-20B   (*continued*)

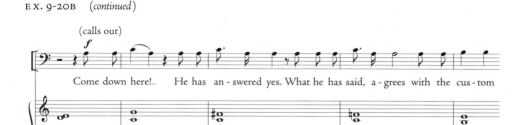

(calls out)

Come down here!_   He has an-swered yes. What he has said, a-grees with the cus-tom

Ultimately, Weill's and Brecht's own attitudes are less important historically than the controversy to which *Der Jasager* gave rise. Once it had left its creators' hands, it led an unpredictable life of its own in the clamorous and unruly political atmosphere of Weimar Germany. Precisely because it had been given an official sanction by a government ministry, the play became the object of furious contention, not all of it to Weill's or Brecht's liking. Conservative Christian writers, and even some on the fascist extreme, praised the play for its moral authoritarianism, and some leftist critics objected to the ease with which it could be given a rightist twist. (And maybe that tells us something about the nature of totalitarian thinking.) It often happened, too, that the schoolchildren engaged in performing the piece objected to the ending.

In theory, open discussion and critique were just what *Lehrstücke* like *Der Jasager* were supposed to provoke. In fact, Brecht revised the text to make it more palatable, and to prevent the sacrifice from being interpreted as favoring the wrong cause. In the first revision, the boy was portrayed as seeking medicine not just for his own mother, but for his whole village, which would suffer if the expedition were delayed on his account; and he asks to be killed in part because he fears being left alone. These changes lessened the chances that his acquiescence might be viewed as unjust.

The second revision, much more radical, produced a sort of counterplay called *Der Neinsager* ("He who says no"). This time the boy refuses to be sacrificed, and the group turns back. His apparent selfishness is mitigated by leaving out the part about the medicine, leaving in its stead only an irrational "Great Custom" that travelers who fall ill must die. The new message, that "great customs" should not be blindly followed, as bourgeois traditionalists might urge, but rather subjected to rational critique, could also serve revolutionary purposes. There was an additional point as well, emphasized by Hinton, who writes that by the early 1930s, the threat of fascism — a political reality in which "nay-sayers would not be tolerated"[28] — was sufficiently real to motivate a play that would advocate their protection. Brecht actually imagined performances of *Der Jasager* and *Der Neinsager* on the same bill, but Weill never wrote a setting for the latter.

THE DEATH OF OPERA?

These debates are worth pondering in detail, not so much for the sake of the issues they raised in their day, but simply as an indication of how seriously artworks were both meant and taken as political expressions in Weimar Germany. The vigor with which *Der Jasager* was discussed, and the frequency with which it was performed, are evidence in turn of a larger historical situation that now seems far more deserving of comment than it could possibly have seemed at the time. The operas and musical plays discussed in this chapter—by Prokofieff, by Berg, by Krenek, by Hindemith, and by Weill—were successful and popular in a way that almost no opera has been since 1933. For the thriving operatic economy of the Weimar Republic was the last truly thriving—that is, consumption-driven—economy in the history of opera.

These composers wrote for a ready market. Their work was in demand. They strove not for eventual immortality but for immediate success. Ephemerality, not immortality, was the order of the day. Sudden eclipse was actually part of the bargain. An opera had its place in the sun if it managed to earn one, and then it moved out of the way. Evanescence was not just the price of a booming operatic economy, it was also the proof; it implied a constant interest in the new. Producers could recoup their investment in new works and sometimes make hefty profits, and so they sought out new works to produce. Premieres were more noteworthy than revivals, and commanded the lively interest of the press.

But all of this came to an end in 1933, when the Nazi regime took power in Germany, and it has never been restored anywhere. In this chapter, that means, we have in effect witnessed the end of opera as a major contemporary genre. There will be operas to discuss in later chapters (and even a couple of important composers who specialized in the genre), but they will be few and far between, and almost none of them will have performance statistics to match any of the ones discussed in this chapter.

So what happened?

Most obviously and proximately, the Great Depression, the economic slump that began with the New York stock market crash in October 1929, and over the next few years encompassed the globe. Beginning in 1931, many theaters in Germany had to close, and even in the theaters that hung on impresarios had to flee the copyrighted contemporary repertory, where expensive royalties had to be paid, and seek refuge in the cheaper public domain. But whereas the spoken theater eventually regained and surpassed its previous artistic and economic levels, contemporary operatic culture was effectively killed, and not only in Germany but worldwide. What killed it?

"Talkies," which were really singies, with or without songs. The movies did not only preempt the operatic audience. At a profound level, the movies became the operas of the mid- to late-twentieth century, leaving the actual opera houses with a closed-off museum repertoire, to which new additions have been exceedingly few, and with a specialized audience of aficionados—"opera buffs," "canary fanciers"—rather than a general entertainment public hungry for sensation. With the advent of the sound film, opera found its preeminence as a union of the arts compromised, and its standing as the grandest of all spectacles usurped.

The kinds of subjects that had been opera's chief preserve—myth and epic, historical costume drama, romance, fast-paced farce—suited the new medium even better. Actors and actresses on film were literally, not just metaphorically, larger than life. The mythic aura of the diva attached itself irrecoverably to them. Cinematic transport to distant times and climes was instantaneous. Evocative atmosphere, exotic or realistic, could be more potently conjured up on film than on the best-equipped operatic stage, and the narrative techniques of the movies were unprecedentedly flexible and compelling. Film, in short, could keep the promise of romanticism, and preserve its flame more effectively than opera, the romantic art par excellence, especially after opera had been invaded by *neue Sachlichkeit*.

To the extent that music gave opera a reason for being by enhancing scale, magnifying characters, providing imaginative transport and "framing" devices that went beyond those of the spoken theater, it now found itself trumped in turn. As to music's hitherto unique powers as a delineator or inducer of moods, as emotional catharsis, as sheer sensuous presence, it turned out that a movie soundtrack could be remarkably like an opera in its function, if not precisely in its means. Both sound-film and opera have the effect of surrounding an action in a metaphorical sonic ambience that represents and objectifies feeling. Like operatic characters, cinematic characters do not hear, as characters, the sounds that attend their behavior. They live in the sounds and through them. When music is actually performed in the course of the action, which happens in almost every opera and every film, a fascinating and endlessly variable tension is set up in both media between two levels of musically represented reality, and the codes that represent them.

It is by no means stretching a point, therefore, to say that movies became the operas of the twentieth century. The creative energy that used to be invested in the opera business now goes into the movie industry, and so do the financial resources. The blockbuster emotional experiences that operas used to deliver are now far more dependably administered by the big screen. All that opera can uniquely claim (and of course it is a big thing) is the charismatic dramatic singer. But since the 1930s, charismatic opera singers have exercised their powers almost exclusively in the museum repertory, not the contemporary one. Most contemporary composers have not even called upon their services, having been convinced by a combination of academic theorizing and sour grapes that they should aim "above" the level of audience appeal.

FROM VIENNA TO HOLLYWOOD

The transmutation of opera into film is neatly — maybe even a little too neatly — epitomized by the career of the Viennese composer Erich Wolfgang Korngold (1897–1957), a composing prodigy on the order of Mozart and Mendelssohn. In 1907, aged ten, he played a cantata he had composed to Mahler, who pronounced him a genius and sent him to Alexander von Zemlinsky — Schoenberg's former mentor — for study. At the age of eleven he composed a ballet that was performed to wide acclaim at the Vienna Court Opera in 1910, when Korngold was thirteen. From then on he was famous. His *Sinfonietta*, op. 5, composed when he was fifteen, aroused "awe and fear" in Richard Strauss, who pronounced Korngold's "firmness of style, sovereignty of form, individuality of expression, and harmonic structure" to be the equal of any living composer's.

Korngold was one of the most active and successful participants in the explosive operatic culture of Weimar Germany. His third opera, *Die tote Stadt* ("The dead city," 1920), on which he began work at the age of twenty, spread his fame throughout the world, with successful productions in Prague, Budapest, Antwerp, Lwów (Poland), and New York, to mention only those outside the German-speaking countries. It is a symbolist drama, with an action that takes place in a space ambiguously located between dream and reality. The music is sophisticated both in structure (the use of leitmotifs) and in sonority, the young Korngold being, among other things, a virtuoso orchestrator. With its gorgeous imagery of death and luxuriant decay, *Die tote Stadt* is often cited, despite the composer's extreme youth (which precluded "genuine" world-weariness), as the supreme monument of musical "decadence."

Decadence was a little old-fashioned in the age of *neue Sachlichkeit*, but that did not impede the opera's success, and Korngold followed up on it with an even more sumptuous expressionist drama, *Das Wunder der Heliane* ("Heliane's miracle", 1927), which contained an eight-minute nude scene for the title character that put even the one in Strauss's *Salome* (not to mention Hindemith's coy bathtub aria) in the shade. The music was an epitome of everything that Asafyev declared outdated: fat, round, heavy, swooning, slow-moving, full of puffy sublimated waltzes. It was the music of romantic "hypnosis" par excellence, and never was a musical hypnotist more adept than Korngold.

He commanded the full panoply of Wagnerian and Straussian resources with a routined virtuosity that exceeded Wagner's and Strauss's, thanks to advances both in orchestral technology and orchestrational know-how. By the use of harp glissandos and brass harmonics, Korngold pioneered effects of orchestral portamento — the illusion of continuously sliding pitch to enhance and intensify modulations — that conspired with perpetual tempo rubato and constantly waxing and waning dynamics to produce (in Ortega's sense) the most "humanized," and (in Hulme's sense) the most "vital" orchestral music ever written. One technical detail is indicative: the celesta, Richard Strauss's *sauce piquante* (to speak in "culinary" terms), which famously adorned the scene of awakening love in *Der Rosenkavalier*, mutates with Korngold into an indefatigably churning section of keyboard and mallet instruments — xylophone, glockenspiel, harmonium, piano, organ, and even the rare *glockenklavier*, a set of tubular bells attached to a keyboard — that oozes endless aromatic goo.

Listeners to Korngold's music were sensually surfeited and emotionally buffeted to a degree that not even Strauss or Scriabin attempted. In his operas, particularly *Heliane*, he applied these hypnotic techniques to subject matter that combined bombastic religiosity and coy eroticism to produce something that might usefully be christened "sacroporn," and that has become very familiar indeed to movie audiences from Hollywood's many mythical and biblical epics. It was very popular with the opera audience that later became the movie audience. During his heyday in the 1920s, Korngold tied with Schoenberg in a newspaper poll to name the greatest living composer.

But his career was abruptly cut short in 1938, when Austria joined Germany in the Nazi Third Reich, and Korngold had to join the great wave of Jewish emigration.

Actually, Korngold was already in America when the Austro-German *Anschluss* (annexation) took place. The theatrical director Max Reinhardt, who as a German rather than an Austrian Jew had to flee from Hitler earlier than Korngold, invited the composer to Hollywood in 1934 to arrange Mendelssohn's music for Reinhardt's film of *A Midsummer Night's Dream*. Korngold accepted a contract as a staff composer at the Warner Brothers studio. Between 1935 and 1946 he furnished original scores for nineteen films, and won two Oscars. After *Die Kathrin* (1939), already in progress when he went to America, Korngold never wrote another opera.

But of course he was writing opera all along. Korngold never had to adapt his style in any way to the exigencies of the new medium; it was perfectly suited. The style of Viennese opera that Korngold inherited and extended became the Hollywood style of the 1930s and 1940s, as established not only by Korngold but by other Central European immigrants like Max Steiner (1888–1971), who was in Hollywood as early as 1929. It was Steiner who pioneered the techniques of "underscoring" or putting continuous, leitmotif-laden music behind the dialogue in a talking picture, and this is what enabled the mutation of opera into cinema in method as well as style.

Perhaps the finest operatic scene that Korngold ever wrote was the love scene from *Anthony Adverse* (1936), his third original score and one of the two that earned him Academy Awards. The opulently swooping, endlessly modulating music could be spliced right into *Das Wunder der Heliane*. The Tristanesque "Night" sequence from *Another Dawn*, Korngold's second Hollywood feature, accompanied the ardent confessions of Kay Francis and Errol Flynn with a solo violin and a quartet of cellos to stand in for the lovers' voices. It later furnished the thematic basis for the first movement of Korngold's Violin Concerto (Ex. 9-21). Composed in 1945 for Jascha Heifetz (1901–87), perhaps the greatest virtuoso violinist of the time, it, too, was a sublimated operatic scene, nostalgically evoking the vanished world that Korngold once inhabited, and that he had helped transform.

A NEW *STILE ANTICO?*

Hollywood, it might seem, had provided a haven for a musical style that had become outmoded in the concert hall and opera house. The phenomenon could be interpreted

EX. 9-21   Erich Korngold, Violin Concerto, beginning of first movement

EX. 9-21 (continued)

FIG. 9-6 Serge Rachmaninoff, caricature by Alfred Bendiner.

in two ways. One could argue that the older style, having lost its contemporaneity (and therefore its authenticity), could only serve in a functional or auxiliary capacity, as an adjunct to the movies, administering emotional stimulation to audiences whose minds were elsewhere. That is how theorists in the tradition of the New German School interpreted it. But one could also argue that the "serious" arts, having fallen victim to the false assumptions of modernism, which measured aesthetic value only in terms of technical innovation, had lost their ability to communicate with any but snob audiences, hence were no longer viable or legitimate. The widening gap between the ordinary concert repertory and the predilections of modernist composers could be cited as evidence for either position: either that audiences were no longer paying due attention, or that modern music was no longer viable.

Both positions had fanatical and prestigious advocates. The most effective antimodernist standard bearer was Rachmaninoff, the virtuoso composer-performer mentioned toward the beginning of this chapter in conjunction with Prokofieff. His position in the public eye and his excellent reputation as an interpreter of the "museum repertory" (not to mention his box-office popularity) allowed Rachmaninoff's very conservative music to join that museum repertory at a time when audiences and concert promoters were often actively resistant to modernist music. There were many, during the 1920s and 1930s, who regarded him as the greatest living composer, precisely because he was the only one who seemed capable of successfully maintaining the familiar and prestigious style of the nineteenth-century "classics" into the twentieth century. The fact that he was in fact capable of doing so, moreover, and that his style was as distinctive as any contemporary's, could be used to refute the modernist argument that traditional styles had been exhausted.

Rachmaninoff's piano concertos, particularly the Second (1901) and the Third (1909), were repertory items at a time when the works of Schoenberg, Stravinsky, Bartók, and all the other modernists were considered specialty items at best; and his *Rhapsody on a Theme of Paganini* for piano and orchestra (1934), a set of variations on the theme of Paganini's Twenty-Fourth Caprice—which had already served Liszt and Brahms as a basis for virtuoso variations—might be called the very latest contribution to the standard (as opposed to the "modern") concert repertory. Modernists derided him: Virgil Thomson, the American composer who in the 1940s was the country's most influential music critic, called Rachmaninoff's music "mainly an evocation of adolescence," and "no part of our intellectual life."[29] But Rachmaninoff's stature was commanding, and his reputation was not only undamaged but, in the eyes of his admirers, even enhanced by modernist abuse.

He could afford to remain largely aloof from the captious criticism he attracted, but one of the variations in the Paganini Rhapsody seems to have been a joke at his critics' expense. The eighteenth variation (Ex. 9-22), which has an independent fame, is the most unabashedly and "anachronistically" romantic of the lot in its expressive gestures. "I wrote it for my manager," the composer (an inveterate jester behind his trademark scowl) sardonically confessed; and indeed, it recalled the manner, if not the style, of Chaikovsky, Rachmaninoff's early mentor, who had died more than forty years previously (and of Chopin's century-old Nocturnes behind Chaikovsky). But it is also the most intellectually and "modernistically" contrived. It uses the device of melodic inversion, which was not only a stock resource of academic counterpoint, but also a mainstay of Schoenberg's "atonal" motivic processes. Perhaps needless to say, though, Rachmaninoff's dissonances were entirely unemancipated.

Yet if Rachmaninoff's eminence and success insulated him from debate, his rather small output during his years of exile after 1917 may reflect discouragement after all

EX. 9-22   Serge Rachmaninoff, *Rhapsody on a Theme of Paganini*, 18th variation

at the reception his music was receiving from connoisseurs, as well as the limits his concert career placed on his composing time. Other traditionalists adopted a more embattled and polemical stance. A curious counterpart to Rachmaninoff was his close friend and fellow émigré Nikolai Medtner (1880–1951), another brilliant piano virtuoso whose composing career, however, lacked the luster—or at least the publicity—of Rachmaninoff's.

While in Russia, Medtner was, as one admirer put it, "Moscow's recognized composer,"[30] especially after the deaths of Chaikovsky and Sergey Taneyev, Medtner's teacher, who was known as the "Russian Brahms." But having left Russia after the revolution, he found himself without an audience. His first destination was Germany; but the Germany he found in 1921 was not the Germany of Brahms or even the Germany of Mahler. It was the Germany of Weill and Hindemith and Schoenberg, and Medtner fled—to Paris. But the Paris he fled to was the Diaghilevized Paris where his countrymen Stravinsky and Prokofieff reigned supreme, and where Medtner for ten years suffered an agony of neglect.

In 1935 he moved again, to England, whose then somewhat provincial musical climate offered him a more congenial environment. He once again became the center of a small but fairly influential coterie cult of fanatical admirers, who gave Medtner's music more exposure on London's concert stages than it ever had in Berlin or Paris. In London, too, he found a somewhat unlikely patron: the Maharajah of Mysore, the rich ruler of an Indian feudal state, who established "The Medtner Society" to subsidize a grandiose project to record the composer's complete works in his own performances. Medtner lived to complete three big sets of 78 RPM discs before his death.

With every move, Medtner found himself further on the margins of Europe's musical life; and his final triumph with the assistance of an eccentric maharajah only underscored that marginality. He was painfully right to see his marginalism in social as well as artistic terms. In Paris, where he suffered most acutely from neglect, what particularly galled him was Stravinsky's snob appeal. He attended the 1924 concert at which Stravinsky unveiled his "neoclassical" Concerto for Piano and Winds, and wrote to Rachmaninoff about it in a rage. The first item on the program was Stravinsky's *Firebird* suite. Medtner found, to his surprise, that he liked it:

> But then the composer appeared with his new concerto and gave me such a box on the ear for my silly sentimentality that I couldn't bear to stay until the end of *The Rite of Spring*, the more so as it showed its stuff right from the start. I walked out. But the public, who had filled the Paris Grand Opera to overflowing, this public who takes it as an insult if someone should appear in its midst in anything but tails or a smoking jacket (for which reason I had to hide myself and my little grey coat in the highest loges)—this public steadfastly withstood every slap in the face and every humiliation, and what is more, rewarded the author with deafening applause. What is all this?![31]

What it was, of course, was irony, something for which neither Medtner nor Rachmaninoff could muster a proper sympathy, which is why they—and all "sincere" romantics—had to suffer after the Great War. Medtner fought back with a book called *Muse and Fashion* (*Muza i moda*, 1935), in which he thunderously defined "modernism" as

The fashion for fashion. "Modernism" is the tacit accord of a whole generation to expel the Muse, the former inspirer and teacher of poets and musicians, and install Fashion in her place, as autocratic ruler and judge. But since only what has been begotten by Fashion can go out of fashion, modernists are eternally the victims of her caprices and changes, victims that are constantly doomed by her to "epigonism" [epigone, from Greek = latecoming mediocrity]. The fear of this "epigonism" compels the cowardly artist to run after Fashion, but she, the artful wench, does not stop in her flight, and always leaves him behind.[32]

But since the book was written in Medtner's native Russian, and found no translator until the year of the author's death (and then into English, not French), it was even easier to ignore than his music. But the music was not negligible. It merits sampling here as much for its intrinsic interest and distinction as for its illustrative value. What it illustrates is what long seemed a musical world irrevocably divided between those who wrote "audience music" and those who wrote "composers' music," those who placed their art at the service of its consumers and those who placed it, so to speak, at the service of its history. It was a situation in some ways reminiscent of the seventeenth century, when the old polyphonic style that Monteverdi called the *prima prattica* hung on (as the *stile antico*) into the age of the *basso continuo* — a "Renaissance" idiom coexisting with the "Baroque" in seeming violation of the "law of stylistic succession."

But of course that "law" was only written in the nineteenth century, and the coexistence of diverse practices in the seventeenth century was peaceful because there was a consensus as to what style served what function. (The "old style" was used exclusively for utilitarian church music.) In the twentieth century coexistence was not peaceful. Those who upheld the "law" and its attendant ideology, and those (like Korngold, Rachmaninoff, and Medtner) who resisted or defied it were factions vying for legitimacy. The upholders always have an edge in the history books, even in this one, because historiography, if it is to be interesting, has to give preference to change over stasis.

But the stasis, it should be emphasized in fairness, was only relative. Even within recognizably "old" styles there was room for freshness and originality as long as imaginative composers were drawn to them; and as long as that was the case, the styles could not be declared dead except as propaganda. Among Medtner's most distinguished pieces was a series of compositions for piano he called *Skazki*, "Tales." It was a time-honored romantic genre, related to the ballade, and practiced particularly by Schumann, who wrote sets of chamber pieces with "*Märchen*" in their titles (*Märchenbilder*, "Pictures from a book of tales," for viola and piano; *Märchenerzählungen*, "Tale-Tellings," for piano, clarinet, and viola). The tale itself was never specified; it was the atmosphere of "telling" that romantic composers liked to evoke.

Medtner's eleven sets of *skazki* were composed between 1905 and 1928, a span of years that encompassed the heydays of both "maximalism" and "neoclassicism." They give no evidence of awareness of either tendency, however, preserving instead the kind of careful miniaturist workmanship and intimate expressivity associated with Chopin, or with the late piano music of Brahms. The set of four *skazki*, op. 26, were written in 1912, contemporaneously with *The Rite of Spring*. The third of them, in F minor, is sampled in Ex. 9-23. It will make a jarring contrast with the rest of the music discussed in this chapter and the last (excepting Korngold's and Rachmaninoff's, of course), and that is part—but only part—of the reason for showing it here.

Looked at superficially or impatiently, or otherwise "from afar," the music may seem stylistically undistinguished, since the limits within which the composer chose to work were familiar—indeed, long-familiar—ones. But a close look, sensitive to particulars, uncovers details of surprising interest. Compare Ex. 9-23a, the opening "perfectly ordinary" 16-measure theme, for example, with Ex. 9-23b, its recapitulation at "Tempo I." The modulation back to the original key, delayed until the theme is more than half over, is handled with a subtlety and aplomb that would have done any composer proud in 1882, and would have earned its author then a reputation for harmonic ingenuity. Is the harmony any less ingenious or the idea any less original because the music was composed thirty years later? Does the music accomplish less, or mean something different, because it comes later? To such questions there can be no simple or categorical answer. They stand here as a symbolic gateway to debate—the most pervasive musical debate of the twentieth century, with ramifications at every level from the most narrowly stylistic to the most broadly political or sociological.

EX. 9-23A   Nikolai Medtner, *Skazka*, Op. 26, no. 3, mm. 1–16

To end the chapter with one last ironic fillip, we may observe that the twentieth-century *stile antico*, represented here by Korngold, Rachmaninoff, and Medtner, did conform after all, in certain respects, to its seventeenth-century "functional" or "utilitarian" prototype. As already suggested by Korngold's career in the movies, the style could function as an emotional illustrator, available to composers, themselves without any personal stylistic commitment, who were adept at manipulating a great range of styles for "semiotic" or signaling purposes in various commercial undertakings from 'B' movies to advertising.

Thus the "Rachmaninoff concerto" style ended up in Hollywood anyway—or, to be more exact, in Ealing, Hollywood's British counterpart. Lots of British movies of the 1940s used the heroic piano concerto idiom as a suitably turbulent device for "underscoring" passionate romantic dialogue. And in one film, *Dangerous Moonlight* (1941), an ersatz Rachmaninoff concerto functions as a major plot element. The main character is a Polish concert pianist in exile, modeled on Ignacy Jan Paderewski (1860–1941), both a great virtuoso and a Polish patriot, who served from 1919 to 1921 as the first prime minister of independent Poland. The movie character uses his concert travels to perform espionage services for the Allies in the early days of World War II. His signature piece, both performed as such in the movie and used

EX. 9-23B   Nikolai Medtner, *Skazka*, Op. 26, no. 3, recapitulation as underscoring material, was a six-minute concerto movement composed by Richard Addinsell (1904–77), England's most prominent film composer of the period. Under the title "Warsaw Concerto" it even became a "pops concert" repertory item (Ex. 9-24).

EX. 9-24   Richard Addinsell, second theme from "Warsaw Concerto"

Theodor W. Adorno, the most vigilant critic of utilitarian music (whether avant-garde *Gebrauchsmusik* or Hollywood romanticism) seized upon what he saw as the generic "devolution" of nineteenth-century styles from the autonomous and absolute artworks of "authentic" romanticism to the commercial and functional soundtracks of capitalist exploitation to support his contention that the styles themselves had become "commodified"—that is, turned from avenues of possibly sincere and spontaneous human expression to mercantile fetishes that manipulate listeners, rob them of emotional authenticity, and reduce them to automatons. Romantic styles, he argued, once co-opted by the movies, could only produce the effects of movie-music, drugging and paralyzing listeners with sensuous pleasure. Such a style was therefore obsolete as art, available only as entertainment, which for Adorno was socially regressive by definition. This was the strongest invective ever mustered on behalf of the "law of stylistic succession."

But the joke turned out to be on Adorno, since (as already hinted above in connection with *Wozzeck*), the modernist styles he regarded as most artistically viable—that is, those least amenable to commercial exploitation because least sensuously appealing to passive consumers—have also long since been annexed by the movies as emotional illustrators, albeit for the opposite sorts of emotions. In 1942, Bertolt Brecht and Hanns Eisler, by then both refugees from Hitler living in Los Angeles, collaborated on

Hangmen Also Die, a Hollywood *filme noir* directed by Fritz Lang, another émigré, about the assassination of Reinhard Heydrich, the officer in charge of the Nazi occupation of the Czech lands. Eisler's score contains many atonal passages to illustrate German brutality and Czech suffering. The earliest twelve-tone movie score was composed in 1955 by Leonard Rosenman, who had studied with Schoenberg at UCLA, for *The Cobweb*, a movie set in an insane asylum. There seems to be nothing inherently more or less exploitable about idioms as such. Nor, given the high premium placed on social function by many disillusioned modernists after the Great War, can one maintain that autonomy was any more an inherent feature of modernism than it had once been of romanticism. As we have seen repeatedly, in many contexts, what looks like inherence within one "discourse" or mode of articulated thought can be easily shown (within another) to be an aspect of use.

The Cult of the Commonplace

SATIE, THE FRENCH "SIX," AND SURREALISM; THOMSON AND THE "LOST GENERATION"

Not long ago, an apple orchard would have suggested to Rimsky-Korsakov, or even to the young Stravinsky, a secret, mysterious place, an impenetrable jungle, whereas in our day the poet seeks an ordinary apple on Olympus, an apple without artifice or complications, which is the most flavorful kind.[1]

—SERGEY DIAGHILEV (1924)

Never any magic spells, reprises, sleazy caresses, fevers, miasmas. Never does Satie "stir up the swamp."[2]

—JEAN COCTEAU (1918)

THE ANTI-*PETRUSHKA*

On 18 May 1917, at the very height of the Great War, Sergey Diaghilev's Ballets Russes unveiled a new work — a "ballet réaliste" in one scene, called *Parade* — at the Théâtre du Châtelet in Paris, where six years earlier Stravinsky's *Petrushka* had premiered. There was nothing at all Russian about this new Ballets Russes offering. The music was by Erik Satie, the scenario was by Jean Cocteau, the sets and costumes were by Pablo Picasso. The choreographer, Leonid Massine, was Russian, it was true (as were all of Diaghilev's choreographers), but the steps he designed were not.

The cast of characters somewhat resembled that of *Petrushka*. A *parade*, in French, means not only what in English is called a parade, but also a sideshow performed outside a vaudeville theater or "music hall" to lure a crowd. So the new ballet featured a conjurer, an oriental entertainer, and other carnival performers. But whereas in *Petrushka* the magically animated characters had interacted in a conventional love melodrama culminating in murder, the characters in *Parade* simply went about their everyday business: the conjurer conjured, the acrobats did acrobatics, a "little American girl" pantomimed a silent movie. Whatever latent drama there was went undramatized.

Except, that is, the drama of art thwarted by the uncomprehending crowd, the perennial self-pitying myth of the avant-garde. Despite the energetic "barking" and gesticulation provided by the managers (or "impresarios") of three competing theaters, the crowd thinks the free samples are the show itself. The managers, having exhorted the dumb yokels in vain, fall in an apoplectic heap. The sideshow performers then try to get the prospective audience to enter the theaters, but again to no avail. The ballet action comes to no conclusion, simply peters out.

The actual audience in the ballet theater, whose members presumably went gladly enough to circuses and music halls to see actual conjurors, dancers, and acrobats, hated *Parade*. Openly they objected to the incongruously "low" level of taste to which it seemed to pander, insulting ballet's proud aristocratic heritage; covertly, they may have resented the rudimentary story line's implied insult to themselves, the dumb yokels, ostensibly the object of the artist's solicitation, but in reality an object of contempt. In any case, the premiere was another succès de scandale to set beside *The Rite of Spring*. People hissed and booed this seemingly bland, innocuous offering just as they had Stravinsky's crashingly dissonant, violent ballet four years ago. Like it, the new ballet had touched a nerve.

Cocteau suggested, indignantly, that the audience had refused to consider that art could be beautiful "without an intrigue of mysticism, of love, or of annoyance."[3] They would have been pleased, he tauntingly protested (recalling *Petrushka*'s great success), only "if the acrobat had loved the little girl and had been killed by the jealous conjuror, killed in turn by the acrobat's wife, or any of thirty-six other dramatic combinations." So banal, he implied, had notions of high art become in the wake of romanticism, and so depraved were the expectations of its audience.

But his words need to be taken with a grain — no, a quarry — of salt. Cocteau knew well enough that artistic frivolity was suspect in a time of bloody conflict. *Parade*'s very insouciance, its "cultivated apathy"[4] (in the words of the cultural historian Daniel Albright), and its flagrant neglect of current events were all deliberate provocations. Its very lack of response, as Albright points out, made it "one of the profoundest artistic responses to the Great War," a display of emotional scar tissue. It was Cocteau's pointed answer to Diaghilev's famous challenge, "Étonne-moi" (Astonish me). He had succeeded in astonishing Diaghilev and the audience alike, precisely by avoiding any conventional attempt to astonish or impress. And so did Satie's primitive, clumsily orchestrated, emotionally aloof score.

There was enough melodrama in ordinary life, *Parade* implied. Let art celebrate ordinariness — "normalcy," to use President Harding's war-weary word — as the precious thing it is. That was the "realism" the ballet's subtitle advertised. But that word, too, carried an ironic freight. For one thing, thanks to technology, contemporary reality now contained a great deal of unreality. Movies (still silent), the newest of the entertainment media and the only specifically twentieth-century one, symbolized this invasion of the real by the imaginary. Movies were a part of everyone's everyday life and yet, at the same time, they were of all media the most instantaneously transporting and manipulative — which is to say the most unreal. They offered an alternative (or what we now call a "virtual") reality through which the imagination could truly supersede the senses.

Parade was the first work of "high art" to pay tribute to the movies. The American girl's routine was a collage of impressions from France's great ally across the sea, most of them carried to the French imagination via celluloid. Cocteau sent this description to Satie to guide him in fashioning the music:

> The *Titanic* — "Nearer My God to Thee" — elevators... steamship gear — *The New York Herald* — dynamos — airplanes... palatial movie houses — the sheriff's daughter — Walt Whitman... cowboys with leather and goat-skin chaps — the telegraph operator from Los Angeles who marries the detective in the end... phonographs... the Brooklyn Bridge — huge automobiles of enamel and nickel... Nick Carter [the detective hero of countless turn-of-the-century American "dime novels"]... the Carolinas — my room on the seventeenth floor... posters... Charlie Chaplin.[5]

To the choreographer, Cocteau sent some more details: the American girl's dance should mime the characteristic poses of silent picture stars Mary Pickford (1893–1979), "America's sweetheart," and Pearl White (1889–1938), the heroine of the *Perils of Pauline* serials: riding a horse, catching a train, driving a Model T Ford, swimming, playing cowboys and Indians, shuffling with feet splayed à la Charlie Chaplin. To accompany these antics, Satie fashioned a motley of ostinatos (perhaps a take-off on the notorious ostinatos of *The Rite of Spring*) surrounding a central *Rag-time du paquebot* ("Passenger-steamer rag") that turns out to be a parody of *That Mysterious Rag*, a popular number by Irving Berlin (1888–1989), a Russian-born composer who was by then already the leading figure in Tin Pan Alley, America's popular song and sheet-music industry. Satie's C-major tune (Ex. 10-1a) matches the rhythm of Berlin's (Ex. 10-1b) exactly, while the melody diverges, though never far.

More evidence of the antirealism (magic realism, dream realism) of *Parade*'s "realism" were Picasso's costumes, especially the huge modernistic constructions — cubist paintings come to life — worn by the "impresarios" (amiable caricatures of Diaghilev, perhaps) as they gesticulated from the sides of the stage (Fig. 10-1). The score contains "parts" for such realistic sounds of modern life (whether as lived or as cinematically experienced) as a lottery wheel, a steamboat whistle, a siren, a pistol, a typewriter, and a "bouteillophone," a row of beverage bottles played like a xylophone. There was also something called *flaques sonores* ("sound puddles"), which Satie never defined. He may have had in mind the sound of a boot stepping in a puddle, common enough on city streets, but he never let on. Every conductor of the score has had to realize the effect somehow. (Ernest Ansermet, who led the premiere, used suspended cymbals struck with sponge-tipped drumsticks.) In

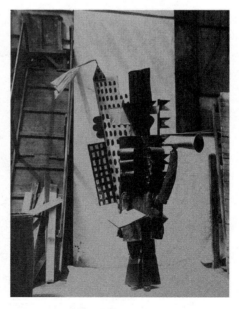

FIG. 10-1 "The American Impresario," costume by Picasso for Satie's *Parade*.

their balletic context, however, these "realistic" sounds were anything but realistic. Abstracted from "life" and placed in a zany world of art, their everyday quality became uncanny.

The poet Guillaume Apollinaire (1880–1918), who at the time was experimenting in his verse with something similar — casual or colloquial language and homely imagery in startling juxtapositions — tried to capture this effect in a promotional piece he wrote

EX. 10-1A   Erik Satie, *Parade, Rag-time du paquebot* episode in piano score

EX. 10-1A (*continued*)

for Diaghilev that appeared in the newspapers in advance of the *Parade* premiere, and then in the program book. This little article became famous for the way it conveyed the enchantment that could arise out of artistic transformations of the ordinary. It being wartime, the article also made a nationalistic appeal: Apollinaire saw in *Parade* a chance to shift the center of artistic gravity permanently away from Germany toward France. Out of these two notions Apollinaire developed and described a new sensibility, to which he gave a name that became a watchword.

First of all, in Satie's music Apollinaire claimed to find "a clarity and simplicity in which you can see the wonderfully lucid mind of France itself."[6] (The phrase "clarity and simplicity" practically became a religious mantra to many French and French-influenced musicians.) Second, Picasso's and Massine's collaboration, in which the impresarios' costumes looked like walking stage sets, succeeded in "consummating for the first time a union between painting and the dance — between the plastic and the mimic — which heralds the arrival of a more complete art." Third, the American girl, "as she cranks an imaginary car, will express the magic of everyday life" and give the audience a chance "to appreciate the grace of modern movement — something they had never suspected." For all these reasons, Cocteau had misnamed his grand collaborative enterprise a "realistic ballet." To communicate the full effect of "this new alliance" of media, Apollinaire decided, a new word was needed: "*sur-réalisme.*"

EX. 10-1B   Irving Berlin, *That Mysterious Rag*

Apollinaire's word immediately shed its hyphen and entered the vocabulary of modern art around the world. It was a brilliant find: the original hyphen made it clear that *surréalisme* had been coined on an analogy with, but in scathing contradistinction to, the standard French word *surnaturalisme* — "supernaturalism," the very thing the new art rejected. The core concept was a collage of ordinary unmagical things from which the supernatural was rigorously excluded. What lent the magic was not the things but the collage itself. The word — from *coller*, "to paste" or "stick together" — had been coined a few years earlier, in 1912, when Picasso began pasting household items into his paintings (at first a swatch of a tablecloth, later bits of newspaper, postage stamps, etc.).

The idea stemmed indirectly from Dada, the movement that sought to extend the concept of art to its limits — or rather, to find out what those limits were — by exhibiting mundane items (most famously, a urinal) as if they were artworks. But in Picasso's collages, and in what eventually became surrealist art, there was no "as if." The assemblage was artful by design: in collage, art was not challenged by reality, but rather the reverse. The recognizable world was subverted by decontextualization — or recontextualization in incongruous juxtapositions — and became a dream world. (Needless to say, the movement has attracted psychoanalytical interpreters, and some of its practitioners — notably the Spanish painter Salvador Dali [1904–89] — studied and ostentatiously quoted the work of Freud.) Given the definition Apollinaire implied, one of everyday reality transfigured by an estranging context, the first surrealist work, in advance of the name, was arguably another ballet produced by Diaghilev: *Jeux* ("Games"), conceived and choreographed by the great dancer Vaslav Nijinsky to music by Debussy (the only ballet the French master ever completed). It was first performed on 15 May 1913, just two weeks before the tumultuous premiere of *The Rite of Spring*, and was more or less forgotten amid the publicity Stravinsky's ballet generated. Debussy's score, which he published as a *poème dansé*, was one of his most sumptuous and shimmering, his ultimate masterpiece of "impressionism." Its harmonic and coloristic subtlety, its narrow but endlessly calibrated dynamic range (out of 700 measures only 150 are marked louder than *piano*) and its kaleidoscopically shifting motivic patterns have all fascinated composers, and the music has had a respectable life in repertory as an orchestral showpiece.

The ballet itself, however, was a fiasco; for the scenario Debussy's mysterious music accompanied consisted of a tennis game played by a boy (Nijinsky) and two girls in ordinary tennis clothes on an ordinary court. The action consists not of tennis but of flirtation, and the ending is deliberately enigmatic: a lost tennis ball from another court suddenly drops into their midst, and the characters all flee the stage. The idea of defamiliarizing the ordinary is apparent enough, but Debussy's impressionist style, thanks especially to *Pelléas et Mélisande*, had been irrevocably marked as *surnaturaliste*. The new ballet's mixture of the natural and the supernatural failed to convince: the danced scenario and the music seemed like oil and water.

"LIFESTYLE MODERNISM"

After the war, or rather after *Parade*, the line initiated by *Jeux* was continued by a new crop of very young French composers who venerated Satie, and who were eager to cast off the trappings of impressionist mystery (by then a cliché and an unwelcome French stereotype) and celebrate the artistically transfigured "everyday." Diaghilev enthusiastically commissioned and produced their work, which was (partly thanks to his patronage) considered the last word in sophistication. Three one-act ballets that received their premieres in 1924 and 1925 typified the new genre, aptly christened "lifestyle modernism"[7] by the ballet historian Lynn Garafola.

First came *Les biches* by Francis Poulenc (1899–1963), presented on 6 January 1924, the eve of the composer's twenty-fifth birthday. (He had received the commission at the age of twenty-two.) The title means, literally, "The Does" (i.e., female deer); in the French idiom of the time it was a term of endearment ("*ma biche*" or "*ma bichette*") a man tendered to a young girl he wished to seduce. In English, Poulenc's ballet is usually called "The House Party." Even more plotless than *Parade*, it simply portrayed a soirée, hosted by a rich society matron, at which girls in summer dresses danced and flirted with young men in bathing suits (and occasionally with their hostess or, more daringly, with each other). Poulenc's music, which included a few songs sung from the pit, was a pastiche of three styles: that of the eighteenth-century dance suite (e.g., Couperin), that of French "classical" (i.e., nineteenth-century) ballet, and that of the contemporary dance hall or ballroom. One characteristic number was a *Rag mazurka* (Ex. 10-2). The action suggests an erotic promiscuity comparable to the stylistic promiscuity of the music.

EX. 10-2 Francis Poulenc, *Les biches*, opening bars of *Rag mazurka*

EX. 10-2 (*continued*)

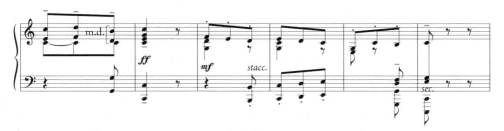

On 13 June 1924, *Le train bleu* ("The blue train") by Darius Milhaud (1892–1974) was unveiled. Composed to a scenario by Cocteau, the ballet depicts an afternoon at a fashionable vacation spot where an elegant train from the capital, "Le Bleu," disgorges new bathers daily. More men in bathing suits do their exercises and practice their favorite sports. That is all. *Les matelots* ("The sailors") by Poulenc's exact contemporary Georges Auric (1899–1983), followed a year later. A simplified and perhaps purposely trivialized version of the story line immortalized in Mozart's *Così fan tutte*, it concerns three mariners who visit the fiancée of one right before departing on what they say will be a long voyage. They soon return, however, and, donning false beards, test her fidelity by trying to seduce her. She refuses them, they remove their disguise, and the loving couple is joyfully reunited. The composer described the music euphemistically as a "fantasia on circus themes." Some of his tunes were readily identified by the audience as songs sung in bars and brothels.

Lifestyle modernism was thus another reversion to a preromantic (hence antiromantic) view of art. Like Mozart's (as described by the American musicologist Wye J. Allanbrook), the new French music offered its audiences a sonorous reflection of their own lives (what Allanbrook called "representations of their own humanity"). But the portrayal was deliberately shallow and not very humane. It pointedly avoided emotional depth and portrayed only the most superficial social activities and amusements; that is why Garafola's seemingly anachronistic adoption of the recent term "lifestyle," which refers implicitly to the routine and material aspects of life, is so appropriate. "Lifestyle," moreover, implies a chosen way of life, which in turn implies comfort and leisure; and indeed, the subject matter of the postwar ballets identified the "reflected audience" explicitly with the moneyed classes who patronized Diaghilev's enterprise. They catered to a revived and newly defined "aristocratic" taste, the somewhat anxiously cynical (or at least insouciant) taste of what was called "the roaring twenties." It was the sensibility of disillusion.

Artists who valued seriousness of purpose were repelled. Karol Szymanowski (1882–1937), for example, the leading composer of newly independent Poland, remained faithful to another kind of modernism, the kind associated before the war with Russia, heavy with that special combination of spiritual elevation and oriental eroticism that evoked the "secret, mysterious places" and "impenetrable jungles" of the soul to which Diaghilev, who had once traded heavily in such items, referred sarcastically in this chapter's epigraph. Szymanowski had offered a ballet to Diaghilev, who rebuffed him with a taunt that his work was a "stew of leftovers." So it is not surprising, perhaps, that Szymanowski became one of the most carping critics of the new Parisian music, denouncing it as "vulgar tavern music"[8] and "mundane trivialities" engineered by that "malicious old man" Satie, who was wreaking revenge on his betters.

Nor did Satie's ballets, or those of his followers, reach the limits of "lifestyle modernism." The malicious old man took the idea to its logical extreme when he conceived of *musique d'ameublement* or "furniture music," described by Milhaud as "background music that would vary like the furniture of the rooms in which it was played," hence, explicitly, "music that would not be listened to."[9] The first experiment, in which Satie and Milhaud dashed off some *ritournelles* (endlessly repeated tunes, some of them quoted from popular concert pieces and operas) to accompany the lobby conversation during the intermissions between the acts of a play by the surrealist poet and painter Max Jacob (1876–1944), was a failure. The audience, obedient to concert decorum, remained seated and paid attention to the music despite Satie's exhortations to "Go on talking! Walk about! Don't listen!"

Later, fulfilling commissions from wealthy friends with little snippets bearing titles like *Tenture de cabinet préfectoral* ("Wall hanging for the boss's office") or *Tapisserie en fer forgé* ("Wrought iron tapestry") or *Carrelage phonique* ("Audible floor tiles"), Satie came closer to fulfilling his intention of actually furnishing a vestibule or salon with music, "adorning it for the ear," as Milhaud put it, "the same way as a still life by Manet might adorn it for the eye."[10] This was art deposed from its pedestal with a vengeance, now assuming a humble utilitarian role of lifestyle-enhancement. One senses a wish to exact penance for the romantic pretensions art had exhibited before the war, and for whatever it might have contributed to the grandiose thinking that had provoked and justified the bloodbath.

That may have been Diaghilev's wish as well; for, although he remained a passionate devotee of Wagner's music to the end of his life, and kept his prewar repertory alive to subsidize his new productions, he never lost an opportunity to mock the work that had made his early reputation, thus (as Poulenc later observed) giving the young artists he now nurtured a lesson in self-renewal. Never before was a generation of artists so exhorted, as Poulenc recalled, "to disown their predecessors, their elders."[11] Whenever Diaghilev would catch Poulenc or Milhaud or Auric at a performance of a prewar ballet, even *Petrushka*, he would taunt them: "You're going to hear that old music? *Mais quel ennui!*" (What a bore!). Triviality was the only escape, frivolity the only salvation.

Penance of another, perhaps related kind is suggested by *Vexations* (Ex. 10-3), a 13-beat, bizarrely notated piece (or fragment) Satie jotted down one day, perhaps as early as 1893, together with its separate bass line, a version with the harmonizing tritones inverted, and a casual note, "play 840 times," all followed by a remark to the effect that if one wants to follow the composer's instructions, one ought to prepare for the ordeal with meditation exercises. Since the time of this little item's posthumous discovery by Robert Caby, one of Satie's disciples, and especially since the famous 1963 concert at which the American composer John Cage (1912–92), leading a team of pianists, gave it a complete performance lasting eighteen hours and forty minutes (now enshrined in the *Guiness Book of World Records*), it has been a cause célèbre and the object of sometimes acrimonious debate.

EX. 10-3 Erik Satie, *Vexations*

Did it (as Cage thought) represent an actual exercise in spiritual transcendence (perhaps plausible in light of the composer's brief involvement in the 1890s with the Rosicrucians, a society of mystics), or was it rather a spoof of such exercises, a disavowal of their connection with the aims of art, and a snare for those humorless enough to take it seriously? That would put the endless little piece in harmony with the antiromantic tenor of lifestyle modernism; and it is hard not to suspect spoofing both in the outlandish note-spelling (B♭♭ "descending" to A♯!) and in the meticulously notated inversions of every tritone, the one interval (aside from the octave) that cannot be acoustically inverted.

Satie's penchant for dadaist cartooning reached its peak in the ballet *Relâche* (1924), his last work, created in collaboration with two early surrealists, the writer Blaise Cendrars (1887–1961) and the painter Francis Picabia (1878–1953). The title is a word (related etymologically to the English "release" or "relax") that was used in French theatrical bills and schedules to denote a night when the theater is not in use (possible English equivalents: "No show," "Theater dark," "Closed") so that unless one reads carefully, a notice of a performance of the work would look like a notice of no performance. Picabia thought that it would symbolize his conviction that all prewar artistic ideas were "out to lunch." Satie claimed credit for the idea, saying that in that way he could have a work of his playing all summer long in every theater in Paris.

As to action, the beginning of the first act set the tone. A ballerina (called Woman in the program) enters, then stops in the middle of the stage, sits down, lights a cigarette and examines the scenery while the orchestra continues playing. Then she gets up and dances while the orchestra stops. The frontispiece to the published score contains a drawing by Picabia in which one gentleman is shown silencing another gentleman (naked except for a top hat and wristwatch) with a note that reads, "When will people get out of the habit of explaining everything?" Between the acts came a little film (shot by René Clair, later a famous director) called *Entr'acte*, that began with Picabia and Satie firing a cannon straight out at the audience and continued with all kinds of strange "automatic" images — boxing gloves fighting with each other, matches lighting themselves — and culminated in a roller coaster ride.

Satie's music was largely a medley of street songs that brought to the audience's mind a collage of offensive or obscene texts to accompany the crazy doings on stage. The connective tissue was supplied by a four-note ostinato that kept coming back, at times somewhat varied in pace and harmony, to furnish an appropriate *musique d'ameublement* (Ex. 10-4). The audience was duly scandalized. This time, however, the attempt to offend seemed labored, and the ballet did not live in infamy like *Parade*. The only part to survive the first performances was Clair's *Entr'acte*, for which Satie had written perhaps the first authentic film score, with musical cues timed precisely to match the length of the shots they accompanied.

EX. 10-4   Erik Satie, *Relâche*, two "Entrées"

(a) Act 1, no. 4 ("Entrée de la Femme"), measures 1-2

(b) Act 2, no. 14 ("Rentrée de la Femme"), measures 1-2

NAKEDNESS

The fifty-eight-year-old Satie thus ended his career, in keeping with the insistently youthful tenor of the time, not like a grand old man but more like a declining *enfant terrible*. The one serious work of his late years was *Socrate*, a "drame symphonique" that consisted of three extracts from the dialogues of Plato, set for a high (preferably female) solo voice and small orchestra. It was written immediately after *Parade* for the American-born Princesse de Polignac (née Winnaretta Singer), the heiress to a sewing-machine fortune who had married into the French aristocracy and set up a famous salon where she presented "chamber-theatricals" for which she commissioned works by many prestigious artists.

Partly by virtue of their source and subject matter, Satie's Platonic settings were regarded as "neoclassical" even though they made no reference at all to old-fashioned musical forms, whether operatic or instrumental. But once the concept of the *style dépouillé* or "stripped-down style" had been named (by Boris Schloezer) in response to Stravinsky's music of the early 1920s (see chapter 8), *Socrate* was seen as its prototype. Its "denuded" or "white" classicism, even if only retrospectively acknowledged, made it Satie's most enduringly influential composition.

The end of the third movement, *Phédon* (Phaedo), which narrates the death of Socrates, is a setting of the most emotionally charged page in all of Plato. The postwar "ban on all pathos," to recall the mandatory irony described in chapter 8, gives way here to a ban on all eloquence, now the only way to preserve any chance of a sincere expression of emotion. From parallel ascending triads (the movement's main leitmotif) through a succession of rigorously diatonic ostinatos, each lasting several measures (but usually an "honest" four), to the harmonically void drumbeats of the final page (Ex. 10-5), the music ostentatiously displays not only its rejection of ostentatious emotional display, but also its eschewal of technical finesse.

The prominent use of the harp in what is otherwise a very spare orchestra (only seven wind players, a timpanist, and a small body of strings) is the only concession to opulence, but a necessary one for the sake of its associations with the classical lyre. The regularity with which ostinato gives way to ostinato lends the setting of Plato's prose an appearance of poetic scansion, turning into chill ritual chanting at the end. The stony-cold, benumbed mood (in accord with the description of the gradually numbing effect of the poison on Socrates' body) is broken only once, when the singer climbs unexpectedly to a high note while reporting Socrates's noncommittal final words ("Crito, we owe a cock to Esculapus"). Obviously an intrusion of the reporter's emotion rather than a depiction of Socrates's, this tiny breach in the otherwise dignified posture of the setting emphasizes that dignity by contrast. "A lesson in greatness and honesty"[12] was Poulenc's judgment of what to many musicians (then and since) has seemed merely skimpy and technically inept.

After Satie's death the mantle of nakedness—of emphatic antirhetoric and sophisticated naïveté—fell on Poulenc and Milhaud. Poulenc was the composer most closely allied with the poets of surrealism, sometimes including himself. His very first piece, *Rapsodie nègre*, op. 1 (1917), for a *Pierrot lunaire*-influenced ensemble of flute, clarinet, string quartet, and piano, brought in a baritone soloist for one movement, *Honoloulou*. The text, according to the composer, was from a book of verses by a Liberian poet named Makoko Kangourou. (No one has ever found this book.) It begins, "Honoloulou, poti lama!/honoloulou, honoloulou,/kati moko, mosi bolou/ratakou sira, polama!" The musical setting contradicts the flamboyant nonsense-exoticism with extreme plainness. The voice part, for example, is a pseudo-chant consisting of a descending minor tetrachord endlessly repeated. That plainness in the face of oddity would remain the surrealist formula.

EX. 10-5   Erik Satie, *Socrate*, III, end

EX. 10-5 (continued)

Cocardes (1919), a more elaborate concoction for voice and instrumental ensemble, became a sort of manifesto for the composers of Poulenc's youthful generation. The title, "Cockades" in English, refers to ribbons worn as an emblem or badge of membership on hats or uniforms. Just so, the Cocardes were a badge of surrealist affiliation. The text, by Cocteau, consisted of three poems — Miel de Narbonne ("Honey of Narbonne"), Bonne d'enfant ("Children's nurse"), Enfant de troupe ("Child of the troupe") — of which the titles were a clue to the sham tour-de-force or gimmick that united the whole. The last syllable of one became the first of the next, and so it was for each line in the poems (including the last, which linked up with the first). Thus, for example, Miel de Narbonne:

> Use ton coeur. Les clowns fleurissent du crottin d'or.
> Dormir! Un coup d'orteil: on vole.
> Vôlez-vous jouer avec moâ?
> Moabite, dame de la croix bleue. Caravane.
> Vanille. Poivre. Confiture de tamarin.
> Marin, cou, le pompon, moustaches, mandoline.
> Linoléum en trompe-l'oeil. Merci.
> Cinéma, nouvelle muse.

Or, in "English":

> Use your heart. The clowns flourish on golden manure.
> To sleep! A kick with the toe; one flies.

Wanna play wiv me?
Moabite, lady of the blue cross. Caravan.
Vanilla. Pepper. Tamarind jam.
Sailor, neck, pompon, moustache, mandolin.
Eye-tricking linoleum. Thanks.
Cinema, new muse.

The translation, since it lacks the wordplay of the original, is a completely arbitrary assemblage of phrases, most of them nouns that bring a crowd of discordant images to mind. The verbal trick of the original, though it lends "form" to the poem, is as meaningless a technical feat as Schoenberg's triple canon in retrograde in *Pierrot lunaire*. In Schoenberg's case it had been the loosening of the constraints of voice leading and dissonance treatment that made the contrapuntal complexities satirically easy to achieve. (Anybody can write canons if they don't have to be consonant.) In Poulenc's, it is the loosening of the constraints of semantics (and spelling!) that make the verbal dexterity a satirically empty display of skill. (Anybody can make puns if they don't have to mean anything.) The absence of semantic logic, made all the more pointed by a perfectly ordinary verbal logic, is the basic surrealist maneuver. The kaleidoscopic linkages of imagery follow no intelligible pattern, thus reminding the reader of the poem (or the hearer of the songs) of the "dialectics" of dreams. And the essential surrealist *musical* device, as Poulenc (following Satie) demonstrated again and again, was to surround the extravagant dream-imagery with a music that sounded insistently "normal" and commonplace in its evocation of the familiar music of one's surrounding "lifestyle." That was the big difference between the "surrealist" cabaret style, as exemplified by the *Cocardes*, and the "expressionist" one exemplified by *Pierrot lunaire*. Schoenberg's music was deliberately "subjective" and strange; Poulenc's deliberately "objective" and commonplace. Shortly before the first performance, Poulenc wrote to a critic that his songs captured the essence of contemporary Paris "without artifice," and that "they will show you that I am no Impressionist!" (i.e., no trafficker in mysterious places or impenetrable jungles).

The third song (Ex. 10-6) most clearly emphasizes what was "realist" in surrealist. The "ritournelle" at the beginning and the end is exactly like those used in vaudeville theaters (or "music halls") to introduce or follow an act, and the original scoring for violin, cornet, trombone, bass drum, triangle, and cymbal gave it an authentic "fairground" color. The ironic return in the middle, marked *triste* (sad), affects the manner of a vaudeville "song stylist." (Poulenc later confided that he was thinking of Maurice Chevalier [1888 – 1972], the star song-and-dance man of the Paris music halls, later a character actor in a number of American films.)

The commonplaces are of course ironic. Their clash with the verbal extravagances makes them extravagant in their own right. That extravagance, that paradoxical excess, is the "sur" in surrealist. To quote Daniel Albright, "Schoenberg worked to emancipate harmonic dissonance, while Poulenc worked to emancipate semantic dissonance"; or, putting it another way, "Poulenc was original, not in the way that his music sounds, but

EX. 10-6   Francis Poulenc, *Cocardes*, no. 3, end

in the way that his music means."[13] Or again, putting it as Apollinaire put it, surrealism demands that the artistic media "marry often without apparent bond as in life."[14] What makes life lively, Apollinaire implies, is the very lack of intelligible correlation between the sensory stimuli that bombard us from all sides. Surrealist art makes that fortuitous unintelligibility purposeful.

GENDER BENDING

Apollinaire's famous definition of surrealism came in the prologue to his play *Les mamelles de Tirésias* ("The breasts of Tirésias," 1918), the first explicitly designated "*drame surréaliste.*" In 1944, at the height of another great war, after turning unexpectedly to religious subject matter in several sober choral works that apparently left his earlier lifestyle modernism behind, Poulenc turned again, just as unexpectedly, to his surrealist roots and set Apollinaire's by-then-forgotten play to music as his first opera. The new war had made it timely again.

The play's title character, a woman named Thérèse when we first meet her, declares to her husband that she would rather be a soldier than a mother, grows a beard forthwith, opens her blouse to release her breasts, which turn out to be rubber balloons, and punctures them. Renamed Tirésias, she becomes a heroic general. In the second act, the husband, still desiring children, decides to have them by himself and manages to give birth to more than forty thousand in a single day. In the end, of course, the

FIG. 10-2   Poulenc, *Les Mamelles de Tiresias* (Metropolitan Opera, New York).

couple is reconciled, but Tirésias still eschews her breasts; when her husband offers her a bunch of balloons from which to select a pair of new ones, she flings the whole bunch out to the audience.

What might at first have appeared to be the drama's antifeminism is recognized in the end to be what is now called an "antiessentialist" argument. At the end of the play it is extended to call many areas of social division into question. Markers of gender—breasts, beards, childbearing—are cast off and assumed at will by characters of both sexes. So, too, are markers of race or class, which only achieve their divisive effect by convention. The artificiality and mutability of all names is the point at issue. At times the point is made ridiculously, as when Thérèse/Tirésias, moving out, throws her belongings out the window. "The piano!" her husband exclaims as the chamber pot comes flying. "The violin!" he bellows, picking up a urinal. At the end, however, the serious purpose is unironically revealed: both world wars having left France with a decimated generation of men, the country must unite and repopulate. "Scratch yourself wherever you may itch," the whole cast sings across the footlights in conclusion. "Love white or black; variety is delight. It is enough if you only learn this lesson, dear audience: Have children!"

Once again Poulenc affirms the special role music can play in the surrealist collage by utterly banishing anything exotic or otherwise extraordinary from his range of stylistic reference. The music does not try to compete in incongruity with the stage antics, but of course in context its apparent ordinariness is the ultimate incongruity. "I don't have Ravel's elfin sense that ennobles the unusual," Poulenc slyly told an interviewer. Instead, he made the commonplace extraordinary. Not *sur-naturel* but *sur-réaliste*.

Poulenc's setting of the prologue (Ex. 10-7), in which the theater manager "preps" the audience to accept the serious message behind the apparent farce, is a study in double irony. By seeming to accept the manager's seriousness at face value, clothing it in a conventionally beautiful aria in a straightforwardly melancholy diatonic idiom (only slightly spiced with Stravinskianisms), Poulenc puts it doubly in doubt. By refusing to admit grotesquerie into his musical language, Poulenc underscores the grotesquerie of the play. But at the same time the sadly lyrical music acknowledges the reality of the pain and horror that gave rise to Apollinaire's frivolities. The music's consonance, in short, is dissonant. Only at the very end, when the manager sinks gravely through a trap door and out of sight, is there a touch of "magic" in the music: the orchestra for an instant becomes a Balinese gamelan to provide a frame (just as actual Balinese gamelans do) for the dramatic action that follows, a passage into the world of the surreal. Once there, however, the music will resume its studied normalcy.

FROM SUBJECT TO STYLE: SURREALIST "CLASSICISM"

Milhaud's version of surrealism, unlike Poulenc's, sought to penetrate the sound-substance of his music and become in itself an attribute of style. For that reason, Milhaud's achievement is often taken more seriously than Poulenc's both by historians in the tradition of the New German School, who place the highest premium on technical innovation, and by neoclassicists who insist on musical "purity." Inspired by some famous passages in the music of Stravinsky (the C/F♯ fanfares in *Petrushka*) and Richard Strauss (the necrophiliac kiss in *Salome*, the ending of *Also sprach Zarathustra*), Milhaud was impelled to devise a systematic theory of "polytonality," which could be described as a technique for creating collages of keys. He gave the theory a thorough, even somewhat pedantic exposition in an article, "Polytonalité et atonalité," which

EX. 10-7 Francis Poulenc, *Les mamelles de Tirésias*, Prologue, 4 to 6

EX. 10-7 (continued)

he published in *La Revue Musicale*, the leading French musicological journal, in 1923. Putting his theory in apposition — hence in competition — with Schoenberg's, Milhaud distinguished them by asserting that "between polytonality and atonality there are the same essential differences as between diatonicism and chromaticism."[15] Polytonality is thus diatonicism multiplied. Milhaud justified it, in time-honored fashion, by tracing it back to Bach (or rather, to strict or "real" counterpoints at intervals other than the octave). But the lineage thus claimed is not convincing: tonal counterpoint is always ready to make adjustments (e.g., "tonal answers") to insure the perceptual ascendancy of a single tonic. At the opposite logical extreme, the mixture of all twelve diatonic tone centers in one stew, polytonality arrives at the same maximum (or meets the same limit) as atonality; to quote Milhaud's article, it "encroaches on the domain of atonality." In Milhaud's actual compositions, however, this never comes close to happening, because, unlike Schoenberg, Milhaud was uninterested in technical maximalism. Instead, as a little survey of Milhaud's polytonal practices will reveal, polytonality made it possible to construct unheard-of harmonies by juxtaposing simple melodies and chords in novel combinations that acquired their piquancy precisely from the recognizability of their homely sources. It was another case of a calculated incongruity that replaced everyday reality with an alternative or magical sur-reality by building fancifully on the real listening experience of real audiences. Rather than polytonality, a term that still offends many theorists who believe (not unreasonably) that combined chords still have single roots, Milhaud's technique might more accurately have been called "polydiatonicism." But the term "polytonality" is probably here to stay, one of the many misnomers that conventional practice has adopted and ensconced in use beyond hope of correction. We have been coping more or less successfully with "Gregorian chant" for a thousand years, so there is no need to complain.

Milhaud's first crop of polytonal experiments dates from around 1918, when the composer returned to France from Brazil, where he had been serving as secretary to his older friend the poet Paul Claudel (1868–1955), a professional diplomat, who had been appointed cultural attaché at the French embassy in Rio de Janeiro. These early works combined polytonality with exotic South American subject matter. They include a mystical ballet, *L'homme et son désir* ("The man and his desire," 1918), to a scenario by Claudel, which portrayed the Brazilian *floresta*, or tropical jungle, in animistic terms, Milhaud's percussion-heavy polytonal score suggesting the luxuriant growth of vegetation. But they also included the entertaining *Saudades do Brasil* ("Memories of Brazil"), a suite of dances for piano in which vivid recollections of urban popular music are given a surrealistic twist.

Ipanema (Ex. 10-8), the fifth item in the suite, is a samba named after one of the districts of Rio de Janeiro. It could be argued that the harmonies at the opening, in which E♭-minor and F-major triads are reciprocally superimposed every two bars, is not polytonal in any functional sense, since neither harmony is established as a functional tonic. In the middle section, however (mm. 35 ff.), the superimposed chords—C and G♭, as in *Petrushka*—are each given dominants. The functional independence is resolved, however, and again, reciprocally, ten bars later.

EX. 10-8A   Darius Milhaud, *Saudades do Brasil*, V (*Ipanema*), mm. 1–9

EX. 10-8B   Darius Milhaud, *Saudades do Brasil*, V (*Ipanema*), mm. 33–55

More abstractly (or at least less exotically) conceived is the Fourth String Quartet, op. 46 (1918). At the outset (Ex. 10-9), the keys of F major and A major are maintained in a functional equilibrium. Neither one is established by harmonic cadence, but the seven-bar diatonic theme, played first in F in the outer voices and then by the inner voices in A, has clearly functional harmonic implications—as it must, if the idea of polytonality is to have any perceptual validity. The third-relation between the tonics is stable throughout the movement. Still, all discrepancies are reconciled at the end, which is unambiguously in F.

Some might argue that only the surrealistic collage technique saves the simple dance tune from banality. But one could just as well turn that around and say that

EX. 10-9 Darius Milhaud, String Quartet no. 4, I, mm. 1–15

only the banality of the dance tune saves the polytonal texture from unintelligibility. As in Poulenc's more conceptual surrealism, Milhaud's functional surrealism depends as much on the ordinariness of the components as on the extravagance of their juxtaposition. The commonplace and the fantastic—or if you prefer, the hackneyed and the preposterous—achieve, ideally, a state of synergy or symbiosis.

Perhaps the ultimate in polydiatonic counterpoint is reached in the third of Milhaud's tiny chamber symphonies, subtitled *Sérénade* (1921), which Milhaud proudly quoted as the culmination of his little theoretical treatise of 1923. Like Stravinsky's *Sérénade en la*, Milhaud's six chamber symphonies, composed between 1917 and 1923, were written so that they could each be recorded on a single 78 RPM side (twelve inches in this case, lasting no more than four minutes). The opening four-bar phrase of the first movement in no. 3 (Ex. 10-10a) pits a simple E-major tune in the clarinet against an equally simple D-major tune in the bassoon. The pair of tunes in differing keys works as a kind of "module," constantly reappearing in various configurations as the basis for the counterpoint. In m. 9 (Ex. 10-10b) it is played down an octave by the bassoon and cello, against a descending scale in the flute and an ascending arpeggio in the viola that by itself would be assigned to the key of B♭ major. According to Milhaud's own analysis in the *Revue Musicale* article, the violin modulates from F major to C major in m. 10, and the clarinet's chromatic scale is to be considered a support for the violin's F major.

In m. 13 the modular pair is transposed and placed in the extreme outer voices: flute in G major against double bass in C. The bassoon can be construed as playing in D major. At m. 23 the upper voice of the modular pair appears alone in F major in the cello, against an A-major tune in the violin. The passage from m. 17 to m. 30, in which this partial appearance is the only direct reference to the modular pair, might be described as a development section, in which case the reappearance of the original modular pair at m. 31 is the recapitulation.

EX. 10-10A   Darius Milhaud, Symphony no. 3 (*Sérénade*), mm. 1–4

The second movement is a study in tritone relationships à la *Petrushka*: B against F, with the F given a "mixolydian" E♭ that concords punningly with the D♯ of B major). The two keys are the mediant and submediant of D, which prepares the way for the finale, in which (a somewhat Lydianized) D major comes through clearly as the dominating key. Thus the whole little symphony can be seen as tending toward its final cadence in good "tonal" fashion, in which case the polytonal texture is perhaps best read as an embellishment or a refreshment of a basic D-major tonality.

EX. 10-10B   Darius Milhaud, Symphony no. 3 (*Sérénade*), mm. 9–16

EX. 10-10B (*continued*)

Refreshment, indeed, seems to have been Milhaud's aim. "The resources of polytonality," he wrote, "enrich the expressive resources of music."[16] Its use "adds subtlety and sweetness to *pianissimi*, while to *fortissimi* it lends greater pungency and force." Above all, it renewed the possibility of writing simple diatonic melodies and ordinary chords that would be transfigured by their context, just as surrealism, with its uncanny juxtapositions, gave new life to figurative painting—the painting of real objects, rendered with craftsmanly verisimilitude—in an age of burgeoning cubism and incipient abstraction. The commonplace, the unremarkable, the stock of everyday life were all "rehabilitated" (the word is Cocteau's) within an art that, recovered from "decadence," no longer sought the rare, the recondite, or the occult, and no longer aspired to high eloquence or grandiosity. With high eloquence and grandiosity went romantic aspirations to the sublime. The French music of the postwar period was a desacralized art, an art brought down to earth, a thing made *pour plaire*—"to please"—that is, to exist in and adorn the lives of its users.

GROUPS

Such music, claimed one of its most articulate devotees, was the only contemporary music that "can be enjoyed and appreciated without any knowledge of the history of music."[17] And, for that reason, its "aesthetic" (that is, the basis of its appeal) was "the only twentieth-century aesthetic in the Western world." This was an ambitious and impressive claim indeed, proclaimed on behalf of a music that seemed to forswear ambition and eschew impressiveness, and offered with the deliberately paradoxical conviction that "the only healthy thing music can do in our century is to stop trying to be impressive."

These words were written not by a Frenchman but by the composer-critic Virgil Thomson (1896–1989), whom we have already met casually (in chapter 9). A Harvard-educated Missourian who came to France as a soldier toward the end of the Great War, Thomson stayed on to study composition with Nadia Boulanger, and remained in Paris until the start of the next war. On his return to the United States in 1940 he was hired as a music critic by the *New York Herald Tribune*. He held the post until 1954, during which time the "interwar" Parisian "aesthetic," as Thomson called it, had a very influential spokesman in frequent word and occasional musical deed.

Thomson was one of many young American artists in all media who lived as expatriates in Europe, mainly in Paris, between the world wars. It was a good time to be an American in Paris. The French regarded America as their wartime savior. French artists and intellectuals like Cocteau, Satie, and the group of younger composers who gathered around the two of them, idolized and absorbed American popular culture. That group, called Les Six ("The Six") on an analogy with the Russian "Five," included Poulenc, Milhaud, and Auric, who (as we have already seen) readily incorporated what they called "jazz"—or, more properly, American dance-band music—as a component in their "lifestyle modernism." The other three members of the group, which was somewhat artificially named by the critic Henri Collet on the basis of their chance appearance together in a concert program in 1920, were somewhat less inclined toward "Americanism" or lifestyle modernism. They included Arthur Honegger (1892–1955), a French-speaking Swiss who inclined, like his native country, to an amalgamation of French and German styles, and who won his chief fame on the strength of his five symphonies and his forceful sacred cantatas; Germaine Tailleferre (1892–1983), whose career eventually foundered on the traditional prejudice against women composers; and Louis Durey (1888–1979), whose left-wing political convictions soon turned him passionately against what he saw as the frivolous values of lifestyle modernism, and to a degree against the values of modern concert music altogether. Durey's music is decidedly obscure, but his lucky charter membership in the celebrated Group of Six (like the membership of the equally shadowy César Cui among the Russian Five) has obliged

FIG. 10-3   Le Group des Six with Cocteau (left to right: Poulenc, Tailleferre, Durey, Cocteau, Milhaud, Honegger; Auric is present as a drawing on the wall, like Mozart's mother in Fig. 30-4).

every subsequent textbook to drop his name, as this one has now done. (In later life Durey wrote workers' choruses on texts by Mao Tse-tung and Ho Chi Minh.)

Having been casually christened by a critic, the Groupe des Six achieved a certain tenuous reality the next year when Cocteau finagled a commission for them (minus the dour Durey) from a Swedish company based in Paris for a collectively composed ballet on a scenario of Cocteau's devising, called *Les mariés de la Tour Eiffel* ("The wedding party on the Eiffel Tower"). As *Parade*'s direct and designated successor, the new ballet synthesized lifestyle modernism with surrealism.

The scenario portrays a perfectly ordinary middle-class wedding party, come to the lowest platform of the Eiffel Tower, where shops and restaurants abound, for a banquet and a group photo. The photographer's "Watch the birdie" — in French, "*Un oiseau va sortir*" ("A bird is about to come out [of the camera]") — is the signal for the surreal juxtapositions to begin. Among the creatures that emerge from the giant prop camera onstage are an ostrich, a lion, a dove, a bathing beauty, and a big fat boy who massacres the wedding party with ping-pong balls and steals their banquet food, some of which he proceeds to feed to the Tower itself. Of course the wedding party recovers from being murdered, and sells its group photo to an art dealer for a fantastic sum.

The special combination of impossible (surreal) and ordinary (lifestyle) components is cemented by a music similarly pervaded by everyday "lifestyle" genres and "surreal" polytonal harmonies. The camera from which animate objects materialize unpredictably was a device, Cocteau wrote, to "extricate objects and feelings from their veils and their mists, to show them suddenly, so naked and so alive that one can scarcely recognize them."[18] Tailleferre's *Quadrille*, whose five tiny sections put five such sudden manifestations together in a collage, best matches its sounds to the effect described by Cocteau. An old-fashioned suite of ballroom dances, it accompanies the antics of a detachment of the *Garde républicaine* who show up after the massacre. They arrest the big boy not for murder but for feeding the Tower outside of feeding time. Then the ostrich is found sleeping in the elevator; the photographer puts a hat on its head, rendering it invisible, and pushes it back through the camera.

As for Virgil Thomson, his Paris years were devoted to translating this French musical surrealism, which incorporated so many faux-Americanisms, back into the authentic American vernacular. The expatriate cohort to which he belonged, a group that included such novelists as F. Scott Fitzgerald (1896–1940) and Ernest Hemingway (1899–1961), and whose major theme was postwar disillusion (or the apathetic frivolity born of it), is often called the "lost generation." The name was invented by Gertrude Stein (1874–1946), an American writer and arts patron who lived in Paris from 1903 until her death, and who maintained a celebrated salon at her home on the Rue des Fleurus that became the informal headquarters of the whole American expatriate arts community. Thomson and Stein, who had attended Radcliffe, Harvard's women's college, hit it off famously ("like Harvard men,"[19] the composer recalled), and the two of them collaborated on an opera, *Four Saints in Three Acts*, that, in terms of its impact on contemporary audiences and their consciousness of modern art, has to be regarded as the principal or "classic" text of musical surrealism.

FINDING ONESELF

The watchword remained collage, in many dimensions: within the text, within the music, and in the relationship of text and music. Having worked at Harvard with the famous psychologist William James, who studied the unconscious mind, Stein was interested in aspects of what is sometimes, erroneously, called "automatic writing" — a style (or method) based on free association that violates norms of semantics, syntax, and grammar while relying on phonic and rhythmic play like puns and jingles to achieve emotional epiphanies ("moments of consciousness,"[20] she called them) independent of time and memory.

This already recalls Thomson's praise of contemporary French music (particularly Satie's) as being music that can be fully understood and enjoyed without knowledge of history. It also recalls the "Surrealist Manifesto" (1924) by André Breton (1896–1966), a French writer who set himself up as the movement's theorist, and who defined surrealism as "pure psychic automatism, by which one proposes to express, either verbally or in writing, or by any other manner, the real functioning of thought; dictation of thought in the absence of all control exercised by reason, outside of all aesthetic and moral preoccupation."[21]

What a true surrealist strove for, Breton insisted, was irreducible and uninterpretable images that could not serve as metaphors, and impossible equations that could be formed by suppressing the word "like" in a simile. Thus, as Daniel Albright remarks, the phrase "breast of crystal"[22] is surrealist only "until somebody comes along to decipher it as a carafe"; and while "a tomato is like a child's balloon" could never qualify as surrealist, "tomato is balloon" does, excellently. "To exhaust the permutations of verbal propositions in the form $x = y$ is to reduce the universe to its essential blobbiness"[23] (or what William James called the "buzzing, blooming confusion"[24] of unmediated reality), minus the illusions of order that our critical faculties insist on imposing on our consciousness.

Now compare Stein on the subject of Susie Asado, a flamenco dancer:

> Sweet sweet sweet sweet sweet tea.
> Susie Asado.
> Sweet sweet sweet sweet sweet tea.
> Susie Asado.
> Susie Asado which is a told tray sure. A lean on the shoe this means slips slips hers. When the ancient light grey is clean it is yellow, it is a silver seller.
> This is a please this is a please there are the saids to jelly. These are the wets these say the sets to leave a crown to Incy.
> Incy is short for incubus.
> A pot. A pot is a beginning for a rare bit of trees. Trees tremble, the old vats are in bobbles, bobbles which shade and shed and render clean, render clean must. Drink pups.
> Drink pups drink pups lease a sash hold, see it shine and a bobolink has pins it shows a nail. What is a nail. A nail is unison.
> Sweet sweet sweet sweet sweet tea.

Writing like this, with its purely sonic associations (*there are the saids/these say the sets; clean must/Drink pups*), its stutters (*A pot. A pot; trees. Trees; bobbles, bobbles; render clean, render clean; Drink pups. Drink pups drink pups*), its puns (*Sweet tea = sweetie*) and its controlling rhythms (e.g., the flamenco hemiola pattern: *A lean on the shoe this means slips slips hers* = ´ ˇ ˇ ˇ ˇ ˇ ˇ / ¯ ¯ ´/) is clearly borrowing a great deal of its "structure" from music, and letting that serve in place of the usual semantic meaning in evoking the imagery promised by the title. What can music add? Ex. 10-11 shows what Thomson thought it could. His first setting of words by Stein, it dates from 1926.

EX. 10-11   Virgil Thomson, *Susie Asado*, beginning

The voice part, meticulously modeled on the rhythms and cadences of conversational English, is little more than a medium for the words, or perhaps a kind of incantation or chant. Thomson, who was just as interested as Stein in the interplay of sound and meaning (or in possibilities arising from the substitution of the one for the other) thought this minimalist approach not only necessary but a heaven-sent opportunity to test his ideas. "My theory," he wrote later,

> was that if a text is set correctly for the sound of it, the meaning will take care of itself. And the Stein texts, for prosodizing in this way, were manna. With meanings already abstracted, or absent, or so multiplied that choice among them was impossible, there was no temptation toward tonal illustration, say of birdie babbling by the brook. You could make a setting for sound and syntax only, then add, if needed, an accompaniment equally functional.[25]

The remark about the birdie and the brook is reminiscent of the surrealist ban on metaphor and simile. Everything is itself only; and at the same time everything equals everything else with no comparison necessary. The music may pursue a semantically parallel rather than subservient path, and all will come out right in the end. Thus Thomson's accompaniment is not merely "functional," but a collage in its own right, a bag of basic musical elements — diatonic arpeggios and scales — that not only holds aloof from the meaning of the text (no flamenco rhythms!), but maintains a freedom of syntax just as daring, in its homely way, as Stein's: the first combination of voice and piano is in blatant harmonic contradiction; the scales move in parallel sevenths or ninths; there is not a single "functional" harmony, or even a full triad. Did Thomson, writing it, think of Gertrude Stein's disclosure that "I like to improvise on a piano I like to play sonatinas followed by another always on the white keys I do not like black keys and never two notes struck by the same hand at the same time because I do not like chords"?[26]

Thomson's second Stein setting, *Capital Capitals* (1927), a little cantata for four men's voices (two tenors, baritone, and bass) and piano, also avoids "harmony" like a plague. The voices take turns in dialogue; they are never once combined. The long text ostensibly consists of a conversation about and among the four capital cities (Aix, Arles, Avignon, and Les Beaux) of ancient Provence. Only four times in fifteen minutes are full triads heard; and when they are, they are deployed in the most hackneyed school-exercise fashion, to accompany (or rather mock) the occurrence of "affective" words like "tenderness." Ex. 10-12a shows the first such passage, which comes on the fourteenth page of the thirty-four-page score.

Far more typical is the opening, a little prologue sung by the baritone before the dialogue as such begins (Ex. 10-12b). The monotonous note-repetitions give a whiff of plainchant, confirmed by the tonally impossible (but "modally" ordinary) cadence in the fourth bar. Thus, if Stravinsky's "neoclassic" manner bracketed off the nineteenth century as a sort of historical wrong turn, Thomson's "neomedieval" manner here brackets off almost the entire history of music, as if to confirm his remark about the possibility, and (one must infer) the desirability, proved by Satie, of composing a new music that required no historical knowledge for its full comprehension and enjoyment.

Composing in defiance of history meant composing in defiance of Germany, the land not only of history but of "historicism" as well.

The opera, on which Thomson began working in 1927 but did not orchestrate until its premiere had been arranged some six years later, actually had four acts, not three, and many more than four saints, although the main character is the great sixteenth-century

EX. 10-12A   Virgil Thomson, *Capital Capitals*, "Cannot express can express tenderness"

mystic, Saint Theresa of Avila. When staged, the opera has action; but that is entirely the director's business. For Stein, "anything that was not a story could be a play," for a play dealt not with the narration of events, but with "the essence of what happened."[27] And that, she said, is why she chose saints as her subject: "A saint a real saint never does anything, a martyr does something but a really good saint does nothing, and so I wanted to have Four Saints who did nothing and I wrote the Four Saints in Three

EX. 10-12B   Virgil Thomson, *Capital Capitals*, opening baritone solo

EX. 10-12B   (*continued*)

Acts and they did nothing and that was everything."[28] A play, she further explained (in a fashion that would have pleased André Breton), is a landscape.

That is not quite the paradox it seems. A landscape exists as a temporal constant, not a sequence or progression; so does heaven, where the saints live; and so does *Four Saints in Three Acts*. It has what the literary critic Joseph Frank christened "spatial form" in a famous essay of 1945, whereby "the time-flow of the narrative [or representation] is halted; attention is fixed on the interplay of relationships within the immobilized time-area."[29] Without using the word (for he is discussing literature rather than painting), he is nevertheless describing collage. Authors like James Joyce and Marcel Proust, in Frank's interpretation, subverted the "linearity" of literature through what amounted to collage techniques. So did Gertrude Stein; and so, in his music, did Thomson.

Among the things "collaged" in Stein's text were the cast of characters, the words (often unassigned to any character in particular), the stage directions, and the scene headings (often nonconsecutive or repetitive). Thomson had no choice but to set it all to music without discrimination, as one can see from the brief last act, "Saints in Heaven" (Ex. 10-13). His creative method, as he described it in his autobiography, was as "automatic" as Stein's:

> With the text on my piano's music rack, I would sing and play, improvising melody to fit the words and harmony for underpinning them with shape. I did this every day, writing down nothing. When the first act would improvise itself every day in the same way, I knew it was set.[30]

FIG. 10-4   Virgil Thomson and Gertude Stein with the score of *Four Saints in Three Acts.*

The Intermezzo that precedes the act is like the accompaniment to *Susie Asado* without the words: a collage of chords, arpeggios, and scales; and also, at times, a collage of keys in the surrealist polydiatonic ("polytonal") mode. The sung music continues in this vein, albeit with a few recurrent vocal phrases for Commère and Compère (Mom and Pop, "characters" invented by Thomson to act as masters of ceremonies)

EX. 10-13   Virgil Thomson, *Four Saints in Three Acts*, IV, intermezzo

EX. 10-13 (*continued*)

that give a semblance of thematic melody. John Cage, in a critical study of Thomson's music, wisely pointed out that the best one could do by way of analyzing the score of *Four Saints in Three Acts* was to cite statistics. "There are 111 tonic-dominants, 178 scale passages, 632 sequences, 38 references to nursery tunes, and one to 'My Country, 'Tis of Thee.'"[31] This is noted in mock-sorrow, as evidence that "the materials of music, in contrast to those of poetry, are becoming impoverished." More seriously critical, perhaps, is the observation that "where the text darts about in unpredictable directions, the accompaniment is merely repetitive, rarely more than linear, monophonic, and harmonic."

But that is Thomson's way, reminiscent of Poulenc's, of offering the text an appropriate "countercollage." Stein's fantastic imagery is countered and anchored, given shape, by Thomson's deliberately plain and unprepossessing music, so that (as Cage shrewdly notes) "the matter-of-fact and the irrational are one." Indeed, Cage might have added (if perhaps still disapprovingly) that when the saints finally get singing, as they do in Ex. 10-13, the music refers openly — and ecstatically — to the idiom of American

Protestant (Southern Baptist) hymns, the commonplace musical vernacular of the Kansas City–born composer's own youthful environment. That finally insures that the idiom of the opera will strike listeners — American listeners, anyway — as genuinely *sur-realistic*. And it resonates poignantly with Thomson's typically "lost generation" recollection that "I wrote in Paris music that was always, in one way or another, about Kansas City."[32]

The ultimate effect of Thomson's surrealism, then, was that of finding oneself, the reassurance any member of a lost generation craves. And that may be the ultimate message (or better, the ultimate massage) that surrealist collage offered the wounded psyches of postwar Europeans and Americans. "If there is one theme that dominates the history of modern culture since the last quarter of the nineteenth century," wrote Joseph Frank with forgivable exaggeration at the end of another World War, "it is precisely that of insecurity, instability, the feeling of loss of control over the meaning and purpose of life amidst the continuing triumphs of science and technics."[33] In the face of reason run amok, the best consolation art could offer was that of irrational acceptance and faith, which, not at all coincidentally, is the only way one can make head or tail of a surrealist collage.

Virgil Thomson spelled it all out when he exhorted listeners, in a note accompanying the first recording of excerpts from *Four Saints in Three Acts* (1947), not "to construe the words of this opera literally or seek in it any abstruse symbolism."[34] Instead, he wrote, "If by means of the poet's liberties with logic and the composer's constant use of the simplest elements in our musical vernacular, something is here evoked of the childlike gaiety and mystical strength of lives devoted in common to a non-materialistic end, the authors will consider their message to have been communicated."

To spell it out in the theater, Thomson cast the original production exclusively for African-American singers, even though, as he freely acknowledged, his work "had nothing whatever to do with Negro life,"[35] and even though the audience to which the work was addressed was unequivocally white and affluent. The implied equation of a Black American sensibility with "childlike gaiety and mystical strength" obviously played into the audience's racial prejudices; its contribution to the work's chic success (a sixty-performance run in a Broadway theater in the season of 1934–1935, unprecedented and rarely paralleled thereafter in the annals of American opera), can only seem in retrospect a fairly cynical calculation, despite Thomson's later protestation that he had chosen the singers "purely for beauty of voice, clarity of enunciation, and fine carriage."[36] But the commercial ploys that went into the casting were not a part of the work's conception, as is evident from the musical style, which refers not to any African-American idiom, but to that of the composer's own upbringing. The irony was that he had to go abroad to discover his American roots. He was not alone.

CHAPTER 11

In Search of the "Real" America

 EUROPEAN "JAZZ"; GERSHWIN; COPLAND; THE AMERICAN
"SYMPHONISTS"

AMERICANS IN PARIS, PARISIANS IN AMERICA

A new chapter in the history of American concert music — of musical "American-ism" — was opened by the generation of composers who, like Virgil Thomson, received their "finishing" in Paris in the 1920s, so often under the tutelage of Nadia Boulanger that their cohort is often called the "Boulangerie," French for bakery. They formed their musical tastes in the period of anti-Germanic backlash that followed World War I, which made them susceptible to the neoclassical and Dada/surrealist currents that dominated in the French capital. But the Parisian atmosphere in which they were coming of age was already seething with "Americanism," and it was this Americanized Paris that brought the new generation of American composers their vision of America. It was one of the characteristic ironies of the time that it should have taken a Parisian apprenticeship to create a viable "American school."

We have already noted the gusto with which the French were then consuming what a shrewd New York journalist, writing in 1925, called "the dance music that the Old World has called American jazz." A harbinger had been Debussy's *Children's Corner* (1908), a suite for piano dedicated to his little daughter Claude-Emma (Chouchou), which ends with "Golliwog's Cakewalk," a piece inspired by her little blackface doll. Cakewalks, strutting dances popularized in blackface minstrel shows, had been known in Europe since the turn of the century. Debussy's is a double parody: of the syncopated blackface dance itself in the outer sections, and of that perennial dartboard, Wagner's *Tristan*, in the middle (Ex. 11-1).

Beginning with the Cocteau-Satie *Parade*, which dates from 1917, the year the United States entered the Great War, a more up-to-date Americanism had begun to infiltrate Parisian concert and theatrical music. It was then that the term "jazz" gradually began showing up in European writings to designate what had formerly been known as ragtime. The etymology of the word and its American origins are obscure: David Schiff sums a complex and thorny matter up when he writes that "the term 'jazz,' first applied around 1916 (in New Orleans) to a rough and sexy strain of African-American music, soon became synonymous with any syncopated mass-marketed popular music."[1]

In 1918 Stravinsky, the greatest trendsetter of the day, wrote two pieces called "ragtime." One (already mentioned in chapter 8) was the last in a suite of three dances (after a tango and a waltz) from a wartime traveling show called *The Soldier's Tale* (*Histoire du soldat*), in which a Russian folktale was somewhat surrealistically updated with contemporary popular music played by an imitation village band consisting of two strings (violin and double bass), two winds (clarinet and bassoon), and two brass (trumpet and trombone), plus percussion. The other piece, called *Rag-time pour onze instruments* ("Ragtime for eleven instruments"), was scored for the same ensemble (minus the bassoon) plus a flute, a horn, a second violin, a viola, and a Hungarian dulcimer or cimbalom. It was finished on 10 November 1918, the very day of the German surrender; the manuscript carries the triumphant notation, *Jour de delivrance. Messieurs les Allemands ont capitulé* ("Day of deliverance; the esteemed Germans have capitulated").

That coincidence neatly symbolized one of the main attractions of American popular genres for the European allies (and also for left-wing "protest music" in Weimar Germany): it was as un-"*boche*" as music could get. That much was already evident in Debussy's double parody. But it received an enormous boost during the war, and was further enhanced in the war's wake by eye- (or ear-) witness contact. The Swiss

EX. 11-1A   Claude Debussy, "Golliwog's Cakewalk," mm. 1–17

conductor Ernest Ansermet, the *chef d'orchestre* for Diaghilev's Ballets Russes and one of Stravinsky's closest friends, wrote back to the Russian composer from America, where the company was touring in 1916, that whereas the American classical-music establishment was hopelessly dominated by Germans (and, he added regrettably, by Jews), nevertheless

> there is at the bottom of this immense country a forgotten or lost soul which has found its way into the *incredible music* you hear in cafes!! And the absence of traditions has forced this people—in their towns, their bridges, their machines—to improvise splendidly and with genius. These two elements are very close to us; they are precisely what we like, and what your work has revealed in Europe. To free this country from the boche imprint, reveal it to itself, and teach it that it belongs with us—and at the same time to take on this wonderful field of activity—would be a fine dream.[2]

E X. 11-1B   Claude Debussy, "Golliwog's Cakewalk," mm. 61–73

Beginning immediately after the war, American popular musicians, many of them African-American, brought their music to Europe and, as Ansermet might have predicted, were lionized in all the allied capitals, but especially by "progressive" musicians in Paris. Some, like the clarinettist Sidney Bechet (1897–1959), came for frequent lucrative tours. Ansermet heard Bechet play in London in 1919 and proclaimed him "an artist of genius."[3] The Swiss conductor's account of the music Bechet played, with an ensemble called the Southern Syncopated Orchestra, shows, perhaps for the first time (as the jazz historian Robert Walser puts it), "a 'serious' musician taking jazz seriously."[4] Ansermet respected what he heard enough to attempt a technical description of it, especially its qualities of rhythm and "modality":

> The desire to give certain syllables a particular emphasis or a prolonged resonance, that is to say preoccupations of an expressive order, seem to have determined in negro singing their anticipation or delay of a fraction of rhythmic unity. This is the birth of syncopation. All the traditional negro songs are strewn with syncopes which issue from the voice while the movement of the body marks regular rhythm . . . .
> In the field of melody, although his habituation to our scales has effaced the memory of the African modes, an old instinct pushes the negro to pursue his pleasure outside the orthodox intervals: he performs thirds which are neither major nor minor and false seconds, and falls often by instinct on the natural harmonic sounds of a given note — it is here especially that no written music can give the idea of his playing.[5]

Other Americans, like the singer Josephine Baker (1906–75), went to Paris to stay. Having originally come over in 1925 to star in a show called *La revue nègre* at the Théâtre des Champs-Elysées (the very hall where, a dozen years earlier, *The Rite of Spring* had had its stormy premiere), she quickly moved over to the Folies-Bergère, the number-one Paris nightspot or "music hall," became the darling of café society, posed for Picasso, opened her own nightclub, became wealthy, and never went back, becoming a French citizen in 1937. Her success was an inspiration to many African-Americans, and in later life Baker was one of the early icons of the American civil rights movement.

A few Europeans even got acquainted, in the early postwar years, with genuine early American jazz at its source. Milhaud was one. Touring America in 1922, he frequented Harlem nightclubs, and "speakeasies" (illicit clubs where alcoholic beverages were served during Prohibition) in New York and Boston, and caused some consternation when he told reporters that European "serious" music was being influenced by American jazz. His memoirs contain a vivid description of what he heard and its invigorating impact:

> Harlem had not yet been discovered by the snobs and aesthetes: we [Milhaud and the singer Yvonne George] were the only white folk there. The music I heard was absolutely different from anything I had ever heard before and was a revelation to me. Against the beat of the drums the melodic lines crisscrossed in a breathless pattern of broken and twisted rhythms. A Negress whose grating voice seemed to come from the depths of the centuries sang in front of the various tables. With despairing pathos and dramatic feeling she sang over and over again, to the point of exhaustion, the same refrain, to which the constantly changing melodic pattern of the orchestra wove a kaleidoscopic background. This authentic music had its

roots in the darkest corners of the Negro soul, the vestigial traces of Africa, no doubt. Its effect on me was so overwhelming that I could not tear myself away. From then on I frequented other Negro theaters and dance halls. In some of their shows the singers were accompanied by a flute, a clarinet, two trumpets, a trombone, a complicated percussion section played by one man, a piano, and a string quintet . . . .

As I never missed the slightest opportunity of visiting Harlem, I persuaded my friends to accompany me, as well as [the Italian composer Alfredo] Casella and [the Dutch conductor Willem] Mengelberg, who were in New York at the time. When I went back to France, I never wearied of playing over and over, on a little portable phonograph shaped like a camera, the Black Swan records I had purchased in a little shop in Harlem. More than ever I was resolved to use jazz for a chamber work.[6]

What eventually emerged from this experience was not the envisioned chamber work but a ballet, *La création du monde* (1923), composed to a scenario by Blaise Cendrars, the surrealist writer, who had traveled widely in China and Africa. It was scored for a small orchestra of seventeen soloists, including a piano, an alto saxophone, and "a complicated percussion section played by one man," like the one Milhaud heard in New York (or, for that matter, like the one Stravinsky employed in *The Soldier's Tale*). The action, based (according to Cendrars) on authentic African mythology, showed first a seething mass of weirdly costumed dancers representing the primal soup from which life would gradually erupt. The section sampled in Ex. 11-2 accompanies the beginning of that process: the inchoate living mass boils in a heaving motion — projections appear — trees shoot up, drop leaves that sprout into prehistoric animals — human forms begin to show (a torso, a great leg, etc.).

Milhaud's music takes the form of a fugue on a subject that embodies a stereotyped jazz "riff" or repeated figure reminiscent of Ansermet's description of "thirds which are neither major nor minor" in its unstable oscillations between F(E♯) and F♯ relative to D

EX. 11-2   Darius Milhaud, *La création du monde*, jazz fugue, beginning

EX. 11-2 (continued)

EX. 11-2   (continued)

as first given out by the bass (later G(Fx) and G♯ relative to E, C(B♯) and C♯ relative to A, etc.) A rapid-fire riff in sixteenth notes first introduced as a countersubject may have been a deliberate quotation from Euday Bowman's "Twelfth Street Rag" (1916), a dance hall favorite of the day (Ex. 11-3).

EX. 11-3   Riff figure from Milhaud's *La création du monde* compared with *12th Street Rag*

Significantly, the prelude that precedes this fugue (played as overture before the curtain is raised), is composed, despite the "jazz band" scoring and occasional syncopated riffs, in a sedately Bachian "chorale-prelude" style. This provides a suitably religious frame for the action to follow, drawing parallels between the African creation myth and the "Western" or biblical one—but also drawing parallels between the new neoprimitivism based on African-American music and other forms of Parisian neoclassicism.

That parallelism was enthusiastically pursued by Maurice Ravel in several of his late works. One was an opera: a *fantaisie lyrique* called *L'enfant et les sortilèges* (*The Child and the Magic Spells*, 1925) to a libretto by the French novelist Colette (1873–1954), who

```
           I
Phrase 1  ‖: / / / / | / / / / | / / / / | / / / / |
           IV                    I
Phrase 2  | / / / / | / / / / | / / / / | / / / / |
           V                     I
Phrase 3  | / / / / | / / / / | / / / / | / / / / :‖
```

FIG. 11-1   Basic harmonic structure of 12-bar blues.

had in her youth appeared on the music-hall stage. A few of the magical apparitions of the title, in particular a foxtrot sung and danced by a teapot and teacup, drew on popular-music idioms for surrealistic effect. (A foxtrot was a slow ragtime dance done with a gliding step, introduced by the team of Vernon and Irene Castle in 1914.) Ravel's most potent jazz stylizations, however, came in generically titled "classical" scores like his two piano concertos (in G, 1929–1931; in D for the left hand alone, 1929–1930) and his three-movement sonata for violin and piano (1923–1927).

The middle movement from the sonata, subtitled "Blues" and sketched in the summer of 1923, was Ravel's earliest essay in jazz effects. "Blues" (or "the blues") is a black-American folk genre that fed into the evolution of jazz around the time of the Great War. The name seems to stem from "the blue devils," a colloquial expression for melancholy or depression that can be traced as far back as Elizabethan English. As a musical term, "blues" can refer generally to a style of expressive performance as well as specifically to a musical form that seems to have been standardized around the turn of the century. As a form, the blues is a framework for poetic and melodic improvisation. The singer improvises three lines of poetry in which the second is a repetition of the first and the third ends with a word that rhymes with the ending-word of the other two. Each line coincides with a four-bar musical phrase in $\frac{4}{4}$ time. The first is supported by the tonic harmony throughout; the second moves from the subdominant (two bars) to the tonic (two bars), and the third is similarly divided between the dominant and the tonic. As a rule, the rhyming word coincides with the third downbeat of a phrase, the rest of the time being filled out by the instrumental accompaniment, usually on guitar or banjo. Fig. 11-1 shows the harmonic frame of a typical "12-bar blues" (each stroke within the measures representing the strummed beat), and Ex. 11-4 shows the opening stanza of *St. Louis Blues* (1914) by the African-American trumpeter and bandleader W. C. Handy (1873–1958), the most famous composed and published (i.e., commercial) example of what was a predominantly oral (folk or nonprofessional) genre.

EX. 11-4   W. C. Handy, *St. Louis Blues*, first stanza

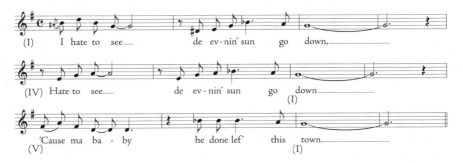

The unstable third degree described by Ansermet and appropriated by Milhaud is conspicuous in Handy's melody, both in the opening melodic "scoop" notated (very approximately) by the use of a grace note, and in the B♭s (also notated approximately) that clash with the B-natural of the tonic triad as cross-relations both direct (in line 1) and oblique (in lines 2 and 3). A folk blues singer will sing these notes sharp, so that they lie "in the crack" between the minor and the major third, and will refer to them as "blue notes." (Also called blue notes are flattened leading tones and fifths, or any note that is "bent out of shape" for expressive purposes.) The characteristic jazz syncopation (also described by Ansermet), in which a long or accented note is made more intensely expressive by placing it ahead of the beat on which it is expected, is also present in Handy's melody, consistently placed at the end of the first measure in every line. (Again the notation gives an exact appearance — displacement by one eighth-note — to what in actual performance is flexible and diverse.)

Ravel's blues movement incorporates — or better, refers to — virtually every feature of blues style as just described, beginning with the twanging pizzicato chords that cast the violin as ersatz banjo, plunking out the rhythmic framework against which the melody will be "improvised" (Ex. 11-5a). The chords are the expected I, IV, and V, although the standard blues pattern is merely suggested, not reproduced. But to score-readers (as opposed to listeners), the clash that occurs at the piano's entrance is implicit from the start in the "bitonal" superimposition of key signatures.

The reason for enclosing the technical term in quotes should be evident if one recalls the nature of a "blue note," poised somewhere between the major and the minor third. The clash of harmonic roots when the piano enters casts the throbbing B-natural at the top of the violin chord simultaneously as major third above G and (in the guise of

EX. 11-5A   Maurice Ravel, Violin Sonata, II ("Blues"), mm. 1–27

EX. II-5A (continued)

C♭) as minor third above A♭. The whole G-major triad, transferred at 1 from the violin to the piano, becomes in effect an implicit appoggiatura; never resolving, it is effectively colored "blue."

Ravel's sophisticated harmonic pun reverses the normal perspective of a blue note: what is ordinarily pitched outside the tempered scale relative to a stable root is pitched stably relative to two competing (hence destabilized) roots. It is the texture at 1 rather than a cadence that establishes A♭, after all, as the functional tonic. The method whereby a distinctive trait is appropriated from an oral tradition to become a device for achieving the renovation of a literate style is reminiscent of the way in which Stravinsky had employed Russian folk music in his early ballets. When the material so deployed is "native," the technique is called "neonationalism." Ravel's adaptation, by analogy, might well be termed "neo-exoticism." Once the violinist picks up the bow and reenters as the "melodist" (the key signature having been appropriately adjusted and the mood identified as "nostalgic"), the solo part is fashioned to give the effect of a blues improvisation on the Handy model. The characteristic blues syncopation, with small note-values tied over the beat to longer ones, becomes the rule; harmonic thirds, fifths, and sevenths constantly waver; that wavering is extended to ever wider melodic intervals by explicitly notated *portamenti* (finger slides) of a kind that was just then going out of style in "classical" playing under the impact of the New Sobriety. (And that might be one of the reasons why Ravel, who grew up with the sliding technique, labeled the portamento-heavy violin solo "nostalgic.")

As the movement nears its climax (Ex. 11-5b), the violin part reverts to an even more plainly indicated banjoistic style, while the piano takes over the portamento wailing as best it can. In the coda (Ex. 11-5c), the two instruments divide the "vocal" line in a sort of hocket; five measures before the end Ravel comes up with a devilishly clever portamento effect for the pianist (second finger literally sliding from black key to white under a tone sustained by the third finger) that could only be put into effect at this point, where the dynamics were soft and the line unaccompanied. The last chord contains another sort of "blue note" in the form of an unresolving, stable seventh that was the stereotyped "jazz" finishing chord. (Its origin was a tag-line, "Good evening, friends," that coincided with the first four notes of the equally stereotypical fugue subject in Ex. 11-2, from Milhaud's *Création du monde*.) Ravel described his "blues" movement to an American audience during his single visit to the United States, a concert tour of 1928. Speaking at the Rice Institute (now Rice University) in Houston, Ravel called attention to his "neo-exotic" technique, or what he called "minute stylization in the manipulation" of "popular forms." The manner in which such stylization is accomplished follows the predilection of the individual composer, Ravel maintained, so that his blues, while based on an American model, "is nevertheless French music, Ravel's music." He elaborated the point by reminding his audience that composers of at least four different nationalities—his French compatriot Milhaud, the Russian Stravinsky, the Italian Casella, and the German Hindemith—had all accomplished "minute stylizations"[7] of American popular music, "while the styles become as numerous as the composers themselves." And this is because "the individualities of these composers are stronger than the materials appropriated."

And yet this did not stop Ravel from turning right around and advising his audience that his neo-exoticist technique, if practiced by Americans, would be ipso facto transformed into a neonationalist one that would at last vouchsafe the emergence of "a veritable school of American music." Acknowledging (or perhaps insisting) that "Negro music is not of purely American origin" (a fact that many European compositions — notably *La création du monde* — also implicitly alleged), Ravel closed by reiterating his belief that

> it will prove to be an effective factor in the founding of an American school of music. At all events, may this national American music of yours embody a great deal of the rich and diverting rhythm of your jazz, a great deal of the emotional expression of your blues, and a great deal of the sentiment and spirit of your popular melodies and songs, worthily deriving from, and in turn contributing to, a noble national heritage in music.

Ravel's prescription is reminiscent of Dvořák's, some thirty years before; and like its predecessor it begs many questions that were of far greater moment to Americans

EX. 11-5B   Maurice Ravel, Violin Sonata, II ("Blues"), mm. 95–100

than they were to Europeans, for whom America was an exotic and still somewhat mythical place. Leaving entirely aside for the moment the highly fraught question of its origins, and granting that jazz (or "jazz") was a distinctively American genre, did that enable it (or entitle it) to represent the diverse population of the United States? Could the music of a minority culture, and an oft-despised one at that, reflect the (often bigoted) majority? Could it even be said that America, as such, had a folk music? And could jazz, a genre that had developed since Dvořák's time and that had (especially in the forms that Europeans knew) long since been "commodified" and commercialized, qualify as folklore? What surely seemed to Ravel a benign (or in any case an innocuous) suggestion led to endless controversy as soon as Americans began taking it up.

And was Ravel's suggestion even all that benign? Or did it still reflect the Old World condescension that many had detected in Dvořák's equally well meaning advice? European enthusiasm for jazz did not entirely efface traditional condescension toward its practitioners. Josephine Baker was surely correct in asserting that black Americans lucky enough to find work there could better escape prejudice and discrimination in Europe than they could at home. (She backed up the point in 1951 when, on a visit to America, she confronted the Stork Club, New York's most exclusive nightclub,

EX. 11-5C   Maurice Ravel, Violin Sonata, II ("Blues"), end

over its racist policies that made it impossible for her, a European celebrity, to obtain service there, even as the club featured many black performers.) And yet her European reputation was won through her willingness to represent herself as an exotic, neoprimitive sex object on terms that might seem degrading now (Fig. 11-2a).

Or consider the illustration that graced the cover of the program book for the "Saison Music-Hall" at the Théâtre des Champs-Elysées in 1925, when Baker made her Parisian début. The pit musicians — thick lips smiling, eyes rolling — are depicted in a style that differed little from the demeaning "Sambo" image common in the States (Fig. 11-2b). The French tendency to associate Negro music with Africa, moreover, although it resonates with the "black nationalism" of a later time, had rather different implications in a country that, as of the 1920s, was still a major colonial power.

Even Ernest Ansermet's rapturous review of Sidney Bechet and the Southern Syncopated Orchestra had a less than judicious side. Having admired jazz melody and rhythm, Ansermet deemed it fitting to temper his remarks with the observation that

> It is only in the field of harmony that the negro hasn't yet created his own distinct expression. Even here, he uses a succession of seventh chords, and ambiguous major-minors with a deftness which many Europeans should envy. But, in general,

FIG. 11-2   (left) Josephine Baker, poster for Casino de Paris. (right) Program for "Saison Music-Hall" at the Théâtre des Champs-Elysées, Paris, 1925.

harmony is perhaps a musical element which appears in the scheme of musical evolution only at a stage which the negro art has not yet attained.[8]

The assumption that the world's cultures and civilizations were all located on a single evolutionary timetable, with Europe out in front, was of course the principle that undergirded and justified Europe's colonial expansion and all its attendant cruelties. Ansermet compounds the colonialist impression with a wishful prediction not unlike Ravel's. Both seem to imply that it will be left to the white Europeans (or the Euro-Americans) to exploit "the negro's" musical resources to the full; and this puts a somewhat different complexion on the Satiean and Stravinskian appropriations that were already taking place by the time Ansermet made his forecast, and even on Ravel's wonderful "minute stylization." Sidney Bechet's true significance, Ansermet suggests, will ultimately be that of forerunner to the more sophisticated talents of the future:

> When one has tried so often to find in the past one of those figures to whom we owe the creation of our art as we know it today — those men of the 17th and 18th centuries, for example, who wrote the expressive works of dance airs which cleared the way for Haydn and Mozart — what a moving thing it is to meet this black, fat boy with white teeth and narrow forehead, who is very glad one likes what he does, but can say nothing of his art, except that he follows his "own way" — and then one considers that perhaps his "own way" is the highway along which the whole world will swing tomorrow.[9]

TRANSGRESSION

So it might be best not to romanticize the European reception of American popular music after the Great War, or to suppose that it indicates any real change in the Old World's attitude toward the culture of the New (let alone belief in the equality of races). In any case it was a very temporary fling; by 1927 Milhaud flatly asserted that there was not a single composer in Europe still interested in American jazz. It was only a minor exaggeration.

Within America the incorporation of "jazz" or popular dance idioms into concert genres, although it was not an entirely new idea, actually became newly controversial in the postwar decade. The most prominent previous exponent of the style, Henry F. Gilbert (1868–1928), was an omnivorous purveyor of exotic Americana after Dvořák's prescription. His *Negro Episode* for orchestra (1896), *Comedy Overture on Negro Themes* (1906, to an opera, *Uncle Remus*, after the ersatz Negro folktales of Joel Chandler Harris), and *The Dance in Place Congo*, a symphonic poem (1908) that was later adapted as a ballet and performed by the Metropolitan Opera Company (1918), took their place in his work list alongside an orchestral suite called *The Intimate Story of Indian Tribal Life; or, The Story of a Vanishing Race* and other "Indianist" compositions, and also alongside several suites of incidental music in an Irish style to accompany plays by W. B. Yeats and J. M. Synge. As for Charles Ives's ragtime "stylizations" (see chapter 5), they remained virtually unknown before Ives's belated "discovery" in the late 1930s.

It was only in the 1920s that jazz or popular idioms became associated with an American music that was overtly "modernist" in style, and thus acquired a challenging

FIG. 11-3 Aaron Copland with the composer Irving Fine (1914–1962) at Brandeis University, 1961.

or threatening edge that could inspire hostility. The chief culprit was Aaron Copland (1900–90), like Virgil Thomson an early pupil of Nadia Boulanger. Copland was in fact the first American to join the Boulangerie, having noticed a magazine advertisement for a school the French government planned to set up in Fontainebleau, a Paris suburb, for American musicians in the summer of 1921 — "a gesture of appreciation to America," as Copland recalled it, "for its friendship during World War I."[10] Nadia Boulanger was on the staff as a teacher of harmony, not composition. She proved, however, to be the one member of the faculty sympathetic to the modernist music Copland wanted to write; and it was her open-mindedness that gave him the courage to experiment, eventually, with what was then called "symphonic jazz." Copland himself associated his serious interest in jazz with an experience he had not in America but in Vienna, during a brief vacation in 1923, while he was studying in Paris. "Defamiliarization" by a foreign environment played a part in awakening that new sympathy: "When I heard jazz played in Vienna, it was like hearing it for the first time," Copland wrote.[11] Even more decisive, though, was Copland's discovery — a discovery that astonished him — that cultured Europeans, unlike their American counterparts, regarded jazz with high respect.

Even before going to Europe, Copland had written one perky little piano piece (called "Jazzy") in a popular style, but had kept it hidden from his early composition teacher in New York, a former Dvořák pupil named Rubin Goldmark (1872–1936), whose uncle, Karl Goldmark (1830–1915), had been Vienna's leading opera composer at the turn of the century. Goldmark maintained Dvořák's advocacy of an "Americanist" idiom for American concert music, had written a Hiawatha overture in 1900, and would even write a Negro Rhapsody in 1923; but the use of popular styles for this purpose was not an option he favored. Dvořák had called for the assimilation of American subject matter to "the beautiful forms of art," and the notion of "the beautiful" did not extend as far as the popular or the demotic in the social circles that then supported the cultivation of art music in America. In retrospect, of course, nothing is easier than to see in that esthetic distinction a covert class discrimination.

Not that Copland's amiable little "Jazzy" (Ex. 11-6) would have challenged it. But the music he wrote with Boulanger's encouragement during his period of study in Paris (1921–24) had taken a defiant turn that reflected European modernist attitudes. A concert by the New York Symphony Orchestra on 11 January 1925 made the young composer notorious. Seeking to placate his audience after the premiere of Copland's

Symphony for Organ and Orchestra (a work commissioned by Boulanger for her American debut), the conductor, German-born Walter Damrosch (1862–1950), announced from the podium that "if a gifted young man can write a symphony like this at twenty-three [*sic*], within five years he will be ready to commit murder!"[12] Virgil Thomson opened the generational gap wide by calling Copland's symphony "the voice of America in our generation."[13] So when Copland began incorporating jazz elements into his compositions after the scandalous Symphony — and doing it, he said, precisely so as the more effectively and authentically to embody the generational voice to which Thomson had called attention — they were read not as an entertaining gesture or an attempt to ingratiate his music with his compatriots, but as something nearer the opposite.

E X. 11-6   Aaron Copland, "Jazzy" (1920)

The work that immediately followed the Symphony was a suite for small orchestra called *Music for the Theatre*, a sort of incidental score to an imaginary play. The ensemble is a typical theatrical (or "pit") orchestra: eighteen players (at a minimum), including piano. The scoring uses only single winds except for a pair of trumpets that already signals brashness. And indeed, the first movement starts right off (Ex. 11-7a) with a cheeky solo for the first trumpet to which the second adds a *Flatterzunge* — a "flutter-tongued" note — that was all too easily heard as an insult of a familiar New York variety (a "Bronx cheer," or "raspberry"). The Molto moderato that follows the introductory fanfares seems to draw in vague and general terms on a "blues" idiom. Its shifting metrical scheme and polytonal harmonic framework — chords "planed" or moved in parallel in two directions (Ex. 11-7b) — refer far more explicitly to the Parisian music (Milhaud, Stravinsky) that made up Copland's sonic environment during his formative years than to jazz. The most specific reference to blues, perhaps, is the syncopated repetitions in the oboe solo (Ex. 11-7c).

The Subito Allegro molto at 5 reinstates the edgy trumpet fanfare motif as the main theme (first in the E♭ clarinet), a study in shifting accents against an ostinato accompaniment. The climax, Molto meno mosso at 11 (Ex. 11-7d), seems to be a calculated attempt at capturing the visceral impact of a certain device enthusiastically described by Ansermet in his review of the Southern Syncopated Orchestra: "When they indulge in one of their favorite effects, which is to take up the refrain of a dance in a tempo suddenly twice as slow and with redoubled intensity and figuration, a truly

EX. 11-7A   Aaron Copland *Music for the Theatre*, I, trumpet solo

gripping thing takes place: it seems as if a great wind is passing over a forest or as if a door is suddenly opened on a wild orgy."[14] The percussion parts here, punctuating the gaps in the melody like hockets, irresistibly evoke a physical response.

FIG. II-4 Entrance to Minsky's Burlesque (locked and guarded by the police), New York, 1930s.

The musical content of the high-spirited fourth movement of Copland's suite, *Burlesque*, is harder to relate to actual jazz; but the title was as deliberate a provocation as the trumpet's flutter-tongue. In French, the word (derived from the Italian *burla*, a joke) simply means comical or grotesque, a meaning that can be extended to encompass the idea of parody or caricature. In American slang, however, the term (often pronounced "burley-cue") had come by 1925 to refer to lewd theatrical entertainments, especially striptease, and to the low-life establishments that displayed them. From there, the term implicitly encompassed all kinds of behavior and social practices that were illicit in Prohibition-era America, from the consumption of alcoholic beverages in speakeasies to the consumption of sexual favors in "houses of ill-repute." These images were exactly what "jazz" connoted to the social circles on which high culture in America depended for patronage. The middle section (Ex. II-8), with its "dirty," low-lying trumpet solo accompanied by sweaty grunts from all the lowest instruments in the band, evoked the strutting ecdysiast "bumping and grinding" her way around the stage.

Copland's suite could thus be construed as biting the hand that fed him—a calculated answer-in-kind to the insult Walter Damrosch had delivered at the Symphony premiere earlier that year. Performed before a stuffy subscription audience, say, at a

EX. II-7B   Aaron Copland *Music for the Theatre*, I, Molto moderato (harmonic "planing")

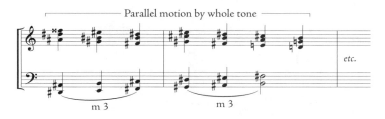

EX. II-7C   Aaron Copland, *Music for the Theatre*, I, oboe solo

EX. 11-7D Aaron Copland, *Music for the Theatre*, I, Molto meno mosso

EX. 11-8 Aaron Copland, *Music for the Theatre*, IV ("Burlesque"), mm. 128–147

Boston Symphony Orchestra concert, it could count on a hostile reception. And that is just where it was performed for the first time, on 10 November 1925, between Beethoven's Fourth Symphony and the Prelude and *Liebestod* from Wagner's *Tristan und Isolde*. It was a typically aggressive modernist bid for public notice, in which Copland was joined by Serge Koussevitzky (1874–1951), the Russian-born conductor of the Boston Symphony Orchestra, to whom *Music for the Theatre* is dedicated.

Koussevitzky, whose marriage to an heiress had made him financially independent, was (like Stravinsky, Prokofieff, and Rachmaninoff) an émigré from the Russian

FIG. 11-5   Boston Symphony Orchestra under Serge Koussevitzky.

revolution. From 1917 to 1924 his base was Paris, where he formed his own orchestra and gave concerts at which, thanks to his self-subsidizing, he could afford to program a great deal of contemporary music and turn his series into a major modernist forum where Stravinsky and Prokofieff (composers whose music Koussevitzky actually published for a while), and many of the younger French generation had important premieres. Koussevitzky also befriended Nadia Boulanger and took an interest in her pupils; so that when he moved to America he was poised to launch their careers with aplomb. In this he was playing a role consciously modeled on the activities of the Russian music patron Mitrofan Belyayev (1836–1904), also the heir to an industrial fortune, who had subsidized the performance and publication of the young Russians of the generation before Stravinsky's.

Thus the careers of the composers in the postwar American generation who studied in Paris quite directly paralleled those of the Russian "nationalist" composers of the late nineteenth century: they had a principal mentor in Nadia Boulanger, paralleling Rimsky-Korsakov (or, before him, Balakirev) and they had a principal promoter in Koussevitzky, paralleling Belyayev, who worked in active collusion with their mentor. But where Belyayev and Rimsky-Korsakov, with their conservative tastes, had acted as a restraining force on the Russian composers of their day, Boulanger and Koussevitzky were committed modernists who abetted every innovative tendency in American music. Where the older influence and the newer one coincided was in their insistence on pronounced national character in whatever music they supported.

Copland's "jazz" works fit the bill to perfection. A review of the Boston premiere of *Music for the Theatre* confirmed the work as an act of mild aggression calculated to win a place for American music as an alternative to the traditional European repertory rather than (as previously) an echo of it. It was, the critic wrote, "a tonal bombshell that left in its wake a mingling of surprise, perplexity, indignation and enthusiasm."[15] After the New York premiere the next week, Olin Downes's review announced that "we do not care if a long time elapses before we listen again to *Music for the Theatre*."[16]

That sort of reaction was in its way an encouragement to Copland and Koussevitzky, who in a larger sense were echoing Europe after all, envisioning as they did the establishment of an authentic modernist school in America on what was by then the established European model: a maximalist nationalism followed by a chic "classical" counterpart. Copland's next work, this time directly commissioned by Koussevitzky, was a Piano

Concerto that he could take around and perform himself, the model being Stravinsky's slightly "jazzy" if more overtly "Bachian" Concerto for Piano and Winds, first performed by the composer at one of the last Parisian Koussevitzky concerts, in May of 1924.

Copland's Piaro Concerto, which had its premiere in Boston in January 1927, aroused all the indignation that *Music for the Theatre* had evoked, but none of the enthusiasm. Nicolas Slonimsky (1894–1995), a Russian émigré musician who was then acting as Koussevitzky's secretary, sent Copland a malodorous bouquet of press clippings and irate letters from subscribers that unnerved the composer enough to elicit a show of bravado in response. "How flattering it was to read that the 'Listener' can understand Strauss, Debussy, Stravinsky — but not poor me," Copland wrote back to Slonimsky.[17] "When the Concerto is played again (O horrid thought!) we must see if we can't get the police to raid the concert hall to give a little added interest to this 'horrible' experiment." The critics were just as "flattering." One called the Concerto an "anti-human outrage"[18]; another characterized it as "barnyard and stable noises."[19] A third, pretending to excuse it, wrote that "some have complained that the work had no spiritual value, only animal excitement; but what else has jazz?"[20]

This last comment points to an ugly undercurrent that now made itself felt in the reception of Copland's music. The second time around, his jazz experiments evoked a racial backlash that expressed itself not directly, with slurs against the composer's musical sources, but in the form of innuendos at Copland's own "racial" or ethnic origins. A Jewish composer trading in the jazz idiom seemed too direct a challenge to Yankee leadership in American musical culture, and aroused renewed controversy, more vehement than ever, as to just what the Americanness of American music should entail.

Who, in short, could truly represent — that is, had the right to represent — America, a nation of immigrants, in folklore? Here is how the journalist Gilbert Seldes posed the question in 1926, even before Copland's Piano Concerto had appeared, in the pages of *The Dial*, a modernist literary magazine: "Can the Negro and the Jew stand in the relation of a folk to a nation? And if not, can the music they create be the national music?"[21] Most answers were dismissive, like the one given by a critic named Paul Fritz Laubenstein in an article, "Race Values in Aframerican Music," published in 1930 in the *Musical Quarterly*, then America's most scholarly musical journal. "As for jazz," he wrote, "the Negro may if he wishes claim the questionable distinction of being its originator."[22] But "the Jewish direption" or exploitation of it made it "a parasitic mannerism preying upon the classics." From the very beginning of modernism (see chapter 1), its opponents associated it with Jewishness. The urban, the commercial, and the Jewish were conflated by those who regarded them, each and all, as a threat. In postwar America, the most vocal musical antimodernist was Daniel Gregory Mason (1873–1953), who from 1929 to 1942 occupied the MacDowell chair in music at Columbia University, where he taught, all told, for almost forty years. The son, nephew, and grandson of distinguished New England musicians, Mason was the foremost living representative of the Yankee strain in American music. His compositions included a "Lincoln Symphony" and a String Quartet on Negro Themes (that is, spirituals). But he drew the line at jazz, which he associated (in an article of 1920) with "the Jewish menace to our artistic integrity."[23]

Ten years later, in a book called *Tune In, America: A Study of Our Coming Musical Independence*, Mason was ready to elaborate. Jazz based its claim to being a representative American music, Mason insisted, on its association with the myth of "American hustle," defined as "a group of qualities induced or encouraged by our present business and industrial life, such as haste, practical 'efficiency,' good humor of a superficial sort, inventiveness, an extrovert preference of action to thought—in short, all that is suggested by such popular slogans as 'Step lively" and 'Keep smiling.' "[24] Quoting an earlier writer named Hiram K. Moderwell, Mason linked jazz with "the 'jerk and rattle' of the American city, 'its restless bustle and motion, its multitude of unrelated details, and its underlying progress toward a vague somewhere,' "[25] all of which could serve equally as a general definition of "the modern."

But jazz was a spurious representation of America, Mason claimed, for the reason that it was

> not, like the varied types of European folk-song to which it is often misleadingly compared, a spontaneous artistic activity of our people; it is a commercial product, like so many others 'put over' upon the people. It does not grow up in simple minds, voicing their feelings; it is manufactured by calculating ones, seeking profit. In a word, it is not an expression at all; it is an exploitation.[26]

All of this was easily read anti-Semitic code. Mason explained the success of the Jewish exploitation of the unsuspecting public in terms of the "pathological state"[27] to which the stresses of modern life have brought the American mind. Jazz, "the product of industrial cities poisoned with nervous fatigue," reflects

> not our health, vitality, and hope, but our restlessness and our despair. It is a symptom of a sick moment in the progress of the human soul: the moment of industrial turmoil, fever, and distress that we can but hope to survive, not to perpetuate. To its tense, false gayety the hearing ear responds never with the joy that comes only in relaxation, but with a sense of depression that may be tinged with tragedy.... Despite its kinship with an undeniable if superficial side of our character, and in spite of its acceptability to Europeans in search rather of new sensations than of living art, the bankruptcy of jazz as a source of serious music is becoming daily more evident.

Surveying the programs of American orchestras during the 1920s for their American content, Mason noted the increasing number of native-born musicians in the latter part of the decade, but noted, too, the increasing prevalence of modernistic styles that rendered the music "a little less representatively American." Copland's Piano Concerto is singled out for dismissal, since the participation of its composer, "a cosmopolitan Jew,"[28] gave the Boston Symphony program in which he played the work "a more European, exotic flavor" than an American one. The inescapable logic of Mason's position was that neither a Negro nor a Jew could be truly an American. The "musical independence" to which the subtitle of his book alluded could only be achieved if such influences were excluded.

Copland may have been unnerved by the backlash. Although, as we shall see, he certainly did not give up the aspiration to represent America in his music, he did discard jazz after the Piano Concerto. It was a conscious decision. He told a Los Angeles interviewer about it before performing the piece in 1928, and the interview ran under a headline, "Copland to Abandon Jazz in Future Compositions."[29] Much later he told another interviewer that "I had been observing the scene around me and sensed it was about to change. Moreover, I realized that jazz might have its best treatment from those who had a talent for improvisation. I sensed its limitations, intended to make a change, and made no secret of the fact."[30]

REDEMPTION

The late recollection is tinged with patronization, typical of "literate" attitudes toward the "limitations" of an oral genre. That was hardly Copland's point of view in the 1920s. In trying to comprehend his decision to abandon jazz, it will be useful to compare the bad reception his jazz-influenced compositions met with the altogether different reception some seemingly similar works by another American composer enjoyed around the same time. What on the surface may appear paradoxical will on investigation prove revealing.

George Gershwin (1898–1937), Copland's near exact contemporary, had a very similar ethnic and family background. Like Copland, he was born in Brooklyn to Jewish parents who had emigrated to the United States from Russia. He even studied briefly with the same teacher, Rubin Goldmark, though at a later stage of life than Copland. Both Copland and Gershwin left school to pursue their musical careers before attending college. But where Copland made the decision voluntarily after graduating from high school, and pursued a full-time musical education at Fontainebleau, Gershwin, who came from a much poorer family, dropped out of high school at fourteen, the youngest age then legal, in order to earn a living.

A precocious pianist, gifted with a remarkable ear, Gershwin found work as a "song-plugger" for a music publisher. His job was to play items of "sheet-music" by request, so that prospective purchasers, both amateur pianists and variety-show ("vaudeville") singers, could hear the songs the firm was offering for sale. The position required a fluent piano technique and a talent for stylish embellishment or improvisation by ear (the very skill Copland lacked and slightly scorned). It was natural that a song-plugger would turn to writing popular songs himself, in the highly standardized format that was the stock-in-trade of "Tin Pan Alley."

Tin Pan Alley was the nickname for the songwriting and music-publishing industry that grew up in New York

FIG. 11-6   George Gershwin, self-portrait in oils (1934).

in the 1890s and lasted roughly until the Second World War. Evoking the sound of the weather-beaten upright pianos on which pluggers like Gershwin plied their trade in publishers' salesrooms on East 14th Street in lower Manhattan, the name was coined by Monroe Rosenfeld (1861–1918), who worked as both a songwriter and a journalist. As a business, Tin Pan Alley was indeed heavily populated if not dominated by Jewish entrepreneurs, and it employed many Jewish songwriters as well. Its products were used not only in domestic parlors but also, and primarily, in the variety theaters on Broadway, and in their Yiddish counterparts on Second Avenue in the Lower East Side.

Within a year of his first employment as a song-plugger, Gershwin had sufficiently distinguished himself as a pianist to find work cutting player-piano rolls for home use, and became a sought-after accompanist for professional entertainers. In 1917 he moved from Tin Pan Alley to the more prestigious theater world uptown, becoming the rehearsal pianist for a "revue" or plotless song-and-dance show called *Miss 1917*, with music by Victor Herbert (1859–1924) and Jerome Kern (1885–1945), who with Irving Berlin (1888–1989) were then the reigning composers on Broadway. The next year, on the strength of a few published songs and piano pieces, Gershwin was put on retainer by Max Dreyfus, the head of T. B. Harms & Co., Tin Pan Alley's biggest publishing firm; for $35 a week, Harms received the "right of first refusal" on anything the young composer might produce.

It was a good bet. In 1920, *Swanee*, a Gershwin song Harms had published in 1919, was recorded by the blackface singer Al Jolson (1886–1950) and became a runaway hit, earning the composer a then fantastic royalty of $10,000 in its first year. More important, it made him a bankable "name" composer for Broadway producers. During the five years 1920–1924, Gershwin wrote the scores for eleven Broadway shows, of which seven were revues, the rest "musical comedies" (later shortened to "musicals"), meaning shows with dramatic plots that emulated operettas. From these shows, seventy-two songs were harvested for publication as sheet music, in addition to sixteen songs that Gershwin wrote for insertion into shows by other composers, and seven "occasional" items that were either dropped from shows or composed directly for sheet-music sale. Added to the songs Gershwin had written up to his first year under contract to Harms, they made a total of well over a hundred songs.

Practically all of them were written according to the same "industrial" formula, a necessity for maintaining such a high commercial productivity. (In this, Tin Pan Alley resembled the Italian opera of a hundred years before, or the early "classical" symphony, other literate genres that required a high volume and that consequently relied on similarly standardized and stereotyped formal designs of a kind more often found in oral cultures.) The standard form was the 32-bar "chorus" or refrain (usually preceded by one or two introductory "verses" that were often omitted). The thirty-two bars were grouped in four eight-bar phrases or "lines" that were cast musically in age-old "fixed" patterns like AABA, ABAB, ABCA, or AABC, of which the first was by far the most prevalent. In its commonest variant, the first two lines had closed and open endings, respectively; the "B" (often called the "bridge" or "release") comprised two 4-bar phrases like the two short lines in a limerick, and the final line repeated the "closed" version of

A, thus: AA'BA. (The remotest literate ancestors of this fixed form, also associated with the *cabaletta* or fast concluding section of an Italian opera aria, were composed by the troubadours, Aquitanian (southern French) poet-musicians of the eleventh century.) As an example of a Tin Pan Alley chorus, "You Don't Know the Half of It, Dearie" (Ex. 11-9), a song from *Lady, Be Good!* (one of four Gershwin shows to open in 1924), will be particularly useful, since it very pointedly illustrates the relationship between Tin Pan Alley and "jazz." It is billed as a "blues" number (marketed as sheet music as "the Half of It, Dearie, Blues") and it appropriates a number of style features from the typical African-American blues as illustrated in Ex. 11-4, by W. C. Handy. The first line, in fact, could have been from an actual blues, both because of its harmony, confined (or confinable) to the tonic triad, and because of its rhythmic structure (all the words concentrated in its first half, with the rest free for "riffing," or for improvisation by the accompanying instrument). There is even a blue note on "Dearie."

EX. 11-9   George Gershwin, *Lady, Be Good!*, "You Don't Know the Half of It, Dearie"

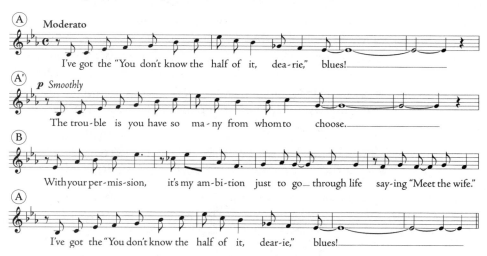

But what was a "12-bar" structure in three lines has been stretched out to meet the requirements of the standard chorus in four, and the distinctive harmonic succession that makes a blues a blues has also been abandoned in favor of a freer set of harmonic "changes." The blues, in short, has become (like all forms of "jazz") one of many flavorings available to the Tin Pan Alley composer. The Tin Pan Alley standard was already a thoroughly hybrid, Europeanized adaptation of jazz, like the ones by Milhaud and Ravel we have already seen; only in place of the modernist insistence on originality of style and form it demanded conformity to a commercial template.

The same year in which he wrote *Lady, Be Good!*, Gershwin was unexpectedly given an opportunity to cross over into more "serious" terrain when Paul Whiteman (1890–1967), a popular bandleader with a classical background who was planning a big concert tour of the United States, invited the young Broadway composer, already known for his remarkable keyboard facility and extraordinary melodic gift, to compose an extended work for piano and large dance orchestra in the form of a "rhapsody." The genre, not really a form but a title popularized by Liszt's *Hungarian Rhapsodies*, was cannily chosen. It connoted at once a romantically "free" form, an opportunity for pianistic display, and a programmatically "nationalistic" statement of a sort that many American composers were then contemplating.

The piece that Gershwin came up with, *Rhapsody in Blue*, was first performed (in an orchestration by Whiteman's arranger, Ferde Grofé) on Lincoln's birthday, 12 February 1924. It came near the end of a long matinee concert called "An Experiment in Modern Music," for which Whiteman had rented Aeolian Hall, a concert venue maintained by a player-piano manufacturing firm, where Walter Damrosch and the New York Symphony gave their concerts (and where Copland's early symphony — plus Damrosch's preposterous comment about it — would be heard a year later). The ticket-selling gimmick was the announcement that a panel of experts — Rachmaninoff, the violinists Jascha Heifetz and Efrem Zimbalist, and the latter's wife, the soprano Alma Gluck — would judge the compositions presented and decide which were the most authentically American.[31] (The fact that three of the panelists were Russian-born and the fourth Romanian seems to have been no impediment to their expertise.)

Other big names in music who were listed as official "patrons" of the event included the Swiss-born composer Ernest Bloch, the Dutchman Willem Mengelberg (then leading the New York Philharmonic), the Vienna-born violinist Fritz Kreisler, the Lithuanian-born pianist Leopold Godowsky, and the Italian-born Metropolitan Opera soprano Amelita Galli-Curci. A prefatory note in the program book, by Whiteman's manager, stated the purpose of the program:

> The experiment is purely educational. Mr. Whiteman intends to point out, with the assistance of the orchestra and associates, the tremendous strides which have been made in popular music from the day of the discordant jazz, which sprang into existence about ten years ago from nowhere in particular, to the really melodious music of today which — for no good reason — is still being called jazz.[32]

"From nowhere in particular . . ." The program was in essence an attempt to sanitize contemporary popular music and elevate it in public esteem by divorcing it from its roots in African-American improvised music and securing endorsements from the classical music establishment. The twenty-five pieces on the program were grouped into sections with slightly pretentious titles like "The True Form of Jazz," "Recent Compositions with Modern Score," "In the Field of Classics," "Flavoring a Selection with Borrowed Themes," and "Adaptation of Standard Selections to Dance Rhythm." Gershwin's culminating *Rhapsody* and Victor Herbert's *Suite of Serenades*, the most ambitious items performed, were sections unto themselves.

Rhapsody in Blue was a huge success with the audience, who had been beginning to show signs of listlessness as its turn approached. The critics were also kind. Deems Taylor (1885–1966), not only a critic but also the successful composer of two operas performed at the Metropolitan, and who had been listed in the program as a "patron" (which made his reviewing the concert a somewhat questionable proposition), allowed that Gershwin's composition "hinted at something new, something that had not hitherto been said in music."[33] Gershwin, he predicted, would provide "a link between the jazz camp and the intellectuals." W. J. Henderson (1855–1937), then the dean of New York critics, saw Whiteman's concert as a milestone, achieving "the total eclipse of the other kind of moderns—all save one, Stravinsky."[34] Mengelberg went further, exclaiming that "Gershwin had succeeded in doing what Stravinsky was [only] trying to do."[35] Olin Downes, who as we know would have harsh words for Copland's *Music for the Theatre*, wrote in the *New York Times*, a little cryptically, that in spite of a certain "technical immaturity," Gershwin's was "a new talent finding its voice, and likely to say something personally and racially important to the world."[36] Given the premises of the concert, as well as the controversies we have already sampled surrounding Copland's Jewishness, Downes's use of the word "racially" may seem dubious or even sinister; in its context, however, it probably referred not to the composer's Jewishness or to the negritude of his models, but more innocently to his music's distinctively New World flavor.

The music critic (and novelist and photographer) Carl Van Vechten (1880–1964), who had already made a name for himself as a proponent of modern music with, among other things, an ebullient account of *The Rite of Spring* premiere, declared *Rhapsody in Blue* "the very finest piece of serious music that had ever come out of America,"[37] and in a letter to the composer he went furthest of all. "Go straight on," he advised Gershwin, "and you will knock all Europe silly."[38] Others seemed to sense this, too: the only discordant notes in the *Rhapsody's* reception came from the proponents of "high" European modernism, who reacted to the "lowbrow" threat with condescension. "You must whisper it softly," wrote Carl Engel, a columnist for the *Musical Quarterly*, "when you dare suggest that at last America has a music all its own," originating not "at the top, in the Hermetic circles of New Music Societies, Manuscript Societies, Associations for the Promotion of Native Talent, and the like, but at the bottom, in the street."[39]

In the wake of *Rhapsody in Blue* Gershwin received a commission from Walter Damrosch and the New York Symphony for a traditional three-movement piano concerto with full orchestra, a far more ambitious and in some ways more sophisticated work, which received its premiere in Carnegie Hall on 3 December 1925. The critics again were welcoming, one going so far as to remark that "of all those writing the music of today," Gershwin "alone actually expresses us."[40] The timing makes it likely that the success of Gershwin's Concerto in F, as he called it, was among the factors that stimulated Copland to compose his own piano concerto. As we know, Copland's work was greeted with a hostile, insulting, and ultimately discouraging reception.

The encouragement Gershwin received, by contrast, steadily increased. *Rhapsody in Blue* turned out to be perhaps the most lucrative piece of concert music ever composed, earning the composer more than a quarter of a million dollars from performance and recording royalties and rental fees during the first ten years of its existence, both in its original scoring for dance band and in its 1926 "symphonic" version (also the work of Ferde Grofé). It is worth noting that much of this income was earned from sales of piano rolls and recordings, and from radio broadcasts, making Gershwin the first composer of concert music to benefit conspicuously from the new mechanized and electronic dissemination-media of the twentieth century. Gershwin readily recognized this. In an essay called "The Composer in the Machine Age," published in 1930 in a volume titled *Revolt in the Arts*, he voiced the soon-to-be-controversial thesis that "the composer, in my estimation, has been helped a great deal by the mechanical reproduction of music."[41] In 1928, shortly after Ravel visited America, Gershwin made the reverse trip, and, as Carl Van Vechten predicted, "knocked all Europe silly." He was lionized everywhere, not only by audiences but by leading modernist composers — Prokofieff, Milhaud, Poulenc, Ravel, Berg—who accepted him as a peer. (Or more than a peer: a famous anecdote has Gershwin asking Ravel for orchestration lessons; after inquiring what Gershwin had earned from his music the previous year, Ravel remarks, "Then it is I who should be taking lessons from you.") No American creative musician ever equaled Gershwin's European conquest, attributable partly—but only partly—to its timing at the height of the "jazz age," when everything American was singularly in vogue in Europe.

The direct issue of Gershwin's trip to Europe was a tone poem, *An American in Paris*, which had its first performance under Damrosch in December 1928. The slower middle section, which according to Gershwin's program note expresses the title character's homesickness, reverts to the idiom of the *Rhapsody in Blue*; the bustling outer sections, however, in which Gershwin worked the sound of taxi horns into his orchestration, shows him aspiring, like the composers of the Boulangerie, toward the general European modernist idiom in its Parisian "neoclassical" version as exemplified by the work of Ravel and Les Six (and, more remotely, by Stravinsky).

All through the late 1920s Gershwin continued working in the Broadway theater and, after the invention of "talkies" around 1930, in Hollywood (where he met and befriended the exiled Arnold Schoenberg). Despite his fame and financial success he continued to take sporadic composition lessons from Rubin Goldmark, Henry Cowell, and Wallingford Riegger (1885–1961), an American composer of an older generation who had studied at the Berlin Conservatory. Finally, in 1932, acting on the advice of Alexander Glazunov, a veteran Russian composer who toured America in 1929, Gershwin sought out Joseph Schillinger (1895–1943), a Russian-born composer and music theorist whose extremely schematic methods were later published in a massive two-volume treatise, *The Schillinger System of Musical Composition* (already sampled in Ex. 6-23).

Schillinger was then enjoying something of a vogue among musicians from the popular-music and theatrical spheres who were looking for technical grounding in serious genres; among his other pupils were the pianist-composer Oscar Levant (1906–72), the jazz clarinettist and bandleader Benny Goodman (1909–86), and the bandleader and jazz trombonist Glenn Miller (1904–44). Gershwin worked with Schillinger for four years, during which time he wrote his most ambitious score, an "American folk opera" called *Porgy and Bess*, after a novel-turned-play by DuBose Heyward about life among the poor black residents of Charleston, South Carolina. The libretto, in Negro-American dialect, was by the composer's brother, Ira Gershwin (1896–1983), who had long been his chief songwriting collaborator.

The four works of Gershwin described in the foregoing sketch have joined the permanent standard concert and operatic repertory, and not only in America. They are, moreover, the only American works of "symphonic jazz" to have done so, all others, including Copland's, having lapsed long ago into obscurity. Though occasionally revived, they now present chiefly a historical interest. In part, the lasting success of Gershwin's contributions is attributable, of course, to their qualities as art works and the pleasure they give audiences. But the enormous discrepancy between the reception accorded Copland and that accorded Gershwin as "jazz" composers requires analysis as a historical phenomenon. That analysis must of course begin with an analysis of Gershwin's music to match the one already given Copland's.

"SOCIOSTYLISTICS"

Gershwin intended his jazz-inflected concert music to reflect contemporary American urban life — that is, American modernity. *Rhapsody in Blue* was conceived on a train, Gershwin wrote in a letter to his first biographer, in response to "its steely rhythms, its rattley-bang," and the composition was "a musical kaleidoscope of America, of our vast melting pot, of our national pep, of our blues, our metropolitan madness."[42] The Concerto in F, for similar reasons, was originally to have been called *New York Concerto*.

Both compositions open, as Copland's *Music for the Theatre* also opens, with what Gershwin called an "icebreaker," a term used on Broadway for a device to grab the audience's attention. In Copland's case it was a trumpet flutter-tongue. In the Concerto in F it was a noisy solo on the kettledrums. The most famous one, at the beginning of *Rhapsody in Blue*, is a clarinet glissando of a type that was pioneered as a special effect by African-American jazz players (based, W. C. Handy wrote, on the "false fingering and incorrect lipping"[43] of self-taught players). It was imparted to Gershwin by Ross Gorman, a player in Whiteman's orchestra, and (in the words of the conductor Maurice Peress) it became "the bane of symphony clarinettists ever since."[44] So far *Rhapsody in Blue* sounds just as aggressively (or "futuristically") modernistic as *Music for the Theatre*.

Thereafter, however, the piece settles down into a medley of five tunes, each resembling a Tin Pan Alley chorus in one way or another, connected by cadenzas and virtuoso roulades, all adhering more or less strictly to the obligatory AA'BA format (Ex. 11-10). Whether because Gershwin selected them with an eye toward the coherence of the whole, or simply because it was such a cliché of the Tin Pan Alley style, four out of five exhibit the same standard ragtime syncopation — ♩♫♩ ♫♩♩ — at some point. Their complete statements are as follows:

> I: mm. 38–54, *72–90*, 225–240
> II: mm. *91–106*
> III: mm. 115–129, *179–194*, 198–213, 486–501
> IV: mm. *138–153* . . . , 257–271 . . .
> V: mm. 300 ff.

The numbers in italics represent statements that conform exactly to the specifications of the 32-bar chorus, here reduced to 16 bars (4 + 4 + 4 + 4) by the use of halved note-values and double measures, typical of instrumental arrangements. Elsewhere the phrase lengths are truncated or extended for the sake of character or variety, just as Haydn and Mozart had varied the symmetrical patterns that typified their "classical" style, by tried-and-true methods that could be compared either with those of the eighteenth-century masters or with those of contemporary pop music performers.

Comparing the "classic" statement of I with its first appearance, for example, one observes how the initial AA′ is extended from eight bars to ten by adding a measure of "riffing" (motivic repetition) to each phrase, just as a blues singer might do. The riff itself, assigned by Grofé to the distinctive timbre of the bass clarinet, is the same standard tag line ("Good evening, friends") that Milhaud had already appropriated in *La création du monde* (Ex. 11-2). Even in its "classic" statement, chorus I is somewhat unconventional thanks to the sudden modulation that takes place at the bridge and is never undone, so that the tune ends in a different key from its beginning. That was a technique routinely employed in musical comedy overtures, in essence tune medleys like *Rhapsody in Blue*, to achieve smooth transitions.

Chorus III, the tune most frequently heard in *Rhapsody in Blue*, and the one usually thought of as its main theme, is also the one most explicitly "bluesy" in character, with

EX. 11-10A George Gershwin, *Rhapsody in Blue* themes, I (mm. 225–240)

EX. 11-10B George Gershwin, *Rhapsody in Blue* themes, II (mm. 91–106)

EX. 11-10C George Gershwin, *Rhapsody in Blue* themes, III (mm. 179–194)

EX. 11-10D George Gershwin, *Rhapsody in Blue* themes, IV (mm. 138–153)

EX. 11-10E George Gershwin, *Rhapsody in Blue* themes, V (mm. 300ff).

its double-inflected seventh degrees ("blue notes") and its measure-long riffs. Chorus II, heard only once, is a "Latin" (or "Cuban") number, with its languorous melodic triplets and its 3 + 3 + 2 accompaniment patterns. Chorus IV is always heard incomplete, its final A dovetailed into a sequential development. These modulatory sequences, which proceed through/ 0 3 6 9 /circles of minor thirds, suggest that Gershwin actually turned to Liszt's rhapsodies for guidance (just as the white-key/black-key opposition elsewhere suggests that he had been playing or listening to Stravinsky's *Petrushka*.)

Another indication that Liszt was the model is the slow "lyrical" theme at m. 300, which suggests Liszt's method of compressing the movements of a traditional concerto (or symphony) into a single temporal span. This theme departs furthest from the 32-bar format, through a process of elision that will again, perhaps surprisingly, bring the techniques of Haydn or Mozart to mind. (But not really surprisingly, given the congruity between the formulas of Tin Pan Alley and those of any "classic" idiom.) The last note of A′ is dovetailed with the first note of B, and the final C is dovetailed with the first A of a wholesale repetition. This theme is the only one in *Rhapsody in Blue* to undergo something akin to a development. Again the tonal trajectory is determined by a root progression that moves through a circle of minor thirds.

This final development (or "developmental coda" à la Beethoven) is balanced at the other end of the Rhapsody by the 37-bar introduction (Ex. 11-11), which juxtaposes fragments or motives from themes I and III with the "Good evening, friends" riff. Opening in B♭ major, it goes through a possibly unprecedented eight progressions along the circle of fifths (E♭ in m. 11, A♭ in m. 16, D♭ (V) in m. 19, G♭ (I) in m. 21, B (V) in m. 27, E (V) in mm. 26–37) to prepare the first full chorus, which comes in at m. 38 in A major, the first key to be fully established as a tonic.

The last key to function as a stable tonic is E♭ major, at the triumphant final reprise of III (m. 486). (The tritone relationship that thus governs the whole trajectory can again be related to Liszt's practice, especially as later adapted by Rimsky-Korsakov.) Thus it seems a little forced and dutiful when Gershwin yanks the key to B♭ at the very end (Ex. 11-12) for a grandiose *Molto allargando*, just so that the ending can parallel the opening gesture and the piece can seem to end in the "right" key, that of the beginning. Since neither the opening nor the closing B♭s play a genuinely defining role in the tonal plan, the effect of the ending, for all its pep and rattlety-bang, is a bit perfunctory or gratuitous, a letdown.

That may seem an overly critical or patronizing way to describe it, but in fact that suggestion of naïveté or clumsiness of construction seems to have been one of the factors that helped win the *Rhapsody* its success — or at least its initial acceptance by the same classical-music establishment that roundly rejected Copland's "jazz"-inspired essays. The fact that the Tin Pan Alley materials in Gershwin's *Rhapsody* were presented in something like their raw state, like the Gypsy tunes in Liszt's *Hungarian Rhapsodies* or in Brahms's *Hungarian Dances* (or the Czech folk songs in Dvořák's *Slavonic Dances*, or the Norwegian folk songs in Edvard Grieg's *Norwegian Dances* of 1881, or the Spanish folk songs in Isaac Albéniz's *Cantos de España* of 1896) lent them the character of folklore rather than commercial art.

Equating the Tin Pan Alley product with "jazz," as white Americans tended to do, Gershwin drew the analogy explicitly in a statement published in 1933: "Jazz I regard as an American folk-music; not the only one, but a very powerful one which is probably in the blood and feeling of the American people more than any other style of folk-music."[45] In this way, *Rhapsody in Blue* could be seen as fulfilling Dvořák's prescription for an American music that would elevate the musical utterances of the folk by means of "beautiful treatment in the higher forms of art." The dynamic — mark it well — was *upward.*

That being so, it did not hurt but actually helped if, in the eyes of the critics, the work fell somewhat short of its goal. Olin Downes preceded his remark about

EX. II-II   George Gershwin, *Rhapsody in Blue,* mm. 1–27

EX. II-II (continued)

Gershwin's "racial importance" by noting that the *Rhapsody* "shows extraordinary talent, just as it also shows a young composer with aims that go far beyond those of his ilk, struggling with a form of which he is far from being master."[46] Going far beyond your "ilk" was one way of defining "upward mobility"—the vaunted American dream. Gershwin's achievement thus fulfilled not only a musical but also a social aspiration, and one that embodied a message of redemption. A remark he made in an interview with a *New York Times* reporter in 1935 shows Gershwin's awareness of the quasi-religious power of literate culture to cleanse, redeem, and "deliver" the oral. "When I wrote the

Rhapsody in Blue," he declared, "I took 'blues' and put them in a larger and more serious form. That was twelve years ago and the *Rhapsody in Blue* is still very much alive, whereas if I had taken the same themes and put them in songs they would have been gone years ago."[47]

A "larger and more serious form" was also (and principally) a textually fixed and determined form, even if, as Gershwin implicitly acknowledged, it remained pretty much a medley of songs. By in effect teaching "jazz" to read he was offering it immortality. And respectability: the classical models to which he aspired as vessels of immortality — the folkloric rhapsodies of the romantic era — were by the 1920s a thoroughly genteel and

EX. 11-12   George Gershwin, *Rhapsody in Blue*, end

EX. 11-12 *(continued)*

domesticated repertory, the very opposite of modernist. The chapter devoted to the concert music in the earliest Gershwin biography — Isaac Goldberg's *George Gershwin: A Study in American Music* (1931), based on interviews with the composer — is called "Lady Jazz in the Concert Hall," and the last chapter is titled "The Wedding of Jazz to Symphonic Art." No wonder a publicity phrase that was widely used to introduce Gershwin to movie and radio audiences in the 1930s described him as "the man who made an honest woman out of jazz."[48] That could never be said of Copland, who was seen, antithetically, as the one who degraded the higher forms of music to the level of the burley-cues. With his elite European education and his sophisticated technique, Copland's assertively modernistic use of jazz represented a *downward* social dynamic. It brought out the fear of jazz as a socially regressive force. When Glazunov heard *Rhapsody in Blue* he described it to Walter Damrosch's wife as "part human and part animal."[49] The remark was taken as a compliment because it was assumed that Gershwin's mission was to humanize the animal instincts of jazz. Yet the very same racist view of American popular music worked against Copland, as we have seen, to the extent of provoking an anti-Semitic backlash. His music threatened to animalize humanistic art.

Perhaps the most pointed comment of all on the "sociostylistics" of American music with respect to jazz — that is, the social implications of stylistic assimilation — came from Edward Burlingame Hill (1872–1960), a composer on the faculty of Harvard University and a leading Francophile. The only critic to make a direct comparison between *Rhapsody in Blue* and the earlier European experiments in jazz appropriation (Copland's concerto not yet having been performed), Hill observed in the *Harvard Graduate's Magazine* that "Mr. Gershwin's works indicate that it may be more profitable for the jazz composer to turn to the larger forms than for the 'high-brow' composer to condescend to jazz."[50] Because his work was so clearly "aspirant" rather than "condescending," Gershwin's reputation never suffered from a racial backlash, not even from the likes of Daniel Gregory Mason; and that is the best evidence of all that, unlike Copland, he was not regarded as a threat — until, that is, he completed his studies with Schillinger and presented himself, in *Porgy and Bess*, as a fully-armed professional, prompting Virgil Thomson to carp somewhat cryptically at its "gefiltefish orchestration"[51] (*gefilte fish*, or "stuffed fish," being a Jewish Sabbath-eve delicacy). But even then, his suppliant stance made Gershwin easy to tolerate, whether by bigots like Mason or by elite modernists like Schoenberg. His message to the establishment was flattering, and room was found for him.

THE GREAT AMERICAN SYMPHONY

What ultimately killed off "symphonic jazz" was not so much snobbery or bigotry as it was the advent of the Great Depression of the 1930s, which abruptly put an end to the "jazz age" or "roaring twenties," the decade of postwar hedonism that had sustained the experimental fusion of genres both in Europe and in America. The times now demanded not "American hustle" and "metropolitan madness," but a music that could sustain faith with eloquence. Again Stravinsky set the tone in Europe, with his *Symphony of Psalms* (1930), an austerely rapt three-movement cantata that he composed in response to a commission from Koussevitzky for a symphony to celebrate the fiftieth anniversary of the Boston Symphony Orchestra.

In America a new national image took hold in the arts. Its earnest optimism and loftiness of expression were epitomized (and affectionately caricatured) by the cliché image of writers aspiring to produce "the Great American Novel." For a Great American Symphony to emerge, greatness itself would have to stage a musical comeback: the ironic mood that was so basic to the postwar esthetic would have somehow to be overcome. "Jazz," among white Americans often an expression of insouciance, would have to be supplanted. Jazz had begun in any case to seem to many American artists too much a mirror of European attitudes toward the New World; its espousal by "sophisticated composers," Henry Cowell argued, was "based on the curious bias of the Parisian's concept of America."

Artistic inspiration tended now to flow not from the industrial centers of the Eastern seaboard but from the traditional mythology of the American West, which in place of bustling urban scenes — crowds, haste, frenzy — emphasized open spaces, imperturbable vision, fortitude, and self-reliance, in other words the "pioneer spirit."

And just as the demand was being felt for such a music, a supplier turned up as if sent by Central Casting. He became for half a dozen years the acknowledged sonic incarnation of the American spirit, hailed by one enthusiastic writer as early as 1931 as "the white hope of the nationalists."[52] That summed it up in more ways, possibly, than the writer had in mind.

He was Roy Harris (1898 – 1979), "an Oklahoma Composer

FIG. 11-7   Roy Harris, undated photo, possibly ca. 1960.

Who Was Born in a Log Cabin on Lincoln's Birthday," to cite (in part!) the bulkily insistent title of an unpublished promotional biography written on Harris's behalf (and Koussevitzky's behest) by Nicolas Slonimsky in the years of the composer's first fame. He could have done even better: the part of Oklahoma (then not yet a state but an "Indian Territory") in which Harris was born on Lincoln's birthday was actually called Lincoln County. But maybe Slonimsky thought that would strain credibility. Harris came honestly by an "image" no press agent would dare invent.

When he was five, his family moved to southern California to farm. Harris worked the land as a youth, drove a truck, and did odd jobs. He received his early musical instruction from his mother on the farm. He did not apply himself seriously to composition until he was in his late twenties, when he sought out as a teacher Arthur Farwell (1877–1952), an "Americanist" composer who had studied in Germany but who in his creative work followed the "other" side of Dvořák's advice and sought to found his personal style on American Indian melodies, many of which he arranged for piano. Harris did not follow Farwell in this practice, but did inherit from his teacher a suspicion of European modernism and an aversion to urbanist styles.

His background, in short, was the very antithesis of Copland's and Gershwin's. Nevertheless, on meeting Copland in 1926, he took the latter's advice and went to Paris to study with Nadia Boulanger. He stayed until 1929, and wrote under Boulanger's tutelage the works that gained him his first professional recognition. In later life, however, he refused to acknowledge her as an influence on his development, and pointedly held aloof from the Boulangerie. Slonimsky, purporting to reproduce a conversation with the composer, reported that

> The first year in Paris was torture to our composer. He was worried and disappointed. He disagreed violently with his great teacher. He came to get *knowledge* and *discipline*. She preached both. But her knowledge was a detailed cataloguing of what had already been done; her discipline, a Royalist-Catholic negation of spontaneity. She taught the doctrine of conservation — the tailor-made article designed from any material to meet the needs of the time and place. He was in search of the machinery with which to release and harness the wild horses within him.[53]

Later still, Harris put things in a less contentious perspective, comparing his obstreperous younger self very aptly to "the rookie who came to France to win the war."[54] But the passage from Slonimsky's biography is an important clue to Harris's brand of Americanism — and, of course, it was not only Harris's. It was a brand that defined itself vehemently against Europe, the realm of authority (royal, papal) and of codified procedure. To be American was to be spontaneous, wild, free. An American was a self-made man.

Harris translated the last phrase directly into an idiosyncratic technical or esthetic vocabulary. In a program note for a "big symphony from the West" that Koussevitzky impulsively commissioned from him at their first meeting in 1933, Harris coined the term *autogenetic* — nothing more or less than a fancy Latinate equivalent of "self-made" — to describe a process of melodic construction that he regarded as innately

Western-American. An ardent supporter, Arthur Mendel (then a young critic, later an eminent American musicologist) attempted an explanation of the autogenetic principle in an article in *The Nation*, then (like most American "general interest" magazines of the time) intensely interested in following and abetting the development of serious musical composition in the United States. "Roy Harris," Mendel wrote,

> is trying to work out an idiom in which the structure shall be based on the self-determined growth of the melodic material, not on any superimposed form . . . . His music must be just as cogent and logical and structurally perfect as he can make it. But its form must be determined by its content. It must grow as a plant or an animal grows, along lines dictated by its own inner necessity, not imposed on it from above.[55]

There is of course nothing specifically American about these ideas. They were boilerplate romanticism and echoed the clichés of "organicism" and "content-determined form" first enunciated as planks in the influential platform of the New German School. But the specific ways in which Harris applied them did produce melodies that could be taken as emblems of Western America. Slonimsky, a noted walking thesaurus, called them "heliotropic," a botanical term that means "growing toward the sun." His prime example was the second theme of the "big symphony from the West" that Koussevitzky and the Boston Symphony performed on 26 January 1934 under the title *Symphony 1933* (Ex. 11-13a). Slonimsky called particular attention to the "ascetic intervals that suggest monastic origin," which, he proposed,

> are reflective in an American composer of the spacious Western deserts. Harris is not a poet of the city and does not take interest in "depicting the age of machinery." In his music he is always a Westerner; his rhythmical verve reflects the dry energy of the mountain air.[56]

The prevalence of quarter-note triplets, usually in a "circumflex" or "anticircumflex" contour, is evidence of Harris's "autogenetic" technique: everything derives from a single

EX. 11-13A   Roy Harris, "autogenetic" melodies, *Symphony 1933*, I, second theme

shape, the arch. As Beth Levy, a historian of musical Americanism, notes, that arch shape pervades the melody at higher levels of structure as well. The whole melody is a composite of overlapping arched figures of varying lengths: mm. 1–4, 4–7, 7–9, 9–10, 10–13, 15–17, 17–18, 18–20, 20–21. And its overall span proceeds from the next-to-lowest note (the initial d″) to a single high point in the middle (the g‴ in m. 11) and down again to the lowest note (d♭″ in m. 21).

That property of "imbricated arches," plus what Levy calls its "casually wandering chromaticism,"[57] lend the melody a quality that led critic after critic to describe Harris's music as deriving, in the words of one, "from the West that bred Mr. Harris and in which he works most eagerly — from its air, its life, its impulses, even its gaits." Nobody seems to have remarked on the resemblance between Harris's technique and Schoenberg's already well-publicized principle of "developing variation" (nor were associations to the American West ever read into Schoenberg's many "heliotropic" melodies). That power of suggestion is significant, however, because it showed that it was possible to create a distinctively American music — that is, a music that would be received and valued by its audience as distinctively American — without recourse to "found objects" of any kind, urban or rural, folk or popular, genuine or simulated. Roy Harris, in short, was living refutation of Dvořák's principles.

He propounded this idea explicitly in "The Growth of a Composer," a short article or manifesto he published in the *Musical Quarterly* in April 1934, in the very wake of the "big symphony from the West." It begins with a declaration that "the creative impulse is a desire to capture and communicate . . . the atavistic burgeonings from the depth of the race-soul,"[58] and ends with a warning that only by maintaining his personal integrity does a composer stand "a good chance of creating music that will be true to his race, to his time, to himself."[59] The extent to which he achieves "an understandable race-expression" will determine "whether he represents a small community, a nation, or mankind."[60] But the means to this achievement lie entirely within the individual creative imagination. A true symbiosis between art and life cannot be mediated by prefabricated (limited and limiting) artifacts, only by a boundless inner process of abstraction Harris calls "metabolism":

> With each successive study (in melody, harmony, counterpoint, form, instrument-ation), he creates a new life for himself. He goes along the streets, in subways, on hiking trips, he talks to people, at the same time seeing, hearing, analyzing, drawing melodic contours, weaving harmonic textures, fashioning contrapuntal designs and patterns, mixing orchestral timbres. Music becomes to him a plastic language of shapes and forms, colors and intensities. Music creates a new world for him, it offers him a new acting philosophy of positive values which he can isolate, examine, and mold.[61]

The next year, Harris put these theories into practice with *A Farewell to Pioneers: Symphonic Elegy*, his first work to embody a program that drew openly, rather than implicitly, on the mythology of the American West. He billed it as

> a tribute to a passing generation of Americans to which my own father and mother belong. Theirs was the last generation to affirm and live by the pioneer standards

of frontiersmen. They were born of and taught by a race of men and women who seemed to crave the tang of conquering wildernesses and wresting abundance from virgin soil.[62]

They were, in a word, "autogenetic." Accordingly, Harris constructed the melodies of this composition to reflect their questing, self-fashioning spirit — and something else as well. In a letter to a pupil who studied with him in the early 1940s, Harris described the theme shown in Ex. 11-13b as embodying "a gentle variation of both pitch and rhythm design so subtly conceived that the auditor is gradually and almost imperceptibly led onward and onward into fresh and new fields of melody." Analogies are drawn now not only to the American character but to the American land — the land of "wide open spaces," to be evoked locally, in melodies like this, by the use of ever-widening intervals (but without any literal repetition), and globally by a systematically ascending ("heliotropic") tessitura. The syncopated rhythms, which Harris took pains never to associate with jazz, reflected, he averred, "our [i.e., American] unsymmetrically balanced melodies (difficult to harmonize with prepared cadences) and our national aversion to anything final, our hope and search for more satisfying conclusions." The opening melody in *Farewell to Pioneers* (Ex. 11-13c) epitomizes everything Harris sought to project as Western-American. Each of its well-demarcated phrases can be read as an autogenic variation of its immediate predecessor (which means, ultimately, of the first phrase). There is no repetition, only forward progression toward the melody's "manifest destiny." The range of the melody widens systematically, eventually to cover more than two octaves. But also note that from the trumpet entry in m. 11 to the end of the flute's first phrase in m. 18, the melody adheres to a pentatonic scale. That is the stuff of folklore, Dvořák territory after all. Its inexorable seepage into Harris's work presages the next (and controversial) stage in the evolution of "Americanist" concert music.

Harris's greatest success as an emblematic American came in February 1939, with the premiere (in Boston, naturally, under Koussevitzky) of his Third Symphony. Like many early-twentieth-century symphonies, perhaps most conspicuously the Seventh (1924) by the Finnish composer Jean Sibelius (1865–1957), then

EX. 11-13B   Roy Harris, "autogenetic" melodies, from *A Farewell to Pioneers* (1935)

EX. 11-13C   Roy Harris, "autogenetic" melodies, *A Farewell to Pioneers*, opening melody

heralded as the greatest living symphonist, it is a sort of programless symphonic poem, in a single movement but with relatively autonomous sections in contrasting tempos.

Or is it programless? A note by the composer for the first performance purported to outline its form, but contained a certain amount of expressive characterization as well (implying, perhaps, that the two were not to be regarded as separable). Measure numbers have been added to Harris's outline as given here to facilitate comparison with the score; also compare Ex. 11-14.

I. Tragic — low string sonorities. [to m. 138]
II. Lyric — strings, horns, woodwinds. [mm. 139–208]
III. Pastoral — woodwinds with a polytonal string background. [209–415]
IV. Fugue — dramatic.

    A. Brass-percussion dominating [416–504]

    B. Canonic development of materials from Section II constituting background for further development of Fugue. [505–566]

V. Dramatic-Tragic.

    A. Restatement of violin theme of Section I: tutti stringsbrass and percussion developing rhythmic motif from climax of Section IV. [567–633]

    B. Coda — development of materials from Sections I and II over pedal timpani. [634–703(end)]

This much was enough to prompt speculation on the part of one critic that, in its uncompromising seriousness, the symphony spoke "of the bleak and barren expanses of Western Kansas, of the brooding prairie night,"[63] and for another critic to assert (in a more "technical" vein) that "although there is no direct use of folksong in this work, the melodic content is clearly rooted in idealized hymnal and secular folk idioms." There is as little evidence for the one conclusion as for the other; on the contrary, what evidence there is indicates that Harris's "hymnic" style was based on a study of Gregorian chant and medieval organum. But both assumptions were understandable and in a way justifiable, even if the most tangible model remained Sibelius, a European.

The lofty rhetorical tone of the Harris Third—in particular, the sense of high peroration as Section IV-B gives way to V-A (Ex. 11-15), with its recapitulation of the "Tragic" violin theme from Section I (another good example of "autogenetic" melody) as a stately dirge in doubled note-values and "heliotropic" upward transposition, its formality underscored by its canonic treatment—made it impressive and gave the "symphonic" manner renewed influence. Sibelius, while acknowledged (especially by American critics) as legitimate heir to the romantic symphonic tradition, was widely regarded as the last of a dying breed; by many Europeans, indeed, he was already thought of as a sort of dinosaur. He had not produced a new symphony in fifteen years; although he lived to the age of ninety-one, he would never do so. His unironized rhetorical eloquence suffered in the general postwar atmosphere of disillusion. Although his later symphonies were decidedly restrained compared with his prewar output, they bore a suspicious taint of bombast.

EX. 11-14 Roy Harris, Symphony no. 3, excerpts demonstrating the main themes: I. Tragic, II. Lyric, III. Pastoral, and IV. Fugue

EX. 11-15   Roy Harris, Symphony no. 3, 6 after fig. 56

EX. 11-15 (continued)

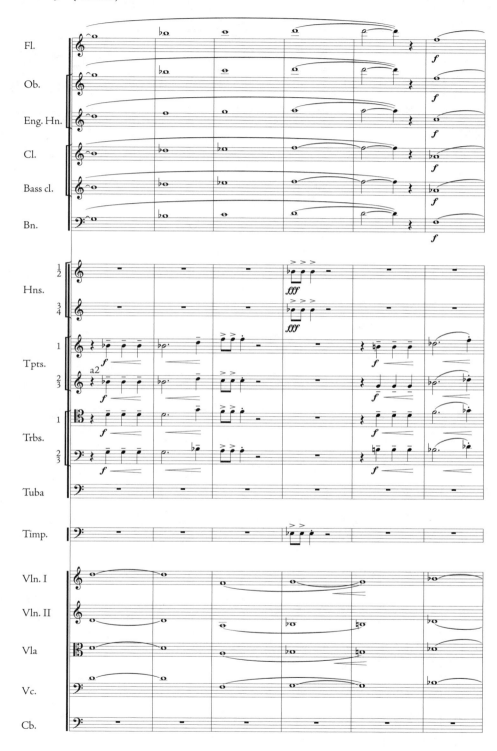

EX. II-I5   (continued)

Virgil Thomson, just back from Paris in his first year as a professional music critic, administered a calculated shock to the American musical establishment in the very first review he published in the *New York Herald Tribune* by declaring Sibelius "vulgar, self-indulgent and provincial beyond all description."[64] Yet even Thomson, orthodox product that he was of the Boulangerie, found himself a bit cowed by Harris, the Boulangerie's most conspicuous renegade, who had so adroitly and, it seems, sincerely captured the mood or self-image of America in depression time — one of ingenuous idealism and commitment. Thomson could wanly note that Harris's rhetoric "invites kidding"[65] and offer some mild reproof: "one would think, to read his prefaces, that he had been awarded by God, or at least by popular vote, a monopolistic privilege of expressing our nation's deepest ideals and highest aspirations."

But he dared not kid the music. On the contrary, he praised it precisely for avoiding, "as if it were of the devil, any colorful accent whatsoever," and for achieving, at its best, an expressive amplitude that has "exactly as much to do with America as mountains or mosquitoes or childbirth have, none of which is anybody's property and none of which has any ethnic significance whatsoever."[66] All of which made Roy Harris's music, and the Third Symphony in particular, "America's most popular (and most exportable) single expression in symphonic form." As evidence of its exportability, and also of the hope that it inspired, one could cite the wondering reactions of many Europeans, not used to taking America seriously as a producer of "important" symphonic music. Italy's Alfredo Casella, for one example: "In producing a composer such as this master, America has placed herself in the front rank amongst those nations who are concerned with building a music for the future."[67]

In Harris's wake, and largely on his legitimizing prestige, a distinctive "school" of American symphonic writing flourished during the depression years. It was borne aloft by a government-subsidized proliferation of orchestras administered by the Works Progress Administration (WPA), part of President Franklin Roosevelt's "New Deal," a policy of fighting unemployment with government spending, and it maintained a high profile well into the 1960s. Its other titular head was Howard Hanson (1896–1981), a Nebraska-born composer of Scandinavian ancestry who, even before Harris, had accepted Sibelius as his chief symphonic model. Koussevitzky and the Boston Symphony commissioned from Hanson two symphonies, the Second ("Romantic," 1930) and the Third (1938), which could be taken equally with Harris's as exemplifying the high symphonic rhetoric of depression-era America, replete with "heliotropisms" (see the horn countermelody in Ex. 11-16). But Harris was the one by whom (or on behalf of whom) the style was explicitly invested with national significance.

As early as 1924, Hanson was appointed director of the newly established Eastman School of Music, a conservatory endowed by George Eastman (the "Kodak" camera manufacturer) and affiliated with the University of Rochester in upstate New York. He held the post for forty years, during which time the Eastman School became a focal point for what might be called the American neoromantic style. Another institutional base was established for it when William Schuman (1910–92), a pupil of Harris, was appointed president of the Juilliard School of Music in New York, America's most distinguished conservatory, in 1945.

Schuman had scored a big public and critical success with his Symphony No. 3 (1941), a massively energetic work in two composite neobaroque movements (Passacaglia and Fugue, Chorale and Toccata). Similarly large and affirmative was the Third Symphony (1947) by Walter Piston (1894–1976), a charter member along with Copland and Thomson of the Boulangerie. Its character, so similar to that of Hanson's, Harris's, and Schuman's "Thirds," suggests that the American symphonists of the "WPA School" still saw themselves in a line that extended back to Beethoven: a Third Symphony had to be an "Eroica." All of these symphonies were accepted as "Americanist" on the strength of stylistic features they all shared with Harris's Third: melodic breadth; a basically diatonic (though often dissonant) harmonic idiom; "asymmetrical" rhythm; sonorous, often percussion-heavy orchestration. With one conspicuous exception to be described later, none employed folk tunes or otherwise "marked" material to establish their national character.

EX. 11-16   Howard Hanson, Symphony no. 2, motto theme

The vitality of the school can be measured by the high productivity of its members: Harris produced thirteen symphonies over the course of his career, Schumann ten, Piston eight, Hanson six. Roger Sessions (1896–1985), who stood somewhat aloof from the other composers named so far thanks to a somewhat more chromatic, more "internationalist" style, was nevertheless an enthusiastic symphonist in a manner that would have been far more unusual in a European composer (except in Russia). He and Peter Mennin (1923–83), a younger member of the group who had studied with Hanson at the Eastman School and who succeeded Schuman as president of the Juilliard School, each logged a "classic" Beethovenian nine.

FERMENT ON THE LEFT

But by the mid-1940s the idea of the All-American (but ethnically unmarked) Symphony as optimum embodiment of the American character had received a powerful challenge from what might be called a resurgent Dvořák faction, yet one colored by contemporary circumstances in a manner that Dvořák never envisioned, and would have surely deprecated. The early 1930s witnessed a renewed interest in American white folklore from the perspective of radical politics, which received a major impetus from the depression, particularly in connection with the labor movement. Folk music, now regarded as the product of the American "proletariat," was researched and performed as an adjunct to political action. It was adopted (and often radically adapted) as agitation and propaganda on behalf of the farmers and workers who were most sorely affected by the economic downturn.

The folk music revival did not immediately affect the composition of "art" music. At first, composers of leftist persuasion modeled their activity on that of their German counterparts like Kurt Weill and Hanns Eisler, as described in chapter 9. Marc Blitzstein (1905–64), the most notable example, was a Philadelphia-born composer whose European study tour took him both to Fontainebleau and the Boulangerie and to Berlin, where he worked briefly with Schoenberg and heard Weill and Brecht's *Three Penny Opera* in its first production. (It would be in Blitzstein's translation that the piece became so popular in America in the 1950s.) Encouraged by the exiled Brecht, whom he met in New York in 1935, Blitzstein composed *The Cradle Will Rock*, a "play in music" (to his own libretto) in ten scenes embodying what the composer called "an allegory about people I hate"[68] that would through a combination of entertainment and political harangue persuade its intended middle-class audience to join the class struggle on the side of the proletariat—or as Blitzstein put it, "to shove those into the progressive ranks who stood on the brink."[69]

The work focuses a general critique of "prostitution" in all walks of American life on an episode involving labor agitation in a place called Steeltown, U.S.A. A group of "upright citizens," all of them in thrall to Mr. Mister, the steelmill boss and the cartoon personification of capitalist evil, have been mistakenly arrested as union organizers, along with one actual (that is, literal) prostitute, a streetwalker named Moll, who is of course the play's only "innocent." One by one the remaining characters—a minister (Reverend Salvation), a newspaperman (Editor Daily), a college president (President

FIG. 11-8   Marc Blitzstein's *The Cradle Will Rock* in rehearsal. The composer is squatting at right.

Prexy), a doctor (Dr. Specialist), and so on — reveal their servile hypocrisy. In the end the righteous workers, led by Larry Foreman the union man, gain the inevitable victory over the forces of reaction.

Among the "prostitutes" are Yasha and Dauber, a pair of artists, who depend on the "cultured" Mrs. Mister, the boss's wife, for patronage. (She summons them with an automobile horn that plays a snatch from Beethoven's supposedly "revolutionary" *Egmont* Overture.) They sing a duet called "Art for Art's Sake" that, in a manner typical of the day, pits ethics against esthetics. A paean to "pure" classical (or neoclassical) art as then trumpeted, above all, by Stravinsky, the duet indicts artists who in their social indifference serve the interests of the exploiting class. *The Cradle Will Rock* achieved a much greater notoriety than expected owing to the circumstances of its first performance, on 17 June 1937. It had been commissioned through the Federal Theatre Project, an arm of the Works Progress Administration; but on the very eve of the premiere, the government contract was rescinded on account of the adverse publicity the work's supposedly subversive character was generating, and the theater was locked. The whole cast, along with the audience, walked to another theater a mile away. The actors' and musicians' unions, fearing reprisals, forbade their members to appear onstage or in the pit at the new venue, so Blitzstein, with the stage to himself, played the score on the piano, while the singers and actors, scattered throughout the auditorium in street dress, performed their roles from their seats. They made theater history, and established the work's performance tradition; it is usually presented as it was on its nearly-thwarted opening night. The full score, it seems, has never been performed.

The cast party afterward took place at the Downtown Music School, a community educational facility administered by the Workers Music League, an adjunct of the American Communist Party, and under its discipline. (That discipline, of course, was international; it was channeled through the so-called Comintern, or Third Communist International Organization, which by the 1930s was an agency of the foreign policy of the USSR.) Among the other organizations the League sponsored was the Composers Collective of New York, a club modeled loosely on the Russian Union of Soviet Composers, where creative musicians met to exchange ideas, hear and critique each other's work, and publish anthologies of labor songs.

Determining its actual membership, or that of any radical political action group in Depression-era America, is difficult now. During the Cold War, when tensions mounted between the United States and Soviet Russia, rival superpowers capable of "mutual assured destruction," membership or former membership in the American Communist Party (driven underground between 1946 and 1966) or any of its affiliated organizations became cause for suspicion and possible legal persecution. As we shall see later, members and sympathizers of the Composers Collective endured reprisals in the 1950s for their idealistic political sympathies in the 1930s.

Many sought protection in denial, or in the exercise of their constitutional right to avoid self-incrimination; to reveal their participation, and even to assert that it had a direct and historically significant impact on their musical output, would at one time have been a hostile and potentially injurious act. Even now such disclosures are unjustly regarded by many, across the political spectrum, as defamatory. But that makes the irony of the situation — that important features of the American national identity in music originated in circumstances that would later be branded "Un-American" — all the more poignant, and all the more needful of elucidation.

The members of the Composers Collective who can be most conclusively identified are the ones who operated within the organization under cover of Party ("revolutionary") pseudonyms. They included Charles Seeger (1886–1979), a minor composer but a very distinguished musicologist, who went by the name Carl Sands, and Elie Siegmeister (1909–91), a recent product of the Boulangerie, whose *nom de guerre* was L. E. Swift. Blitzstein, who boldly used his own name, was listed in official publications as the organization's secretary. The Collective's most concrete musical legacy was the *Workers' Songbook*, two volumes of "mass songs" (agitation-and-propaganda songs to be sung by amateur choruses in unison or as rounds), issued in 1934 and 1935. The Collective also sponsored concerts devoted largely, but not solely, to the performance of such works.

One such concert, presented in March 1934 at the organization's New York headquarters, called the Degeyter Club (after Pierre Degeyter, a French woodcarver who in 1888 had composed the music to the Communist hymn "Internationale"), was Aaron Copland's first "one-man show," the first full-length program anywhere devoted exclusively to his music. Since his abortive jazz experiments, Copland had been writing in an abstractly modernistic and decidedly "urban" idiom unmarked by any specifically Americanist coloration. The program presented by the Collective included a two-piano arrangement of the jazzy Concerto with Copland as the soloist; an early piano Passacaglia; a pair of pieces ("Nocturne" and "Ukelele Serenade") for violin and piano; a piano trio (1928) based on a Yiddish theme, called "Vitebsk" after one of the major centers of Eastern European Jewry; and—the most recent composition, as well as the most abstract one—a rigorously worked-out and aggressively dissonant set of *Piano Variations* (1930; the opening bars or "theme" is given in Ex. 11-17).

Seeger reviewed the concert in the *Daily Worker*, the Communist Party newspaper, and hailed Copland's new sound, equating musical with political militancy as was then the fashion among artists with leftist leanings but elite training. Thanks to its uncompromising dissonance and its use of quarter tones, even the "Vitebsk" trio was seen as politically progressive despite its incorporation of what might otherwise have looked like religious subject matter, normally equated by Communists with reactionary politics. Allowing himself some chronological liberty, Seeger charted Copland's course as moving steadily and inevitably leftward:

> From the "genteel seclusion" of the earlier works, through an intermediate stage of almost religious rage or, better, rage at religion, and of a flirtation with Broadway, he emerged by 1930 as the composer of one of the most undeniably revolutionary pieces of music ever produced here—the Piano Variations. That he was not "conscious" of this at the time he wrote the work is merely to say that in 1930 he had progressed further in musical than in language development.[70]

EX. 11-17   Aaron Copland, *Piano Variations* (theme)

EX. II-17 (continued)

The last comment was a reference to a disclaimer Copland had made before the concert, which, Seeger contended, had been disproved not only by the music but also by an exchange he had in a follow-up discussion period, during which a steelworker had commented that the *Piano Variations* reminded him of his work environment. Copland replied that, while he had not imagined "riveters and subways" while composing, he did write the piece over the noise of a New York street, and felt that his music was therefore "able to stand up against modern life." That gave Seeger the grounds for a ringing peroration:

> For one of the finest definitions of revolutionary musical content yet made, we hail Aaron Copland's "Up Against!" And with vigor, too — that is the essence of the Piano Variations. Their chief shortcomings seem to be that they are almost too much "against" — against pretty nearly everything. So some day, Aaron, write us something "for." You know what for![71]

Although it would be rash to offer this one incident as an explanation, it is nevertheless telling that, beginning exactly then, in the spring and summer of 1934, positive political commitment shows up in Copland's work (and in other public activities as well: during that summer he made speeches on behalf of Communist politicians in Minnesota, and campaigned for the Communist presidential ticket in 1936). In the fall of 1934, he wrote a one-act ballet called *Hear Ye! Hear Ye!* that in Blitzsteinesque fashion satirizes an obviously corrupt American courtroom at a time when the Communist Party was actively engaged in protesting such miscarriages of justice as the trial of the "Scottsboro boys," nine black youths in Alabama who had been tried and, with one exception, convicted and condemned on trumped-up charges of rape in 1931. (Their appeals continued until 1937 so that the case was still in the news.) The score, which incorporates an orchestrated version of the "Ukelele Serenade," begins and ends with a dissonant parody of the "Star-Spangled Banner."

In 1935, Copland completed a set of short symphonic studies called *Statements for Orchestra*, of which several ("Militant," "Dogmatic," "Jingo") simulated political oratory, and in one case parodied it, thus giving an ideological focus (as Seeger had "demanded") to Copland's aggressive modernism. The "Dogmatic" statement actually quotes the theme of the *Piano Variations* as its middle section, not in self-parody (for Communists, like religious fundamentalists, used the word "dogma" without irony), but as if spelling out the content that Seeger had discerned in it the year before. The parody item is the "Jingo" statement. The word, no longer much in use, was slang for a blustery chauvinist or warmonger; the music (replete with brainless "polytonal" quotations from "The Sidewalks of New York," a song often appropriated by New York "machine" politicians for campaign purposes) is a send-up of the sort of American patriotic rhetoric — the "Fourth of July" rhetoric Charles Ives nostalgically idealized (see chapter 5) — that was derided by the left in those days as a mask for political reaction.

Copland's most direct response to his reception at the Degeyter Club, however, was a contribution to the genre that the organization sponsored: a mass song called "Into the Streets, May First!" (Ex. 11-18). It was the winning entry in a contest sponsored by the *New Masses*, another Communist organ, for the best setting of a poem for May Day, the international workers' holiday. Copland's song was performed at an exercise called the "Second Annual American Workers' Music Olympiad," published in the paper's 1 May edition, reprinted that August in *Sovetskaya muzïka*, the organ of the Union of Soviet Composers, and reissued the next year in the second volume of the *Workers' Songbook*, alongside works by "Sands," "Swift," Wallingford Riegger (using the pseudonym "J. C. Richards"), the Soviet mass song specialist Alexander Davidenko, and Hanns Eisler, the acknowledged master of the genre (see chapter 9), who had just come to America as a refugee from the Nazi regime and given some seminars on mass songs at the Degeyter Club.

EX. 11-18   Aaron Copland, "Into the Streets, May First!"

EX. 11-18   (continued)

Come with a storm of ban-ners Come with an earth-quake tread

Bells ring out_ of your bel-fries Red flag leap out your red

Out of the shops and fac-tor-ies Up with the sic-kle and_ ham-mer

Com-rades these are our tools A song and a ban-ner.

Copland's song exemplifies the position he had staked out when reviewing the first volume of the *Workers' Songbook* in *The New Masses*, a month after winning the contest. Perhaps responding to some misgivings Seeger had expressed when his rather "difficult" song was picked as the winner, Copland addressed the problem of an appropriate style for proletarian art. He conceded that "to write a fine mass song is a challenge to every composer," and that for the sake of achieving "a first-line position on the cultural front" some stylistic compromise was both necessary and well compensated, "for every participant in revolutionary activity knows from his own experience that a good mass song is a powerful weapon in the class struggle."[72]

And yet he did not hesitate to criticize the songs on "aesthetic" grounds, calling the work of one Collective member "flatfooted and unimaginative," and that of another "unnecessarily conventional in spirit." He argued against excessive simplicity or familiarity in style, since (as Seeger himself had claimed) revolutionary content demanded a revolutionary style, even within the limits set by the abilities and experience of amateur performers. He had traditional Communist theory on his side: both folklore (a remnant of "feudalism") and commercial music ("jazz") were considered reactionary political expressions by the orthodox. This was the position adopted in the USSR by the radical Russian Association of Proletarian Musicians (RAPM). Within the Collective, Eisler and Blitzstein preached vehemently against employing idioms that were tainted by capitalist exploitation.

In his own song Copland strove to maintain a striking modern idiom, full of unexpected modulations and pungent harmonies, while staying within the capacities of amateur performers. Each phrase of the melody is diatonic and largely conjunct. Motion between phrases (that is, over tonal modulations) is always conjunct until the last eight measures, which remain within the confines of C major. The tune is expertly crafted to produce a steady rise in tessitura, each succeeding phrase hitting a higher climax than the last. It was a fine specimen of its type, at least theoretically, and was chosen unanimously by the Collective membership (including Eisler) to be its standard bearer.

But traditional Communist esthetic theory was just then being subjected to a massive review that would ultimately doom both the Collective and its approved "revolutionary" style. The first inkling of the change was the way in which Michael Gold, a proletarian writer who had a regular column called "Change the World!" in the *Daily Worker*, reacted to Elie Siegmeister's setting of his "Strange Funeral in Braddock," an angry lament for the victim of a horrifying steel mill accident who had to be buried encased in a block of steel that had spilled over him in its molten state. Siegmeister had sought to express the fury of Gold's poem in a typically modernist way, with dissonant tone-clusters in the piano part and operatic *parlando* effects in the voice. Performed at a New York concert in December 1935, the song was well received by critics and was soon published in Henry Cowell's *New Music Quarterly*, but Gold savagely attacked it in the *Daily Worker*: "I think a new content often demands a new form, but when the new form gets so far ahead of all of us that we can't understand its content, it is time to write letters to the press."[73]

Gold demanded that workers' music henceforth adopt rural folk music as its primary model, citing as precedent the activity of Joe Hill (Joseph Hillstrom, 1879–1915), Ella May Wiggins (martyred by a mob in 1929), and Aunt Molly (Mary) Jackson (1880–1960), union organizers who used folk-song parodies and original songs in traditional style — for example, Hill's popular "Casey Jones," a call to railway workers — as agitational propaganda. It was hard to argue with Gold's position from within the movement: Hill and Wiggins, actual victims in the struggle for workers' and farmers' rights, were hallowed names on the left. And yet it might have seemed a somewhat paradoxical or quixotic demand, given that most industrial workers were urban and many of them foreign-born. But Gold was not speaking only for himself. He was expressing a new Party line.

FIG. 11-9   Earl Robinson, "Joe Hill," as it appears in *The Fireside Book of Folk Songs*, ed. Margaret B. Boni (New York: Simon and Schuster, 1947).

"TWENTIETH-CENTURY AMERICANISM"

When the Soviet leadership liquidated both the RAPM and its modernist rival, the Association for Contemporary Music, and replaced them with the Union of Soviet Composers in 1932 (a story that will be more fully told in chapter 13), it prescribed a compromise between their positions: a professional contemporary art music that would remain accessible to workers and peasants because it would draw on familiar folk and popular idioms. Stalin himself summed up the new ideal in a phrase, "an art national in form and socialist in content."[74] Seeger paraphrased it slightly in the *Daily Worker* when he called for a music that was "national in form, proletarian in content."[75]

This line was exported to Communist parties throughout the world as part of an overall policy known as the Popular Front, announced by Georgi Dimitrov, the Bulgarian-born General Secretary of the Comintern, at its Seventh Congress held in Moscow in August 1935. In an effort to unite the left against the rise of fascism in Germany, and thereby promote the security of the Soviet Union, Communist parties were instructed to form alliances and coalitions with more moderate, nonrevolutionary progressive or liberal groups, and to shift their tactics from an appeal to international working-class solidarity to one that invoked national or patriotic resistance against the foreign fascist threat.

To achieve these aims, Communist parties would have to look less "foreign" themselves. They would need to soft-pedal their international ties (in the first place to Moscow) and emphasize their indigenous roots. They would have to stop using the international jargon of political radicalism and start couching their doctrines in terms familiar to those they sought to persuade. That is exactly what Mike Gold was calling for when he rejected the musical radicalism of Siegmeister's *Strange Funeral in Braddock* and asserted the need for a popular musical idiom to clothe revolutionary messages.

On the face of it, the American Communist Party had an easier task than most in implementing Popular Front directives, since it could draw directly on the revolutionary founding myth of the United States. At its nominating convention in June 1936, the Party adopted the slogan "Communism is Twentieth Century Americanism." A pamphlet with that title by Earl Browder, the Party's general secretary and candidate for president, supported the motto with adroitly culled "revolutionary" quotations from the founding fathers (especially Jefferson) and above all from Abraham Lincoln, whose mythic status as the Great Emancipator fit in with the Communist stake in the struggle for racial as well as social justice.

One such quote, from Lincoln's First Inaugural Address, became the basis for an immensely popular "ballad" by Earl Robinson (1910–91), the youngest member of the Composers Collective, one of the few who favored a folkloristic idiom even before the Popular Front directives came down. A classically trained pianist and violinist who studied composition with Eisler and Copland, Robinson taught himself guitar in 1934 and began performing as a "troubadour" at political meetings, providing a model for Charles Seeger's son Peter (or Pete, b. 1919) a Harvard dropout whose distinguished career as a folksinger and political songwriter began around 1941.

Robinson's *Abe Lincoln* was a remarkable stylistic synthesis: its verse alluded to the style and structure of a folk or country (i.e., pre-"jazz") blues, an African-American genre, while its refrain embodied the march cadence of an Eisler *Kampflied* or socialist "fight song" (see chapter 9), all tinged with catchy American colloquialisms in the rhythm of its text-setting to imprint Lincoln's "revolutionary" message in the singers' memories. One of the earliest musical by-products of the Popular Front, Robinson's song was a masterpiece of agitational propaganda.

Abe Lincoln settled the stylistic matter as far as the Communist Party was concerned, and put the Composers Collective out of business. The former members, to a greater or lesser extent, all began to incorporate American rural folklore into their creative work, whether through actual quotation or in the guise of "neonationalism," the abstraction of its stylistic features into a personal expressive idiom. In a pamphlet, *Music and Society*, published in 1938, a chastened Elie Siegmeister wrote that the task of the contemporary composer must be that of "breaking down the age-old division between learned or art music on the one hand, and folk or popular music on the other," for "in doing this he will be helping to break down the class division which these musical divisions have symbolized and helped to perpetuate."[76]

No other composer on the left, however, equaled Robinson's feat of actually composing a folk song — that is, writing a song that became accepted into the American oral tradition and sung by multitudes who did not know its origin. Robinson's *Joe Hill*, set to a poem by a Communist journalist named Alfred Hayes (who also wrote the words to Copland's *Into the Streets, May First!*) and first published in the *Daily Worker* in

1936, passed from mouth to mouth at union meetings and on picket lines, went overseas with the American volunteers who fought under the banner of the "Abraham Lincoln Brigade" in the Spanish Civil War, and even turned up, sung by Joan Baez (b. 1941), a latter-day political troubadour, at the Woodstock Music and Arts Fair, an enormous outdoor festival of folk and popular music, in August 1969, whence it experienced a new round of "folk" currency.

Fig. 11-3 shows the song as it appears in *The Fireside Book of Folk Songs*, a mass-marketed anthology (ed. Margaret B. Boni) published in 1947. The music is attributed to Robinson, but the words are unattributed. The composer, in a half-proud, half-rueful memoir, recalled seeing it published in a labor songbook with the legend, "Words: Earl Robinson, Music: Traditional."[77] An anthology called *Songs That Changed the World* (ed. Wanda W. Whitman; New York, 1969), published in the wake of the Woodstock Festival, called it, simply, "the 'spiritual' of the union movement." By then it had even found its way back into serious, scholarly, "field-collected" folklore anthologies.

In other words, it joined the contents of the sort of book that, with the Popular Front directives in mind, composers who had been writing mass songs began consulting for models and actual melodies. The earliest such popular anthology, *The American Songbag*, was published in 1927 by Carl Sandburg (1878–1967), a newspaperman and poet and sometime socialist politician (and the author of a monumental biography of Lincoln), who played the guitar after a fashion and liked to end his public readings with songs. During the depression years there was, predictably, an explosion of publications of this type, culminating in a vastly enlarged 1938 reissue of John A. Lomax's classic anthology *Cowboy Songs and Other Frontier Ballads* (1910), revised in collaboration with the compiler's son Alan Lomax (1915–2002), who went on to become the century's foremost collector of American folk songs.

Even before that, the father-son team had issued a popular collection, *American Ballads and Folksongs* (1934) that follows the example of the original Lomax publication by furnishing piano accompaniments to the songs as an aid to popularization. Southern Baptist hymnody or "Sacred Harp" singing was popularized by the literary historian George Pullen Jackson in *White Spirituals in the Southern Uplands*, a treatise illustrated with settings drawn from early-nineteenth-century hymnbooks. Another collection based on early published sources (also by a literary historian) was S. Foster Damon's *Series of Old American Songs* (1936–37), an annotated collection in facsimile of one hundred American folk and popular songs from before the Civil War.

Elie Siegmeister, formerly of the Composers Collective, came out with an anthology of his own (*Treasury of American Song*, edited with Olin Downes) in 1940. The book became the basis for a Broadway musical, *Sing Out Sweet Land!*, in 1944. By then, white rural folk song had been "mainstreamed" into American popular culture, no longer associated exclusively or automatically with protest movements or the political left. But the political origins of the folklore movement in the Popular Front are still reflected, if only vestigially, in the show's authorship.

The same can be said about the absorption of rural folklore into the concert repertory. The earliest, somewhat isolated instance was Virgil Thomson's *Symphony on a Hymn Tune* (1928), the first American symphony to emerge from the Boulangerie. A compositional tour de force in that its four traditional movements were all based on a single melody (*How Firm a Foundation*, a hymn of Scottish origin with which Southern Baptists traditionally brought their convocations to a close), it eschewed the Germanic technique of motivic extraction and transformation ("developmental" writing, as it was then called) in favor of the more harmonically static or "polytonal" collage techniques that, as shown in chapter 10, were associated with French surrealism. As in *Four Saints in Three Acts*, the opera sampled there, Thomson laced his music with deliberate commonplaces and mock-realistic touches, like the doubling of lines in near-octaves that call to mind the sound of malfunctioning organs (Ex. 11-19).

EX. 11-19   Virgil Thomson, *Symphony on a Hymn Tune*

Although, as Thomson told a biographer, he meant the symphony to be "an ambitious and noble work," he encountered the same difficulty with it that Satie faced when he meant to be serious. His commonplaces were heard as parodies or arch "wrong-note" effects, which prevented the work from meeting the expectations of the traditional audience he was addressing the way Harris's heroic symphonies eventually would. Nor could a music so deliberately refined and esoteric serve the socially utilitarian purposes promoted on the American left during the depression years.

Eventually Thomson shelved it and reused parts of it a decade later to represent the Old South in a documentary film score (*The River*, 1937) commissioned by the United States government through the WPA, to accompany a stern propaganda film directed by poet turned documentary film maker Pare Lorentz (1905–92) that showed the sorry aftermath of floods on the Mississippi caused by greedy exploitation of the land, and made a pitch for the Roosevelt administration's public works programs that many were resisting as "socialistic." All at once the seemingly trivial symphony of 1928 had "social significance," to cite a catchphrase of the thirties. Elsewhere Thomson used southern hymns procured for him by George Pullen Jackson.

The River was Thomson's second government commission. The first was for a score to accompany an earlier Lorentz documentary, *The Plow That Broke the Plains*, on the effects of soil erosion. For one section, Thomson contrived a collage of three cowboy songs — "Houlihan" (a.k.a. "I Ride an Old Paint"), "Git Along Little Dogies," "The Streets of Laredo" — from the 1934 Lomax anthology. As a movement in an orchestral suite drawn from the movie score and first performed in 1936, it marked the first use of specifically Western-American folklore by a composer in the Euro-American "art" tradition — the first of many.

The most successful and lasting ones were by Aaron Copland. The first dated from 1936, the same year as *The Plow That Broke the Plains*, when Copland was commissioned by the Henry Street Settlement, a New York child welfare organization that had recently sponsored a performance of Weill and Brecht's *Der Jasager* (see chapter 9), to write a "school opera" in a similar didactic vein. The opera, called *The Second Hurricane*, concerns a group of stranded schoolchildren who learn cooperation in the face of danger. Siegmeister, in his Popular Front tract, praised it alongside works of "social music" by Shostakovich, Blitzstein, and Eisler as "a children's opera teaching solidarity."[78] Their socialization having been accomplished, the children keep their spirits up while waiting to be rescued by joining in a singing game based on "The Capture of Burgoyne" (1777), an "excellent revolutionary song"[79] (in the compiler's words) that Copland found in Damon's *Old American Songs*. It forms the musical climax of the play.

The Second Hurricane was first performed at the Settlement Music School in April 1937. Three months later, another work commissioned in 1936 was first performed, this time over the radio. Copland was one of six composers who had been invited by the CBS network to write orchestral pieces for national broadcast. His working title was *Radio Serenade*, but to stimulate interest in the program the network substituted the generic name *Music for Radio*, and announced that the piece had a secret program that listeners were invited to guess by proposing titles, the winning entry to be selected by the composer. In this way the piece became known as *Saga of the Prairie*, the winning listener (a housewife named Ruth Leonhardt) having been reminded of "the intense courage — the struggles and final triumphs — of the early settlers, the real pioneers." Copland assumed she was reacting to the clarinet solo marked "simply, in the manner of a folk song" in the 1968 published score (retitled *Prairie Journal*: Ex. 11-20).

EX. 11-20   Aaron Copland, *Prairie Journal*, clarinet solo

In an interview published in 1984, Copland identified the melody as "a cowboy tune," which made "the western titles" submitted by listeners "seem most appropriate."[80] There is no evidence from the time of the work's composition to corroborate his statement, and as a matter of fact most listeners who wrote in suggested titles having to do with the usual modernistic imagery of machinery and urban life. Howard Pollock, Copland's biographer, has suggested that the composer's recollection may have been misled by memories of the many cowboy songs that he and many others would be using in various pieces composed over the coming decade. But even if it is not an actual cowboy song, the clarinet tune does bear an authentic whiff of the kind of Anglo-American folklore that Popular Front artists were assiduously mining at the time.

What makes the folklike quality of the tune historically significant is the fact that, as Wayne Shirley of the Library of Congress discovered, the marchlike section that both precedes and follows the clarinet solo was based on an unfinished mass song Copland had composed to Langston Hughes's "Ballad of Ozie Powell," a poetic tribute to one of the Scottsboro boys whose legal fate, as of 1936, was still undecided.[81] Again we see the conjunction, previously exemplified by Earl Robinson, between the stylistic appropriation of American folklore and the political aims of the Popular Front. (Meanwhile, Robinson continued to expand his range with the "Ballad for Americans," a 1938 cantata in folk style that recounted the founding myth of the United States and related its revolutionary spirit to contemporary events; first performed on the radio with the African-American basso Paul Robeson as soloist, it achieved such popularity that it was sung at the 1940 nominating convention of the Republican Party.)

PRAIRIE NEONATIONALISM

"Anglo-folklorism" reached its peak, and exerted its maximum impact on the American musical mainstream, in three ballets that Copland wrote between 1938 and 1944, the most successful works of their kind since Stravinsky's prewar ballets for Diaghilev. They finally made Copland, in a succession that can be traced from Gershwin through Harris, the "exemplary" American composer, the commonly accepted (if not quite undisputed) standard bearer of musical Americanism.

The first of them, *Billy the Kid*, was commissioned by Lincoln Kirstein (1907–96), the director of a company called Ballet Caravan, who also wrote the scenario. It portrays the title character (real name William H. Bonney, 1859–81), a notorious New Mexico cattle rustler and murderer, in his legendary light as a Robin Hood (or Joe Hill) figure, his violent death at the hands of a former friend turned lawman thus becoming a martyrdom. For this ballet "Western," Copland mined the contents of several anthologies of cowboy songs that Kirstein had supplied him with. The Copland scholar Jessica Burr has demonstrated the highly imaginative way Copland fashioned his own thematic material from the songs, sometimes leaving them recognizable though changed, sometimes absorbing them into the fabric of his own music so that without the evidence of the source books they would pass undetected.[82]

Copland's basic source was *The Lonesome Cowboy*, a compilation edited by John I. White and George Shackley (New York, 1930); but as Burr discovered, he compared the settings there with others in his possession and was open to influences not only from the original tunes but from the various arrangements as well. A case in point is Copland's adaptation of "Git Along, Little Dogies," one of the most famous cowboy ballads (already used by Thomson), for the ballet's opening scene, "Street in a Frontier Town," in which Billy's mother is shot and he, avenging her, embarks on his life of crime.

In Ex. 11-21, the setting from *Lonesome Cowboy* is set, first, alongside a rather fancy harmonization of the tune from the Lomax collection by Oscar J. Fox (a separate sheet music publication in Copland's archive at the Library of Congress), and, second, alongside Copland's adaptation. Traces of both arrangements are visible in Copland's tune. The big downward leap of a ninth, Burr suggests, is Copland's response to the shout on "Whoopee" in *Lonesome Cowboy*, indicated with diamond noteheads to represent the approximate pitch (as the editors write) of "a man-sized 'Whoopee-e-e'"; and the dissonant seconds in Copland's setting are a harsher version of the appoggiaturas in Fox's accompaniment. (That Copland's first semitone clash, E♯/F♯, approximates a "blue note" as conventionally rendered by piano arrangers may well have attracted his ear, despite the resulting stylistic miscegenation.)

The very opening of *Billy the Kid*, with its striking "white key" or strictly diatonic dissonances, set another sort of standard for Copland's "prairie" idiom. This one reached a peak in *Rodeo*, Copland's second ballet Western, commissioned in 1942 for the choreographer Agnes de Mille by the Ballet Russe de Monte Carlo, the successor organization to the Diaghilev Ballet. A nearly plotless, "classical" ballet or divertissement on a cowboy theme, it is devoid of the political subtexts that characterized Copland's Popular Front period. (What plot there is concerns the efforts of a hapless cowgirl to attract a beau; some found subtexts of sexual domination here, others have found parallels with the "absent" generation of American men in the first year of wartime).

The use of folklore is more pervasive in *Rodeo*, a simpler score, than in *Billy the Kid*, and for the most part the familiar tunes are allowed to appear in their entirety and (as Howard Pollock puts it) "in relatively traditional settings." For that very reason, the score's slow section, "Corral Nocturne" (Ex. 11-22), the one extended portion in which no folk tunes are known to be quoted, takes on an extra significance, since its style is

EX. 11-21A   "Git Along, Little Dogies" as transcribed by John Lomax

EX. 11-21B   "Git Along, Little Dogies" as arranged by White and Shackley in *The Lonesome Cowboy*

completely consistent with the folklore-saturated sections of the ballet, showing to what an extent Copland had absorbed the folk idiom into his own increasingly distinctive and influential Americanist style.

The music is a veritable tour de force of simplicity and "accessibility," and to that extent could be said to keep faith with the Popular Front's call for a music that resisted the mannerisms and complications of elite modernism. Awareness of the extent to which Copland had formerly displayed those mannerisms makes his compliance with the call seem a knowing one. But to an extent unmatched by any of his contemporaries, Copland succeeded in maintaining both stylistic individuality and a high level of interesting technical detail (both of them prime modernist values) without compromising the "naturalness" and easy comprehensibility of his new style. In his hands, the new simplicity seemed an innovation.

The reasons for that freshness of effect are elusive (a longstanding critical riddle, in fact) but some of them can perhaps be accounted for in terms of "voicing" (i.e., chord spacing) and orchestration, while others seem to reflect a flair for the "neonationalist" assimilation of folklore at a very basic level of style (which, as we recall, was Stravinsky's

EX. 11-21C   "Git Along, Little Dogies" as harmonized by Oscar J. Fox

EX. 11-21D   "Git Along, Little Dogies" as adapted by Aaron Copland in *Billy the Kid*

EX. 11-22 Aaron Copland, *Rodeo*, "Corral nocturne" in the composer's piano score, beginning

secret, too). The strictness with which C-major diatonicism is maintained is in itself a bit shocking, given the time. Out of fifty-three measures, only sixteen have any sharps or flats; and when accidentals are present they usually signal quick forays into new key areas that are maintained as strictly as the original one. (Only twice, in mm. 14 and 52 at opposite ends of the piece, are there direct chromatic inflections.)

It had surely been a long time since a piece of modern music had begun with six bars of nothing but Is, IVs, and Vs. The first modification on the scheme consists of Stravinskyesque superimpositions (e.g., I over IV in m. 7) that maintain diatonic purity while introducing some harmonic novelty and a whiff of counterpoint. At 2, when the music from mm. 3–6 is given a varied reprise, the "wide open" spacing recalls Harris's "heliotropic" manner, already typed as "American"; in combination with the primary-colors harmonization it became a Copland trademark. The most characteristic and convincing touch comes in m. 9 and at analogous points thereafter. The introduction at these points of "mixolydian" B♭s to neutralize the dominant chord recapitulates the tonal progression of "Git Along Little Dogies" (most clearly seen in John Lomax's transcription, Ex. 11-21a) — as telling an example of "neonationalism" as Stravinsky had ever milked from Russian folklore. The source tune is nowhere to be found, but its style has been absorbed as bedrock.

The two-part counterpoint at 4 (Ex. 11-23) also recalls Stravinsky's earlier achievement in the way it posits a strict diatonic style in which parallel fifths and even sevenths are made to sound "correct." That invented yet compelling neoprimitivist style reached its fullest development in Copland's third Americanist ballet, *Appalachian Spring* (1944), composed for the eminent "modern dance" choreographer Martha Graham, in which a set of variations on the Shaker hymn '"Tis the Gift to Be Simple" became something of an emblem for Copland's uncomplicated yet technically sophisticated manner. (It was widely played *in memoriam* after his death at the age of ninety.)

EX. 11-23   Aaron Copland, *Rodeo*, "Corral nocturne" in the composer's piano score, mm. 33–37

The most concentrated (and equally emblematic) assertion of Copland's neonationalism was *Fanfare for the Common Man* (Ex. 11-24), composed in 1942, the first year of World War II so far as America was concerned, as part of a series of nineteen orchestral fanfares commissioned by the English conductor Eugene Goossens (1893–1962), then heading the Cincinnati Symphony Orchestra, as concert-openers during the wartime seasons. Copland's, performed in March 1943, was the only contribution to the series — which included compositions by Hanson, Harris, Thomson, Piston, Cowell, Deems Taylor, Milhaud (then living as a refugee in California), and Daniel Gregory Mason — to survive the circumstances of its commission and join the repertory.

The theme, given out unharmonized at first by three trumpets in unison, and then with three horns in two-part counterpoint, takes the homespun "wide open" style to extremes. Absolutely diatonic and contoured in great soaring arches, it is projected in its solo statement over nearly two octaves, and in its duet form over nearly three. The trumpet part has only four instances of conjunct motion, the horn part none. Phrases typically end in wide descents through multiple skips. The counterpoint is entirely homorhythmic and proceeds entirely by similar motion. The closest the two parts ever

EX. 11-24   Aaron Copland, *Fanfare for the Common Man*, mm. 1–21

EX. 11-24   (continued)

get to one another is a perfect fourth. For the most part they sound sixths, tenths, fifths, and—just as "consonant" in its treatment—a seventh.

These are the traits—mined in equal measure from Western (or otherwise rural) folklore and from the wide intervals and angular contours of Copland's earlier modernistic style—that at last began to communicate a generic (or generalized) "America" to concert audiences both at home and abroad. Needless to say, they were quickly copied not only by other composers of concert music, but also by film and commercial composers in need of methods of instantaneous evocation. In this way they quickly became a stereotype, and "Coplandesque" became an adjective denoting a certain range of moods—pastoral, wistful, sanguine, domesticated—that in turn conjured up a comforting vision of home to depression-era and wartime America.

The most overtly patriotic use to which Copland put his "prairie" style was *A Lincoln Portrait*, yet another product of the banner year 1942. It was commissioned by the conductor André Kostelanetz, a specialist in summertime "pops" concerts, shortly after the Japanese attack on Pearl Harbor, and was first performed in Cincinnati in May. It uses two very familiar songs: Stephen Foster's *Camptown Races* (1850) to lend period flavor to the quick middle section, and *On Springfield Mountain* (or, *The Pesky Sarpent*), from the Damon collection, a natural for evoking Lincoln both because Lincoln had made his political name in Springfield, Illinois, and because the text of the song laments the loss of a man cut down, as Lincoln was, in the prime of life.

After the middle section, the solemn opening returns, this time accompanied by a speaker reading quotations from Lincoln's speeches chosen for their bearing on the predicament of a nation thrust into a military conflict that would test its resolve and its democratic principles. Inevitably, the last of these extracts (Ex. 11-25) is the peroration of the most famous Lincoln speech of all, the Gettysburg Address, accompanied by a trumpet recalling *On Springfield Mountain*, the opening phrase of which coincides with one of the phrases of "Taps," the bugle call sounded at military funerals. When the speaker finishes, the orchestra provides a coda that develops the same multivalent phrase from the folk song into an epitome of "heliotropism."

"I've stolen your thunder,"[83] Copland joked to Earl Robinson, who had followed up on his *Abe Lincoln* of 1936 with a Lincoln cantata of his own, called *Lonesome Train*, in that same early wartime season of 1942. Like Copland's, Robinson's also contains parts for speaking voices (six of them, plus eight solo singers and chorus). But where Robinson's effort remained within the sectarian confines of "progressive" and labor circles, Copland's became a staple of the mainstream concert repertory. That does nothing to alter the fact that *A Lincoln Portrait* was as much a product of the Popular Front esthetic as *Lonesome Train*, even if (as Howard Pollock points out) Lincoln exerted an appeal for all Americans, "especially as a symbol of democracy in action" that "transcended partisan politics."[84]

That, of course, was exactly the reason for his partisan exploitation. Lincoln was the radical left's passport to general acceptability; and this was even more the case after

EX. 11-25   Aaron Copland, *A Lincoln Portrait*, mm. 257–264

EX. 11-25 (continued)

1941, when the United States and Soviet Russia unexpectedly found themselves allied in a war against Nazi Germany and Imperial Japan. During the war, and for a short while thereafter, friendship toward the Soviet Union was official American policy (even as, between 1939 and 1941, friendship toward Nazi Germany was official Soviet policy). One of the fanfares Goossens commissioned for the Cincinnati Symphony, by Deems Taylor, was called "Fanfare for Russia," and it quoted "Dubinushka" ("The cudgel"), an old Russian revolutionary song that had been banned under the tsars.

Taylor was never associated with the political left, and his composing a Fanfare for Russia in wartime did not in itself make for such an association. In the case of Copland's *Lincoln Portrait*, however, those associations went deep: not only to the Lincoln music of Earl Robinson or the writings of Carl Sandburg (who was the first to record the speaker's part, with Kostelanetz, shortly after the premiere), but to the Soviet genre of oratorios with speaker, singled out in Elie Siegmeister's Popular Front tract for its capacity "to focus and intensify a sense of solidarity among great masses of people."[85]

Indeed, according to the threefold definition to be given in chapter 13, Copland's *Lincoln Portrait* perfectly exemplified what in the Soviet Union was called "socialist realist" art. It had a pronounced national character, conveyed both through citations of actual folk and popular songs and by means of a personal style that drew heavily on an idealized folk idiom. It had a strong ideological component, conveyed both explicitly in words, and implicitly by virtue of its accessibility to a wide and heterogeneous audience, which it sought to unite behind an idea. And yes, it served the purposes of the Communist Party as then enunciated, which at that time of crisis were barely distinguishable from the aims of American society at large.

Those aims were later sharply differentiated, of course, and during the 1950s and beyond, to be identified as a Communist carried a ruinous stigma in the United States. The stigma was not unjustified in the case of the many Communist operatives who actively engaged in espionage on behalf of the Soviet Union; but it was also applied indiscriminately to members and sympathizers who were associated with the Party out of sincere idealism in the 1930s and 1940s, when radical politics was not considered to be at all incompatible with American patriotism. As we shall see, Copland was forced to disavow his earlier political affiliations, and claim that his Americanist style was a purely esthetic construct. His music was sufficiently popular, and he was sufficiently esteemed as a musician, for the claim to be accepted. But the connection between his widely emulated Americanist idiom and the Popular Front is a historical fact. Unless it is taken into account, the development of American music during the depression years cannot be adequately understood. There is no reason to assume that Anglo-American folklore would have achieved its emblematic status in American concert music under other circumstances.

As in the case of "jazz," the authenticity of Copland's folklore appropriations was challenged. Roy Harris, whose Americanist style had been a stimulant to Copland's, but who had kept proudly aloof from "quotational" methods, was stirred to compete with Copland after the success of *Billy the Kid* threatened his status as premier Americanist. (It is possible, too, that Harris was stimulated more directly by the Popular Front line; although he was never institutionally affiliated with radical politics, he was an enthusiast of Soviet music and dedicated his Fifth Symphony, first performed shortly after the German defeat at Stalingrad in February 1943, to "the heroic and freedom-loving people of our great Ally, the Union of Soviet Socialist Republics, as a tribute to their strength in war, their staunch idealism for world peace, their ability to cope with stark materialistic problems of world order without losing a passionate belief in the fundamental importance of the arts.") Harris's Fourth Symphony, originally conceived as a "Folksong Jamboree" for nonprofessional chorus and orchestra (and retitled "Folksong Symphony" at his publisher's insistence after two purely instrumental movements were added to it) is a medley of famous American songs. Three movements are based on single songs, including, as finale, "When Johnny Comes Marching Home Again," a Civil War song on which Harris had already composed an overture on commission. The second movement, titled "Western Cowboy," is a tapestry woven of three songs from the Lomax collection, and the next-to-last, called "Negro Fantasy," conflates two well-known spirituals. Two of the cowboy songs in the second movement had already been used by Copland in *Billy the Kid*. The Symphony was first performed in April 1940, and in its revised and expanded form received another well-publicized premiere in December.

In between, Harris published a testy article called "Folksong—American Big Business," in which he made two big claims. First, that the integrity of American folklore was threatened by commercial exploitation; and second, that only those for whom folk songs were the stuff of daily life had any business incorporating them into artworks. In support of the first claim, Harris warned of "urban charlatans"[86] (as Beth Levy puts it): "America," Harris prophesied:

> will have many folksong vendors in the next few years. Some city boys may take a short motor trip through our land and return to write the Song of the Prairies—others will be folksong authorities after reading in a public library for a few weeks.[87]

"Song of the Prairies," *Saga of the Prairie*—it was clear who Harris was trying to impugn. In support of his second claim, he offered himself as evidence: the composer as great Westerner, the first of a breed who

> will absorb and use the idioms of folk music as naturally as the folk who unconsciously generated them. They will have learned that folk song is a native well-spring, an unlimited source of fresh material; that it can't be reduced to a few formulas to stir and mix to taste. Those composers who are drawn to and richly satisfied with folksong will inherit the privilege of using it with the professional's resources and discipline and the amateur's enthusiasm and delight.[88]

To solidify the claim that he came to folk song as a birthright, rather than as a commodity to be exploited, Harris began the article with autobiographical ruminations, recalling how "Idaho Bill," a cowboy friend, complained to the composer about the professionalization of the rodeo at a Cowboy's Reunion they had attended together. "You know there's somethin cussed-ornery about that, somehow," said Idaho Bill.[89] "Taint decent to be ridin your heart out for pay." "Now that," the composer commented, "is what folksong is all about: singing and dancing your heart out for yourself and *the people you were born among*" (italics added).

But though a Westerner, the California-bred Harris was no cowboy; his attempt to construct a self-serving mystique of authenticity was as spurious as it was pernicious. And it did not work. It was precisely the novelty and the originality, rather than the literal authenticity, of Copland's folk-song treatments that gained them their acceptance as American emblem in the context of the concert hall; as always, the only authenticity that counts is perceived authenticity.

The decisive success that a left-leaning, homosexual Jew from Brooklyn, triply marginalized by birth and temperament from anyone's definition of an all-American hero, finally enjoyed in defining America musically is further testimony to what has already emerged many times over as a musical-historical truth: in art, the national is a socially negotiated discourse rather than a natural essence. Popular acceptance, as evidenced both by audience reaction and by professional emulation, is what determines the authenticity of musical nationalism; and popular acceptance is a complicated transaction into which many historical factors inevitably — and unpredictably — play.

CHAPTER 12

In Search of Utopia

SCHOENBERG, WEBERN, AND TWELVE-TONE TECHNIQUE

PROGRESS VS. RESTORATION

O n the evening of 23 February 1928, Arnold Schoenberg went to the opera. A new work by Stravinsky was having its local premiere, and attendance, so to speak, was mandatory. Stravinsky, at forty-five, had yet to make a name for himself as a composer of opera. Having made his reputation as a composer of ballets, he affected coolness toward music theater encumbered (as he maintained) with words. "Music can be united with action or with words," he once told a reporter, "but not with both without bigamy."[1]

To date he had written only a couple of one-acters. *The Nightingale*, based on a tale by Hans Christian Andersen, had had its Paris premiere in 1914 during Diaghilev's last prewar season. As befitted its performance by a ballet troupe, it was more a pageant than a conventional opera, very long on stage spectacle and very short on sung content. *Mavra*, a trifling "opéra bouffe" based on a funny little story in verse by the Russian poet Alexander Pushkin, performed (again in Paris and again by Diaghilev) in 1922, was Stravinsky's first downright flop. The scuttlebutt was that the great Russian composer, who ironically enough was the son of a star opera singer, just wasn't cut out for opera (or "lacked melodic invention").

But the new work, *Oedipus Rex*, had had a big success when first performed in Paris in 1927, and came to Berlin preceded by a formidable reputation. Like the other Stravinsky operas it was a terse one-act affair, and like the others it was extremely unconventional in its dramatic methods. But otherwise it was very different from them, in ways that were expressly calculated by the composer to be seen as a sign of the times. Having decided not to go back to Russia after the Bolshevik coup d'état, Stravinsky had renounced the Russian language as a medium for his music. Instead—and very much in keeping with the postwar "neoclassical" idea—he composed the opera on a "universal" myth (for

FIG. 12-1   Stravinsky, by Picasso, 1925.

such was the prestige enjoyed by the culture of ancient Greece, the original "classical" culture), and in Latin, a "universal" and "classical" language. He probably chose Latin over the original Greek because, unlike Greek, it signified religious ritual to modern Western Europeans, especially the Roman Catholics among them, and this further emphasized notions of universality and authority.

The fact that the language was unintelligible to modern audiences anywhere in the world did not worry Stravinsky. He solved the problem, at least to his own satisfaction, by having the librettist — the ubiquitous Jean Cocteau, whose text had been translated into Latin by a scholarly priest (later a cardinal) named Jean Daniélou — furnish a little précis of the action that could be announced to the audience in advance of each scene by "Le Speaker" (as the part was identified in the score), in the language of the country where the opera was performed. There could hardly be any greater "distancing" of a drama than that. But as Stravinsky's strange methods of course assumed, myths were well-known stories; nobody, he could reasonably suppose, would go to see an *Oedipus* opera for the plot. In that sense attending a mythological opera really was, or could be, like attending a religious service. It provided an occasion for an audience to come together in worship: not of God, precisely, in this case, but of an artifact of "universal" culture that bore a "universal" message.

But what *was* that message? By the time Stravinsky wrote his opera, the myth of Oedipus, the tale of a ruler who unwittingly kills his father and marries his mother, was well on its way to being appropriated and transformed by Sigmund Freud and his followers in psychoanalysis into an allegory of family relationships and the guilt anxieties they produce in modern men. For the Greeks, especially as embodied in the famous tragedy by Sophocles, it was an allegory of fate, which took revenge on the great and powerful king by revealing to him the horrible and unacceptable circumstances of his ascent to the throne: a "classic" case of skeletons in the closet and a chilling reminder that good fortune is precarious and provisional. Because he must acknowledge crimes he has unwittingly committed, the lofty Oedipus is cast down; Sophocles's chillingly memorable last line, spoken (or sung) by the moralizing "Greek chorus," exhorts the audience to "count no mortal happy till he has passed the final limit of his life secure from pain."[2]

For Stravinsky, the play was less a "family romance" or a parable of fate than an allegory of insubordination and submission — precisely the haughty lesson we have seen him impose on musical performers in his Harvard lectures, applied now on a "universal" scale. Not fate but Oedipus's pride brings him down, for it causes him to tempt fate and pursue dangerous knowledge. At the beginning of the opera his musical utterances are placed high and are richly and ostentatiously ornate. At the end his voice is brought low and his lines are stark.

But that is not all. To symbolize and ratify the offended universal order, Stravinsky resurrected in glory every stiff traditional convention of the eighteenth-century musical stage (da capo arias, monolithic choruses, accompanied recitatives) and every seemingly outmoded harmonic cliché (arpeggiated triads, diminished seventh chords, formulaic cadences). It was (to put it Greekly) as if Apollo himself, the god of formal beauty and repose in whose honor Stravinsky had recently composed a ballet, were beating back the "Wagnerian revolution" (here standing in for revolution in general) with its vaunting individualistic hubris and its frenzied overthrow of conventions as if in the name of Dionysus, the god of wine and orgies, for the sake of untrammeled emotional arousal and expression.

In the Harvard lectures, Stravinsky connected the theme of his *Oedipus* with the objectives of his musical neoclassicism. He invited his audience to receive his words as "dogmatic" and "objective" confidences, delivered "under the stern auspices of order and discipline,"[3] virtues that are finally associated, in the fourth lecture, with their "best example" in music, a Bach fugue: "A pure form in which the music means nothing outside of itself. Doesn't the fugue imply the composer's submission to the rules? And is it not within those strictures that he finds the full flowering of his freedom as a creator?"[4] The artist must "submit to the law," to ordained values that transcend individuals, because, Stravinsky finally said explicitly, "Apollo demands it."[5]

Needless to say, Stravinsky's *Oedipus* made Schoenberg ill. He vented his rage at it, and at Stravinsky, in his diary the next day. "This work is nothing," he noted in exasperation; and yet he also noted, with impressive candor, that he feared it, for "the works which in every way arouse one's dislike are precisely those the next generation will in every way like."[6] The *Oedipus* premiere came at the end of a period that Schoenberg later remembered as the worst in his life as an artist, "the first time in my career," as he put it, "that I lost, for a short time, my influence on youth."[7] The reason? A French journalist summed it up: "Schoenberg is a romantic; our young composers are classic."[8] That sense of vulnerability conditioned Schoenberg's furious rejection of neoclassicism.

By 1928, Schoenberg's polemics against Stravinsky were nothing new; and the mutual antagonism of the two composers' followers were approaching proportions that became legendary in the annals of twentieth-century music. Two years earlier, Schoenberg had fired off a little squib called "Igor Stravinsky: Der Restaurateur,"[9] the punning title of which compared Stravinsky, who claimed to be restoring timeless musical values, to somebody who ran a restaurant (and merely catered, that meant, to trivial "culinary" taste).

Stravinsky, for his part, liked to poke fun at those (beginning, he supposed, with Wagner) who claimed to be writing the music of the future. Stravinsky claimed, instead, to be writing the true music of the present. He went around telling interviewers, tongue in cheek, that "modernists have ruined modern music." One reporter, in New York in January 1925, asked him who he had in mind:

> Stravinsky smiled. "I shan't mention any names," said he. "But they are the gentlemen who work with formulas instead of ideas. They have done that so much they have badly compromised that word 'modern.' I don't like it. They started out by trying to write so as to shock the bourgeoisie and finished up by pleasing the Bolsheviks. I am not interested in either the bourgeoisie or the Bolsheviks."[10]

It is not entirely obvious that Stravinsky had Schoenberg (certainly no Bolshevik, though often touted as a revolutionary) in mind, but Schoenberg had no doubt about it. Who else could Stravinsky have meant, Schoenberg thought, but he, the extreme maximalizer of Romantic individualism in music, the composer who brought the art of psychopathology to its final shriek in *Erwartung*? It is reasonable to believe that Schoenberg was at least among Stravinsky's targets, because (as he put it elsewhere) "atonality" implied "anarchy,"[11] a state of lawlessness against which Stravinsky wanted to dictate the Bachian reaction. It must have seemed to an uprooted Russian aristocrat an analogue to the "Bolshevik" straits in which his native land was foundering.

But if Stravinsky was writing the music of the present (and Schoenberg was by implication a thing of the past), then why, Schoenberg wanted to know, did Stravinsky look to the even more distant past for models? That was the nub of the issue as far as Schoenberg was concerned: Stravinsky was trying to turn back the clock on the development of music, substituting restoration for the progress it was every artist's obligation to advance. It was not just an esthetic but a moral issue, involving not just taste but the artist's responsibility. After reading Stravinsky's New York interviews, Schoenberg retorted not only in word but in musical deed. In November and December of 1925 he composed (to his own texts) a set of Three Satires, opus 28, for chorus, of which the first two were unaccompanied canons and the last a little cantata called *Der neue Klassizismus* ("The new classicism").

In the cantata Schoenberg, like Stravinsky, named no names, but spoofed those who say (with the tenor at the outset), "No longer will I stay Romantic. I hate Romantic! From tomorrow on I am writing only the purest Classical!" or who aver, with the chorus at the end, "Classical perfection — that's the latest style!" But in the text of the second canon (a clever piece called *Vielseitigkeit* ("Versatility") that can be turned upside down and performed with the same results as rightside up) he could not resist a direct hit:

Ja, wer trommelt denn da?	But who's that drumming away there?
Das ist ja der kleine Modernsky!	Why, it's little Modernsky!
Hat sich ein Bubizopf schneiden	He's had his hair cut in an
lassen;	old-fashioned queue,
sieht ganz gut aus!	And it looks quite nice!
Wie echt falsches Haar!	Like real false hair!
Wie eine Perücke!	Like a peruke [pigtail wig]!
Ganz (wie sich ihn der kleine	Just like (or so little Mo-
Modernsky vorstellt),	dernsky likes to think)
ganz der Papa Bach!	Just like Papa Bach!

By 1928, then, the lines seemed pretty well drawn between those who were still committed to perpetual progress in art and those who wanted to make new contact with old wellsprings.

DISCOVERY OR INVENTION?

But only in rhetoric. For the amazing and ironic fact is that, despite their mutual disdain and their bombastically expressed differences, Schoenberg and "little Modernsky" were in the 1920s caught up as participants in the same postwar reaction; and Schoenberg's technical breakthrough of those years, the main subject of this chapter and for a long time the very emblem of musical progress, was as much a neoclassicizing or restorative effort as anything done in the name of Papa Bach.

No composer suffered a graver creative crisis in the years surrounding the Great War than Schoenberg. The war itself, oddly, was not (at least consciously) a trauma for him. He enlisted enthusiastically in the Austrian army as a private despite his relatively advanced years (he was forty) and his fame in civilian life. He claimed to have enjoyed the anonymity, or at least the respite from notoriety, that the army gave him. "The war years were my peace years," he later quipped. But maybe he also found relief in the time-consuming, mentally undemanding routines of army life from his creative problems.

For a period of a decade or more, Schoenberg composed only fitfully when not entirely blocked. In November 1913 he completed a one-act opera, *Die glückliche Hand* ("The lucky hand"), op. 18, sometimes translated "The Golden Touch," on which he had been working since 1910. Between November 1914 and July 1916 he managed to complete three little orchestral songs to join a previously composed one in a set of four, published as opus 22. Opus 23, a set of five pieces for piano, was not even begun until July 1920 and not finished until February 1923. For four years, this means, Schoenberg did not complete a single composition, although he started many. When opus 23 was published in 1923, it was the first new composition by Schoenberg to appear since 1914. The long silence signaled an impasse.

Such a turn in any famous artist's career (and especially an expressionist's!) calls forth all kinds of biographical speculation. Doubtless psychological factors played a significant role, but there were also musical issues to be solved—or at least Schoenberg deeply felt that there were. If one compares *Die glückliche Hand*, the opera that arduously preoccupied him between 1910 and 1913, with *Erwartung*, the opera that he had written with seeming effortlessness and at white heat in the late summer of 1909, one can see (at least in suitably bespectacled hindsight) the makings of the crisis.

The glory of *Erwartung* had been its imaginative abandon: Schoenberg "trusted his hand,"[12] as he later put it, to compose an "athematic" and "atonal" music that not even his own rational mind could comprehend at the time. In chapter 6 we saw that its touted avoidance of motivic and thematic repetition was not perfect, and that there were aspects of the score (particularly its harmony) that could be rationalized in retrospect; but the basic effort to avoid the appearance of rationalized routine and yet achieve a coherently expressive result was impressively successful. The music of *Die glückliche Hand*, while still atonal and in principle athematic (as any genuinely expressionistic music ought by rights to be), far more frequently resorted to rationalized (and therefore analytically transparent) procedure. There are extensive passages in imitative counterpoint. There is a lot of ostinato. One might say that the devices that resurfaced in *Pierrot lunaire* under cover of irony persisted in the new opera without the ironic pretext, and were therefore problematical.

The difference between the two operas is sometimes explained as a difference in gender portrayal. *Erwartung*, the portrait of a feminine psyche under stress, conformed to the misogynistic ideas of contemporary Viennese psychologists and sexologists like

Otto Weininger, whose widely read *Geschlecht und Charakter* ("Sex and character," 1903) defined women as "logically insane," and attributed their often admired "intuition" to "a lack of definiteness in their thinking capacity," which "gives the widest scope to vague associations."[13] These descriptive slogans are easy to apply by analogy to the music of *Erwartung*: "tingling and spasmodic, sensual, without structure or direction,"[14] in the words of critic and composer David Schiff. The obvious organizing factors in the music of *Die glückliche Hand*, which concerns a masculine paragon (pretty obviously the composer's own ego-surrogate) threatened by feminine guile, could then be seen as devices for portraying the superior mental and ethical equipage of the male.

Schoenberg knew Weininger's crackpot writings and admired them. He even cited Weininger in the preface to his *Harmonielehre* as an example to his pupils and readers of "one who has thought earnestly."[15] Schoenberg's creative crisis, in both its musical and personal (ethical, spiritual) dimensions may have had something to do with the composer's need to lessen his reliance on "intuition," stigmatized by Weininger as feminine (as well as Jewish, another category applicable to the recently converted and therefore squeamish Schoenberg). What had seemed a creative ideal and a glorious liberation had become something he now felt a need to exorcise.

NOMOS (THE LAW)

Whatever its source, Schoenberg did express discomfort with what music historian Joseph Auner has called the "intuitive aesthetic"[16] that produced *Erwartung*. His creative trough was a response to this dilemma. Outwardly Schoenberg cast the dilemma as one involving the autonomy of music rather than the spiritual health of the composer. Composing *Erwartung* — that is, a thirty-minute stretch of athematic atonal music — would have been impossible without a text to hang it on. Could a way be found to compose such music without an extramusical crutch?

Die glückliche Hand was a first tentative step in dealing with the problem of musical autonomy, but ultimately unsatisfactory: first, of course, because as in any opera there was still a text to lean on; but also because the traditional contrapuntal textures and the ostinatos could only be understood as a retreat from a problematical extreme rather than progress toward a new ideal. Schoenberg did not come out of the ditch, so to speak, until he had found a means of rationalizing his technique that did not depend on the kind of outworn traditional methods that satisfied the likes of Stravinsky. These new means were first displayed in the piano pieces he began composing around 1920. They provided a new "principle capable of serving as a rule,"[17] in the words of the architect Le Corbusier (1887–1965), whose quest was retrospectively compared with Schoenberg's by the British music critic Donald Mitchell, in an influential discussion published in 1963.

The sources of Schoenberg's new technique have been variously described and furiously disputed. One of his pupils, the composer and musicologist Egon Wellesz (1885–1974), claimed some credit for stimulating its discovery.[18] In 1916, Wellesz wrote, he met Josef Matthias Hauer (1883–1959), a composer who had just received a medical discharge from the army and was working as an elementary school teacher. Hauer showed Wellesz some short keyboard compositions dating back to around

1912 — technical studies, really — in which he was experimenting with a novel technique that Hauer chose to call *Nomos*, after the ancient Greek word for "law." A *Nomos* consisted of a particular ordering of the twelve tones of the chromatic scale that served as the basis for a particular composition. In Hauer's pieces, each such melodic sequence was divided into four groups of three notes each, which furnished a harmonic vocabulary for the composition in question.

Wellesz showed these little studies by Hauer to his fellow students, and eventually to his teacher. By then Schoenberg had experimented (as we already know) with "aggregate compositions" that would display and exploit the total chromatic spectrum in various ways, and he was by no means the only composer to have done so. (See the discussions of Scriabin and Ives, as well as Schoenberg, in chapters 4–6.) Along with Webern, Schoenberg had already written some tiny pieces in which the completion of the aggregate marked important formal divisions or even defined the work's limits (chapter 6). Nor were Hauer's *Nomos* studies absolutely the first pieces to be based consistently on particular orderings of the twelve pitch classes. Gregory Dubinsky, a scholar who has researched the origins of the technique, has proposed some earlier candidates, including works by two Russians: Nikolai Obouhov, whom we met in chapter 4, and Yefim Golyscheff (1897–1970).[19] But in Wellesz's recollection, Hauer's had a decisive effect on Schoenberg: they "showed him the way out of his crisis; they came to him as the right impulse at the right moment."[20] Wellesz's account is not only overly simple but also vague and factually inexact. Still, its basic contention probably holds water.

A brief look at Hauer's *Nomos*, op. 19 (composed not in 1912 but 1919) will confirm several points of interest. The first page, given in Ex. 12-1, displays an exhaustive sequence of twelve pitch-classes (B♭ E♭ F D♭ G E A C F♯ D B A♭) that is repeated five times. It is parsed not into groups of three or four notes, which divide the twelve pitches evenly, but into rhythmically identical groups of five, which overlap the pitch series rather in the manner of a medieval isorhythmic tenor, so that no two melodic phrases have identical pitch content. The main innovation is the constant circulation of the exhaustive chromatic series so that no pitch class ever recurs until the other eleven have intervened.

The strictness of this procedure in Hauer's op. 19 is not maintained past the first page. But now compare a work of Schoenberg's composed in February 1923: "Walzer" (waltz), published as the last piece in op. 23, the set of five that marked Schoenberg's return to productivity (Ex. 12-2). The note sequence played by the right hand in mm. 1–4, which exhausts the chromatic aggregate, is quite rigorously maintained as a sort of ostinato from beginning to end. Since the pitch-classes always follow one another in the same order, it will be convenient to number them for ready reference in the discussion that follows:

1	2	3	4	5	6	7	8	9	10	11	12
C♯(D♭)	A	B	G	A♭(G♯)	F♯(G♭)	A♯(B♭)	D	E	E♭(D♯)	C	F

Except for the curious way the left-hand part begins with a chord consisting of notes 6–8 (and then continues to the end of the series), the relationship of the little

EX. 12-1   Josef Matthias Hauer, *Nomos*, Op. 19, beginning

scheme just given and the music of the waltz is practically self-evident. (And even the little anomaly at the outset will find an explanation before we are done.) The left-hand Db in m. 2 is the beginning of a new statement of the series that continues in the left hand until E in m. 5 (note no. 9), whereupon it is taken up and completed by the right hand, beginning with the Eb at the end of the same measure.

From this point on, the circulation of the pitch sequence is entirely straightforward, with both hands participating in each statement. Although a tedious exercise, numbering all the pitches in the composition according to our makeshift analytical scheme enables one to retrace all of Schoenberg's compositional decisions in a fashion rarely so accessible to analysis. Following through in this way will reveal the resourcefulness and variety of Schoenberg's treatment of the series. It is not a melody, although it gives rise to all the melodies; nor is it a harmony, although it gives rise to all the harmonies as well.

Various manners of dividing it up produce many kinds of texture from homophonic (melody + accompaniment) to homorhythmic (chordal) to intricately contrapuntal. The unaccompanied statement in the right hand, beginning toward the end of m. 17,

EX. 12-2   Arnold Schoenberg, Op. 23, no. 5 (Walzer), mm. 1–60

EX. 12-2 *(continued)*

is the most purely melodic (that is, monophonic) incarnation the series is given, reminiscent of Hauer's portentous octaves *all'unisono*; but note that Schoenberg's does not exhaust the series, and that the left hand's "harmonizing" entrance in m. 19 (on notes 11 and 12) both completes the statement begun by the right hand in m. 17 and dovetails into the next statement without any articulation of an ending. Thus we learn that in this piece the series is not in itself any kind of formal marker, and that it would be naive therefore to call the composition a theme and variations (although everything that happens in it, being derived from a common source, could be called "developing variation").

One spot invites special comment. The passage from m. 44 to m. 55, in what an eighteenth-century keyboard player would have called the "broken" (or arpeggiated) style, presents three statements of the series in which each measure introduces three notes, so that four measures exhaust the series. Because of that evenness of distribution, the pitches presented in m. 44 are the same as those presented in mm. 48 and 52; m. 45 corresponds to mm. 49 and 53; and so on, only the registers being varied to maintain a sense of continual evolution (or "developing variation").

The series, in other words, has been divided into four recurrent "trichords," or three-note groups, just as Wellesz had (erroneously) described Hauer's procedure in his *Nomos* pieces. Schoenberg's passage, in fact, conforms more closely to Wellesz's description of Hauer's pieces than any composition by Hauer. Evidently, Schoenberg's waltz had replaced Hauer's actual *Nomos* in Wellesz's memory. This may lessen the reliability of Wellesz's factual details, but it actually strengthens the plausibility of the general connection Wellesz drew between the two composers' explorations.

The only place in the waltz where Schoenberg departs from strict adherence to the order presented at the outset comes at the very end (Ex. 12-3), when the left hand suddenly puts the series in reverse, starting with note 12 (F) and running back to note 1 (C♯ in m. 106). That C♯ is paired in a "dyad" or two-note harmony with A (note 2). The fact that a dyad presents two pitches as a single simultaneous attack enables Schoenberg to create an elaborate musical pun, starting a series in forward motion with the same dyad. That series continues in m. 106 in the right hand, and is pitted contrapuntally against another reversed series that begins in the left hand in m. 107. The B♭D dyad on the downbeat of m. 108 again does double duty, participating both in the right hand's forward series and the left hand's backward one. Because both series are in continuous motion around the common dyad, measures 107–108 display a pitch palindrome. Putting the music, as it were, in reverse, letting it run backward (or "run down") shortly after the formal recapitulation of the opening melodic idea in m. 100, punningly reinforces the expectation of the end.

And the "anomalous" beginning? It is explained by the ending. The last three statements of the series, beginning with the C♯ and A tied over into m. 111, are increasingly chordal for "cadential" effect. The big eight-note chord in m. 112 contains notes 9–12 of a finishing statement and notes 1–4 of the next one. It is surrounded on either side by notes 5–8. The five-note chord on the downbeat of the last measure is the beginning of the last statement of the series. The F♯D dyad that ends the piece leaves the series hanging on notes 6 and 7. Now look back at the beginning of the piece and see how the left hand picks up those very notes and continues the series to the end. Perhaps in keeping with the use of the reversed series in mm. 104–111, the end of the piece is linked to the beginning as if the composition described a kind of circle in time.

EX. 12-3   Arnold Schoenberg, Op. 23, no. 5 (*Walzer*), mm. 104–end

It is possible that these "bending time" effects (or rather, the idea of such effects) harked back to the mystical thinking that had guided Schoenberg's prewar strivings toward the infinite and universal — hence toward the aggregate. Perhaps more likely, by 1923, it was a typically "Ortegan" jest to delight the minds of analysts, and therefore indicative of the "poietic" bias (the emphasis on the "making" of the composition rather than on its "effect") that increasingly characterized advanced composing-practice after the Great War. And it was precisely in its highly sophisticated, concentrated, and elaborated *making* that Schoenberg's music so thoroughly transcended whatever technical example Hauer's naive *Nomos* pieces had set for him.

Hauer, whose career amounted to so much less than Schoenberg's, became embittered over what he regarded (or at least advertised) as Schoenberg's intellectual theft. Schoenberg's followers and biographers, in retaliation, have tended to minimize or dismiss (and even deride) Hauer's putative input. It is not so difficult, at our present historical remove, to take a nonpartisan view, acknowledging that Hauer probably gave Schoenberg an important idea, but that Schoenberg, who did far more with that idea than its originator, lent it a prestige (hence an influence and historical importance) that Hauer's own efforts could not have accomplished.

The notorious *Prioritätstreit* ("battle over priority"), as Schoenberg's future biographer Hans Heinz Stuckenschmidt was calling it as early as 1925, can only strike us now as a tempest in a teapot.[21] But at the time it mattered greatly, to Schoenberg as much as to Hauer. Indeed, Schoenberg recalled in a memoir that "when I gathered about twenty of my pupils together to explain to them the new method in 1923, I did it because I was afraid to be taken as an imitator of Hauer."[22] Precisely because the matter of priority was taken so seriously at the time, not only by the parties involved but also by onlookers, it can serve us now as a symptom of the "rush to the patent office" that was such an integral component of modernism — especially the German brand that descended from the ideology (and the rhetoric) of the mid-nineteenth-century New German School.

GIVING MUSIC AN AXIOMATIC BASIS

The strictness of Schoenberg's adherence to the ordered twelve-note series in his compositional practice, and the consequent pervasiveness with which the series informed the musical substance thus created, elevated the series in Schoenberg's usage to the status of a *Grundgestalt*, the "basic shape" or intervallic constellation that informs an entire composition down to its smallest details and gives it its "organic" motivic consistency. Indeed, the use of an exhaustive twelve-note series makes the *Grundgestalt* function, and the organic unity thus guaranteed, virtually automatic. And that, of course, was the great breakthrough, the "principle capable of serving as a rule," which allowed the composition of large-scale, abstract, and autonomous atonal music of constant and at-all-times-demonstrable motivic coherence despite its renunciation of predefined tonal hierarchies, and despite its frequent "athematicism."

But beware! As soon as any musical characteristic becomes the automatic result of a method, it stops being a compositional achievement. As long as Schoenberg's atonal music was based on "working with the tones of a motive," meaning an unordered collection of intervals, the kind of tightly controlled motivic organization visible (to cite one especially rich instance) at the beginning of the first piece in op. 23, composed in July 1920, is an impressive compositional tour de force (Ex. 12-4).

EX. 12-4   Arnold Schoenberg, Op. 23, no. 1 (*Sehr langsam*), mm. 1–5

The strict three-part contrapuntal texture is supersaturated with versions of the intervallic *Grundgestalt* (or basic cell, to use an "organicist" metaphor) first expressed as the opening harmony (F♯ A♭ A), which contains a major second, a minor second, and a minor third. The first three notes in the middle voice (A♭ G B♭) are a "linearization" of the same cell, immediately echoed by the top voice in m. 2 (E♭ D F). Meanwhile, the first three notes in the bottom voice (A C B) present a variant of the same linearization, in which the same intervals occur in the opposite order and with the contour reversed (a "retrograde inversion"). The bass B in the second measure is a pivot linking two sequential statements of this manner of presenting the basic cell. In m. 3 the middle voice repeats the three-note beginning of the bass in diminution at the octave, while in mm. 4–5, the bass reciprocates with a transposition of the middle voice's opening cell (B♭ A C), with the final interval inverted from a rising minor third to a falling major sixth.

(Note, incidentally, the "hairpins" in m. 5 over a single note, A. They are obviously impossible to perform on the piano, as Schoenberg surely knew perfectly well. The expressive swell on a single note, typical of vocal and string music, is part of the "idea" of the piece, rather than its sound—and so, it might be argued, is the motivic consistency we are now accounting for, which is far more likely to reveal itself fully to the analytical eye than to the listening ear. Again we see the composer characteristically preoccupied with "poietics" over "esthesics," with input over output, manufacture over effect.)

Meanwhile, another variant of the basic cell, in which the minor third and the minor second go in the same direction, covering a major third's total distance, has been enjoying a similar "developing variation." The first three notes in the top voice (F♯ E♭ D) are its first presentation, echoed in the middle voice in m. 3 (C B G♯). It, too, gets a "harmonic" presentation, on the downbeat of m. 4. But even before the middle voice has echoed it, the top voice reverses it (D♯ E G in mm. 2–3), and that reversal is also echoed in the middle voice (G♯ A C in m. 4). Both the initial statement of this variant in the top voice and its echo in the middle voice overlap with presentations of the variant previously described. Thus the first four notes of the "soprano" (F♯ E♭ D F) and the four sixteenth notes in the "tenor" in m. 3 (A C B G♯) each present the two variants of the basic cell (but in opposite order) with the middle pair of notes doing double duty.

The head swims, not only at the thought of such motivic density (which the foregoing description has by no means fully accounted for) but also at the thought of the mental labor it must have required to contrive it. One can easily sympathize with the wish to find the kind of labor-saving device Schoenberg adopted in the final waltz from the same set of pieces, even if the lessened labor can seem to lessen the intellectual accomplishment. In any case, from 1921 on, virtually every one of Schoenberg's atonal compositions would adopt a chromatically exhaustive twelve-note series like the one in the waltz (or in Hauer's 1919 *Nomos*) as its basis.

Schoenberg called such a series a *Tonreihe*, using a German word for series, *Reihe*, that has "row" as its English cognate; hence the term "tone row" has become standard in British and American usage. At first he called the method on which he now relied *Reihenkomposition*, "composition with rows" or "serial composition." English usage in this case has favored Hauer's term *Zwölftontechnik*, "twelve-tone technique." (More pretentious writers sometimes call it "dodecaphony" from the Greek for twelve.) Eventually Schoenberg also came round to using this nomenclature, calling his method "composition with twelve tones related only to one another" (rather than to a predefined tonic).

And yet the term "twelve-tone", although we are certainly stuck with it, remains something of a misnomer; for what gives a tone row its distinction is not its pitch content (for every tone row has that in common with every other tone row) but its ordered interval content. That is what enables a row, like any basic cell or *Grundgestalt*, to maintain its identity when transposed. Indeed, it was transposition, as an outgrowth of his earlier *Grundgestalt* or "developing variation" technique, that now became Schoenberg's primary technical preoccupation: more specifically, the question of how transpositions (and precisely which transpositions) may help realize the form-defining or harmony-defining properties of particular tone rows. That is where Schoenberg will henceforth engineer his tours de force of compositional planning and motivic saturation.

The first major work of Schoenberg's that was written using twelve-tone row technique throughout was a five-movement Suite for Piano, published as opus 25 in 1925. The pieces in it — Präludium, Gavotte and Musette, Intermezzo, Menuett, Gigue — had accumulated over an eighteen-month period between July 1921 and March 1923, during which Schoenberg was also working on other compositions, but all were based on a single twelve-tone row, albeit treated with a bit more variety than Schoenberg had allowed in the waltz, the first twelve-tone piece to be published.

There, as we recall, Schoenberg had contented himself (partly as a technical challenge, partly in an effort to outdo Hauer) with a single "row form" until the end, when he ran it backwards a couple of times. The row was never even transposed, so that in this case it was indeed literally a row of tones as well as intervals. The technical challenge, of course, was to disguise the fact that the piece consisted of what in less sophisticated hands might have sounded like a relentless melodic ostinato. The suite was based on a complex consisting of a row, its inversion, and the transposition of each by a tritone (Ex. 12-5). Inverting a row, like inverting any motive or Grundgestalt, maintains the same intervallic sequence as if seen in a mirror. Transposition, of course, has no effect at all on intervallic sequence. So the four rows in Ex. 12-5 are merely four ways of representing a single intervallic succession (i.e., a single *Grundgestalt*).

EX. 12-5   Row complex from Arnold Schoenberg, Suite, Op. 25

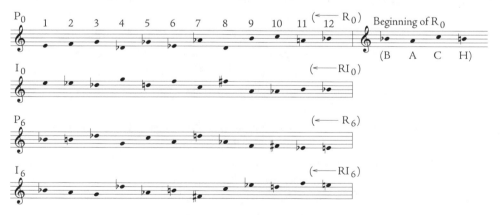

NB: In analyzing twelve-tone compositions, row transpositions are often counted by semitones. Thus the four row forms in Ex. 12-5 are labeled P (for "prime," the form heard first), I ("inversion"), P_6 (prime transposed up six semitones) and I_6 (inversion transposed up six semitones). For extra clarity, untransposed row forms are usually designated as having been transposed by "zero" semitones, thus: P_0 and I_0. In the diagram, the arrows running right to left are a reminder that rows can be freely reversed for additional variety within the same interval-determined unity.

Even before looking at or listening to the music, the row complex gives us a foretaste of its harmonic world. The row has been deliberately constructed so as to create close relationships between exactly these four forms, so as to produce an even more pervasive unity than a single row form could achieve. In other words, the row has been constructed with its role as a *Grundgestalt* in mind, and the character of the composition will be to a significant degree determined by the relationships that have been built into the structure of the row. And what are these relationships? By now they will seem very familiar, having appeared in the work of so many of the "maximalist" composers of the early twentieth century, including Schoenberg himself along with Stravinsky, Bartók, Webern, and Berg. But here they have been sublimated or abstracted into a formal and methodical context that accords with the cool ironic mood of postwar modernism.

It will take no more than a glance at the beginnings and ends of all the row forms in Ex. 12-5 to establish harmonic symmetry based on the "invariance" properties of the tritone as the principle Schoenberg's rows have been designed to exploit. The first and last notes in the untransposed prime form of the row are a tritone apart. Since the tritone reproduces itself when inverted, and since the only transposition invoked in Ex. 12-5 is that of the tritone itself, E and B♭ are the invariant framing pitches of every row form employed in the Suite. That is already a giant step toward defining a consistent (if contextual) "tonality" for the piece.

But there is more. Since any tritone can be embedded in a circle of minor thirds that shares its invariance properties (reproducing itself when inverted or when transposed by its generating interval), the notes G and D♭ will have the same invariance properties within this row complex as do the notes E and B♭. And that is the reason why Schoenberg made sure that those two notes would occupy adjacent positions in the untransposed prime form. They occupy order positions 3 and 4 in every form shown in Ex. 12-5, and hence will also function as an invariant pair within the actual music of the Suite. (When reversed forms of the row are employed, of course, the G and D♭ will just as invariably occupy positions 9 and 10.) In addition, the first pair of notes in each row form in Ex. 12-5 has a counterpart in one of the reversed forms: EF begins both P_0 and RI_6; EE♭, I_0 and R_6; B♭B, P_6 and RI_0; B♭A, I_6 and R_0. And ending pairs coincide similarly, as they must. These, too, are invariance relationships, the invariant pairs linking not only forward and backward row forms, but also transposed and untransposed ones.

By seeking out abstract invariance relationships like these within the row forms, it is easy to create concrete musical relationships in which some aspect of a musical configuration changes while some other aspect remains the same. That is the essence of the "developing variation" technique that Schoenberg had long insisted was implicit in Brahms's motivic textures. And that is one of the features of twelve-tone composition, as Schoenberg practiced it, which allowed him to claim that this method, no less than his earlier "atonal" style, was a "natural" (or even an inevitable) evolution of "classical" or "mainstream" techniques rather than a break with them, despite its rejection of the most salient — indeed, the defining — feature of "tonal" music. Indeed, twelve-tone techniques, by rationalizing the composition of atonal music and making it more orderly and "plannable," significantly strengthened the bonds that connected atonal music with the formal methods of the "classical mainstream." In this sense, it too was a "neoclassical" move, another response to the postwar "call to order."

IRONY CLAIMS ITS DUE

All the more obviously was this the case when Schoenberg, for all the scorn he poured on "little Modernsky" and his false "Papa Bach" peruke, found himself writing his own allotment of minuets and gavottes. Explaining that away has cost his "defenders" a lot of sweat. Usually the difference between Schoenberg's pastiches and Stravinsky's turns on the absence in Schoenberg's of any actual diatonic melody or triadic harmony. Despite the recourse to eighteenth-century forms, the musical content was still novel, still resembled the melodic and harmonic idiom of the older "expressionist" music. "If Schoenberg does call into service older form types," one such defender has argued, "it is not because he considers them to be 'ideal,' but because he sees in them usages which should not be dispensed with until the novel and more difficult aspects of his musical language are better understood."[23]

But this is clearly an equivocation. Before the war he had no such scruples, nor did he offer listeners any such help with "the novel and more difficult aspects of his musical language." However one tries to explain it, the contradiction between Schoenberg's "older form types" and his "novel language" after the war greatly magnified his distance from his former self. Indeed, his first published twelve-tone composition had cast the tortured musical language of *Erwartung* in the form of a waltz — not merely an "older formal type" but a "light music" genre! And the gigues and musettes he was now turning out had more familiar repertory counterparts in the work of Ambroise Thomas, Saint-Saëns, Chaikovsky, or Prokofieff than in Bach, even though Schoenberg invoked Papa Bach in person (and far more explicitly than Stravinsky) by embedding his very name in

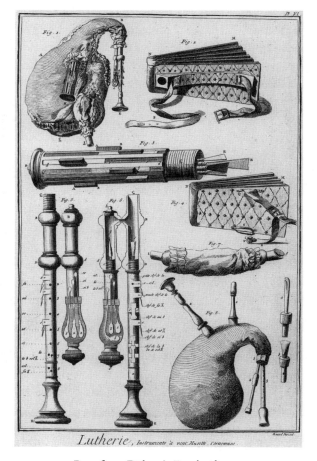

Lutherie, Instruments à vent Musette, Cornemuse.

FIG. 12-2   Page from Diderot's *Encyclopédie*: musettes are at upper left and lower right.

the op. 25 tone row. (See the beginning of R$_0$ in Ex. 12-5, bearing in mind that in German "B" means B♭ and B-natural is "h.") It was, all of it, "mock-light" music. And while little pieces in sectional forms were always good for working out a technical discipline, if technical studies were all that they were it is not likely that Schoenberg would have published them.

Some of the early twelve-tone pieces are quite obviously "jesting," and not only in Ortega's sense of the word. Another suite, for an instrumental septet that included three clarinets (op. 29, 1926), was to have included a movement called "Foxtrot," before Schoenberg recoiled from *neue Sachlichkeit* and changed the title to the more neutral "Tanzschritte" (dance steps). Op. 24 (1923), a Serenade for chamber septet, uses a pair of literal serenader's instruments (guitar and mandolin) that are rarely employed in "classical" music without parodic intent (most recently, as we may remember, in Mahler's Seventh Symphony, a Schoenberg favorite that Webern had already emulated in his *Five Pieces for Orchestra*).

Two movements in the Serenade are based on tone rows. One of them, in which a baritone voice (the serenader himself) joins the instrumental group, is a parody in many ways. For one thing, it parodies love songs: the text, a sonnet by the fourteenth-century Italian poet Petrarch, is no tender entreaty but a fantasy of violent revenge on a cold mistress. For another, it parodies the "emancipated-dissonance" style, implying that if your poem is about mayhem you have no other choice. And for a third, it parodies the new twelve-tone technique itself—or rather, perhaps, Hauer's version of it as set out in Ex. 12-1.

The singer's part, like the waltz in op. 23, is based throughout on a single untransposed row, treated as a sort of ostinato. Because the text is an Italian sonnet, it is cast in undecasyllabic (11-syllable) lines. There are fourteen lines in all, the last two being an "envoy" in a different meter. Now because Schoenberg's snickering setting is strictly syllabic, each eleven-syllable line leaves a remainder of one note from the tone row. The grim poem constantly gains on the music (see Ex. 12-6), so that the first line uses notes 1–11, the second 12–10, the third 11–9, and so forth, so that each line of the text (like each 5-note phrase in Hauer's *Nomos*, op. 19) is a unique melodic statement. Things come full circle after exactly twelve lines, just in time for the envoy.

The persistent contrast between Schoenberg's heavy content and its feather-light containers was perhaps the most vivid example of postwar irony to be found in all of modernist music. It gave his early twelve-tone music a crooked side that is not only useless to deny, but makes the music all the more genuinely a reflection of its time, all the more genuinely interesting, therefore, as a historical document, and all the more esthetically appealing. As we embark now on a closer look at the Suite for Piano and investigate the multifaceted relationship between its *Grundgestalt* (that is, the complex of twelve-tone row forms in Ex. 12-5) and the music derived from it, that irony will provide the essential link between the technical means and the expressive ends.

The most straightforwardly composed of the five movements is the last one, the Gigue (Ex. 12-7). The tonality-defining properties of the row are best displayed here, since the features we have already remarked on the basis of the row diagram function

EX. 12-6 Arnold Schoenberg, *Serenade*, Op. 24, IV (*Sonett No. 217 von Petrarch*), voice part

Ah! That my vengeance soon be flaunting
On her who has destroyed me with her glances,
And who, by leaving me, my woe enhances
and hides from me her eyes, so sweet, so haunting . . . *etc.*

EX. 12-7   Arnold Schoenberg, Suite, Op. 25, Gigue, mm. 1–13

very obviously and audibly as stable, prominent, and therefore normative aspects of the tonal organization. Most of the time row forms and measures coincide, one-to-one. Thus measure 1 presents P_0, m. 2 I_6, m. 3 I_0, and m. 4 P_6. In mm. 10–13, the reversed row forms pass in review: R_0, RI_6, RI_0, and R_6. And so on. This means that, owing to the tritone invariance, every measure moves either from E to B♭ or from B♭ to E. Measures 1–4 also exploit the other stable invariance property: note that the third eighth-note position in each measure is occupied by the GD♭ tritone that crops up in order positions 3 and 4 in Ex. 12-5. In mm. 10–13, the GD♭ tritones are avoided, but the tritones that appear in order positions 7 and 8 (there are two : DA♭ and F♯C) are ferreted out and placed consistently on the fourth eighth-note position. The combination of constant and changing factors again produces that sense of constant progression that Schoenberg dubbed "developing variation."

The funniest moment in the Suite, surely, is the Trio of the Menuett movement (Ex. 12-8), in which normal and inverted row forms (beginning with P_0 in the left hand and I_6 in the right) are consistently played off one another in a strict rhythmic and contour imitation, producing a strict "mirror canon" (canon by inversion). As in *Pierrot lunaire*, the composer gets no technical points for constructing a contrapuntal tour de force (a poodle with basic twelve-tone training could do so as easily as Schoenberg), but the wildly exaggerated angularity of the writing, wide intervals like ninths and tenths careening up and down, shines such a garish spotlight on the contour inversion as to leave no doubt that the composer is in on the joke.

EX. 12-8   Arnold Schoenberg, Suite, Op. 25, Trio, mm. 34–44

Another overtly joking piece is the Musette that is paired with the Gavotte as the Suite's second movement (Ex. 12-9). *Musette* was the eighteenth-century French word for bagpipe, and a keyboard piece so titled was a mock-bucolic number that imitated the bagpipe drone with an ostinato bass. The GD♭ tritone, which turns up in the same place in every row form in Ex. 12-5, functioned within the row itself as a sort of ostinato, and easily assumed the drone function the Musette required. In the first strain the G alone serves as drone; the full tritone is reserved for the longer second half, where it lends a sense of harmonic closure. With its staccato articulations, its harmonic clarity, and its high tessitura, this clever, jaunty little piece might plausibly have been signed "Prokofieff." As usual, the dire split between Schoenberg and his circle and the "Franco-Russians" can be much better substantiated in their verbal polemics than in their actual music.

More complex textures are created in the Suite by pitting row forms against one another in counterpoint, often with punning ambiguities that arise out of their

EX. 12-9 Arnold Schoenberg, Suite, Op. 25, Musette, beginning

invariance properties. At the very outset, the beginning of the Präludium (Ex. 12-10), the prime form is given complete in the right hand against P_6, its transposition at the tritone, in the left. The texture is thickened to three parts in mm. 2–3 by running the second and third four-note segments (tetrachords) of P_6 simultaneously. The multiply repeated B♭ in m. 3, like every B♭ or E in the piece, is of course a boundary note. And, as is usually the case, it does double duty, as the last note of P_0 and the first of I_6. (The repeated E in the bass in mm. 6–7 is another boundary note doing double duty, linking RI_0 and P_0.)

EX. 12-10   Arnold Schoenberg, Suite, Op. 25, Präludium, beginning

The most-analyzed movement in the Suite is the Menuett (Ex. 12-11), partly because of the "license" with which Schoenberg seems to be breaking his own rules. That license is immediately apparent in the fact that, uniquely, the Menuett does not begin with a "boundary note." The continuation is reassuring, however: following G♭ with E♭, then

A♭, then D, identifies it as the fifth note in P₀. Schoenberg himself acknowledged this in an article on twelve-tone composition, and minimized the apparent departure from strict twelve-tone "orthodoxy" with the "excuse" that, the Menuett being the fourth movement of the Suite, "the row has already become familiar" to the listener.

EX. 12-11   Arnold Schoenberg, Suite, Op. 25, Menuett, beginning

He also cites the more interesting fact that the four-note group or tetrachord with which the piece begins (i.e., order positions 5–8) ends with a tritone, just as the first tetrachord does, and that this correspondence or invariance justifies treating the two tetrachords "like independent small sets." If we mentally label the three tetrachords in the row as A, B, and C, the first two measures of the piece pit B and C (right hand in m. 1 and m. 2 respectively) against A (left hand). The whole Menuett, as Schoenberg implies, treats the set as a collection of three quasi-independent tetrachords throughout.

But Schoenberg has been coy. He quotes the first two measures of the Menuett as an illustration to his remarks, but not the third and fourth, or any of the others, since only in the first measure do the notes of each tetrachord come in the order determined by the tone row as a whole. In mm. 3–4, based on I₆, the tetrachords interact just as they do in mm. 1–2 (B and C in the right hand over A in the left) but the notes of A come in the order 4 2 1 3, the notes of B in the order 5 8 6 7, and those in C in the order 12 11 10 9. In mm. 5–6, based on P₆, the tetrachords come in a different order, B + A in the right hand over C in the left, and the notes within each tetrachord are again presented in a permuted order. In effect, Schoenberg has divided his row into three "independent small sets" that are not truly independent, as none can appear without the others, but which are in effect *unordered*, an even greater "deviation" from what is normally looked upon as strict twelve-tone procedure.

These "licenses," as the Mexican music historian Maria Luisa Vilar-Paya has pointed out, have a purpose — one that is even more strikingly at odds with conventional notions of the "nature" of twelve-tone music.[24] That purpose is the creation of a hierarchy among the pitches in the row, most easily seen at the very end (Ex. 12-12), where the two boundary pitches, E and B♭, appear in close proximity, each participating in what looks — and sounds! — like a traditional "tonal" progression from leading tone to tonic. But under such conditions the B♭ would be a functional tonic, and therefore stable, while the E would be a functional leading tone, and therefore unstable. The B♭, in other words, has been effectively promoted to a position of priority over E (which conspicuously begins every movement of the suite except the Menuett) as the definer of the contextually created tonality that governs the Suite.

EX. 12-12   Arnold Schoenberg, Suite, Op. 25, Menuett, mm. 31–33

Its status as the pitch of priority can be confirmed in other ways, one of the most interesting (as Vilar-Paya has shown) being the subtle organization of the harmony around B♭ as an axis of symmetry, in which the ubiquitous GD♭ tritone, its notes equidistant from B♭, plays a decisive supporting role. There are even a couple of loose pages among the sketches for the Suite that support this interpretation. (Before Vilar-Paya produced her analysis, significantly enough, nobody suspected the relationship of these sketches to the finished piece.) They are charts that map equidistant intervals surrounding the note C (traditionally the "neutral" theoretical starting point), showing the kind of relationships that may actually be plotted around B♭ in the Menuett. This puts Schoenbergian tonality, even his twelve-tone tonality, in line with that of much if not most of the modernist music we have already encountered, a line that goes back — by way of Bartók and Stravinsky — beyond modernism to Liszt and even Schubert. All of this only gives us more good reason to view the institution of twelve-tone procedures as not only a radical but, in equal measure, a profoundly conservative development.

BACK AGAIN TO BACH

These desultory remarks on a few salient features of the Suite for Piano, op. 25, could easily be amplified into a complete analysis of the piece — indeed a more complete analysis, in the sense that it can more fully trace the composer's decisions in the very act of composing, than in any other kind of music. That analytical transparency, making twelve-tone technique perhaps the easiest of all compositional methods to demonstrate and teach, and which therefore gave it an aura of uprightness in the spirit of scientific "positivism" (open empirical inquiry), was an important spur to its spread, just as its "artificiality" and "arid intellectualism" (the very same qualities, of course, viewed from a less welcoming perspective) incited resistance.

In any case, from the most arcane of compositional methods, "atonal" composition all at once became the most lucid. It withheld no secrets at all from a determined analyst (although the naked ear might still be baffled). Like a scientific proof, a twelve-tone composition proceeded logically, by inference from an axiomatic premise (the row). No music better illustrated the debunking, materialist, objective, and antimetaphysical spirit of postwar disillusion than this ironic descendant of expressionism, of all prewar styles the most subjective and mystique-ridden. And yet the gnawing tension between poietic transparency and esthesic opacity would never be entirely dispelled.

And there was something else, too, that made twelve-tone music permanently controversial. A tiny hint of it comes at the beginning of the Gavotte (Ex. 12-13), in which the prime form of the row is split, at the outset, between the two hands. The right hand plays the first eight notes of P_0 as a typically grotesque little tune, which the left hand accompanies with notes 9 – 12. But once the boundary note 12 is reached, it does typical double duty and serves as the fulcrum for a reversal. The B, C, and A that had preceded the B♭ in m. 1 come back in reversed order, producing the beginning of R_0: B♭ A C B, which, as we have long known, in German spells "Bach." Schoenberg does not pursue R_0 beyond this point. Like the extra little incipit in Ex. 12-5, its beginning is there just to "say hello" and make its point.

EX. 12-13   Arnold Schoenberg, Suite, Op. 25, Gavotte, beginning

This time the point is made *sotto voce*, in a witty whisper, for the analysts alone. In the Variations for Orchestra, op. 31 (1928), Schoenberg's first large-scale "public" twelve-tone composition and anything but a jest, the tandem declaration of innovation and birthright is ostentatious and hortatory. The theme on which the variations are based encompasses one complete complex, so to speak, of row forms: first a prime, next a double mirror or retrograde inversion, third an order mirror or retrograde, and finally a contour mirror or inversion, accompanied by another prime. Ex. 12-14a shows the theme as it first appears in the Variations, played by the cellos (joined at the end by the first violins) and harmonized by another complex of row forms, whose special complementary relationship to the melody it accompanies will be something to return to.

EX. 12-14A   Arnold Schoenberg, Variations for Orchestra, Op. 31, the theme

Once, in a radio address, Schoenberg stressed the kinship between the drooping contours of his theme and the typically appoggiatura-rich themes of late Romantic compositions by half-jestingly giving it a "tonal" accompaniment (Ex. 12-14b) in "a quite good F major that insistently courts G-flat major."[25] He further commented, "Some people will prefer this treatment to the original. I don't like it, but that is a matter of taste. Why now, if I can also do it that way, do I write a different accompaniment, which is bound to have a less general appeal? All I can say now is that it is not out of malice." Rather than malice, of course, it was commitment to "New German" ideals of evolutionary progress that, as always, impelled Schoenberg's stylistic development. But in the actual music of the Variations he contrived another, far more pointed, reminder of his stylistic heritage. In the Introduction — that is, the section preceding the first statement of the theme — Schoenberg contrived a pair of measures, each of which corresponded, like many measures in the Piano Suite, to a statement of a single row form. Together, they put P_0 and I_1 in counterpoint (Ex. 12-14c). The four circled notes in Ex. 12-14c, which occupy corresponding order positions (1 and 6) in both row forms, are the notes Schoenberg entrusts to the traditionally portentous trombone (having allowed himself many liberties in the order of presentation of I_1). When so intoned, and doubled by the cellos using "hairpin" dynamics, the BACH motif is difficult to miss (Ex. 12-14d). It is a sort of time bomb.

EX. 12-14B   Arnold Schoenberg, Variations for Orchestra, Op. 31, theme as harmonized over Radio Frankfurt in 1931

EX. 12-14C   Arnold Schoenberg, Variations for Orchestra, Op. 31, prime and inverted row forms

EX. 12-14D   Arnold Schoenberg, Variations for Orchestra, Op. 31, mm. 24–25

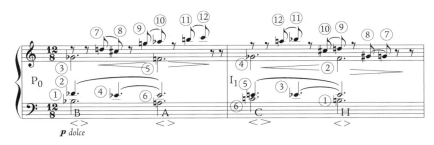

EX. 12-14E   Arnold Schoenberg, Variations for Orchestra, Op. 31, the row forms in Ex. 12-14c transposed to reveal additional BACH ciphers

EX. 12-14F   J. S. Bach, main subject from *The Art of Fugue*

cf P₀ order positions: 7   6   5   7   8   7   5   9 5

The tone row, indeed, has been covertly tailored to a Bachian purpose. The notes in order positions 2–5 in any statement of the row or its inversion (or in positions 8–11 in any reversed statement) are a transposition of the BACH set (albeit presented in the easily "correctable" order BCAH/HACB; see Ex. 12-14e). Not only that, but as Schoenberg scholar Ethan Haimo has pointed out,[26] the notes in order positions 5–9 in P_0 correspond to the notes in the subject of Bach's crowning testament of his mastery, the *Art of Fugue* (see Ex. 12-14f), venerated by all the Schoenbergians as an epitome of "organicism." The grandiose finale to the Variations, whose 210 measures nearly equal all the rest combined (252), flaunts dozens of BACH allusions, some dramatic (like the ones introduced near the beginning by a double bass recitative in the manner of Beethoven's Ninth Symphony), some woven into tight contrapuntal textures, others building at the end to a blazing climax. Schoenberg's Variations aggressively proclaim the composer's special line of descent from the composer who — and this is in itself significant — was as much everybody's asserted forebear after the Great War as Beethoven had been before it.

But who *was* Bach to Schoenberg? Not at all the same man as "kleine Modernsky's" Papa Bach, whose archaism represented timelessness, and whose abstract mastery represented universality. Schoenberg's Bach was not a universal figurehead but a national one. Bach, for Schoenberg, was above all a German, indeed the greatest of Germans and the fountainhead of German musical art; hence the special venom with which Schoenberg derided "Franco-Russian" attempts to appropriate him. Schoenberg's neoclassicism was uniquely laced with nationalism — the particularly embittered nationalism of a defeated and resentful nation.

His writings abound in passages that underscore this connection. "It was mainly through J. S. Bach," Schoenberg alleged in an essay called "National Music," "that German music came to decide the way things developed, as it has for 200 years."[27] What vouchsafed German domination, moreover, was precisely the technique that Schoenberg saw himself as having inherited from Bach and, through the twelve-tone system, perfecting: namely, "contrapuntal art, i.e., the art of producing every audible figure from one single one."[28] Lest anyone miss the point, Schoenberg spelled out his truculent claims. First, with respect to twelve-tone music: "If at the climax of contrapuntal art, in Bach, something quite new simultaneously begins — the art of development through motivic variation — and in our time, at the climax of art based on harmonic relationships, the art of composing with 'twelve tones related only to each other' begins, one sees that the epochs are very similar."[29] And with reference to himself: "My music, produced on German soil, without foreign influences, is a living example of an art able most effectively to oppose Latin and Slav hopes of hegemony and derived through and through from the traditions of German music"[30] — traditions that went "back to Bach," as the saying went, but a route that in Schoenberg's insistent view only Germans could legitimately take.

The Variations for Orchestra—one of a number of early twelve-tone pieces by Schoenberg and his pupils to invoke the BACH motif, if by far the most impressive—asserted these claims in a manner that went beyond words. This view of his twelve-tone compositions and their heritage had informed what is now Schoenberg's most notorious remark, which he made in conversation with his teaching assistant, the musicologist Josef Rufer, in the summer of 1921 or 1922: "Today I have discovered something which will assure the supremacy of German music for the next hundred years."[31] Needless to say, ever since Rufer published it in 1959 this has been one of the most pounced-upon assertions in the history of European music. A representative defense of Schoenberg's position (by George Perle, already familiar to us as an analyst, and one of many European and American composers who have devoted their careers to enlarging on the Schoenbergian legacy) excuses the rhetorical excess by placing it in historical context. "There was much speculation, in the years immediately following the First World War, on the likelihood that the great Austro-German tradition, to which we still owe the major part of our standard orchestral repertory, was coming to an end," Perle wrote. "Why should we be surprised that a post-bellum Austro-German composer would hope that that tradition had not 'had its day'?"[32] Others have not found it so easy to overlook the distinction between survival and supremacy, especially after the Second World War, which was fought precisely over the issue of Germany's claim to world supremacy in an arena much larger than music.

CONSOLIDATION

Whatever the motivation, Schoenberg's career was dedicated henceforth to justifying the claims he had made for his method, elaborating and standardizing procedures so that its neoclassical principles could indeed become law. The greatest emphasis was placed on whatever might enhance the status of the row as *Grundgestalt*, with the result that principles of symmetry and complementation, already noticeable in Schoenberg's earliest twelve-tone works, would become the basic determinants of structure. Thus twelve-tone music, for all that it descended from expressionism (at least insofar as some leading composers of the one tendency became leading composers of the other), quickly metamorphosed into a haven for technical research and compositional tours de force. Sharing the predilection of all other neoclassicists for abstract or generic forms, twelve-tone composers went further than any others in ordering the content of their work according to rational structural principles, making content in effect tantamount to form.

An important structural principle that Schoenberg hit upon at the time of the Variations (one of the earliest works to exemplify it) could only be described in exceedingly cumbersome terms during his lifetime. Richard S. Hill, for example, a music scholar and librarian who in an article of 1936 gave the first comprehensive description of twelve-tone technique in English, spoke of "pieces in which the 'row' is divided into two six-note groups, the first of which in the prime contains the same notes as the second half of the mirror, but in a different order, the other halves being necessarily related similarly."[33]

Schoenberg himself, in a letter to Rufer dating from 1950, the year before his death, tried to explain his purposes as well as (still cumbersomely) describing the method: "Personally I endeavour to keep the series such that the inversion of the first six tones a fifth lower gives the remaining six tones. The consequent, the seventh to twelfth tones, is a different sequence of these second six tones. This has the advantage that one can accompany melodic phrases made from the first six tones with harmonies made from the second six tones, without getting doublings."[34] Doublings were to be avoided, in Schoenberg's oft-stated view, because they strengthened some tones at the expense of others, compromising the implied equality of "twelve tones, related only to each other" under the aegis of emancipated dissonance. Yet we have already seen that Schoenberg's actual practice admitted tonal hierarchies. They always would. As with most theorist-composers, his stated principles (or at least the principles he stated to outsiders) were purer than his deeds — which is less to accuse him of hypocrisy than to suggest we seek the reasons for the technique in question in his most basic, and therefore unarticulated, assumptions. What may seem at first an anachronistic or extrinsic approach has in fact proved the most revealing.

Nowadays, following a nomenclature first proposed by Milton Babbitt, a mathematically adept American theorist and composer, rows that meet the criteria defined by Hill and Schoenberg are called "combinatorial," and the technique of contriving and employing them, "combinatoriality." In mathematics, combinatoriality is a branch of probability theory that analyzes permutations (i.e., the reordering of sets) and combinations (i.e., principles of sampling from sets). It is a useful analogy for studying the properties of twelve-tone rows, since all rows are permutations of a single set (the "aggregate," as we have been calling it, or more simply but vaguely, the contents of the chromatic scale).

A row is combinatorial if from its various row-forms corresponding samples can be drawn that, when combined, produce invariant relationships that can be exploited as "basic shapes" (in this case harmonic constants) in the composition. In the most consummate instance, noted by Hill and Schoenberg, the corresponding segments of combinatorially related row forms complete the aggregate. Schoenberg sought out such rows because he considered them to offer a basis for a true — that is to say distinctive, consistent, and self-contained — twelve-tone harmonic system.

Look again at Ex. 12-14a, the theme from the Variations for Orchestra, op. 31, together with its harmonization. At the beginning, P_0 is pitted against I_9, the former providing the melody, the latter the harmony. In Ex. 12-15, the two row forms, labeled A and B, are notated abstractly, one atop the other, with their respective six-note segments or hexachords labeled with subscripts $_1$ and $_2$. The pitch content of A_1 and A_2, two halves of a single row, are of course by definition mutually exclusive. But in this particular combination of inversion and transposition, so are A_1 and B_1. And from this it must follow that A_1 and B_2 have identical pitch content (as must A_2 and B_1). Segments A_1 and B_2, in other words, are permutations of a single (six-note) set. They have the same relationship to one another as the row forms of which they are a part. And—the converse of this relationship—A_1 and B_1, though mutually exclusive in pitch content, have identical intervallic orders—another combination of constancy and difference that can be compositionally exploited.

When P_0 is put in counterpoint with I_9 all of these reciprocal and complementary relationships can be turned to structural account. Aggregates are completed in two dimensions: horizontal (A_1+A_2, B_1+B_2) and vertical (A_1+B_1, A_2+B_2). In addition, the cross pairs A_1 and B_2, or B_1 and A_2, being identical in pitch content but different in ordering, can be exploited either as harmonic constants or as variations on a basic shape. With all of these features in play, the motivic consistency of the music—its "relatedness quotient"—is vastly enhanced. Within an esthetic that valued music according to precisely this criterion (even to the point of declaring it an emblem of national supremacy), combinatoriality produced a self-evidently superior music; its discovery constituted incontrovertible musical progress.

But there is an even more particular consistency in play here. The row forms in Ex. 12-15 have been contrived and selected to produce harmonic symmetry at another level of combinatoriality. A_1 begins with a tritone, B♭E, that is automatically mirrored by GC♯ in B_1, the inversion. But since a tritone contains six semitones, and B_1 is at a transposition of 9 semitones from A_1, the /0 6/ tritone in A_1 is answered by /3 9/, giving a sum of /0 3 6 9/, a symmetrical division of the octave known to us since the days of Liszt as the circle of minor thirds. But Schoenberg has also included the reciprocal tritone (C♯G) in the second hexachord of the P_0, so that the /0 3 6 9/ coincidence happens twice when the two row forms are put in counterpoint, forming another harmonic constant.

EX. 12-15   Combinatorial row forms in Arnold Schoenberg, Variations for Orchestra, Op. 31

What is true of P_0 and I_9 must necessarily also be true of the next pairing in the harmonized theme, R_0 and RI_9 (the same two row forms reversed). But now the reciprocal tritones will be found in the reciprocal order positions: 4–5 and 11–12 rather than 1–2 and 8–9. This kind of relationship can be exploited for its punning resemblances to more familiar, functional harmonies: by combining P_0 and I_9 at the very outset, Schoenberg contrives to begin the Variations on a "diminished seventh chord," a traditional evoker of portent or suspense. But the relationship also produces an abstract and internal consistency: every phrase of the theme as harmonized displays the same basic shape (the constant C♯EGB♭, or sum of two tritones) and surrounds it with a different intervallic configuration. It is this extreme (and extremely controllable) consistency, which Schoenberg did not attempt to explain to his radio audience in 1931, that led him to prefer (or to argue in favor of) the twelve-tone harmonization of his theme over the "tonal" one. It is secured by combinatoriality.

Having discovered these possibilities, Schoenberg went back to the laboratory, so to speak, and gave them a concentrated investigation in a pair of piano pieces, op. 33a and 33b, that resembled the ones in op. 23 and opus 25 except that now he felt secure enough in his new structural principles not to tie the pieces to familiar or archaic genres, preferring, in the use of the neutral designation *Klavierstück*, to imply that the working out of the row relationships sufficed to generate the form. Ex. 12-16 shows the first page of each piece (the first published in Vienna in 1929, the second published in San Francisco by Henry Cowell's New Music Edition in 1932), together with the combinatorial row forms that in their interaction have engendered the musical shapes.

It was in these pieces that Schoenberg made it a rule of his own combinatorial practice, as stated in his letter to Rufer, to have the prime and inverted row forms stand at the distance of a perfect fifth. As we have seen in the case of the Variations, where the interval of transposition was a minor third, transposition by a fifth is not the only one that can produce the desired complementation. As Schoenberg confided to Rufer, he wished to ally his twelve-tone practice with what he considered to be "an acoustical law of nature — that between a note and its strongest and most frequent overtone."[35] Nor can we fail to recall that the fifth relation, as embodied in harmonically defined binary structures like "sonata form," is the one that traditionally governed the form of "tonal" music.

This is symptomatic of Schoenberg's postwar ambivalence. It has been apparent since our first comparison of his twelve-tone music with his rival Hauer's that Schoenberg's immediate inclination was to synthesize the novel technique with as many aspects of traditional practice as possible (and that he regarded multiplying its points of contact with tradition as technical progress), while Hauer, in his very primitiveness, displayed a tendency that was (even if only superficially or trivially) far more radical than Schoenberg's.

Hauer's *Nomos* pieces are nothing if not formally idiosyncratic and antitraditional. Seeking to place them in relation to a relevant cultural context, Gregory Dubinsky associates them not with any other contemporary music but with the public poetry readings of the time, highly declamatory affairs at which revolutionary sentiments were often given veiled expression. Dubinsky compares Hauer's monophonic or primitively homophonic compositions with declaimed poems, each musical phrase corresponding with a line of poetry, larger groupings with stanzas. The paucity of performance directions in Hauer's *Nomos* pieces, such as dynamics, articulation, and tempo markings, were an invitation, Dubinsky suggests, "to deliver a natural, affecting

EX. 12-16   Opening of Arnold Schoenberg, *Klavierstücke*, Op. 33a and 33b with a summary of its combinatorial row forms

EX. 12-16 *(continued)*

declamation of Hauer's lines of music"[36] according to the rhythms of heightened public speech.

But of course nothing could have been further from Schoenberg's expressive purposes than that sort of staged improvisation. Schoenberg saw in twelve-tone music an instrument for ever-greater control over those "organic" shaping functions that had always defined the greatness of the German musical tradition, and that Schoenberg saw epitomized in his own technique of developing variation. These principles are given a bravura display in the progressively denser, more elaborate combinatorial relations on which the piano pieces of opus 33 are based.

The beginning of op. 33a, for example, consists of a series of six four-note chords, the first three (m. 1) representing a harmonic segmentation of P_0 and the second a segmentation of its combinatorial mate, I_5. The next time the chordal idea is sounded, P_0 and I_5 are juxtaposed vertically (m. 10) and answered by their retrogrades, R_0 and

RI_5, in m. 11. Measures 1 and 2 each contain a single aggregate. Measures 10 and 11 contain four aggregates apiece: one in the right hand, one in the left hand, and two formed by the combinations $A_1 + B_1$ and $A_2 + B_2$. Each note in these measures has a double function, participating in two aggregate-completions, one horizontal and the other vertical.

SPREAD

The first composers after Schoenberg to adopt his twelve-tone methods were, naturally enough, his former pupils Berg and Webern. Berg's first essay using aspects of the new technique was the Chamber Concerto for violin, piano, and an ensemble of thirteen wind instruments (1925), the first piece he composed after finishing *Wozzeck*. It was a fiftieth-birthday offering to Schoenberg, and, as we saw in chapter 6, its row material incorporated the names Schoenberg, Berg, and Webern as pitch ciphers. As in some of Schoenberg's early twelve-tone compositions like the *Serenade*, op. 24, Berg's use of tone rows in the Chamber Concerto was sporadic.

The first composition in which Berg attempted a thoroughgoing application of Schoenbergian principles of *Reihenkomposition* ("serial composition") was a tiny song, *Schliesse mir die Augen beide* (1925; Berg had already made a "tonal" setting of the same poem by Theodor Storm in 1907). Here Berg adopted a row of a type his own pupil Fritz Heinrich Klein (1892–1977) had "discovered" the year before and published in a quasi-scientific article called "Die Grenze der Halbtonwelt" ("The frontiers of the semitone world"): namely, a symmetrical all-interval series (Ex. 12-17a). Each of the hexachords in the row contains all of the intervals from semitone to perfect fourth (or when inverted, from the perfect fifth to the major seventh), with the self-inverting tritone coming once, in the middle, as the boundary between the two hexachords. As a by-product of the row's structure, pitches flanking the central tritone (order positions 6/7) form tritone-related — hence self-inverting — pairs: GD♭ (positions 5/8), AE♭ (positions 4/9), CG♭ (3/10), EB♭ (2/11), FC♭[B] (1/12). One could say that this row maximized the tritone-symmetrical properties of the row on which Schoenberg had built his Suite for Piano, op. 25.

Berg used the row again as the basis for his next major work, the *Lyric Suite* for string quartet (1926). As he set it out in his sketches this time (Ex. 12-17b), Berg treated the inversions independently, so that every interval from the semitone to the major seventh is represented exactly once. And then (like Schoenberg in the Menuett from

FIG. 12-3   Berg and Schoenberg in 1914.

his Suite for Piano, op. 25), Berg reordered the set to emphasize its cognates with "tonal" practice: first into a circle of fifths, then into a diatonic scale. When the row is reordered in these ways, the tritone pairs no longer radiate out from the center but occupy analogous positions in the two hexachords (1/7, 2/8, 3/9, 4/10, 5/11, 6/12). Finally (and most "licentiously" with respect to the original order), in various movements Berg exchanged the positions of certain notes so as to produce new rows (Ex. 12-18). Again we see the role of playful "research" or "precompositional work" in the elaboration of the twelve-tone method.

EX. 12-17A   All-interval row in Alban Berg, *Schliesse mir die Augen beide*

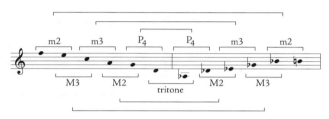

EX. 12-17B   All-interval row in Alban Berg, *Lyric Suite*

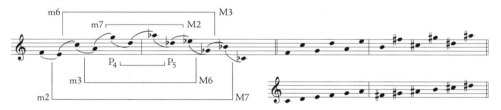

But all of these idiosyncratic row-manipulations and permutations (as well as equally meticulous rhythmic and tempo calculations) are placed at the service of an expressivity as intense as anything in *Wozzeck*. The very titles of the six movements in the *Lyric Suite* — *Allegretto gioviale* ("jolly allegro"), *Andante amoroso* ("lovestruck andante"), *Allegro misterioso* and *Trio ecstatico*, *Adagio appassionato*, *Presto delirando* ("delirious Presto"), *Largo desolato* ("broken-hearted Largo") — and the use of musical quotations (including a famous one from the Prelude of *Tristan und Isolde* in the final movement) have always struck listeners and critics as the makings of a "latent opera," as Berg's pupil, the critic Theodor Wiesengrund Adorno, called it.[37] During the 1970s, a group of scholars, working independently, pieced together the opera's libretto and its dramaturgy.

One of them, Douglass Green, discovered a sketch that revealed the last movement — the *Largo desolato*, which contained the *Tristan* quotation — to be a secret setting of a despairing poem by Baudelaire, *De profundis clamavi* ("Out of the depths have I cried unto thee" [Psalm 130]), as translated by the German poet Stefan George (Ex. 12-19).[38] A year later, George Perle discovered the printed score in which Berg wrote out, for the benefit of his secret lover, Hanna Fuchs-Robettin, all of the coded symbolic occurrences of her initials and his (HF/AB =BF/AB♭ as named in German). Looking back at

EX. 12-18   Permutations of *Lyric Suite* row

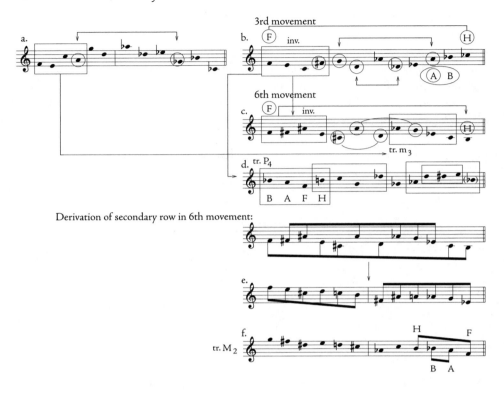

Ex. 12-18, it is easy now to see that the puzzling "licenses" Berg took with the order of the twelve-tone row were all contrived to produce conjunctions of the lovers' initials (hence, symbolically, the conjunction of their persons).

Hanna Fuchs's tritone-related initials were already the boundary notes of the original all-interval row "discovered" by F. H. Klein (as were his own), and this is probably what gave Berg the idea for the hidden program. The first permutation, the exchange of A and F♯G♭ in Ex. 12-18b, puts the composer's initials together. The inversion-plus-permutation in Ex. 12-18c, while keeping HF at the boundaries, produces an initial tetrachord that if transposed up a fourth would give the two sets of initials side by side. The transposition in Ex. 12-18d achieves this, and the three additional boxes identify other places where other transpositions would have the same effect. The elaborate transformation-plus-transposition in Exx. 12-18ef, which corresponds to the section of the movement that contains the *Tristan* quote, manages to put the symbolic tetrachord at the end, meanwhile folding (or "couching") AB within HF. As the music of the Largo proceeds to its desolate conclusion, the tetrachord is transposed to pitch levels at which the musical intervals lose their association with the lovers' initials, as if to suggest their loss of identity in death (or in the ecstasy of love)—a clear reference to the myth of Tristan and Isolde.

It is fair to ask whether any of this truly enhances the meaning of the *Lyric Suite* for anyone not a party to the affair. We knew about the presence of *Tristan* in the *Lyric Suite*, after all, before we knew about AB and HF. Does the particular reference add resonance to the general, or vice versa? Professor Perle himself has cautioned that to suggest that the meaning of the music is confined to the note symbolism is vastly to diminish it. Only in the case of the last movement, with an actual text that becomes an ineluctable subtext to anyone aware of its presence, do the new discoveries "change" the music (or rather, change the way in which a listener apprehends it). Our purpose in discussing them here is not interpretive but historical: the new discoveries shed additional light on

EX. 12-19 *Largo desolato* from *Lyric Suite*, with Baudelaire-George text underlaid, end

EX. 12-19 (*continued*)

> To you, you dear one, my cry rises
> Out of the deepest abyss in which my heart has fallen.
> There the landscape is dead, the air like lead
> And in the dark, curse and terror well up.
>
> Six moons without warmth stands the sun.
> During six darkness lies over the earth.
> Even the polar land is not so barren —
> Not even brook and tree, nor field nor flock.
>
> But no terror born of brain approaches
> The cold horror of this icy star
> And of this night, a gigantic Chaos!
>
> I envy the lot of the most common animal
> Which can plunge into the dizziness of a senseless sleep...
> So slowly does the spindle of time unwind!
>
> — Trans. Douglass M. Green

what the earliest practitioners thought to be the advantage of the twelve-tone method, not only in insuring the pervasive presence of a musical *Grundgestalt*, but also in finding new ways of relating the form and the meaning of a musical composition.

The fact, moreover, that both Schoenberg and Berg were drawn, in their twelve-tone music, to rows that exhibited intervallic symmetries was far from coincidental; for such harmonic symmetries were easily projected, at least conceptually, as structural symmetries to guide the composing hand and govern the resultant form. Berg's fascination with the liminal—with the border, that is, between the tonal and the atonal—was also well served by the twelve-tone technique, since now the harmonic consonances and occasional linear functions that had impinged (often with parodic effect) on the otherwise nonfunctional motivic texture in *Wozzeck* could be integrated into the row material itself, becoming part of the *Grundgestalt* rather than a graft or a hybrid, and thus come closer to the traditional ideal of "organic" unity.

Berg exploited these resonances in his second opera, *Lulu* (after a pair of plays about a ruthless femme fatale by Frank Wedekind, a German writer born in San Francisco), of which the last act was left unorchestrated at his death. (The act was completed by the Austrian composer Friedrich Cerha and first performed in 1979.) Berg brought them to an eloquent culmination in his last finished work, a concerto that had been commissioned by the American violinist Louis Krasner early in 1935, and that Berg wrote as a memorial to his young friend Manon Gropius—the daughter of Gustav Mahler's widow by her second husband, Walter Gropius, a famous architect—who died of polio, aged eighteen, in April of that year. Dedicated "to the memory of an angel," the Concerto makes no secret of its programmatic content, with a third movement that reaches a truly catastrophic climax, and a finale full of the pathos of mourning, and finally of acceptance.

Where the *Lyric Suite* had managed to educe allusions to works of Wagner and Zemlinsky from its twelve-tone strategies, the Violin Concerto alludes to even more frankly diatonic material: a South Austrian folk song to represent Manon's carefree early life (and possibly, as some commentators have suggested, Berg's as well), and a chorale, *Es ist genug* ("It is enough"), adapted from a striking harmonization by Bach, the text of which, entered in the score at the appropriate point in the finale, has an appropriately funereal import.

What made it possible to integrate this material into a twelve-tone context was the nature of the row, which consists mainly of an alternation of major and minor thirds. As first played by the violin during the introductory measures, it takes the form shown in Ex. 12-20a. By the time it is played, the listening ear has been conditioned, by the passage immediately preceding it (Ex. 12-20b) to interpret it as a succession of triads in a "reverse circle-of-fifths," followed by a whole tone tetrachord that coincides with the beginning of the chorale tune (Ex. 12-20c).

The next time the violin enters, it plays the inversion of its initial statement (hence the inversion of the row itself, Ex. 12-20d), and in so doing reveals its extraordinary properties. If the row and its inversion are linked up by reversing the latter (Ex. 12-20e), and if the gap that is left between the A at one end and the F at the other is plugged by the G with which both row forms begin, then a perfectly symmetrical pitch circle is achieved (Ex. 12-20f), in which any prime form of the row coincides with the reversed inversion at a transposition of a major third down, and any inverted row coincides with the reversed prime at a complementary transposition of a major third down. In effect, the reversed rows have been eliminated as an independent form. The row is its own

E X. 12-20A   Alban Berg, Violin Concerto, entrance of solo violin (mm. 15 – 18)

E X. 12-20B   Alban Berg, Violin Concerto, mm. 11 – 15

E X. 12-20C   J. S. Bach, harmonized chorale, "Es ist genug!"

Es   ist   ge - nug!   Herr,   wenn   es   Dir   ge - fällt

It is enough! Whenever you please, Lord, take me . . .

retrograde. Writing out the prime form so that it starts and ends on the Eb, which splits the whole-tone tetrachord down the middle, produces an intervallic palindrome that shows this effect most clearly (Ex. 12-20g).

EX. 12-20D   Alban Berg, Violin Concerto, mm. 24–27 (solo violin)

EX. 12-20E   Alban Berg, Violin Concerto, symmetrical pitch circle formed by prime and inverted row forms

EX. 12-20F   Alban Berg, Violin Concerto, symmetrical circle laid out as a melodic palindrome

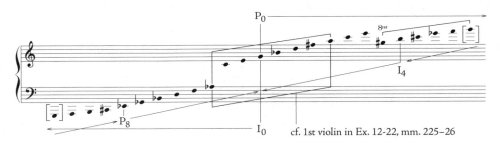

EX. 12-20G   Alban Berg, Violin Concerto, intervallic palindrome condensed

(Adapted from Perle, *The Operas of Alban Berg*, Vol. 2, p. 251.)

Several passages in the Concerto exploit these symmetries through transpositions by major thirds, but more conspicuous are the passages in which Berg transposes the row by minor thirds to emphasize cognates between its structure and the structural functions of traditional harmony. The very beginning of the concerto is the best example of this, and its recapitulation at the end to produce the concerto's final cadence shows that Berg thought of the effect not only as an expressive resource, but also as a structural principle to unify the concerto tonally. (As we have already seen in *Wozzeck*, though, the distinction between the structural and the expressive in Berg's music is ultimately as gratuitous as it is invidious.)

The first eight measures, shown in Ex. 12-21a, have a traditional (neoclassical?) "preluding" character, produced by the steadily rocking arpeggios, reminiscent of the old *style brisé*, the "broken (chord) style" of the baroque lute or keyboard suite. The violin alternates throughout with a harp, standing in for the lute/harpsichord, that is doubled by a group of three clarinets which sometimes follow the harp notes, at other times pull tones out of the arpeggios to sustain them as background harmony. The violin's first arpeggio, cunningly enough, consists of the four open strings, as if to emphasize the preludizing (or "ricercata") effect, a mock-aimless improvisation in which one noodles on the instrument in search of an idea.

To isolate the pitches of the open violin strings, Berg "samples" the row, selecting order positions 1, 3, 5, and 7 — that is, every other note. The violin's next arpeggio consists of the complementary sample: 2, 4, 6, and 8. The "chord" produced this time is a whole-tone tetrachord to match the one at the row's end. The implied progression of the starting pitches — G to B♭ — suggests a traditional tonal move from the tonic minor to the relative major, and Berg reinforces the parallel (as well as foreshadowing the eventual key of the Bach chorale in the finale) by deriving the harp's arpeggios from P_3, the row transposed up a minor third. The two row forms are thus juxtaposed in a sort of hocketing counterpoint, as set forth in Ex. 12-21b, which forges a link between them that will hold throughout the Concerto.

The coda of the finale, given in Ex. 12-22, consists of one last full statement of the chorale tune but without its internal repeats. The first phrase (mm. 214–219) is played by the winds; the second (mm. 220–222) by the winds plus pizzicato strings; and the last, falling phrase (F-D-C-B♭), to which the words "Es ist genug" are repeated, is assigned first, *molto adagio*, to the solo violin, thence to the trumpet (accompanied by the traditional "brass chorale"), and finally, in augmentation, *espressivo e amoroso*, to the French horns. The accompaniment to the chorale consists of phrases extracted from the row.

At m. 215 the violin is given a sequence of rising whole-tone tetrachords that echo the chorale's beginning; its flourish before it takes up the tune in m. 222 consists of the first tetrachord of I_2 (=R_{10}, positions 4–7). The last chorale phrase is accompanied by ribbons of arpeggios in many transpositions, all of them referable to the array given in Ex. 12-20f. The last of these, in the solo violin (mm. 226–228), after a preliminary pair of notes (D♭-F) that apes the preceding entrance (solo orchestral violin in m. 225) at the fourth, consists of one last statement of the row, at P_2, which allows it to end, rather than begin, on G. The French horn, having finished the last chorale phrase, appends a final muted statement of the whole-tone tetrachord, inverted so that it descends to another G. The harp and winds sound the chorale's tonic for the last time, in an "added-sixth" variant that admits the concluding G as a consonance.

The chord thus created, B♭DFG, had an important poetic resonance: Mahler had ended the finale of *Das Lied von der Erde*, his "symphony with voices," on a similar added-sixth chord; that movement was called "Der Abschied" ("The farewell"). But there is an "introversive" echo as well: the chord combines the first pair of notes in each of the opening arpeggios (see Ex. 12-21a). That this reference is intended to function at once as closure and summation on both poetic and tonal levels is confirmed by the explicit echoes of the opening arpeggios in the orchestral violins and the double bass, which supply the concerto's concluding notes.

EX. 12-21A   Alban Berg, Violin Concerto, mm. 1–8

EX. 12-21B   Alban Berg, Analytical sketch for Violin Concerto, mm. 1–8

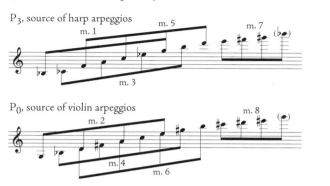

P_3, source of harp arpeggios

P_0, source of violin arpeggios

In keeping with the predilections we observed in *Wozzeck*, Berg used the resources of twelve-tone technique so as to achieve an integration of eclectic ingredients that continually cross the threshold between the functionally tonal and the motivically atonal. His art remained one of affective association, his expressive aims remained traditionally humanistic, concerned with the representation, and possible transmission, of subjective feelings like erotic love (in the *Lyric Suite*), or grief and consolation (in the Concerto). It was to these ends that Berg sublimated the intellectual curiosity that attracted him to technical tours de force. His obsession with motivic and harmonic symmetries acted as a useful counterfoil to his representational bent, enabling his music to be at once eclectic and economical in a way that interests analysts, and giving his music, to a perhaps greater degree than that of the other early Viennese atonalists, strong appeal on both the poietic and esthesic planes.

CLARIFICATION

With Webern the situation has been somewhat different. Drawn even more strongly than Schoenberg or Berg to symmetrically constructed rows, he was also drawn to extremes of structural rigor and economy that vastly exceeded theirs, reflecting his own personal predilections as we have already come to know them from the radically compressed "expressionistic" works encountered in chapter 6. "Adherence to the row is strict, often burdensome," Webern wrote, "but it is *salvation!*"[39] It provided a "new law" — *Nomos* — that made larger forms possible again. But even Webern's larger forms were tiny. And his utopian vision of twelve-tone music as a discipline for musicians and a salvation for music has come, for reasons

FIG. 12-4   Webern in the Ötztal Alps, July 1937.

neither he nor any other composer could have predicted during his lifetime, to characterize the technique in the eyes of those who have cast themselves as his creative progeny, and to limit its scope.

Webern's first twelve-tone composition was a little piano piece called *Kinderstück* ("Children's piece"), composed in 1924. His next twelve-tone study, a piano piece in the form of a minuet (1925), again underscored the close relationship between the new technique and the general "disciplinary" aims of neoclassicism. Over the course

EX. 12-22   Alban Berg, Violin Concerto, coda

EX. 12-22 (*continued*)

of the next twenty years Webern completed a round dozen works intended for publication—two orchestral, three choral, one for piano, four for chamber ensembles, and two sets of songs—using the technique his teacher had invented. Their total duration is less than the combined length of Berg's *Lyric Suite* and Violin Concerto. But their impact would be extraordinary. While Schoenberg invented (or, as he preferred to say, "discovered") the twelve-tone technique, it was Webern who provided the paramount model for its later development and use.

It may have been Webern's training in musicology, then primarily an antiquarian field, that predisposed him to take a more purely intervallic view of twelve-tone

EX. 12-23   Jacob Obrecht, *Missa Graecorum*, cantus firmi from Gloria, Agnus I and Agnus III

a. Gloria

b. Agnus I (inversion)

c. Agnus III (retrograde), middle to end

composition than the other members of his circle. He was aware of the many works by such fifteenth-century masters as Henricus Isaac (on whom he wrote a doctoral dissertation), Jacob Obrecht, Josquin des Prez, and others, in which a cantus firmus was turned upside down or back to front for the sake of variety or for the display of a sometimes hermetic virtuosity, and liked to claim the "Netherlanders," as they were then called, as his immediate forebears. Comparison of three versions of the tenor in Obrecht's *Missa Graecorum* (Ex. 12-23), a "Webernian" work dating from around 1490, might almost seem to validate the whimsical claim.

But the properties that ideally remained "occult" in the work of the Netherlanders, buried in the middle of the texture, often played on the crystal-clear surface in Webern's work. The first and second movements of his Variations for Piano, op. 27 (1936), for example, of which the row is given in Ex. 12-24a, respectively "foreground" or "thematize" intervallic symmetry in two dimensions. In the first movement, row forms are consistently paired with their retrogrades and juxtaposed in counterpoint to form little palindromes that are nothing if not salient to the ear.

The first such palindrome (Ex. 12-25) can serve as paradigm. The right hand begins with P_0, the left with R_0; at the halfway point, when each has completed one hexachord, the hands reverse their assignments so that the left completes the prime, the right the retrograde. Not only the registral distribution of the two row forms and the pitch succession, but also the rhythm is exactly reversed around the fulcrum symbolized in notation by the sixteenth rest in m. 4; that is what makes the mirror-writing so easily observable. And so it remains throughout. Note that the row has been deliberately constructed so as to make the distinctively thematic alternation of dyads (sevenths and ninths) and single notes all but unavoidable. And note, too, that the trichord produced by order positions 6–8, which crosscut the hexachords, can be arranged to form the equally distinctive "atonal triad," a chord that by the 1930s had (as we know) a distinguished history. Again, a distinctive sonority is given a distinctive (in this case conjunctive) function.

In the second movement (Ex. 12-26), row forms are paired contrapuntally with their inversions around an axis of symmetry that can just as easily be discerned by ear: the first full measure has the first of four pairs of As played by the two hands in succession. (The others are in mm. 9, 13, and 19; they come once per "cursus," or

EX. 12-24A   Anton Webern rows and their properties: Variations for Piano, Op. 27 (1936)

EX. 12-24B   Anton Webern rows and their properties: Symphony, Op. 21 (1928)

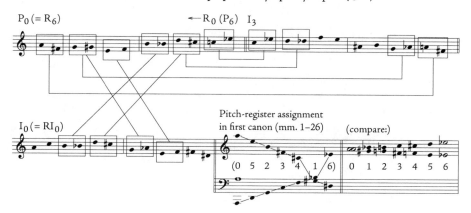

EX. 12-24C   Anton Webern rows and their properties: Quartet, Op. 28 (1938)

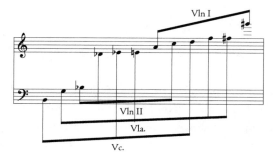

EX. 12-24D   Anton Webern rows and their properties: Concerto, Op. 24 (1934)

EX. 12-24E   Anton Webern row forms arranged in magic square: Concerto, Op. 24

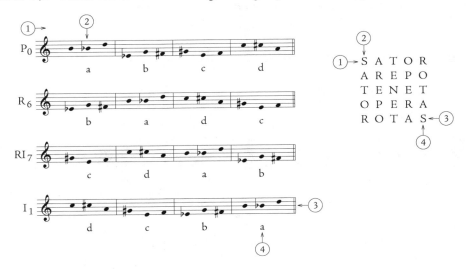

```
S A T O R
A R E P O
T E N E T
O P E R A
R O T A S
```

EX. 12-25   Anton Webern, Variations for Piano, Op. 27, I, mm. 1–7

run-through, of the paired rows.) Thus A is identified as the axis of a fully elaborated symmetrical array such as we first encountered in Richard Strauss in chapter 1, and in Bartók in chapter 7 (but also, incipiently, in early Webern in chapter 6):

```
A  Bb  B  C  C#  D  Eb  E  F  F#  G  G#
A  G#  G  F#  F   E  Eb  D  C#  C  B  Bb
```

Any Bb in one hand will be paired with a G# in the other, B with G, and so on. Not only the As at the axis, but every pitch is assigned a specific "hypostatized" register in this composition such as we have already observed in some of Stravinsky's earlier music, radiating out from the axis (see Ex. 12-24a). The only consistent exception to this rule is the note Eb, which appears in three different registers. Eb, of course, is the tritone-antipode of A, and the only other note that pairs with itself in the array shown above. Precisely for that reason Webern went out of his way to minimize its role in the movement. In m. 6 it occurs in both hands (in octaves) as a grace note to a main note played *fortissimo*. That is one way of sweeping it under the rug. The other way is to make it the last pitch of the first pair of row forms and the first pitch of the second; in this way the single grace note can do double duty in the row-count, and thus appear only once in the whole first section.

EX. 12-26   Anton Webern, Variations for Piano, Op. 27, II

In the second half, the E♭ appears twice. In m. 21 it does what it did in m. 6; in m. 15, it appears as part of a three-note chord, where its own specific identity is muted by the overriding harmonic color (as usual, an "atonal triad"; in fact, all the three-note chords in this movement, as in the first, are drawn from order positions 6–8, so that the atonal triad is the only chord that appears). The systematic minimizing of E♭ leaves

A as the perceptually undisputed tone center of the movement. We could not have a better illustration of the way in which the twelve-tone system was seen by its early practitioners not as a way of excluding pitch hierarchies (or "tonal" references), but as a way of asserting them in new, context-specific ways.

The third movement is the most straightforwardly composed of the three, and the most conventionally laid out as a set of variations. It consists of a theme and five variations, set off from one another by tempo and texture. The theme (Ex. 12-27), consisting of R_4, RI_4, and P_4 laid end to end, sums up within itself the inverse and reverse symmetries of the preceding two movements; its middle part is a contour-mirror of the first, and the last is the first reversed. Not by accident, the starting (and hence the finishing) note is E♭, the suppressed tritone complement from the preceding movement, now given its complementary place in the sun.

EX. 12-27   Anton Webern, Variations for Piano, Op. 27, III, mm. 1–12

It is with reference to this movement, and particularly to the theme, that the stems and beams have been added to the usual note-heads in the row as given in Ex. 12-24a, for it is here that the row is partitioned most rigorously into its constituent semitones, presented always in inverted or compound form (that is, as sevenths or ninths). The very beginning of the theme, which uses the reversed row, shows most clearly the way the two semitones in order positions 9–12 (grouped 9/12 + 10/11) are associated (or, if one prefers, differentiated) by means of texture and articulation: the outer pair are long and detached, the inner pair short and legato. In m. 3 the two semitone pairs that occupy order positions 3–6 (3/5 + 4/6) are similarly associated. For the rest, the variations consist of additional studies in inverse and reverse symmetry, using the restricted harmonic vocabulary with which we have become familiar: single notes, sevenths and ninths, and "atonal triads." Only the last variation (Ex. 12-28) introduces a new chord: /0 3 4/, sometimes called the "double-inflected third" since it combines /0 3/ (a minor third) with /0 4/ (a major third).

E X. 12-28   Anton Webern, Variations for Piano, Op. 27, III, mm. 56–end

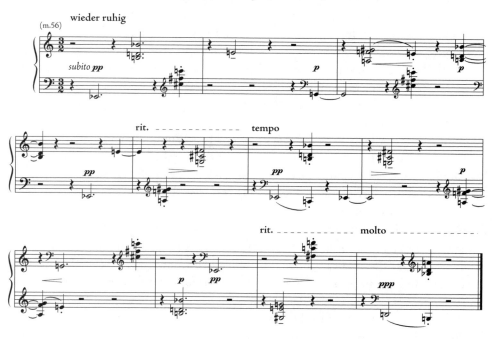

As a succession, these intervals are found in two places in the row: order positions 1–3 and 9–11. Webern seizes the opportunity this coincidence offers for constructing symmetries. Since 1–3 can do double duty as the beginning of a prime or end of a retrograde, Webern begins with the latter, R$_4$ (the row form with which the theme had originally begun), and follows it with P$_4$ (with which the theme had originally ended), allowing the first right-hand chord in m. 58 (AFG♯) to serve as fulcrum for a pitch palindrome such as formed the substance of the first movement.

Another pitch palindrome begins at the upbeat to m. 60. This time, Webern chooses to begin with a transposition of the retrograde-inversion, RI$_5$, that allows the two /0 3 4/ trichords to exchange places and functions when followed by the similarly pitched inversion, I$_5$. The E♭ that closes I$_5$ in m. 64 does double duty as the first note of RI$_6$, with which the variation, and the Variations, come to an end. Beginning with that E♭ in m. 64, then, the last three measures of the piece are, in effect, mm. 60–61 transposed down a "cadential" semitone. More importantly, the transposition allows the Variations to end with A, the pitch center of the second movement and the tritone complement of E♭, in the melodically exposed top voice.

EPITOME

Even more economical are the Webern compositions in which the row itself is so contrived as to do "double duty," reducing the number of independent row forms and multiplying the field of potential relationships among them. In the two-movement Symphony, op. 21 (1928), the second hexachord is the first reversed at the tritone, as tracing them from the middle out to the ends will quickly show. But this means that the entire row is an intervallic palindrome: its retrograde form is the same as the prime transposed by a tritone, so that $P_0 = R_6$ and $R_0 = P_6$. This eliminates the retrograde as an independent row form, leaving only twelve possible primes and twelve possible inversions (=retrograde inversions).

With the row its own retrograde, and with inversion therefore the only meaningful transformation of it, the Symphony became inevitably ("by nature") what the Piano Variations were by artful design: a study in tightly controlled multidimensional symmetry. That seems in fact to be what Webern meant by calling the work a symphony. There is little or nothing in its formal procedures to compare with those of the traditional symphony; but the texture, as we are about to discover it, is maximally "harmonious" or "sym-phonic" in the etymological sense (well known to antiquarian musicologists) that everything in it fits ideally with everything else.

The first movement of the Symphony consists of three elaborately worked out double canons that pit two prime forms against two inversions. The three canons are presented in a binary form in which the first repeated part consists of the first canon (mm. 1–26), and the second contains the other two (mm. 25–44, 43–66). This may in fact have been a "neoclassical" reference to the traditional first-movement form, in which the section up to the first double bar was the exposition, while the section up to the second double bar contained both a development and a recapitulation.

By constructing canons by inversion on a self-reversing row, Webern assures a constant multidimensional intervallic symmetry throughout the movement, combining the palindrome effect from the first movement of his Piano Variations with the invariant harmonic axis of the second (again located on A, the starting note of P_0). The first canon by inversion (Ex. 12-29) begins in the horns at the unison: the second player enters first with P_0 (=R_6) and the first answers with I_0 (=RI_6). After the first four pitches have been sounded, the *dux* or leading voice moves to the clarinet for the next four and the cello for the last four, while the *comes* or following voice moves to the bass clarinet for the next four and the viola for the last four. The second canon shadows the first at the major third, both below (I_8) and above (P_4). Both of these row forms begin in the harp, I_8 in m. 2 (continuing in the cello) and P_4 in m. 4 (continuing in the viola).

The fact that both canons begin with similar tone colors but then shift to others, and the fact that some of the same colors are used in both canons, suggests that

EX. 12-29   Anton Webern, Symphony, Op. 21, I, mm. 1–25

EX. 12-29   (*continued*)

Webern was not interested in having his canons perceived by the listener as coherent lines. Instead, they are absorbed into a kaleidoscopically fragmented texture that has often been compared with the painterly technique known as pointillism, in which solid objects are rendered as multitudes of individual daubs and dots of pigment, and become unrecognizable when viewed up close.

It may not be the best analogy for Webern's fragmentation technique, since there is no standpoint from which the linear coherence of his canons becomes salient. But that is not surprising. As we have long since observed, a canon as such is of no particular interest (and shows no particular skill on the part of the composer) once dissonance has been "emancipated." Webern has simply relied on the device in order to generate a profusion of symmetrically related intervals that can be mined for motivic connections. It was the patterning of these smaller units — as a means for achieving what Webern called "the greatest possible unity in music," and "the utmost relatedness between all component parts"[40] — that provided the point and purpose of this or any twelve-tone composition. That is what we need, however briefly, to investigate.

The reason the beginnings and ends of the three canons — mm. 1–26, 25–44, 43–66 — overlap by a measure is that throughout the movement Webern proceeds from row form to row form by a sort of punning process that the structure of the row was designed to make possible. The C and E♭ in the cello in mm. 11–12, for example, are at once the last two pitches of P_0 and the first two in I_3, while the F♯ and E♭ in the viola in mm. 13–14 are simultaneously the last two pitches in I_0 and the first two in P_9. (Note, by the way, that the new row forms are now shadowing P_0 at the minor third, another potential axis of harmonic symmetry.) But these correspondences are only the beginning. As Ex. 12-24b shows, four dyads in I_3 have exact counterparts in P_0 (and so will all the other P/I pairs at a transposition of a minor third in either direction). And as the same example also shows, any P/I pair at the unison will also have four dyads (two the same, two different) in common.

And that is why Webern so elaborately fixed (or "hypostatized") the relationships between pitch and register and between pitch and rhythm in this movement. For the duration of the first canon, pitches are assigned registers strictly according to the symmetrical distribution shown in Ex. 12-24b, which is derived from the ordinary axis of symmetry around A by transforming the chromatic scale (or "circle of minor seconds") into a circle of fifths (here represented, by inversion, as fourths). Only E♭, the antipode to A, appears in two registers (and in the actual music, always in harmony with A: see the harp in mm. 7 and 9, the viola in m. 19, the cello in m. 21). All the other pitches appear in one register only.

Comparing the actual music now with the abstract representation of the row forms in Ex. 12-24b, we find the paired dyads expressed as actual recurring motives: the GA♭ in the horn in mm. 3–4 (from P_0) is answered in the bass clarinet in mm. 9–10 (from I_0), using the exact same pitch placement and rhythm: similarly the BB♭ in the first horn in mm. 5–6 (from P_0) and in the clarinet in mm. 7–8 (from I_0), the DC♯ in the bass clarinet in m. 8 (from I_0), in the cello in m. 10 (from P_0), and again in the cello in m. 13 (from I_3). And so it goes throughout the movement.

In the second double canon, all of these conditions continue to hold (although the particular pitch-register distribution changes somewhat), and in addition, the two canons use the identical sequence of rhythms. These reverse midway, like the rhythms in the first movement of the Piano Variations but on a much larger scale, so that the whole section from m. 25 to m. 44 (Ex. 12-30) is a pitch-rhythm palindrome that reverses around the downbeat of m. 35. Another way of putting it would be to say that mm. 35–44 are a literal retrograde of mm. 25–34.

It has been claimed, on the basis of movements like this, that (unlike Schoenberg and Berg) Webern sought what Milton Babbitt once described as "a completely autonomous conception of the twelve-tone system," in which all components of a composition "would be determined by the relations and operations of the system."[41] But while Webern was obviously more concerned than his colleagues were to systematize all the details of his works, and while he achieved a sometimes astoundingly thorough organization of their textures, his conception of twelve-tone music was not completely "autonomous," if by that one means completely independent of traditional criteria of "tonal" coherence.

The pitch-register distribution in the first canon, for example, with its ascending fourths in the bass, could not have been selected without awareness of the "tonal" properties of such progressions. Indeed, Webern seems to have gone out of his way to emphasize them by the frequent placement of the low Ds and Gs in strong metrical

EX. 12-30   Anton Webern, Symphony, Op. 21, I, mm. 27–42 (the pitch-rhythm palindrome minus the ends, which overlap with other material)

EX. 12-30 (continued)

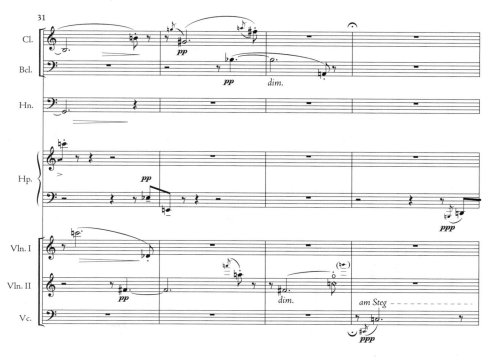

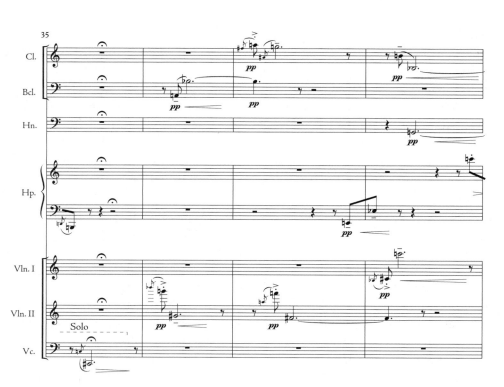

EX. 12-30   *(continued)*

positions: for example, in the bass clarinet (mm. 8–9), the cello and harp in mm. 13–14 (the harp's low G not only metrically strong but unaccompanied), or even at the very outset, where the second horn's repeated F♯ in m. 2 acts as an upbeat (ineluctably suggesting the leading-tone function) to the strongly placed G in m. 3.

This residual or reflexive bond with "tonal" tradition was a facet of the early twelve-tone composers' high consciousness of their role, within their idiosyncratic conception of music history, as custodians of a great tradition who kept faith with it by maintaining it in a state of incessant stylistic and technical evolution. The "progressive" and the "traditional" were thus held in a conceptual or "dialectical" balance that made it possible for the Viennese dodecaphonists to disdain with equal fervor both those who (in the name of conventional standards of beauty) resisted the progress that atonality exemplified and those who (in the name of primitivism or in that of radical politics) denigrated tradition.

We have seen Schoenberg declare his loyalty to that tradition, and also assert leadership within it, by quoting the B-A-C-H cipher in his Variations for Orchestra, op. 31 (1928). Ten years later, Webern brought that assertion to a characteristic climax in his String Quartet, op. 28, by basing the entire composition on a row consisting of three statements of the cipher, which thus became its all-pervasive *Grundgestalt* (Ex. 12-24c). The first and last statements are related by simple transposition both to the original BACH cipher and to each other. The middle tetrachord employs a version that could be described either as the inversion of the cipher or as the retrograde, since the cipher happens to be structured in such a way that the two forms coincide. And therefore the row constructed from it will also have remarkably "redundant" properties of a kind that, as we already know, Webern loved to exploit.

The BACH tetrachords that make up the row have been ingeniously chosen so that the two halves of the row — that is, its hexachords — reproduce one another by inversion if one proceeds from the middle out to the ends. The interval separating them at the midpoint is a minor third. Thus the entire row is its own retrograde inversion, a minor third "up" (and its retrograde is its own inversion by a complementary transposition of a minor third "down"). But at the same time the first and last tetrachords stand a major third apart, so that row forms at that transposition will overlap by an entire tetrachord. The implications of this unique feature are shown in Ex. 12-24c, where the three versions of P(=RI) and the three versions of R(=I) that may be related by transpositions of a major third are shown to break down into a fund of only three constituent tetrachords, each of which occurs in two orderings. That is the material out of which the first movement of the quartet is constructed.

In a lecture that he gave in March 1932, Webern exulted in the tightness of structure he had achieved in his Symphony thanks to the palindromic row on which it had been based: "Greater unity is impossible. Even the Netherlanders didn't manage it."[42] But in the Quartet he did manage to exceed it, and in the first movement he went even further in limiting his material to recurrent motives by hypostatizing not only the registers in which pitches could occur, but also the instruments to which they were assigned. The first section of the movement (Ex. 12-31) uses the scheme shown in Ex. 12-24c, in which the first violin plays only two pitches, a′ and g♯″; the second violin only b♭, d♭, and c′; the viola only g, e, f′, and f♯′; and the cello only b, e♭, and d′.

Webern's Quartet thus epitomizes the Janus-faced aspect of early twelve-tone music. It goes further than any other composition of its time in the tightly organized direction that Webern and his colleagues identified as progress — that is, the inevitable fate of music as mandated by its history — at the same time that it asserts, in every single note, its claim of lineal descent from Bach (or from the "Netherlanders"), from whom that history was traced. And yet it was another, slightly earlier composition of Webern's from the same period that would have the greatest influence of all on the later development of twelve-tone music, although no one at the time foresaw it.

Webern worked on his seven-minute Concerto, op. 24, for nine instruments (flute, oboe, clarinet, horn, trumpet, trombone, violin, viola, and piano) over a three-year period, from 1931 to 1934. Ex. 12-24d shows its row, perhaps the most famous individual tone row ever devised, and Fig. 12-5 shows a sketch page, dating from February 1931, on which Webern worked toward fashioning it. At the end of the first day's work (4 February), at the beginning of the seventh staff, Webern entered what looks something like a tritone transposition of the row he finally adopted: F E G♯ A C C♯ D B♭ B G G♭ E♭. The next day he made two minute adjustments, exchanging the positions of the CC♯ and GG♭ pairs, and then he had it: a row that could be divided into four trichords that would sum up among them all the standard "operations" of the twelve-tone technique.

EX. 12-31   Anton Webern, String Quartet, Op. 28, I, mm. 1–15

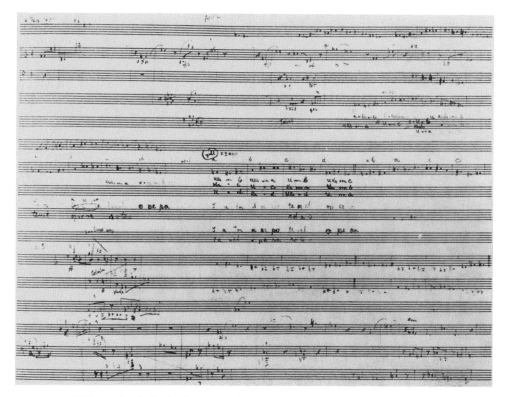

FIG. 12-5   Webern, sketch for the first movement of *Concerto*, op. 24.

Labeling the trichords *a*, *b*, *c*, and *d*, and using the German abbreviations U (for *Umkehr*, inversion), Kr (for *Krebs*, "crabwise" or retrograde), and Ukr (for *umgekehrter Krebs*, or inverted retrograde), Webern noted with schoolmasterly meticulousness that *a* was the Ukr of b, the Kr of c, and the U of d; that *b* was the Ukr of a, the U of c, and the Kr of d; that *c* was the U of b, the Kr of a, and the Ukr of d; and that *d* was the Ukr of c, the Kr of b, and the U of a. Next he wrote out the retrograde form of the whole row, and noted its corollary property: that applying the four operations to the whole row reproduced the four trichords in a different order and at a uniform transposition (in this case, a tritone). Restoring the original order of the constituent trichords at the pitch of the retrograde produced the row form with which the composition would eventually start, and which is therefore now regarded as the prime form.

The strange inscription entered twice beneath these musical sketches — "Sator Arepo tenet opera rotas" — is a famous Latin palindrome that had served as Webern's inspiration in deriving his row from a single trichord. Near-gibberish, it may be translated into English in a number of equally cryptic ways: "The sower Arepo holds the works of his hoe," and "The sower Arepo keeps the work circling" are among the translations that have been proposed. But its meaning is altogether secondary to its "structure": for it is more than a palindrome. When arranged as a square, thus —

```
S   A   T   O   R
A   R   E   P   O
T   E   N   E   T
O   P   E   R   A
R   O   T   A   S
```

— its five five-letter words can be read from left to right starting at the top, from right to left starting at the bottom, down the columns starting at the left, or up the columns starting at the right, producing a very suggestive analogy, made explicit in Ex. 12-24e, to the U, Kr, and Ukr trichords and the way they reconstitute themselves in various permutations of the row.

As might easily be inferred simply from knowing the properties of the row, the music of the Concerto (so called, evidently, on the basis of the way in which the piano interacts with the instrumental group) is a kaleidoscope of trichords, all of which have the identical intervallic shape of the *Grundgestalt*: a semitone and a major third, with "circumflex" contour, or a chord (like the ones near the end of the Piano Variations) with a double-inflected third. The first five measures (Ex. 12-32) are a paradigm: the oboe, flute, trumpet, and clarinet give the four trichords of the prime form, their contrasting tone colors and implied speeds (in a ratio of 8:4:6:3) giving the contrapuntal texture maximum clarity. Then the piano, with its uniform tone color, plays the row's retrograde inversion with the rhythm reversed and at the transposition of a minor third, which reproduces the pitch contents of the trichords in their original order of succession but with their internal pitch orders reversed.

It is notoriously easy to overestimate the complexity of this music. Both its highly rationalized compositional (or "precompositional") methods, and the immense sum total of motivic relationships to which nearly everything else is sacrificed, lend themselves to exhaustive verbal or graphic description that, like any other kind of detail-heavy programmatic paraphrase, can all too readily replace the sound-object so described as focus of attention. But the sound-object as such is neither dense nor arcane. Webern's textures are famously spare and transparent, and in terms of events-per-unit-time, his music is far less heavily laden than Schoenberg's — or, especially, Berg's, whose music has always been regarded by audiences as far more "accessible." It is the description, not the music, that boggles the mind. The music lays everything bare. The description all too easily covers it up again. And that may be because the description is usually cast entirely in "poietic" terms — in terms, that is, of the relationship between the music and its maker — or else in what is sometimes called "neutral" terms (in terms, that is, of an "objective" inventory of its "purely musical" content). As there has already been occasion to observe, the "esthesic" aspect — the relationship between the music and its audience, or the impact the composer seeks to make on a hearer — is rarely addressed.

In part this has been a deliberate strategy. Surrounding modernist art with a cult of difficulty has been a trusty protective measure, keeping the hostile crowd at bay. As the hostility of the crowd became more and more overtly political, in the context, first,

EX. 12-32 Anton Webern, Concerto, Op. 24, I, mm. 1–5

of "Weimar culture" (not limited, of course, to Weimar or even to Germany) and later in that of the totalitarian Nazi state, which threatened and eventually swallowed up Webern's Austrian homeland, resistance of this kind was hardened. Webern himself tended to cast the difficulty of his art in heroic terms, as a bulwark of embattled high culture. "It's nonsense to advance 'social objections'" to the difficulty of the new music, Webern told a lecture audience in 1932, when most of the opposition came from the political left. "Why don't people understand that? Our push forward *had* to be made, it was a push forward such as never was before. In fact we have to break new ground with each work: each work is something different, something new . . . . How do people hope to follow this? Obviously it's very difficult."[43] But in private correspondence, and in one exceptional case in an article meant for publication (but unpublished until 1978), Webern described his music "esthesically"—and with enormous emotional excitement—in terms of the impact his achievements had on himself as an ideally informed listener. The article, significantly enough, concerned the String Quartet and its total governance by the BACH cipher. It had been commissioned in 1939 by Erwin Stein (1885–1958), a close friend of Webern's and a fellow former pupil of Schoenberg, who had been forced to emigrate to England as a result of the Nazi annexation of Austria in 1938. Stein had become a music editor for the London firm of Boosey and Hawkes, which had agreed to publish the Quartet. He commissioned an analysis from Webern to appear in *Tempo*, the firm's house organ. Webern sent it off for translation during the summer. But the publication both of the Quartet and of the analysis were thwarted by the outbreak of the Second World War in September, which made commerce, or even correspondence, between London and Vienna impossible.

From this article, which runs about 2,500 words, three selected paragraphs will suffice to give the extravagantly hyperbolic flavor. The first concerns the structure of the third movement, which Webern describes as a synthesis of two "classical" or academic forms that are usually deemed incompatible.

> Formwise, this structure is but a *periodic scherzo subject* in the shape of the third exposition of a *double fugue*; that is to say (with reference to my fugue subject which begins in the development of the Scherzo): a stretto of "subject" and "countersubject." As far as I know, this had *never* been done before; as a double canon *in retrograde, moreover,* it had never been done at all!!! Therefore, does this not justifiably constitute also the third exposition of a double fugue? And to repeat it once more, it is yet but nothing other than a period, in compliance with the principles of construction of a *scherzo subject,* as in Beethoven. Thus, it obeys the laws of *horizontal* construction. But as the stretto, the third exposition of a double fugue, at the same time it is also in compliance with the principles of *vertical* construction, as in Bach. Now then, is this or is this not a synthesis of the two styles?[44]

A little later, Webern reveals the intimate relationship between his success in fashioning an unprecedented canon in retrograde and the structure — but not only the structure! — of his row:

> The question could be raised how this is possible, I mean the canon just described: one pair of voices has Notes 5–12 and the other pair Notes 1–8. And is a strict canon among all four parts possible in spite of this? Well, now I must finally reveal how the "row" is constructed; this is, indeed, one of the most important concerns in this Quartet, perhaps the most fundamental one! You see, the second four notes of the row fashion their *intervals* from the *retrograde* of the first four, and the last four notes relate to the second four in the same way. But this means that the entire Quartet is based on nothing else than this specific *succession of four pitches*! Now it so happens that the first four notes of the "original" form of the row, transposed to B♭, yield the four letters BACH. Thus, my fugue subject presents this name three times (with the subject's three motives of four notes each making up the 12 notes of the row), but only *secretly* because, on the other hand, the original form NEVER occurs in this ostentatious transposition!!! All the same though, the *four notes* do underlie the *entire Quartet*!![45]

And here is the conclusion:

> Perhaps one could ask: what does the fugue subject "really" have in common with the scherzo subject, so that the reprise of the latter can also function as the third exposition of the fugue? Answer: in both cases the 12 notes of the row; that is, what rules here is altogether the MOST FAR REACHING RELATIONSHIP which can exist between two forms: they are *identical*!!! In both cases, moreover, the grouping of 3×4 notes; for it is also present in the subject of the Scherzo, even if it is not so conspicuous there. But it is there — and this I still would like to say in closing —, even reaching as far as it does in the row itself. Namely, as each successive four notes in the row constitute the *retrograde* of the preceding four, so is such a relationship given also in the scherzo subject's *rhythmic structure* from four-note group to four-note group, even if it does not become so clearly visible there because of the variations. For such a relationship within the row must also

carry an *obligation* for everything else that follows!! And with this I am saying that the subject is based not only on a group of FOUR PITCHES, but also on their rhythmic configuration![46]

The italics, the capitals, the double and triple exclamation points (all of which would surely have been edited out for publication in English) convey tremendous pride in authorship, of course; and there is also the specific combination of satisfaction in the achievement of structural consistency and triumph at its concealment from the uninitiated that was so typical of elitist modernism, and that reached its peak in the literature dealing with twelve-tone music. There is also the familiar joy in synthesizing the two great Bs — something that goes back at least as far as the "third B," Brahms, and constitutes the composer's claim to a place in an anointed line of succession.

What there is not is the thing one always finds in Berg: the assurance that the elaborate compositional means were a conduit to a cathartic emotional payoff. Webern's esthetic had become as "dehumanized" and impersonal as Stravinsky's. The joy he sought (and sought to convey) was the joy of wondrous contemplation. After the experience of Webern's sparse and attenuated sound-patterns one is not surprised to learn that his great passion outside of music was mountain climbing. If Schoenberg's expressionist music proffered a whiff of "air from another planet," Webern's rarefied twelve-tone compositions exuded the atmosphere of a solitary Alpine peak.

But there is something else as well in Webern's exuberant description of his creative produce — something that goes beyond esthetics into the domain of ethics — in all the talk of constraint, obedience, compliance, and obligation. We have circled back to the veneration for the Law with which we started (with Stravinsky's *Oedipus Rex* as our example); and it is hard not to connect Webern's artistic vision, in the context of the turbulent 1930s, with the Utopian or Arcadian (futuristic or nostalgic) cravings that dominated European social and political thought. Like Stravinsky's contemporaneous parables of submission, Webern's musical Utopias, the most orderly and disciplined worlds of music ever to have been conceived and realized by that time, seem in their tidy beauty of conception and their ruthlessly exacting realization to broach a theme that was on the mind of every artist then alive: the theme — ominous to some, inspiring to others — of art and totalitarianism.

CHAPTER 13

Music and Totalitarian Society

CASELLA AND RESPIGHI (FASCIST ITALY); ORFF, HINDEMITH, HARTMANN (NAZI GERMANY); PROKOFIEFF AND SHOSTAKOVICH (SOVIET RUSSIA)

It is as though mankind had divided itself between those who believe in human omnipotence (who think that everything is possible if one knows how to organize masses for it) and those for whom powerlessness has become the major experience of their lives.[1]

—HANNAH ARENDT, ORIGINS OF TOTALITARIANISM

Is it conceivable that certain historico-political conditions can have a profound and beneficial influence on art? Does it make any sense whatsoever to expect an artistic rebirth to come from a political rebirth? Can the work of a man of politics, however exceptional, influence that most intimate, personal and jealously guarded thing which is artistic creation?
Counter to every Romantic prejudice, our answer to this question is yes.[2]

—ALESSANDRO PAVOLINI, *CRITICA FASCISTA* (1 NOVEMBER 1926)

MASS POLITICS

With the destruction of the great imperial states of Europe, the great political question was what kind of state should replace them. The question was answered in Russia even before the end of the Great War, when the Bolshevik (Communist) party, led by Vladimir Ilyich Lenin (1870–1924), took power, in a coup d'état engineered on 25 October 1917, from the so-called Provisional Government that had been set up by liberal politicians, many of them noblemen, after the Russian revolution in February of that year, which had forced the abdication of the tsar. (The date of Lenin's coup is given here according to the "Old Style" or Julian calendar, then still used in Russia, which had long since been replaced in the rest of Europe and America by the "New Style" or Gregorian calendar, according to which the date of the coup was 7 November; the new Russian government adopted the New Style in 1918, but continued to celebrate its coming to power as the "October Revolution," even though the celebrations now took place in November.) The government that emerged from the coup called itself the government of Soviets, after the Russian word for council, the nominal seat of power under the new regime. In 1922, after the victorious conclusion of a civil war through which the Soviet government was able to reconsolidate

FIG. 13-1   Russia, the February Revolution: wives of soldiers and sailors marching on the Duma (parliament).

under its rule most of the territory of the former Russian Empire, the name of the country was changed to Union of Soviet Socialist Republics (USSR or Soviet Union for short). The Soviet Union lasted until 1991, when the power of the Communist Party collapsed and the country fell apart into its constituent republics, which then adopted various forms of government. Its hold of seventy-plus years made the Soviet Union the twentieth century's most durable totalitarian state.

Totalitarianism is the concentration of total political power into the hands of a ruling elite, in the most extreme case into the hands of a single person, who exercises that power in the name of a totalized, all-encompassing worldview or ideology that gives government a totalizing purpose: the achievement of a "total and perfected"[3] social order (to quote Massimo Bontempelli, a theorist of Italian fascism) through the imposition of direct state control in all areas of public and even private life; the total solution of economic problems; the total "reeducation" of citizens to erase the distinction between the political and any other potentially competing source of power (such as religious authority or the "romantic" concept of inherent human rights), the total mobilization of the population in a single plan of action (enforced by coercion and, if necessary, by terror), and often the total domination of the totalitarian state's weaker neighbors.

It is a term (coined in 1925 by Giovanni Gentile, an Italian philosopher) — and a definition — that has arisen out of the twentieth century's historical experience. There were coercive regimes in the past, to be sure, and many of the coercive techniques employed by the modern totalitarian states, such as the use of terror tactics and professional informers ("secret police"), had precedents in revolutionary France and later in the post-Napoleonic reaction. The term totalitarian is reserved for regimes that, having the use of modern surveillance technology and mass media, were able to operate on a far grander (more "totalizing") scale than their predecessors. The three great totalitarian powers that arose in postwar Europe, of which the Soviet Union was the first, often touted themselves as the world's only truly modern states, a claim that was based on their power to manipulate and mobilize mass psychology through propaganda. Thus totalitarianism thrived on "mass politics," rabble-rousing writ large.

The Soviet form of totalitarianism was, or purported to be, the realization of a social vision put forth by the political economist Karl Marx (1818–83) in a number of treatises, culminating in the massive *Das Kapital* ("Capital"), issued in three volumes (two of them posthumous) between 1867 and 1895. Marx's purportedly scientific analysis of capitalism, the entrepreneurial system through which the advanced societies of Europe and America had amassed their wealth, had concluded with a prediction that its built-in contradictions must engender a revolt from below that would put political and economic power in the hands of the social classes who actually produced the wealth that capitalists exploited for the sake of their own selfish enrichment.

An earlier document, *The Communist Manifesto*, which Marx and Friedrich Engels, another German economic theorist, issued in the great revolutionary year 1848, had ended with a prediction that ultimate revolutionary success would be enjoyed not by the bourgeois politicians who were leading the political disturbances that year, but by the urban workers who thus far had lacked the organization that would allow them to mobilize their collective strength. "Working men of all countries, unite!" the *Manifesto* ended; "You have nothing to lose but your chains." The outcome of proletarian revolution, Marx and Engels prophesied, would be a "classless" society — a perfected and homogenized democracy toward which the whole history of mankind had been striving, a utopia that would make all existing states and nations obsolete.

Marx and Engels, who had to flee to England after the revolutions in which they had participated were crushed, never dreamed that Russia would be the first country to witness a communist revolution such as they had predicted. Their doctrine assumed that the world revolution would begin in the countries where capitalist development had proceeded furthest, and where there was consequently a large urban "proletariat" or working class. Russia was economically backward and largely agrarian; indeed, not until 1861 were the laws of serfdom, the last official remains of feudalism, legally abolished in Russia. And by no stretch of the imagination (except the stretch of imagination that became mandatory in the Soviet Union) could the Leninist coup be called a mass revolution from below such as Marx and Engels had foreseen.

Instead, the Soviet Union was a country in which a communist revolution was decreed, from above, by an oligarchy that wielded total power in the name of "the masses" — the proletariat and the peasantry — and with the promise, never kept, that power would eventually pass into the hands of those whom Marx had envisioned as the actual revolutionary agents. The nominal source of Soviet political ideology in Marxism enabled the Soviet government to claim, all contradictions notwithstanding, that it was acting in accordance with Marx's "Hegelian" philosophy of historical necessity (a notion we have already seen applied to the history of music).

In the turmoil that followed the Great War, there was a great deal of communist agitation in the countries that emerged out of the defeated empires of Austria and Germany. The Soviet Communists were briefly successful, in fact, in exporting their brand of revolution abroad. "Soviet republics" were set up in 1919 through coups d'état in the Southern German state of Bavaria and in Hungary. Both were suppressed by bloody military interventions: in Bavaria by the German army, and in Hungary by a counterrevolutionary force led by Admiral Nicholas Horthy, who had been the commander of the Austro-Hungarian naval fleet during the Great War. The Bavarian state was reincorporated into the so-called Weimar Republic, a short-lived experiment in democracy that lasted until 1933, while Horthy proclaimed the reinstatement of the old kingdom of Hungary — which, however, he continued to rule as autocratic regent rather than allowing the return of the crown to the former Austrian emperor (thus the new, and land-locked, Hungarian state became a totalitarian but anti-Communist kingdom without a king, ruled by an admiral without a navy).

Faced with totalitarian threats from the Soviet Union (which, following Marx, declared "world revolution" to be its goal), racked by internal political agitation, and beset by economic chaos, the fledgling democracies of Central Europe were insecure and unstable. There was considerable sentiment everywhere that revolution could only be resisted by counterrevolution, or by a preemptive counter-totalitarianism to resist the spread of Soviet power. The looming presence of the Soviet Union on the world scene was thus among the factors that brought the other totalitarian regimes to power.

The first country in which such a counter-totalitarian regime was established turned out to be Italy, where a semi-legal political organization called the *Partito Nazionàle Fascista*, led by Benito Mussolini (1883–1945), seized power in a coup d'état (preceded by a dramatic "march on Rome") on 29 October 1922. Fascism began as a doctrine of nationalist resistance to revolutionary internationalism ("world revolution"). It took its name from the *fasces* (bundles), tightly wound gatherings of wooden rods from which axe heads projected, that were carried by imperial guards to symbolize unity and power in ancient Rome. Fascism upheld the role of elites in political leadership, and the ideal of social hierarchy.

Fascist society was to be ordered by syndicates, groups representing economic and social roles (skills, trades, professions), with ultimate political power residing in the managerial syndicate, which alone represented the interests of the society as a whole, or what was called the "corporate state." As in the case of Russian Communism, Italian Fascism ultimately devolved in practice into an autocratic dictatorship propped up by an enormous bureaucracy. The difference was that Fascist authoritarian power did not challenge or deny the right of individual enterprise, but sought instead to discipline or co-opt it. Its core constituency, in sharp contrast to Soviet power, was the bourgeoisie. Where Soviet Communism (or "Bolshevism") could be simplistically described as the use of directed force and violence to overthrow established hierarchies, Italian Fascism could be (just as simplistically) described as the use of directed force and violence to maintain them.

During the first decade of its existence, Italian Fascism was widely admired from afar. "Mussolini has made the trains run on time," ran the familiar refrain. His admirers in the 1920s included some leading politicians in the democratic governments of western

Europe and America. Even Winston Churchill, who as prime minister of the United Kingdom would eventually lead his nation in war against Mussolini, had warm words for him in the twenties. And he was downright popular among artists, particularly elite modernists who felt threatened by the empowerment of the uneducated working class.

Stravinsky, an uprooted Russian nobleman who had been personally impoverished as a consequence of the Bolshevik coup, was particularly vociferous in his praise of Mussolini, called *Il Duce* ("The Leader") by his followers. In 1931, Stravinsky allowed himself to be described in print by one of his spokesmen as "the dictator of the reaction against the anarchy into which modernism has degenerated."[4] Thus the "neoclassical" Stravinsky had consciously cast himself as the Mussolini of music, who wanted to do for modern music what the Duce promised to do for modern Europe. Nor was Stravinsky the only composer to draw an explicit connection, in the twenties, between the ideals of neoclassicism and those of Fascism. Alfredo Casella (1883–1947), an Italian composer educated in France and a great admirer of both Mussolini and Stravinsky, wrote of the "close affinity between the beneficial if sometimes chimerical objectives pursued by 'Mussolinism,' and the goal of intellectual restoration sought by the best Italians of the present day."[5] Both Fascism and the new currents in music, Casella wrote, were "movements full of audacity and life," which together were bringing about a national reawakening. He compared his country and its political renewal with "a young composer" of his acquaintance, "who, formerly involved, muddled and postromantic, has suddenly turned classical: that is to say, concerned with imitating Frescobaldi."[6] Invoking the name of Italy's great seventeenth-century organist, Casella was describing the Italian equivalent of the Franco-German "back to Bach" movement, but even better because, evoking a "still more remote past," it was more truly classical.

"Classicism is the natural form of Italian thought," Casella declared, "inherited directly from the Greeks, through Rome"[7] — the glorious Rome that Mussolini was reviving. "And this modern classicism," he went on, "far from being an artificial thing" like that of some composers he could name, "is with us an enforced result of language, tradition and daily contemplation of nature." That was why Italian neoclassicism, a "deep and fertile love of the past that now stirs young Italian musicians," had nothing in common with those "famous 'returns' to other geniuses with which Paris (and Berlin too) have so heaped us during the last years,"[8] for these were but the flabby goods of flabby and indolent democracies that lacked a glorious classical past of their own on which to draw.

What changed everything, ending the romance of Fascism forever, was Mussolini's eventual alliance with Adolf Hitler (1889–1945), his counterpart in Germany, who came to power in 1933 with a platform of barefaced racial intolerance; who practiced repressions and betrayals that rivaled and in some ways even exceeded those of the Soviet government, on which (many think) they were covertly modeled; whose insatiable territorial aggression led to the outbreak of the Second World War, the bloodiest military conflict in history; and who eventually committed the century's most horrendous acts of politically rationalized and legalized mass murder.

What brought Hitler and his National Socialist (Nazi) Party to power was, once again, the threat of Soviet-style subversion. As we already know from its potent propaganda impact on the arts, and especially on opera and music theater (see chapter 9), the German Communist Party had become very strong during the latter phases of the democratic Weimar Republic, which led many to mistrust democracy as a safeguard of their interests. It was his party's strong showing in the free parliamentary elections of 1932 that led to Hitler's being appointed Reichskanzler (Chancellor), the equivalent of prime minister, by Paul von Hindenburg, the last president of the Weimar Republic.

By the end of the next year, Hitler had done away with the democratic institutions that had allowed his rise to power and had begun the systematic persecutions, not only of political opponents but of minority groups such as Jews, Gypsies, homosexuals, and the mentally retarded. Nazi fury was especially vehement toward the Jews, who unlike the other targeted minorities had been politically active, culturally prominent, and therefore disproportionately powerful in the democratic republic, and who were easy scapegoats for the adverse economic conditions that led to the political unrest for which Hitler had promised a remedy. By the end of 1933, both Arnold Schoenberg and Kurt Weill, composers who had virtually nothing in common except their Jewish heritage, had fled Germany for their lives. (It is a measure of the then-perceived differences between totalitarian states that in retrospect seem kin that Schoenberg, who eventually went to the United States by way of France and Spain, first considered seeking refuge in the Soviet Union.) The Fascist and Nazi regimes lasted only until the end of the war Hitler had provoked and lost. The Soviet Union, though briefly Hitler's ally, had ended up on the other side of that conflict as a result of Hitler's betrayal. The wartime ally of the United States, Great Britain, and France, the Soviet Union emerged from the war badly scarred (since its territory had seen much of the worst fighting) but politically much strengthened. It almost immediately became the rival "superpower" to the United States. The period of international tension thus initiated, which lasted from about 1948 until the Soviet collapse some forty years later, was known as the Cold War. Its repercussions in music are a story in itself; for now we will consider music in the totalitarian countries chiefly in their "interwar" heyday.

MUSIC AND MUSIC-MAKING IN THE NEW ITALY

The most conspicuous feature of interwar totalitarianism as it affected music was the obvious fact that the two countries that had more or less dominated the international musical scene in the eighteenth and nineteenth centuries, Italy and Germany, were to be found among the totalitarian powers. It is also an obvious historical fact that Italy and Germany lost their commanding musical positions during the twentieth century. The obvious question, then, is how, and to what degree, these two facts may be related.

Italy's arts policy during the period of Fascist rule was far less intrusive than the policies of the other totalitarian states. This was in keeping with the principles of the corporate state, which respected individual initiative and the autonomy of the professions, and was therefore not inherently hostile to modernism. Stravinsky's cordial relationship with Mussolini is already evidence of this tolerance. In fact it was more than tolerance: Mussolini took pride in his advanced artistic views and was glad to have

Italy play host to international festivals of contemporary music like the one in Venice in 1925 at which Stravinsky performed his *Sonate* for piano "sotto il patronato di S. E. Benito Mussolini" (under the patronage of His Excellency Benito Mussolini).

Fascist cultural bureaucrats might be as philistine as their counterparts anywhere, issuing blustery, well-publicized manifestos against "atonal and polytonal honking" and "so-called objective music."[9] But Schoenberg, atonal honker par excellence, toured Italy with *Pierrot lunaire* in 1924, and his music continued to be performed there under prestigious auspices until 1938, five years after the composer had been forced out of Germany. Alban Berg's concert aria *Der Wein* had its Italian premiere at the Venice Biennale (biennial festival) in 1934; the composer, in attendance, was resoundingly fêted. *Wozzeck* was given at the Rome Opera as late as 1942, with the war raging. (By then it had been banned not only in Germany but in Berg's native Austria as well.)

Also performed during that wartime season was the ballet *The Miraculous Mandarin*, the most modernistic composition by Bartók, the most outspoken anti-Fascist among modernists, who by then had for two years been a voluntary exile from Europe. These examples of artistic tolerance, moreover, were more than matched by the racial tolerance that the Fascist government exhibited, in pointed contrast with Germany, until 1938. Refugees from Hitler like the conductors Bruno Walter (1876–1962) and Otto Klemperer (1885–1973) regularly performed in Mussolini's Italy. The *Sacred Service*, a setting of the Reform Jewish liturgy by Ernest Bloch (1880–1959), a Jewish composer of Swiss birth, had its world premiere over Radio Turin in 1934.

In contrast to Soviet Russia and Nazi Germany, where the banning of artworks was common, Mussolini's government actually suppressed a musical composition only once, in 1934. The unlucky work was an opera, *La favola del figlio cambiato* ("The fable of the changeling son") by Gian Francesco Malipiero (1882–1973), to a libretto by Pirandello. The ban was provoked not by the music, but by the setting of the second act, which takes place in a brothel. It exemplified the prudery that all totalitarian regimes have in common, regarding sexual license as a certain path to political disorder.

Still and all, the Fascist period did lend a new and unique coloration to Italian music. It was no coincidence, to begin with, that the most eminent composer of the period, and the one most lavishly promoted by the government, was known best (especially abroad) not for his operas but for his

FIG. 13-2   Ernest Bloch with his children: Lucien, Suzanne (who became a pioneering scholar and performer of early music), and Ivan.

symphonic music. Ottorino Respighi (1879–1936) did write operas, of course—ten of them. Few composers from opera's birthplace did not. (Even Casella wrote three, one of them in honor of Mussolini's imperialist campaign in Ethiopia.) But all agreed that Respighi's operas were a "secondary and uneven" branch of his output, to quote John C. G. Waterhouse,[10] the foremost English expert on twentieth-century Italian music. What brought him international fame were his superbly scored programmatic suites for orchestra: *Fontane di Roma* ("Fountains of Rome," 1916), *Pini di Roma* ("Pines of Rome", 1924), *Vetrate di chiesa* ("Church windows," 1925), *Trittico botticelliano* ("Botticelli triptych," 1927), *Feste romane* ("Roman festivals," 1928).

As their very titles suggest, these works were pictorial in character rather than narrative. As an orchestral colorist Respighi was rivaled during his lifetime only by Ravel. He developed his skills by studying the scores of Richard Strauss and by submitting his early attempts for critique to Rimsky-Korsakov, the best possible teacher, during the musical seasons of 1900–1901 and 1902–1903, which Respighi spent in St. Petersburg as leader of the viola section in the orchestra of the Maryinsky Theater. He prided himself particularly (as did Strauss) on the precision of his musical depictions.

The most famous instance of Respighi's precision—the use of a phonograph recording of a singing nightingale in the *Pines of Rome*—has become controversial. Such literalness, it is often argued, misses the artistic point. (Indeed, as long ago as the first century CE, the Greek writer Plutarch, in his biography of King Agesilaus of Sparta, recounted how the king, "being invited once to hear a man who admirably imitated the nightingale, declined, saying he had heard the nightingale itself.") More darkly, it has been suggested that both the recourse to what in 1924 was "high technology," and the extreme resort to realism (to the point of coercing the listener's imagination), were indicative of a Fascist mentality.

That may be overstating the case in retrospect. But the extravagantly vivid nationalism of Respighi's scores, sentimental and aggressive by turn, and almost unprecedented in Italian music, is less easy to disengage from the clamorous politics of the day. Some of it was nostalgic or archaic, in the neoclassical fashion. Respighi arranged three orchestral suites (1917, 1923, 1931) of *Antiche arie e danze per liuto* ("Ancient airs and dances for the lute") based on transcriptions by the pioneering Italian musicologist and early-music performer Oscar Chilesotti. More interesting were the works in which Respighi took his thematic material from Gregorian chant. These included the *Church Windows* for orchestra, but also several nonprogrammatic compositions, like the *Concerto gregoriano* for violin and orchestra (1921), the *Quartetto dorico* ("String quartet in the dorian mode," 1924) and the *Concerto in modo misolidio* ("Concerto in the mixolydian mode") for piano and orchestra (1925).

And then there is *Feste romane*, Respighi's most modernistic score, full of polytonal and polyrhythmic effects and heavy with somewhat belated reminiscences of Stravinsky's neoprimitivist ballets. Its first movement, "Circus Maximus," gives full rein to the pre- or anti-Christian sentiments that the Fascist regime glorified in the name of Il Duce, the new Caesar. Deploying a huge orchestra with virtuoso facility, Respighi evokes the sadistic spectacles of ancient Rome. In its central episode, a band of Christians (identifiable by their hymn) is stalked and set upon by lions (identifiable by their cacophonous snarling and roaring) while the crowd goes wild and the *bucinatores* (trumpeters) rend the air with fanfares. The ending, seemingly modeled on the blaring chords that bring Berlioz's "March to the Scaffold" (from the *Symphonie fantastique*) to its grisly conclusion, lacks the saving irony of its prototype.

The abnegation of Christian meekness and humility in favor of Roman aggression and audacity was an explicit plank in the Fascist platform. Its musical analogue, equally explicit, was the brash orchestral virtuosity Respighi's scores exemplified. In 1931, Mussolini sent around a circular to Italian diplomats abroad on the need for projecting a new image of Italy — spartan, ruthless, militaristic. Aware of the historic importance of music in framing the national reputation, the Duce gave it special attention, heaping special scorn on the recently deceased Enrico Caruso (1873 – 1921), the great tenor who had in his time been Italy's chief musical ambassador:

> I prescribe that from now on, no favor be shown in any way to musical initia-
> tives — operas, vocal recitals, concerts or musical soirées — and that they be treated
> icily. Exceptions will be made for symphony orchestras, whose performances give
> an idea of collective group discipline. All the rest must be ignored. It is high time
> that the world — that is, hundreds of millions of men — get to know a different
> type of Italian from that of yesterday — the eternal tenor and mandolinist for the
> entertainment of others. Caruso and the like were or are the old Italy.[11]

The chief musical representative of the new Italy, by Mussolini's implied definition, was Arturo Toscanini, in the opinion of many the century's most important conductor, who (among many greater accomplishments) was instrumental in popularizing the work of Respighi and other modern Italians abroad. Toscanini revolutionized orchestral performance precisely in the way that Mussolini emphasized (undoubtedly with Toscanini in mind), and in a way that also exemplified the ideal of objective performance practice identified in chapter 8 with neoclassicism. A Toscanini performance, to a degree previously unprecedented, was a display of "collective group discipline" that aimed above all for a scrupulous ("uninterpreted") realization of the musical text.

At the time Mussolini came to power, Toscanini was known primarily as a conductor of opera, in which field he was already supreme. Since 1898, though with several interruptions for engagements and residencies abroad (including a seven-year stint at New York's Metropolitan Opera), he had been the artistic director of La Scala, the Milan opera theater and Italy's premiere performing arts institution. His range was broad, encompassing Wagner, Debussy, and Chaikovsky in addition to the full Italian repertoire. He had given the world premieres of Leoncavallo's *I pagliacci* (1892) and of two operas by Puccini: *La bohème* (1896) and *La fanciulla del west* ("The girl of the golden West," 1910). He was the first non-German to be invited to conduct at the yearly Wagner Festival in Bayreuth.

Unlike most opera specialists, Toscanini had a longstanding interest in the symphonic repertoire. He conducted the Municipal Orchestra of Turin from 1898, and gave with it the world premiere of Verdi's last major work, *Quattro pezzi sacri* ("Four sacred pieces," including a Stabat Mater and a Te Deum) for chorus and orchestra. He first achieved world celebrity as a symphonic conductor during the 1920–1921 season, when, already past the age of fifty, he made a tour of Europe and America with a newly constituted La Scala Orchestra (called the Orchestra Arturo Toscanini for the occasion). In under eight months they gave 133 performances before audiences totaling over a quarter of a million.

These concerts were received everywhere as a revelation, in part for purely technical reasons. The crisp attacks and cutoffs, the transparent textures, the rhythmic precision of Toscanini's performances far exceeded contemporary standards, as may be corroborated by listening to the recordings he made with his orchestra at the Victor Talking Machine studios in Camden, New Jersey. Critics used to the Germanic approach to Beethoven and Brahms complained about Toscanini's relentless tempos and his "small, short-breathed and over-detailed"[12] conceptions (to quote Richard Aldrich, the reviewer for the *New York Times*). But audiences found the approach irresistible, and so, in consequence, did concert managers.

By 1926 Toscanini was dividing his time between La Scala and the New York Philharmonic Orchestra (which had been led, from 1909 to 1911, by Gustav Mahler, the supreme apostle of the elastic German Romantic tradition). After two years as guest and associate conductor of the orchestra, Toscanini was appointed music director of the Philharmonic, which had just merged with its chief rival, the New York Symphony, to become the New York Philharmonic-Symphony Orchestra. The next year he resigned from La Scala; except for guest appearances at festivals, his opera days were over.

He led the New York orchestra, which he took on triumphal tours of Europe, until 1936. He retired at the age of sixty-nine and returned to Italy; but the very next year, in 1937, he received an invitation from David Sarnoff, the head of the National Broadcasting Company, to return to America to lead a handpicked orchestra that would be created for him, that would do its performing on the radio rather than in the concert hall, and that would record the entire standard symphonic repertoire for Victor, the producers of Toscanini's first records, which was by then a subsidiary of Sarnoff's corporation. Toscanini led the NBC Symphony for seventeen years, until he re-retired, in 1954, at the age of eighty-seven. He died in New York in January 1957, two months short of his ninetieth birthday.

For the culminating phase of his career, then, Toscanini worked almost exclusively through the broadcast and recording media, achieving through technology a fame no "classical" musician had ever previously known (except, perhaps, and ironically, Caruso). He fulfilled, and then some, Mussolini's musical prediction for the New Italy, which is also ironic, since Toscanini and Mussolini had fallen out in the 1920s (leading indirectly to the conductor's retirement from La Scala), and during the 1930s and 1940s, decades spent almost entirely in America, Toscanini traded heavily on his anti-Fascist credentials and lent his celebrated name and priceless services to Allied wartime propaganda.

For this reason it may seem bizarre to discuss Toscanini in the context of totalitarianism. And yet the kind of performances he achieved were attributable as much to the dominating force of his personality, and his dictatorial behavior, as they were to his musical insight. Musicians who played under him, and who were subject to summary dismissal, experienced a veritable reign of terror that is documented not only in anecdotes but in recordings that were surreptitiously made of Toscanini's appalling outbursts of temper. Toscanini justified his behavior precisely the way political dictators do, by claiming that the ends justified the means. "Gentlemen, be democrats in life but aristocrats in art,"[13] he told his orchestras. Only the strictest hierarchy of command could achieve the precision results for which Toscanini became famous, and which the musical world has treasured ever since. But if Mussolini cannot be excused his violations of human rights because he made the trains run on time, is it right to excuse Toscanini's tyrannical behavior because he made his orchestras play in time, or submit more obediently to the composer's notations?

Toscanini's hostility toward Mussolini, and his fortuitous situation as an American "exile," made the double standard easier to maintain; but with historical distance it is clear that Toscanini was no political resister. He actually declined his one documented opportunity to give public voice to principled political opposition to the dictator, when he refused to sign an anti-Fascist manifesto circulated in 1925 by the philosopher Benedetto Croce. His run-ins with Mussolini had mainly to do with the Duce's attempts to infringe upon the conductor's authority at La Scala. It was a matter of symbolic trifles, like playing the Fascist hymn (*La Giovinezza*, "Youth") before performances, or displaying the leader's portrait in the foyer. The story of Toscanini vs. Mussolini was the tale of two Duci engaged in a protracted battle of wills.

And so the difficult problems raised by the relationship between Toscanini's methods and his results continue to nag. It is a particularly crisp and concentrated instance of the old, perpetually renegotiated dilemma concerning the relationship between the competing, possibly incompatible ideals of equality and excellence. Toscanini's revolutionary transformation of orchestral performance, amounting to the creation of a new standard of clean, efficient, uncomplicated (in a word, streamlined) execution, chimed well with Fascist ideals of polity. He contributed more than anyone else toward turning the art of musical performance into an "Art of Being Ruled," to borrow the title of a book of essays by Wyndham Lewis, a British modernist writer and painter who was notoriously a Fascist sympathizer in the years preceding the Second World War. Can we now endorse the artistic results and at the same time ignore or reject the political parallel? If we cannot, is artistic excellence achievable within a democratic society, or is it to be regarded as politically tainted?

DEGENERACY

In any case, a stance of high moral dudgeon is harder to maintain with respect to Mussolini's Italy than it is with respect to the other twentieth-century totalitarian states, whose histories were incomparably bloodier. Fascist Italy entered the phase that now inspires universal condemnation — primarily for its imperialist adventures in Africa and Albania, and its persecution of minorities — in its last decade, beginning in the mid-1930s, chiefly in consequence of its military alliance with Nazi Germany, with whose policies it had to maintain a united front.

FIG. 13-3 Lothar Heinemann, "Germany, the Land of Music" (1935), a poster that strongly conveys the subordination of art to totalitarian political power.

The Nazis' arts policies were motivated by the same horridly explicit racial and ethnic biases as their political policies. Indeed there was no separate or separable arts policy: arts censorship in Nazi Germany was merely an application of Nazi race theory to art, for which reason the idea of "Nazi esthetics" is entirely incoherent both as theory and as practice. What follows, therefore, is no more than a selection of tragicomic vignettes from the history of that application.

Insofar as Nazi esthetics had a theory, it followed the theory of "degeneracy" put forth by the nineteenth-century Italian psychiatrist Cesare Lombroso (1836–1909), who ended his career as a professor of criminal anthropology at the University of Turin. Lombroso sought through empirical science to account for criminal tendencies — and thus (the chilling part) to predict and preemptively control them — by identifying the "born criminal" (*l'uomo deliquente*) as a distinct anthropological "type" with measurable physical and mental "stigmata." (Lombroso checked particularly for imperfections in the shape of the outer ear.) Such "stigmata," Lombroso alleged, were the product of a morbid genetic regression brought about by inbreeding (the Nazis added miscegenation, interracial mating), or by what we now call substance abuse.

The application of these theories to art and literature was first made by Lombroso's disciple Max Nordau (1849–1923), a Hungarian physician, in a massive two-volume treatise called *Entartung* ("Degeneration"), which appeared in 1893 and went through many printings. Nordau drew many sensational connections — or rather, asserted many facile analogies — between genetic mental or physiological decay as described by Lombroso and fin-de-siècle "decadence" in the arts, which amounted, from Nordau's middle-class perspective, to "contempt for traditional views of custom and morality." Nordau maintained that the eroticized mysticism and egomania of contemporary art (in music, say, Scriabin's), its overrefined estheticism (as in, say, Debussy), or its gruesome naturalism (as in, say, Strauss or Stravinsky) all had the same pathological basis.

That this was pseudoscience in the service of philistinism is apparent from the nature of the "evidence" that Nordau adduced, entirely speculative and tautological:

> There might be a sure means of proving that the application of the term "degenerates" to the originators of all the *fin de siècle* movements in art and literature is not arbitrary, that it is no baseless conceit, but a fact; and that

would be a careful physical examination of the persons concerned, and an inquiry into their pedigree. In almost all cases, relatives would surely be met who were undoubtedly degenerate, and one or more stigmata discovered which would indisputably establish the diagnosis of "degeneration." Science has found, together with these physical stigmata, others of a mental order, which betoken degeneracy quite as clearly as the former; so that it is not necessary to measure the cranium of an author, or to see the lobe of a painter's ear, in order to recognize the fact that he belongs to the class of degenerates.[14]

For the Nazis, the process of verification became even easier: all that was needed was evidence of "Jewish blood." Ironically enough, Max Nordau himself was not only Jewish but also an early Zionist leader; his prime example of artistic degeneracy was Wagner, and his prime diagnostic symptoms were anti-Semitism and "Teutomaniacal Chauvinism." But any number can play the same pseudoscientific game, and the theory of degeneracy was easily adapted to a new set of politically predicated stigmata. The adaptation became notorious in 1937, when the German government sponsored a huge show of otherwise unshowable modern art in Munich under the title *Entartete Kunst*, "Degenerate Art." It was followed the next year by a somewhat smaller exhibition in Düsseldorf, called *Entartete Musik*.

A deliberately ape-like caricature of the blackface title character from Ernst Krenek's *Jonny spielt auf*, the wildly popular "Zeitoper" of a decade before (see chapter 9) graced the cover of the 1938 exhibition catalogue(Fig. 13-1), which contained a list or index of banned Jewish musicians, including a few who were either mistakenly or deliberately made honorary Jews for the occasion: Alexander Glazunov, Maurice Ravel, Erik Satie, Camille Saint-Saëns. (Krenek himself was listed as *jüdisch versippt*, Jewish by marriage.)

There were a couple of somewhat more serious errors of classification. Because he was of Slavic blood and a naturalized Parisian, Igor Stravinsky was assumed to be a foe of the Nazis, and his portrait was displayed at the exhibit with the insulting caption, "Who ever invented the story that Stravinsky is descended from Russian noble stock?" The mortified composer, through his German publisher, protested to the German Bureau of Foreign Affairs at his inclusion, explicitly disavowing any taint of "Jewish cultural Bolshevism."[15] As he had previously taken the precaution of submitting an affidavit to his publisher, in lieu of the official Nazi questionnaire establishing Aryan heredity, and as the publisher had placed an item in the papers quoting Richard Strauss on Stravinsky's enthusiasm for Hitler's ideas, Stravinsky received a declaration from the German government affirming its "benevolent neutrality" toward him. (The 74-year-old Richard Strauss was not only Germany's musical elder statesman, but also for a time the figurehead president of the official Nazi musical supervisory organization, the *Reichsmusikkammer*.)

And because he was a citizen of Hungary, an ally of Germany, Béla Bartók was assumed, like the composers of Mussolini's Italy, to be a friend of the "Reich," and was therefore left out of the *Entartete Musik* exhibit. The mortified composer, who had refused his publisher's request to file what he called "the questionnaire about grandfathers,"[16] protested his exemption, attached the E-word to himself, and tried to prevent the performance of his music in Germany and Italy. He wrote to an official of the German Radio in 1939, about his own First Piano Concerto, that he was "astonished that such 'degenerate' music should be selected for — of all things — a radio broadcast"[17] in the Nazi state. But of course the broadcast went on as scheduled: as these examples show, for the Nazis the first question about a work of art was never, What does it say? It was, rather, Who is speaking, friend or foe?

There was no principle to override this double standard. Erich Wolfgang Korngold's opera *Das Wunder der Heliane*, mentioned in chapter 9, aroused Nazi antipathies almost as strongly as *Jonny spielt auf*. Almost the minute it came to power, Hitler's government banned it. The stated reason both for the original antipathy and for the ban was the opera's "decadent" nude scene. But Reichsmusikkammerpräsident Strauss's *Salome* also had a nude scene, even more brazen (and certainly more garish) than Korngold's, not to mention a libretto by Oscar Wilde, the archdegenerate of all degenerates, and yet it played steadily to good Aryan audiences throughout the Hitler years.

True, Salome perishes at the end of "her" opera, while Heliane triumphs at the end of "hers," but the real reason for the ban on the latter was the Jewishness of its composer, who had to flee as soon as the Nazis annexed Austria to the German Reich; and the reason for *Salome*'s survival was the venerable name of *its* composer — "international celebrity, German, late romanticist, advocate for copyright protection and senior citizen,"[18] in the words of Pamela Potter, the best-informed historian of the Nazi musical establishment. It was his interest in lengthening the term of copyright for composers that induced Strauss to accept from Hitler a bureaucratic post. Strauss's collaboration — like that of the great conductor Wilhelm Furtwängler (1886–1954), Toscanini's only rival in fame and authority from within the Germanic-romantic "mainstream" — offered the Nazis the most potent insurance they could buy against the charge of barbarism.

YOUTH CULTURE

That charge was frequently leveled against the music of Carl Orff (1895–1982), the foremost German composer to achieve international eminence during the Nazi years, and the only one whose music has survived in the international repertory. The work that made him famous was *Carmina burana* (1936), a "scenic cantata" (sometimes staged as a ballet with singing, like Stravinsky's *Les noces*) based on "Goliard" poems — Latin poems by German students of the late middle ages that lustily celebrated the vagabond life. The largest extant collection of Goliard poems is a manuscript now kept at the Bavarian State Museum in Munich, but which had belonged for centuries to the Catholic monastery at Benediktbeuren, a town nearby; *Carmina burana* means "Songs of Beuren.") Orff, who lived all his life in Munich, made a selection of songs from the manuscript, which he knew from a nineteenth-century edition that contained only the texts, and grouped them into "scenes" on the basis of their subject matter: songs of fatalism under the heading *Fortuna imperatrix mundi* ("Dame Fortune, the ruler of the world"); nature songs (*Primo vere*, "In early spring"); carousing songs (*In taberna*, "In the tavern"); songs of love (*Cour d'Amours*, "At Venus's court"). The music — scored for eight soloists, three choruses, and a huge orchestra including five percussionists, full of diatonic melodies in a vaguely antique ("modal" or at least "leading-toneless") style, and driven by vigorous, unyielding ostinatos — was a streamlined "populist" (in German, *Völkisch*) adaptation of Stravinsky's neoprimitivist manner that made its appeal to a much wider audience than did the modernist ("elitist") original.

The opening number ("O Fortuna," Ex. 13-1a), which also serves as the finale, sets the tone. Although written out in full, it is a strophic song in three stanzas (the first a bit truncated, the last somewhat embellished) to a tune that until the final melisma uses only the first five degrees of a D-minor (or, arguably, a "Dorian") scale. Although composed by Orff, it is meant to sound like an authentic medieval tune (of which the Benediktbeuren manuscript actu-ally contains many). The climactic number

FIG. 13-4   Carl Orff, 1930.

("Tempus est iocundum," "It is the time of joy"; Ex. 59-1b) is of a similar design, this time in five slightly varied strophes, and followed by a melismatic soprano solo — "Dulcissime" (O Sweetie!; Ex. 13-1c) — that, without actually saying so, is as

EX. 13-1A   Carl Orff, *Carmina burana*, no. 1, "O fortuna," mm. 5–28

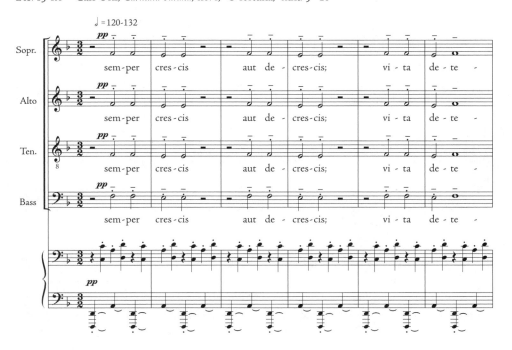

EX. 13-1A (continued)

unmistakably a portrait of feminine sexual ecstasy as the preceding chorus, with its huffing and puffing ("oh, oh, oh . . .") had been one of masculine potency.

After its 1937 premiere, at which a certain amount of unofficial discomfort was expressed at the frank sexual innuendoes, *Carmina burana*'s instant popularity and international success won it official approval as a display piece celebrating Nazi "youth

EX. 13-1A (continued)

EX. 13-1B   Carl Orff, *Carmina burana*, no. 22, "Tempus est iocundum"

EX. 13-1B (continued)

culture." In 1943, at the height of the war, Orff followed up with a sequel, *Catulli carmina* ("Songs of Catullus"), a setting of erotic poems by the Roman poet named in the title. Subtitled "Ludi scaenici" ("scenic games"), it was another ballet with songs, consisting of twelve *a cappella* choruses framed by a huge choral-instrumental number that in its scoring for soloists, chorus, four pianos, and a huge battery requiring the services of a timpanist and a dozen assistant percussionists, announced even more plainly its

EX. 13-1B   *(continued)*

EX. 13-1C   Carl Orff, *Carmina burana*, no. 23, "Dulcissime"

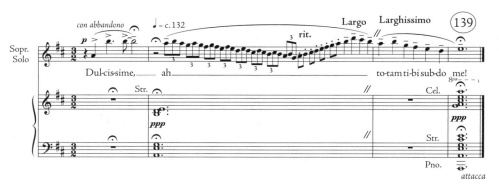

derivation from Stravinsky's *Noces*. (Stravinsky was by this time banned again in Nazi Germany, not for musical or ethnic reasons but simply because he was an "enemy national" living in the United States.) Somehow Orff managed to strip the already virtually denuded style of *Carmina burana* even further down in the new piece, producing an even franker, ruder, more athletic eroticism.

In the passage shown in Ex. 13-2, for example, the poet hymns at length the beauty of his beloved's breasts. Just like medieval churchmen confronted with the Hebrew psalms or the Song of Songs, the puritanical critics of the official Nazi press managed to reconcile themselves to the content of Orff's cantatas by giving them allegorical, "politically correct" interpretations. The critic of the *Zeitschrift für Musik*, since Schumann's day the leading German musical paper, claimed that *Carmina burana* was "in terms of expression, a Song of Songs praising the strength of the unbroken life-instinct," hence an antidote to "decadence," and exulted that "German musical creativity in our day can produce such a work."[19] The *Völkischer Beobachter* ("People's observer"), the Nazi Party's official organ, pointed to Orff's cantatas as "the kind of clear, stormy, and yet always disciplined music that our time requires."[20]

Stravinsky, when he came to know these imitations of his own youthful style, dismissed them with a snicker as "Neo-Neanderthal."[21] (More recently it has been described as "pop Gothic.") There were many who saw Orff's celebrations of youthful vitality as debased (if not newly—and hypocritically—"decadent"), and saw their popularity as evidence of that fact. And there were just as many who dismissed such criticism as a remnant of high-modernist snobbery and greeted the simple music for its infectiousness, its ability to bond an audience in the spirit of *Gemeinschaft*, "community." Such defenders of Orff could remind his critics that not only Nazis, and not only

EX. 13-2   Carl Orff, *Catulli carmina*, "mammae molliculae"

EX. 13-2 *(continued)*

totalitarians, had called for art to fulfill a communitarian aim and carry a social message. (In Weimar Germany, we may recall from chapter 9, Weill and Eisler, not to mention Brecht, had made a similar appeal from the political left, and might well have welcomed music like Orff's had it been set to a different sort of text.)

Back at them comes the argument that in Nazi Germany the spirit of *Gemeinschaft* had been hopelessly tainted by *Volksgemeinschaft*, "ethnic communalism," a tribalism that was as much an exclusionary as a communitarian sentiment. In its insistent simplicities and its hypnotic rhythmic monotony, Orff's music, which so effectively roused primitive, unreflective enthusiasm in millions, was inviting (or compelling) its listeners, to put it as Hitler did, to "think with their blood" instead of their brains, and was thus humanly as well as artistically debasing. Historically, the best (or most specifically) grounded approach to the question of Orff's place within the culture of Nazism would situate the reception of his orgiastic and "paganistic" cantatas within the context of the propaganda war the Nazi Party was waging against the Christian churches of Germany, both Catholic and Protestant, which resisted the Nazi doctrine of hatred as long as possible.

The controversy, which reached a head in 1936–37 (the period of *Carmina burana*'s genesis and premiere), ended with a ban on all political activities by clergymen outside their houses of worship. In the decree silencing the churches, promulgated on 12 September 1938, Hitler's deputy Rudolf Hess (1894–1987) emphasized the need to combat Christianity ("a doctrine from the Near East and Jewish through and through") not by direct polemics but by counterexample:

> The more we National Socialists avoid religious controversies, abstain from Church ceremonies, but on the other hand win the confidence of the people by our dutifulness, justice, and loyalty, the more men will feel that they belong to National Socialism. The more National Socialism is seen as a blessing as a result of our work and the conviction spreads that Providence is with us and with our work, the more people will recognize that National Socialism is a God-ordained order and institution. Thus they will gradually become increasingly alienated by the Churches and their dogmas in the degree to which the latter stand in our way.[22]

After the outbreak of the war in 1939, the Nazi government actually tried to set up a competing anti-Christian and explicitly neo-Pagan religious denomination, that of the *Gottgläubige* ("Believers in God"). Beginning in 1940, Orff's cantata was performed at Party and government functions, and received the status of a quasi-official anthem.

The continuing popularity of Orff's cantatas since the war, both in and outside of Germany, has worked to counteract the taint of association. Debate has proceeded on a new footing, the main question now being whether the origin or original context of an artwork has a decisive bearing on its interpretation or its effect, or whether works like *Carmina burana* and *Catulli carmina* can now be taken at face value and enjoyed as innocently mindless fun and games. Orff's continued popularity has also quickened postwar debate as to whether hermetic, difficult modernist art, insofar as it is so much less easily exploited for possibly unsavory or even criminal political purposes, might after all be morally superior to "accessible" art. (Whatever Schoenberg may have been, to put it bluntly, at least he was no rabble-rouser.) One of the things that make these questions hard is the fact that they cannot be answered simply on the basis of the composer's intention. Nothing that has been said about Orff's work is evidence of his own political or social beliefs. After the war, like most Germans, he claimed to have been opposed to the Hitler regime. The present discussion has not accused him of Nazism, just as the discussion of Respighi made no claims about his personal commitment to Mussolini's policies. (We have far stronger evidence of Stravinsky's commitments in that regard than we do of Respighi's or Orff's.) Were it established that Orff was anti-Nazi and Respighi anti-Fascist, the information would be relevant to their biographies, but not of decisive import in interpreting their works, which left their hands the moment they were performed and have in any case outlived their authors. The question of political meaning is as much or more a question about reception as it is a question about intention.

But neither intention nor reception alone can be decisive. If an author's intention were the sole criterion for evaluating his work, Wagner's *Ring* would surely draw picket lines today (as it does in the state of Israel); and if reception were the sole criterion, then Beethoven and Bruckner would draw picket lines, since the Nazis claimed them, along with Wagner, as spiritual forerunners. In any case, musical life in Nazi Germany continued to function at a high professional level. The performance traditions that had previously been established for the German classics reached new heights of achievement, as recordings that continue to circulate, and to be enjoyed everywhere, attest.

This, too, has made for aesthetic quandaries: since the Second World War it has been much more difficult to claim that exposure to the greatest masterpieces of art is inherently ennobling. The Germans continued to be sincere and discriminating lovers of their finest music (and thanks to Furtwängler, experienced the finest performances of it) all through the period of Nazi atrocity. It did not inhibit the prevailing barbarism of the period in any way. (And in this sad observation may unexpectedly lie Orff's best defense; for if Bach and Beethoven could not prevent Nazi barbarity is it hard to claim that Orff could have inspired it.)

VARIETIES OF EMIGRATION

The only musicians who could avoid questions of complicity with the Nazi regime were the many who emigrated from Germany during the dozen years of its ascendancy. But even emigration had its degrees and nuances. Some emigration was forced, like that of Jews or Communists or others for whom remaining in Germany would have been fatal. The most celebrated forced emigrant was of course Schoenberg, formerly an ardent German cultural chauvinist, who defiantly reconverted to the Hebrew faith of his ancestors in Paris in 1933, and who went on from there to the United States, where he spent the last seventeen years of his life, eight of them (1936–44) on the faculty of the University of California at Los Angeles. Other famous forced emigrés included Weill, Eisler, and Brecht, the conductors Bruno Walter and Otto Klemperer, the cellist Emanuel Feuermann (1902–42), and the music scholars Alfred Einstein (1880–1952) and Curt Sachs (1881–1959). All of them ended up in the United States, the musical life of which was enormously enriched by their presence, and which willy-nilly found itself at the end of the war with the greater part of the former European musical élite among its citizens.

For Bartók, Stravinsky, and Hindemith were also in America at war's end. They were voluntary emigrés. Bartók alone was purely a principled exile; as we have already seen he was a committed anti-Fascist and an outspoken opponent of the Nazi regime. He did not have to fear for his life or livelihood in Hungary, and he suffered many hardships in America, where he was not yet by any means a celebrity. He had to eke out a living as a piano teacher and occasional performer, and as the holder of a research sinecure in folklore that was tendered to him by Columbia University as an act of charity, at the instigation of Paul Henry Láng (1901–91), a Hungarian-born professor of musicology there. (Bartók's stature as a composer rose tremendously, ironically enough, almost immediately after his death in New York from leukemia in September 1945.)

Stravinsky's emigration was more opportunistic than voluntary. The beginning of the war found him already in the United States, at the invitation of Harvard University, which had offered him a guest professorship to deliver the lectures that were later published as *Poetics of Music*. Although his political sympathies at the time of the war's outbreak were equivocal to say the least, Stravinsky decided to remain in America after his Harvard tenure expired, so as to avoid the turbulent conditions on the European continent that would have made concentration on his work difficult. (He had sought neutral territory during World War I as well, which he sat out in Switzerland.) He bought a house in Hollywood, California, in 1940, not far from where Schoenberg was living, and took American citizenship in 1945. Their physical proximity did not lead to any lessening of the personal and esthetic tensions that had divided Schoenberg and Stravinsky in Europe. During the eleven years that they lived as neighbors they met only twice, by chance.

The Hindemith case was complicated. By the time the Nazis came to power he was not only a famous performer but was also long established as the foremost composition teacher in Berlin next to Schoenberg, and it was inevitably "next to Schoenberg" that he was viewed. Thus despite his avant-garde reputation he was deemed, at least by comparison, acceptable to the new regime, and there is evidence of his early wish to accommodate it. The more radical Nazi contingents opposed him, however, and launched a press campaign in 1934 to discredit him on the basis of his earlier associations

with leftist musicians and his continuing associations with Jewish playing partners, not to mention his scandalous early operas and a chamber concerto in which he was accused of parodying a favorite Nazi march.

Furtwängler came to his defense in a widely disseminated newspaper article, "Der Fall Hindemith" ("The Hindemith case"), in which the conductor put Hindemith forth as the model for German composers of the day. The result was an intensified backlash against him in the press and at public Nazi functions. Although he suffered no material reprisals or personal threats, Hindemith decided in 1937 that he had best leave the country, in part because his wife was Jewish and he expected eventually to lose his professorship on that account. After three years in Switzerland

FIG. 13-5   Paul Hindemith with viola, photo ca. 1930.

he came to America. In 1941 he was appointed Battel Professor of the Theory of Music at Yale University, a position he held (eventually part time) until 1953, when he returned to Europe, spending his last decade again in Switzerland.

Hindemith did not consider himself a voluntary émigré, but felt that he had been hounded out of Germany. He left resentfully, and worked out his feelings of alienation on his American colleagues and pupils, with whom he achieved a legendary reputation for haughty arrogance and disparagement. (He awarded only twelve students masters' degrees in composition during his entire tenure at Yale.) Although his reputation gave him considerable authority, and he had an impact both on music education and on American composing styles, Hindemith held himself aloof from the musical life of his adopted country despite his accepting American citizenship in 1946 and holding it to the end of his life. His most public (and possibly his most influential) activity in America, curiously, was in organizing and leading a Collegium Musicum at Yale—that is, a performing group not for contemporary but for "ancient" music, with which he made his only American appearances as a performer during his period of residence there, and with which he made some records. In short, his life in America ironically paralleled the sort of life he would have led had he remained in Germany: one of withdrawal from public life, or what was known in Germany as "inner emigration."

That Hindemith had inner emigration on his mind even while still in Germany is evident on the basis of his most celebrated work, the three-act opera *Mathis der Maler* ("Matthias the painter"), composed to his own libretto, which he began writing in 1934, the year of his disillusionment, and which received its premiere in Switzerland in 1938, after he had gone into exile. (A symphony on themes from the opera, also called *Mathis der Maler*, was actually composed in advance of the rest; Furtwängler gave it its very successful premiere in March 1934, and it became the focal point of his attempted defense of the composer.) Ostensibly based on the life and times of Matthias Grünewald, the fifteenth-century German religious painter, the opera depicts an artist who retreats, spiritually wounded, from the turbulent world of contemporary politics—a world replete with class warfare and book burnings—into the timeless world of art.

It was in fact an allegory of the composer's own inner emigration, as Hindemith pointedly implied in his program essay for the premiere, in which the expatriated composer identified himself not only with Mathis, who "decides in his work to develop traditional art to its fullest extent," but also, and predictably, with J. S. Bach, who "two centuries later proves to be a traditionalist in the stream of musical development."[23] At a time of anxiety and threat (in Hindemith's day political, in Bach's, presumably, merely stylistic), the true artist serves his art by withdrawal, enabling its preservation.

This was a new conception of Bach's role as universal model, born of a new twist in the politics of the twentieth century. Hindemith, who by the rather embittered end of his life was considered a very conservative composer indeed, would remain faithful to his new image of Bach for the duration of his composing career. In a sentimental lecture called *Johann Sebastian Bach: Heritage and Obligation*, delivered in Hamburg to honor Bach's bicentennial in 1950, the former prophet of *neue Sachlichkeit* located Bach's crowning achievement in the complete transcendence of the worldly: his "activity has become pure thought, freed from all incidents and frailties of structural manifestation, and he who ascended relentlessly has defeated the realm of substance and penetrated the unlimited region of thought."[24] In the works that followed *Mathis der Maler*, and especially in those of his American years, Hindemith tried his best to follow "his" Bach into the realm of pure speculation. During his brief Swiss exile he tried his hand at speculative theory, coming up with a revised tonal system to save the "natural" or "acoustic" basis of harmony in an age of "artificial" systems like Schoenberg's. His system, embodied in a textbook called *Unterweisung in Tonsatz* (1937–39; published in English in 1942 as *The Craft of Musical Composition*), replaced the circle of fifths with a new tonal hierarchy, purportedly derived from the overtone series, that arranged the degrees of the chromatic scale "concentrically," in intervallic pairs of increasing functional distance from the keynote (Ex. 13-3): dominant/subdominant, submediant/mediant, flat mediant/flat submediant, supertonic/flat subtonic, "Neapolitan" supertonic/leading tone, tritone (equidistant from the keynote in both directions).

EX. 13-3   Paul Hindemith, "Series I" from *Unterweisung in Tonsatz*

One of the first works Hindemith completed in America, *Ludus tonalis* ("The game [or play] of tones," 1942), subtitled "Studies in Counterpoint, Tonal Organization, and Piano Playing," was a systematic practical application of his theories in emulation of Bach's *Well-Tempered Clavier*. Instead of Bach's twenty-four preludes and fugues, Hindemith presents twelve fugues (since his system did not distinguish major and minor modes), framed by a Preludium and a Postludium (the Preludium in mirror inversion) and connected by eleven interludes that bridge their keys and moods. The keys are presented in an order corresponding to Ex. 13-3, which Hindemith called "Series I." (Series II is an array of harmonic intervals that assigns a root to each so that logical progressions can be plotted.) As one can see from the way in which Fugue No. 5 ends (Ex. 13-4)—somewhat willfully or wistfully, perhaps—on a plain and placid major triad, Hindemith has indeed withdrawn from the mad stylistic rat-race of the twentieth century in which he had played a very conspicuous role before the commotions and coercions of the times had overwhelmed him, in favor of an imagined tonal utopia—a far, far better (or at least more orderly) place than the one history had wrought.

EX. 13-4   Paul Hindemith, *Ludus tonalis*, Interlude and Fugue no. 5 (in E)

Even more tellingly, Hindemith revised some of his earlier, expressionistic or new-objective works so that they might enter his timeless tonal paradise. The most radical and striking revision of this kind involved the song cycle *Das Marienleben* ("The life of Mary"), op. 27 (1923), to ecstatic poems by Rainer Maria Rilke. The religious subject matter of this particular work made its compliance with timeless values and verities especially urgent. Hindemith began revising it in 1936, just as he was formulating his new rules of harmony, and finished the new version in 1948. The cycle's key sequence was reordered in conformity with Series I, its harmonies were clarified in conformity with Series II, and its melodic writing was tamed to make it more practicable for the singer.

The two versions of *Das Marienleben* have become a touchstone for criticism; one's preference for the original (composed as an act of passionate engagement with the novelties and challenges of the day) or the revision (composed as an act of withdrawal from the same, amounting to an inner emigration) says a lot about one's attitude toward modernism. The endings of both versions of the final song, "Vom Tode Mariä III" ("Third song on the death of Mary") are given for comparison in Ex. 13-5.

SHADES OF GRAY

The most noteworthy and literal case of inner emigration among composers who remained in Germany was that of the Munich composer Karl Amadeus Hartmann

(1905–63). By the time of the Nazi takeover, Hartmann had already made a name for himself with a few piano and chamber pieces of a "new-objective" character, including a *Jazz-Toccata und Fuge* (1928) and two works for wind ensemble — *Tanzsuite* (1931) and *Burleske Musik* (1930) — that drew upon the composer's experience, both in wind playing and in contemporary dance music, as a professional trombonist. From 1933 to 1945 not

EX. 13-5A   Paul Hindemith, *Das Marienleben,* "Vom Tode Mariä III," 1923 version, end

EX. 13-5B   Paul Hindemith, *Das Marienleben*, "Vom Tode Mariä III," 1948 version, end

a note of Hartmann's was played in Germany. Between 1933 and 1939 he submitted his music to competitions and festivals in neighboring countries (France, Austria, Czechoslovakia, Switzerland, Belgium), but with the coming of the war Hartmann's withdrawal from public life became absolute.

During the war years Hartmann composed three symphonies in a newly "subjective" or neoromantic style, all of them bitterly lamenting or remonstrative works at a time when

FIG. 13-6   Karl Amadeus Hartmann and his wife with (at right) Stravinsky, in Munich; photo 1956.

official Nazi art, like all totalitarian art, was invincibly optimistic. One of them — *Sinfonia dramatica: China kämpft* ("Dramatic Symphony: China struggles," 1942) — would have counted as politically seditious had it been performed. They were written, however, "for the drawer." In the fall of 1942, Hartmann traveled to Vienna and took lessons from Webern, but never adopted the twelve-tone technique.

Immediately after the war Hartmann founded Musica Viva, a performing organization for new music, which made a specialty of acquainting audiences with music that the Nazi regime had banned. His wartime works were performed there, and also at other new music centers that were cropping up in Germany, and won him enormous acclaim and prestige. By the time of his fairly early death he had composed another eight symphonies, and was widely credited with reviving the Austro-German symphonic tradition, dormant since the death of Mahler. Between 1948 and 1961, Hartmann was awarded major prizes practically on a yearly basis. He was honored not only as a musician but also as a heroic political resister at a time when Germany was in dire need of new role models.

Of course the situation was more complicated than that. Hartmann was able to sustain his much-admired stance of principled if passive opposition during the war, composing prolifically but refusing to participate in the musical life of his corrupted homeland, because he was economically privileged. He lived off the generosity of his father-in-law, a wealthy factory manager, who provided Hartmann and his family with a spacious apartment, the use of a suburban summer home where they lived full-time at the height of the war when Munich was subjected to aerial attacks, and freedom from the need to seek salaried employment.

To take these factors into consideration is by no means to impugn the sincerity of Hartmann's dissidence; but it paints his story, like those of Orff and Hindemith, in shades of gray. As Michael Kater, a sympathetic but unsentimental historian of the arts in Nazi Germany, has put it, Hartmann's situation mixes elements of sacrifice with elements of "self-centeredness, sometimes to the point of narcissism,"[25] especially as regards the claims of wartime suffering on which the composer's postwar reputation as a moral paragon were largely based. One's tendency in retrospect is to imagine life under totalitarianism in terms of stark choices and moral extremes. Real-life conditions and alternatives are seldom so clear-cut.

Most poignant of all, perhaps, was the case of Webern. From the time of the German annexation of Austria in 1938 until his dreadful death, on 15 September 1945, in the aftermath of the German defeat (shot by an American soldier in the course of a raid on his home on account of his son-in-law's black-market activities), Webern, shorn of performance prospects for his "degenerate" music, was altogether shut out of public musical life. He subsisted on private lessons and a small pension. He continued to compose for the drawer at his slow devoted pace, completing his last three compositions (Variations for Orchestra, op. 30, and two Cantatas to texts by his poet friend Hildegard Jone, opp. 29 and 31) in conditions of virtual seclusion.

Considering not only the conditions in which he worked but also the esoteric, utopian qualities of his music, Webern would seem the archetypal "inner emigrant," retreating from his adverse surroundings into a purer world of art and scholarship. So, indeed, he was regarded in the immediate postwar decades, when his music became for many a shining model of transcendent artistry surviving in a time of depravity, thence a symbol of pertinacious resistance to evil. The uncompromising character of his music, its commitment to reviled but unsullied artistic ideals, became an emblem of uncompromising ethics.

It was therefore an agonizing discovery for many when evidence began mounting in the late 1970s that Webern had been a supporter of the Nazi regime. Hartmann had already found this out in 1942. He cut his studies with Webern short because, as he wrote back to his wife,

> The conversation kept returning to politics. I would not have steered it there, for I learned things that I would rather not have heard. He seriously defended the viewpoint that, for dear order's sake, *any kind* of authority should be respected and that the State under which one lives would have to be recognized at any price.[26]

That much sounds like resignation, but Webern's letters show him reading Hitler's autobiography *Mein Kampf* ("My struggle") with exhilaration, and exulting in Germany's prosecution of the war. "Are things not going forward with giant steps?" he wrote a friend in 1940, still using the hyperbolic tone and style we may recall from his lectures and writings on music, quoted in chapters 6 and 12:

> This is Germany today! But the *National Socialist* one, to be sure! This is the *new* state, for which the seed was already laid twenty years ago. Yes, a *new state* it is, one that has never existed before!! *It is something new!* Created by this unique man!!![27]

There are elements here of hysteria and denial that require a sort of analysis far beyond the scope of a book like this. But that we are hopelessly in a realm of comfortless moral grays is evident. Webern's tragicomic powers of dissociation were not at all unusual at the time, however difficult it may be at half a century's remove to empathize with them. There was, to begin with, the dissociation of the Nazi regime from the anti-Semitic policies that had made an exile out of Schoenberg, Webern's beloved mentor. Webern, who was not personally anti-Semitic, continued as long as possible his association with Jewish musicians, and even deplored official persecutions, though he usually ascribed reports of them to anti-German propaganda.

Stranger yet, perhaps, was his inability to grasp the fact that the music to which he was committed was considered socially unacceptable beyond all petition or appeal by the new rulers of his country. Webern persisted in the quixotic belief that the historical inevitability of dodecaphonic music paralleled the historical inevitability of Nazism, that both were the fruits of German greatness, and that eventually he (or someone) would be able "to convince the Hitler regime of the rightness of the twelve-tone system."[28] It would be far too simple, as well as invidious, to draw direct parallels between the order that Webern sought in his art and the order that, to Hartmann's dismay, he upheld in political discussions. But here, too, Webern was not alone. Although Schoenberg would have been persecuted for his ethnic background no matter what kind of music he wrote, twelve-tone music was indeed tainted by association in Nazi eyes as "Jewish" as well as "Bolshevik." Or so many official documents proclaimed. And yet, amazingly enough, there was an officially tolerated cadre of twelve-tone composers in the Third Reich. Its members included Winfried Zillig (1905–63), a former pupil of Schoenberg, who had a successful career as an opera conductor in German-occupied Poland during the war; and Paul von Klenau (1883–1946), a Danish composer who made his career in Germany, and whose historical operas — *Michael Kohlhaas* (1933), *Rembrandt van Rijn* (1937), and *Elisabeth von England* (1939) — were successfully produced there despite his use of twelve-tone procedures.

Nor did von Klenau keep them hidden. On the contrary, exactly as Webern might have wished, he proclaimed the virtues — the specifically Nazi virtues — of twelve-tone music in the public press, openly touting the method as "totalitarian," and claiming that its strict discipline made it "entirely appropriate to the future direction of the 'National Socialist World.'" He justified it further as "consistent with Nazi insistence on technical competence," and, in its strictness, as an antidote to the "individualistic arbitrariness" that had formerly plagued modern music.[29]

So was it inherently "degenerate" or inherently "totalitarian"? Inherently Jewish or inherently Nazi? The questions, one must surely recognize by now, are silly. Musical techniques do not have political sympathies or ethnic backgrounds; the people who use them are the ones that do. And as people are inconstant and inconsistent, their means of expression are shaped and colored by their expressive aims. Twelve-tone music has been interpreted in many cultural contexts and in the light of many subtexts. The most contentious period of such readings, of course, took place after the war.

One foreshadow of it is relevant here. In his *Doktor Faustus* (1949), an allegory of the Nazi period in the form of the biography of a fictitious composer who is the complete inner emigrant, the war-exiled German novelist Thomas Mann (1875–1955) made an elaborate, though implicit, comparison between the twelve-tone system and the Nazi political regime. Its point was a dual paradox: as Hitler enslaved the German people so as to liberate "Germany," so the twelve-tone system regimented the notes in a musical composition to an unprecedented degree in order to achieve the ultimate artistic "autonomy." (In a note added to the English translation at the insistence of its infuriated inventor, Mann called the twelve-tone system "the intellectual property of a contemporary composer and theoretician, Arnold Schoenberg"; Schoenberg's rejoinder: "We will see who is whose contemporary!")[30]

SOCIALIST REALISM AND THE SOVIET AVANT-GARDE

Inner emigration, by and large, was not an option for the artists of Soviet Russia. While the overtly genocidal policies of the Nazi regime have earned it supremacy in the annals of human horror, most historians agree that the Soviet regime, particularly during the reign of Joseph Stalin (1879–1953), its most adamant dictator, was the most oppressive of the twentieth-century totalitarian states in terms of general regimentation of the population, and the most intrusive into the daily lives of its inhabitants. In a bitterly ironic twist, it was precisely the egalitarian and communitarian ideals on which the Communist regime was founded — "from each according to his ability; to each according to his needs,"[31] in the words of Marx — that eventually justified what may have been the bloodiest political terror the world had ever seen. It was a replay of the aftermath of the French Revolution, but on a scale only twentieth-century technology could enable.

Principled or alienated withdrawal from public affairs in such a society was impossible. Anyone not engaged in productive, salaried employment (and all citizens were in effect the government's employees) was judged a social parasite and prosecuted under law. Nowhere were the demands of citizenship more pervasive or more zealously enforced, and artists were citizens above all. Neither in Fascist Italy nor in Nazi Germany were the arts so policed and watchdogged as in the Soviet Union, nor did the Italian or German governments ever promulgate a theory that would effectively transform the arts into a delivery system for state propaganda, as did the Soviet government under Stalin.

That theory was called "socialist realism." It was defined in countless encyclopedias and dictionaries as "a creative method based on the truthful, historically concrete artistic reflection of reality in its revolutionary development."[32] The wording was framed by Andrey Alexandrovich Zhdanov (1896–1948), a member of the Central Committee of the Soviet Communist Party with responsibilities for overseeing the arts, and was enunciated in 1932, at the first Congress of the Union of Soviet Writers, by the famous novelist Maxim Gorky (1868–1936), who had just returned from emigration, and who allowed himself to be used as a figurehead for the dissemination of official doctrine.

It is from that year, 1932, in which official unions were set up for writers, graphic and plastic artists, and composers, that stringent Stalinist controls over the arts are usually said to date. During the first decade and a half after the Russian revolution, the arts were far less subject to direct state intervention. Nor was modernism discouraged, since revolutionary politics was seen as a

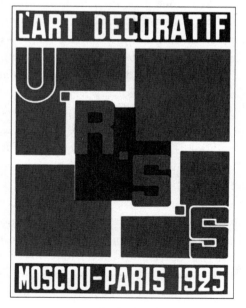

FIG. 13-7   Poster by Alexander Rodchenko for the Soviet section of the Paris Art Deco Exposition, 1925.

form of avant-gardism that sought an appropriately maximalistic reflection in art. "You are revolutionaries in art, we are revolutionaries in life" said Anatoly Lunacharsky, the first Soviet commissar of culture and education, to Prokofieff when the latter announced his intention to emigrate. "We ought to work together."[33]

The most spectacular instances of this collaboration occurred in the visual arts, not in music, and took the form of Soviet propaganda posters and placards designed by the most advanced—"futurist," "suprematist," "constructivist"—painters and photographers of the day, like Kazimir Malevich (1878–1935), Lazar (El) Lissitsky (1890–1941), and Alexander Rodchenko (1891–1956). At the Exposition Internationale des Arts Décoratifs et Industriels Modernes (International Exhibition of Modern Decorative and Industrial Arts) in 1925—the event from which the term "art-deco" was derived—the Soviet contingent made a colossal impression on viewers and critics in Paris, the very nerve center of international modernism.

Amazed by it, Sergey Diaghilev commissioned from one of the Soviet artists exhibited there, Georgiy Bogdanovich Yakulov (1884–1928), a "constructivist" set for a ballet, to be composed by Prokofieff, that would celebrate Soviet industrialization. The cacophonous work that emerged from this collaboration, *Le pas d'acier* ("The leap of steel," 1928), was best seen in its Parisian modernist context as an exercise in "radical chic." (Stravinsky, from whose *The Rite of Spring* it poached a bit, but who was by then completely cold to Russia and to primitivism, declared that it made him ill.) But it gave Prokofieff specious reassurance that the atmosphere back home would be hospitable to his work, and was one of the first nudges in the direction of his eventual return to Russia.

With one exception, however, the early Soviet musical scene was devoid of a real avant-garde. And that is because, owing to a combination of powerful patronage incentives and a strong educational establishment, there had been virtually no musical avant-garde to speak of in the immediate prerevolutionary period, with Scriabin prematurely dead and Stravinsky already living abroad. Not even Prokofieff, conservatory-trained and proud of it, was truly an avant-garde artist. His technique, like Stravinsky's or Scriabin's, may have been "advanced" by conservatory standards, but it was elite, highly professionalized, and, like all maximalism, committed to extending a tradition. That implies loyalty to the tradition one is extending, even if one is extending it to the point of "decadence." An avant-garde is something else. The term is military, and it implies belligerence: countercultural hostility, antagonism to existing institutions and traditions. That was indeed the fear among traditional artists, no matter how advanced, in the aftermath of the revolution. It seemed at first inevitable that a "workers' and peasants'" government would be hostile to the art institutions of the aristocracy and the bourgeoisie, which had harbored the art of what Lenin called the "bored upper ten thousand."[34] It seemed to elite establishmentarians that the handwriting was on the wall, and they left—the Rachmaninoffs and the Prokofieffs alike.

But if Prokofieff was no true revolutionary in art, neither, it turned out, were Lenin or Lunacharsky. They too were committed traditionalists in art. On reflection that should not be surprising since, although the Soviet government was set up in the name of the workers and the peasants, the revolution that produced it was led not "from below" by workers or peasants but "from above," by the descendents of the urban intelligentsia, whose tastes were formed within the social class from which they had emerged. In a famous conversation with the German Communist Clara Zetkin, Lenin had no hesitation in proclaiming himself a philistine with respect to modern art movements, and even derided the sentiment Lunacharsky expressed to Prokofieff. "We are good revolutionaries," he said, "but somehow we feel obliged to prove that we are on a par with 'contemporary culture.' But I have the courage to declare myself a 'barbarian.' I am unable to count the works of expressionism, futurism, cubism, and similar 'isms' among the highest manifestations of creative genius. I do not understand them. I do not derive any pleasure from them."[35] If Lenin had gone on to say that therefore the art of the traditional high culture was corrupt and had to be replaced with a proletarian culture, he would have qualified as an avant-gardist. But he said nothing of the kind. In fact, he said, "We must preserve the beautiful, take it as a model, use it as a starting point, even if it is 'old.' Why must we bow low in front of the new, as if it were God, only because it is 'new'?" That traditionalism, under the paradoxical (or hypocritical) cover of revolutionary rhetoric, would later be canonized in the doctrine of socialist realism.

But during the 1920s, the period of the so-called New Economic Policy (a limited free-market economy that Lenin reintroduced in 1921 and that lasted until 1929), a genuine Soviet avant-garde emerged. In 1923, two major professional associations of musicians were organized on the initiative of their memberships. One, the Association of Contemporary Music (called the ASM after its Russian initials) comprised the traditional establishment, including the traditional modernists. Its leading creative figure, Nikolai Yakovlevich Myaskovsky (1881–1950), became the Soviet "classicist" par excellence with twenty-seven symphonies and thirteen string quartets to his credit. Its fierce and frightening adversary, the Russian Association of Proletarian Musicians (RAPM), was the Soviet avant-garde. Militantly countercultural, hopelessly doctrinaire, intolerant, self-righteous, these radical proletarians (and not the Soviet government) were the ones who wanted to throw out all sophisticated traditions and build the new Soviet music on the rubble.

RAPM defined itself by what it opposed: it was antimodernist, anti-Western, and anti-jazz, but also anti-folklore and antinationalist in the spirit of Marxist internationalism. In place of all existing classical, popular, and folk music (except revolutionary songs and a few works of Beethoven, the "voice of the French revolution") RAPM proffered revolutionary utilitarian music — what in "new-objective" Germany would have been called *Gebrauchsmusik*: mainly marchlike "mass songs" for group singing, set to agitational propaganda (*agitprop*) lyrics. For six years ASM and RAPM contended, until in 1929 the NEP came to an end and the country entered its harsh totalitarian phase with the inauguration of the first Five Year Plan. As part of the general centralization of authority now imposed, RAPM was given administrative control over Soviet musical institutions.

This was the period during which the Moscow Conservatory was renamed the Felix Kon School of Higher Musical Education, after a firebrand politician of the period who edited the newspaper *Rabochaya gazeta*, The Workers' Gazette. A nonmusician, Boleslaw Przybyszewski, the doctrinaire Marxist son of a famous symbolist writer, was installed as rector. Myaskovsky, together with Reinhold Glière (1875–1956) and Mikhail Gnesin (1883–1957), his fellow stalwarts of the prerevolutionary creative elite, were denounced and fired from the faculty. Grades and examinations were abolished, and admission restricted to students of acceptable class background. Composers were exhorted to spurn all styles and genres that had flourished under the tsars. The only politically correct concept of authorship was collective, epitomized in the so-called Prokoll, a group of Moscow Conservatory students who banded together to produce revolutionary operas and oratorios that were in essence medleys of mass songs.

The joyous declaration after three years of a prematurely successful completion to the first Five Year Plan was the Soviet (now firmly Stalinist) leadership's way of retreating from a ruinous situation without admitting error. The country was in misery — a misery that could be blamed on local administrators and "wreckers" in the case of the real tragedies like forced collectivization of agriculture, in which millions had died as a result of mass starvation tactics. This was the beginning of the era of Soviet "show trials," in which scapegoats were subjected to orchestrated campaigns of denunciation and coerced confessions that deflected popular discontent away from the real culprits, the economic planners themselves and their enforcers. On the artistic and intellectual fronts, all excesses were blamed on "left deviationism" from the true Party line.

The same Party that installed the proletarianists in 1929 suppressed them in 1932 in the name of a benign administrative *perestroyka* or "restructuring." The RAPM and its sister organizations in the other arts were "liquidated," along with ASM, and replaced by the all-encompassing creative unions. The RAPMists were stripped of power and forced to make public recantations. Nominal power reverted to the old guard, from whose standpoint the 1932 *perestroyka* meant salvation from chaos and obscurantism. The grateful old conservatory professors were given back their classrooms and installed as willing figureheads in the organizational structure of the Composers' Union. To all appearances, the union was a service organization, even a fraternal club.

The real power, of course, lay elsewhere, and the real purpose of the organization, though this was not immediately apparent, was to be a conduit of centralized authority and largesse. As the guarantor of its members' right to work, as the channeler of state patronage through commissions, and as dispenser of material assistance, the union was ostensibly engaged in protecting the interests of composers, but by the same token it was implicitly endowed with the power to enforce conformity. Its chief social functions were the so-called internal *pokazї* — meetings at which composers submitted their work in progress to comradely peer review in the spirit of idealistic "Bolshevik self-criticism," and open forums at which composers and musical intellectuals shared the floor discussing topics like Soviet opera or "symphonism" for eventual publication in *Sovetskaya muzïka* (Soviet Music), the union's official organ.

Early discussions of Socialist Realism and the problems of its application to music, the least inherently "realistic" of the arts, were also carried by the journal. As in the case of literature and the fine arts, the nature of the doctrine was fully revealed in its application rather than its theory. It turned out to have far less to do with Marxist socialism than with more traditional Russian attitudes to the arts, particularly those associated most recently with the Christian doctrines of Count Leo Tolstoy, and more remotely with the doctrine of official nationalism that was promulgated a round century before in the early reign of Tsar Nikolai I.

It may seem bizarre to trace a militantly atheistic ideology like Socialist Realism back to a militant Christian thinker, but their common militancy, and their shared contempt for "art for art's sake," provided the link. In his tract *What Is Art?* (1898), Tolstoy asserted that all art must contain the Good and the Important. If these are present, a work of art is "moral" and satisfies one of Tolstoy's three criteria for consideration as art, the others being intelligibility and sincerity. Tolstoy defined the Good as "that which is always necessary to all people,"[36] namely "feeling that can unite people with God and with one another."[37] The Important, for Tolstoy, was "that which causes people to understand and to love what previously they did not understand or love."[38] Thus, in order to deserve its existence and dissemination, art must be communitarian, didactic, and comprehensible to all.

Modernism, socially divisive and "elitist," is immediately excluded. Substitute the words Socialist for Christian, Socialism for Christianity, political for religious, and the following passage from Tolstoy could easily have issued from the pen of a Gorky, a Lunacharsky, or a Lenin:

> The art of our time should be appraised differently from former art chiefly in this, that the art of our time, that is, Christian art (basing itself on a religious perception which demands the union of man), excludes, from the domain of art good in subject-matter, everything transmitting exclusive feelings which do not unite men but divide them. It relegates such work to the category of art that is bad in its subject-matter; while on the other hand it includes in the category of art that is good in subject-matter a section not formerly admitted as deserving of selection and respect, namely, universal art transmitting even the most trifling and simple feelings if only they are accessible to all men without exception, and therefore unite them. Such art cannot but be esteemed good in our time, for it attains the end which Christianity, the religious perception of our time, sets before humanity.[39]

Here in embryo is the essence of Socialist Realism as expressed by a trio of terms that was fashioned by Zhdanov as if expressly to echo the trio — *pravoslaviye* (Orthodoxy), *samoderzhaviye* (autocracy), *narodnost'* (nationality) — that had characterized Russian official nationalism a century before. The last term, *narodnost'*, remained the same. Like the earlier concept, Socialist Realism demanded that art be rooted in folklore, or at least in styles familiar and meaningful to all without special preparation. The other terms were *partiynost'* and *ideynost'*. The former means loyalty to the Communist Party and conformity with its official line — which, though it claimed to be a stable point of political and moral reference, proved to be as changeable as the weather, and therefore dangerous to artists. The latter term, *ideynost'*, means "being full of ideas," which in practice amounted to a requirement that works of art have a content that is easily grasped and paraphrased.

This last was a difficult demand to enforce in the case of textless music. The difficulty had two consequences. At times it led to the catastrophic downgrading of the instrumental genres in the Soviet scheme of musical value. At other times it led to theorizing the means whereby the ideological content of instrumental music could be rendered "objectively" intelligible (and therefore censorable). The chief theorizer was Boris Asafyev (1884–1949), a mediocre composer but a brilliant musicologist, in a book called *Muzïkal'naya forma kak protsess* ("Musical form as process"), first issued in 1930 and continually reworked and reissued as Asafyev refined his thinking according to changing political demands.

Asafyev theorized that instrumental music contained semantic units comparable to what linguists call morphemes — minimal bearers of meaning. Asafyev's term for his musical morphemes was "intonation" (*intonatsiya*); in combination, intonations produced musical "imagery" (*obraznost'*) that could be verbally paraphrased just as iconographical codes might be invoked to translate the meaning of a painting into words. Ironically enough, these formulations of Asafyev's were all adaptations of theories associated with "Russian formalism," a school of criticism that flourished in the 1920s, which interpreted works of literature "semiotically" (according, that is, to a "sign language" of tacit codes and signaling "devices" that made form as meaningful as content). Formalism as a literary practice was officially banned as modernist in the 1930s; indeed the very word "formalist" became an all-purpose and much dreaded term of Stalinist abuse. But as adapted by Asafyev (not, originally, with any political purpose in mind), and called by another name, it remained viable for music, because it could in principle help render instrumental music policeable.

PROTAGONIST OR VICTIM?

So much for theory. The story of Stalinist totalitarianism in practice, where music was concerned, can best be told — in fact, in some ways can *only* be told — in terms of the creative biography of Dmitriy Dmitriyevich Shostakovich (1906–75), the Soviet Union's emblematic composer. Shostakovich was the one composer wholly formed in the Soviet Union to achieve unquestionable world eminence. In that sense his work was not only regarded, but was actively promoted by the regime, as an emblem of Soviet cultural achievement and a vindication of the theory of socialist realism. His actual biography, containing as it did dramatic collisions and painful compromises with Soviet authority, is emblematic in another way, symbolizing the plight of artists who are subject to direct political control under uniquely modern conditions. And the controversies that have swirled about his legacy since his death (and especially since the collapse of the Soviet Union) are emblematic in yet a third way, exemplifying the contests over the meaning of art to which conditions of censorship and political manipulation inevitably give rise.

Shostakovich was a composing prodigy. He became nationally famous at the age of nineteen, when his First Symphony, his conservatory graduation piece, was publicly performed in Leningrad (the former Russian capital, St. Petersburg, renamed in honor of Lenin) on 12 May 1926. (Shostakovich celebrated the date for the rest of his life as a personal holiday.) World fame followed less than a year later, when Bruno Walter

FIG. 13-8 Dmitriy Shostakovich at a rehearsal of Vladimir Mayakovsky's *Bedbug* in Leningrad, 1929. Seated beside the composer is the director Vsevolod Meyerhold. Standing behind are (left) the designer, Alexander Rodchenko; and (right) Mayakovsky.

performed the symphony with the Berlin Philharmonic Orchestra on 5 May 1927. The American premiere, by Leopold Stokowski and the Philadelphia Orchestra, took place in November 1928. By then Shostakovich had won international recognition as a pianist as well, receiving a prize at the International Chopin Competition in Warsaw.

The precocious symphony, very much a sign of its times, shows Shostakovich to have been well abreast of all the fashionable currents in European music. In form it was impeccably "neoclassical," while in content it was full of "new-objective" irony in its allusions to "subartistic" or utilitarian genres and its sarcastic tendency to take things to laughable expressive extremes. The first and second themes in the opening movement, for example, are a cheeky military march and a shyly coquettish waltz. The second movement, nominally a scherzo and trio, contrasts a maniacal galop (in which the piano takes a leading part) with some sort of weirdly antiquated hymn or ersatz medieval organum. The finale, another galop (or possibly a circus march), brazenly and explicitly mocks the pathos of the affecting slow movement — and implicitly mocks the listener who had been taken in by it. The main sentiment of *neue Sachlichkeit* — "We won't be fooled again!" — is written all over this icily brilliant score.

The piano's conspicuous mischief-making in the second and fourth movements is perhaps a reminder of the composer's apprenticeship, during the hard days following the Bolshevik coup and the ensuing civil war, as low-paid pianist in a cold silent movie theater, where he may have acquired his lifelong taste for satirical intrusions of "low" genres, and for abrupt quasi-cinematic "cuts" in lieu of smooth transitions, to undermine the dignity of classical instrumental forms. His keen insolence seems to reflect that of early Soviet society, which saw itself very much as a buoyantly renewed culture injecting vigor into a decadent world.

Shostakovich's early satirical vein reached a peak in his first opera, *The Nose*, on which he embarked in the summer of 1927 and finished a year later, aged twenty-one. It is based on a famously hilarious but inscrutable tale by the novelist Nikolai Gogol (1809–52), in which a pompous civil servant awakens one morning to find that his nose has left his face; later he encounters his nose gallivanting around the city in a uniform that outranks his own. By the end of the opera all St. Petersburg is chasing after the nose, which is apprehended, beaten back to its normal size, and returned to its owner, who tries in vain to affix it to his face, but wakes up the next day to find it has returned there of its own accord. The story can support any number of interpretations ranging from the sexual to the political to the religious. The opera attempts none at all, aping Gogol's own deadpan (or "objective") manner and leaving the task of "reading" to others — another lifelong habit of the composer's.

Instead, the music seeks out every conceivable opportunity to underscore Gogol's extravagant sense of the absurd. Toward the end of the second scene in act I, for example, a policeman, grotesquely cast as a tenor falsettist (as close to a castrato as a twentieth-century composer could come) and incongruously accompanied by an ensemble of balalaikas (a folk instrument entirely out of place in an urban street scene), tries to apprehend a barber, who has discovered the nose in a freshly baked roll and is trying to dispose of it (Ex. 13-6). The stage is abruptly plunged in darkness, and an entr'acte ensues that has become famous as perhaps the earliest example in modern music of a composition scored entirely for unpitched percussion instruments. (It was often performed as a separate piece, and is included as one of the movements in an instrumental suite Shostakovich extracted from the opera after its 1930 premiere; among other claimants to patent-office primacy is the all-percussion scherzo from the First Symphony by another young Russian composer,

EX. 13-6   Dmitriy Shostakovich, *The Nose* in vocal score, end of Act I, scene 2

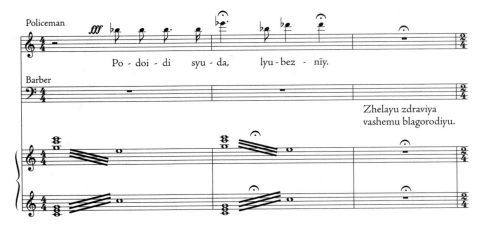

EX. 13-6 (continued)

EX. 13-6   (continued)

Policeman: Come here, kind sir.
Barber (*spoken*): I wish your lordship good health.
Policeman: No! No! My good fellow, I'm no lordship; tell me, though, what were you doing standing by the river?
Barber: I swear, guv'nor, I was on my way to give a shave and just looked down to see how fast the river was going.
Policeman: You're lying, yes you're lying, and you won't get away with it. Please be so kind as to answer.
Barber: I'll gladly shave your grace twice or even three times a week — without the slightest demur.
　　　　　　　— Trans. R.T.

Alexander Tcherepnin, also composed in 1927 and actually performed earlier than *The Nose*.)

The curtain goes up on the third scene to find Kovalyov, the civil servant, asleep in bed. He gets up to wash and sees his noseless face in the mirror. His "cavatina" (Ex. 13-7), consisting of nothing but grunts and gargles, is a pointed satirical counterpart to the tuneless percussion entr'acte. The whole opera burlesques the conventions of the genre in a similarly broad, unsubtle yet impressively inventive manner. More than any other composer of the time, perhaps, the young Shostakovich comes across as someone out to debunk and discredit the musical status quo from within. It was at the time an authentically and typically "Soviet" attitude toward "bourgeois" traditions.

The radical proletarianists (RAPMists) opposed Shostakovich's opera, for it still honored those traditions "in the breach," displayed elite virtuosity in its composing, and demanded a sophisticated audience for its appreciation. Once in power they managed to get the work taken off the boards, not to be revived until the 1960s. But their opposition was as yet a factional, not an official one. Until the end of his third decade, Shostakovich was regarded everywhere as the brash young musical genius of a brash young society, thriving in the din of its social upheavals, and pampered by its artistic elite.

Like most Soviet artists, Shostakovich greeted the 1932 *perestroyka*, which removed RAPM from the scene, as a great boon. His confidence restored, he embarked on another opera. This one was based on another famous nineteenth-century novella, but a serious one: *The Lady Macbeth of the Mtsensk District* by Nikolai Leskov (1831–95), not a fantastical writer like Gogol but an adherent of the naturalist school. It is the story

EX. 13-7   Dmitriy Shostakovich, *The Nose* in vocal score, Act I, scene 3, Kovalyov's "cavatina"

EX. 13-7   (*continued*)

of Katerina Izmailova, a childless merchant's wife in the middle of the great Russian nowhere, who rebels against her patriarchal surroundings by murdering her husband, her father-in-law, and her husband's saintly nephew. She and her lover, Sergey, are discovered in the act of killing the little boy and sentenced to exile in Siberia. On the way there, Sergey takes a shine to another woman, whom Katerina duly murders by jumping with her into a freezing river in which both of them drown.

Shostakovich and his librettist Alexander Preys (with whom he had collaborated on *The Nose* as well) tried to turn Leskov's creepy "sketch" of ungovernable passion and mayhem into a Soviet morality play. The objective conditions under which Katerina was forced to live, they argued in a program essay, justified her acts of violence. They were presented not as crimes but as acts of liberation. (Still, the third murder had to be eliminated because, as Shostakovich put it in the program, "killing a child always makes a bad impression.")[40] By emphasizing Katerina's awakened libido as her motivation, moreover, Shostakovich and Preys purported to turn her into a feminist icon. Shostakovich announced the opera as the first in a trilogy that would glorify

F I G. 13-9   Shostakovich, *The Lady Macbeth of the Mtsensk District*, act I, scene 2.

Russian womankind, first as rebel against the tsarist order, then as revolutionary, finally as the fully emancipated and productive heroine of Soviet society.

As befitted its loftier if morally distorted theme, Shostakovich's music balanced his earlier satirical manner against a more lyrical and conventionally beautiful idiom. The latter he reserved for Katerina, the former for her victims, so that the dubious heroine of this very inhumane opera becomes the only character with whom it is possible for the audience to identify as a human being. Katerina's is the only music in the opera that has emotional "life," as traditionally (that is, romantically) portrayed. It waxes and wanes; it has rhythmic and dynamic flexibility; it reaches climaxes. All the other characters are portrayed as subhuman. Their singing and, above all, their movements are accompanied by trudging or galloping ostinatos whose inflexible pulsations characterize them as soulless, insensate automatons, comic-strip creatures incapable of experiencing or evoking an emotional response.

The technique of dehumanizing victims operates most effectively in the crucial fifth scene of the opera, which depicts the murder of Katerina's husband, a well-meaning, ineffectual chap who (unlike his father) has done her no harm. The scene opens with Katerina in bed with Sergey, surrounded by the opera's lushest, most lyrical orchestral music. The mood lasts until the husband's offstage approach, signaled by a typical "trudging" ostinato. Once he arrives on stage, the trudge gives way to one of Shostakovich's signature galops. The whole scene of confrontation and murder is played against its unremitting oompah (Ex. 13-8).

When this scene has been performed abroad, many have found it puzzling. The American composer Elliott Carter, who saw *The Lady Macbeth of the Mtsensk District* in Berlin, wrote that "the relation of the music to the action is unaccountable," since he could not imagine why Shostakovich would have "the heroine and her lover strangle her husband on a large stage-sized four-poster bed to a lively dance tune."[41] Within the semiotic codes of socialist realism, however, the reason is clear enough: the dance tune is there to dehumanize the husband and mitigate the heroine's crime to one of cruelty to animals at worst. What condemns him is nothing more than his being part of Katerina's hated environment. He is dehumanized and dispatched not for anything he has done but for what he is: a beneficiary of the social system that oppressed his wife, or in Marxian terms, a "class enemy." That is enough "objectively" to justify his

EX. 13-8   Dmitriy Shostakovich, *The Lady Macbeth of the Mtsensk District*, Act I, scene 5

EX. 13-8 (continued)

Zinovy: for my wife's honor! Tell me the truth! Tell me the whole truth! Well, then! Well, then! Take that! What? What Sergey? Who's that? What Sergey? Bastards!

Katerina: What for? I don't even want to talk to you, I don't care, you lousy merchant, you'll never understand! Ai! Ai! Sergey! Sergey! I'm getting beaten! Come out, protect me! Sergey, my love!

liquidation. And all of this is conveyed, as in any successful opera, by the music, read through its appropriate codes by a properly attuned audience.

The Lady Macbeth of the Mtsensk District was a huge success with audiences and critics alike after its nearly simultaneous premieres in Leningrad, the composer's hometown, and Moscow, the Soviet capital, in January of 1934. It played to full houses for two years and toured the Western world as well, where, if it was not understood quite the way it was understood at home, it nevertheless captivated audiences, as *Wozzeck* did, with its strong doses of sex and violence. (The scene in which Sergey rapes Katerina — musically quite similar to the murder scene — became especially famous when a New York critic, quoted later in a national news magazine, dubbed it an exercise in "pornophony.")[42] No one foresaw its now emblematic fate.

In January 1936, a festival of Soviet music was held in Moscow. The Little Opera Theater of Leningrad lent its two most successful productions to Moscow's Bolshoi Theater for the occasion. One was *Quiet Flows the Don*, a corny "song opera" (a uniquely Soviet genre somewhat similar to a Broadway musical but sung throughout) by a hack named Ivan Dzerzhinsky, which was based on Mikhail Sholokhov's famous novel of the postrevolutionary civil war. The other was *Lady Macbeth*. On the evening of January 17, Stalin attended a performance of Dzerzhinsky's opera in the company of a close aide, and, in the words of an official press communiqué, called the composer, the conductor, and the director to his box, where he "gave a positive assessment of the theater's efforts on behalf of Soviet opera and noted the considerable ideological and political merits of the production."[43] On the evening of January 26, Stalin returned to the theater, together with a somewhat larger entourage that included Andrey Zhdanov, to see *Lady Macbeth*. Shostakovich, alerted by telegram, was in the audience. He left the theater perturbed (as he wrote to a friend) about "what had happened to Dzerzhinsky, and what didn't happen to me."[44] For Stalin and his retinue had left without comment before the end. Two days later, what soon became known all over the Soviet Union as the Historic Document appeared in *Pravda*, the Soviet Communist Party's official organ. It was an unsigned editorial titled "Muddle Instead of Music," and a historic document it was indeed. At a time when newspaper campaigns were already rife against the "left deviationism" of old Bolsheviks in preparation for the show trials and mass executions that were then in the planning stage, the same merciless rhetoric of political denunciation was leveled, for the first time anywhere, at an artist.

The opera was excoriated both for its libretto and its music. The main thrust of the invective was puritanical: no surprise, since totalitarian regimes fear nothing so much as an unleashed libido. "The music croaks and hoots and snorts and pants in order to represent love scenes as naturally as possible," *Pravda* fumed; "and 'love,' in its most vulgar form is smeared all over the opera."[45] That, the editorial insinuated, was why the opera had enjoyed its sensational international success. It was a capitulation to "the depraved tastes of bourgeois audiences," whom it titillated with its "witching, clamorous, neurasthenic music." But then the attack turned from the opera's subject to its style. "The composer," *Pravda* ranted, "seems to have deliberately encoded his music, twisted all its sounds so that it would appeal only to aesthetes and formalists who have lost all healthy tastes." And now came the threat. "Left deviationism in opera grows out of the same source as left deviationism in painting, in poetry, in pedagogy, in science," the newspaper asserted, using the very term that was a death sentence to political losers. In a phrase that must have scared the poor composer half out of his wits, the chief organ of Soviet power denounced him for "trifling with difficult matters," and hinted that "it might end very badly."

Lady Macbeth, until then the jewel of the Soviet operatic stage, was summarily banned, not to return until 1961, in a revised version stripped of pornophony (but also with an expanded final scene depicting the convoy en route to Siberia, which many read as Shostakovich's oblique reference to the threats he had endured). The premiere of Shostakovich's monumental Fourth Symphony was canceled on its very eve. (It would not be performed until 1962.) There have been many attempts to find a rationale for these bans on the basis of musical content, or on that of Stalinist taste (or even the personal taste of the dictator, who had been a seminarian in his youth and perhaps retained a prospective clergyman's squeamishness about sex).

It is more likely that Shostakovich was singled out for attack not because his works gave particular offense, but because of his preeminence among the Soviet composers of his generation. If Shostakovich could be summarily silenced and brought low, then nobody was safe. It was a demonstration of the omnipotence of Soviet power over the arts in the wake of the 1932 *perestroyka*, which by dissolving all musical institutions not directly administered by the government at the behest of the Party, removed all impediments to the exercise of Stalin's arbitrary rule.

Some of Shostakovich's surviving friends have stated since his death that at the time of the *Pravda* editorial, the composer fully expected to be arrested and imprisoned, and packed a suitcase. That never happened, but for the rest of his life, or at least until the end of Stalin's reign, he had to live with the threat of a "bad end." That this tortured figure continued to function as an artist and a citizen has lent his career, and many of his works, a heroic luster that no "benignly neglected" modernist composer in the West can hope to rival.

READINGS

The first work to be so regarded, the Fifth Symphony, was also the work that won Shostakovich his rehabilitation and return to official favor. It was first performed in Leningrad, on 21 November 1937, at the very height of Stalin's so-called "purge" of the Party and government, in the midst of mass arrests, disappearances, and executions, to an audience that, according to reliable reports, had been weeping openly during the slow movement and cheered the symphony for fully half an hour when it was over. The history of its reception is a most revealing narrative, not only in the context of Soviet music, but in the more general context of music created, presented, and interpreted under conditions of modern totalitarianism at its most stringent.

The most conspicuous difference between the Fifth Symphony and its composer's earlier works is the total suppression of the satirical mode, formerly one of Shostakovich's most distinctive features. The scherzo, where formerly one might have expected a madcap caricature of a march or galop, was a rather heavy, traditionally Germanic (hence "classical") triple-metered affair — perhaps a waltz, perhaps a *Ländler*, perhaps even a somewhat cloddish minuet — in an idiom seemingly derived from that of Mahler's early symphonies (particularly the First, in which the scherzo shares the key of D major with that of Shostakovich's Fifth). The change was noted with satisfaction by the critic for *Sovetskaya muzïka*, who approvingly contrasted the scherzo's "new traits of fresh, hearty humor, naivety, and even tenderness" with Shostakovich's previous "pretentious urbanity," his "flaunting of cheap effects."[46] The work was taken on high as a recantation. The composer, at least outwardly, sought (or allowed himself to appear to seek) to abet the impression. The very "iffy" language is necessary since no public utterance by a public figure in Stalinist Russia can be presumed actually to come from its ostensible source. In the present case the utterance took the form of a newspaper article called "My Creative Answer," which was published in a Moscow newspaper on the eve of the Symphony's premiere in the capital, 25 January 1938. The author of the article announced that in the wake of the Leningrad premiere, "among the often very substantial responses that have analyzed this work, one that particularly gratified me said that 'the Fifth Symphony is a Soviet artist's practical creative answer to just criticism.'" He went on to state that "at the center of the work's conception I envisioned *a man* in all his suffering," and that "the Symphony's finale resolves the tense and tragic moments of the preceding movements in a joyous, optimistic fashion."

That man, the Symphony's hero, is explicitly identified with the composer and his recent past: "If I have really succeeded in embodying in musical images all that I have thought and felt since the critical articles in *Pravda*, if the demanding listener will detect in my music a turn toward greater clarity and simplicity, I will be satisfied."[47] In keeping with the explicit demands of Socialist Realism, a special effort was made to dissociate the Symphony's "tense and tragic moments" from any hint of "pessimism," an impermissible message for art to convey since it promoted passivity and low productivity. "I think that Soviet tragedy, as a genre, has every right to exist," the author of the article published over Shostakovich's name declared,

> *but:* its content must be suffused with a *positive idea,* comparable, for example, to the life-affirming ardor of Shakespeare's tragedies. In the literature of music we are likewise familiar with many inspired pages in which, for example, the severe images of suffering in Verdi's or Mozart's Requiems manage to arouse not weakness or despair in the human spirit but courage and the will to fight.

The official press, which may have actually authored this interpretation of the symphony, naturally accepted it at its face value, even if some of the stricter critics, like the one in *Sovetskaya muzïka,* faulted Shostakovich for occasionally falling short of his intentions as set forth in "My Creative Answer." The slow movement, which had provoked the epidemic of weeping in the hall, was a failure, in the critic's view, because instead of arousing "courage and the will to fight," it seemed to depict instead a state of "torpor, numbness, a condition of spiritual prostration, in which the will is annihilated along with the strength to resist or overcome. This numbness, this torpor is the very *negation* of the life-affirming principle."[48] And it would have made the Symphony unacceptable, one feels after reading the review, had not the finale saved the day — or tried to — by breaking the objectionable mood, and especially with its insistently, earsplittingly yea-saying D major coda (Ex. 13-9). The critic ended his review with cautious approval, but with a question in his mind: had Shostakovich truly succeeded in dispelling the torpor he so vividly portrayed (and possibly conveyed) in the Largo?

With that, the critic unwittingly (or — who knows? — perhaps wittingly) signaled the real story of the Fifth's reception, in which the official reading contended with a sort of folk tradition of "dissident" readings that put the symphony's supposed message in quite another light. This tradition, carried on in private (or in coded language), has to be pieced together from scattered documents and reminiscences, beginning with a notation that Alexander Fadeyev, the very orthodox head of the Soviet Writers' Union, made in his diary after hearing the 1938 Moscow premiere and published posthumously, in 1957: "A work of astonishing strength. The third movement is beautiful. But the

EX. 13-9   Dmitri Shostakovich, Symphony no. 5, IV, coda

EX. 13-9 *(continued)*

ending does not sound like a resolution (still less like a triumph or victory), but rather like a punishment or vengeance on someone. A terrible emotional force, but a tragic force. It arouses painful feelings."[49]

This turned the official reading on its head, judging most successful the very movement that the official critic had called the least, and hinting that the finale may have "failed" on purpose. Myaskovsky, writing to Prokofieff (who was traveling abroad), confessed that he was surprised that Shostakovich could have come up with a finale so "utterly flat,"[50] and Yevgeniy Mravinsky, the conductor of the Leningrad premiere, wrote much later that despite the composer's "great effort to make the finale the authentic confirmation of an objectively affirmative conclusion," the confirmation was unconvincing since it was achieved by transparently artificial means: "Somewhere in the middle of the movement the quick tempo spends itself and the music seemingly leans against some sort of obstacle, following which the composer leads it out of the cul-de-sac, subjecting it to a big dynamic buildup, applying an 'induction coil' "[51] — that is, an externally administered electric shock.

Were these writers using code? And was even Georgiy Khubov, the "official critic," using code when he called such insistent attention to the slow movement's "torpor"? By now a whole library of late- and post-Soviet memoirs, accounts by émigrés, and clandestinely published dissident writings attests that that was precisely the mood that reigned among the populace during the political terror — the "Yezhovshchina," as it was called, after Nikolai Yezhov, the commissar who directed it — whose very peak coincided with the symphony's premiere. The Russian poet Anna Akhmatova (1889–1966) used that very word — torpor (otsepeneniye) — in the prose preface to her poem "Requiem" (composed and memorized at the time, committed to paper and published after Stalin's death) to characterize the endless queues of women who gathered daily at the prisons of Leningrad to learn the fates of their arrested loved ones:

> In the terrible years of the Yezhovshchina I spent seventeen months in the Leningrad prison lines. One day someone "fingered" me. Then the blue-lipped woman standing behind me, who of course had never heard my name, roused herself out of the torpor we all shared and whispered in my ear (for everyone there spoke in whispers): "But can you describe this?" And I said, "I can." Then something like a smile slid across what had once been her face.

There are many now, both in and out of Russia, who believe that Shostakovich's Fifth Symphony was a similar act of witness. In 1979, four years after the composer's death, a book called *Testimony* was published in New York, purporting to be memoirs of Shostakovich as transcribed from conversations with an émigré journalist named Solomon Volkov. It contains this unequivocal characterization of the symphony that had once been called Shostakovich's creative response to just criticism:

> I think it is clear to everyone what happens in the Fifth. The rejoicing is forced, created under threat, as in [the first scene of Musorgsky's opera] *Boris Godunov*. It's as if someone were beating you with a stick and saying, "Your business is rejoicing, your business is rejoicing," and you rise, shaky, and go marching off, muttering,

"Our business is rejoicing, our business is rejoicing." What kind of apotheosis is that? You have to be a complete oaf not to hear that.[52]

The authenticity of *Testimony* has been seriously questioned, but in the end it is not relevant to the point at issue here, which is the way in which the folk reading has triumphed, both in Russia and abroad, over the official one as Soviet power grew weaker and eventually collapsed. We may never know what Shostakovich intended, but (as is always the case with instrumental music) multiple readings were available to listeners despite all attempts to control interpretation by means of Socialist Realism, and those who wished to believe in the work's dissident message had a consolation that was otherwise unavailable under conditions of Soviet censorship. And that is why nowhere on earth was symphonic music ever valued more highly by multitudes of listeners than in the Soviet Union.

That high social value was purchased at an exorbitant price in suffering, one that neither the composer nor his audience, given the choice, might willingly have paid. But it illustrates more poignantly, perhaps, than any other episode in the history of music just what it is that has made music so special among the arts. It was something that the Romantics had valued in all art. As early as 1794, when the idea of the esthetic was in its infancy, the German poet Friedrich Schiller observed that "the real and express content that the poet puts into his work remains always finite; the possible content that he allows us to contribute is an infinite quality."[53] But it was a quality that, inevitably, became especially associated with the art that had the least, or most weakly specified, semantic content. A century and a half later, in a country and a society undreamt of by Schiller, the truth of his statement received its greatest validation when it allowed the formerly sarcastic, "objective" and often somewhat trivial music of a chastened and newly serious Dmitriy Shostakovich to become the secret diary of a nation.

Notes

CHAPTER 1: REACHING (FOR) LIMITS

1 Ezra Pound, "Arnold Dolmetsch" (1914), in *Literary Essays of Ezra Pound* (New York: New Directions, 1968), p. 434.

2 *The American College Dictionary* (New York: Random House, 1950), p. 781.

3 Richard Specht, *Johannes Brahms* (Hellerau, 1928), p. 382.

4 See Erica Mugglestone, "Guido Adler's 'The Scope, Method, and Aim of Musicology' (1885): An English Translation with an Historico-Analytical Commentary," *Yearbook for Traditional Music* XIII (1981): 1–22.

5 Cited in Harmann Danuser, *Die Musik des 20. Jahrhunderts* (Laaber: Laaber-Verlag, 1984), p. 24.

6 Gustav Mahler to Anna von Mildenburg, 18 July 1896 (on his Third Symphony), *Selected Letters of Gustav Mahler*, ed. Knud Martner, trans. Eithne Wilkins and Ernst Kaiser (New York: Farrar, Straus, Giroux, 1979), p. 190.

7 Mahler to Max Marschalk, 26 March 1896; Piero Weiss, *Letters of Composers Through Six Centuries* (Philadelphia: Chilton Books, 1967), p. 393.

8 *Ibid.*

9 See Stephen E. Hefling, "Mahler's 'Todtenfeier'" and the Problem of Program Music," *Nineteenth-Century Music* XII (1988–89): 27–53.

10 Mahler to Max Marschalk, 17 December 1895; *Selected Letters of Gustav Mahler*, p. 172.

11 *Gustav Mahler in den Erinnerungen von Natalie Bauer-Lechner*, eds. Herbert Killian and Knud Martner (Hamburg, 1984), pp. 170–71; quoted in Hefling, "Mahler's Totenfeier," p. 43.

12 Donald Mitchell, *Gustav Mahler: The Wunderhorn Years* (Boulder, Colo.: Westview Press, 1986), p. 183.

13 Weiss, *Letters of Composers*, p. 394.

14 Guido Adler, *Gustav Mahler* (Leipzig: Breitkopf und Härtel, 1916), p. 23.

15 Debussy to André Caplet, 29 May 1913; Debussy, *Letters*, eds. François Lesure and Roger Nichols (Cambridge: Harvard University Press, 1987), p. 270.

16 Cf. Theodor W. Adorno, *Alban Berg: Master of the Smallest Link*, trans. Juliane Brand and Christopher Hailey (Cambridge: Cambridge University Press, 1991). (Originally published in 1968 as *Alban Berg: Der Meister des kleinsten Übergangs*).

17 Joris-Karl Huysmans, *Against Nature*, trans. Robert Baldick (Baltimore: Penguin Books, 1959), p. 204.

18 Friedrich Nietzsche, *Der Fall Wagners* (1888); in Friedrich Nietzsche, *The Birth of Tragedy* and *The Case of Wagner*, trans. Walter Kaufmann (New York: Vintage Books, 1967), p. 165.

19 Richard Aldington, ed. *The Portable Oscar* Wilde, (New York: The Viking Press, 1947), p. 280.

20 Oscar Wilde, *The Picture of Dorian Gray* (London: Ward, 1891), Chap. 6.

21 Vasiliy Yastrebtsev, *Nikolai Andreyevich Rimskiy-Korsakov: Vospominaniya, 1886–1908*, Vol. II (Leningrad: Muzgiz, 1960), p. 468.

22 Richard Dehmel, *Bekentnisse* (1926); quoted in Walter Frisch, *The Early Works of Arnold Schoenberg, 1893–1908* (Berkeley and Los Angeles: University of California Press, 1993), p. 93.

23 Richard Strauss, *Betrachtungen und Erinnerungen*, ed. Willi Schuh (Zürich, 1949), p. 184; trans. Piero Weiss in P. Weiss and R. Taruskin, *Music in the Western World: A History in Documents* (2nd ed., Belmont, CA: Thomson/Schirmer, 2007), pp. 353–54.

24 Willi Reich, *Schoenberg: A Critical Biography*, trans. Leo Black (New York: Praeger Publishers, 1971), p. 25.

25 Robert P. Morgan, *Twentieth-Century Music* (New York: Norton, 1991), p. 33.

26 *Ibid.*, p. 35.

27 Bram Dijkstra, *Idols of Perversity: Fantasies of Feminine Evil in Fin-de-siècle Culture* (New York: Oxford University Press, 1986).

28 Huysmans, *Against Nature*, pp. 65–66.

CHAPTER 2: GETTING RID OF GLUE

1 Charles Baudelaire to Arsène Houssaye; Baudelaire, *Oeuvres completes* (Paris: Pléiade, 1956), p. 291.

2 Claude Debussy to Eugène Vasnier, 19 October 1885; quoted in Stefan Jarocinski, *Debussy: Impressionism and Symbolism*, trans. Rollo Myers (London: Eulenburg Books, 1976), p. 172n50.

3 Cf. José Ortega y Gasset, *La Deshumanización del arte e Ideas sobre la novela* (Madrid: Revista del Occidente, 1925).

4 Ortega y Gasset, *The Dehumanization of Art*, trans. Helene Weyl (Princeton: Princeton University Press, 1968), p. 12.

5 *Ibid.*, p. 6.

6 *Ibid.*, p. 12.

7 Quoted in Andrey Nikolayevich Rimsky-Korsakov, "Lichnost' Lyadova," *Muzïkal'nïy sovremennik*, Vol. II, no. 1 (September 1916), p. 33.

8 Alan M. Gillmor, *Erik Satie* (New York: Norton, 1992), p. 10.

9 Vladimir F. Odoyevsky, *Literaturno-muzïkal'noye naslediye* (Moscow: Muzgiz, 1956), p. 343.

10 Gillmor, *Erik Satie*, p. 37.

11 Ortega y Gasset, *The Dehumanization of Art*, p. 14.

12 "La Musique Russe et les Compositeurs Français," *Excelsior* (9 March 1911); quoted in Malcolm H. Brown, "Modest Petrovich Musorgsky, 1881–1981," in *Musorgsky: In Memoriam 1881–1981*, ed. M. H. Brown (Ann Arbor: UMI Research Press, 1982), p. 4.

13 Quoted in Edward Lockspeiser, *Debussy: His Life and Mind*, Vol. I (London: Cassell, 1962), p. 208.

14 Report by the Permanent Secretary of the Académie des Beaux-Arts, 1887; quoted in Jarocinski, *Debussy*, p. 11.

15 Debussy, *Monsieur Croche Antidilettante*, trans. B. N. Langdon Davies; in *Three Classics in the Aesthetics of Music* (New York: Dover Publications, 1962), p. 8.

16 Debussy, "Why I Wrote Pelléas" (1902); in *Debussy on Music*, ed. François Lesure, trans. Richard Langham Smith (New York: Knopf, 1977), p. 75.

17 Quoted in Jarocinski, *Debussy*, p. 8.

18 Baudelaire, *Petits poèmes en prose* (1862); quoted in Baudelaire, *Pages choisis* (Classiques Larousse, 1934), p. 14n5.

19 Michel Foucault, *The Order of Things* (New York: Vintage Books, 1973), pp. 25–26; quoted in Gary Tomlinson, *Music in Renaissance Magic* (Chicago: University of Chicago Press, 1993), p. 55.

20 Edouard Schuré, *Histoire du drame musical* (Paris, 1882); quoted in Jarocinski, *Debussy*, p. 36.

21 Baudelaire, *Salon de 1859*; quoted in Jarocinski, *Debussy*, p. 29.

22 Jarocinski, *Debussy*, p. 130.

23 *Debussy on Music*, p. 75.

24 Debussy to Ernest Chausson; *Letters*, eds. François Lesure and Roger Nichols (Cambridge: Harvard University Press, 1987), p. 62.

25 Debussy to Pierre Louÿs, 20 August 1894; *Letters*, ed. Lesure, p. 72.

26 Debussy, *Letters*, ed. Lesure, p. 62.

27 Debussy to Chausson, 2 October 1893; *Letters*, ed. Lesure, p. 54.

28 *Debussy on Music*, p. 74.

29 Carolyn Abbate, "*Tristan* in the Composition of *Pelléas*," *Nineteenth-Century Music* V (1981–82): 117–40.

30 Richard Strauss and Romain Rolland, *Correspondance; Fragments de Journal* (1951); quoted in Edward Lockspeiser, *Claude Debussy: His Life and Mind*, Vol. II: *1902–1918* (Cambridge: Cambridge University Press, 1978), p. 88.

31 *Gabriel Fauré: A Life in Letters*, trans. and ed. J. Barrie Jones (London: B. T. Batsford, 1989), p. 84.

32 Émile Vuillermoz, *Gabriel Fauré*, trans. Kenneth Schapin (Philadelphia: Chilton Books, 1969), p. 75.

33 Aaron Copland, "Fauré Festival at Harvard" (1945); in *Copland on Music* (New York: Norton, 1963), p. 126.

34 Vuillermoz, "Gabriel Faure", *Revue musicale* III, no. 11 (1922): 14.

35 *Le Temps*, 24 March 1908; quoted in Debussy, *Letters*, eds. François Lesure and Roger Nichols, trans. Roger Nichols (Cambridge: Harvard University Press, 1987) p. 190.

36 *Debussy on Music*, pp. 322–23.

37 See A. Suschitzky, "*Ariane et Barbe-Bleue*: Dukas, the Light and the Well," *Cambridge Opera Journal* IX (1997): 133–61.

38 Debussy to Vittorio Gui, 25 February 1912; Debussy, *Letters*, ed. Lesure, p. 256.

39 Debussy to Henri Lerolle, 17 August 1895; *Letters*, p. 80.

40 "Maurice Ravel's Opinion of Modern French Music," *The Musical Leader* (16 March 1911); in *A Ravel Reader*, ed. Arbie Ornstein (New York: Columbia University Press, 1990), p. 410.

41 See Pieter Van den Toorn, *The Music of Igor Stravinsky* (New Haven: Yale University Press, 1983).

42 Nikolai Rimsky-Korsakov, *My Musical Life*, trans. Judah A. Joffe, ed. Carl Van Vechten (London: Eulenburg Books, 1974), p. 78.

43 Elliott Antokoletz, Review of Pieter Van den Toorn, *The Music of Igor Stravinsky*, *JAMS* XXXVII (1984): 429.

44 Mikhail Fabianovich Gnesin, *Mïsli i vospominaniya o N. A. Rimskom-Korsakove* (Moscow: Muzgiz, 1956), p. 207.

45 Alma Mahler Werfel, *And the Bridge Is Love* (London: Hutchinson, 1959), p. 148.

46 See Steven Baur, "Ravel's 'Russian' Period: Octatonicism in His Early Works, 1893–1908," *JAMS* LII (1999): 376–77.

47 The two main texts are Harold Bloom, *The Anxiety of Influence: A Theory of Poetry* (New York: Oxford University Press, 1973), and Bloom, *A Map of Misreading* (New York: Oxford University Press, 1975).

48 Linda Nochlin, "Why Have There Been No Great Women Artists?" (1971); in Nochlin, *Women, Art, and Power and Other Essays* (New York: Harper and Row, 1988), p. 167.

49 Annegret Fauser, "*La Guerre en dentelles*: Women and the *Prix de Rome* in French Cultural Politics," *JAMS* LI (1998): 122.

50 *Ibid.*, p. 127.

51 Marc Blitzstein, "Music's Other Boulanger," *Saturday Review*, 28 May 1960, p. 60.

Chapter 3: Aristocratic Maximalism

1 Arnold Haskell, *Ballet* (Harmondsworth: Penguin Books, 1938), p. 22.

2 *L'Art du théâtre*, January 1903; quoted in Ivor Guest, *The Romantic Ballet in Paris* (Middletown, Conn.: Wesleyan University Press, 1966), p. 11.

3 *La Presse* (Paris), 5 July 1841; quoted in Guest, *The Romantic Ballet*, p. 206.

4 *La Presse*, 1 July 1844; quoted in Guest, *The Romantic Ballet*, p. 10.

5 Prince Peter Lieven, *The Birth of the Ballets-Russes* (London: George Allen & Unwin, 1936), p. 56.

6 A. A. Grigoryev, "Russkiy teatr v Peterburge," in *Epokha* (1864), no. 3: 232.

7 Rimsky-Korsakov to Semyon Kruglikov, 2 February 1900; N. A. Rimsky-Korsakov, *Polnoye sobraniye sochineniy: literaturnïye proizvedeniya i perepiska*, Vol. VIIIb (Moscow: Muzïka, 1982), p. 105.

8 Sergey Taneyev to Chaikovsky, 18 March 1878; M. Chaikovsky, *Life and Letters of Tchaikovsky*, Vol. I (New York: Vienna House, 1973), pp. 292–93.

9 Chaikovsky to Taneyev, 27 March 1878; *Ibid.*, p. 293.

10 Memoir by Alina Bryullova; *Vospominaniya o P. I. Chaikovskom* (2nd ed., Moscow: Muzïka, 1973), p. 132.

11 Solomon Volkov, *Balanchine's Tchaikovsky: Interviews with George Balanchine* (New York: Simon and Schuster, 1985), p. 127.

12 Chaikovsky to Pyotr Jurgenson, 3 June 1891; P. I. Chaikovsky, *Perepiska s P. I. Yurgensonom*, Vol. II (Moscow and Leningrad: Muzgiz, 1952), p. 212.

13 Roland John Wiley, *Tchaikovsky's Ballets* (Oxford: Clarendon Press, 1985), p. 376.

14 Alexandre Benois, *Reminiscences of the Russian Ballet*, trans. Mary Britnieva (London: G. P. Putnam's Sons, 1941), p. 372.

15 Alexandre Benois, "Beseda o balete," in V. Meyerhold, et al., *Teatr* (St. Petersburg: Shipovnik, 1908), p. 100.

16 *Ibid.*, p. 103.

17 *Ibid.*, p. 106.

18 Mikhail Fokine, *Memories of a Ballet Master*, trans. Vitale Fokine, ed. Anatole Chujoy (Boston: Little, Brown, 1961), p. 161.

19 Cf. Jean Cocteau, "La Difficulté d'être" (Monaco: Éditions du Rocher, 1947), p. 45.

20 Typescript, dated 1927, in the Igor Stravinsky archive, Paul Sacher Stiftung, Basel, Switzerland.

21 Korney Chukovsky, *Futuristï* (1922); quoted in I. V. Nestyev, *Prokofiev*, trans. Florence Jonas (Palo Alto: Stanford University Press, 1960), p. 91.

22 Igor Stravinsky, *An Autobiography* (New York: Simon and Schuster, 1936), p. 31.

23 Florent Fels, "Un entretien avec Igor Stravinsky à propos de l'enregistrement au phonographe de *Pétrouchka*," *Nouvelles littéraires*, 8 December 1928; François Lesure, ed., *Stravinsky: Études et témoignages* (Paris: Éditions Jean Claude Lattès, 1982), p. 248.

24 Yakov Tugenhold, "Itogi sezona (pis'mo iz Parizha)," *Apollon* (1911), no. 6: 74.

25 Charles Hamm, "The Genesis of *Petrushka*," in Igor Stravinsky, *Petrushka*, ed. Hamm (Norton Critical Scores; New York: Norton, 1967), p. 12.

26 Edith Sitwell, "The Russian Ballet in England," in *The Russian Ballet Gift Book* (London, 1921); rpt. in *Petrushka*, ed. Hamm, pp. 187–88.

27 *Ibid.*, p 189.

28 *The Russian Primary Chronicle*, trans. Samuel Hazzard Cross and Olgerd P. Sherbowitz (Cambridge: Cambridge University Press, 1953), p. 56.

29 Chaikovsky, diary entry for 27 June 1888; quoted in David Brown, *Glinka* (London: Oxford University Press, 1974), p. 1.

30 Vyacheslav Karatïgin, "Sed'moy kontsert Kussevitskogo," *Rech'*, 14 February 1914.

31 Rimsky-Korsakov, *My Musical Life*, p. 165.

32 Igor Stravinsky and Robert Craft, *Expositions and Developments* (Garden City, N.Y.: Doubleday, 1962), pp. 161–62.

33 Leonid Sabaneyev, "Vesna svyashchennaya," *Golos Moskvï*, 8 June 1913.

34 Stravinsky to Maximilian Steinberg, 3 July 1913; in I. F. Stravinskiy: Stat'i i materialï, ed. L. Dyachkova (Moscow: Sovetskiy kompozitor, 1973), p. 474.

35 Louis Vuillemin, "Le Sacre du Printemps," *Comoedia* 7, no. 2068 (31 May 1913); in Truman C. Bullard, "The First Performance of Igor Stravinsky's *Sacre du Printemps*," Vol. I (Ph.D. diss., University of Rochester, 1971), p. 144.

36 Jacques Rivière, "Le sacre du printemps," *La Nouvelle revue française*, November 1913; Bullard, *The First Performance*, Vol. III, pp. 271, 274.

37 Michel Georges-Michel, "Les deux Sacres du printemps," *Comoedia* (11 December 1920); Bullard, *The First Performance*, Vol. I, pp. 2–3.

38 Theodor W. Adorno, *Philosophy of New Music* (1948), trans. Anne G. Mitchell and Wesley V. Blomster (New York: Seabury Press, 1973), p. 155.

CHAPTER 4: EXTINGUISHING THE "PETTY 'I'" (TRANSCENDENTALISM, I)

1 The first of Babbitt's published articles in which this term appeared was "Twelve-Tone Invariants as Compositional Determinants," *Musical Quarterly* XLVI (1960): 246–59; rpt. in *Problems of Modern Music*, ed. P. H. Lang (New York: Norton, 1960), pp. 108–21.

2 Quoted by Robert Craft in the notes accompanying Columbia Masterworks MS 6103 (1959).

3 Milton Babbitt, untitled memoir in "Stravinsky: A Composers' Memorial," *Perspectives of New Music* IX/2–X/1 (1971): 107.

4 William Carlos Williams, introduction to "The Wedge" (1944), in *Selected Essays of William Carlos Williams* (New York: New Directions, 1969), p. 256.

5 Christopher Williams, "Of Canons and Context: Toward a Historiography of Twentieth-Century Music," *Repercussions*, 2–1 (spring 1993): 42.

6 Willi Reich, *Alban Berg. Mit Bergs eigenen Schriften und Beiträgen von Theodor Wiesengrund-Adorno und Ernst Krenek* (Vienna: Herbert Reichner Verlag, 1937), p. 47.

7 Schoenberg, "Old Forms in New Music," unpublished essay quoted in Alan Lessem, "Schoenberg, Stravinsky, and Neo-Classicism: The Issues Reexamined," *Musical Quarterly* LXVIII (1968): 538.

8 Varvara Dernova, *Garmoniya Skryabina* (Leningrad: Muzïka, 1968).

9 Vyacheslav Ivanov, "Skryabin" (1919), in *Pamyatniki kul'turï: Novïye otkrïtiye, 1983* (Leningrad: Nauka, 1985), p. 114.

10 Ivanov, "Vzglyad Skryabina na iskusstvo" (1915), *Pamyatniki kul'turï 1983*, p. 103.

11 James A. Baker, *The Music of Alexander Scriabin* (New Haven: Yale University Press, 1986), p. 270.

12 *Pamyatniki kul'turï 1983*, p. 115.

13 Dernova, *Garmoniya Skryabina*, p. 352.

14 L. Sabanejew, "'Prometheus' von Skrjabin," *Almanach der blaue Reiter*, eds. W. Kandinsky and F. Marc (Munich: Piper Verlag, 1912).

15 Arthur Eaglefield Hull, *Scriabin: A Great Russian Tone-Poet* (1916); (2nd ed., London: Kegan Paul, 1927), p. 106.

16 Igor Boelza, "Filosofskiye istoki obraznego stroya 'Prometeya,'" *Razlichnïye aspektï tvorchestva A. N. Skryabina* (Moscow: Scriabin Museum, 1992), p. 19.

17 See Andrey Bely, "Realiora," *Vesï* V, no. 5 (May 1908): 59.

18 Simon Morrison, "Skryabin and the Impossible," *JAMS* LI (1998): 314.

19 Boris de Schloezer, *Scriabin: Artist and Mystic*, trans. Nicolas Slonimsky (Berkeley and Los Angeles: University of California Press, 1987), p. 269.

20 Morrison, "Skryabin and the Impossible," pp. 326–27.

21 Rose Lee, "Dmitri Szostakovitch: Young Russian Composer Tells of Linking Politics with Creative Work," *New York Times*, 20 December 1931; reproduced in facsimile in Eric Roseberry, *Shostakovich: His Life and Times* (New York: Hippocrene Books, 1982), p. 79.

22 Olivier Messiaen, *The Technique of My Musical Language*, trans. John Satterfield (Paris: Leduc, 1956), p. 8.

23 Messiaen, *Technique*, p. 13.

24 Anthony Pople, "Messiaen's Musical Language: An Introduction," in *The Messiaen Companion*, ed. Peter Hill (Portland: Amadeus Press, 1995), p. 21.

25 Olivier Messiaen, *The Technique of My Musical Language* (1944), trans. John Satterfield (Paris: Alphonse Leduc, 1956), Vol. I, p. 58.

26 John Milsom, "Organ Music I," *The Messiaen Companion*, p. 55.

27 Messiaen, *Technique*, p. 21.

28 Wilfrid Mellers, "Mysticism and Theology," in *The Messiaen Companion*, p. 228.

Chapter 5: Containing Multitudes (Transcendentalism, II)

1 *Emerson's Essays* (London: Oxford University Press, 1901), p. 31.

2 *Emerson's Essays*, p. 188.

3 William Lyon Phelps, *Music* (New York: E. P. Dutton, 1930), p. 3.

4 *Emerson's Essays*, p. 39.

5 Michael Moran, "New England Transcendentalism," in *The Encyclopedia of Philosophy*, Vol. V (New York: Macmillan, 1967), p. 479.

6 Emerson, "The Transcendentalist," quoted in Moran, p. 479.

7 Octavius Brooks Frothingham, *Transcendentalism in New England: A History* (1876); (New York: Harper and Brothers, 1959), p. 136.

8 *Ibid.*, p. 355.

9 Charles E. Ives, *Memos*, ed. John Kirkpatrick (New York: Norton, 1972), pp. 115–16.

10 Stuart Feder, *Charles Ives: "My Father's Song"* (New Haven: Yale University Press, 1992), p. 174.

11 Frank R. Rossiter, "Charles Ives: Good American and Isolated Artist," in *An Ives Celebration*, eds. H. Wiley Hitchcock and Vivian Perlis (Urbana: University of Illinois Press, 1977), p. 16.

12 *Ibid.*, p. 17.

13 Henry and Sidney Cowell, *Charles Ives and His Music* (New York: Oxford University Press, 1955), p. 106. The Cowells' source was an unpublished typescript, "A Connecticut Yankee in Music," by Lucille Fletcher, who heard it from Ives himself

(see Maynard Solomon, "Charles Ives: Some Questions of Veracity," *JAMS* XL [1987]: 466).

14 Rossiter, p. 18.

15 Ives, *Memos*, p. 74.

16 Boris Schwarz, "Elman, Mischa," in *New Grove Dictionary of Music and Musicians*, Vol. VIII (2nd ed., New York: Grove, 2001), p. 157.

17 Charles Ives, *Essays Before a Sonata* (1920); in *Essays Before a Sonata and Other Writings by Charles Ives*, ed. Howard Boatwright (New York: Norton, 1964), p. 84.

18 Lawrence Kramer, *Classical Music and Postmodern Knowledge* (Berkeley and Los Angeles: University of California Press, 1995), p. 184.

19 Harding coined the term in a campaign speech given on 14 May 1920, in which he announced that the nation needed "not nostrums but normalcy."

20 See, for example, *Essays Before a Sonata*, p. 75.

21 Robert M. Crunden, "Review Essay: On Charles Ives," *Modernism/Modernity* IV, no. 3 (September 1997): 155.

22 Lawrence Gilman, "A Masterpiece of American Music Heard Here for the First Time," *New York Herald Tribune*, 21 January 1939, p. 9.

23 Wayne Shirley, "Gilman, Lawrence," in *New Grove Dictionary of Music and Musicians*, Vol. IX (2nd ed., New York: Grove, 2001), p. 870.

24 Vivian Perlis, ed., *Charles Ives Remembered: An Oral History* (New Haven: Yale University Press, 1974), p. 138.

25 Maynard Solomon, "Charles Ives: Some Questions of Veracity," *JAMS* XL (1987): 453.

26 *Ibid.*, p. 466.

27 *Ibid.*, p. 470.

28 *Essays Before a Sonata*, pp. 72–73.

29 Elliott Carter, "The Case of Mr. Ives" (1939), in *The Writings of Elliott Carter*, eds. Else Stone and Kurt Stone (Bloomington: Indiana University Press, 1977), p. 48.

30 Edward Burlingame Hill, *Modern French Music* (Boston: Houghton Mifflin, 1924), p. 36.

31 *Essays Before a Sonata*, p. 36.

32 J. Peter Burkholder, *All Made of Tunes: Charles Ives and the Uses of Musical Borrowing* (New Haven: Yale University Press, 1995), p. 195.

33 J. Peter Burkholder, *Charles Ives: The Ideas Behind the Music* (New Haven: Yale University Press, 1985), p. 75.

34 William Lyon Phelps, *Music*, pp. 19–20.

35 *Ibid.*, pp. 27–28.

36 See Richard Hofstadter, *The Age of Reform: From Bryan to F.D.R.* (New York: Knopf, 1955), p. 62.

37 Jan Swafford, *Charles Ives: A Life with Music* (New York: Norton, 1996), p. 208.

38 Ives, *Memos*, p. 61.

39 *Essays Before a Sonata*, p. 3.

40 Ives, *Memos*, p. 84.

41 Ives, *Memos*, pp. 139–40.

42 Cowell, *Charles Ives and His Music*, pp. 144–45.

43 Draft of a letter to Paul Rosenfeld (1940); quoted in Jan Swafford, *Charles Ives: A Life with Music* (New York: Norton, 1996), p. 3.

44 *Essays Before a Sonata*, p. 94.

45 Quoted in Feder, *Charles Ives: "My Father's Song,"* p. 294.

46 Ives, *Memos*, p. 108.

47 Ives, *Memos*, p. 107.

48 Harry Partch, Introduction to *Photographs of Instruments Built by Harry Partch and Heard in His Recorded Music* (Champaign, Ill.: Gate 5, 1962), n.p.

49 Ives, "Some Quarter-Tone Impressions," *Essays Before a Sonata and Other Writings*, p. 108.

50 *Ibid.*, p. 109.

51 *Ibid.*, pp. 111–12.

52 *Ibid.*, p. 113.

53 *Ibid.*, p. 117.

54 *New York Times*, 15 February 1925; rpt. J. Peter Burkholder, ed., *Charles Ives and His World* (Princeton: Princeton University Press, 1996), p. 293.

55 David Hall, *The Record Book: International Edition* (New York: Oliver Durrell, Inc., 1948), p. 439.

56 Paul Rosenfeld, *An Hour with American Music* (1929), quoted in Judith Tick, "Ruth Crawford's 'Spiritual Concept': The Sound-Ideals of an Early American Modernist," *JAMS* XLIV (1991): 235.

57 Quoted in *Ibid.*, pp. 239–40.

58 Quoted in Judith Tick, "Ruth Crawford's 'Spiritual Concept': The Sound-Ideals of an Early American Modernist," *Journal of the American Musicological Society* XLIV (1991): 244.

59 Michael Hicks, "Cowell's Clusters," *Musical Quarterly* LXXVII (1993): 428, 440.

60 Michael Hicks, *Henry Cowell, Bohemian* (Urbana: University of Illinois Press, 2002), p. 184n64.

61 Louise Vermont, "A Musical Note Butchers Paper and Cold Feet," *Greenwich Villager*, 15 April 1922.

62 "Public Unafraid of New Music, Composer Says," *Houston Post*, 15 November 1955; quoted in Hicks, "Cowell's Clusters," p. 450.

63 Nicolas Slonimsky, "Henry Cowell," in *American Composers on American Music*, ed. Henry Cowell (Palo Alto: Stanford University Press, 1933), p. 62.

64 Hicks, "Cowell's Clusters," p. 452.

CHAPTER 6: INNER OCCURRENCES (TRANSCENDENTALISM, III)

1 Arnold Schoenberg, "Aphorismen," in *Schöpferische Konfessionen*, ed. Willi Reich (Zürich, 1964), p. 12; translation adapted from that of Leo Black, in Reich, *Arnold Schoenberg: A Critical Biography* (New York: Praeger, 1971), pp. 56–57.

2 Arnold Schoenberg, "Criteria for the Evaluation of Music" (1946); *Style and Idea: Selected Writings of Arnold Schoenberg*, trans. Leo Black, ed. Leonard Stein (Berkeley and Los Angeles: University of California Press, 1984), p. 132.

3 Schoenberg to Wassily Kandinsky, 24 January 1911; *Arnold Schoenberg/Wassily Kandinsky, Letters, Pictures and Documents*, ed. Jelena Hahl-Koch, trans. John C. Crawford (London: Faber and Faber, 1984), p. 23.

4 Schoenberg, *Theory of Harmony* [*Harmonielehre*, 1911], trans. Roy E. Carter (Berkeley and Los Angeles: University of California Press, 1978), p. 18.

5 *Arnold Schoenberg/Wassily Kandinsky, Letters*, p. 23.

6 Schoenberg, Program note to the first performance of *Five Orchestra Pieces*, op. 16 (1909); Nicolas Slonimsky, *Music since 1900* (4th ed., New York: Scribners, 1971), p. 207.

7 Schoenberg, "Problems in Teaching Art" (1911); *Style and Idea*, p. 365.

8 Schoenberg, *Theory of Harmony*, p. 18.

9 *Ibid.*, p. 21.

10 The term as such appears for the first time in "Opinion or Insight?," an essay of 1926 (*Style and Idea*, p. 260).

11 Schoenberg, *Theory of Harmony*, p. 330.

12 *Ibid.*, p. 384.

13 Alban Berg to Schoenberg, 9 February 1925; Juliane Brand, Christopher Hailey, and Donald Harris, eds., *The Berg-Schoenberg Correspondence* (New York: Norton, 1987), pp. 334–37.

14 See Allen Forte, "Schoenberg's Creative Evolution: The Path to Atonality," *Musical Quarterly* LXIV (1978): 133–76.

15 Schoenberg, "Analysis of the Second Quartet" (1949), in *Schoenberg, Berg, Webern: The String Quartets: A Documentary Study*, ed. Ursula von Rauchhaupt (Hamburg: Deutsche Grammophon Gesellschaft, 1971), booklet accompanying LaSalle Quartet recording, DG 2713 006, p. 48.

16 Pieter van den Toorn, *The Music of Igor Stravinsky* (New Haven: Yale University Press, 1983), p. 332.

17 Schoenberg, "Composition with Twelve Tones (II)" (1948); *Style and Idea*, p. 248.

18 Anton Webern, "Schönberg's Musik," in Alban Berg, et al., *Arnold Schönberg* (Munich: Piper Verlag, 1912); quoted in John C. Crawford and Dorothy L. Crawford, *Expressionism in Twentieth-Century Music* (Bloomington: Indiana University Press, 1993), pp. 79–80.

19 Robert P. Morgan, *Twentieth-Century Music*, p. 73.

20 Charles Rosen, *Arnold Schoenberg* (New York: Viking Press, 1975), pp. 57–58.

21 Herbert Buchanan, "A Key to Schoenberg's *Erwartung*, op. 17," *JAMS* XX (1967): 434–49.

22 Schoenberg to Kandinsky, 19 August 1912; *Letters*, p. 54.

23 Honoré de Balzac, *Séraphîta* (Blauvelt, N.Y.: Freedeeds Library, 1986), p. 173.

24 Schoenberg, *Theory of Harmony*, pp. 421–22.

25 Schoenberg to Nicolas Slonimsky, 3 June 1937; *Music since 1900*, p. 1316.

26 Webern, *The Path to the New Music*, trans. Leo Black (Bryn Mawr, Pa.: Theodore Presser Co., 1963), p. 37.

27 Schoenberg, "Composition with Twelve Tones (I)" (1941); *Style and Idea*, p. 223.

28 Schoenberg, "Analysis of the First Quartet" (1936); Rauchhaupt, *Documentary Study*, p. 36.

29 Alban Berg, "Why Is Schoenberg's Music So Difficult to Understand?" (1924); in *Contemporary Composers on Contemporary Music*, eds. Elliott Schwarz and Barney Childs (New York: Holt, Rinehart and Winston, 1967), pp. 68–69.

30 Webern, *The Path to the New Music*, p. 51.

31 Lawrence Gilman, *New York Herald Tribune*, 29 November 1926; quoted in Nicolas Slonimsky, *Lexicon of Musical Invective* (2nd ed., Seattle: University of Washington Press, 1969), pp. 249–50.

32 [Alban Berg], Society for Private Musical Performance in Vienna: Statement of Aims; Slonimsky, *Music since 1900*, pp. 1307–8.

33 Franz Liszt, "John Field and His Nocturnes"; in P. Weiss and R. Taruskin, *Music in the Western World: A History in Documents* (2nd ed., Belmont, CA: Thomson/Schirmer, 2007), p. 312.

34 Schoenberg, "New Music, Outmoded Music, Style and Idea" (1946); *Style and Idea*, p. 124.

35 Quoted in Reich, *Schoenberg: A Critical Biography*, p. 49.

36 Webern, *The Path to the New Music*, p. 36.

37 Morgan, *Twentieth-Century Music*, p. 1.

38 Donald Jay Grout, *A History of Western Music* (New York: Norton, 1960), p. 647.

39 Morgan, *Twentieth-Century Music*, pp. 1–2.

40 Joseph N. Straus, *Remaking the Past: Musical Modernism and the Influence of the Tonal Tradition* (Cambridge: Harvard University Press, 1990), p. 22.

41 Robert Craft, "Schoenberg's Five Pieces for Orchestra," in *Perspectives on Schoenberg and Stravinsky*, eds. Benjamin Boretz and Edward T. Cone (Princeton: Princeton University Press, 1968), p. 8.

42 Adorno, *Philosophy of New Music* (1948), trans. Anne G. Mitchell and Wesley V. Blomster (New York: Seabury Press, 1973), p. 32ff.

43 Webern, *The Path to the New Music*, p. 33.

44 Quoted in Hans Moldenhauer and Rosaleen Moldenhauer, *Anton von Webern: A Chronicle of His Life and Work* (New York: Knopf, 1979), p. 444.

Chapter 7: Socially Validated Maximalism

1   Ferenc Bónis, "Mosonyi, Mihály," in *New Grove Dictionary of Music and Musicians*, Vol. XVII (2nd ed.; New York: Grove, 2001), p. 184.

2   Franz Liszt, *Des Bohémiens et de leur musique en Hongrie* (1859); quoted in Jonathan Bellman, *The Style Hongrois in the Music of Western Europe* (Boston: Northeastern University Press, 1993), p. 179.

3   Bellman, *Style Hongrois*, p. 179.

4   Judit Frigyesi, "Béla Bartók and Hungarian Nationalism: The Development of Bartók's Social and Political Ideas at the Turn of the Century (1899–1903)" (Ph.D. diss., University of Pennsylvania, 1989), p. 117.

5   Bellman, *Style Hongrois*, p. 215.

6   Frigyesi, *Béla Bartók and Hungarian Nationalism*, p. 138ff.

7   Bartók and Kodály, *Magyar Népdalok* (Budapest: Rozsnyai Károly, 1906), Introduction; trans. Klára Móricz.

8   Bartók, "The Influence of Peasant Music on Modern Music," in *Béla Bartók's Essays*, ed. Benjamin Suchoff (New York: St. Martin's Press, 1976), p. 341.

9   Bartók, "Autobiography"; *Béla Bartók's Essays*, p. 410.

10 "The Influence of Peasant Music on Modern Music"; *Béla Bartók's Essays*, pp. 341–44.

11 Bartók, "The Folk Songs of Hungary" (1928); *Béla Bartók's Essays*, p. 331.

12 *Ibid.*, p. 338.

13 Bartók, *Music for String Instruments, Percussion and Celesta* (London: Boosey & Hawkes, 1939), p. iii.

14 László Somfai, *The New Grove Modern Masters* (London: Macmillan, 1984), p. 62.

15 Elliott Antokoletz, "Principles of Pitch Organization in Bartók's Fourth String Quartet," in *Theory Only* III, no. 4 (September 1977): 4.

16 George Perle, "Symmetrical Formations in the String Quartets of Béla Bartók," *The Music Review* XVI (1955): 309ff.

17 Leo Treitler, "Harmonic Procedure in the *Fourth Quartet* of Béla Bartók," *Journal of Music Theory* III (1959): 292–97.

18 Theodor W. Adorno, *Philosophy of New Music*, pp. 35–36n5.

19 Mirka Zemanová, ed., *Janáček's Uncollected Essays on Music* (London: Marion Boyars, 1989), p. 61.

20 Desmond Shawe-Taylor, "Jeritza, Maria," in *New Grove Dictionary of Opera*, Vol. II (London: Macmillan, 1992), p. 893.

21 *Janáček's Uncollected Essays on Music*, p. 61.

22 *Ibid.*

23 Michael Beckerman, *Janáček as Theorist* (Stuyvesant, N.Y.: Pendragon Press, 1994), p. 133.

24 *Janáček's Uncollected Essays on Music*, pp. 121–22.

25 *Ibid.*, p. 56.

26 John Tyrrell, *Czech Opera* (Cambridge: Cambridge University Press, 1988), p. 255.

27 Tyrrell, *Czech Opera*, pp. 294, 296.

28 Tyrrell, *Leoš Janáček: Kat'a Kabanová* (Cambridge Opera Handbooks; Cambridge: Cambridge University Press, 1982), p. 13.

29 Arnold Schoenberg to Prince Egon Fürstenberg, April 1924; *Arnold Schoenberg's Letters*, ed. Erwin Stein, trans. Eithne Wilkins and Ernst Kaiser (Berkeley and Los Angeles: University of California Press, 1987), p. 108.

30 Béla Bartók to Jenö Takács, 31 December 1925; Béla Bartók, *Letters*, ed. János Demény (New York: St. Martin's Press, 1971), p. 168.

Chapter 8: Pathos Is Banned

1 Aaron Copland, *The New Music 1900/60* (London: Macdonald, 1968), p. 72.

2 *Ibid.*

3 Chaikovsky to Nadezhda von Meck, 25 August 1878; P. I. Chaikovsky, *Perepiska s N. F. fon-Mekk*, Vol. I (Moscow: Academia, 1934), p. 421.

4 Engelbert Humperdinck to a Dr. Distl, 2 November 1898; quoted in Edward F. Kravitt, *The Lied: Mirror of Late Romanticism* (New Haven: Yale University Press, 1996), p. 87.

5 Egon Wellesz, *Arnold Schoenberg: The Formative Years* (London: Galliard, 1971), pp. 7–8.

6 Charles Rosen, *Arnold Schoenberg* (New York: Viking Press, 1975), p. 55; or Wellesz: "in the whole range of modern music I have nowhere found [anything] to place beside it" (*Schoenberg: The Formative Years*, p. 142).

7 José Ortega y Gasset, *The Dehumanization of Art*, trans. Helene Weyl (Princeton: Princeton University Press, 1968), p. 25.

8 *Stravinsky: An Autobiography* (New York: Simon and Schuster, 1936), p. 67.

9 "Romanticism and Classicism," in T. E. Hulme, *Speculations: Essays on Humanism and the Philosophy of Art*, ed. Herbert Read (London: Routledge, 1924), p. 115.

10 Hulme, "Modern Art and Its Philosophy," *Speculations*, p. 80.

11 Hulme, *Speculations*, pp. 126–27.

12 Jacques Rivière, "Le Sacre du Printemps," *La Nouvelle Revue française*, 1 November 1913; trans. adapted from Truman C. Bullard, "The First Performance of Stravinsky's *Sacre du Printemps*," Vol. II (Ph.D. diss., Eastman School of Music, 1971), pp. 269–308.

13 Boris de Schloezer, "La musique," *La Revue contemporaine*, 1 February 1923; quoted in Scott Messing, *Neoclassicism in Music from the Genesis of the Concept through the Schoenberg/Stravinsky Polemic* (Ann Arbor: UMI Research Press, 1988), p. 130.

14 *Stravinsky: An Autobiography*, pp. 83–84.

15 Igor Stravinsky, *Poetics of Music in the Form of Six Lessons*, trans. Arthur Knodel and Ingolf Dahl (New York: Vintage Books, 1956), p. 62.

16 Quoted in Deems Taylor, *Of Men and Music* (New York: Simon and Schuster, 1937), pp. 89–90.

17 Quoted in Tony Judt, "The End of the World," *New York Times Book Review*, 27 June 1999, p. 12.

18 David Lowe, "Bourbon County" (1973); quoted in Paul Fussell, *The Great War and Modern Memory* (New York: Oxford University Press, 1975), p. 24.

19 John Keegan, *The First World War*; quoted in Judt, "The End of the World," p. 10.

20 Judt, "The End of the World," p. 10.

21 Quoted in Fussell, *The Great War and Modern Memory*, p. 8.

22 Philip Gibbs, *Now It Can Be Told* (1920); quoted in Fussell, *The Great War*, p. 8.

23 Ernest Hemingway, *A Farewell to Arms* (New York: Charles Scribner's Sons, 1929), p. 191.

24 Fussell, *The Great War in Modern Memory*, pp. 21–22.

25 Hulme, *Speculations*, p. 85.

26 *Ibid.*

27 *Ibid.*, pp. 86–87.

28 Stravinsky, *Poetics of Music*, p. 128.

29 *Ibid.*, p. 129.

30 Ortega y Gasset, *The Dehumanization of Art*, pp. 6–8.

31 Alberto Gasco, *Da Cimarosa a Stravinsky* (Rome, 1939); quoted in Harvey Sachs, *Music in Fascist Italy* (New York: Norton, 1988), p. 168.

32 *Il Piccolo*, May 1935; quoted in Vera Stravinsky and Robert Craft, *Stravinsky in Pictures and Documents* (New York: Simon and Schuster, 1978), p. 552.

33 Prokofieff to Nikolai Myaskovsky, 5 March 1925; *S. S. Prokof'yev i N. YA. Myaskovskiy: Perepiska*, ed. M. G. Kozlova and N. R. Yastenko (Moscow: Sovetskiy kompozitor, 1977), p. 211.

34 Prokofieff to Myaskovsky, 4 August 1925; *Perepiska*, p. 218.

35 Igor Stravinsky and Robert Craft, *Conversations with Igor Stravinsky* (Garden City, N.Y.: Doubleday, 1959), p. 18.

36 Igor Stravinsky, "Some Ideas about My Octuor," *The Arts*, January 1924; reprinted in Eric Walter White, *Stravinsky: The Composer and His Works* (Berkeley and Los Angeles: University of California Press, 1966), p. 528.

37 Charles Koechlin, "Le 'Retour à Bach,'" *La Revue musicale* VIII (1926): pp. 1–2.

38 Stravinsky, "Some Ideas," pp. 529–31.

39 *Ibid.*, p. 528.

Chapter 9: Lost — or Rejected — Illusions

1 Samuel Taylor Coleridge, *Biographia Literaria* (1817), Chap. 14.

2 Sergei Prokofieff, "Avtobiografiya," in *S. S. Prokof'yev: Materialï, dokumentï, vospominaniya*, ed. S. I. Shlifshteyn (Moscow: Muzgiz, 1961), p. 177.

3 *Useless Memoirs of Carlo Gozzi*, trans. John Addington Symonds (London, 1962), p. 168.

4 Vsevolod Meyerhold, *Lyubov' k tryom apel'sinam, zhurnal Doktora Dapertutto*, Vol. I (1914), p. 32.

5 Alban Berg, lecture on *Wozzeck* (1929); Hans Redlich, *Alban Berg: Versuch einer Würdigung* (Vienna: Universal Edition, 1957), p. 327.

6 José Ortega y Gasset, *The Dehumanization of Art*, trans. Helene Weyl (Princeton: Princeton University Press, 1968), pp. 14–19.

7 Joseph Kerman, *Opera as Drama* (New York: Vintage Books, 1956), p. 231.

8 George Perle, *The Operas of Alban Berg*, Vol. I: *Wozzeck* (Berkeley and Los Angeles: University of California Press, 1980), p. 89.

9 Igor Stravinsky and Robert Craft, *Dialogues and a Diary* (Garden City, N.Y.: Doubleday, 1963), p. 24.

10 Alban Berg, "A Word about *Wozzeck*" (*Das Opernproblem*, 1928); *Composers on Music*, ed. Sam Morgenstern (New York: Bonanza Books, 1956), p. 462.

11 Roger Sessions, "Music in Crisis: Some Notes on Recent Musical History," *Modern Music* X (1932–33): 75.

12 See George Perle, "Berg's Master Array of Interval Cycles," *Musical Quarterly* LXIII (1977): 1–30.

13 Quoted in Herbert Lindenberger, *Georg Büchner* (Carbondale: Southern Illinois University Press, 1964), p. 129.

14 Lindenberger, *Georg Büchner*, p. 129.

15 T. S. Eliot, "Poetry and Drama"; quoted in Kerman, *Opera as Drama*, p. 8.

16 Boris Asafiev, *A Book about Stravinsky*, trans. Richard F. French (Ann Arbor: UMI Research Press, 1982), p. 97.

17 Asafiev, *A Book about Stravinsky*, p. 99.

18 Quoted in Stephen Hinton, *The Idea of Gebrauchsmusik: A Study of Musical Aesthetics in the Weimar Republic (1919–1933) with Particular Reference to the Works of Paul Hindemith* (New York and London: Garland Publishing, 1988), p. 181.

19 Quoted in Hinton, *The Idea of Gebrauchsmusik*, p. 186.

20 "Der Musiker Weill," *Berliner Tageblatt*, 25 December 1928, as translated in *The Musical Times* 70 (1 March 1929): 224.

21 *Brecht on Theatre*, trans. and ed. John Willett (New York: Hill and Wang, 1964), p. 39.

22 Cf. Weill, "Über den gestischen Charakter der Musik," *Die Musik* 21 (March 1929), 419–23; translated in Kim H. Kowalke, *Kurt Weill in Europe* (Ann Arbor: UMI Research Press, 1979), pp. 491–96.

23 *Brecht on Theatre*, pp. 44–45; quoted in W. Anthony Sheppard, *Revealing Masks: Exotic Influences and Ritualized Performance in Modernist Music Theater* (Berkeley and Los Angeles: University of California Press, 2001), p. 88.

24 Arnold Schoenberg, "Linear Counterpoint" (1931); *Style and Idea*, p. 294.

25 Brecht, "Über die Verwendung von Musik für ein episches Theater"; *Brecht on Theatre*, p. 89.

26 Weill, "Über meine Schuloper *Der Jasager*" (1930); Kowalke, *Kurt Weill in Europe*, p. 530.

27 Stephen Hinton, "Jasager, Der," in *New Grove Dictionary of Opera*, Vol. II (London: Macmillan, 1992), p. 885.

28 *Ibid.*

29 Virgil Thomson, "On Being Discovered" (1965); *A Virgil Thomson Reader*, ed. John Rockwell (Boston: Houghton Mifflin, 1981), p. 410.

30 Leonid Sabaneyeff, *Modern Russian Composers* (New York: International Publishers, 1927), p. 135.

31 Nikolai Medtner to Sergei Rachmaninoff, 28 May 1924; N. K. Medtner, *Pis'ma*, ed. Z. A. Apetyan (Moscow: Sovetskiy kompozitor, 1973), p. 271.

32 Nicolas Medtner, *The Muse and the Fashion*, trans. Alfred J. Swan (Haverford, Pa.: Haverford College Bookstore, 1951), p. 100.

Chapter 10: The Cult of the Commonplace

1 Sergey Diaghilev to Boris Kochno, 22 July 1924; Boris Kochno, *Diaghilev and the Ballets Russes* (New York: Harper and Row, 1970), p. 226.

2 Jean Cocteau, *A Call to Order*, trans. Rollo H. Myers (London: Faber and Gwyer, 1926), p. 25.

3 *Ibid.*, pp. 25–26.

4 Daniel Albright, *Untwisting the Serpent: Modernism in Music, Literature and Other Arts* (Chicago: University of Chicago Press, 2000), p. 197.

5 Quoted in Nancy Perloff, *Art and the Everyday: Popular Entertainment and the Circle of Erik Satie* (Oxford: Clarendon Press, 1991), p. 113.

6 Guillaume Apollinaire, "Parade," *Excelsior*, 11 May 1917.

7 Lynn Garafola, *Diaghilev's Ballets Russes* (New York: Oxford University Press, 1989), p. 98ff.

8 Quoted in Stephen Downes, "The Polish Polemicist," *Times Literary Supplement*, 15 October 1999, p. 23.

9 Darius Milhaud, *Notes without Music*, trans. Donald Evans (New York: Alred A. Knopf, 1953), pp. 122–23.

10 *Ibid.*, p. 123.

11 Francis Poulenc, *My Friends and Myself* (London: Dennis Dobson, 1978), p. 127.

12 *Ibid.*, pp. 69–70.

13 Albright, *Untwisting the Serpent*, p. 288.

14 Apollinaire, *Les Mamelles de Tirésias* (1916); quoted in Albright, *Untwisting the Serpent*, p. 246.

15 Darius Milhaud, "Polytonalité et atonalité," *Revue musicale*, Vol. IV (1923); trans. R. Taruskin in P. Weiss and R. Taruskin, *Music in the Western World: A History in Documents* (2nd ed., Belmont, CA: Thomson/Schirmer, 2007), pp. 400–01.

16 *Ibid.*, p. 401.

17 Virgil Thomson, "French Music Here" (1941); *A Virgil Thomson Reader*, ed. John Rockwell (Boston: Houghton Mifflin, 1981), pp. 207–8.

18 Jean Cocteau, *Les mariés de la Tour Eiffel* (1923); quoted in Albright, *Untwisting the Serpent*, p. 280.

19 Virgil Thomson, *Virgil Thomson* (New York: Alfred A. Knopf, 1967), p. 89.

20 *The Columbia Encyclopedia* (6th ed.; New York: Columbia University Press, 2000), p. 2710.

21 André Breton, "Surrealist Manifesto" (1924), in André Breton, *Manifestoes of Surrealism*, trans. Richard Seaver and Helen R. Lane (Ann Arbor: University of Michigan Press, 1972), p. 26.

22 Albright, *Untwisting the Serpent*, p. 268.

23 *Ibid.*, p. 269.

24 William James, *The Principles of Psychology* (New York: Henry Holt, 1890).

25 Thomson, *Virgil Thomson*, p. 90.

26 Gertrude Stein, *Everybody's Autobiography*; quoted in Albright, *Untwisting the Serpent*, p. 322.

27 Gertrude Stein, *Lectures in America* (New York: Vintage Books, 1975), p. 119.

28 Quoted in Albright, *Untwisting the Serpent*, p. 328.

29 Joseph Frank, "Spatial Form in Modern Literature," in J. Frank, *The Idea of Spatial Form* (New Brunswick, N.J.: Rutgers University Press, 1991), p. 17.

30 Thomson, *Virgil Thomson*, p. 104.

31 Kathleen Hoover and John Cage, *Virgil Thomson: His Life and Music* (New York: Thomas Yoseloff, 1959), p. 157.

32 Virgil Thomson, program note for *The Seine at Night* (1947); quoted in Kathleen Hoover and John Cage, *Virgil Thomson: His Life and Music* (New York: Thomas Yoseloff, 1959), p. 108.

33 Frank, "Spatial Form," p. 58.

34 Liner note to RCA Victor DM-1244 (released 1948); quoting a radio talk given in 1942.

35 Virgil Thomson, "About 'Four Saints,'" liner note to Nonesuch Records 79035–1 X (1982).

36 *Ibid.*

CHAPTER 11: IN SEARCH OF THE "REAL" AMERICA

1 David Schiff, *Gershwin: Rhapsody in Blue* (Cambridge: Cambridge University Press, 1997), p. 83; increasingly accepted among scholars is an etymology relating the term to "jizz," an African-American slang word for seminal ejaculate.

2 Quoted in Stephen Walsh, *Stravinsky: A Creative Spring: Russia and France, 1882–1934* (New York: Knopf, 1999), p. 264.

3 Ansermet, "Sur un Orchestre Nègre" (1919); Robert Walser, ed., *Keeping Time: Readings in Jazz History* (New York: Oxford University Press, 1999), p. 11.

4 Walser, *Keeping Time*, p. 9.

5 Ansermet, "Sur un Orchestre Négre"; *Keeping Time*, pp. 10–11.

6 Darius Milhaud, *Notes without Music*, trans. Donald Evans (New York: Knopf, 1953), pp. 136–37.

7 Maurice Ravel, "Contemporary Music," in *The Rice Institute Pamphlets*, Vol. XV (1928); P. Weiss and R. Taruskin, *Music in the Western World*, 2nd ed., pp. 407–8.

8 Ansermet, "Sur un Orchestre Nègre"; *Keeping Time*, p. 11.

9 *Ibid.*

10 Aaron Copland and Vivian Perlis, *Copland: 1900 through 1942* (New York: St. Martin's/Marek, 1984), p. 35.

11 Quoted in Howard Pollack, *Aaron Copland: The Life and Work of an Uncommon Man* (New York: Henry Holt, 1999), p. 113.

12 Copland and Perlis, *Copland: 1900 through 1942*, p. 104.

13 *Ibid.*

14 Ansermet, "Sur un Orchestre Nègre"; *Keeping Time*, p. 10.

15 Warren Storey Smith in *The Boston Post*, 21 November 1925; Perlis and Copland, *Copland: 1900 through 1942*, p. 121.

16 Olin Downes in *New York Times*, 29 November 1925; *ibid.*

17 Aaron Copland to Nicolas Slonimsky, March 1927; in *Letters of Composers*, ed. Gertrude Norman and Miriam Lubell Shrifte (New York: Grosset and Dunlap, 1945), p. 401.

18 Unsigned editorial, *Boston Evening Transcript*, 5 February 1927; Nicolas Slonimsky, *Lexicon of Musical Invective* (Seattle: University of Washington Press, 1965), p. 87.

19 Samuel Chotzinoff, *New York World*, 4 February 1927; Slonimsky, *Lexicon*, p. 86.

20 John Tasker Howard, *Our Contemporary Composers* (New York: Thomas Y. Crowell, 1941), p. 149.

21 Gilbert Seldes, "The Negro's Songs," *Dial*, March 1926; quoted in Macdonald Smith Moore, *Yankee Blues: Musical Culture and American Identity* (Bloomington: Indiana University Press, 1985), p. 144.

22 Fritz Laubenstein, "Race Values in Aframerican Music"; quoted in Moore, *Yankee Blues*, p. 143.

23 Daniel Gregory Mason, "Is American Music Growing Up? Our Emancipation from Alien Influences," *Arts and Decoration*, November 1920; quoted in D. G. Mason, *Tune In, America: A Study of Our Coming Musical Independence* (1931; rpt. Freeport, N.Y.: Books for Libraries Press, 1969), p. 160.

24 Mason, *Tune In, America*, p. 162.

25 Hiram K. Moderwell, *The New Republic*, 16 October 1915; quoted in Mason, *Tune In, America*, p. 163.

26 Mason, *Tune In, America*, pp. 163–64.

27 *Ibid.*, pp. 164–65.

28 *Ibid.*, p. 28.

29 *Los Angeles News*, 20 July 1928; Copland and Perlis, *Copland: 1900 through 1942*, p. 134.

30 Copland and Perlis, *Copland: 1900 through 1942*, p. 134.

31 "Whiteman Judges Named: Committee Will Decide 'What Is American Music?' (*New York Tribune*, 4 January 1924); photo inset in Edward Jablonski and Lawrence D. Stewart, *The Gershwin Years* (Garden City, N.Y.: Doubleday, 1973), p. 89.

32 Hugh C. Ernst, introduction to the Whiteman program book; quoted in Thornton Hagert, "Jazz Invades Aeolian Hall," liner insert to *An Experiment in Modern Music: Paul Whiteman at Aeolian Hall* (The Smithsonian Collection R 028, 1981).

33 Quoted in Joan Peyser, *The Memory of All That: The Life of George Gershwin* (New York: Simon and Schuster, 1993), p. 84.

34 *New York Herald*, 13 February 1924; quoted in Carol J. Oja, "Gershwin and American Modernists of the 1920s," *Musical Quarterly* LXXVIII (1994): 653.

35 H.O. Osgood, *So This Is Jazz* (1926); quoted in Oja, "Gershwin and American Modernists," p. 652.

36 Quoted in Peyser, *The Memory of All That*, p. 84.

37 *Vanity Fair*, March 1925; quoted in Oja, "Gershwin and American Modernists," p. 653.

38 Quoted in Schiff, *Gershwin: Rhapsody in Blue*, p. 89.

39 Carl Engel, "Views and Reviews," *Muiscal Quarterly* XII (1926): 306.

40 Samuel Chotzinoff (*New York World*); quoted in Peyser, *The Memory of All That*, p. 107.

41 George Gershwin, "The Composer in the Machine Age," *Revolt of the Arts* (1930); rpt. in Gilbert Chase, *The American Composer Speaks* (Baton Rouge: Louisiana State University Press, 1966), p. 144.

42 George Gershwin to Isaac Goldberg; quoted in Peyser, *The Memory of All That*, pp. 80–81.

43 W. C. Handy, *Father of the Blues* (1941); Ruth Halle Rowen, *Music through Sources and Documents* (Englewood Cliffs, N.J.: Prentice-Hall, 1979), p. 341.

44 Maurice Peress, liner note to *The Birth of Rhapsody in Blue: Paul Whiteman's Historic Aeolian Hall Concert of 1924* (Musical Heritage Society MHS Stereo 827531Y, 1987).

45 George Gershwin, "The Relation of Jazz to American Music," in *American Composers on American Music*, ed. Henry Cowell (Palo Alto: Stanford University Press, 1933), p. 187.

46 Quoted in Jablonski and Stewart, *The Gershwin Years*, p. 95.

47 "Rhapsody in Catfish Row: Mr. Gershwin Tells the Origin and Scheme for His Music in That New Folk Opera Called 'Porgy and Bess,'" *New York Times*, 20 October 1935; quoted in Charles Hamm, "Towards a New Reading of Gershwin," in Wayne Schneider, ed., *The Gershwin Style: New Looks at the Music of George Gershwin* (New York: Oxford University Press, 1999), p. 9.

48 Cf. Rudy Vallee Hour, broadcast 10 November 1932, on *Gershwin Conducts Excerpts from Porgy and Bess*, Mark 56 Records 667 (1974).

49 Quoted in the *Alexander Glazunov Society Quarterly Newsletter* II, no. 1 (July 1986): 12.

50 Edward Burlingame Hill, "Jazz," *Harvard Graduates' Magazine*, March 1926; Oja, "Gershwin and American Modernists," p. 654.

51 Virgil Thomson, review of Porgy and Bess in *Modern Music* XIII, no. 1 (November 1935): 18.

52 John Tasker Howard, *Our American Music* (New York: Thomas Y. Crowell, 1931), p. 572; quoted in Beth E. Levy, "'The White Hope of American Music'; or, How Roy Harris Became Western," *American Music* XIX (2001): 161n1.

53 Nicolas Slonimsky, "Roy Harris: The Story of an Oklahoma Composer Who Was Born in a Log Cabin on Lincoln's Birthday" (unpublished MS at the Music Division, Library of Congress); quoted in Levy, "White Hope," p. 137.

54 Roy Harris, "Perspective at 40," *The Magazine of Art* XXXII, no. 11 (Nov. 1939): 667; quoted in Beth E. Levy, "Frontier Figures: American Music and the Mythology of the American West, 1895 — 1945" (Ph.D. diss., University of California at Berkeley, 2002), p. 108.

55 Arthur Mendel, "Music: A Change in Structure," *The Nation*, 6 January 1932; quoted in Levy, *Frontier Figures*, p. 152.

56 Slonimsky, "From the West: Composer New to Bostonians," *Boston Evening Transcript* 24 January 1934; quoted in Levy, "White Hope," p. 146.

57 Levy, "White Hope," p. 148.

58 Roy Harris, "The Growth of a Composer," *Musical Quarterly* XX (1934): 188.

59 *Ibid.*, p. 191.

60 *Ibid.*, p. 188, 191.

61 *Ibid.*, pp. 189–90.

62 Program note for the Philadelphia première; quoted in Levy, *Frontier Figures*, p. 154.

63 George Henry Lovett Smith, "American Festival in Boston," *Modern Music* XVII, no. 1 (October–November 1939): 44.

64 Virgil Thomson, "Age without Honor," *New York Herald Tribune*, 11 October 1940; rpt. in Virgil Thomson, *Music Reviewed 1940–1954* (New York: Vintage Books, 1967), p. 4.

65 Virgil Thomson, "Music from Chicago" (21 November 1940); *Music Reviewed*, p, 15.

66 *Ibid.*, p. 16.

67 Quoted in Moore, *Yankee Blues*, p. 163.

68 Marc Blitzstein, "City College Presents 'Cradle Will Rock' Tonight," *Daily Worker*, 29 November 1940; Barbara Zuck, *A History of Musical Americanism* (Ann Arbor: UMI Research Press, 1980), p. 211.

69 Edith Hale, "Author and Composer Blitzstein," *Daily Worker*, 7 December 1938; *Ibid.*

70 "Carl Sands" (Charles Seeger), "Copeland's [*sic*] Music Recital at Pierre Degeyter Club," *Daily Worker*, 22 March 1934; Pollack, *Aaron Copland*, p. 275.

71 *Ibid.*

72 Aaron Copland, "Workers Sing!" *New Masses* XI, no. 9 (1934): 28–29.

73 Quoted in Ronald D. Cohen and Dave Samuelson, *Songs for Political Action: Folk Music, Topical Songs and the American Left* (Hambergen: Bear Family Records, 1996), p. 67.

74 Joseph Stalin, Report to the XVI Congress of the Communist Party of the Soviet Union (Bolshevik); J. V. Stalin, *Works*, Vol. XII (Moscow: Foreign Languages Publishing House, 1952) p. 379.

75 "Carl Sands" (Charles Seeger), "Proletarian Music Is a Historical Necessity," *Daily Worker*, 6 March 1934; Zuck, *A History of Musical Americanism*, p. 123.

76 Elie Siegmeister, *Music and Society* (New York: Critics Group Press, 1938), pp. 58–59.

77 Earl Robinson and Eric Gordon, *Ballad of an American: The Autobiography of Earl Robinson* (Lanham, Md.: Rowman & Littlefield, 1997) p. 51.

78 Siegmeister, *Music and Society*, p. 59.

79 S. Foster Damon, *Series of Old American Songs* (Providence: Brown University Library, 1936), no. 5.

80 Copland and Perlis, *Copland: 1900 through 1942*, p. 255.

81 Pollack, *Aaron Copland*, pp. 312–13.

82 Jessica Burr, "Arranging 'Git Along, Little Dogies': A Case Study Using Aaron Copland's Cowboy Songbooks," paper presented at the Sixty-Fifth Annual Meeting of the American Musicological Society, Kansas City, Missouri, 4 November 1999.

83 Robinson and Gordon, *Ballad of an American*, p. 65.

84 Howard Pollack, *Aaron Copland*, p. 358.

85 Siegmeister, *Music and Society*, p. 59.

86 Levy, "White Hope," p. 158.

87 Roy Harris, "Folksong — American Big Business" (1940); *Contemporary Composers on Contemporary Music*, eds. Elliott Schwartz and Barney Childs (New York: Holt, Rinehart and Winston, 1967), p. 163.

88 *Ibid.*, p. 164.

89 *Ibid.*, p. 161.

CHAPTER 12: IN SEARCH OF UTOPIA

1 *The Daily Mail* (London), 13 February 1913; Eric Walter White, "Stravinsky in Interview," *Tempo*, no. 97 (1971): 7.

2 *Oedipus the King*, trans. David Grene; Sophocles, *Three Tragedies* (Chicago: University of Chicago Press, 1954), p. 76.

3 Igor Stravinsky, *Poetics of Music in the Form of Six Lessons*, trans. Arthur Knodel and Ingolf Dahl (New York: Vintage Books, 1956), pp. 5–8.

4 *Ibid.*, p. 79.

5 *Ibid.*, p. 83.

6 Arnold Schoenberg, "Stravinsky's *Oedipus*" (1928); *Style and Idea*, p. 483.

7 Schoenberg, "How One Becomes Lonely" (1937); *Style and Idea*, p. 52.

8 Paul Landormy, "Schönberg, Bartók, und die französische Musik," *Musikblätter des Anbruch*, May 1922; quoted in Scott Messing, *Neoclassicism in Music from the Genesis of the Concept through the Schoenberg/Stravinsky Polemic* (Ann Arbor: UMI Research Press, 1988), p. 126.

9 *Style and Idea*, pp. 481–82.

10 Henrietta Malkiel, "Modernists Have Ruined Modern Music, Stravinsky Says," *Musical America*, 10 January 1925, p. 9.

11 See Arthur Lourié, *Sergei Koussevitzky and His Epoch* (New York: Knopf, 1931), p. 196.

12 Egon Wellesz, *Arnold Schoenberg: The Formative Years* (London: Galliard, 1971), p. xii.

13 Otto Weininger, *Sex and Character: An Investigation of Fundamental Principles* (Bloomington: Indiana University Press, 2005), p. 379.

14 David Schiff, "Schoenberg's Cool Eye for the Erotic," *New York Times*, Arts and Leisure, 8 August 1999, p. 30.

15 Schoenberg, *Theory of Harmony*, p. 2.

16 See Joseph Auner, "Schoenberg's Aesthetic Transformations and the Evolution of Form in 'Die gluckliche Hand,'" *Journal of the Arnold Schoenberg Institute* XII (1989): 103–28.

17 Donald Mitchell, *The Language of Modern Music* (New York: St. Martin's Press, 1970), chap. 1.

18 Wellesz, *Arnold Schoenberg: The Formative Years*, pp. xiii–xiv.

19 Gregory Dubinsky, "Six Essays on the Dissemination of Twelve-Tone Composition, 1921–1945" (Ph.D. diss. in progress, University of California at Berkeley).

20 Wellesz, *Arnold Schoenberg: The Formative Years*, p. xiv.

21 H. H. Stuckenschmidt, "Zwölftöne-Musik," *Melos*, Vol. IV (1925), p. 520; cited in Dubinsky, *Six Essays*, Chap. 1.

22 Schoenberg, "Schoenberg's Tone-Rows" (1936), *Style and Idea*, p. 213.

23 Alan Lessem, "Schoenberg, Stravinsky, and Neo-Classicism: The Issues Reexamined," *Musical Quarterly* LXVIII (1982): 538.

24 Maria Luisa Vilar-Paya, "Schoenberg's Re-centerings: Pitch Organization and Formal Processes in Early Twelve-Tone Music," paper read at the fifty-eighth annual meeting of the American Musicological Society, Pittsburgh, 6 November 1992.

25 Arnold Schoenberg, "Variations for Orchestra, op. 31," *The Score* (July 1960); quoted in Glenn Watkins, *Soundings: Music in the Twentieth Century* (New York: Schirmer, 1988), p. 335.

26 Ethan Haimo, *Schoenberg's Serial Odyssey: The Evolution of His Twelve-Tone Method, 1914–1928.* (Oxford: Clarendon Press, 1990), p. 162.

27 Schoenberg, "National Music" (1931), *Style and Idea*, p. 170.

28 *Ibid.*, p. 171.

29 *Ibid.*

30 *Ibid.*, p. 173.

31 Josef Rufer, *The Works of Arnold Schoenberg: A Catalogue of His Compositions, Writings, and Paintings*, trans. Dika Newlin (New York: Free Press of Glencoe, 1963), p. 45.

32 George Perle, "The Dark Side of Musicology" (letter to the editor in answer to R. Taruskin, "The Dark Side of Modern Music," *The New Republic*, 5 September 1988).

33 Richard S. Hill, "Schoenberg's Tone-Rows and the Tonal System of the Future," *Musical Quarterly* XXII (1936): 14–37.

34 Arnold Schoenberg to Josef Rufer, 8 April 1950; Josef Rufer, *Composition with Twelve Notes Related Only to One Another*, trans. Humphrey Searle (2nd ed., London: Barrie & Jenkins, 1961), p. 95.

35 Rufer, *Composition with Twelve Tones*, p. 95.

36 Gregory Dubinsky, *Six Essays*, Chap. 1.

37 Theodor W. Adorno, *Alban Berg: Master of the Smallest Link*, trans. Juliane Brand and Christopher Hailey (Cambridge: Cambridge University Press, 1991), p. 104.

38 Douglas Green, "Berg's De Profundis: The Finale of the *Lyric Suite*"; George Perle, "The Secret Program of the *Lyric Suite*"; both in the *International Alban Berg Society Newsletter*, no. 5 (April 1977).

39 Anton von Webern, *The Path to the New Music*, trans. Leo Black (Vienna: Universal Edition, 1963), p. 54.

40 "The Path to Twelve-Note Composition," in Webern, *The Path to the New Music*, ed. Willi Reich, trans. Leo Black (Bryn Mawr, Pa.: Theodore Presser Co., 1963), p. 42.

41 Milton Babbitt, "Some Aspects of Twelve-Tone Composition," *The Score*, no. 12 (June 1955), p. 53.

42 Webern, *The Path to the New Music*, p. 56.

43 *Ibid.*, p. 45.

44 Anton von Webern, "Analysis of the String Quartet, op. 28," trans. Zoltan Roman, in Hans Moldenhauer and Rosaleen Moldenhauer, *Anton von Webern: A Chronicle of His Life and Work* (New York: Knopf, 1979), p. 754.

45 *Ibid.*, pp. 755–56.

46 *Ibid.*, p. 756.

CHAPTER 13: MUSIC AND TOTALITARIAN SOCIETY

1 Hannah Arendt, *The Origins of Totalitarianism* (San Diego: Harvest/Harcourt Brace Jovanovich, 1968), p. vii.

2 Trans. Elizabeth MacIntosh and Barbara Spackman, in Jeffrey Schnapp and Barbara Spackman, "Selections from the Great Debate on Fascism and Culture: *Critica fascista* 1926–27," *Fascism and Culture, Stanford Italian Review* VIII (1990): 242.

3 *Critica fascista*, 15 November 1926; *Ibid.*, p. 248.

4 Arthur Lourié, *Sergei Koussevitzky and His Epoch* (New York: Knopf, 1931), p. 196.

5 Alfredo Casella, "Music and Politics in Italy," *Christian Science Monitor*, 19 September 1925, p. 8.

6 Casella, "Neoclassicism in Italy," *Christian Science Monitor*, 7 January 1928, p. 12.

7 *Ibid.*

8 Casella, "About 'Returns,'" *Christian Science Monitor*, 13 October 1928, p. 12.

9 "A Manifesto of Italian Musicians for the Tradition of Nineteenth-Century Romantic Art" (signed by, among others, Ottorino Respighi, Ildebrando Pizzetti, Riccardo Zandonai and Riccardo Pick-Mangiagalli), *La Stampa* (Turin), 17 December 1932; Harvey Sachs, *Music in Fascist Italy* (New York: Norton, 1987), p. 24.

10 John C. G. Waterhouse, "Respighi," in *New Grove Dictionary of Opera*, Vol. III (London: Macmillan, 1992), p. 1295.

11 Benito Mussolini, *Opera omnia* XLI (Rome, 1979): 424; Sachs, *Music in Fascist Italy*, p. 17.

12 Richard Aldrich, *New York Times*, 12 January 1921; Joseph Horowitz, *Understanding Toscanini: How He Became an American Culture-God and Helped Creat a New Audience for Old Music* (New York: Knopf, 1987), p. 86.

13 Quoted in G. Barblan, *Toscanini e la Scala* (Milan, 1972); Sachs, *Music in Fascist Italy*, p. 213.

14 Max Nordau, *Degeneration* (New York: D. Appleton and Co., 1895), p. 17.

15 See Igor Stravinsky, *Selected Correspondence*, Vol. III, ed. Robert Craft (New York: Alfred A. Knopf, 1985), pp. 265–70.

16 Béla Bartók to Frau Professor Dr. Oscar Müller-Widmann, Basle, 13 April 1938; Béla Bartók, *Letters*, ed. János Demény (New York: St. Martin's Press, 1971), p. 268.

17 Béla Bartók to Hans Priegnitz, 12 January 1939: *Béla Bartók's Letters*, ed. János Demény (New York: St. Martin's Press, 1971), p. 274.

18 Pamela M. Potter, "Strauss and the National Socialists," in *Richard Strauss: New Perspectives on the Composer and His Work*, ed. Bryan Gilliam (Durham: Duke University Press, 1992), p. 109.

19 Horst Büttner, "Hochkultur und Volkskunst: 68. Tonkünstlerversammlung des Allgemeinen Deutschen Musikvereins vom 8. bis 13. Juni in Darmstadt und Frankfurt a. M.," *Zeitschrift für Musik* CIV, no. 8 (August 1937), 873; trans. Steven Moore Whiting.

20 *Völkischer Beobachter* 7 October 1940; trans. S. M. Whiting.

21 Igor Stravinsky and Robert Craft, *Memories and Commentaries* (Berkeley and Los Angeles: University of California Press, 1981), p. 123.

22 Rudolf Hess, address to the Gauleiters of Nuremberg, 12 September 1938; Peter Matheson, *The Third Reich and the Christian Churches: A Documentary Account of Christian Resistance and Complicity during the Nazi Era* (Edinburgh: T. and T. Clark, 1981), p. 75.

23 Program note to the première production of *Mathis der Maler* (28 May 1938); rpt. in the libretto booklet accompanying the Angel recording (SZCX-3869, 1979).

24 Paul Hindemith, *Johann Sebastian Bach: Heritage and Obligation* (trans. of *J. S. Bach: Ein verpflichtendes Erbe*) (New Haven: Yale University Press, 1952), pp. 40–41.

25 Michael H. Kater, *Composers of the Nazi Era: Eight Portraits* (New York: Oxford University Press, 2000), p. 97.

26 Karl Amadeus Hartmann, *Kleine Schriften* (Mainz Schott, 1965), "Lektionen bei Anton Webern"; quoted in Hans Moldenhauer and Rosaleen Moldenhauer, *Anton von Webern: A Chronicle of His Life and Work* (New York: Knopf, 1978), pp. 540–41.

27 Anton Webern to Joseph Hueber, May 1940; Moldenhauer, *Anton von Webern*, p. 527.

28 Moldenhauer, *Anton von Webern*, p. 474 (reporting a conversation with Hans Erich Apostel).

29 Quoted in Erik Levi, "Atonality, 12-Tone Music and the Third Reich," *Tempo*, no. 178 (1991), p. 21.

30 Arnold Schoenberg, letter to the editor, *Saturday Review of Literature*, 1 January 1949; quoted in H. H. Stuckenschmidt, *Arnold Schoenberg: His Life, World and Work*, trans. Humphrey Searle (New York: Schirmer, 1977), p. 494.

31 Karl Marx, *Critique of the Gotha Program* (1875).

32 Quoted from Yuriy M. Keldïsh, et al., eds., *Muzïkal'naya èntsiklopediya*, Vol. V (Moscow: Sovetskaya èntsiklopediya, 1981), p. 226.

33 Sergey Prokofieff, *Autobiography, Articles, Reminiscences*, trans. Rose Prokofieva (Moscow: Foreign Languages Publishing House, n.d.), p. 50.

34 V. I. Lenin, "Party Organization and Party Literature" (1905), in *Selected Works* (New York: International Publishers, 1971), p. 151.

35 Klara Zetkin, *Reminiscences of Lenin* (London: Chatto and Windus, 1929), p. 14.

36 Leo Tolstoy, *What Is Art? and Essays on Art*, trans. Aylmer Maude (London: Oxford University Press, 1930), p. 55.

37 *Ibid.*, p. 240.

38 *Ibid.*, p. 55.

39 *Ibid.*, p. 241.

40 Dmitri Shostakovich, "Moyo ponimaniye 'Ledi Makbet,'" in *Ledi Makbet Mtsenskogo uyezda: Opera D. D. Shostakovicha* (Leningrad: Gosudarstvennïy Akademicheskiy Malïy Opernïy Teatr, 1934), p. 6.

41 Elliott Carter, "Current Chronicle: Germany, 1960," *Musical Quarterly* XLVI (1960); *The Writings of Elliott Carter*, eds. Else Stone and Kurt Stone (Bloomington: Indiana University Press, 1977), p. 213.

42 "The Murders of Mtsensk," *Time*, 11 February 1935, p. 35.

43 "Beseda tovarishchey Stalina i Molotova s avtorami opernogo spektaklya 'Tikhiy Don,'" *Sovetskaya muzïka* IV, no. 2 (1936): 3.

44 Shostakovich to Ivan Sollertinsky, 28 January 1936; quoted in Lyudmila Mikheyeva, "Istoriya odnoy druzhbï," *Sovetskaya muzïka* LV, no. 9 (1987): 79.

45 "Sumbur vmesto muzïki," *Pravda*, 28 January 1936.

46 This and following quotations from Georgiy Khubov, "5-ya simfoniya D. Shostakovicha," *Sovetskaya muzïka* VI, no. 3 (1938): 16.

47 "Moy tvorcheskiy otvet," *Vechernyaya Moskva*, 25 January 1938, p. 30.

48 Khubov, "5-ya simfoniya," p. 22.

49 Alexander Fadeyev, *Za tridtsat' let* (Moscow: Sovetskiy pisatel', 1957), quoted in *Dmitriy Shostakovich*, eds. G. Ordzhonikidze et al. (Moscow: Sovetskiy kompozitor, 1967), p. 43.

50 S. S. Prokofieff and N. Ya. Myaskovsky, *Perepiska* (Moscow: Sovetskiy kompozitor, 1977), p. 455.

51 "Tridtsat' let s muzïkoy Shostakovicha," in Ordzhonikidze, et al., *Dmitriy Shostakovich*, p. 109.

52 *Testimony: The Memoirs of Dmitri Shostakovich as Related to and Edited by Solomon Volkov*, trans. Antonina W. Bouis (New York: Harper and Row, 1979), p. 183.

53 Friedrich Schiller, review of Friedrich Mattheson's landscape poetry, quoted in Charles Rosen, *The Romantic Generation* (Cambridge: Harvard University Press, 1995), p. 93.

Art Credits

3-5b   Cliché Bibliothèque Nationale de France. *Le sacre du printemps,* "Danse sacrale," Sketches, 1911–1913. Facsimile reproductions from the autographs by Igor Stravinsky. Boosey and Hawkes, 1969.

3-6   Valentine Hugo, 1913. AKG Images, Artists Rights Society (ARS), New York/ADAGP, Paris.

4-1   Collection of the author.

4-2   Glinka State Central Museum of Musical Culture. In *The New Grove Dictionary of Music and Musicians,* ed. Stanley Sadie, Grove, New York, 1980, vol. 17, p. 372.

4-3   Photograph by Marion Kalter, Paris, 1983. AKG Images/Marion Kalter.

4-4   Lambertus, *Liber Floridus,* Flemish, MS 724, fol.12, Musée Condé, Chantilly, France. © Réunion des Musées Nationaux/Art Resource, NY.

5-1   MSS 14, Photo 57, Charles Ives Papers in the Irving S. Gilmore Music Library of Yale University, New Haven, Conn.

5-2   MSS 14, Photo 68, Charles Ives Papers in the Irving S. Gilmore Music Library of Yale University, New Haven, Conn.

5-3   New York, ca. 1917. Yale University, AKG Images.

5-4   Photograph by Ray Fisher, 1958. Time Life Pictures/Getty Images.

5-5a   Hulton Archive/Getty Images.

5-5b   Images of Yale individuals, ca. 1750–1976 (RU 684). Manuscripts and Archives, Yale University Library.

5-6   Ives, *Universe* Symphony, Prelude no. 2, "Birth of the Ocean Waters," sketch (f 1843). Charles Ives Papers, Yale University Music Library. © Peer International/Charles Ives.

5-7a   Photograph by Fernand de Gueldre. In Judith Tick, *Ruth Crawford Seeger: A Composer's Search for American Music,* Oxford University Press, Oxford and New York, 1997, jacket illustration and frontispiece. By permission of Judith Tick.

5-7b   Program from Judith Tick, *Ruth Crawford Seeger: A Composer's Search for American Music,* Oxford University Press, Oxford and New York, 1997, following p. 128. By permission of Judith Tick.

5-8   Courtesy of BMI Archives.

6-1   Egon Schiele, 1917, IMAGNO/Austrian Archives.

6-2   AKG Images.

6-3   © Arnold Schoenberg Center, Vienna.

6-4   © Giraudon/Art Resource, NY

6-5   © Arnold Schoenberg Center, Vienna.

7-1   Library of Congress.

7-2   Photograph made at Darázs, annotated on back: Kósa Gyula nyitrai amatör fényképész ("Gyula Kósa, amateur photographer, of Nyitra"). By permission of Peter Bartók.

7-3	Aladar Székely, 1910. © Archivo Iconografico, S.A. /CORBIS.
7-4	Hugo Boettinger, 1928. Music Division, New York Public Library for the Performing Arts, Astor, Lenox, and Tilden Foundations.
7-5	Moravske Museum, Brno. AKG Images.
8-1	*Les Noces.* Photographer: Anthony Crickmay. Jerome Robbins Dance Division, New York Public Library for the Performing Arts, Astor, Lenox, and Tilden Foundations.
8-2	© Arnold Schoenberg Center, Vienna.
8-3	Berlin, 1912. © Arnold Schoenberg Center, Vienna.
9-1	Piotr Konchalovsky, Tretyakov Gallery, Moscow. © Scala/Art Resource, NY.
9-2	Library of Congress.
9-3	Irving S. Gilmore Music Library of Yale University. Title page (H24 H662+ op.26). © 1992 by Schott Musik International, copyright renewed, all rights reserved.
9-4	Associated Press, World Wide Photos, and Weill-Lenya Research Center, Kurt Weill Foundation for Music, NY.
9-5	Stiftung Archiv der Akademie der Künste, Berlin, Bestandsbezeichnung.
9-6	Alfred Bendiner, National Portrait Gallery, Smithsonian Institution, Washington, DC. © National Portrait Gallery, Smithsonian Institution/Art Resource, NY.
10-1	Cliché Bibliothèque Nationale de France, Estate of Pablo Picasso/Artists Rights Society (ARS), New York.
10-2	Courtesy of the Metropolitan Opera.
10-3	Roger Viollet/Getty Images.
10-4	Photograph by Therese Bonney, Paris, ca. 1932. Yale Collection of American Literature, Beinecke Rare Book and Manuscript Library.
11-1	Rendered by A Good Thing, Inc.
11-2a	Photographs and Prints Division, Schomburg Center for Research in Black Culture, New York Public Library, Astor, Lenox, and Tilden Foundations.
11-2b	Collection of the author.
11-3	Library of Congress, Music Division, Irving Fine Collection.
11-4	© Bettmann/ CORBIS.
11-5	Music Division, New York Public Library for the Performing Arts, Astor, Lenox, and Tilden Foundations.
11-6	George Gershwin, 1934. National Portrait Gallery, Smithsonian Institution, Washington, DC. © National Portrait Gallery, Smithsonian Institution/Art Resource, NY.
11-7	AKG Images.
11-8	Theatre of the Thirties Collection, Special Collections and Archives, George Mason University Libraries.

11-9   Musical arrangement and art for "Joe Hill" are reprinted with permission of Simon & Schuster Adult Publishing Group from *The Fireside Book of Folk Songs*, edited by Margaret Bradford Boni. Arrangements by Norman Lloyd. Illustrations by Alice and Martin Provensen. Copyright 1947, and renewed ©1975, by Simon & Schuster, Inc., and Artists and Writers Guild, Inc. Music copyright Bob Miller, Inc. (successor, Universal/MCA).

12-1   Pablo Picasso, 1920. Musée Picasso, Paris. © Réunion des Musées Nationaux/Art Resource. NY. ©2004 Estate of Pablo Picasso/Artists Rights Soceity (ARS), New York.

12-2   General Research Division, New York Public Library, Astor, Lenox, and Tilden Foundations.

12-3   © Arnold Schoenberg Center, Vienna.

12-4   Paul Sacher Foundation, Anton Webern Collection, Basel.

12-5   In Anton von Webern, *Sketches (1926–1945): Facsimile Reproductions from the Composer's Autograph Sketchbooks in the Moldenhauer Archive* (commentary by Ernst Krenek, foreword by Hans Moldenhauer), C. Fischer, New York, 1968. By permission of Carl Fischer, LLC, NY.

13-1   Library of Congress.

13-2   Library of Congress, George Grantham Bain Collection.

13-3   © Bildarchiv Preussischer Kulturbesitz, Berlin, 2003.

13-4   Photograph 1930, AKG Images.

13-5   Photograph ca. 1930, AKG Images.

13-6   Photograph ca. 1956, AKG Images.

13-7   Photograph © Scala/Art Resource, NY. Art © Estate of Aleksandr Rodchenko/RAO, Moscow/VAGA, NY.

13-8   © Snark/Art Resource, NY.

13-9   Courtesy of the Metropolitan Opera.

Further Reading

The Early Twentieth Century

Chapter 1   Reaching (for) Limits

Adorno, Theodor W. *Mahler: A Musical Physiognomy*, trans. Edmund Jephcott. Chicago: University of Chicago Press, 1992.

Bauer-Lechner, Natalie. *Recollections of Gustav Mahler*, ed. Peter Franklin, trans. Dika Newlin. Cambridge: Cambridge University Press, 1980.

Blaukopf, Herta, ed. *Gustav Mahler, Richard Strauss: Correspondence, 1888–1911*, trans. Edmund Jephcott. Chicago: University of Chicago Press, 1984.

Blaukopf, Kurt, ed. *Mahler: A Documentary Study*. New York: Oxford University Press, 1976.

Butler, Christopher. *Early Modernism: Literature, Music and Painting in Europe, 1900–1914*. Oxford: Clarendon Press, 1994.

Dahlhaus, Carl. *Between Romanticism and Modernism*, trans. Mary Whittall. Berkeley and Los Angeles: University of California Press, 1980.

De la Grange, Henri-Louis. *Gustav Mahler: Vienna: The Years of Challenge (1897–1904)*. Oxford: Oxford University Press, 1995.

_____. *Gustav Mahler: Vienna, Triumph and Disillusion (1904–1907)*. Oxford: Oxford University Press, 2000.

Del Mar, Norman. *Richard Strauss: A Critical Commentary on His Life and Works*. 3 vols. Ithaca: Cornell University Press, 1986.

Floros, Constantin. *Gustav Mahler: The Symphonies*, trans. Vernon Wicker. Portland, Ore.: Amadeus Press, 1993.

Franklin, Peter R. *The Life of Mahler*. Cambridge: Cambridge University Press, 1997.

_____. *Mahler: Symphony No. 3*. Cambridge: Cambridge University Press, 1991.

Frisch, Walter. *The Early Works of Arnold Schoenberg, 1893–1908*. Berkeley and Los Angeles: University of California Press, 1993.

Gilliam, Brian. *The Life of Richard Strauss*. Cambridge: Cambridge University Press, 1999.

_____. *Richard Strauss's 'Elektra.'* Oxford: Oxford University Press, 1991.

_____. *Richard Strauss: New Perspectives on the Composer and His Work*. Chapel Hill: University of North Carolina Press, 1992.

Gilliam, Brian, ed. *Richard Strauss and His World*. Princeton: Princeton University Press, 1992.

Hartmann, Rudolf. *Richard Strauss: The Staging of His Operas and Bellets*. New York: Oxford University Press, 1981.

Jefferson, Alan. *Richard Strauss: Der Rosenkavalier*. Cambridge: Cambridge University Press, 1986.

Kennedy, Michael. *Mahler*. London: J. M. Dent, 1974.

_____. *Richard Strauss: Man, Musician, Enigma*. Cambridge: Cambridge University Press, 1999.

_____. *Strauss Tone Poems*. London: British Broadcasting Corporation, 1984.

Kravitt, Edward F. *The Lied: Mirror of Late Romanticism*. New Haven: Yale University Press, 1996.

Lebrecht, Norman, ed. *Mahler Remembered*. New York: Norton, 1987.

Mahler, Alma. *Gustav Mahler: Memories and Letters*, trans. Basil Creighton, ed. Donald Mitchell. London: J. Murray, 1973.

Mann, William. *Richard Strauss: A Critical Study of the Operas*. London: Cassell, 1964.

Martner, Knud, ed. *Selected Letters of Gustav Mahler*, trans. Eithne Wilkins, Ernest Kaiser, and Bill Hopkins. New York: Farrar, Straus and Giroux, 1979.

Mitchell, Donald. *Gustav Mahler: The Early Years*. Rev. ed., London: Boydell Press, 2003.

_____. *Gustav Mahler: Songs and Symphonies of Life and Death. Interpretations and Annotations*. Rev. ed., London: Boydell Press, 2002.

_____. *Gustav Mahler: The Wunderhorn Years*. 3rd ed., London: Boydell Press, 2004.

Myers, Rollo, ed. *Richard Strauss and Romain Rolland: Correspondence*. Berkeley and Los Angeles: University of California Press, 1968.

Painter, Karen, ed. *Gustav Mahler and His World*. Princeton: Princeton University Press, 2002.

Puffett, Derrick. ed. *Richard Strauss: Elektra*. Cambridge: Cambridge University Press, 1990.

_____. *Richard Strauss: Salome*. Cambridge: Cambridge University Press, 1989.

Roman, Zoltan. *Gustav Mahler's American Years, 1907–1911: A Documentary History*. Stuyvesant, N.Y.: Pendragon Press, 1989.

Samson, Jim. *Music in Transition*. London: J. M. Dent, 1977.

Samuels, Robert. *Mahler's Sixth Symphony: A Study in Musical Semiotics*. Cambridge: Cambridge University Press, 1995.

Schorske, Carl. *Fin-de-siècle Vienna: Politics and Culture*. New York: Random House, 1980.

Strauss, Richard. *The Correspondence between Richard Strauss and Hugo von Hoffmansthal*, trans. Hanns Hammelmann and Ewald Osers. London: Collins, 1961.

_____. *Recollections and Reflections*, ed. Willi Schuh, trans. L. J. Lawrence. London: Boosey & Hawkes, 1953.

Wilhelm, Kurt. *Richard Strauss: An Intimate Portrait*. London: Thames & Hudson, 1989.

Williamson, John. *Strauss: 'Also Sprach Zarathustra.'* Cambridge: Cambridge University Press, 1993.

Chapter 2   Getting Rid of Glue

Austin, William W., ed. *Debussy: Prelude to "The Afternoon of a Faun."* Norton Critical Scores. New York: Norton, 1970.

Brody, Elaine. *Paris: The Musical Kaleidoscope, 1870–1925.* New York: George Braziller, 1987.

Debussy, Claude-Achille. *Letters*, ed. François Lesure and Roger Nichols, trans. Roger Nichols. Cambridge: Harvard University Press, 1987.

Fulcher, Jane. *Debussy and His World.* Princeton: Princeton University Press, 2001.

_____ . *French Cultural Politics and Music from the Dreyfus Affair to the First World War.* New York: Oxford University Press, 1999.

Gillmor, Alan M. *Erik Satie.* Boston: Twayne, 1988.

Grayson, David. *The Genesis of Debussy's Pelléas et Mélisande.* Ann Arbor, Mich.: UMI Research Press, 1986.

Harding, James. *Erik Satie.* London: Secker and Warburg, 1975.

Holloway, Robin. *Debussy and Wagner.* London: Eulenburg Books, 1979.

Huebner, Steven. *French Opera at the 'Fin de Siècle': Wagnerism, Nationalism, and Style.* Oxford: Oxford University Press, 1999.

Jarocinski, Stefan. *Debussy, Impressionism and Symbolism*, trans. Rollo Myers. London: Eulenburg Books, 1976.

Koechlin, Charles. *Gabriel Fauré*, trans. L. Orrey (1946). New York: AMS Press, 1976.

Lesure, François, ed. *Debussy on Music*, trans. Richard Langham Smith. Ithaca: Cornell University Press, 1988.

Lockspeiser, Edward. *Debussy: His Life and Mind.* 2 vols. Cambridge: Cambridge University Press, 1962.

Mawer, Deborah. *The Cambridge Companion to Ravel.* Cambridge: Cambridge University Press, 2000.

Meister, Barbara. *Nineteenth-Century French Song: Fauré, Chausson, Duparc, and Debussy.* Bloomington: Indiana University Press, 1980.

Myers, Rollo. *Emmanuel Chabrier and His Circle.* London: J. M. Dent, 1969.

_____ . *Erik Satie.* London: Dobson, 1948.

_____ . *Modern French Music: Its Evolution and Cultural Background from 1900 to the Present Day.* Oxford: Oxford University Press, 1971.

Nectoux, Jean-Michel. *Gabriel Fauré: A Musical Life*, trans. Roger Nichols. Cambridge: Cambridge University Press, 1991.

Nectoux, Jean-Michel, ed. *Gabriel Fauré: His Life through His Letters*, trans. J. A. Underwood. St. Paul, Minn.: Consortium Book Sales, 1984.

Nichols, Roger, ed. *Claude Debussy: Pelléas et Mélisande.* Cambridge: Cambridge University Press, 1989.

_____ . *Debussy Remembered.* Portland, Oreg.: Amadeus Press, 1992.

_____ . *The Life of Debussy.* Cambridge: Cambridge University Press, 1998.

_____ . *Ravel Remembered.* New York: Norton, 1988.

Noske, Frits. *French Song from Berlioz to Duparc*, revised by Frits Noske and Rita Benton, trans. Rita Benton. 2nd ed., New York: Dover Publications, 1970.

Orledge, Robert. *Debussy and the Theatre.* Cambridge: Cambridge University Press, 1982.

_____ . *Gabriel Fauré.* London: Eulenberg Books, 1979.

_____ . *Satie the Composer*. Cambridge: Cambridge University Press, 1990.

Orledge, Robert, ed. *Satie Remembered*. Portland, Ore.: Amadeus Press, 1995.

Ornstein, Arbie. *Ravel: Man and Musician*. New York: Columbia University Press, 1975.

Ornstein, Arbie, ed. *A Ravel Reader: Correspondence, Articles, Interviews*. New York: Columbia University Press, 1990.

Roland-Manuel, Alexis. *Maurice Ravel*, trans. C. Jolly. London: Dennis Dobson, 1947.

Shattuck, Roger. *The Banquet Years*. New York: Random House, 1955.

Stuckenschmidt, Hans Heinz. *Maurice Ravel: Variations on His Life*, trans. Samuel R. Rosenbaum. Philadelphia: Chilton Books, 1968.

Trezise, Simon. *The Cambridge Companion to Debussy*. Cambridge: Cambridge University Press, 2003.

Volta, Ornella. *Satie: His World through His Letters*, trans. Michael Bullock. London: Marion Boyars, 1989.

Vuillermoz, Émile. *Gabriel Fauré*. Philadelphia: Chilton Books, 1969.

Whiting, Steven Moore. *Satie the Bohemian: From Cabaret to Concert Hall*. Oxford: Oxford University Press, 1999.

Wilkins, Nigel, ed. *The Writings of Erik Satie*. London: Eulenburg Books, 1980.

Chapter 3   Aristocratic Maximalism

Asafiev, Boris. *A Book about Stravinsky* (1929), trans. Richard F. French. Ann Arbor, Mich.: UMI Research Press, 1982.

Cross, Jonathan, ed. *The Cambridge Companion to Stravinsky*. Cambridge: Cambridge University Press, 2003.

Druskin, Mikhail. *Igor Stravinsky: His Personality, Works, and Views* (1974), trans. Martin Cooper. Cambridge: Cambridge University Press, 1983.

Garafola, Lynn. *Diaghilev's Ballets Russes*. New York: Oxford University Press, 1989.

Guest, Ivor. *The Romantic Ballet in Paris*. Middletown, Conn.: Wesleyan University Press, 1966.

Hill, Peter. *Stravinsky: The Rite of Spring*. Cambridge: Cambridge University Press, 2000.

Kochno, Boris. *Diaghilev and the Ballets Russes*. New York: Harper & Row, 1970.

Lederman, Minna, ed. *Stravinsky in the Theatre*. New York: Pellegrini and Cudahy, 1949.

Press, Stephen D. *Prokofiev's Ballets for Diaghilev*. Aldershot: Ashgate, 2004.

Roslavleva, Natalia Petrovna. *Era of the Russian Ballet*. New York: Da Capo Press, 1979.

Schouvaloff, Alexander, and Victor Borovsky. *Stravinsky on Stage*. London: Stainer and Bell, 1982.

Searle, Humphrey. *Ballet Music*. 2nd ed., New York: Dover Publications, 1973.

Smith, Marian. *Ballet and Opera in the Age of Giselle*. Princeton: Princeton University Press, 2000.

Stravinsky, Igor, and Robert Craft. *Dialogues and a Diary*. Garden City, N.Y.: Doubleday, 1963.

_____ . *Expositions and Developments*. Garden City, N.Y.: Doubleday, 1962.

_____ . *Memories and Commentaries*. Garden City, N.Y.: Doubleday, 1960.

_____ . *Retrospectives and Conclusions*. New York: Knopf, 1969.

_____ . *Themes and Episodes*. New York: Knopf, 1966.

Stravinsky, Vera, and Robert Craft. *Stravinsky in Pictures and Documents*. New York: Simon and Schuster, 1978.

Taruskin, Richard. *Stravinsky and the Russian Traditions*. Berkeley and Los Angeles: University of California Press, 1996.

Van den Toorn, Pieter. *The Music of Igor Stravinsky*. New Haven: Yale University Press, 1983.

_____ . *Stravinsky and "The Rite of Spring": The Beginnings of a Musical Language*. Berkeley and Los Angeles: University of California Press, 1987.

Vershinina, Irina. *Stravinsky's Early Ballets*, trans. L. G. Heien. Ann Arbor, Mich.: UMI Research Press, 1989.

Walsh, Stephen. *The Music of Stravinsky*. London: Routledge and Kegan Paul, 1988.

_____ . *Stravinsky: A Creative Spring: Russia and France, 1882–1934*. New York: Knopf, 1999.

White, Eric Walter. *Stravinsky: The Composer and His Works*. 2nd ed., Berkeley and Los Angeles: University of California Press, 1979.

Wiley, Roland John. *Tchaikovsky's Ballets*. Rev. ed., Oxford: Clarendon Press, 1991.

Chapter 4 Extinguishing the "Petty 'I'" (Transcendentalism, I)

Baker, James. *The Music of Alexander Scriabin*. New Haven: Yale University Press, 1986.

Bowers, Faubion. *Scriabin: a Biography of the Russian Composer, 1871–1915*. Tokyo and Palo Alto, Calif.: Kodansha International, 1969.

Griffiths, Paul. *Olivier Messiaen and the Music of Time*. Ithaca, N.Y.: Cornell University Press, 1985.

Hill, Peter, ed. *The Messiaen Companion*. London: Faber & Faber, 1995.

Johnson, Robert Sherlaw. *Messiaen*. London: J. M. Dent, 1975.

Messiaen, Olivier. *Music and Color: Conversations with Claude Samuel*, trans. E. T. Glasgow. Portland, Oreg.: Amadeus Press, 1994.

_____ . *The Technique of My Musical Language*, trans. John Satterfield. Paris: Leduc, 1957.

Morrison, Simon. *Russian Opera and the Symbolist Movement*. Berkeley and Los Angeles: University of California Press, 2002.

Nichols, Roger. *Messiaen*. London: Oxford University Press, 1975.

Pople, Anthony. *Messiaen: Quatuor pour la fin du temps*. Cambridge: Cambridge University Press, 1998.

Rischin, Rebecca. *For the End of Time: The Story of the Messiaen Quartet*. Ithaca, N.Y.: Cornell University Press, 2003.

Roberts, Peter D. *Modernism in Russian Piano Music: Skriabin, Prokofiev and Their Contemporaries*. Bloomington: Indiana University Press, 1993.

Schloezer, Boris de. *Skryabin: Artist and Mystic*, trans. Nicolas Slonimsky. Berkeley and Los Angeles: University of California Press, 1987.

Scott, Cyril. *Music: Its Secret Influence throughout the Ages* (1933). Rev. ed., New York: Samuel Weiser, 1976.

Chapter 5   Containing Multitudes (Transcendentalism, II)

Block, Geoffrey. *Ives: Concord Sonata.* Cambridge: Cambridge University Press, 1996.

Burkholder, J. Peter. *All Made of Tunes: Charles Ives and the Uses of Musical Borrowing.* New Haven: Yale University Press, 1965.

_____. *Charles Ives: The Ideas behind the Music.* New Haven: Yale University Press, 1985.

Burkholder, J. Peter, ed. *Charles Ives and His World.* Princeton: Princeton University Press, 1996.

Cowell, Henry. *New Musical Resources.* New York: Knopf, 1930.

Feder, Stuart. *Charles Ives: "My Father's Song": A Psychoanalytic Biography.* New Haven: Yale University Press, 1992.

_____. *The Life of Charles Ives.* Cambridge: Cambridge University Press, 1999.

Hicks, Michael. *Henry Cowell: Bohemian.* Urbana: University of Illinois Press, 2002.

Higgins, Dick, ed. *Essential Cowell: Selected Writings on Music by Henry Cowell, 1921–1964.* Kingston, N.Y.: McPherson, 2002.

Hisama, Ellie M. *Gendering Musical Modernism: The Music of Ruth Crawford, Marion Bauer, and Miriam Gideon.* Cambridge: Cambridge University Press, 2001.

Hitchcock, H. Wiley. *Ives.* London: Oxford University Press, 1977.

Ives, Charles. *Essays before a Sonata, The Majority, and Other Writings,* ed. Howard Boatwright. New York: Norton, 1970.

_____. *Memos,* ed. John Kirkpatrick. New York: Norton, 1972.

Mead, Rita H. *Henry Cowell's New Music, 1925–1936: The Society, the Music Edition, and the Recordings.* Ann Arbor, Mich.: UMI Research Press, 1981.

Miller, Leta E., and Fredric Lieberman. *Lou Harrison: Composing a World.* New York: Oxford University Press, 1998.

Nicholls, David. *American Experimental Music, 1890–1940.* Cambridge: Cambridge University Press, 1990.

Nicholls, David, ed. *The Whole World of Music: A Henry Cowell Symposium.* Amsterdam: Harwood Academic Publishers, 1997.

Oja, Carol. *Making Music Modern: New York in the 1920s.* New York: Oxford University Press, 2000.

Perlis, Vivian, ed. *Charles Ives Remembered: An Oral History.* New York: Norton, 1976.

Rich, Alan. *American Pioneers: Ives to Cage and Beyond.* London: Phaidon Press, 1995.

Rossiter, Frank. *Charles Ives and His America.* New York: Liveright, 1975.

Saylor, Bruce, and William Lichtenwanger, eds. *The Writings of Henry Cowell.* Brooklyn, N.Y.: Institute for Studies in American Music, 1986.

Swafford, Jan. *Charles Ives: A Life with Music.* New York: Norton, 1996.

Tick, Judith. *Ruth Crawford Seeger, a Composer's Search for American Music.* New York: Oxford University Press, 1997.

Ziffrin, Marilyn J. *Carl Ruggles: Composer, Painter and Storyteller.* Urbana: University of Illinois Press, 1994.

Chapter 6   Inner Occurrences (Transcendentalism, III)

Auner, Joseph. *A Schoenberg Reader: Documents of a Life*. New Haven: Yale University Press, 2003.

Behr, Shulamith, David Fanning, and Douglas Jarman, eds. *Expressionism Reassessed*. Manchester: Palgrave-Macmillan, 1994.

Brand, Juliane, and Christopher Hailey, eds. *Constructive Dissonance: Arnold Schoenberg and the Transformations of Twentieth-Century Culture*. Berkeley and Los Angeles: University of California Press, 1997.

Crawford, John C., and Dorothy L. Crawford. *Expressionism in Twentieth-Century Music*. Bloomington: Indiana University Press, 1993.

Dahlhaus, Carl. *Schoenberg and the New Music*, trans. Derrick Puffett and Alfred Clayton. Cambridge: Cambridge University Press, 1987.

Dale, Catherine. *Tonality and Structure in Schoenberg's Second String Quartet, op. 10*. New York: Garland Publishing, 1993.

Forte, Allen. *The Atonal Music of Anton Webern*. New Haven: Yale University Press, 1998.

Hahl-Koch, Jelena. *Arnold Schoenberg and Wassily Kandinsky: Letters, Pictures and Documents*. London: Faber & Faber, 1984.

Hicken, Kenneth L. *Aspects of Harmony in Schoenberg's Six Little Piano Pieces, op. 19*. Winnipeg: Robert P. Frye and Co., 1984.

Lessem, Alan Philip. *Music and Text in the Works of Arnold Schoenberg: The Critical Years, 1908–1922*. Ann Arbor, Mich.: UMI Research Press, 1982.

Newlin, Dika. *Bruckner, Mahler, Schoenberg*. Rev. ed., New York: Norton, 1978.

Reich, Willi. *Arnold Schoenberg: A Critical Biography*, trans. Leo Black. London: Longman, 1971.

Reti, Rudolf. *Tonality, Atonality, Pantonality: A Study of Some Trends in Twentieth-Century Music*. New York: Macmillan, 1958.

Ringer, Alexander. *Arnold Schoenberg: The Composer as Jew*. Oxford: Oxford University Press, 1990.

Rosen, Charles. *Arnold Schoenberg*. Baltimore, Md.: Penguin USA, 1975.

Schoenberg, Arnold. *Letters*, ed. Erwin Stein, trans. Eithne Wilkins and Ernst Kaiser. London: Faber & Faber, 1964.

———. *Style and Idea*, trans. Leo Black. 2nd ed., Berkeley and Los Angeles: University of California Press, 1975.

———. *Style and Idea: Selected Writings of Arnold Schoenberg*, ed. Leonard Stein, trans. Leo Black. Expanded ed., Berkeley and Los Angeles: University of California Press, 1984.

———. *Theory of Harmony (Harmonielehre, 1911)*, trans. Roy E. Carter. Berkeley and Los Angeles: University of California Press, 1978.

Shawn, Allen. *Arnold Schoenberg's Journey*. New York: Farrar Straus & Giroux, 2002.

Simms, Bryan. *The Atonal Music of Arnold Schoenberg*. New York: Oxford University Press, 2000.

Smith, Joan Allen. *Schoenberg and His Circle: A Viennese Portrait*. New York: Schirmer, 1986.

Stuckenschmidt, Hans Heinz. *Arnold Schoenberg: His Life, World, and Work*, trans. Humphrey Searle. London: Calder, 1977.

Chapter 7   Socially Validated Maximalism

Antokoletz, Elliot, *The Music of Béla Bartók: A Study of Tonality and Progression in Twentieth-Century Music*. Berkeley and Los Angeles: University of California Press, 1984.

Beckerman, Michael. *Janáček as Theorist*. Stuyvesant, N.Y.: Pendragon Press, 1994.

Beckerman, Michael, ed. *Janáček and His World*. Princeton: Princeton University Press, 2003.

Bellman, Jonathan. *The Style Hongrois in the Music of Western Europe*. Boston: Northeastern University Press, 1993.

Eösze, László. *Zoltán Kodály: His Life and Work*, trans. Istvan Farkas and Gyula Gulyas. London: Collet's, 1962.

Evans, Michael. *Janáček's Tragic Operas*. London: Faber and Faber, 1977.

Frigyesi, Judit. *Béla Bartók and Turn-of-the-Century Budapest*. Berkeley and Los Angeles: University of California Press, 1998.

Gillies, Malcolm, ed. *The Bartók Companion*. London: Faber & Faber, 1994.

––––––. *Bartók Remembered*. London: Faber & Faber, 1990.

Horsbrugh, Ian. *Leoš Janáček: The Field That Prospered*. Newton Abbot and London: David & Charles, 1981.

Janáček, Leoš. *Leaves from His Life*, ed. and trans. Vilem and Margaret Tausky. London: Kahn and Averill, 1982.

––––––. *Letters and Reminiscences*, ed. Bohumir Stedron, trans. Geraldine Thomsen. Prague: Artia, 1955.

Kodály, Zoltán. *Folk Music of Hungary*, trans. Ronald Tempest and Cynthia Jolly. 2nd ed., London: Barrie & Jenkins, 1971.

Laki, Peter. *Bartók and His World*. Princeton: Princeton University Press, 1995.

Leafstedt, Carl S. *Inside Bluebeard's Castle: Music and Drama in Béla Bartók's Opera*. New York: Oxford University Press, 1999.

Legány, Dezso. *Liszt and His Country*, trans. G. Gulyas. Budapest: Corvina Press, 1976.

Lendvai, Ernő. *Béla Bartók: An Analysis of His Music*. London: Kahn and Averill, 1971.

––––––. *Symmetries of Music*, ed. M. Szábo and M. Mohay. Kecskemét, 1993.

––––––. *The Workshop of Bartók and Kodály*. Budapest: Editio Musica, 1983.

Sárosi, Bálint. *Gypsy Music*, trans. F. Macnicol. Budapest: Corvina Press, 1971.

Somfai, László. *Béla Bartók: Composition, Concepts, and Autograph Sources*. Berkeley and Los Angeles: University of California Press, 1996.

Stevens, Halsey. *The Life and Music of Béla Bartók*, ed. Malcolm Gillies. 3rd ed., Oxford: Oxford University Press, 1993.

Suchoff, Benjamin, ed. *Béla Bartók's Essays*. New York: St. Martin's Press, 1976.

Szabolcsi, Bence. *A Concise History of Hungarian Music*, trans. Sára Karig. Rev. ed., Budapest: Corvina Press, 1974.

Tallián, Tibor. *Béla Bartók: The Man and His Work*. Budapest: Corvina, 1981.

Tyrrell, John. *Janáček's Operas: A Documentary Account*. London: Faber & Faber, 1992.

Tyrrell, John, ed. *Janáček: Kat'a Kabanova*. Cambridge: Cambridge University Press, 1982.

Walsh, Stephen. *Bartók's Chamber Music*. London: British Broadcasting Corporation, 1982.

Chapter 8   Pathos Is Banned

Andriessen, Louis, and Elmer Schönberger. *The Apollonian Clockwork: On Stravinsky*, trans. Jeff Hamburg. Oxford: Oxford University Press, 1989.

Boehm, Gottfried, Ulrich Mosch, and Katharina Schmidt, eds. *Canto d'Amore: Classicism in Modern Art and Music, 1914–1935*. London: Merrell Holberton, 1996.

Carr, Maureen A. *Multiple Masks: Neoclassicism in Stravinsky's Works on Greek Subjects*. Lincoln: University of Nebraska Press, 2002.

Cocteau, Jean. *A Call to Order*, trans. Rollo H. Myers. London: Faber and Gwyer, 1926.

Daviau, Donald G., and George J. Buelow. *The "Ariadne auf Naxos" of Hugo von Hofmannsthal and Richard Strauss*. Chapel Hill: University of North Carolina Press, 1975.

Dunsby, Jonathan. *Schoenberg: Pierrot Lunaire*. Cambridge: Cambridge University Press, 1992.

Forsyth, Karen. *'Ariadne auf Naxos' by Hugo von Hofmannsthal and Richard Strauss: Its Genesis and Meaning*. London: Oxford University Press, 1982.

Lambert, Constant. *Music Ho!* London: Faber and Faber, 1934.

Levitz, Tamara. *Teaching New Classicality: Ferruccio Busoni's Master Class in Composition*. Frankfurt: Peter Lang, 1996.

Messing, Scott. *Neoclassicism in Music from the Genesis of the Concept through the Schoenberg/Stravinsky Polemic*. Ann Arbor, Mich.: UMI Research Press, 1988.

Oja, Carol J. ed. *Stravinsky in "Modern Music," 1924–1946*. New York: Da Capo Press, 1982.

Stravinsky, Igor. *An Autobiography (Chroniques de ma vie, 1935–36)*. New York: Norton, 1962.

———. *Poetics of Music in the Form of Six Lessons (1939)*, trans. Arthur Knodel and Ingolf Dahl. New York: Knopf, 1960.

Watkins, Glenn. *Proof through the Night: Music and the Great War*. Berkeley and Los Angeles: University of California Press, 2003.

Chapter 9   Lost — or Rejected — Illusions

Appel, David H., ed. *Prokofiev by Prokofiev*, trans. Guy Daniels. New York: Doubleday, 1979.

Bazelon, Irwin. *Knowing the Score: Notes on Film Music*. New York: Van Nostrand Reinhold, 1975.

Bertensson, Sergei, and Jay Leyda. *Sergei Rachmaninoff*. New York: New York University Press, 1956.

Betz, Albrecht. *Hanns Eisler: Political Musician*, trans. Bill Hopkins. Cambridge: Cambridge University Press, 1982.

Cook, Susan. *Opera during the Weimar Republic: The "Zeitopern" of Ernst Krenek, Kurt Weill, and Paul Hindemith*. Ann Arbor, Mich.: UMI Research Press, 1989.

Culshaw, John. *Sergei Rachmaninov*. London: Dobson, 1949.

Drew, David. *Kurt Weill: A Handbook*. Berkeley and Los Angeles: University of California Press, 1987.

Eisler, Hanns. *A Rebel in Music: Selected Writings*, ed. Manfred Grabs, trans. Marjorie Meyer. New York: International Publishers, 1978.

Eisler, Hanns, and Theodor W. Adorno. *Composing for the Films* (1947). London: Athlone Press, 1994.

Flinn, Caryl. *Strains of Utopia: Gender, Nostalgia, and Hollywood Film Music*. Princeton: Princeton University Press, 1992.

Gorbman, Claudia. *Unheard Melodies: Narrative Film Music*. Bloomington: Indiana University Press, 1987.

Hinton, Stephen. *The Idea of Gebrauchsmusik: A Study of Musical Aesthetics in the Weimar Republic (1919–1933) with Particular Reference to the Works of Paul Hindemith*. New York: Garland Publishing, Inc., 1989.

_____. *Kurt Weill: The Threepenny Opera*. Cambridge: Cambridge University Press, 1990.

Jarman, Douglas. *Alban Berg: Wozzeck*. Cambridge: Cambridge University Press, 1989.

_____. *Kurt Weill: An Illustrated Biography*. Bloomington: Indiana University Press, 1982.

Kemp, Ian. *Paul Hindemith*. London: Oxford University Press, 1970.

Kowalke, Kim H. *Kurt Weill in Europe*. Ann Arbor, Mich.: UMI Research Press, 1979.

Neumeyer, David. *The Music of Paul Hindemith*. New Haven: Yale University Press, 1986.

Nice, David. *Prokofiev — A Biography: From Russia to the West, 1891–1935*. New Haven: Yale University Press, 2003.

Norris, Geoffrey. *Rakhmaninov*. 2nd ed., revised, New York: Oxford University Press, 2001.

Palmer, Christopher. *The Composer in Hollywood*. London: Marion Boyars, 1990.

Perle, George. *The Operas of Alban Berg*, Vol. I: *Wozzeck*. Berkeley and Los Angeles: University of California Press, 1980.

Prendergast, Roy M. *Film Music: A Neglected Art*. New York: Norton, 1977.

Schmalfeldt, Janet. *Berg's "Wozzeck."* New Haven: Yale University Press, 1983.

Skelton, Geoffrey. *Paul Hindemith: The Man behind the Music*. New York: Crescendo, 1975.

Stewart, John L. *Ernst Krenek: The Man and His Music*. Berkeley and Los Angeles: University of California Press, 1991.

Thomas, Tony. *Music for the Movies*. Cranbury, N.J.: A. S. Barnes, 1973.

Chapter 10   The Cult of the Commonplace

Axsom, Richard H. *Parade: Cubism as Theatre*. New York: Garland Publishing, 1979.

Buckland, Sidney, and Myriam Chimènes, eds. *Francis Poulenc: Music, Art, and Literature.* Aldershot: Ashgate, 1999.

Clair, René. *A nous la liberté and Entr'acte: Classic Film Scripts.* London: Lorimer, 1970.

Collaer, Paul. *Darius Milhaud.* San Francisco: San Francisco Press, 1988.

Daniel, Keith W. *Francis Poulenc: His Artistic Development and Musical Style.* Ann Arbor, Mich.: UMI Research Press, 1982.

Drake, Jeremy. *The Operas of Darius Milhaud.* New York: Garland Publishing, 1989.

Harding, James. *The Ox on the Roof: Scenes from Musical Life in Paris in the Twenties.* London: Macdonald, 1972.

Mellers, Wilfrid. *Poulenc.* Oxford: Oxford University Press, 1993.

Milhaud, Darius. *Notes without Music,* trans. Donald Evans. London: Dobson, 1952. Rev. ed. (titled *My Happy Life*), ed. Rollo H. Myers. London: Calder & Boyers, 1967.

Perloff, Nancy. *Art and the Everyday: Popular Entertainment and the Circle of Erik Satie.* Oxford: Oxford University Press, 1991.

Poulenc, Francis. *Diary of My Songs,* trans. Winifred Radford. London: Gollancz, 1985.

_____ . *Echo and Source: Selected Correspondence 1918–1963,* ed. Sidney Buckland. London: Trafalgar Square, 1991.

_____ . *My Friends and Myself,* trans. James Harding. London: Dobson, 1978.

Rostand, Claude. *French Music Today* [*La Musique française contemporaine,* 1952], trans. Henry Marx. New York: Merlin Press, 1955.

Shead, Richard. *Music in the 1920s.* New York: St. Martin's Press, 1976.

Thomson, Virgil. *Virgil Thomson by Virgil Thomson.* New York: Knopf, 1966.

Watson, Steven. *Prepare for Saints: Gertrude Stein, Virgil Thomson, and the Mainstreaming of American Modernism.* New York: Random House, 1998.

Chapter 11   In Search of the "Real" America

Alpert, Hollis. *The Life and Times of Porgy and Bess: The Story of an American Classic.* New York: Random House, 1990.

Berger, Arthur. *Aaron Copland: This Work and Contribution to American Music.* New York: Oxford University Press, 1955.

Copland, Aaron, and Vivian Perlis. *Copland: 1900 through 1942.* New York: St. Martin's Press, 1984.

Cowell, Henry. *American Composers on American Music: A Symposium.* New York: Ungar, 1933. Reprint, Palo Alto: Stanford University Press, 1962.

Gordon, Eric A. *Mark the Music: The Life and Work of Marc Blitzstein,* New York: St. Martin's Press, 1989.

Heyman, Barbara. *Samuel Barber: The Composer and His Music.* New York: Oxford University Pres, 1992.

Jablonski, Edward. *Gershwin: A Biography.* Rev. ed., New York: Da Capo Press, 1998.

_____ . *Gershwin Remembered.* Portland, Ore.: Amadeus Press, 1992.

Jablonski, Edward, and Lawrence D. Stewart. *The Gershwin Years: George and Ira*. Rev. ed., New York: Da Capo Press, 1996.

Levy, Alan Howard. *Musical Nationalism: American Composers' Search for Identity*. Westport, Conn.: Greenwood Press, 1983.

Mason, Daniel Gregory. *Tune In, America: A Study of Our Coming Musical Independence* (1931). Freeport, N.Y.: Books for Libraries Press, 1969.

Moore, Macdonald Smith. *Yankee Blues: Musical Culture and American Identity*. Bloomington: Indiana University Press, 1985.

Pollack, Howard. *Aaron Copland: The Life and Work of an Uncommon Man*. New York: Henry Holt & Co., 1999.

Saminsky, Lazar. *Living Music of the Americas*. New York: Howell, Soskin and Crown, 1949.

Schiff, David. *Gershwin: Rhapsody in Blue*. Cambridge: Cambridge University Press, 1997.

Schneider, Wayne J., ed. *The Gershwin Style: New Looks at the Music of George Gershwin*. New York: Oxford University Press, 1999.

Stehman, Dan. *Roy Harris: An American Musical Pioneer*. Boston: Twayne, 1984.

Tawa, Nicholas E. *Serenading the Reluctant Eagle: American Musical Life, 1925–1945*. New York: Schirmer, 1984.

Tischler, Barbara L. *An American Music: The Search for an American Musical Identity*. Oxford: Oxford University Press, 1986.

Zuck, Barbara A. *A History of Musical Americanism*. Ann Arbor, Mich.: UMI Research Press, 1980.

Chapter 12   In Search of Utopia

Adorno, Theodor W. *Alban Berg: Master of the Smallest Link*, trans. Juliane Brand and Christopher Hailey. Cambridge: Cambridge University Press, 1991.

Bailey, Kathryn. *The Life of Webern*. Cambridge: Cambridge University Press, 1998.

———. *The Twelve-Note Music of Anton Webern: Old Forms in a New Language*. Cambridge: Cambridge University Press, 1991.

Brande, Juliane, Christopher Hailey, and Donald Harris, eds. *The Berg-Schoenberg Correspondence*. New York: Norton, 1986.

Carner, Mosco. *Alban Berg: The Man and His Work*. 2nd ed., London: Holmes and Meier, 1983.

Doctor, Jennifer. *The BBC and Ultra-Modern Music, 1922–1936: Shaping a Nation's Tastes*. Cambridge: Cambridge University Press, 1999.

Haimo, Ethan. *Schoenberg's Serial Odyssey: The Evolution of His Twelve-Tone Method*. Oxford: Oxford University Press, 1990.

Headlam, Dave. *The Music of Alban Berg*. New Haven: Yale University Press, 1996.

Hyde, Martha M. *Schoenberg's Twelve-Tone Harmony: The Suite Op. 29 and the Compositional Sketches*. Ann Arbor, Mich.: UMI Research Press, 1982.

Jarman, Douglas. *The Music of Alban Berg*. Berkeley and Los Angeles: University of California Press, 1979.

Jarman, Douglas, ed. *The Berg Companion*. Boston: Northeastern University Press, 1990.

John, Nicholas. *Igor Stravinsky: Oedipus Rex, The Rake's Progress*. English National Opera Guides. New York: Riverrun Press, 1991.

Kolneder, Walter. *Anton Webern: An Introduction to His Work*, trans. Humphrey Searle. Berkeley and Los Angeles: University of California Press, 1968.

Milstein, Silvina. *Arnold Schoenberg: Notes, Sets, Forms*. Cambridge: Cambridge University Press, 1992.

Moldenhauer, Hans, and Rosaleen Moldenhauer. *Anton von Webern: A Chronicle of His Life and Work*. New York: Knopf, 1979.

Perle, George. *The Operas of Alban Berg*, Vol. II: *Lulu*. Berkeley and Los Angeles: University of California Press, 1985.

_____. *Serial Music and Atonality*. 6th ed., Berkeley and Los Angeles: University of California Press, 1991.

Pople, Anthony. *Berg: Violin Concerto*. Cambridge: Cambridge University Press, 1991.

Pople, Anthony, ed. *The Cambridge Companion to Berg*. Cambridge: Cambridge University Press, 1997.

Redlich, Hans. *Alban Berg: The Man and His Music*. London: John Calder, 1957.

Reich, Willi. *Alban Berg*, trans. Cornelius Cardew. London: Thames and Hudson, 1965.

Rufer, Joseph. *Composition with Twelve Notes*, trans. Humphrey Searle. London: Rockliff, 1954.

Rognoni, Luigi. *The Second Vienna School: Expressionism and Dodecaphony*, trans. Robert W. Mann. London: John Calder, 1977.

Shreffler, Anne C. *Webern and the Lyric Impulse: Songs and Fragments on Poems of Georg Trakl*. Oxford: Oxford University Press, 1994.

Walsh, Stephen. *Stravinsky: Oedipus Rex*. Cambridge: Cambridge University Press, 1993.

Webern, Anton. *The Path to the New Music*, trans. Leo Black. Bryn Mawr: Theodore Presser, 1963.

Whittall, Arnold. *Schoenberg Chamber Music*. London: British Broadcasting Corporation, 1972.

Chapter 13   Music and Totalitarian Society

Applegate, Celia, and Pamela Potter, eds. *Music and German National Identity*. Chicago: University of Chicago Press, 2002.

Bartlett, Rosamund, ed. *Shostakovich in Context*. Oxford: Oxford University Press, 2000.

Blokker, Roy, and Robert Dearling. *The Music of Dimitri Shostakovich: The Symphonies*. London: Tantivy Press, 1979.

Brinkmann, Reinhold, and Christoph Wolff. *Driven into Paradise: The Musical Migration from Nazi Germany to the United States*. Berkeley and Los Angeles: University of California Press, 1999.

Brown, Malcolm H., ed. *A Shostakovich Casebook*. Bloomington: Indiana University Press, 2004.

Bruhn, Siglind. *The Temptation of Paul Hindemith: Mathis Der Maler As a Spiritual Testimony*. Stuyvesant, N.Y.: Pendragon Press, 1998.

Cooper, David. *Bartók: Concerto for Orchestra*. Cambridge: Cambridge University Press, 1996.

Fanning, David. *The Breath of the Symphonist: Shostakovich's Tenth*. London: Royal Musical Association, 1988.

——. *Shostakovich: String Quartet No. 8*. Aldershot: Ashgate, 2004.

——. *Shostakovich Studies*. Cambridge: Cambridge University Press, 1995.

Fay, Laurel E. *Shostakovich: A Life*. New York: Oxford University Press, 1999.

——. *Shostakovich and His World*. Princeton: Princeton University Press, 2004.

Grigoryev, Lev, and Yakov Platek, eds. *Dimitry Shostakovich about Himself and His Times*. Moscow: Progress Publishers, 1981.

Hakobian, Levon. *Music of the Soviet Age, 1917–1987*. Stockholm: Melos, 1998.

Kater, Michael H. *Composers of the Nazi Era: Eight Portraits*. New York: Oxford University Press, 2000.

——. *The Twisted Muse: Musicians and Their Music in the Third Reich*. New York: Oxford University Press, 1997.

Levi, Erik. *Music in the Third Reich*. London: Macmillan, 1994.

Meyer, Michael. *The Politics of Music in the Third Reich*. New York: Peter Lang, 1991.

Nestyev, Israel. *Prokofiev*, trans. Florence Jonas. Palo Alto, Calif.: Stanford University Press, 1960.

Norris, Christopher, ed. *Shostakovich: The Man and His Music*. London: Laurence & Wishart, 1982.

Olkhovsky, Andrey. *Music under the Soviets*. London: Routledge and Kegan Paul, 1955.

Potter, Pamela M. *Most German of the Arts: Musicology and Society from the Weimar Republic to the End of Hitler's Reich*. New Haven: Yale University Press, 1998.

Prokofieff, Sergei. *Autobiography, Aricles, Reminiscences*. Moscow: Foreign Languages Publishing House, n.d. Reprint, University Press of the Pacific, 2000.

——. *Selected Letters*, ed. Harlow Robinson. Boston: Northeastern University Press, 1998.

——. *Soviet Diary 1927 and Other Writings*, ed. Oleg Prokofiev. Boston: Northeastern University Press, 1992.

Russolo, Luigi. *The Art of Noises*, trans. Barclay Brown. New York: Pendragon, 1986.

Sachs, Harvey. *Music in Fascist Italy*. New York: Norton, 1987.

Schuh, Willi, ed. *A Confidential Matter: The Letters of Richard Strauss and Stefan Zweig, 1931–1935*, trans. Max Knight. Berkeley and Los Angeles: University of California Press, 1977.

Schwarz, Boris. *Music and Musical Life in Soviet Russia*. 2nd ed., Bloomington: Indiana University Press, 1983.

Sollertinsky, Dimitri, and Ludmilla Sollertinsky. *Pages from the Life of Dimitri Shostakovich*. London: Hale, 1981.

Steinberg, Michael P. *The Meaning of the Salzburg Festival: Austria as Theater and Ideology, 1890–1938*. Ithaca, N.Y.: Cornell University Press, 1990.

Steinweis, Alan E. *Art, Ideology, and Economics in Nazi Germany: The Reich Chambers of Music, Theater, and the Visual Arts.* Chapel Hill: University of North Carolina Press, 1993.

Volkov, Solomon. *Shostakovich and Stalin: The Extraordinary Relationship between the Great Composer and the Brutal Dictator.* New York: Knopf, 2004.

_____. *Testimony: The Memoirs of Dmitri Shostakovich as Related to and Edited by Solomon Volkov.* New York: Harper & Row, 1979.

Wilson, Elizabeth. *Shostakovich: A Life Remembered.* Princeton: Princeton University Press, 1994.

Index

Page numbers in *italics* indicate illustrations.